Juvenile Justice in America

EIGHTH EDITION

Clemens Bartollas

- University of Northern Iowa

Stuart J. Miller

- Washington & Jefferson College

PEARSON

Boston Columbus Indianapolis New York San Francisco Hoboken Amsterdam
Cape Town Dubai London Madrid Milan Munich Paris Montréal Toronto
Delhi Mexico City São Paulo Sydney Hong Kong Seoul Singapore Taipei Tokyo

Editorial Director: Andrew Gilfillan
Senior Acquisitions Editor: Gary Bauer
Editorial Assistant: Lynda Cramer
Director of Marketing: David Gesell
Marketing Manager: Thomas Hayward
Marketing Assistant: Les Roberts
Program Manager Team Lead: Laura Weaver
Program Manager: Tara Horton
Project Manager Team Lead: Bryan Pirrmann
Project Manager: Susan Hannahs
Operations Specialist: Deidra Smith
Creative Director: Andrea Nix
Art Director: Diane Six

Manager, Product Strategy: Sara Eilert
Product Strategy Manager: Anne Rynearson
Team Lead, Media Development & Production:
Rachel Collett
Media Project Manager: Maura Barclay
Cover Designer: Melissa Welch, Studio Montage
Cover Image: Shutterstock
Full-Service Project Management: Philip Alexander, Integra
Software Services Private, Ltd.
Composition: Integra Software Services Private, Ltd.
Printer/Binder: R. R. Donnelley/Owensville
Cover Printer: Lehigh/Phoenix Color Hagerstown
Text Font: ITC Century Std

Credits and acknowledgments borrowed from other sources and reproduced, with permission, in this textbook appear on the appropriate page within the text.

Acknowledgements of third party content appear on page with the borrowed material, which constitutes an extension of this copyright page.

Many of the designations by manufacturers and sellers to distinguish their products are claimed as trademarks. Where those designations appear in this book, and the publisher was aware of a trademark claim, the designations have been printed in initial caps or all caps.

Library of Congress Cataloging-in-Publication Data
Bartollas, Clemens.
    Juvenile justice in America/Clemens Bartollas, Stuart J. Miller.—Eighth edition.
        pages cm
    ISBN 978-0-13-416375-8 (alk. paper)—ISBN 0-13-416375-3 (alk. paper)
    1. Juvenile justice, Administration of—United States.   2. Juvenile delinquency—United States.
    3. Juvenile delinquents—United States.   I. Miller, Stuart J.,   II. Title.
    HV9104.B347 2016
    364.360973—dc23
                                                                    2015030733

10 9 8 7 6 5 4 3 2 1

ISBN 10:   0-13-416375-3
ISBN 13: 978-0-13-416375-8

To Irie Sky Bell
A Beautiful Granddaughter

Brief Contents

Contents

PART III *The Environmental Influences on and the Prevention of Delinquency*

Preface

Juvenile justice is part of a broader human rights movement that is concerned with far more than society's response to juvenile lawbreaking. Indeed, as globalization, urbanization, industrialization, and communications quickly spread across the globe, the world's attention increasingly is directed to the plight of all children, regardless of circumstances. This concern is extremely late in coming. Approximately **twenty-five percent** of the world's population today is age 15 or younger, and the magnitude of the problems these youths face is staggering. Poverty, racism, sexism, ethnocentrism, and religious differences all influence how children are treated. The reality is that in many societies, children are considered to be economic hindrances and expendable. Local, municipal, state, provincial, territorial, and national governments often lump together the needy, the dependent and neglected, the status offender, those who are mentally ill or violent, and the victims of abuse. These children are discriminated against, victimized, persecuted, and sometimes executed by citizens, police, and paramilitary forces. The problems youths face go to the core of cultural thinking, far beyond the needs of societies simply to fine-tune agencies and the rules already in place for the handling of youths in need.

English-speaking countries such as the United States provide many of the ideals that are behind current worldwide efforts to reform the world's approach to juvenile justice. Unfortunately, even world leaders often fall far short of their own ideals. In this regard, the United States is an excellent case study of what is and what could be in juvenile justice in the world today.

Goals and Objectives

Our primary purposes in writing this edition are as follows:

1. To give students an intimate look at the lives of juveniles, their experiences in society, and the consequences of those experiences
2. To present the structures, procedures, and philosophies of juvenile justice agencies in the United States
3. To explore and define the important components of and debates over juvenile justice in the United States
4. To examine the issues and challenges facing juvenile justice agencies today
5. To maintain a balance between theory, evidence-based findings, law, and practice in our examination of juvenile justice
6. To provide the most up-to-date materials possible and, at the same time, to make this text interesting for the student.

Although no author is totally value-free, every attempt has been made to be fair and provide a balanced presentation of the juvenile justice system. Before juvenile justice can develop more just systems and a more humane present and future for juveniles, its characteristics, procedures, policies, and problems must be carefully examined. That is the task of this text.

What's New in This Edition

- New chapter openers are provided for a number of chapters.
- Chapter 1 has a new section on the juvenile court today.
- Chapter 1 has a new table on the minimum age of juvenile court jurisdiction by state.
- Chapter 1 has a new career box on the judge.
- Chapter 1 has an article on the recent reforms in juvenile justice in a number of states.
- This 2013 article is reflective of using new up-to-date publications through the text.
- Chapter 1 has a new Focus on Offenders describing a youth who ended up on death row.
- Chapter 1 has a new theme of the text, delinquency prevention. Most chapters in this text retains this theme.
- Chapter 1 concludes with another new emphasis—that of the importance of theory—research (usually evidence-based practices)—and policy in generating effective policy in juvenile justice. This emphasis reappears throughout the text.
- Chapter 1 has a new topic in the summary section—Working with Juveniles. This topic is found throughout the remainder of the text.
- Chapter 2 has updated statistics on the measurement of delinquent behavior.
- Chapter 2 has a new career box on the court referee.
- Chapter 2 has a new topic on Thinking Like a Correctional Professional; this topic is found in most chapters of the text.
- Chapter 2 has the section on the victimization of juveniles moved in an expanded form to the final chapter.
- Chapter 3 has a new section on why we punish.
- Chapter 3 has a new section on the goals and philosophy of punishment, divided into general deterrence, specific deterrence, incapacitation, rehabilitation, and restorative justice.
- Chapter 3 has a new career box on the juvenile justice officer.
- Chapter 3 has a new section on social policy in juvenile justice: PHDCN/LAFANS.
- Chapter 4 has a new focus on gender roles and delinquency, including the female delinquent, why adolescent females become involved in offending, and the most important dimensions of female delinquent behavior.
- Chapter 4 has a new career box on the juvenile psychotherapist.
- Chapter 4 has a new section that examines the programs for girls sponsored by the Girls, Inc. (formerly called the Girls Club of America).
- Chapter 4 also has a section on Gender Across the Life Course.
- Chapter 5 has a new section on Police Attitudes Toward Youth Crime.
- Chapter 5 has a new policy section on school police district (Los Angeles) agreed to rethink court citations for students.
- Chapter 5 has a new career box on the juvenile school resource officer (SRO).
- Chapter 5 further discusses the Baltimore Outward Bound Police Insight Program, which brings officers and middle school students together for a unique one day program.
- Chapter 6 has a new career box on the juvenile court defense attorney.
- Chapter 6 has a new section on the dangers of detention, based on the recent report by the Justice Policy Institute.
- Chapter 7 has updated figures on transfer procedures.
- Chapter 7 has a new career box on the juvenile court prosecutor.
- Chapter 7 has a new table on state prisons and age of responsibility.
- Chapter 7 has a new table on juveniles under 18 executed from January 1, 1973 until the *Roper* decision

- Chapter 8 has a new exhibit on Categories Depicting a Probation Officer.
- Chapter 8 has a new exhibit on differences between probation and aftercare.
- Chapter 8 has a new career box on the gang intelligence officer.
- Chapter 9 has new materials on youth courts, drug courts, and mental health courts.
- Chapter 9 discusses a new day treatment program, the Family Centered Treatment program in Maryland.
- Chapter 9 has a new career box on the substance abuse counselor.
- Chapter 10 has updated statistics on juvenile institutionalization.
- Chapter 10 has a new career box on the superintendent of a training school.
- Chapter 10 has a new section on racial differences in juvenile justice processing.
- Chapter 11 has a new section on the Assessment of Those on Aftercare, including a discussion of the Level of Service Inventory-Revised (ISI-R).
- Chapter 11 has a new exhibit on the Powelton Aftercare in Philadelphia.
- Chapter 11 has a new career box on the juvenile aftercare or parole officer.
- Chapter 12 has a new career box on the institutional social worker.
- Chapter 13 has a new exhibit on gang scholars.
- Chapter 13 has a new exhibit on Father Greg Boyle, S. J.—A Man with a Vision
- Chapter 13 has a new career box on residential staff members.
- Chapter 14 is a new chapter on juvenile offender populations. It examines the juvenile drug user, juvenile gang delinquent, violent youthful offender, mentally ill juvenile offender, the crossover youth, and the homeless youth. The backgrounds, types, offenses, and treatment of these offenders are covered.
- Chapter 14 has a new career box on the recreational therapist.
- Chapter 15 begins with a section on the context of juvenile victimization, including the family and the victimization of children, the school and victimization, bullying, brothels and the streets, and mass media and delinquent behavior.
- The next section of chapter 15 includes an expanded section of professionalism in juvenile justice.
- Chapter 15 has an expanded section on careers in juvenile justice.
- Chapter 15 has a new section on internships in juvenile justice and corrections.

Organization of the Text

The eighth edition of *Juvenile Justice in America* has fifteen chapters:

- Chapter 1 presents the history of juvenile justice and several historical themes of juvenile justice, examines juvenile justice agencies and functions, and reviews the most widely held philosophies and strategies on correcting juveniles.
- Chapter 2 examines the measurement of juvenile crime and considers the dimensions of law-violating behavior.
- Chapter 3 provides a broad review of the causes of juvenile crime as they developed over the past century.
- Chapter 4 focuses on gender and delinquency. It examines the causes of female delinquency, behaviors that female offenders become involved in, and racial and class dimensions of female delinquency behaviors.
- Chapter 5 discusses the role of the police in dealing with juveniles. It covers police attitudes, juvenile attitudes towards the police, the legal rights of juveniles in dealing with the police, how police process juveniles, and the role of community-oriented policing.

- Chapter 6 examines the main U.S. Supreme Court cases related to the handling of juveniles who come before the juvenile court, considers how status offenders have been handled, presents information on the judge and other key personnel in the juvenile court, and discusses the pretrial procedures of the juvenile court. This chapter also focuses on the adjudicatory hearing, disposition hearing, and judicial alternatives of the juvenile court and looks at the rights of appeal a juvenile has and the current juvenile sentencing structure. Then it provides a defense of the juvenile court and suggestions concerning what is needed for the juvenile court to achieve excellence.

- Chapter 7 extends the discussion to juveniles who are waived to adult court. The issue of transfer receives major attention, but discussions are also provided on the youthful offender system, life for a juvenile in prison, changes in the death penalty for juveniles, and current evaluation of the situation in which juveniles are sentenced to life without the possibility of parole.

- Chapter 8 considers the administration, functions, and risk control focus of probation today. The job of the probation officer is described, and the rights of probationers, the role of volunteers, and the effectiveness of probation are considered.

- Chapter 9 examines the various aspects of community-based programs, including prevention, diversion, day treatment, and residential programs.

- Chapter 10 evaluates the various aspects of institutionalization, both short-term and long-term, for juveniles.

- Chapter 11 delves into aftercare in juvenile justice. Using current research, it places a major emphasis on reentry programs.

- Chapter 12 considers and evaluates the various types of treatment modalities.

- Chapter 13 extends the discussion to juvenile gangs, revealing their history, the types and background of urban and emerging gangs, and the toxicity of gang involvement. The chapter concludes by considering what communities can do to prevent and control youth gangs.

- Chapter 14 examines six offender populations: drugs user, the sex offender, gang delinquent, violent offender, medically ill youthful offender, the crossover youth, and the homeless offender.

- Chapter 15 opens with a context of juvenile victimization, now, considers what juvenile justice will look like in the future, looks at the new technologies emerging in corrections and security procedures, examines how professionalism impacts juvenile justice, and discusses whether juvenile justice is a good career.

Learning Tools

This text contains a number of features that are designed to help students in the learning process.

For Students

Evidence-Based Practice Boxes. A new box in each chapter (except for Chapter 1) highlights real-life examples of evidence-based practices and programs currently in operation.

Focus Boxes. Each chapter contains one or more boxes relating to aspects of juvenile justice, such as laws, social policy, intervention programs, and insights into offenders' thoughts and motivations.

Nearly all chapters have a Thinking Like a Corrections Professional box. This feature provides an opportunity for the student to think how, as a professional, he or she would handle an issue or challenge in juvenile justice.

Nearly all the chapters include a section on the prevention of delinquency.
Effective programs, theories, and practices are featured in these sections.

Summary. The chapter concepts are summarized and organized according to the
chapter's learning objectives to help students learn the material.

Critical Thinking and Review Questions. These are found at the end of some boxes
and at the end of each chapter.

Group Exercises. Each chapter includes exercises for small group discussions,
writing exercises, and/or suggestions for class debate topics.

**All of the chapters have a Section in the Summary Called Working with
Juveniles.** What is suggested are important ingredients or characteristics of
effective workers with juveniles.

Instructor Resources

Voices in the Juvenile Justice System.   Victims, delinquents, and professionals contribute
thirty-five "stories"; twenty-one are from individuals who talk about their childhoods, the crimes
they committed, the contacts they had with the police and juvenile justice system, and a victim
of sex slavery. The other statements are from those who either have worked or presently work
with youthful offenders, ranging from police officers to a juvenile court judge, a chief of juvenile
probation, a deputy director of a detention center, a community mental health coordinator, a
forensic psychiatrist, and a practicing clinical psychologist. The founder and director of a residential facility, two staff members in residential facilities, a therapist who has worked with sex
offenders, a former juvenile court prosecutor from New York City, and a Deputy Commissioner of
Probation in New York City. These are identified in the margins of the text and can be accessed from
www.pearsonhighered.com/careers.

Instructor Supplements

Instructor's Manual with Test Bank.   Includes content outlines for classroom discussion, teaching suggestions, and answers to selected end-of-chapter questions from the text.
This also contains a Word document version of the test bank.

TestGen.   This computerized test generation system gives you maximum flexibility in creating and administering tests on paper, electronically, or online. It provides state-of-the-art
features for viewing and editing test bank questions, dragging a selected question into a test
you are creating, and printing sleek, formatted tests in a variety of layouts. Select test items
from test banks included with TestGen for quick test creation, or write your own questions
from scratch. TestGen's random generator provides the option to display different text or
calculated number values each time questions are used.

PowerPoint Presentations.   Our presentations offer clear, straightforward outlines and
notes to use for class lectures or study materials. Photos, illustrations, charts, and tables
from the book are included in the presentations when applicable.

To access supplementary materials online, instructors need to request an instructor access code. Go to **www.pearsonhighered.com/irc**, where you can register for an
instructor access code. Within 48 hours after registering, you will receive a confirming
email, including an instructor access code. Once you have received your code, go to the site
and log on for full instructions on downloading the materials you wish to use.

Alternate Versions

eBooks.   This text is also available in multiple eBook formats. These are an exciting new
choice for students looking to save money. As an alternative to purchasing the printed
textbook, students can purchase an electronic version of the same content. With an eText-
book, students can search the text, make notes online, print out reading assignments that

incorporate lecture notes, and bookmark important passages for later review. For more information, visit your favorite online eBook reseller or visit **www.mypearsonstore.com**.

REVEL™ is Pearson's newest way of delivering our respected content. Fully digital and highly engaging, REVEL replaces the textbook and gives students everything they need for the course. Seamlessly blending text narrative, media, and assessment, REVEL enables students to read, practice, and study in one continuous experience—for less than the cost of a traditional textbook. Learn more at **pearsonhighered.com/revel**.

Acknowledgments

Many individuals have contributed to the writing of this book. I am profoundly grateful to my wife, Linda Dippold Bartollas. She was a constant source of support and encouragement throughout the many phases involved in the publication of this eighth edition. She also conducted interviews with juvenile offenders in three states.

At the University of Northern Iowa, we thank Wayne Fauchier for all the tasks that he and his staff performed to keep the manuscript moving without interruption. Cassidy Myers did the career boxes for this book as well as the research and development of Chapter 14 on Special Juvenile Offender Populations. Other staff at UNI that made a contribution toward this text were Wendy Christensen, Shana Skay, and Ashley Beaird. Finally, we are grateful to our development editor, Margaret McConnell, and our editor, Gary Bauer.

We would also like to thank the reviewers of the manuscript for their time and valuable feedback. This includes: Brian Agnitsch, Marshalltown Community College; Ryan Alexander, Washburn University; Michael Bisciglia, Southeastern Louisiana University; Janet Foster Goodwill, Yakima Valley Community College; Jay Kramer, Central Georgia Technical College; Barry McCrary, Western Illinois University; and Brittany Rodriguez, Tarleton State University.

Juvenile Justice
An Overview

THE STOCKS (16TH CENTURY).

Learning Objectives

1. Retrace the journey of juvenile justice in the United States.
2. Summarize the history of juvenile confinement.
3. Summarize the historical themes that guided the development of juvenile justice in the United States.
4. Present the structure and procedures of juvenile justice agencies in this nation.
5. Examine the various philosophies and strategies for correcting juveniles.

In 2010, Mark W. Lipsey and colleagues published Improving the Effectiveness of Juvenile Justice Programs[1]:

> *We now have research on best practices for juvenile justice–involved youth and the policies that support the practices. We find this reflected in the increased use of evidence-based practices and programs, in the growth of the science of risk and protective factors and criminogenetic factors and characteristics, and in the development and use of validated risk and needs assessment instruments. We have learned about the importance of advancing our work on an ecological platform, serving youth closer to home, and better connecting youth to family, school, community, and pro-social peers while utilizing a strength-based approach. The true challenge is not, therefore, a lack of knowledge of what works, but rather is in translating the robust body of knowledge into practice.[2]*

Evidence-based research provides reason to be positive about the future of juvenile justice in the United States. All of the remaining chapters of this text discuss evidence-based practices in juvenile justice. "Gold standard" programs that have recently been developed to benefit youthful lawbreakers are Blueprints for Violence Prevention developed by Dr. Delbert Elliott, the Office of Juvenile Justice and Delinquency Prevention's Model Programs guide, and the Substance Abuse and Mental Health Services Administration's National Registry of Evidence-Based Programs and Practices.[3]

In the midst of these hopeful program innovations in the juvenile justice system, there remains wide criticism of juvenile justice in the United States. Some of the criticism focuses on the juvenile court, as well as on the court's rehabilitative **parens patriae** ("the state as parent") philosophy. Indeed, one characteristic of juvenile justice today is the proposal, from both liberals and conservatives, to reduce the scope of the juvenile court's responsibilities. Conservatives want to refer more law-violating youths to adult court, while many liberals recommend divesting the juvenile court of its jurisdiction over **status offenders** (juveniles who have engaged in behaviors for which adults would not be arrested). Some also believe that the adult court could do a much better job than the juvenile court with youthful offenders. Juvenile offenders, according to this position, would at least receive their constitutionally guaranteed due process rights.

The fact is that the juvenile justice system will experience major changes in the next few years. How it will change and whether the changes will be helpful to the youth of this nation are critical questions to be answered. In the chapters of the current volume, positive changes are recommended to improve the functioning of the juvenile justice system.

The juvenile justice system is responsible for controlling and correcting the behavior of troublesome juveniles. What makes this mission so difficult to accomplish in the twenty-first century are the complex forces that intrude on any attempt either to formulate goals or to develop effective programs. Juvenile violence remains a serious problem, although homicides committed by juveniles began to decline in the mid-1990s. Even though juvenile gangs declined in numbers and membership across the nation in the final four years of the twentieth century, these gangs continue to be a problem in many communities. Juveniles' increased use of weapons has also become a serious concern, and there are those who believe that "getting the guns out of the hands of juveniles" is the most important mandate that the juvenile justice system currently has. The use of drugs and alcohol among the juvenile population declined in the final decades of the twentieth century, but beginning in the mid-1990s and continuing to the present, there is evidence that the use of alcohol and drugs, especially marijuana and methamphetamine, is rising in the adolescent population. Furthermore, conflicting philosophies and strategies for correcting juvenile offenders have combined with the social, political, and economic problems that American society faces today—this combination presents other formidable challenges to the juvenile justice system.

Yet, let it be clear that while presenting the challenges of juvenile justice and the often disturbing results of working with youth in trouble, the authors are not promoting a "nothing works" thesis. There are stirring accounts of youths who started out in trouble and

Focus on Offenders 1–1

In a biography I am writing on Rico Johnson, or as he is known, Rahim, Minister of Justice, the head of the Vice Lord nation in Chicago, I learned how his childhood was one of becoming involved in one juvenile caper after another. When he was sent to St. Charles Training School in Illinois, he became involved with an emerging group that eventually became the Vice Lords.

Upon his return to Chicago, he attempted to bring money home because he was the oldest child, the only boy with several daughters, and he felt responsible for helping his mother, a nurse, feed her family. This commitment on his part of helping his mother financially required him to become involved with robbery, sometimes with a weapon. It was not long before he appeared again in court and was sent to an institution in Joliet, Illinois, a facility for older juveniles involved in serious forms of offending.

The Vice Lord gang was starting to expand beyond its neighborhood to other parts of Chicago, and with its growth, came increased involvement of "Little Rico," as he was called. It was not long before he was recognized as one of the gang leaders, and he was sent to an adult facility for a short sentence.

Upon his return, he returned to gang involvement and family "overseer." One of his sisters had married, and her husband became involved in domestic violence from time to time. Finally, Rico had had enough; he went over to the home and warned the husband that this behavior had to cease or there would be dire consequences. Then, not long after that, his sister called again and informed her brother that her husband had beaten her with a firing pan, and she was really "messed up." Rico returned to the sister's house determined to get the situation resolved, whatever it took. The husband was sitting on the sofa in the living room, and in the noisy exchange between the two men, he drew a weapon. Before he had a chance to discharge it, Rico fatally shot him.

On the face of it, it appeared to be self-defense, but in Chicago in those days, gang leaders sometimes got "different justice." He was convicted of murder and given a long prison sentence. He was sent to Stateville Penitentiary, a maximum-security prison in Joliet, Illinois.

During his stint there, while he was gaining in gang credibility, he became friends with a Muslim prisoner and before too many months he was converted to Islam. Rico's standing with the gang was such that he was able to persuade the entire Vice Lord Nation to become practicing adherents of Allah.

In 1980, after being in prison for a decade, he was granted parole. He had had a clean record, avoiding disciplinary offenses. It seemed to be apparent that redemption had taken place in his life. However, redemption was not part of his time on parole; he became a terror on the streets. And a few months later, he was arrested for armed robbery and return to the Illinois' Department of Corrections to finish his sentence.

Rico Johnson was to remain in prison from late 1980 to August 2012, eventually serving forty-one years in confinement. It was during this time that I visited him in prison and even appeared in several of his parole hearings. While it appeared to me that he would not be released, this now second-in-command of the Vice Lord Nation, assumed an extremely positive role in the lives of those who claimed to be Vice Lords. Having interviewed fifteen individuals who were in prison with Rico, they claimed to have returned home and never again resumed criminal behavior, drug using, or drug trafficking. All these individuals claimed that Rico Johnson had changed their lives.

Then, much to my surprise, he was released in August 2012. He had to wear an ankle bracelet from August to December. In the more than three years he has been out, his mission in life has been to impact young people in positive ways. There have been no problems with criminal behavior or conflict with law enforcement; instead, there are continuous programs that he has been involved with, providing positive guidance to young people, in order to help them avoid criminal behavior or drug involvement and use. He is attempting to help young people avoid the mistakes he made as an adolescent.

Source: The story of Rico Johnson's life will be found in his forthcoming biography. I hope to have this published in 2016.

were able to turn things around. In some cases, it was a program that worked with them; in others, it was an adult who made a difference in their lives; and in still others, it was the youths themselves who made the decision to live a crime-free life. As previously noted, with the current emphasis on evidence-based practices and other model programs, it is hoped that juvenile justice programs will be more effective in the future.

A heartwarming success story is found in Focus on Offenders 1–1. The youth in this case had more than his share of troubles with the law as an adolescent. He ended up in and out of juvenile institutions and became a member of an emerging Vice Lord gang. Incarcerated for forty-one years in Illinois' prisons, he became a positive force to inmates while incarcerated and during his three years since his parole, he is committed to helping juvenile people in the community stay out of trouble.

This chapter examines four topics: a historical sketch of juvenile justice, several historical themes, the organizational structure of juvenile justice agencies, and the philosophical approaches to treating youthful offenders. What these topics have in common is that they present the contexts (past and present) that have shaped juvenile justice in the United States.

What Are the Roots of Juvenile Justice?

Throughout history, there has rarely been an emphasis on the special needs of juveniles. Adults and juveniles who violated the law were typically processed in the same manner and were subject to the same types of punishments, including whippings, mutilation, banishment, torture, and death.

Early Europe

In the fifth century A.D., the age was fixed at seven for determining whether youths would be exempted from criminal responsibility under certain conditions. With the onset of puberty, at the age of twelve for girls and fourteen for boys, youths were held totally responsible for their socially unacceptable behaviors.

This understanding of children and criminal responsibility continued in medieval Europe. For example, during the entire period between 700 and 1500 A.D., children were not viewed as a distinct group with special needs and behaviors. Although little is known about the peasant families of the Middle Ages, it is clear that children were expected to assume adult roles in the family early in life and apprentice themselves in crafts or trades to wealthier families. The landowners of the country, then, assumed control over children and their welfare and, at the same time, lifted the burden of child care from their parents.

These early medieval traditions eventually influenced the shaping of juvenile justice in England. Both the Chancery court, which eventually became responsible for overseeing the general welfare of the citizenry, and the concept of *parens patriae*, which focused on the sovereign as the one who protected his or her subjects, played a prominent role in the shaping of English juvenile justice.

Because children and other incompetents were under the protective control of the sovereign, it was not difficult for English kings to justify interventions in their lives. With the passage of time, the concept of *parens patriae* was increasingly used to justify interventions in peasants' families.

The common law tradition in England eventually concurred with earlier law that children under seven should not face legal penalties. Children between seven and fourteen were deemed another matter, and their responsibility was determined by other considerations: severity of the crime, maturity, capacity to distinguish between right and wrong, and evidence of blatant malice.

A sad page in the history of English juvenile justice is that some 160 to 200 capital offenses were listed in the statutes for which children could be executed. Although many juveniles sentenced to die were later pardoned or transported to another country, some children were executed. For example, eighteen of the twenty people executed in London in 1785 were under the age of eighteen.[4] The executions of children continued, but only occasionally, into the 1800s.

The Colonies and Later

Juvenile justice in the United States began in the colonial period and continued English practices. In the colonial period, juvenile justice was shaped principally by the cultural and religious ideas of the Puritans. The family, the cornerstone of the community in colonial times, was the source and primary means of social control of children. The law was uncomplicated; the only law enforcement officials were town fathers, magistrates, sheriffs, and watchmen; and the only penal institutions were jails for prisoners awaiting trial or punishment. Juvenile lawbreakers did not face a battery of police, probation, or **aftercare officers** (the juvenile equivalent of adult parole officers), nor did they have to worry that practitioners of the juvenile justice system would try to rehabilitate or correct them. They only had to concern themselves with being sent back to their families for punishment.[5]

As children got older, however, the likelihood increased that they would be dealt with more harshly by colonial law. The state, even in those early days, clearly was committed to raising its children correctly and making them follow society's rules. If children were still recalcitrant after harsh whippings and other forms of discipline from their families, they could be returned to community officials for more punishment, such as public whippings, dunkings, or the stocks, or in more serious cases, expulsion from the community or even the use of capital punishment.[6]

The state became even more concerned about the welfare of its children in the 1800s. Increased urbanization, industrialization, and bureaucratization were changing the face of America. In the cities particularly, increasing numbers of youths were seemingly out of control. Reformers searched for ways to teach them traditional values, and the asylum and the training school were developed to help the state maintain its control.

The courts were by now heavily involved with the juvenile problem. The concept of *parens patriae* was formalized by *ex parte Crouse* in 1838 and gave the courts a legal basis for intervening in the lives of children. The Bill of Rights, the court ruled, did not apply to minors, and the state could legitimately confine minors, who, according to the ruling, did not have the right to counsel or trial by jury, and who could be confined even in the absence of criminal behavior.

By the end of the 1800s, much of the U.S. population lived in urban areas and worked in factories. Cities were large and growing, and waves of immigration were inundating the nation's shores with millions of people destined to remain poor. Conditions in the cities were shocking; there was much poverty, crime, disease, mental illness, and dilapidation. The cities' children were viewed as unfortunate victims of the urban scene.

How Did the Juvenile Court Develop?

Anthony Platt, in *The Child Savers*, adds greatly to our understanding of the origins of the first juvenile court in Chicago. The Chicago court was created, he argues, partly because the middle and upper classes wanted to control the increasing numbers of immigrants and the poor. Platt claims that the juvenile court was established in Chicago and later elsewhere because it satisfied several middle-class interest groups. He sees the juvenile court as an expression of middle-class values and of the philosophy of conservative political groups.[7]

There is a somewhat different interpretation of the development of the juvenile court. The conditions of the Cook County Jail and the Chicago House of Correction, in which children were placed with adults, were deplorable. Increased numbers of youths were being confined with hardened adult felons who corrupted and exposed them to debauchery, crime, and sin. A group of middle- and upper-class women who had achieved a certain amount of power and freedom wanted to relieve children from confinement with adults in deplorable conditions. Women such as Jane Addams, Louise Bowen, and Julia Lathrop were committed to rescuing the urban American family and its youth by restoring rural values to them. They wanted to reaffirm parental authority, restore the role of the woman in the home, ensure the proper training of youths, and, most important, save youths from the sins they were exposed to on the streets.[8] Focus on the Law 1–2 reveals the prohibited behaviors that the early juvenile courts attempted to correct in the youth brought before them.

The reformers were aided in their quest by a new emerging philosophy. In the past, the classical school of criminology had argued that laws were violated because people willfully chose to violate them. People were presumed to operate on the basis of free will, having total control over their actions; punishment was required to get them to follow the law. The emerging **positivist** school, in contrast, contended that people were pushed into crime by forces beyond their control. It argued that the causes of crime could be discovered through the use of the scientific method and that the biological, psychological, social, economic, political, and other environmental causes of crime could be discovered through rigorous and precise measurement. Once the causes of crime were discovered, this school argued, experts could then step in and cure the offender of his or her problem. Proponents of this philosophy believed that the juvenile court should use these assumptions in attacking the problems of youth.

Everything was in place. The *parens patriae* doctrine had been accepted by the courts for more than a half century. Social conditions had generated an underclass of people who appeared unable to help themselves. Conservative, humanitarian, and religious philosophies had justified the need and had provided the power necessary for change. Jails and prisons clearly were no places for children. And finally, the positivist philosophy held out the promise that if the right mechanism could be developed, wayward children could be saved.

▲ Beheadings and the amputations of limbs of adults and children were undertaken in public squares to act as deterrents to crime in the Middle Ages—and even today in some countries.

Focus on the Law 1–2
Prohibited Behaviors in Early Juvenile Codes

- Violating any law or ordinance
- Being habitually truant from school
- Associating with vicious or immoral persons
- Being incorrigible
- Demonstrating behavior that is beyond parental control
- Leaving home without consent of parents
- Growing up in idleness or crime
- Participating in behavior that injures or endangers the health, morals, or safety of self or others
- Using vile, obscene, or vulgar language in public
- Entering or visiting a house of ill repute
- Patronizing a place where liquor is sold
- Patronizing a gaming place
- Wandering in the streets at night while not at lawful business (curfew violations)
- Engaging in immoral conduct at school or in other public places

- Smoking cigarettes or using tobacco in any form
- Loitering
- Sleeping in alleys
- Using intoxicating liquor
- Begging
- Running away from a state or charitable institution
- Attempting to marry without consent, in violation of law
- Indulging in sexual irregularities
- Patronizing public pool rooms
- Wandering about railroad yards or tracks
- Jumping a train or entering a train without authority
- Refusing to obey a parent or guardian

CRITICAL THINKING QUESTIONS

Which of these offenses do you believe should be defined as delinquent behavior today? How many of these behaviors did you engage in when you were a teenager? How should you have been punished?

The Cook County Juvenile Court was founded in 1899. Its premises were that the *parens patriae* doctrine permitted it to take charge of children in need, that the causes of the children's problems could be discovered and treated, and that the court had to develop a different set of procedures and terminology from those of the adult courts to achieve these goals.

Accordingly, the Illinois court was set up to operate on an *informal* basis. First, this meant that traditional courtrooms were not used; all that was actually required were a table and chairs where the judge, the child, and his or her parents and probation officers could sit together and discuss the case. Second, children could be brought before the court on the basis of complaints of citizens, parents, police, school officials, or others. Third, the children's hearings were not public, and their records were kept confidential because children coming before the court were not considered criminal. Fourth, proof of the child's criminality was not required for the child to be considered in need of the court's services. Fifth, the court had great discretion in determining what kinds of services the child required and had wide latitude in determining a disposition. Sixth, lawyers were not required because the hearings were not adversarial. Finally, the standards and procedures long in use in adult courts were missing in the juvenile courts; the standard of proof beyond a reasonable doubt was not required, and hearsay evidence was permitted.

The attractiveness of the juvenile court philosophy resulted in almost all states setting up juvenile courts. In fact, by 1928, only two of thirty-one states had not passed a juvenile court statute.[9] Those that did closely followed the wording and intent of the Chicago statute and its amendments. These were civil courts, usually a family court, and their purpose was rehabilitation, not punishment. The neglected, the dependent, the misbehaving youngster, the status offender, and the delinquent were all subject to the courts' dictates. But the public was assured that programs would be developed to solve the problems of wayward youth so that they would be released to the community as respectable citizens.

Juvenile courts attempted to live up to their mandate for the next sixty years. For about the first twenty years, the court was aided by religiously motivated volunteers who brought strong moral commitments to their work with juveniles. Confidence in the juvenile court began to erode in 1911 and 1912, with exposés detailing the court's deplorable conditions and practices.[10] Another negative influence on the juvenile court following World War I was the general disenchantment with the idea that society was improving.

Immediately following World War I, volunteers were replaced with paid social work professionals called "social adjusters." The social work orientation of these professionals enabled them to help redefine the juvenile court as a social agency and to lobby successfully for more paid social workers. In the 1920s, the field of social work adopted Freudian psychoanalysis, which focused on the client's emotional feelings. Thus, instead of attempting to deal with social environmental problems as the cause of delinquency, as the earlier reformers did, social workers began to focus on the inner mental workings of the child.

The Juvenile Court Today

Juvenile court codes, which exist in every state, define what constitutes delinquency and specify the conditions under which states can legitimately interfere in a juvenile's life. The juvenile court usually specifies that the court has jurisdiction in relationship to the three categories of delinquency, dependency, and neglect. First, the court may intervene when the youth has been accused of committing an act that would be a misdemeanor or felony if committed by an adult. Second, the court may intervene when the juvenile commits certain status offenses. Third, the court may intervene in cases involving dependency and neglect; for example, if the court determines that a child is being deprived of needed support and supervision, it may decide to remove the child from the home for his or her own protection.

Some controversy has surrounded the issue of how long a juvenile should remain under the jurisdiction of the juvenile court. The age at which a juvenile offender is no longer treated as a juvenile ranges from fifteen to eighteen years. In 37 states and the District of Columbia, persons under eighteen years of age charged with a law violation are considered juvenile. In ten states, the upper limit of juvenile court jurisdiction is sixteen years, and in three states, the upper limit is fifteen years. See Table 1–1 for the minimum age of juvenile court jurisdiction by state.

A status offense, as previously noted, is behavior that is an offense only because a person involved is a juvenile. In various jurisdictions, status offenses are known as minors in need of supervision (MINS), children in need of supervision (CHINS), juveniles in need of supervision (JINS), children in need of assistance (CHINS), persons in need of supervision (PINS), children in need of protection and services (HIPS), or members of family in need of supervision (FINS). They may also be called predelinquent, incorrigible, beyond control, and ungovernable, or wayward. What these terms and acronyms have in common is that they view the status offender as in need of supervision or assistance. For a list of status offenses, see Table 1–2.

What Is the History of Juvenile Confinement?

At the time of the American Revolution, the penal system in the colonies was modeled after the one in England. The larger urban jails, county jails, and prisons contained men, women, and juveniles, whether they were felons or misdemeanants, insane or sane—sometimes all mixed together. Smaller rural counties, however, had less need for large jails and prisons and temporarily housed their wayward citizens in small rural jails.

TABLE 1–1
Minimum Age of Juvenile Court Jurisdiction by State

Age	States
15	New York, North Carolina
16	Georgia, Louisiana, Massachusetts, Michigan, Missouri, New Hampshire, South Dakota, Texas, and Wisconsin
17	Alabama, Alaska, Arizona, Arkansas, California, Colorado Connecticut, Delaware, District of Columbia, Florida, Hawaii, Idaho, Illinois, Indiana, Iowa, Kansas, Kentucky, Maine, Maryland, Minnesota, Mississippi, Montana, Nebraska, Nevada, New Jersey, New Mexico, North Dakota, Ohio, Oklahoma, Oregon, Pennsylvania, Rhode Island, South Dakota, Tennessee, Utah, Vermont, Virginia, Washington, West Virginia, and Wyoming

Source: OJJDP Statistical Briefing Book. Online, accessed January 5, 2015.

> **TABLE 1–2**
> **Status Offenses**
>
> Drinking alcohol
> Incorrigibility at home
> Ungovernable at school
> Running away from home
> Truancy
> Smoking cigarettes and using smokeless tobacco

In neither city nor county, however, were youths expected to get into trouble. If they did, they were subject to the same punishments as were adults. Beyond that, normal community processes were thought to be sufficient to keep them in line. Community norms were enforced through gossip, ridicule, and other informal social pressures, and little formal social control was needed. Local enforcers consisted of watchmen, magistrates, and sheriffs. All those who were caught, including youths, received fines, beatings, and floggings; were put in stocks; were driven through town in carts to be ridiculed by the citizenry; and in extreme cases were hanged, burned, mutilated, or banished from the community. After punishment, some youths were apprenticed to local craftsmen; until the mid-1800s, others were sent on extended whaling voyages; and still others were placed with relatives or farm families.[11]

In the late 1700s and early 1800s, the United States was in a period of transition. The rural way of life was threatened, and the changes were having an irreversible effect on the structure of society. Concern about what to do with the growing number of juveniles who were abandoned, were runaways, or had run afoul of community norms increased and placed the young nation in a dilemma. On the one hand, thinkers reasoned that the natural depravity of humans made attempts at rehabilitation useless and that banishing the guilty was simpler than either punishment or rehabilitation. On the other hand, some hoped to find specific causes for deviancy, and the family was believed to be the primary source of the problem. Common sense and the examination of case histories indicated that older offenders usually had been problem children. The idea emerged that if institutions could be used for the poor, perhaps similar institutions could be set up for children using the well-adjusted family as the model.[12]

Juvenile Judge

PREPARATION FOR THE JOB

This person almost always starts out as a licensed lawyer who has practiced law for a period of time. Juvenile court judges have an enormously important and difficult job. The most traditional role of the juvenile court judge is to decide the legal issues that appear before the court.

QUALIFICATION AND EDUCATIONAL REQUIREMENTS

The judge must first be selected, and juvenile judges are chosen by a variety of methods. In some states, the governor appoints candidates chosen by a screening board. In other states, judges are chosen through partisan elections, and in still other states, judges run for office without party affiliation. The legislature appoints judges in a few states.

DUTIES AND RESPONSIBILITIES

The judge must determine, whether certain facts are true, whether a child should be removed from a parent, what types of services should be offered to the family and whether the child should be returned to the family and the community or placed permanently in another setting. The judge must also be an advocate for the youth making certain they receive all their constitutional safeguards.

JOB OUTLOOK

There is high demand for the highly prestigious job, but there is little turnover because the available jobs are already filled and are not being replaced until a person steps down, retires, or is not reappointed.

SALARY

In the United States, the average juvenile judge's salary on June 5, 2015 was $78,000.

Source: Pay.state.com.

Regardless of the source of the problem, the situation demanded a solution. The growing number of delinquents and other children running in the streets of larger cities, the increasing population, and the changing character of U.S. society were all putting greater pressure on existing facilities. Conditions in the jails and prisons were deplorable. Youths were sentenced for fixed periods of time and were confined with the worst criminals society had to offer. Some youths died of disease, and morals were corrupted as children ten to eighteen years old were confined with adult felons.

The House of Refuge

When citizens and reformers first became concerned about these inhumane conditions, their solution was the **house of refuge**. This facility was for all children, not just delinquents. Benevolence and compassion, along with concern over the degrading conditions in the jails and prisons, motivated the reformers to establish the houses of refuge.

New York City started the first school for males in 1825, followed by Boston in 1826 and Philadelphia in 1828. Other cities, including Bangor, Richmond, Mobile, Cincinnati, and Chicago, followed suit over the years. Twenty-three houses of refuge were built in the 1830s and thirty more in the 1840s. Of these, the vast majority were for males, with an occasional institution reserved for females. Their capacity ranged from ninety at Lancaster, Massachusetts, to 1,000 at the New York House of Refuge, with a median number of 210. The promise of these institutions seemed so great that youths with every type of problem were placed in them. The New York House of Refuge accepted children adjudicated guilty of committing crimes as well as those who simply were in danger of getting into trouble. The poor, the destitute, the incorrigible, and the orphaned were all confined. Admission policies were obviously quite flexible, and little concern was shown for due process; some youths simply were kidnaped off the streets. Not until later did these institutions begin to limit their rosters to those who had committed crimes.

The children generally were confined for periods ranging from less than six weeks to about twenty-four months, although some stayed longer. In some institutions the youths were taught trades, such as manufacturing shoes, brushes, and chairs, or were readied for apprenticeships to local craftsmen. Sentences were indeterminate, and superintendents of the institutions decided whether the apprenticed youths would be released or returned to the institution.

These juvenile institutions accepted the family model wholeheartedly, for reformers desired to implant the order, discipline, and care of the family in institutional life. The institution, in effect, would become the home, peers would become the family, and staff would become the parents. Orphanages and houses of refuge substituted a rigorous system of control and discipline for the disordered life of the community.

Discipline was severe when the rules were disobeyed, but the reformers believed that once the authority of the superintendents was established, they would be looked on admiringly and as friends. Belief in these principles was so great that parents for the first time had to surrender their authority to superintendents and could not participate in the upbringing of their unruly children.

Treatment of the youths paralleled the routine nature of the facility's physical plant. When the youths entered, they were dressed in institutional clothing and given identical haircuts. Troublemakers were punished; placing offenders on a diet of bread and water or depriving them of meals altogether were milder forms of discipline, but they were coupled with solitary confinement if a severe punishment was deemed necessary. Corporal punishments, used alone or in combination with other corrections, consisted of whipping with a cat-o'-nine-tails or manacling with a ball and chain. The worst offenders were shipped off to sea.

The specific order of daily events varied from institution to institution, but all followed the same basic schedule and routine. In some, youths were counted frequently to make sure that none had escaped, and in many facilities silence was maintained at all times, even during the recreation and exercise periods. Eating at times other than regularly scheduled mealtimes was forbidden, and youths who wanted extra food had to raise their hands. In school, everyone recited in unison.

Reformers were enthusiastic about the houses of refuge, but the residents apparently did not share their positive feelings. Hutchins Hapgood, sent to the New York House of Refuge in the nineteenth century, viewed this setting as a "school for crime," because "unspeakably bad habits were contracted there. The older boys wrecked the younger ones," and children who were orphans had an especially hard time. The residents, he added, were overworked while making overalls and were beaten frequently. He bluntly concluded, "I say without hesitation that lads sent to an institution like the House of Refuge, the Catholic Protectory, or the Juvenile Asylum might better be taken out and shot."[13]

The Reformatory or Training School

Reformatories, also called *training schools* or *industrial schools*, developed in the mid-nineteenth century. The new reformatories were essentially a continuation of the houses of refuge, although they did stress a longer period of schooling, usually half a day. Another change was that the contracting of inmates' labor became more exploitative, as manufacturers often inflicted cruelty and violence on juveniles during working hours. The cat-o'-nine-tails, for example, was used on youths who slacked off on their work in the reformatory shops.

In spite of the questionable nature of these institutions, states continued to build reformatories or training schools. In 1847, Massachusetts opened the first state-operated training school, the Lyman School for Boys, and in 1856, established the State Industrial School for Girls at Lancaster. New York built an industrial school in 1849, and by 1870, Connecticut, Indiana, Maryland, Nevada, New Hampshire, New Jersey, Ohio, and Vermont had opened training schools for delinquents. By 1890, nearly every state outside of the South had established a training school.[14]

The Cottage System

Introduced in 1854, the **cottage system** spread throughout the country. Reformers had succeeded in placing the industrial schools outside cities, their rationale being that youths on farms would be reformed when exposed to the rural virtues, the simple way of life, and the bounty of Mother Nature. With the new cottage system, the process of individual reform could be furthered, as residents were housed in separate buildings, usually no more than twenty to forty per cottage. The training schools were no longer supposed to be fortress-like either in physical design or in the relationships among residents and staff. The first cottages were log cabins; later ones were made of brick or stone. This form of organization was widely accepted and is the basic design for many juvenile facilities even today.

Three major changes began to affect juvenile institutions in the closing decades of the nineteenth century: the increasing size of institutional populations, a decrease in funding from state legislatures, and the admission of more dangerous offenders. As a result, the industrial school became custodial, and superintendents had to accept custodianship as an adequate goal.[15] Yet faith in the industrial school continued into the twentieth century.

How Did Probation Develop?

John Augustus, a Boston cobbler, is considered to be the father of probation in this country. He spent considerable time in the courtroom, and in 1841, accepted his first probation client, whose offense was "yielding to his appetite for strong drink."[16] Beginning with this "common drunkard," he was able to devote himself to the cause of probation as he became convinced that many lawbreakers needed only the interest and concern of another to be able to stop drinking, straighten out their lives, and become model citizens. Augustus worked with women and children as well as with male offenders; in fact, he was willing to work with all types of offenders—drunkards, petty thieves, prostitutes, and felons—as long as he met a contrite heart. Augustus instigated such services as investigation and screening, supervision of probationers, interviewing, and arranging for relief, employment, and education—all of which are still provided today.

The state of Massachusetts, very much impressed with Augustus's work, established a visiting-probation-agent system in 1869. The philosophy of this system, which was set up to assist both youths and adults, was that first offenders who showed definite promise should be released on probation. Youths would be allowed to return to their parents and to live at home as long as they obeyed the injunction, "Go and sin no more."[17]

Probation was regulated by statute for the first time in 1878, when the mayor of Boston was authorized to appoint a paid probation officer to the police force, to serve under the police chief. In 1880, the authority to appoint probation officers was extended to all cities and towns in Massachusetts. By 1890, probation had become statewide, with the authority to appoint officers resting with the courts rather than with municipal authorities. Soon thereafter, Vermont, Missouri, Illinois, Minnesota, Rhode Island, and New Jersey enacted probation statutes.

Although probation was radically extended in the wake of the juvenile court movement, probation systems varied from one jurisdiction to another. Probation officers generally considered themselves servants of the juvenile court judge rather than defenders of the rights of children. Thus, they would gather relevant facts and opinions on each case to help the judge make his decision, sometimes blatantly disregarding the due process safeguards of the law. Judges, in turn, saw nothing objectionable about returning children to the care of the probation officer who had placed them at the court's mercy in the first place. Most juvenile courts relied at first on volunteer juvenile probation officers. One observer said that their work "is the chord upon which all the pearls of the Juvenile Court are strung. It is the keynote of a beautiful harmony; without it the Juvenile Court could not exist."[18] Probation volunteers, however, largely disappeared by the second decade of the twentieth century, not to return until the late 1950s.

The spread of probation was marked by the founding in 1907 of the National Association of Probation Officers (renamed the National Probation Association in 1911). Homer Folks, one of the early advocates of probation, summarized the perception of probation in the early twentieth century: "Probation provides a new kind of reformatory, without walls and without much coercion."[19] Nevertheless, the idea of coercion lurked close to the surface, and force was used without hesitation if the delinquent continued to disobey the law. "When sterner treatment was demanded," said one officer, "the friendly advisor became the official representative of the court with the demand that certain conditions be observed or that the probationer be returned to the court."[20]

After World War I, there was an ever-increasing demand for trained social workers to serve as probation officers. In addition to a greater concern for treating children's problems, twentieth-century probation theory also includes the idea of more responsibility for the delivery of services to probationers, a greater consciousness of standards, and a desire to upgrade the probation officer and restore the volunteer to probation services.

What Is the History of Aftercare?

Juvenile aftercare is as old as the juvenile institution. Superintendents of the early houses of refuge had the authority to release youths when they saw fit. Some youths were returned directly to their families; others were placed in the community as indentured servants and apprentices. After such service, they were released from their obligations and reentered the community as free citizens. For some, placement amounted to little more than slavery. They were sent to stores, factories, or farms that needed cheap labor. For others, the situation was more favorable, and some youths in trouble benefited from placement with caring and responsible families. Nevertheless, the system was not at all formalized; only in the 1840s did states begin to set up inspection procedures to keep watch on those with whom youths were placed.[21]

Parole, the period of time after institutional release when offenders are still under the control of the courts or state, continued to be used throughout the 1800s and into the 1900s. With the formation of the juvenile court, parole generally was called *aftercare*. In the early 1900s, professionally trained individuals were added to the juvenile court to deal with released juveniles. In addition, aftercare officers generally mirrored probation officers in trying to utilize current popular treatment modalities. Aftercare officers' caseloads were generally extremely high, and few resources were available to them. Even today, aftercare officers in many jurisdictions have the task of monitoring extremely large caseloads.

The development of aftercare programs was far from rapid, and the system remains underdeveloped even today. Citizens and professionals perhaps thought that institutionalization was sufficient for youth, or they might have been more concerned about adults,

FIGURE 1–1
Historical Stages in the Development
of Juvenile Justice

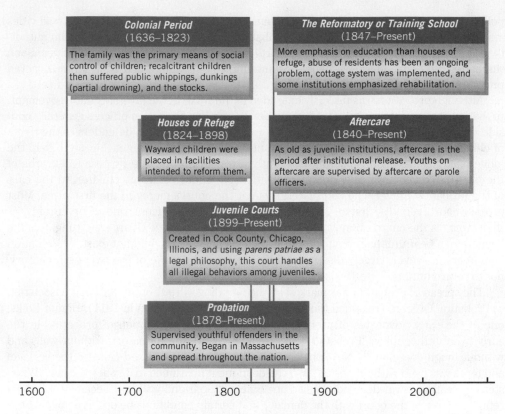

whom they feared and mistrusted more. Whatever the reason, not until fairly recently have
innovative efforts been undertaken to improve juvenile aftercare systems. See Figure 1–1
for the historical stages in the development of juvenile justice.

What Are the Historical Themes of Juvenile Justice?

The roots of today's juvenile justice extend back through the European experience and the
norms and values of agricultural societies. As societies change socially, technologically, and economically, from nomadic communities to agricultural societies, from villages to cities, from feudal
systems to industrialized societies and into the "postindustrial" world, their structures change
as do their citizens' assumptions and perceptions about youths, their roles, and motivations.
Of concern in all societies is what causes misbehavior on the part of youths and what should
be done to solve the problem. Some of the major themes that run through this history include
discovering the child, the rising power of the state, reform and retrenchment, the get-tough and
go-slow approaches, the threat of the dangerous poor, and the unsolvable nature of youth crime.

Discovering the Child

The background of juvenile justice illustrates well the difficulties societies faced in defining
children and their place in society. For most of history, the special needs of juveniles were
never considered, with the possible exception of children ages two and under in the earliest
eras and under the age of seven later in history. Subsistence living in the earliest societies
required children to take on whatever productive roles necessary to help their families and
themselves survive. In some societies, children were looked upon as adults in miniature and
were subject to the same punishments as were adults. Eventually, children were classified
by whether they were under the age of seven, between seven and fourteen years of age, or
fourteen and older. Members of society began to debate children's "age of responsibility" in
considering the seriousness and extent of their undesirable behavior.

Increased Authority of the State

Ever since the colonial period, society has gradually *taken authority away from the family* and given it to the state for correcting the behavior of children. There is little reason to

believe that the three-hundred-year-old legacy of taking authority away from the family is likely to change in the near future. Even if the state were receptive to relinquishing some of its power (all indicators point to the fact that the state wants to increase rather than decrease its power over citizens), the American family is under greater pressure now than ever before. Its mounting problems include high rates of divorce and single-parent families, alarming rates of abuse and neglect of children, problems with drug and alcohol abuse among both parents and children, and large numbers of adolescent and out-of-wedlock births.

Reform and Retrenchment

It is sometimes claimed that the history of juvenile justice has been a steady march toward more humane and enlightened conceptions of childhood and democracy, but a more reliable reading of history shows that a period of reform has inevitably led to a period of retrenchment.[22] To express this another way, the history of juvenile justice appears to go through cycles of reform and retrenchment. Thomas J. Bernard's *The Cycle of Juvenile Justice* is a perceptive analysis of what drives these cycles of reform and retrenchment. According to Bernard, a cycle begins when both juvenile officials and the general public believe that youth crime is at an exceptionally high level and that many harsh punishments are used but few lenient treatments exist for youthful offenders. In this context, many minor offenders avoid punishment because justice officials believe that harsh punishment will make them worse. A period of reform arrives when the solution is seen as introducing lenient treatments for youthful offenders.[23]

The period from the 1960s to the mid-1970s was characterized by a liberal agenda. This reform agenda emphasized the reduced use of training schools, the diversion of status offenders and minor offenders from the juvenile justice system, and the reform of the juvenile justice system.

The liberal agenda ended in the 1990s and was followed by a get-tough approach. One of the contributing causes of this shift from reform to repression was the failure of the reform agenda of the 1970s to address violent youth crime and repeat offenders. Thus, the inability of the reformers to provide meaningful programs and policies aimed at persistent and serious youth crime proved to be the Achilles heel of the reform process.[24] The get-tough approach continued into the 1980s. The main thrusts of the Reagan administration's crime control policy for juveniles were preventive detention, transfer of violent and repeat juvenile offenders to the adult court, mandatory and determinate sentences for serious and repeat juvenile offenders, increased long-term confinement for juveniles, and enforcement of the death penalty for juveniles who commit "brutal and senseless" murders.

The get-tough attitude toward youth crime led to a number of federal juvenile justice initiatives in the 1990s that went beyond those implemented in the 1980s. These initiatives consisted of (1) establishing curfews, (2) passing parental responsibility laws, (3) increasing efforts to combat street gangs, (4) moving toward graduated sanctions, (5) creating juvenile boot camps, (6) maintaining and strengthening current laws restricting juveniles' use of guns, (7) opening juvenile proceedings and records, (8) transferring juveniles to criminal or adult courts, and (9) expanding sentencing authority over juveniles. The popularity of the get-tough approach was reflected in the fact that in the 1990s nearly every state enacted legislation incorporating these federal initiatives into the social policy for handling juveniles.[25]

In a 2013 article, The Justice Policy Institute examines recent reforms including reducing the use of incarceration in the juvenile justice system across the nation, improving the conditions of juvenile facilities, and expanding community-based corrections that can be used instead of confinement. The top performers are Connecticut, Tennessee, Louisiana, Minnesota, and Arizona. In fact, juvenile correctional populations have dropped by about a third across the nation since 1999, when they peaked at over one hundred thousand youths.[26] Commonalities among these top performers include the following:

- the state was a target of class action litigation concerning conditions of confinement or other legal or administrators scrutinies;
- juvenile corrections split from the adult system and/or partnered with child welfare;
- there was improved interagency collaboration and communication, often through the formulation of a high-level task force or commission; and

• state leaders recommitted their system to a holistic juvenile justice ideal that acknowledged that youthful behavior is inherently different from adult behavior and that it requires different intervention and services.[27]

In sum, the cyclical relationship between reform and retrenchment in juvenile justice seems to hinge upon society's dissatisfaction with the ill-fated promises of reform, followed, a generation or two later, by rejection of retrenchment's lack of benevolence. Perhaps the key to this shift is that society and its policy makers want social order, but, at the same time, they want special treatment for children.

Get-Tough and Go-Soft Approaches

Although reform and retrenchment alternate as official policies for juvenile justice in this nation, the get-tough approach for serious juvenile offenders and the go-soft strategy for minor offenders and status offenders have characterized the sentencing practices of juvenile courts in recent decades. The **least-restrictive** (or go-soft) **approach** first became popular in the 1960s. When professionals and students became aware of the extent of youth crime, the negative impact of delinquency labels, and the criminogenic and violent nature of juvenile institutions, many of them began to reappraise what should be done with juvenile lawbreakers. Studies on hidden delinquency and middle-class lawbreaking also taught a valuable lesson—nearly all juveniles break the law, but only a few are caught.[28]

For these reasons, supporters of this approach urge a least-restrictive philosophy—do not do any more than necessary with youthful offenders. If possible, leave them alone.[29] If their offense is too serious to permit this course of action, use every available resource before placing them in detention or in institutions. Keeping status offenders (juveniles who run away, violate a curfew, are ungovernable at home, or are truant from school) out of the juvenile justice system is one of the predominant concerns of proponents of this philosophy. Providing juveniles with all the procedural safeguards given to adults is also a vital concern. Adherents, of course, urge the use of community resources in working with juvenile offenders, an approach believed by many to be the best for juvenile justice.

On the other end of the spectrum, however, juveniles who commit serious crimes or continue to break the law are presumed to deserve punishment rather than treatment because they possess free will and know what they are doing. Their delinquencies are viewed as purposeful activity resulting from rational decisions in which the pros and cons are weighed and the acts that promise the greatest potential gains are performed. See Figure 1–2 for three approaches to delinquency control.

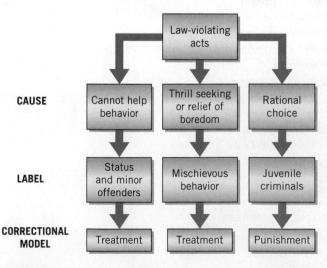

FIGURE 1–2
Three Approaches to Delinquency Control

Threat of the Dangerous Poor

Early in the history of this nation, crime was blamed on the poor, especially on those who were newcomers to America. The fact that these individuals came from different cultural, ethnic, and religious backgrounds also made them appear dangerous. It was reasoned that institutions were needed to protect society against the behavior of these so-called **dangerous poor**.

Significantly, until the late nineteenth century, each succeeding wave of immigration that brought impoverished newcomers was perceived as threatening a new crime wave. Anthony Platt's classic work, *The Child Savers*, makes the point that the behaviors the child savers selected to be penalized—sexual license, roaming the streets, drinking, begging, fighting, frequenting dance halls and movies, and staying out late at night—were found primarily among lower-class children. From the very beginning, according to this interpretation, juvenile justice engaged in class favoritism that resulted in poor children being processed through the system while middle-class children were more likely to be excused.[30] The association of poverty with dangerousness has continued to the present day. It is expressed, especially, with the fear of violence and gang behaviors from African American and Hispanic underclass children.

Thinking like a Correctional Professional

The governor has appointed you chairperson of a task force to bring reform to the juvenile justice system. She is particularly concerned with the brutality and corruption that the institutions of that state have experienced. She also wants you to reduce the population of the training schools, without compromising public safety. Whom will you appoint to your committee? What is your strategy for developing this plan of reform? Where do you plan to disseminate the results of your report?

The Unsolvable Nature of Youth Crime

The get-tough and go-soft policies illustrate that the United States has a history of seeking cure-alls to solve the crime problem. Unfortunately, no simple solution to this age-old problem exists. The search for a panacea began in the early nineteenth century—the Jacksonian period—when the young American nation was thought to have an unlimited capacity to solve its social problems.[31] The institutions that emerged to create better environments for deviants represented an attempt to promote the stability of society at a time when traditional ideas and practices seemed to be outmoded, constricted, and ineffective.

Legislators, philanthropists, and local officials were all convinced that the nation faced both unprecedented dangers and unprecedented opportunities. It was hoped that the penitentiary for adults and the house of refuge for juveniles, as well as the almshouse for the poor, the orphan asylum, and the insane asylum, would restore a necessary balance to the new republic and, at the same time, eliminate long-standing problems. The fact that these institutions eventually came to be viewed as failures did not prevent another generation of reformers from seeking new ways to cure the crime problem.[32] Table 1–3 summarizes the historical themes of juvenile justice.

TABLE 1–3
Historical Themes of Juvenile Justice

Theme	What Has Taken Place in Society	Effects on Juvenile Justice
Discovering the Child	Society began the process of defining children and their place in society	Enabled the development of the juvenile system, where juveniles would be treated differently than adults
Increased Authority of the state	Society took authority away from the family and gave it to the state	With the development of the juvenile court and its *parens patriae* philosophy, the state assumed authority over juveniles
Reform and Retrenchment	Society changed its mind about the juvenile justice system depending upon which cycle of reform and retrenchment currently seemed effective	Juvenile justice appears to go through cycles of reform and retrenchment
Get-Tough and Go-Soft Approaches	Society is apt to excuse the behavior of minor forms of delinquency and to desire punishment for serious forms	The juvenile justice system likewise excuses or punishes depending on the seriousness of delinquent acts
Threat of the Dangerous Poor	Beginning with immigration, certain groups are perceived as the dangerous class	African Americans and Hispanic children are more likely to be given this label
Unsolvable Nature of Youth Crime	Society has long pursued solutions to both juvenile and adult crime	No panacea has been found

What Are the Juvenile Justice Agencies and Functions?

The Constitution of the United States gives both the federal government and the states the authority to draw up laws and the mechanisms for enforcing those laws. The primary laws with which this book is concerned are laws governing delinquent and criminal behaviors and the three subsystems—the police, the courts, and correction departments—that carry out the mandates of the laws.

These three subsystems have between 10,000 and 20,000 public and private agencies, with annual budgets totaling hundreds of millions of dollars. Many of the 40,000 police departments have juvenile divisions, and more than 3,000 juvenile courts and about 1,000 juvenile correctional facilities exist across the nation. More than 30,000 of the 50,000 employees in the juvenile justice system are employed in juvenile correctional facilities; 6,500 are juvenile probation officers, and the remainder are aftercare officers and residential staff in community-based programs. Several thousand more employees work in diversion programs and privately administered juvenile justice programs.[33]

The Police

The functions of the three subsystems are somewhat different. The basic responsibilities of the police consist of enforcing the law and maintaining order. The law enforcement function requires that the police deter crime, make arrests, obtain confessions, collect evidence for strong cases that can result in convictions, and increase crime clearance rates. The maintenance of order function involves such tasks as settling family disputes, directing traffic, furnishing information to citizens, providing emergency ambulance service, preventing suicides, giving shelter to homeless persons and alcoholics, and checking the homes of families on vacation. Police–juvenile relations require the police to deal with juvenile lawbreaking and to provide services needed by juveniles.

The Juvenile Courts

The juvenile courts must dispose of cases referred to them by intake divisions of probation departments, make detention decisions, deal with child neglect and dependency cases, and monitor the performance of juveniles who have been adjudicated delinquent or status offenders. The *parens patriae* philosophy, which has undergirded the juvenile court since its founding at the end of the nineteenth century, charges that juvenile judges treat rather than punish juveniles appearing before them. This treatment arm of the juvenile court generally does not extend to those committing serious crimes or persisting in juvenile offenses, however; such hard-core juveniles may be sent to training schools or transferred to the adult court.

Correction Departments

The agency responsible for the care of juvenile offenders sentenced by the courts is called a variety of names—one of the more popular ones is the Department of Youth Services. Juvenile probation departments supervise offenders released on probation by the courts, ensuring that they comply with the courts' imposed conditions of probation and refrain from unlawful behavior in the community. Day treatment and residential programs have the responsibility of preparing juveniles for their return to the community.

Training schools have similar responsibilities, but the administrators of these programs are generally also charged with deciding when each juvenile is ready for institutional release and with ensuring that residents receive their constitutionally guaranteed due process rights. Aftercare officers are delegated the responsibility of supervising juveniles who have been released from training schools to ensure that they comply with the terms of their

FIGURE 1–3
Basic Subsystem of the Juvenile Justice System

Subsystem	Function
Police	Maintaining order and enforcing the law
Juvenile Court	Disposing of cases referred to them by intake divisions of probation departments, supervising juvenile probationers, making detention decisions, dealing with cases of child neglect and dependency, monitoring the performance of youths who have been adjudicated delinquent or status offenders
Corrections	Caring for youthful offenders sentenced by the courts, supervising offenders released to probation by the courts, and using day-treatment and residential programs, as well as short- and long-term juvenile facilities, to prepare youths for release to the community

aftercare agreements and avoid unlawful behavior. See Figure 1–3 for the basic subsystem of the juvenile justice system.

Juvenile justice agencies, because they have been developed by more than fifty state and federal government legislative bodies, do differ rather significantly across the nation. The structure of the juvenile court, as well as its administrative responsibilities, varies widely from one state to the next. Most juvenile probation departments emphasize restitution and community service programs as conditions of probation, but some provide intensive supervision programs and may even have house arrest and electronic monitoring programs. Some states hire private agencies to implement community-based programs, and most states are increasingly using private institutional placements for status offenders. Finally, a number of organizational structures are in use to administer juvenile correctional institutions and aftercare services.

Much similarity exists between the juvenile and adult justice systems. Both consist of three basic subsystems and interrelated agencies. The flow of justice in both is supposed to be from law violation to police apprehension, judicial process, judicial disposition, and rehabilitation in correctional agencies. The basic vocabulary is the same in the juvenile and adult systems, and even when the vocabulary differs, the intent remains the same.

The following terms refer to both the juvenile and adult systems:

An **adjudicatory hearing** is a trial that can result in a conviction.

Aftercare is parole.

A **commitment** is a sentence to confinement.

Detention is holding in jail.

A **dispositional hearing** is a sentencing hearing.

Juvenile court officer is a probation officer.

A **minor** is a defendant.

A **petition** is an indictment.

A **petitioner** is a prosecutor.

A **respondent** is a defense attorney.

Taking into custody is the act of **arresting** a suspect.

Both the juvenile and adult systems are under fire to get tough on crime, especially on offenders who commit violent crimes. Both must deal with excessive caseloads and institutional overcrowding, must operate on fiscal shoestrings, and face the ongoing problems of staff recruitment, training, and burnout. Focus on Practice 1–3 further describes the common ground and differences between the juvenile and adult justice systems.

Focus on Practice 1–3
Similarities and Differences Between the Juvenile and Adult Justice Systems

SIMILARITIES

- Police officers use discretion with both juvenile and adult offenders.
- Juvenile and adult offenders receive Miranda and other constitutional rights at time of arrest.
- Juveniles and adults can be placed in pretrial facilities.
- The juvenile court the adult court's use proof beyond a reasonable doubt as a standard for evidence, except when a juvenile court hearing matters such as status offenses, beyond a reasonable doubt is not required.
- Plea-bargaining may be used with both juveniles and adult offenders.
- Convicted juvenile and adult offenders may be sentenced to probation services, residential programs, or institutional facilities.
- Boot camps are used with juvenile and about adult offenders.
- Released institutional juvenile and adult offenders may be assigned to supervision in the community.

DIFFERENCES

- Juveniles can be arrested for acts that would not be criminal if they were adults (status offenses).
- Age does not affect the jurisdiction of the adult court.
- Parents are deeply involved in the juvenile process but not in the adult process.
- Juvenile court proceedings are informal, whereas adult court proceedings are informal and open to the public.
- Juvenile court proceedings, unlike adult proceedings, are not considered criminal.
- Juvenile records are generally sealed once the age of majority is reached.
- Juvenile courts cannot sentence juveniles to jail or prisons, only adult courts issue such sentences.

CRITICAL THINKING QUESTIONS

How much harm would it do to juveniles if juvenile proceedings were abolished and juveniles were handled in adult court? What would the advantages be to juvenile offenders if they were handled with adult proceedings and procedures?

How Are Juvenile Offenders Processed?

The means by which juvenile offenders are processed by juvenile justice agencies are examined throughout this text. The variations in the juvenile justice systems across the nation make describing this process difficult. The process begins when the youth is referred to the juvenile court; some jurisdictions permit a variety of agents to refer the juvenile, whereas others charge the police with this responsibility. The more common procedure is that the youth whose alleged offense has already been investigated is taken into custody by the police officer who has made the decision to refer the juvenile to the juvenile court. After adjudication, a youth is placed in juvenile detention or moved out of detention and into probation, residential placement, or the adult system, and then released (see Figure 1–4).

The intake officer, usually a probation officer, must decide whether the juvenile should remain in the community or be placed in a shelter or detention facility. A variety of options exist for determining what to do with the youth, but in more serious cases, the juvenile generally receives a petition to appear before the juvenile court.

The juvenile court judge, or the referee in many jurisdictions, hears the cases of those juveniles referred to the court. The transfer of a juvenile to the adult court must be done before any juvenile proceedings take place. Otherwise, an adjudicatory hearing, the primary purpose of which is to determine whether the juvenile is guilty of the delinquent acts alleged in the petition, takes place. The court hears evidence on these allegations. The *In re Gault* case (see Chapter 6) usually guarantees to juveniles the right to representation by counsel, freedom from self-incrimination, the right to confront witnesses, and the right to cross-examine witnesses. Some states also give juveniles the right to a jury trial.

A disposition hearing takes place when a juvenile has been found delinquent in the adjudicatory stage. Most juvenile court codes now require that the adjudicatory and disposition hearings be held at different times. The number of dispositions juvenile judges have available to them varies from one jurisdiction to the next. In addition to the standard dispositions of warning and release, placement on juvenile probation, or adjudication to the department of youth services or corrections, some judges can place juveniles in a publicly or privately administered day treatment or residential program. Some jurisdictions even grant juvenile judges the authority to send a juvenile to a particular correctional facility.

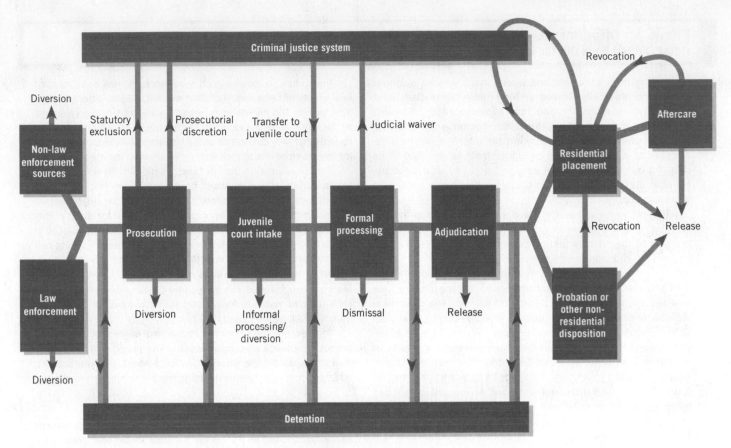

FIGURE 1–4

The Stages of Delinquency Case Processing in the Juvenile Justice System

Note: This chart gives a simplified view of case flow through the juvenile justice system. Procedures vary among jurisdictions.

Source: Howard N. Snyder and Melissa Sickmund, *Juvenile Offenders and Victims: 2006 National Report* (Washington, DC: Office of Juvenile Justice and Delinquency Prevention, 2006), 105.

A juvenile adjudicated to a training school is generally treated somewhat differently in small and large states. In small states with one training school for males and usually one for females, a youth adjudicated to a training school is usually sent directly to the appropriate school. But large states that have several facilities for males and perhaps more than one for females may send the youth to a classification, or diagnostic, center to determine the proper institutional placement. Training school residents currently are not confined for as long a period as they were in the past and are often released within a year. Institutional release takes place in a variety of ways, but a juvenile released from a training school is generally placed on aftercare status. To be released from this supervision, the juvenile must obey the rules of aftercare and must avoid unlawful behavior.

What Are the Most Widely Held Philosophies and Strategies on Correcting Juveniles?

Four basic correctional models exist in juvenile justice: the treatment model, the justice model, the crime control model, and the balanced and restorative justice model. These conflicting strategies handicap juvenile justice and are a major reason why no single policy or set of policies presently guide the handling of offenders. Indeed, nearly everyone has an opinion on what can be done to correct the behavior of law-violating youths; pet theories and folk remedies abound throughout society. In Focus on Offenders 1–4 there is the sad story of an individual who has been through the juvenile system and who is now waiting to be executed.

Focus on Offenders 1–4
It Just Did Not Work Out for Tony

Tony came from a background where there was an alcoholic father who physically abused all his children, especially Tony. The mother was passive and Tony experienced considerable neglect from her. However, Tony was not an easy child. He set his parents' bed on fire when he was five, with his father taking a nap. He then hid under the bed and had to be dragged out from under the bed by his father who woke up. He also stabbed his sister in the eye with scissors when he was also five.

Tony was referred to the welfare system at an early age. Nothing seemed to work with him, and he eventually was referred to the juvenile justice system. When programs in the community did not seem to control his behavior, he began his commitments to juvenile institutions. The major problem with juvenile institutional placements is that he did not stay at a facility long enough to accomplish any positive outcomes. He was what you called a "runner," and this began a process of sending him to more secure facilities. Finally, at sixteen-years-of-age, he ended up in the maximum-security facility of an urban state. The problem he faced was that this facility typically housed youths aged seventeen to twenty-one, and he found himself forced to deal with youths who were older and more aggressive than he was.

He did not have a positive experience, and it was decided to grant him an early release. Within a couple years, Tony was in a bar, and apparently intoxicated, was asked to leave by the bartender. He refused to leave; the bartender pulled out a gun, but before he could discharge it, Tony shot him first. He was convicted of murder and sent to prison for twenty years.

Prison has not been a good experience. He has been involved in a variety of behaviors, including assault, suicide attempts, and drug abuse. And he has been extremely unstable. As an example of the latter, he persuaded another inmate to take their anger out toward what they defined as unfair treatment by the state by sending the governor one of their fingers, which each inmate had cut off.

Then, because he did not have a cellmate, he was informed that a particular inmate would be moving in the following weekend. Knowing this inmate's reputation as one of the largest sexual victims in the prison (he apparently traded sex for drugs), Tony reacted. He said that he would kill this inmate if he was placed in his cell. He also sent a kite (letter) to the warden informing him what would happen if this inmate was placed in his cell.

When he was placed in his cell that Friday, Tony was true to his word. He stabbed him sixty-three times with a shank (small knife) he had made. Before prison staff could extract the inmate from his cell, he was dead.

Tony experienced physical abuse and neglect at home. His school experience was unsuccessful. The public welfare system failed him, as did the juvenile justice system. His years as an adult prisoner have been a disaster, leading to his current charge.

CRITICAL THINKING QUESTIONS

What could have been done to turn this young man around? With his early abusive background, do you believe the state should have given him a death sentence for a prison homicide?

Source: Experiences and knowledge that one of the authors has had with this individual over the span of his life course.

The Treatment Model

Parens patriae, the philosophical basis of the **treatment model**, emerged with the founding of the juvenile court. The state, represented by the juvenile court, was to deal with children differently than it did with adults by substituting a more informal and flexible procedure. In the juvenile court, a fatherly and benevolent juvenile judge would gently, and in a friendly manner, probe the roots of the child's difficulties. The court, acting in lieu of a child's parents, was to engage in individualized justice; delinquency was viewed as a symptom of some underlying personality problem.

The juvenile court, then, was to serve as a social clinic. Its task was to call up the scientific expert to provide the necessary treatment for the child. *Child-saving reformers*, a term used by Anthony Platt, were confident that the combination of *parens patriae* philosophy and the treatment provided by the scientific expert would lead to the salvation of wayward children.[34]

The treatment model, or rehabilitation model, is based on the belief that the basic mission of juvenile justice is to rehabilitate youthful offenders. The treatment model also proposes that the legal definition of delinquency should be broad and that victimless crimes and status offenses, as well as crimes against victims, should remain on the books. Proponents of this model do not believe in the frequent use of detention facilities; these facilities should be reserved for children who need special care and custody.

How Does the Treatment Model Work?

The mental, physical, and social needs of the child are the focus of the treatment model, and many rehabilitation efforts are implemented before the juvenile is processed into the system. Police officers may recommend community programs to youths and their parents that help youths in need with their specific problems. Intake officers, probation officers, prosecutors, judges, and aftercare officers also may either informally or formally request that juveniles—status as well as delinquent offenders—attend drug and alcohol, tutoring, anger management, and other after-school programs; youths who are institutionalized also often receive drug and alcohol, sexual offending, and other treatment modalities. The treatment model encountered considerable criticism in the late twentieth century, but it is experiencing a resurgence of research and interest in the early twenty-first century.

The Justice Model

The *parens patriae* philosophy has been challenged by due process philosophy since the very founding of the juvenile court. Those promoting the due process approach wanted to give juveniles better protection through due process provisions and procedural safeguards. In the 1970s, proponents of due process were troubled by the contradictions of juvenile justice philosophy and by the inequities and inadequacies of juvenile justice law, policy, and practice.[35] These reformers turned to David Fogel's **justice model** and its concept of **just deserts**. Fogel believes that both juvenile and adult offenders are volitional and responsible human beings and, consequently, deserve to be punished if they violate the law. The punishment they receive, however, must be proportionate to the seriousness of the offense. Fogel also proposed the end of the indeterminate sentence and parole, the initiation of uniform sentencing, and the establishment of correctional programming based solely on the compliance of inmates.[36] Fogel reasons, "If we cannot coercively treat with reliability, we can at least be fair, reasonable, humane, and constitutional in practice."[37]

How Does the Justice Model Work?

Proponents of the justice model are now advocating a number of changes to bring more fairness to juvenile justice:

- Limit the enormous discretion granted to juvenile justice practitioners.
- Divert increasing numbers of youthful offenders from the justice system to voluntary services.
- Remedy common deficiencies in due process to ensure greater fairness in the transactions among the justice system, the family, and the juvenile offender.
- Curb indeterminate sentencing practices of juvenile courts and give juveniles a fixed sentence by the court at the time of disposition.
- Decriminalize status offenses.
- Change the governing principle of sentencing to one of *proportionality*, which means that there must be a relationship between the seriousness of the offense committed and the severity of the sanction imposed.
- Make training schools safer and more humane.
- Allow programs offered in training schools to be voluntary in nature and to have nothing to do with the release of a youth.
- Require restitution and community service sanctions of more juvenile lawbreakers; these sanctions have the potential for fairness because they give youthful offenders opportunities to atone or make amends for the damage or harm they have inflicted on others.[38]

The mandatory sentencing law for violent juvenile offenders in the state of New York, the determinate sentencing law for juveniles in the state of Washington, and the institutional release policy adopted in the state of Minnesota are other indicators of the national acceptance of the justice model.

The Crime Control Model

The **crime control model** emphasizes punishment as the remedy for juvenile misbehavior. Punishment philosophy actually originated well before the eighteenth century, but it gained popularity in the 1970s because of the assumed rise of youth crime. Although this approach has had different connotations at various times, supporters today maintain that punishment is beneficial because it is educative and moral. Offenders are taught not to commit further crimes, whereas noncriminal citizenry receive a demonstration of what happens to a person who breaks the law; punishment, proponents believe, deters crime.

The supporters of punishment philosophy claim that the juvenile court has abandoned punishment in favor of individual rehabilitation. They argue for severity and certainty of punishment and advocate a greater use of incarceration. Other fundamental assumptions of punishment philosophy propose that those who become involved in unlawful behavior are abnormal and few in number; that this unlawful behavior reflects a character defect that punishment can correct; that punishment can be helpful in teaching a youth to be responsible, diligent, and honest; and that the deterrence of youth crime depends on the juvenile justice system apprehending and punishing youthful offenders with greater speed, efficiency, and certainty.

How Does the Crime Control Model Work?

The crime control model holds that the first priority of justice should be to protect the life and property of the innocent. Accordingly, proponents of this model support the police and are quick to isolate juvenile offenders, especially those who have committed serious crimes, in detention homes, jails, and training schools. The increased use of transfers to adult court and the adoption of mandatory sentencing laws specifying extended confinements for serious crimes are recent crime control policies. Many states are now using a combination of the crime control and justice models to deal with violent and hard-core juvenile offenders.

The Balanced and Restorative Justice Model

A traditional New Zealand approach to juvenile offending, the **balanced and restorative justice model**, is rapidly expanding throughout the United States and, indeed, throughout the world. "Balanced" refers to system-level decision making by administrators to "ensure that resources are allocated equally among efforts to ensure accountability to crime victims, to increase competency in offenders, and to enhance community safety." These three goals are summarized in the terms *accountability, competency,* and *community protection.*[39]

Accountability refers to a sanctioning process in which offenders must accept responsibility for their offenses and the harm caused to victims, and make restitution to the victims, assuming that community members are satisfied with the outcome. *Competency* refers to the rehabilitation of offenders, that is, when offenders improve their educational, vocational, emotional, social, and other capabilities and can perform as responsible adults in the community. *Community protection* refers to the ability of citizens to prevent crime, resolve conflict, and feel safe because offenders have matured into responsible citizens. Subsequently, the overall mission of the balanced and restorative justice model is to develop a community-oriented approach to the control of offenders rather than rely solely either on punishment by confinement or on individual rehabilitation through counseling. The juvenile justice system, in implementing this model, meets the needs of the community, the victim, and the offender in the most cost-effective manner possible. See Focus on Practice 1–5 for the objective, practice, and location of the balanced and restorative justice model.

How Does the Balanced and Restorative Justice Model Work?

This approach is an alternative to processing youths through the juvenile justice systems of their communities. Once a juvenile is identified as being a perpetrator of a delinquent act, a police officer, probation officer, community volunteer, or other designated person initiates the restorative process. The victim, the offender, the offender's family, a law enforcement representative, or a volunteer brings all the parties together to begin discussing the problem at hand.

This model, in other words, calls for a new framework of community organization and a restructuring of practitioner roles throughout the juvenile justice system. It calls for a new set of values that emphasize a commitment to all—the offender, the victim, and the community. Importantly, offenders are viewed as clients whose crime is a symptom of family breakdown, community disorganization, and community conflict, and these problems must be addressed if juvenile crime is to be reduced.

Focus on Practice 1–5
Balanced and Restorative Justice Model

Restorative justice intervention includes a wide variety of programs and practices that may be applied at virtually any point in the juvenile justice process, or in the community.

Objective/Focus	Practice	Location
Conflict resolution; prevention; peacemaking	Community mediation; alternative dispute resolution; school and neighborhood conferencing; victim awareness education; youth development	Schools; neighborhoods; churches; civic groups
Provide decision-making alternatives to formal court or other adversarial process for determining obligations for repairing harm	Victim offender dialog; family group conferencing circles; reparation boards: other restorative conferencing	Police and community diversion; court diversion; dispositional/sentencing alternatives; postdispositional planning; residential alternative discipline; conflict resolution; postresidential reentry
Victim and community input to court or formal decision making	Written or oral impact statement to court or other entity	Court; probation; residential
Provide reparative sanctions or obligation in response to crime or harmful behavior	Restitution; community service to victims; and payment to victims service funds	Diversion; court sanction; probation condition; residential program; postincarceration
Offender treatment; rehabilitation; education	Victim impact panels; victim awareness education; Mothers Against Drunk Driving panels; community service learning project designed to build offender competency and strengthen relationships with law-abiding citizens	Probation; residential facilities; diversion program; jails
Victim services and support groups	Counseling; volunteer support groups; faith community groups	Multiple settings
Community building	Family support and discussion groups	Neighborhood and community

Source: Gordon Bazemore, Jay S. Zaslaw, and Danielle Riester, "Behind the Walls and Beyond: Restorative Justice, Instrumental Communities, and Effective Residential Treatment," *Juvenile and Family Court* (Winter 2005), 58.

Comparison of the Four Models

The treatment model, or rehabilitation model, is most concerned that juvenile offenders receive therapy rather than institutionalization. The crime control model emphasizes punishment because it argues that juveniles must pay for their crimes. Proponents of this model support long-term, rather than short-term, confinements for juvenile offenders. The justice model strongly supports the granting of procedural safeguards and fairness to juveniles who have broken the law. Yet proponents of this model also believe that the punishment of juveniles should be proportionate to the gravity of their crimes. The balanced and restorative justice model also contends that juveniles have free will and know what they are doing and, therefore, should receive punishment for their antisocial behavior. The advantages of this model, according to its proponents, are that it includes the punishment approach of the crime control and justice models, supports the due process emphasis of the justice model, and places consequences on behavior to encourage juveniles to become more receptive to treatment.

Each of the models has supporters. The crime control model, or the hard line, is used with violent and repetitive juvenile offenders. The treatment model, or the soft line, is primarily used with status offenders and minor offenders. Some jurisdictions show support for the justice model in juvenile justice, but the balanced and restorative justice model is making the most extensive advances. Nevertheless, on a day-to-day basis, juvenile justice practitioners continue to pick and choose from each of the four models in designing how

TABLE 1–4
Comparison of Key Elements of the Rehabilitation, Justice, Balanced and Restorative, and Crime Control Models

Elements	Models			
	Rehabilitation	**Justice**	**Crime Control**	**Balanced and Restorative**
Theory of why delinquents offend	Behavior is caused or determined; based on positivism	Free will; based on the classical school	Free will; based on the classical school	Free will; based on the classical school
Purpose of sentencing	Change in behavior or attitude	Justice	Restoration of law and order	Community protection
Type of sentencing advocated	Indeterminate	Determinate	Determinate	Determinate
View of treatment	Goal of correctional process	Voluntary but necessary in a humane system	Ineffective and actually coddles offenders	Voluntary but necessary in a humane system
Crime control strategy	Use therapeutic intervention to eliminate factors causing crime	Provide fairness for victims, for offenders, and for practitioners in the system	Declare war on youth crime by instituting "get-tough" policies	Make juvenile offenders accountable for their behavior

they work with juvenile offenders. These conflicting approaches, as well as the intolerance of those who follow a different course of action, create inefficiency and confusion in juvenile justice. Table 1–4 compares the key elements of the rehabilitation, justice, balanced and restorative, and crime control models.

Themes in the Study of Delinquency

Before concluding this introductory chapter, it is important to discuss the three themes that flow through the text. The first theme is *delinquency prevention*. The second theme is the *use of evidence-based practice and juvenile justice*. The third theme is *juvenile justice and social policy.*

Delinquency Prevention

The prevention of delinquency is something that can be accomplished by effective social programs, or it may involve personal characteristics that shield young people from negative environmental influences. In terms of the individual level, one of the most important concepts in the area of delinquency prevention is **resiliency**. We know that many of today's youth face a host of negative influences in their lives—substance abuse, gang affiliations, teenage pregnancy, school violence, and many others. Despite these and other hardships, some youth remain resilient, that is they are able to persevere in the face of difficulty and become productive community citizens. Why is it that some youth thrive despite being in auspicious beginnings, while others do not?[40]

Youth are generally considered resilient when they are able to rely on apparently innate characteristics to fend off or recover from life's misfortunes. Some proponents contend that youth best learn human resiliency when they reside in environments that offer caring and supportive relationships, that hold high expectations for behavior and attitudes for themselves and others, and that provide opportunities for meaningful participation. Others believe that children who survived risky environments benefit in large part from personal qualities such as strong self-confidence, coping skills, and the ability to avoid risky situations. Some experts suggest that we are all born with the innate capacity for resilience through which we are able to develop social competence, problem-related skills, critical consciousness, sense of autonomy, and sense of purpose and accountability.

Evidence-Based Practices and Juvenile Justice

Evidence-based practices, as previously mentioned, are the most effective intervention in juvenile justice and are supported by evidence of achievement. Peter Greenwood's recent study of evidence-based practices or EBP, defines them as practice that "involves the use of scientific principles to access the various evidence on program effectiveness and develop principles for best practices in any particular field."[41] Evidence-based programs and their ways of assessing outcome-related evidence have been growing trends in the field of juvenile justice prevention and intervention for at least the past decade. For example, the OJJP offers 200 evidence-based prevention and intervention programs, encompassing the entire continuum of youth services. The online guide can be used to assist juvenile justice practitioners, administrators, and researchers seeking to enhance accountability, ensure public safety, and reduce recidivism. To stress its importance, nearly every chapter will include an example of an EBP.

Social Policy and Juvenile Justice

Social policy in juvenile justice is our third theme, one that inquires about what can be done to improve the quality of young people's lives, and to provide ideas for effectively treating and controlling youth crime. The Children's Defense Fund publication, titled *State of America's Children 2012,* is quick to remind us of the cost of society letting vast numbers of young people grow up without realizing their full potential.[42] To stay on the path to successful adulthood, the publication says that it is necessary to champion policy and programs that lift children out of poverty, protect them from abuse and neglect, and ensure their access to health care, quality education, and a solid moral and spiritual foundation. What this type of success requires is healthy communities, constructive peer relationships, and productive aftercare and summer programs, and positive role models. The pressing and exciting challenge for all of us is to design policy recommendations that provide helpful directions for daily work effectively with adolescents in general and with youth crime in particular.

Effective policy will merge when well-thought-out theoretical assumptions are supported by sound research. Another way to say this is that there are two basic tools of social science, research and theory, each helps to guide and direct the other. Research identifies appropriate variables for collecting data, helps to identify variables to be studied, analyzes related variables, and suggests new directions for theory development. Research collects and theory analyzes. Most importantly, policy recommendations will be taken more seriously by policymakers if they are based on sound theory and evidence-based practices. See Figure 1–5, on the relationship between research, theory, and social policy.

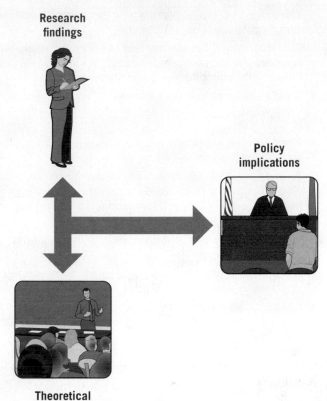

Research findings

Policy implications

Theoretical assumptions

FIGURE 1–5
The Relationship Between Research, Theory, and Social Policy

SUMMARY

LEARNING OBJECTIVE 1: Retrace the journey of juvenile justice in the United States.

- The influences affecting the juvenile justice system can be traced back to the Middle Ages.

- The common law tradition in England eventually concluded that children under age seven should not face legal penalties.

- However, the responsibility of children between ages seven and fourteen was determined by such considerations as the severity of the crime, maturity, capacity to distinguish between right and wrong, and evidence of blatant malice.

- The family was the source and primary means of social control of children in the colonial period.

- The concept of *parens patriae* gave the courts a legal basis for intervening in the lives of children.

- The premises of the *parens patriae* doctrine permitted the juvenile court to take charge of children in need so that the causes of their problems could be discovered and treated.

- The juvenile courts had to develop different procedures and terminology from those of the adult courts to achieve their goals.

- The attractiveness of the juvenile court philosophy resulted in almost all states setting up juvenile courts.

- Juvenile confinement goes back to the nineteenth century, when houses of refuge were established to separate juveniles from adult offenders in jails and prisons.

- The cottage system, in which residents were housed in separate buildings, usually included no more than twenty to forty juveniles per cottage.

- Later nineteenth-century juvenile institutions were called *reformatories* or *industrial schools.*

- Probation and aftercare were also early developments of juvenile justice; their focus was on treating youthful offenders in the community.

LEARNING OBJECTIVE 2: Summarize the history of juvenile confinement.

The history of juvenile confinement began with the house of refuge in the early 19th century, followed by the reformatory or training school. The collage system, in which residents were housed in separate facility, was a change in juvenile confinement. Another significant change in the final decades of the nineteenth century was the increased size of institutional populations.

LEARNING OBJECTIVE 3: Summarize the historical themes that guided the development of juvenile justice in the United States.

The historical themes of juvenile justice include discovering the child, increased authority of the state, reform and retrenchment, get-tough and go-soft approaches, threat of the dangerous poor, and the unsolvable nature of youth crime.

LEARNING OBJECTIVE 4: Present the structure and procedures of juvenile justice agencies in this nation.

- The juvenile justice system has been given the mandate to correct and control youthful offenders. The U.S. Constitution gives both the federal government and the states the authority to make laws and the mechanisms for enforcing the law. The primary laws with which this book is concerned are laws governing delinquent and criminal behaviors in the three subsystems—the police, the courts, and correction departments—that carry out the mandates of the laws.

- The juvenile is typically referred to the juvenile court, which first decides whether to leave the juvenile in the system or not. The juvenile court decides in what is called an adjudicatory hearing whether the juvenile is guilty of the delinquent acts alleged in the petition. A disposition hearing takes place when a juvenile has been found delinquent in the adjudicatory stage. A delinquent youth might be referred to probation or one of the residential programs in the community or might be referred to a training school.

LEARNING OBJECTIVE 5: Examine the various philosophies and strategies for correcting juvenile offenders.

- The treatment model is most concerned that juvenile offenders receive therapy rather than institutionalization.

- The justice model supports the granting of procedural safeguards and fairness to juveniles who have broken the law.

- The crime control model emphasizes punishment because it argues that juveniles must pay for their crimes. The crime control policies of the past twenty years have proposed a get-tough strategy, especially with violent juveniles.

- The balanced and restorative justice model called for a new framework of community organization and a new set of values that emphasizes a commitment to all—the offender, the victim, and the community.

- The conflicting philosophies and methods of correcting juvenile offenders make it difficult to succeed in correcting juveniles in trouble.

KEY TERMS

adjudicatory hearing, p. 17
aftercare, p. 17
aftercare officers, p. 4
arrest, p. 17
balanced and restorative justice
    model, p. 22
commitment, p. 17
cottage system, p. 10
crime control model, p. 21
dangerous poor, p. 14

detention, p. 17
dispositional hearing, p. 17
house of refuge, p. 9
just deserts, p. 21
justice model, p. 21
juvenile court officer, p. 17
least-restrictive approach, p. 14
minor, p. 17
parens patriae, p. 2

parole, p. 11
petition, p. 17
petitioner, p. 17
positivist, p. 5
resiliency, p. 24
respondent, p. 17
status offenders, p. 2
taking into custody, p. 17
treatment model, p. 20

GROUP EXERCISES

1. Write a single paragraph describing each of the following: the history of the juvenile court, probation, juvenile confinement, and aftercare. Critique and revise.
2. *Group Work:* Describe each of the juvenile justice agencies and their functions.

3. *Class Debate:* Divide the class into four groups. Each group will be assigned one of the four models found in juvenile justice today. Each group should learn its essentials and argue for its model as being the best model for the United States today. Groups may not compromise in the defense of their models.

REVIEW QUESTIONS

1. The juvenile justice system has devised four ways to deal with youth crime: the treatment model, the justice model, the crime control model, and the balanced and restorative justice model. Which do you think works the best? Why?
2. Why is justice so important to the juvenile justice system? How can the juvenile justice system become more just, fair, and effective?

3. What do you believe can be done about reconciling the different approaches to juvenile justice?
4. What do you think would be the result of abolishing the juvenile justice system and having the adult courts deal with all youthful offenders?

THE EFFECTIVE WORKER WITH JUVENILES

Passion is a key ingredient in working with juvenile offenders. For the worker who has passion, it is easier for the juvenile to believe that he or she cares, and that he or she is committed to having positive things happen in the juvenile's life. There is no question that some staff members are burned out or no longer care. It is simply a job and perhaps in their minds not a very good job. But for staff members who have passion, they will make a difference in the lives of many over the span of their lives.

NOTES

1. Mark W. Lipsey, James C. Howell, Marion R. Kelly, Gabrielle Chapman, and Darin Carver, *Improving the Effectiveness of Juvenile Justice Programs: A New Perspective on Evidence-Based Practice* (Washington, DC: Georgetown University, Center for Juvenile Justice Reform, 2010).
2. Ibid., 1.
3. S. Mihalic, K. Irwin, D. Elliott, A. Fagan, and D. Hansen, *Blueprints for Violence Prevention* (Washington, DC: U.S. Department of Justice, Office of Justice Programs, Office of Juvenile Justice and Delinquency Prevention, 2001); Office of Juvenile Justice and Delinquency Prevention, *Model Programs Guide (MPG)*, accessed at http://www.ojjdp.gov/mgg; and Substance Abuse and Mental Health Services Administration, *SAMHSA Bulletin: National Registry of Evidence-Based Programs and Practices* (Washington, DC: SAMHSA, 2009).
4. Leon Radzinowicz, *A History of English Criminal Law and Its Administration from 1750–1833* (London: Stevens and Sons, 1948), 14.
5. David Rothman, *The Discovery of the Asylum* (Boston: Little, Brown, 1971), 46–53.
6. Ibid.
7. Anthony M. Platt, *The Child Savers* (Chicago: University of Chicago Press, 1969), 121–36.
8. Ibid.

9. Ibid., 98.
10. Sanford J. Fox, "Juvenile Justice Reform: An Historical Perspective," *Stanford Law Review* 22, no. 6 (June 1970), 1187–239.
11. Rothman, *The Discovery of the Asylum.* See also Barbara M. Brenzel, *Daughters of the State* (Cambridge, MA: MIT Press, 1983) and Alexander W. Pisciotta, "Treatment on Trial: The Rhetoric and Reality of the New York House of Refuge, 1857–1935," *American Journal of Legal History* 29 (1985), 151–81.
12. Rothman, *The Discovery of the Asylum,* 53–54. For the origins of juvenile justice in California, see Daniel Macallair, "The San Francisco Industrial School and the Origins of Juvenile Justice in California: A Glance at the Great Reformation," *UC Davis Journal of Juvenile Law & Policy* 7 (Winter 2003), 1–60.
13. Hutchins Hapgood, *Autobiography of a Thief* (New York: Fox, Duffield, 1903), 71–72.
14. National Conference of Superintendents of Training Schools and Reformatories, *Institutional Rehabilitation of Delinquent Youth: Manual for Training School Personnel* (Albany, NY: Delmar, 1962).
15. For this same tendency in the State Industrial School for Girls in Lancaster, Massachusetts, see Brenzel, *Daughters of the State.*

16. John Augustus, *John Augustus: First Probation Officer* (Montclair, NJ: Patterson-Smith Company, 1972), 4–5.

17. Board of State Charities of Massachusetts, *Sixth Annual Report, 1869,* 269.

18. Robert M. Mennel, *Thorns and Thistles* (Hanover: University of New Hampshire Press, 1973), 140.

19. Homer Folks, "Juvenile Probation," *NCCD Proceedings, 1906,* 117–22.

20. Mennel, *Thorns and Thistles,* 142.

21. Frederick Howard Wines, *Punishment and Reformation: Rise of the Penitentiary System* (Boston: Thomas Y. Crowell, 1985), 222.

22. Barry Krisberg and James Austin, *The Children of Ishmael: Critical Perspectives on Juvenile Justice* (Palo Alto, CA: Mayfield, 1978), 569.

23. Thomas J. Bernard, *The Cycle of Juvenile Justice* (New York: Oxford University Press, 1992), 3.

24. Barry Krisberg et al., "The Watershed of Juvenile Justice Reform," *Crime and Delinquency* 32 (January 1986), 40.

25. National Crime Justice Association, *Juvenile Justice Reform Initiatives in the States, 1994–1996* (Washington, DC: Office of Juvenile Justice and Delinquency Prevention, 1997), 9.

26. Justice Policy Institute, Common Ground: Lessons Learned from'/Five States That Reduced Juvenile Confinement by More Than Half (Washington, DC: Justice Policy Institute, 2013).

27. Ibid.

28. See David Matza, *Delinquency and Drift* (New York: Wiley, 1964); Edwin M. Schur, *Radical Non-Intervention: Rethinking the Delinquency Problem* (Upper Saddle River, NJ: Prentice Hall, 1973).

29. Schur, *Radical Non-Intervention.*

30. Platt, *The Child Savers.*

31. Rothman, *The Discovery of the Asylum,* 78.

32. Ibid.

33. *Sourcebook of Criminal Justice Statistics—2009* (Washington, DC: Bureau of Justice Statistics, 2010).

34. Anthony M. Platt, *The Child Savers,* 2nd ed. (Chicago: University of Chicago Press, 1977).

35. Charles Shireman, "The Juvenile Justice System: Structure, Problems and Prospects," in *Justice as Fairness,* edited by David Fogel and Joe Hudson (Cincinnati: W. H. Anderson, 1981), 136–41.

36. David Fogel, *"…We Are the Living Proof…": The Justice Model for Corrections* (Cincinnati: W. H. Anderson, 1975).

37. Fogel, "Preface," in *Justice as Fairness,* viii.

38. Adapted from Shireman, "The Juvenile Justice System."

39. Adapted from D. Maloney, D. Romig, and T. Armstrong, "Juvenile Probation: The Balanced Approach," *Juvenile and Family Court Journal* 39 (1988), 5; G. Bazemore, "On Mission Statements and Reform in Juvenile Justice: The Case for the Balanced Approach," *Federal Probation* 56 (1992), 64–70. G. Bazemore, "What's 'New' about the Balanced Approach?" *Juvenile and Family Court Journal* 48 (1997), 2, 3.

40. Toney Bissett Ford, *A Glance Backwards:An Analysis of Youth Resiliency Through Autoethniological anf Life History, Ph.D Dissertation, 2010.*

41. Peter W. Greenwood andBrandon C. Welsh, "Promoting Evidence-Based Practice in Delinquency Prevention at the State Level: Principles, Progress, and Policy Directions," *Criminology & Public Policy* 22 (2012): 491–92.

42. Children Defense Fund, *The State of American Children* (Washington, DC: Children Defense Fund, 2012).

Measurement and Nature of Juvenile Crime

Karramba Production/Shutterstock

Learning Objectives

1. Summarize juvenile crime trends, and how the data is categorized, measured, and reported.

2. Describe the methods, l benefits, and limitations of self reporting.

3. Interpret the variables and patterns of offending.

4. Analyze evidence-based policy and the prevention of delinquency.

On December 11, 2013, Ethan Couch, a sixteen-year-old Texas teenager, received a ten-year probationary sentence for causing quadruple fatalities while driving his truck in an intoxicated state. He had previously pleaded guilty of intoxicated manslaughter and two counts of assault causing serious bodily injury. The crash occurred six months earlier while Couch was driving a Ford F3 50 pickup truck. Couch and two of his friends had stolen beer from a nearby Walmart and while fleeing the scene, rammed into a disabled vehicle that had been parked inside beside the road while going 70 mph Couch had a .24 blood alcohol content, which is triple the legal limit in Texas, and was also high on valium. The judge explained her seemingly light sentence by saying that Couch's wealthy parents had never taught him right from wrong. She may have been influenced by a psychologist who had interviewed Couch and entitled "Affluenza" as an affliction from which he suffered. Affluenza, a word the psychologist coined, was meant to indicate that some people are so financially privileged while growing up that they don't acquire the fundamental values that the rest of us have. At this writing, Couch remained at a juvenile detention center and his defense attorney continues to argue that he needs counseling, not hard time.[1]

Sensational crimes committed by juveniles, like that involving Couch have fueled public concerns over juvenile crime. Even greater concern is cited with misgivings miscarriages of justice seem to occur, and the 2013 Texas case discussed here fueled public outrage across the nation with many people questioning how a juvenile who had caused so much harm could end up with a relatively minor punishment.

Major Data Sources in Delinquency

Juveniles are studied by a wide variety of agencies. Traditionally, the **Uniform Crime Reports**, collated by the Federal Bureau of Investigation (FBI), were known as **official statistics** and were the primary source of our knowledge. Today, these data are referred to as the CIUS or *Crime in the United States*. During the past seventy-five years, however, many more data collection sources have been developed that contribute to our knowledge of juveniles and their problems. **Juvenile Court Statistics** were developed to show what happens to juveniles who come to the attention of authorities. Victimization surveys focus on "hidden" or non-reported crime. Other governmental agencies such as the National Center for Education Statistics, the National Clearinghouse on Child Abuse and Neglect, and the Office of Juvenile Justice and Delinquency Prevention also do research on juveniles. In addition, research funded by federal and state governments and private foundations takes place in private research institutes and in universities and hospitals across the nation. This chapter looks at these research efforts and their findings on children in trouble. Table 2–1 lists major sources of data about juvenile delinquency.

Uniform Crime Reports

The *Uniform Crime Reports* have been our major source of information since 1930 on the amount of crime in the United States. In an effort to better understand the nature and extent of crime, the International Association of Chiefs of Police recommended that national crime statistics be collected and reported. The FBI was chosen as the clearinghouse for these data, and police departments across the United States were requested to report all arrests to the FBI. This information is currently published by the FBI on both a quarterly and a yearly basis and is probably the most popular of all the crime statistics. Reports of offenses, however, are not always sent from the local police directly to the FBI. Some states have state reporting agencies; the local police report to the state agency, which, in turn, reports to the FBI.

The UCRs classify crimes into Part I and Part II offenses. This classification is used to differentiate very serious from less serious crimes for the purpose of national statistics.

Part I offenses include murder, rape, aggravated assault, robbery, burglary, larceny, auto theft, and arson. Part II offenses include all crimes not listed as Part I, such as simple assaults; buying, receiving, and possessing stolen property; carrying and possessing

TABLE 2–1
Major Sources of Data About Delinquency

Data Source	Sponsoring Agency	Type of Information	General Findings
Uniform Crime Reports program *National Crime Victimization Study*	Federal Bureau of Investigation Statistics	Arrest Statistics Interview data	Youth crime is widespread in U.S. society. The number of victimization discovered is much higher than the number of offenses reported to the police.
Juvenile Court Statistics	Office of Juvenile Justice and Delinquency Prevention	Delinquency cases processed in juvenile courts	Most youths come into juvenile court as a result of the filing of a petition or complaint.
Self-report surveys	Universities/ academic researchers and crime	Individual self-report involvement in delinquency	A large amount of hidden delinquency occurs and is not reported to the police.

weapons; fraud; forgery; and counterfeiting. All states classify these behaviors as crimes and call for their prosecution.

In addition to reporting arrest data, the UCRs provide data on the age, sex, and race of offenders, as well as on the amount of crime they commit. Information is available on whether the total amount of crime is increasing or decreasing, as well as on the amount of crime by size of city and by the gender and race of the offenders. In addition to the FBI, the Office of Juvenile Justice and Delinquency Prevention and the Bureau of Justice Statistics use these data in their analysis of juvenile crime.

In evaluating the measurement of the extent and nature of delinquency in this chapter, one of the important considerations is the **validity** and **reliability** of the data sources. *CUC S* data provides numerous problems. In terms of the validity, one of the most serious complaints is that the police can report on crimes that come to their attention. Many crimes are hidden or not reported to the police, therefore, the UCR Program vastly underestimates the actual amount of crime in the United States. Some critics also charge that because the police arrest only juveniles who commit serious property and personal crimes and ignore most of the other offenses committed by young people, the statistics tell us more about official police policy and practice and about the amount of youth crime. Moreover, youthful offenders may be easier to detect in the act of committing a crime than older offenders, with a resulting inflation of the rates for juveniles. Finally, there is a reliability issue: Do local police departments often manipulate the statistics that are reported to the FBI? The intent may be to make the problem appear worse or better, depending on the reporting agency's agenda.

The CIUS program examines the extent of juvenile crime; compares youth crime to adult crime; considers gender and rural variations in youth crime; and presents urban, suburban, and ruled differences in youth crime. Following are the chief findings of the CIUS 2012 data reporting on juveniles[2]:

1. Youth crime is widespread in U.S. society. For example, the CIUS 2012 data reveal that 968,534 juveniles under age eighteen were arrested that year. Youths between the ages of ten and seventeen constituted about 25 percent of the total population of the United States.[3] Of those arrested, 11.7 percent were arrested for violent crimes and 18 percent for property crimes.[4]

2. The percentages of total arrests involving juveniles are highest for curfew breaking, loitering, disorderly conduct, liquor law violations, drug abuse violations, vandalism, and larceny-theft.[5]

FIGURE 2–1
Juvenile Arrests

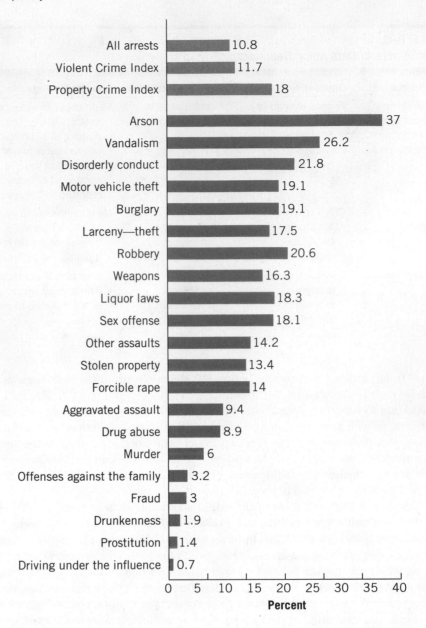

3. Juveniles are arrested for serious offenses as well. As Figure 2–1 indicates, Juveniles were arrested for 19.1 percent of all burglaries, 20.6 percent of robberies, 16.3 percent of weapons offenses, 6.0 percent of murders, and 9.4 percent of aggravated assaults in 2012.[6]

4. Juvenile murder rates increased substantially between 1987 and 1993. In the peak year of 1993, approximately 3,800 juveniles were arrested for murder; between 1993 and 2003, however, juvenile arrests for murder declined, with the number of arrests in 2012 (560) averaging less than one-fifth of the 1993 figure.[7]

5. Juvenile female arrests in 2012 represented 25.5 percent of all female arrests that year.[8]

6. As Figure 2–2 shows, not all types of juvenile crime are declining. Since 1980, for example, the number of juvenile arrests for minor assaults has almost tripled, while arrests for drug abuse violations and disorderly conduct have more than doubled.[9]

Juvenile Court Statistics

Most information about the number of children appearing before the juvenile court each year comes from the *Juvenile Court Statistics* publication, released annually by the Office of Juvenile Justice and Delinquency Prevention (OJJDP), an arm of the U.S. Department of Justice.

The number of children appearing before the juvenile court significantly increased from 1960 until the early 1980s, when it began to level off. It then started to rise again and continued to rise until the late 1980s, when it began to level off again. In 2014, OJJDP released 2010 delinquency data. Juvenile courts in the United States handled an estimated 1.4 million delinquency cases—a significant decline from 15 years earlier (Figure 2–3). Thirty-seven percent of these were property cases, 25 percent were person offenses, 26 percent were public order offenses, and 12 percent were drug offenses. The largest percentage of person offenses consisted of simple assaults, followed by aggravated assaults, and then robberies. Larceny-theft made up the largest number of property offenses, followed by burglary and vandalism; and obstruction of justice and disorderly conduct comprised the largest percentage of public order offenses.[10]

OJJDP describes what happens to the cases brought into the system. For example, 55 percent of the delinquency cases were petitioned. That is, these youths came into the juvenile court system as a result of someone filing a petition or issuing a complaint requesting the court to declare the youths delinquent or dependent or to transfer the youths to an adult court. In terms of nonpetitioned cases, 46 percent were informally handled cases in which authorized personnel for the court screened the cases prior to the filing of a formal petition and decided not to prosecute the offenders.[11] Figure 2–1 shows the case processing of delinquency cases in juvenile courts nationwide in 2009, and Figure 2–4 shows the general downward trend of offenses, and how these cases are processed.[12]

▲ White supremacists are potentially the most dangerous "home grown" terrorists in the United States. Many want to overthrow the U.S. Government.

A summary of the findings of the juvenile court statistics is as follows:

1. Older delinquents are referred to the court more often than are younger delinquents.

2. The number of cases appearing before the juvenile court increased until the mid-1970s, leveled off until the late 1980s, rose dramatically from the late 1980s to the mid-1990s, and then declined 11 percent to the 2008 level (see Figure 2–3).

3. Of status offenses, truancy and ungovernability rates peak at age sixteen, while liquor law violations increase continuously with age.

4. Males are more frequently referred to the juvenile court than are females.

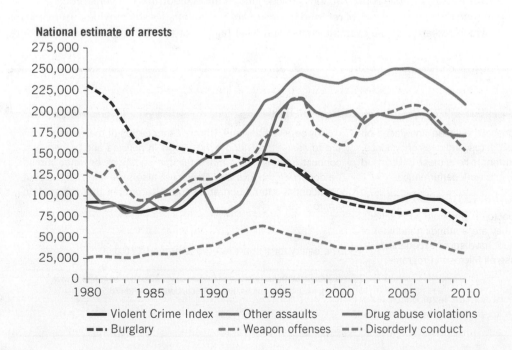

National estimate of arrests

Legend: — Violent Crime Index — Other assaults — Drug abuse violations --- Burglary --- Weapon offenses --- Disorderly conduct

FIGURE 2–2
Juvenile Arrests by Offense, 1985–2010.

Source: National Research Council, Reforming Juvenile Justice: A Developmental Approach (Washington, DC: National Academies Press, 2014), pp. 3–34.

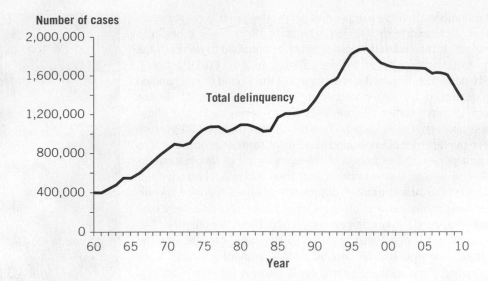

FIGURE 2-3
Delinquency Cases in Juvenile Courts,
1960–2010.

Source: Office of Juvenile Justice
and Delinquency Prevention,
Statistical Briefing Book.

5. Females are referred to juvenile court for truancy and ungovernability at about the same rate as males; across the board, female rates are increasing relative to male rates.

6. White males are referred to the juvenile court roughly in proportion to their numbers in the population; black males are referred to the juvenile court at rates highly disproportionate to their numbers in the population.

The findings of juvenile court statistics parallel those of the UCRs. The advantage of the court statistics, however, is that they reveal not only who the offenders are but also what types of dispositions are handed down. The juvenile court statistics are also able to track the number of offenders coming to the courts over specific periods of time and to follow trends in the changing characteristics of offenders and the dispositions handed down. The latter data are helpful in determining the success of suggested and mandated social policy changes that determine who should come to court and what should happen to them.

Juvenile court statistics do have serious limitations. The usual time lag in the publication of the statistics lessens their usefulness. In addition, these cases make up only a small percentage of the total number of juvenile offenses. Moreover, the data collected by the OJJDP represent only an estimate of the total number of juvenile crimes that come to the attention of juvenile courts. Finally, juvenile court statistics provide limited information about juvenile court transactions and the characteristics of referred juveniles. Yet these statistics still provide a useful means by which researchers can examine youths and what happens to them relative to juvenile court.

Court Referee
Preparation for the Job

This job will require that the person have a broad knowledge on juvenile cases, family law, judicial procedures, and rules of evidence. When preparing for this job, it is important to have these skills: good time management, high attendance, and work performance.

QUALIFICATION AND EDUCATIONAL REQUIREMENTS

A court referee usually has a Juris Doctor degree from a law school. Some states will also require that they are a standing member of that states bar association. They must have some experience with juvenile casework, and be able to use all Microsoft Programs.

DUTIES

The duties of a court referee are to analyze legal documents, organize information, and be able to present this information clearly both verbally and written. Other duties of the court referee are to assist the Friend of the Court in policies and procedures, conduct hearings, and make recommendations on what should be done with the juvenile. They must also have knowledge about confidential information and be able to protect that information appropriately.

SALARY

The salary for a court referee is around $70,140.

Source: "Job Descriptions," accessed November 18, 2014, http://www
.stclaircounty.org/offices/hr/jobdescriptions.aspx?id=76

Juvenile court processing for a typical 1,000 delinquency cases, 2009

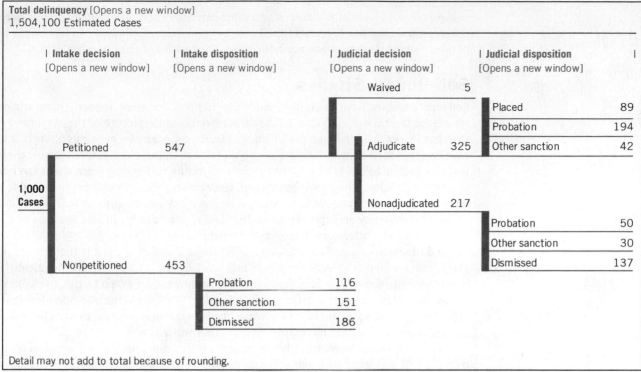

Detail may not add to total because of rounding.

- Cases referred to juvenile court are first screened by an intake department (either within or outside the court). The intake department may decide to dismiss the case for lack of legal sufficiency or to resolve the matter formally (**petitioned**) or informally (**nonpetitioned**).

   o In 2009, 55% (547 of 1,000) of all delinquency cases disposed by juvenile courts were handled formally while 45% (453 of 1,000) were handled informally.

   o Among nonpetitioned cases, 41% (186 of 453) were dismissed at intake, often for lack of legal sufficiency. In the remaining cases (59%, or 266 of 453), youth voluntarily agreed to informal sanctions, including referral to a social service agency, informal probation, or the payment of fines or some form of voluntary restitution.

- If the intake department decides that a case should be handled formally within the juvenile court, a petition is filed and the case is placed on the court calendar (or docket) for an adjudicatory hearing. On the other hand, the intake department may decide that a case should be removed from juvenile court and handled instead in criminal (adult) court. In these cases, a petition is usually filed in juvenile court requesting a waiver/transfer hearing, during which the juvenile court judge is asked to waive jurisdiction over the case.

   o In 2009, 59% (325 of 547 cases) of all formally processed delinquency cases resulted in the youth being adjudicated delinquent. In 40% (217 of 547) of these cases, the youth was not adjudicated and 1% (5 of 547) were judicially waived to criminal court.

- At the disposition hearing, the juvenile court judge determines the most appropriate sanction, generally after reviewing a predisposition report prepared by the probation department. The range of options available to a court typically includes commitment to an institution; placement in a group or foster home or other residential facility; probation (either regular or intensive supervision); referral to an outside agency, day treatment, or mental health program; or imposition of a fine, community service, or restitution.

   o Youth in 27% (89 of 325) of adjudicated delinquency cases were placed in a residential facility. In another 60% (194 of 325) of these adjudicated cases, youth were placed on formal probation.

FIGURE 2–4
Case Flow by Detailed Offense

What Are Self-Report Measures of Juvenile Crime?

Self-report and cohort studies are other main sources of information on delinquent behavior. Self-report studies ask juveniles to tell about offenses they committed in a previous period of time. Cohort studies utilize raw police files along with a variety of other data.

Self-Report Studies

Self-report studies have been used since the 1940s to measure hidden youth crime. The reason for their use is to obtain a fuller and more accurate picture of the amount of crime than can be obtained through the UCRs. The UCRs, for example, generally show that lower-class youths commit more crime than do middle- or upper-class youths. Researchers can test this finding by going to different classes of youths and asking them about the number and type of offenses they have committed. Researchers also can obtain considerable information on offender characteristics such as age, gender, and race, as well as on the amount of gang delinquency and the extent of drug and alcohol abuse. In this section, we look at self-reporting and offenders' demographic characteristics.

One of the most significant findings of all the self-report studies is that the amount of youth crime is much greater than that indicated by the UCRs. Indeed, practically every youth commits some type of crime. Very few, however, ever come to the attention of the authorities. This means that little reason exists for dividing youths into offenders and non-offenders, as many students of the juvenile justice system are prone to do. The self-report studies contradict or expand on the UCRs in other ways as well.

The logic of self-report studies is based on the fundamental assumption of survey research: "If you want to know something, ask." Researchers have gone to juveniles and asked them to admit to any illegal acts they have committed. However self-report studies have been criticized for three reasons. The research designs have been deficient, resulting in the drawing of false inferences, the varied nature of social settings in which studies have been undertaken make it difficult for investigators to test hypothesis, and the studies of validity and reliability are questionable.[13]

Validity and Reliability of Self-Report Studies

The most serious questions about self-report studies relate to their validity and reliability. In terms of validity, how can researchers be certain that juveniles are telling the truth when they fill out self-report questionnaires? The evidence tends to suggest that self-report studies underestimate the illegal behavior of seriously delinquent youth, because any juvenile who commits frequent offenses is less likely to answer questions truthfully than the youth who is less delinquent.[14]

Reliability gauges the consistency of a questionnaire or an interview; that is, the degree in which administration of a questionnaire or an interview will elicit the same answers from the juveniles where they are questioned two or more times. After analyzing the reliability of self-report studies, Hindelang and colleagues concluded that "reliability measures are impressive, and the majority of studies produce validity coefficients in the moderate to strong range."[15]

Self-Report Studies and Race

Official statistics tend to show that the differences between African Americans and whites are greater than self-report studies indicate. In looking at race, for example, David Huizinga and Delbert S. Elliott's examination of the National Youth Survey concluded that "there are few if any substantial and consistent differences between the delinquency involvement of different racial groups."[16] Two other national studies reported involvement in seventeen delinquent behaviors with similar frequencies, but further analysis of the data revealed that the seriousness of self-reported delinquency was slightly greater for African American males than for white males.[17] Elliott and Suzanne Ageton's study revealed that the offense rate was greater for African Americans because they were more likely to be involved in serious property crime and because they were more likely to be chronic or repeat offenders.[18]

Self-Report Studies and Gender

Similar discrepancies appear between official data and self-report studies when examining the gender of youthful offenders. Self-report studies show that female delinquency is higher than reported in official data.[19] Between 1989 and 1993, the relative growth in juvenile arrests for females was more than double the growth for males (23 percent vs. 11 percent). Self-report studies do show that females are less likely to be involved in serious crime.

Social Class and Delinquency

The finding that unlawful behavior is unrelated or only slightly related to a juvenile's social class is one of the most significant findings of self-report studies.[20] Travis Hirschi's survey of four thousand junior and senior high school students in Richmond, California, found little association between self-reported delinquencies and income, education, and occupation.[21] Richard E. Johnson, in redefining social class as underclass and earning class, added: "The data provide no firm evidence that social class, no matter how it is measured, is a salient factor in generating delinquent involvement."[22]

Elliott and Ageton's national study, however, found a different pattern when youths were asked how many times they had violated the law during the previous year. The average number of delinquent acts reported by lower-class juveniles, according to these researchers, exceeded that reported by working- or middle-class youths. Indeed, the average number of crimes against persons reported by lower-class youths was one and one half times greater than that reported by working- or middle-class youths.[23]

Focus on Research 2–1
Highlights from the Denver, Pittsburgh, and Rochester Youth Surveys

DENVER

The Denver study follows 1,527 boys and girls from high-risk neighborhoods in Denver who were seven, nine, eleven, thirteen, and fifteen years old in 1987. In exploring the changes in the nature of delinquency and drug use from the 1970s to the 1990s, the Denver study's findings are as follows:

- Overall, there was little change in the prevalence rates of delinquency, including serious delinquency and serious violence. However, the prevalence rate of gang fights among males doubled (from 8 to 16 percent).
- The level of injury from violent offenses increased substantially.
- The prevalence of drug use decreased substantially: alcohol, from 80 to 50 percent; marijuana, from 41 to 18 percent; and other drug use, from 19 to 4 percent.
- The relationships between drug use and delinquency have changed in that a smaller percentage (from 48 to 17 percent) of serious delinquents are using hard drugs other than marijuana, and a greater percentage (from 27 to 48 percent) of hard drug users are serious offenders.
- More than half (53 percent) of the youth in the study ages eleven through fifteen in 1987 were arrested over the next five years.

PITTSBURGH

The Pittsburgh study, a longitudinal study of 1,517 inner-city boys, followed three samples of boys for more than a decade to advance knowledge about how and why boys become involved in delinquency and other problem behaviors. Its chief findings are as follows:

- There were no differences between African American and white boys at age six, but differences gradually developed, the prevalence of serious delinquency at age sixteen reaching 27 percent for African American boys versus 19 percent for white boys.
- As prevalence increased, so did the average frequency of serious offending, which rose more rapidly for African American boys than for white boys.
- The onset of offending among the boys involved in serious delinquency occurred by age fifteen, when 51 percent of African American boys and 28 percent of white boys committed serious delinquent acts.
- The boys generally developed disruptive and delinquent behavior in an orderly, progressive fashion, with less serious problem behaviors preceding more serious problem behaviors.
- Three groups of developmental pathways were identified that displayed progressively more serious problem behaviors:

  Authority Conflict: Youths on this pathway exhibit stubbornness prior to age twelve, then move on to defiance and avoidance of authority.

  Covert: This pathway includes minor acts, such as lying, followed by property damage and moderately serious delinquency.

  Overt: This pathway includes minor aggression followed by fighting and violence.

(continued)

ROCHESTER

The Rochester study, a longitudinal study of 1,000 urban adolescents, investigates the causes and consequences of adolescent delinquency and drug use by following a sample of high-risk urban adolescents from their early teenage years through their early adult years. Its chief findings are as follows:

- Attachment and involvement were both significantly related to delinquency. Children who were more attached to and involved with their parents were less involved in delinquency.
- The relationship between family process factors and delinquency was bidirectional—poor parenting increased the probability of delinquent behavior, and delinquent behavior further weakened the relationship between parent and child.
- The impact of family variables appeared to fade as adolescents became older and more independent of their parents. Weak school commitment and poor school performance were associated with increased involvement in delinquency and drug use.
- Associating with delinquent peers was strongly and consistently related to delinquency, in part because peers provide positive reinforcements for delinquency. There is a strong relationship between gang membership and delinquent behavior, particularly serious and violent delinquency.

CRITICAL THINKING QUESTIONS

What do the findings of these three studies have in common? How do they differ? What would you say are the most important findings overall?

Sources: Katharine Browning, Terence P. Thornberry, and Pamela K. Porter, "Highlights of Findings from the Rochester Youth Development Study," *OJJDP Fact Sheet* (Washington, DC: Office of Juvenile Justice and Delinquency Prevention, 1999); Katharine Browning and Rolf Loeber, "Highlights from the Pittsburgh Youth Study," *OJJDP Fact Sheet* (Washington, DC: Office of Juvenile Justice and Delinquency Prevention, 1999); and Katharine Browning and David Huizinga, "Highlights from the Denver Youth Study," *OJJDP Fact Sheet* (Washington, DC: Office of Juvenile Justice and Delinquency Prevention, 1999).

Evaluation of Self-Report Studies

The realization that official statistics on juvenile delinquency have serious limitations led to a growing reliance on the use of self-report studies. These studies have revealed the following conclusions:

1. A significant amount of undetected delinquency exists in the United States, and police apprehension is low—probably less than 10 percent.
2. Juveniles in both the middle and lower classes are involved in considerable illegal behavior.
3. Not all hidden delinquency involves minor offenses; a significant number of serious crimes are committed each year by juveniles who elude apprehension by the police.
4. The differences between the offenses of African Americans and those of whites are less visible in self-reports than in official statistics.
5. Girls commit more delinquent acts than official statistics indicate, but boys commit more delinquent acts and commit more serious youth crimes than girls do.

Thinking like a Correctional Professional

You are a district judge. A thirty-year-old public school teacher appears before you. She is accused of having sex with two male high school students, both of whom are juniors, and she has pleaded guilty. The teacher is six months pregnant and has been divorced for a number of years.

What will be your sentence? What are the most important factors leading you to your sentence? Is it important that you make an example of her so that other similar cases will not take place in nearby school districts?

Victimization Surveys

In 1972, the U.S. Bureau of the Census began victimization studies to determine as accurately as possible the extent of crime in the United States. This type of data was needed because the UCRs measured police activity, that is, the number of arrests that police made, not the actual amount of crime committed. The volume of "hidden crime" has long been known to be great, because many crimes go unreported to the police. The **National Crime Victimization Survey** was set up to overcome this problem, and it gives policy makers a better idea of just how much crime is actually committed.

The *National Crime Victimization Survey* is conducted annually by the Bureau of Justice Statistics and administered by the U.S. Census Bureau. The 2012 survey shows that persons twelve years or older suffered more than 18 million crime victimizations, of which nearly 15 million were property crimes, 5.2 million were violent crimes, and 1 more than 11 million were crimes of theft.[24] Overall, the number of victimizations discovered was much higher than the number of offenses reported to the police. Figure 2-5 shows changes in reported property and violent crime victimization rates between 1999 and 2010. Data from these individuals reported by the NCR were used to measure all crimes—whether or not reported to the police—in the previous six-month period. To collect the data, representatives of the Bureau of the Census interviewed all household residents twelve years of age or older in the selected sample.

The *National Crime Victimization Survey* reported that in 2012, juveniles were highly overrepresented in comparison to other age groups in the population of those victimized. Juveniles between the ages of twelve and fourteen experienced the highest rape victimization rate of any age group for all violent crimes, and youths between the ages of fifteen and seventeen have the next highest rate, with rates dropping as the victims' age increased. Data also showed that adolescents are more likely than adults to commit violent crimes against peers and to report knowing their assailants. Crimes against adolescents are also less likely to be reported to the police than are crimes against adults.[25]

Within the adolescent population, males are more likely than females to become victims of violent crime, but females are much more likely to be victims of sexual assault (see Figure 2-6). The survey also revealed that African Americans are several times more likely than Caucasians to be victims of violence overall, including rape, sexual assault, aggravated assault, and robbery.[26]

Victimization surveys are not as widely used in analyzing youth crime as are the other means of measuring youth crime, but they do add to what is known about delinquency in the United States. Some of the principal findings of victimization surveys are as follows:

1. Much more crime is committed than is recorded.

2. The discrepancy between the number of people who say they have been victimized and the number of crimes known to the police varies with the type of offense.

3. The probability of being victimized varies with the type of crime and one's place of residence. The centers of U.S. cities are the more probable sites of violent crimes.

4. Juveniles are more likely to be victimized than any other age group.

Victimization studies do have limitations: information on status offenses is not included, victims may forget the victimization they experienced, or victims may state that a specific crime took place within the research year when it took place before or after that period.

What Are the Dimensions of Law-Violating Behaviors?

A century of study has enabled researchers to identify variables and patterns that are important to the understanding of juvenile crime. The age of onset, escalation of offenses, specialization of offenses, desistance from crime, and transition to adult crime all help focus attention on some key patterns in juvenile crime and provide some guidelines for understanding the causes of crime and the recidivism of offenders.

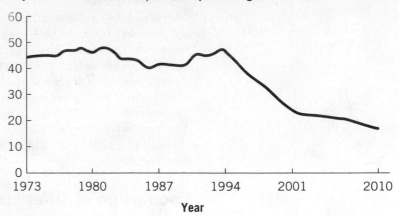

Adjusted victimization rate per 1,000 persons aged 12 or older

FIGURE 2-5
Juvenile Victimization in Recent Years

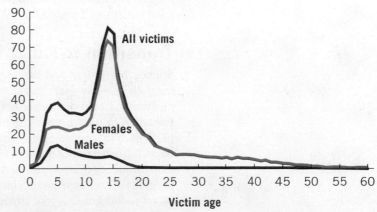

Victims (per 1,000 total sexual assault victims)

FIGURE 2-6
Victimization and Assaults

Age of Onset

Several studies have found that the earlier the juveniles began law-violating behaviors (the **age of onset**) the more likely they were to continue such behaviors. Marvin E. Wolfgang, Terence P. Thornberry, and Robert M. Figlio followed a 10 percent sample of Cohort I (of the Philadelphia cohort study) to the age of thirty and found that the average number of offenses tended to decline almost uniformly as the age of onset increased.[27] Alfred Blumstein, David P. Farrington, and Soumyo Moitra also showed that one of the factors predicting who became chronic offenders was offending at an early age.[28] Farrington further found that those who were first convicted at the earliest age (ten to twelve years) consistently offended at a higher rate and for a longer time period than did those who were first convicted at later ages.[29]

Escalation of Offenses

The findings on **escalation of offenses** (an increase in the number of crimes committed by an individual) are less consistent than those on age of onset. Official studies have typically found that the incidence of arrest accelerates at age thirteen and peaks at about age seventeen, but this pattern is less evident in self-report studies. For example, Ageton and Elliott found that the incidence of some offenses, such as assault and robbery, increased with age, whereas that of others peaked between ages thirteen and fifteen.[30]

Specialization of Offenses

The findings on **specialization of offenses** (the tendency to repeat one type of crime) are more consistent than those on escalation. The cohort studies, especially, revealed little or no specialization of offenses among delinquents.[31] Some evidence exists, however, that specialization is much more typical of status offenders. Susan K. Datesman and Michael Aickin's examination of a sample of status offenders found that the majority, regardless of gender and race, were referred to court within the same offense category 50 to 70 percent of the time. Females, especially white females, were referred to court for the same offenses, a sizable proportion of them for running away.[32]

Desistance from Crime

Desistance from crime, or the age of termination of delinquency, has become a recent concern of researchers. A major problem in establishing desistance is the difficulty of distinguishing between a gap in a delinquent career and true termination. Crime-free intervals are bound to be present in the course of delinquent careers. Two of the most popular theories of desistance are (1) the maturation and aging out of deviance, which suggests that individuals pursue a conventional lifestyle when they deal with the undesirability of continuing with unlawful activities; and (2) the decision to give up or continue with crime is based on a person's conscious reappraisal of the costs and benefits of criminal activity. See Table 2–2 for the dimensions of delinquent behavior.

Transition to Adult Crime

Studies have identified three groups of criminal offenders. One group offends only during their juvenile years; a second group offends only during adult years; and a third group persistently offends during both periods.[33] Some scholars argue that juvenile offenders' **transition to adult crime** is due to their prior participation in unlawful activities. This prior participation, according to this position, reduces inhibitions against engaging in future unlawful behavior. Other scholars contend that some individuals have a higher propensity to delinquency than do others and that this higher propensity persists over time. This higher propensity is related to such factors as poor parental supervision, parental rejection, parental criminality, delinquent siblings, and low IQ.[34] For an examination of chronic offenders, the group of youthful offenders who violate the law more frequently and seriously and are more likely to go on to adult crime, see Focus on Offenders 2–2.

TABLE 2–2
Dimensions of Delinquent Behavior

Dimensions of Behavior	Finding	Consensus
Age of onset	It is the best predictor of length of continuity of delinquent behavior.	Mixed
Escalation of Offenses	Offense studies have generally found that the instance of arrest accelerates at age 13 and peaks about age 17.	Mixed
Specialization	The majority of studies have found little or no specialization.	Fairly strong
Chronic offender	A small group of offenders commits the most serious offenses.	Strong
Youth crimes and adult criminality	Some childhood factors have been identified as contributing to the continuity of criminality.	Very mixed
Lengths of criminal careers	Careers tend to be longer for violent offenses, for those with early convictions, and for minority offenders.	More studies are needed to determine outcomes.

Evidence-based practices (EBPs) in juvenile justice are featured throughout this text. EBP forms an important part of the knowledge of what we know and do not know about the efficacy of juvenile justice programs. The EBP feature for this chapter, however, alerts the reader to the limits of these best practice research programs.

Focus on Offenders 2–2
Chronic Offenders: Notes on Their Backgrounds

The **chronic offender** is known by many labels: *serious delinquent, repeat offender, violent offender, dangerous offender, hard-core delinquent,* and *career delinquent.* Whatever the label, the predominant characteristics of these youths are their commitment to crime and their involvement in one crime after another, often very serious crimes against persons and property. Their initial participation in crime constitutes the budding of a lifestyle centered on violence and "making it big" in the criminal world. Chronic offenders expect to engage in criminal careers for at least several years, if not for the rest of their lives.

Chronic offenders become committed to criminal careers through one of two routes. In the first, noncriminal and situational offenders move from casual involvement with other offenders on the streets, to being processed with them through the system, to perceiving crime as a way of life, and finally to being willing to stand up for this involvement. Usually these youths have been picked up by the police many times, have been in courts and detention halls several times, and have had one or more institutional stays. The decisions they make at each stage move them closer to a delinquent career.

The second route is quite different. Some youths become absorbed in crime before they have contact with the justice system. These offenders often grow up in a ghetto area and, surrounded by vice and crime, become involved, along with peers, in unlawful acts at an early age. Frequently, they come from impoverished families. They tend to feel that life is a struggle and that only the strong survive; therefore, they are always on guard against being hurt or exploited by others, and they develop a hostile and suspicious view of the world around them. They seem to accept a commitment to crime without any apparent episodes of decision making.

Chronic offenders typically come from lower-class backgrounds and in many cases have grown up in urban pockets of poverty. They most often are minority males who have lived on the streets with insufficient parental support and with a history of failure in social institutions. An inability to function in school either in acceptable academic performance or in satisfactory relationships with teachers and peers characterizes their school experiences. A history of school dropout is followed by a pattern of unemployment. Part of this inability to find jobs is the lack of marketable skills. These juveniles contribute to the disturbingly high rates of unemployment among urban African Americans.

The attitudes of chronic offenders, of course, do vary. Some are more bitter or angry than others, and this variation seems to be affected greatly by the amount of love and acceptance they received at home and the injustices they experienced. In addition, some chronic offenders have more hope than others. Youths with

(continued)

histories of drug addiction generally do not demonstrate the positive attitudes of those without such histories. Chronic offenders who are closest to institutional release, not surprisingly, are more hopeful than those who face long periods of confinement. Chronic offenders who have developed positive goals for the future are also more hopeful than those who lack such goals. Finally, the more the chronic offenders see life as a "give me" experience, the less they seem able to develop positive relationships with others or to pursue noncrime options.

Prevention of Delinquency

Positive Youth Development (PYD) is a comprehensive way of thinking about adolescents that challenges the traditional deficit-based perspective (which holds that adolescents become delinquent by virtue of some personal flaw) by pointing out that youth can sometimes thrive in the presence of multiple risk factors. It provides an alternative model and prefers approaching adolescents and their issues. Supporters of this model claim that traditional approaches to the problems of young people and the society" interventions that are intended to address them are based on a deficit—based perspective. Instead, PYDD advocates say that youth development activities at organizations should build on youths' resistance and competencies. PYD uses the term *resilience* (introduced in chapter 1) to describe the qualities that support healthy adolescent development in the face of adversity.

Evidence-Based Practice
Evidence, Emotions, and Criminal Justice: The Limits to Evidence-Based Policy

In 2008, Australian Prime Minister Kevin Rudd, in addressing the heads of agencies and members of the senior executive of the Commonwealth Public Service, set out as one of his goals a "robust, evidence-based policy-making process" that would lead to government by reason rather than ideology, "by facts rather than fads."

In making this commitment, the prime minister was joining a long line of politicians and other policy makers who had shared similar ideas before him. In one way or the other, evidence-based policy is as old as the state itself. For example, Davies, Nutley, and Smith have charted its history from Bacon's seventeenth-century vision of the New Atlantis where "policy is formed by knowledge, truth, reason, and facts." Evidence-based policy can be described as an approach that "helps people make well-informed decisions about policies, programs, and projects by putting the best available evidence from research at the heart of policy development and implementation."

There is no question that the phenomenon of evidence-based policy has truly arrived. Evidence-based policy and practice have spawned dozens of specialist journals, and evidence-based institutes, generally attached to universities, have also flourished in recent times. The more self-conscious approaches to evidence-based policy in criminology can probably be traced to the development of an evaluation literature, especially the meta-analysis evaluation studies of correctional effectiveness. The theory of evidence-based policy, however, has been most fully developed in the field of crime prevention where the cycle of experimentation/evaluation/improvement has been most widely used and resourced.

Reasons exist to explain why the rational model in itself is inadequate to describe the policy process:

- *Economic and financial factors:* In view of the limits on resources, the decision for policy makers is not just "What works," but "How much does it cost and can we afford it?"
- *Time and tactical versus strategic factors:* Decision makers often operate in conditions of uncertainty and must make their decisions within strict time constraints that may be related to budget cycles, electoral cycles, or institutional requirements.
- *Lack of a research-oriented culture:* There may not be a culture in the organization that understands the nature of research and its role in policy development.
- *Habit, tradition, and bureaucratic logic:* It is more comfortable to hold to the old rather than venture out into the new.
- *Politics:* Decision makers have the right to reject or ignore evidence if there are other more pressing or politically convincing reasons to act in a particular way.

In the field of policy studies, the role of emotion in the shaping of governmental decisions must be taken into account. The point is made that criminal justice policies are more likely to be adopted if they recognize the importance of the roles of emotions, symbols, faith, belief, and religion in the criminal justice system.

CRITICAL THINKING QUESTION

What insights does this paper leave to the person committed to using evidence-based practices in juvenile justice?

Source: Arie Freiberg and W. W. (Kit) Carson, "Evidence, Emotion and Criminal Justice: The Limits to Evidence-Based Policy," paper presented before the New South Wales Bureau of Crime Statistics and Research, 40th Anniversary Symposium, February 18–19, 2009.

From the perspective of PYD, adolescents are seen not as objects need to be acted upon, but as self-directed, independent individuals who may deserve special care and who merit the autonomy and dignity accorded to other members of the community. The concepts of PYD appeal why do you propose that youth will flourish and develop when they are connected to the right mix of relationships, opportunity cobblers, and social-action assets? The concepts PYD propose that youths will develop and flourish when they are connected to the right mix of relationships, opportunities, and social assets.[35]

The PYD approach has long been present in the field of juvenile justice and its influence can be seen in many prevention programs implemented throughout the nation. Recently, however, the principles of P1 ID were championed using federal resources to include the backing of the White House through the helping of American Youth initiative, launched by the Bush administration. The final report of the White House Task Force for disadvantaged youth highlighted research that showed that healthy adolescent development requires youth to have "caring adults in their lives, opportunity to learn marketable skills,…and opportunities to contribute meaningfully in their communities and society."[36]

The basic principles of P1 ID practice all:

- Youth developments must strive to enhance individual and community capacities. One is not possible without the other.
- Youth development is predicated on youths exercising meaningful choices over the programs in which they participate.
- Youth developments must break down racial/ethnic, gender, disability, sexual orientation, and class barriers and stereotypes.
- Youth developments must build bridges between community-based organizations, formal and informal.
- Youth development activities must transform the communities in which youths' live.
- Youth developments must provide participants with an opportunity to learn and at the same time to have fun.
- Youth developments must product provide use with opportunity to serve their communities.
- Youth developments must provide youths with the necessary knowledge and skill that can be converted into meaningful lifelong employment.
- Youth developments must actively integrate as many core elements as possible into all activities.[37]

PYD seems to be a particularly desirable approach for prevention programs as well as for those youths accused of less serious and nonviolent offenses, and who make up three quarters of the youths referred annually to juvenile justice authorities in the United States.

Juvenile Justice and Social Policy

Of the most important issues facing juvenile justice at the present time is the continued reduction of youth violence. The national epidemic of youth violence began in the mid-1980s, peaked in the 1990s, and then began to decline. There is common agreement that this outburst of youth violence was as deadly as it was because more guns were carried and used than ever before. Homicide death rates of males to seventeen years old triple, primarily because of gun assaults.[38]

The studies also reported the following findings:

- Youths who carried guns were more likely to live in communities that have a high presence of gun ownership.
- Youths who lived in communities with high rates of violence were more likely to carry guns than those who lived in communities with low rates of violence.
- Youths who carried guns were significantly more likely to engage in serious assaults and robberies than those who did not have guns.
- Youths who sold large amount of drugs at an early age were more likely to carry guns than those who did not sell drugs.

- Youths who were dealing in large amounts of drugs and money that could be stolen were more likely to carry guns because they believed that gun carrying was necessary to protect themselves and their investment.

- Youths who were heavy drug users were also more likely to carry guns because they believed that buying drugs from armed drug dealers made it necessary for them to be armed themselves.

- Youths who were members of gangs had a higher probability of carrying a hidden gun than those who were not members of gangs.

- Youths who were chronic offenders and were involved in gangs played some part in most youth homicides, both as offenders and as victim.

The police have played a major role in the decline of guns use by juveniles. Their efforts have resulted in the reduction of firearm violence in Atlanta, Boston, Detroit, Indianapolis, Los Angeles, and St. Louis. The Boston Gun Project had been one of the most successful projects; the two main elements of Operation Ceasefire were a direct law enforcement attack on firearms traffickers supplying juveniles with guns and an attempt to generate a strong deterrent to gang violence. Youth homicides decreased dramatically following the first day of intervention in May 1996 and have remained below to the present.[39]

The office of Juvenile Justice and Delinquency Prevention (OJJDP) implemented the partnership to Reduce Juvenile Gun Pilot Program to put focus on gun violence and juveniles.

FIGURE 2–7
Reduced Gun Violence

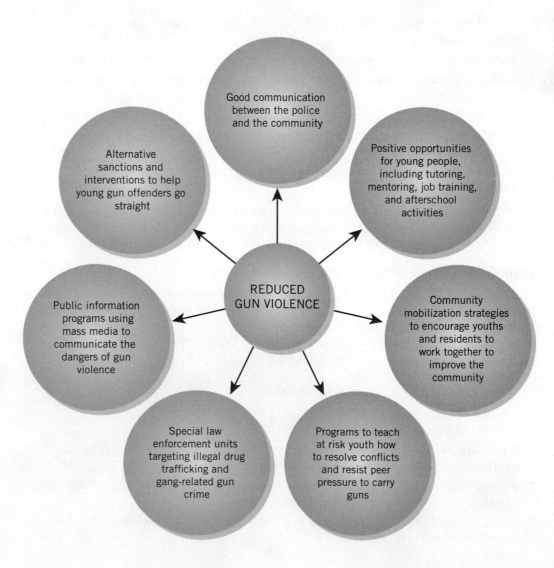

Gun, ownership, possession, and carrying guns have led to violence and drug transactions in schools and gangs. After examining 400 gang violence programs throughout the United States, it was decided that the implementation of the seven strategies shown in Figure 2–7 would be required if the program is to achieve its goals.[40]

SUMMARY

LEARNING OBJECTIVE 1: Summarize juvenile crime trends and how the data is categorized, measured, and reported.

The *Uniform Crime Reports, Juvenile Court Statistics, National Crime Victimization Data*, and self-report surveys are the major sources of data on juvenile crime.

Official statistics have contributed important findings about youth crime in American society:

- Juveniles commit a disproportionate number of property and violent offenses.

- Lower-class youths are involved in slightly more frequent and more serious offenses than are middle-class youths.

- African American youths commit more frequent and more serious offenses than do white youths.

- Urban youths commit more frequent and more serious offenses than do suburban or rural youths.

- A small group of youthful offenders, primarily lower-class minority youths, commit at least half of the serious offenses in urban areas.

- The interventions by the juvenile justice system frequently make youths worse rather than better.

The findings of unofficial studies of juvenile lawbreaking include the following:

- Self-report studies have revealed that most youths are involved in delinquent behavior and that almost 90 percent of delinquent acts are undetected or ignored.

- Self-report studies also indicate that girls commit more delinquent acts than are recorded in official accounts of delinquency, but boys still appear to commit more serious crimes than girls do.

- Victimization surveys reveal nearly four times as many victims each year as the UCR statistics show.

- Surveys also reveal that juveniles are more likely than adults to become victims.

- Together, these unofficial measurements of delinquency add to what is known officially about juvenile crime in the United States. As we continue to seek out the parameters of youth crime, important data are being developed in the area of drug use, and comprehensive data are beginning to emerge on school violence and bullying.

LEARNING OBJECTIVE 2: Describe the methods, benefits, and limitation of self reporting.

In self reporting studies, juvenile tell about offenses they committed in a previous period. A major benefit of self report studies is that it is possible to obtain a more complete picture of the amount of crime that could be obtained through the UCRs data.

Self report studies have been helpful in discovering the relationship between race, gender, and social class and juvenile offending. The most serious weaknesses about self-report studies relate to their validity and reliability. in terms of validity, how it is possible to be certain that juveniles are telling the truth when they fill out self-report questionnaires? Also, there seems to be some evidence that juveniles who have committed more serious behaviors are less likely to answer questions truthfully than those youths who are less delinquent.

LEARNING OBJECTIVE 3: Interpret the variables and patterns of offending.

The most important factors in understanding the variables and patterns of offending are age of onset, escalation o offenses, specialization of offenses, desistance from crime, and transition to adult crime.

The evidence is mixed on some of these variables, but together they constitute the most important dimension of delinquent behavior. The latter two, desistance from crime and the transition to adult crime, are the most important to researchers because they examine those who are exiting from youth crime and those who are going on to adult crime.

LEARNING OBJECTIVE 4: Analyze Evidence-Based Policy and the Prevention of Delinquency.

Evidence-based policy is examined throughout this text and it constitute an important means to evaluate and improve juvenile justice programs and practices. But there are limits to evidence-based policy, especially because the rational model is inadequate to fully describe the policy process and the role of emotion with policy makers cannot be dismissed.

The section on the prevention of delinquency examines positive youth development (PYD) Instead of a deficit-based perspective which holds that youths become delinquents because of some personal flaw. PYD advocates say that youth development activities and organizations build on youths' resistance and competencies.

KEY TERMS

REVIEW QUESTIONS

1. What do the UCRs generally show about youth crime in the United States?
2. What do juvenile court statistics show about youth crime in the United States?
3. What can self-report studies tell us that official accounts of youth crime cannot?
4. What do you believe the connection is between the maltreatment of children in their homes and on the streets and their involvement in crime and delinquency?

GROUP EXERCISES

1. *Group Work:* First, identify and describe the different types of research methodologies used to collect data on crime and offenders. After discussions die down, you may open your books and spell out in considerably more detail the different types of research methodologies used to collect data.
2. *Group Work:* First, all groups are, without looking at the data in the text, to discuss with each other the findings of the different research methods. After initial discussions, open the text and describe the findings of the different research methodologies.
3. *Writing to Learn:* Write on one or more of the following topics: the UCRs, victimization surveys, self-report studies, or cohort studies. Critique and revise.
4. *Class Debate:* Divide the class into two parts. Assign one group to argue the benefits and advantages of the UCRs, victimization studies, and *Juvenile Court Statistics* in understanding crime. Assist the other group to argue, supported by the chapter's introductory comments by Dr. Zahn and her excerpt in *Voices of Delinquency: A Researcher Speaks Out*, that the data on school and family victimization are the most worthwhile data for use in juvenile justice.
5. *Writing to Learn:* Write on the nature of juvenile victimization in the school and in the family (about 10 minutes for a paragraph on each). Critique and revise.

WORKING WITH JUVENILES

The ability to listen is an Important skill in working with juveniles. It may take time for the youth to open up to you, but when he or she they does, it is necessary to listen carefully. Many times youths wanted to talk to someone, but they never had anyone who would listen to them.

NOTES

1. Philip Caulfield, "The Rich Kid Who Killed 4 in Drunken Car Crash Spared Jail," *New York Times*, December 11, 2013; "Texas Teen Gets Probation for DU Crash that Killed Four," *Toronto Sun*, December 11, 2012.
2. Federal Bureau of Investigation, *Crime in the United States,* 2010, accessed at http://www.fbi.gov/about-us/cjis/ucr/crime-in-the-u.s/2010/crime-in-the-u.s.-2010/persons-arrested.
3. Ibid., Table 41.
4. Ibid.
5. Ibid., Table 38.
6. Ibid., Table 41.
7. Ibid., Table 32.
8. Ibid., Table 40.
9. Ibid., Table 32.
10. Adapted from *Juvenile Court Statistics 2009* (Pittsburgh, PA: National Center for Juvenile Justice, 2012), accessed May 1, 2012, at http://www.ojjdp.gov/ojstatbb/court/qa06201.asp?qaDate=2009. Special thanks goes to Benjamin Adams for his assistance in directing the authors to these data sets. Special thanks goes to Benjamin Adams for his assistance in directing the authors to these data sets.
11. Ibid.
12. Ibid.
13. Michael J. Hindelang, Travis Hirschi, and Joseph P. Wise, *Measuring Delinquency* (Beverly Hills, CA: Sage, 1981), 22.
14. Ibid.
15. Ibid., 129.
16. David Huizinga and Delbert S. Elliott, "Juvenile Offenders: Prevalence, Offender Incidence, and Arrest Rates by Race," *Crime and Delinquency* 33 (April 1987), 208, 210; Franklin W. Dunford and Delbert S. Elliott, "Identifying Career Offenders Using Self-Report Data," *Journal of Research in Crime and Delinquency* 21 (February 1984), 57–82, 215.
17. J. R. Williams and Martin Gold, "From Delinquent Behavior to Official Delinquency," *Social Problems* 20 (1972), 202–29; Martin Gold and David J. Reimer, *Changing Patterns of Delinquent Behavior Among Americans*

13 to 16 Years Old (Ann Arbor, MI: Institute for Social Research, University of Michigan, 1974).

18. Delbert S. Elliott and Suzanne S. Ageton, "Reconciling Race and Class Differences in Self-Reported and Official Estimates of Delinquency," *American Sociological Review* 45 (February 1980), 103.

19. Gary Jensen and Raymond Eve, "Sex Differences in Delinquency: An Examination of Popular Sociological Explanations," *Criminology* 13 (1976), 427–88; Michael Hindelang, "Age, Sex, and the Versatility of Delinquent Involvements," *Social Problems* 18 (1979), 522–35; James F. Short, Jr. and F. Ivan Nye, "Reported Behavior as a Criterion of Deviant Behavior." *Social Problems* 5 (Winter 1957–1958).

20. Short and Nye, "Reported Behavior as a Criterion of Deviant Behavior," 211; F. Ivan Nye, James Short, Jr., and Virgil Olsen, "Socio-Economic Status and Delinquent Behavior," *American Journal of Sociology* 63 (1958), 381–89; Robert Dentler and Lawrence Monroe, "Social Correlates of Early Adolescent Theft," *American Sociological Review* 26 (1961), 733–43.

21. Travis Hirschi, *Causes of Delinquency* (Berkeley: University of California Press, 1969).

22. Richard E. Johnson, "Social Class and Delinquent Behavior: A New Test," *Criminology* 18 (May 1980), 91.

23. Elliott and Ageton, "Reconciling Race and Class Differences."

24. Jennifer Truman, *Criminal Victimization, 2010* (Washington, DC: Bureau of Justice Statistics, 2011).

25. Ibid.

26. Ibid.

27. Marvin E. Wolfgang, Terence P. Thornberry, and Robert M. Figlio, eds., *From Boy to Man, from Delinquency to Crime* (Chicago: University of Chicago Press, 1987), 37, 39.

28. Alfred Blumstein, David P. Farrington, and Soumyo Moitra, "Delinquency Careers: Innocents, Amateurs, and Persisters," in *Crime and Justice: An Annual Review*, 6th ed., edited by Michael Tonry and Norval Morris (Chicago: University of Chicago Press, 1985), 187–220.

29. D. P. Farrington, "Offending from 10 to 25 Years of Age," in *Prospective Studies of Crime and Delinquency*, edited by K. T. Van Dusen and S. A. Mednick (Boston: Kluwer-Nijhoff, 1983).

30. Suzanne S. Ageton and Delbert S. Elliott, *The Incidence of Delinquent Behavior in a National Probability Sample of Adolescents* (Boulder, CO: Behavioral Research Institute, 1978).

31. See Wolfgang et al., *Delinquency in a Birth Cohort* and Hamparian et al., *The Violent Few*.

32. Susan K. Datesman and Michael Aickin, "Offense Specialization and Escalation Among Status Offenders," *Journal of Criminal Law and Criminology* 75 (1984), 1260–73.

33. See Wolfgang et al., *From Boy to Man*, 21.

34. Daniel S. Nagin and Raymond Paternoster, "On the Relationship of Past to Future Participation in Delinquency," *Criminology* 29 (May 1991), 163, 165.

35. Jeffrey A. Butts, *Beyond the Tunnel Vision: Addressing Cross-Cutting Issues That Impact Vulnerable Youth* (Chicago: University of Chicago: Chapin Hall Center for Children, 2008).

36. *White House Task Force Final Report*, October 2003, 11.

37. Melvin Delado, *New Frontier for Youth Development in the Twenty-First Century* (New York: Columbia University Press, 2008), 164.

38. Alan J Lizotte, Melvin D. Krohn, John C. Howell, Kimberly Tobin, and Gregory J. Howard, "Factors Influencing Gun Varying Among Young Urban Male Over the Adolescent-Young Life Course," *Criminology* 28 (2000), 811–34.

39. Ibid.

39. David Kennedy, Anthony Braga, and Anne M. Pichi, *Reducing Gun Violence: The Boston Gun Project's Operation Ceasefire* (Washington, DC: National Institute of Justice, 2011).

40. Office of Juvenile Justice and Delinquency, *Partnership to Reduce Gun Violence Programs*, accessed December 22, 2012, at http/wwwojjd.gov/pubs/96/juvgung.htm.

Causes of Juvenile Crime

David Grossman/Alamy

Learning Objectives

1. Summarize the principles and influences of the classical school of criminology.
2. Describe biological theories of juvenile crime and delinquency.
3. Describe psychological theories of juvenile crime and delinquency.
4. Describe sociological theories of juvenile crime and delinquency.
5. Explain why delinquency across the life course is important in studying theories of juvenile crime.
6. Summarize integrated theories of juvenile crime and delinquency.

A few years ago, researchers at Shippensburg University in Pennsylvania released results of a study showing that unpopular first names are frequently associated with juvenile delinquency for children of all races.[1] The researchers concluded that unpopular names are probably not the direct cause of crime but are instead correlated with socioeconomic factors that increase the tendency toward juvenile crime, such as disadvantaged home environment, low income, place of residence, and acquisition of cultural values supportive of delinquency. At the same time, it is possible to imagine that some people are unconsciously influenced by the need to live up to their name. The study's authors reviewed other literature that showed that job applicants with certain first names were more likely to receive callbacks from potential employers, even when their skills and other qualifying attributes were similar to those of other job candidates. The authors suggested that juveniles with unpopular names may be treated differently by their peers, making it more difficult for them to form positive relationships and that they may turn to crime or delinquency when their names result in a negative employment bias. Finally, as noted by the study authors, their findings have "potential implications for identifying . . . who may engage in disruptive behavior or relapse into criminal behavior."[2]

I n this chapter, we offer some possible explanations for juvenile crime. In contrast to the unconscious influence exerted by unpopular first names, described in the chapter's opening story, some authors suggest that much delinquency is caused not by factors beyond the offender's control but by a conscious thought process that considers the cost and benefits of particular behavior and once with some degree of planning and foresight goes on for reasons whether the behavior is desirable or not.

On the other hand, if something as simple as first names can impact people's behavior, then they might not be able to make fully conscious choices. This kind of deterministic view—that delinquents cannot stop themselves from committing socially unacceptable behavior because of some overpowering influence—build on your perspective known as **positivism**, a major theoretical position in criminology.

However, whether talking about youth crime arising from free will, biological or psychological inferiority, social causes, or integrated explanations (two or more existing theories), it is clear that any particular theory only accounts for some of the reasons for juvenile offenses. Some explanations are more powerful than others in explaining youth crime, but even the most powerful amounts to only a small piece in the larger puzzle of juvenile offending.

The association between criminal behavior and the rationality of crime has its roots in the eighteenth-century classical school of criminology. More recently, a number of approaches to the rationality of crime, especially the rational choice theory, have emerged.

Classical School of Criminology

Cesare Beccaria and Jeremy Bentham were the founders of the classical school of criminology. These scholars viewed humans as rational creatures who are willing to surrender enough liberty to the state so that society can establish rules and sanctions for the preservation of the social order.

In 1763, Cesare Bonesana Beccaria, Marquis of Beccaria, then only twenty-six and just out of law school, published *On Crimes and Punishment*. This essay was read avidly and translated into the languages of Europe.[3] Beccaria based the legitimacy of criminal sanctions on the social contract. The authority of making laws rested with the legislator, who should have only one view in sight: "the greatest happiness of the greatest number." Beccaria also saw punishment as a necessary evil and suggested that "it should be public, immediate, and necessary: the least possible in the case given; proportioned to the crime; and determined by the laws."[4] He then defined the purpose and consequences of punishment as being "to deter persons from the commission of crime and not to provide social revenge. Not severity, but certainty and swiftness in punishment best secure this result."[5]

FIGURE 3–1
Founders of the Classical School

1747	1764	1780
Charles de Secondat, Baron De Montesquieu argued against severe punishments for crime in the book, *On the Spirit of the Laws.*	**Cesare Bonesana, Marquis of Beccaria** developed the notion of the social contract, and suggested that the purpose of punishment should be "to deter persons from the commission of crime and not to provide social revenge."	**Jeremy Bentham** contended that punishment would deter criminal behavior, provided it was made appropriate to the crime.

In 1780, the Englishman Jeremy Bentham published *An Introduction to the Principles of Morals and Legislation*, which further developed the philosophy of the classical school. Believing that a rational person would do what was necessary to achieve the maximum pleasure and the minimum pain, Bentham contended that punishment would deter criminal behavior, provided it was made appropriate to the crime. He stated that punishment has four objectives: (1) to prevent all offenses if possible, (2) to persuade a person who has decided to commit an offense to commit a less rather than a more serious one, (3) "to dispose [a person who has resolved upon a particular offense] to do no more mischief than is necessary to his purpose," and (4) to prevent the crime at as small a cost to society as possible.[6] See Figure 3–1.

The basic theoretical constructs of the classical school of criminology were developed from the writings of Beccaria and Bentham:

- Human beings were all looked on as rational creatures who, being free to choose their actions, could be held responsible for their behavior. This doctrine of **free will** was substituted for the widely accepted concept of theological determinism, which saw humans as predestined to do certain actions.

- Punishment was justified because of its practical usefulness, or utilitarianism. No longer was punishment acceptable on the grounds of vengeful retaliation or as expiation on the basis of superstitious theories of guilt and repayment. The aim of punishment was the protection of society and its dominant theme was deterrence.

- The human being was presumed to be a creature governed by a **felicific calculus** oriented toward obtaining a favorable balance of pleasure and pain.

- A rational scale of punishment was proposed that should be painful enough to deter the criminal from further offenses and to prevent others from following his or her example of crime.

- Sanctions should be proclaimed in advance of their use; these sanctions should be proportionate to the offense and should outweigh the rewards of crime.

- Equal justice should be offered to everyone.

- Proponents of the classical school urged that individuals should be judged by the law solely for their acts, not for their beliefs.

According to the principles of the classical school then, juveniles who commit serious crimes or continue to break the law are presumed to deserve punishment rather than treatment, because they possess free will and know what they are doing. Their delinquencies are viewed as purposeful activity resulting from rational decisions in which the pros and cons are weighed and the acts that promise the greatest potential gains are performed.[7]

Rational Choice Theory

Rational choice theory, largely borrowed primarily from the utility model in economics, is one of the hottest present-day topics in criminology. This approach makes the assumption that the delinquent chooses to violate the law and has free will. In its pure form, rational choice theory is reviewed, at least in part, as an extension of the deterrence doctrine found in the classical school to include incentives as well as deterrence and to focus on the rational calculation of payoffs and costs before delinquent and criminal acts are committed.[8]

Lawrence E. Cohen and Marcus Felson are guided by ecological concepts and the presumed rationality of offenders in developing a **routine activity approach** for analyzing crime rate trends and cycles. This approach links the dramatic increase in crime rates since 1960 to changes in the routine activity structure of U.S. society and to a corresponding increase in target suitability and a decrease in the presence of "guardians," such as neighbors, friends, and family. The decline of the daytime presence of adult caretakers in homes and neighborhoods is partly the result of a trend toward increased female participation in the labor force.[9]

Steven F. Messner and Kenneth Tardiff used the routine activities approach to help interpret patterns of homicides in Manhattan (New York City) and found that the routine activities approach does indeed provide a useful framework for interpreting the social ecology involved in urban homicides. They found that people's lifestyles affected their chances of being victimized. People who tended to go out frequently were more often victimized by strangers, whereas those who preferred to stay at home were more likely to be killed by someone they knew.[10]

▲ The purchasing of drugs between two adolescents. Is this rational behavior?
Marie-Reine MATTERA/Glow Images

In sum, rational choice theory in criminology has recently moved away from the strictly rational, reasoning model of behavior to a more limited and constrained role for rational thought. Rational choice theory does not even assume that all or even most delinquent or criminal acts result from clear, planned, well-informed, and calculated choices.[11] It can still be argued, of course, that the rational choice model places more emphasis on rationality and free will than do other theories of delinquent behavior and that this degree of rationality is not present in most juvenile crimes.[12]

Rational Choice and Delinquency

Some youthful offenders clearly engage in delinquent behavior because of what they see as a low risk of such behavior. Hence, some delinquency can be interpreted as a form of problem-solving behavior in response to the pressures of adolescents. Finding themselves struggling with issues of perceived control, seeking positive self-evaluation, and facing the negative impact of others who punish, sanction, or reject them, delinquents solve such problems by deriving short-term pleasures from delinquent involvements.[13] Conversely, offenders may also decide on rational grounds that the risk of continued delinquent behavior is not justified by the rewards. Even more to the point, most persistent offenders appear to desist from crime as they reach their late teens or early twenties, claiming that continued criminality is incomparable with the demands of holding a full-time job or settling down to marriage and the family. Desistance from crime, or maturing out of crime, is a process of deciding that the benefits of crime are less than the advantages of ceasing to commit crime.

Yet, important issues arise when assuming too much rationality in delinquent behavior. Rational choice theory is based on the notion that delinquent behavior is planned—at least to some degree. Planning has to do both with (1) formulating a scheme or a procedure for doing something before doing it or having an intention of acting and (2) assessing the possible alternative courses of action available, choosing a particular course, and constructing a complex set of facts to achieve the intended result. But many studies of delinquency have reported that most delinquent behavior is not planned; spur of the moment decision making most frequently characterized juvenile wrongdoing.[14]

The concept of rationality also assumes that individuals have free will and are not controlled by their emotions, but many youngsters do not appear to have such control. Youths who are mentally ill or who engage in obsessive compulsive acts, such as compulsive arsenics, kleptomaniacs, or sex offenders, seem to be held in bondage by their emotions. Furthermore, in examining the actual process of rational choice, it is apparent that there are degrees of freedom for all juveniles and that juveniles' rationality is contextually oriented. The notion of degrees of freedom suggests, then, that delinquents "are neither nearly wholly nor completely constrained but fall somewhere in between."[15] Because the ability to make rational decisions and act on them depends to a considerable degree on the social situation, delinquents do have some control over their actions in some situations but in others they may have little or no control.

Emory University professor Robert Agnew's examination of hard and soft determinism led him to conclude that freedom of choice varies from one individual to another. It is dependent on factors—such as biological, psychological, or social nature—that exist prior to the choices that arise. For example, one individual may be forced to choose between two different alternatives because of psychological limits but another may have six different alternatives available to him or her because that person is less limited in his or her perceptions. The latter, Agnew says, has greater freedom of choice.[16]

Why Do We Punish?

The purpose of punishment has changed over time. What purpose is served when a fellow human being suffers punishment? After all, punishment involves applying pain, often long after the evil deed has been committed. At its core, criminal punishment results in harm to another human being—something that is in opposition to the moral values of modern society. But nonetheless, criminal punishment is considered justified because it is applied by a duly authorized governmental body on someone who has violated the laws of society. Yet, how can a practice that results in the loss of personal liberty and freedom be justified in a nation such as ours? Punishment is considered justified in modern society for the following reasons:

- *Punishing law violators provides beneficial consequences.* Although it can be harsh and demeaning, punishment of all violators is believed to create benefits from all abiding citizens. Both the threat and application of criminal punishment are cost-effective means to an end: protecting the public, preventing disorder, and reducing social harm.

- *Punishment is deserved.* Criminal sanctions are justified because those who voluntarily break the law forfeit some of the rights claimed by citizens. They are made blameworthy: their wrongdoing justifies treatment that under other circumstances would be considered coercive and, or, a violation of civil rights. And according to **just desert** philosophy, punishment is justified only when it confirms to what the guilty deserve, no more and no less.

- *Punishment expresses public outreach.* Criminal punishment is a method of expressing public outrage over the commission of a hideous crime. Because such wrongdoing provokes anger and sorrow, the public demands the perpetrator suffer to "pay for their sins."

- *Punishment teaches a lesson.* By punishing wrongdoers, the state demonstrates its disapproval of their behavior and in so doing, teaches them not to repeat their misdeeds. Just as a parent punishes a misbehaving child, so she won't repeat her behavior, so does the government punish a juvenile who violates its rules. The educative effect of punishment is not lost on the general population, which learns from the mistakes of others.

- *Punishment helps maintain the government, the social structure, and society.* A state cannot survive unless it maintains a set of rules that creates, supports, and protects its structure and process. As a government becomes more structured, the rules are formalized into laws designed to control behavior that threatens the state security and well-being. The law provides that people may be corrected or punished if they engage in socially prescribed wrongs—the conduct is condemned as wrong and threatens social norms.

Goals and Philosophy of Punishment

While criminal punishments are ideally designed to maintain the social order, there is no single vision of who should be punished, how the sanctions should be administered, and the ultimate goals that justify the application of punishment. Today the object of criminal punishment can be grouped into seven distinct areas: general deterrence, specific deterrence, in capitation, rehabilitation, retribution/just desserts, restoration, and equity/restitution.

General Deterrence

Deterrence is the goal of punishment designed to prevent others from committing similar crimes. The public application of punishment produces a **general deterrent effect**, designed to signal the community at large that crime does not pay. The logic is quite simple. By severely punishing those juveniles convicted of crime, others who are contemplating delinquency will be frightened, deterred, and discouraged from their planned actions.

Specific Deterrence

The philosophy of specific deterrence focuses on the fact the individual offender should learn first-hand that crime does not pay when he or she experiences harsh criminal penalties. What this position suggests is that the suffering caused by punishment shall inhibit future criminal activities. Although a few research efforts have found that punishment can have significant specific deterrence on future criminal behavior, these studies are balanced by research that has failed to uncover specific deterrent effects.

Incapacitation

Another goal of punishment is to incapacitate dangerous people so that they don't have the opportunity to harm others. Offenders are sentenced to a training school to restrain them physically, so during the time they are confined, society is protected, a concept known as incapacitation.

Rehabilitation

The rehabilitation aspect of sentencing suggests that people who violate the law are the victims of society. They had been mistreated by their families, forced to live in poverty, or suffered some life trauma, which through no fault of their own has forced them into a life of crime. They will refrain from further criminal activity if they can be successfully helped and treated rather than condemned and punished.

Retribution/Just Desserts

A retributionist position is that punishment is justified if and only if it is deserved because of a past crime. Similarly, the theory of just deserts holds that it is unfair to deprive a person of liberty as a consequence of committing a criminal act for any other reason than the act they engaged in deserves to be punished

Restorative Justice

Restorative justice goal of sentencing is designed to reintegrate the criminal offender back into the community. Restorative justice has its roots in the concept of report preparation, sometimes something done or paid to make amends for harm or loss.

Beginning with a brief introduction to the theoretical constructs of the positivist school, we examine the biological, psychological, and sociological explanations of delinquency and crime in this section.

Development of Positivism

According to **positivism**, human behavior is but one more facet of a universe that is part of a natural order, but human beings can study behavior and discover how natural laws operate. Two positions diverge at this point of natural law. One view states that because a natural order with its own laws exists, to change human behavior is impossible. The other view

> ### TABLE 3–1
> ### Three Assumptions of the Positivist Approach
>
> - First, the character and personal backgrounds of individuals explain delinquent behavior. Positivism, relegating the law and its administration to a secondary role, looks for the cause of deviancy in the actor.
>
> - Second, the existence of scientific determinism is a critical assumption of positivism. Delinquency, like any other phenomenon, is seen as determined by prior causes; it does not just happen. Because of this deterministic position, positivism rejects the view that the individual exercises freedom, possesses reason, and is capable of making choices.
>
> - Third, the delinquent is seen as fundamentally different from the nondelinquent. The task then is to identify the factors that have made the delinquent a different kind of person. In attempting to explain this difference, positivism has concluded that wayward youths are driven into crime by something in their physical makeup, by aberrant psychological impulses, or by the meanness and harshness of their social environment.

is that just as laws operate in the medical, biological, and physical sciences, laws govern human behavior, and these laws can be understood and used. The causes of human behavior, once discovered, can be modified to eliminate or ameliorate many of society's problems. This second position is the one most scientists accept. The concept, as it applies to juvenile justice, is called positivism.

Positivism became the dominant philosophical perspective of juvenile justice at the time the juvenile court was established at the beginning of the twentieth century. During the Progressive Era (the period from about 1890 to 1920), the wave of optimism that swept through U.S. society led to the acceptance of positivism.

U.S. society led to the acceptance of positivism. The doctrines of the emerging social sciences assured reformers that through positivism their problems could be solved. The initial step was to gather all the facts of the case. Reformers were then expected to analyze the important questions in a scientific fashion and discover the right solution using objective data.[17]

Armed with these principles, reformers set out to deal with the problem of delinquency, feeling confident that they knew how to find its cause. Progressives looked first to environmental factors, pinpointing poverty as the major cause of delinquency. Some progressives were attracted also to the doctrine of eugenics and believed that the biological limitations of youthful offenders drove them to delinquency. But eventually the psychological origins of delinquency came to be more widely accepted than either the environmental or the biological origins.[18] Table 3–1 lists three assumptions of positivism.

Biological Positivism

The belief that there is a biological explanation for criminality has a long history. For example, the study of physiognomy, which attempts to discern inner qualities through outward appearance, was developed by the ancient Greeks. The attention given to **biological positivism** in the United States can be divided into two periods.

Early Forms of Biological Positivism

The first period was characterized by the nature–nurture debate during the latter part of the nineteenth century and the early twentieth century. Cesare Lombroso's theory of physical abnormalities, genealogical studies, and theories of human somatotypes represent early approaches relating crime and delinquency to biological factors to the study of crime.

- *Lombroso and biological positivism.* Lombroso, a nineteenth-century Italian forensic psychiatrist, is frequently regarded as the father of criminology and the founder of biological positivism. In the process of examining prisoners before and after their deaths, he became convinced that there was a "criminal man" distinct from other human beings. According to Lombroso, the **born criminal** was atavistic, someone who reverts to an earlier evolutionary form or level; in other words, the characteristics of primitive men periodically reappeared in certain individuals.[19]

- *Genealogical studies and delinquency.* Henry Goddard's finding that at least half of all juvenile delinquents had mental deficits sparked intense debate for more than a decade.[20] But the findings of Edwin Sutherland discouraged future investigations of the correlation between intelligence and delinquency. Sutherland, evaluating IQ studies of delinquents and criminals, concluded that the lower IQs of offenders were related more to testing methods and scoring than the offenders' actual mental abilities.[21]

- *Body type theory.* Ernst Kretschmer, a German, first developed the theory that people have one of two body types: the schizothyme or the cyclothyme. Schizothymes are strong and muscular, and according to Kretschmer, they are more likely to be delinquent than are cyclothymes, who are soft-skinned and lack muscle.[22] William Sheldon,[23] Sheldon Glueck and Eleanor Glueck,[24] and Juan B. Cortes and Florence M. Gatti also supported body type theory. Cortes and Gatti even drew on body type theory to develop a biopsychosocial theory of delinquency.[25]

Biological Positivism Today: Sociobiology

In the second half of the twentieth century, **sociobiologists** began to link genetic and environmental factors; they claimed that criminal behavior, like other behaviors, has both biological and social aspects. These sociobiologists have investigated the relationship between antisocial behavior and biological factors and the environment through studies of twins and adoption, chromosomal abnormalities, electrodermal activity, chemical imbalances, and psychopathy. The focus of these studies was on minimal functioning, intelligence, and physique.

In the twenty-first century, the two areas of sociobiology that are receiving the most attention are neuropsychological factors and delinquency and the relationship between temperament and negative behavior. Activity and emotionality are two behaviors that identify a child's temperament. *Activity* refers to motor movements, such as the movement of arms and legs, crawling, or walking. Children who exhibit an inordinate amount of movement as compared with peers are often labeled *hyperactive* or as having an attention deficit disorder (generally referred to as *attention deficit hyperactivity disorder* or ADHD). *Emotionality* ranges from very little reaction to intense emotional reactions that are out of control.

The hyperactive child remains a temperamental mystery. Three common behaviors in such children are impulsivity (shifts quickly from one activity to another), inattention (is easily distracted and does not want to listen), and excessive motor activity (cannot sit still, runs about, is talkative and noisy). Educators note that ADHD children have difficulty staying on task, sustaining academic achievement in school, maintaining control over their behavior, and remaining cognitively organized.[26]

In sum, early biological positivism was replaced by sociobiology, which has more support in the criminological community. However, criminologists generally are reluctant to place much credence in biological explanations of delinquent behaviors because social factors are often needed to trigger and/or interact with the physiological characteristics of the brain and nervous system.

Psychological factors have always been more popular in the United States in explaining juvenile offending than were biological or sociobiological factors. An early psychological explanation of juvenile offending was the psychoanalytic explanation. More recently, sensation seeking, reinforcement theory and psychopathic indicators are receiving considerable attention.

Psychoanalytic Explanations

Sigmund Freud's psychoanalytic theory, although not positivistic because of the inability to measure his concepts, was based on a biological determinist view of human behavior. In developing **psychoanalytic theory**, he contributed three insights that have shaped the handling of juvenile delinquents: (1) Children who have not yet learned to control primitive drives are pushed by the raw instincts and primitive drives of the id and cannot distinguish socially acceptable behavior from socially unacceptable behavior.[27] (2) Children must learn to control their sexual and aggressive drives, which create inner tensions that children must learn to resolve in socially acceptable ways.[28] (3) What a child has experienced emotionally by the age of five affects that child for the rest of his or her life. Emotional traumas experienced in childhood are especially likely to cause lifelong psychological problems.[29]

Other psychologists have taken the insights of psychoanalysis and applied them to the situations of delinquents:

- William Healy focused on mental conflicts that originate in unsatisfactory family relationships.[30]
- August Aichhorn thought that delinquents had considerable hatred toward their parents because of the conflicted nature of family relationships and that children transfer this hatred to other authority figures.[31]
- Kate Friedlander focused on the development of antisocial characteristics in the personality, such as selfishness, impulsiveness, and irresponsibility, which she defined as the results of disturbed ego development in early childhood.[32]

Sensation Seeking and Delinquency

Sensation seeking is defined "as an individual's need for varied, novel, and complex sensations and experiences and the willingness to take physical and social risks for the sake of such experience."[33] Derived from optimal arousal theory, this construct assumes that organisms are driven or motivated to obtain an optimal level of arousal.[34]

Jack Katz's controversial book, *Seductions of Crime*, conjectures that individuals who commit crime are involved in "an emotional process—seductions and compulsions that have special dynamics." It is this "magical" and "transformative" experience that makes crime "sensible," even sensually "compelling." For example, he states that for many adolescents, shoplifting and vandalism offer an exciting experience, not because of the act, but because if adults see the youths do something wrong and the kids still can get away with it, the youths will feel they have proved their competence in society.[35]

Katz is arguing that instead of approaching criminal or delinquent behavior from the traditional focus on background factors, what needs more consideration are the foreground or situational factors that directly precipitate antisocial acts and reflect crimes' sensuality. According to Katz, offenders' immediate social environment and experiences encourage them to conceive of crimes as sensually compelling.[36]

The Psychopath

The psychopath (also known as the **sociopath**, *person with a conduct disorder*, and a host of other names) is acknowledged as the personality of the hard-core juvenile offender. According to the DSM-IV, these individuals are usually diagnosed with a conduct disorder. The claim is made that these are chiefly the unwanted, rejected children, who grow up but remain undomesticated "children" and never develop trust in or loyalty to other adults.[37] Hervey Cleckley gave a very complete clinical description of this type of personality.[38] More recently, Robert D. Hare developed a new checklist for the antisocial personality; some of the most significant items on the list are the following:

- Cunning and manipulativeness
- Giving false impressions to others
- Lack of remorse or guilt
- Callousness and lack of empathy
- Lack of realistic long-term goals
- Impulsivity
- Failure to accept responsibility for their actions[39]

The continuity between childhood symptoms of emotional problems and adult psychopathic behavior emerged in Lee N. Robins' thirty-year follow-up of 526 white children who were patients in a St. Louis, Missouri, guidance clinic in the 1920s. Robins was looking for clues to the adult "antisocial personality," or "sociopathy."[40] Excluding cases involving organic brain damage, schizophrenia, mental retardation, or symptoms that appeared only after heavy drug or alcohol use, she found that the adult sociopath is almost invariably an antisocial child who has grown up. Indeed, she found no case of adult sociopathy without antisocial behavior before the age of eighteen. Over 50 percent of sociopathic males showed an onset of symptoms before the age of eight.[41]

What percentage of the juvenile offender population can be classified as psychopathic? It depends on what population of delinquents is being considered. The percentage is very low with status offenders and youthful offenders with minor violations and it increases as hard-core youthful offenders sentenced to long-term training schools come under examination. One study of adult prison inmates found that only 15 to 25 percent met the criteria for psychopathy.[42] Based on the experience of working with inmates for several years in a maximum-security juvenile institution, one of the authors would agree that those numbers seem reasonable for delinquents who commit serious personal and property offenses.

Reinforcement Theory

James Q. Wilson and Richard Herrnstein's *Crime and Human Nature* combines biosocial factors and psychological research with rational choice theory to redevelop reinforcement theory.[43] Wilson and Herrnstein consider potential causes of crime and of noncrime within the context of **reinforcement theory**, that is, the theory that behavior is governed by its consequent rewards and punishments, as reflected in the history of the individual.

The rewards of crime, according to Wilson and Herrnstein, are found in the form of material gain, revenge against an enemy, peer approval, and sexual gratification. The consequences of crime include pangs of conscience, disapproval of peers, revenge of the victim, and, most important, the possibility of punishment. The rewards of crime tend to be more immediate, whereas the rewards of noncrime generally are realized in the future. The authors are quick to dismiss evidence that is inconsistent with their theoretical framework but, as few have done in the field of criminology, they are able to show how gender, age, intelligence, families, schools, communities, labor markets, mass media, and drugs, as well as variations across time, culture, and race, influence the propensity to commit crimes, especially violent offenses.[44]

Wilson and Herrnstein's theory does have serious flaws. Most important, it consistently shows a disdain for the social context in which crime occurs. What Wilson and Herrnstein do, in effect, is to factor society out of their considerations of crime. Instead of examining criminal behavior as part of complex social mechanisms and attempting to understand the connection, they typically conclude that no conclusion is possible from the available data, and therefore no programs for reducing criminality among groups perceived as major sources of crime are worth their costs.[45]

Sociological Positivism

Social structure, social process, and conflict theories are the three main divisions of the sociological explanations of crime and delinquency. The basic flaw of explanations based on the individual, according to these sociological theories, is that such interpretations fail to come to grips with the underlying social and cultural conditions giving rise to youthful offending. These sociological theories add that the overall crime picture reflects conditions requiring collective social solutions; therefore, social reform, rather than individual counseling, must be given the highest priority in efforts to reduce crime problems.

Social Structural Theories

Using official statistics as their guide, social structure theorists claim that such forces as social disorganization, cultural deviance, and status frustration are so powerful that they induce lower-class individuals to become involved in criminal and delinquent behaviors. Social structural theories include the following:

1. *Social disorganization theory.* Clifford R. Shaw and Henry D. McKay's **social disorganization theory** views crime as resulting from the breakdown of social control by

▲ Disorganized, dilapidated, and unkempt areas of cities both produce and attract delinquency and violent behaviors.

JeffHaynesAFP/Getty Images

the traditional primary groups, such as the family and the neighborhood, because of the social disorganization of the community. Shaw and McKay's studies revealed that high-delinquency areas are found in disorganized communities characterized by physically deteriorated and condemned buildings, economic dependence, population mobility, heterogeneous populations, high rates of school truancy, infant mortality, and tuberculosis.[46]

2. *Cultural deviance theory.* Walter B. Miller contends that the lower class has its own cultural history and that the motivation to become involved in criminal activities is intrinsic in lower-class culture. Miller's **cultural deviance theory** argues that the lower-class culture is characterized by a set of focal concerns, or values, that command widespread attention and a high degree of emotional involvement. The focal concerns consist of trouble, toughness, smartness, excitement, fate, and autonomy.[47]

Trouble: Getting into and out of trouble represents a major preoccupation of the lower class, and fighting, drinking, and sexual adventures are basic causes of trouble for this class.

Toughness: The "tough guy" who is hard, fearless, undemonstrative, and a good fighter is the ideal personality in the eyes of lower-class males.

Smartness: This value among the lower class involves the desire to outsmart, outfox, con, and dupe others.

Excitement: The quest for excitement leads to the widespread use of alcohol and drugs by both genders and to extensive gambling.

Fate: Lower-class individuals feel that their lives are subject to a set of forces over which they have little control.

Autonomy: Desire for personal independence is an important concern for lower-class persons because they feel controlled so much of the time.[48]

3. *Status frustration theory.* In an early version of **strain theory**, Robert K. Merton theorized that cultural goals and the means to achieve these goals must be reasonably well integrated if a culture is to be stable and smooth running. If individuals feel that a particular goal is important, they should have legitimate means of attaining it. The cultural goal of American society, according to Merton, is success, but the inequality of life in this nation produces structural pressures toward deviation to criminal behavior. In Table 3–2, types of individual adaptation are listed: a plus (+) signifies acceptance, a minus (−) signifies rejection, and a plus-and-minus (±) signifies a rejection of the prevailing values and a substitution of new ones.

Two of the most important delinquency theories are those by Cloward and Ohlin and by Cohen. Richard A. Cloward and Lloyd E. Ohlin's insight is that lower-class cultures

---

TABLE 3–2
Merton's Theory of Anomie

	Means	Ends
1. Conformity	+	+
2. Innovation	−	+
3. Ritualism	+	−
4. Retreatism	−	−
5. Rebellion	±	±

Source: This material appears in Robert K. Merton, "Social Structure and Anomie," *American Sociological Review* 3 (1938), 676.

Focus on Offenders 3–1
Staying Out of Trouble

"I made up my mind the last time I was released from Fairfield that I was going to stay out of trouble. I went home and told my friends that I was going to stay clean. Then, my mother got sick, needed an operation, and couldn't work. I am older than my brothers and sisters and someone had to put food on the table. Instead of telling my friends to stay out of my face, I agreed to pull an armed robbery with them. We got caught and here I am."

This young man could be said to have several explanations for his antisocial behavior. It was rational behavior—he did it because his mother needed surgery and there was no money. He was from a disorganized community, and he was influenced by the lack of positive support from others. Cloward and Ohlin's opportunity appears to be at play here because he was unable to make the money he needed through legitimate means, so he turned to illegitimate means. Furthermore, Sutherland's differential association theory can be seen in his history of learning crime from others.

CRITICAL THINKING QUESTIONS

If you were his institutional social worker, as I was, how would you work with him? Would you have short- and long-term goals? What would you hope to accomplish?

are asked to orient their behavior toward the prospect of accumulating wealth while being denied the means of doing so legitimately. Thus, delinquent subcultures develop as collective social adjustments to the strains of blocked opportunity.[49] See Figure 3–2. Cloward and Ohlin's Opportunity Theory.

Cohen's frustration (or strain) theory suggests that the destructive and malicious behavior of lower-class delinquent subcultures is a reaction to their failure to achieve middle-class norms and values.[50] See Figure 3–3.

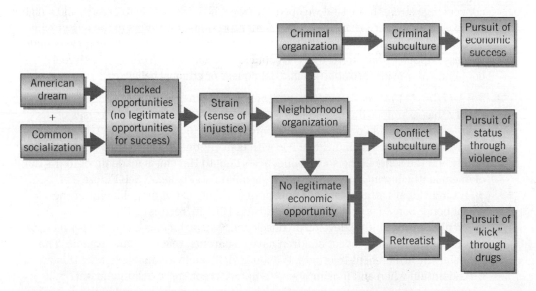

FIGURE 3–2
Cloward and Ohlin's Opportunity Theory

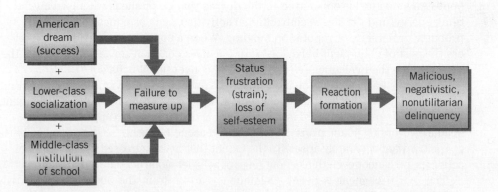

FIGURE 3–3
Cohen's Theory of Delinquent Subcultures

▲ Lil' MoJo. Children growing up in a culture of gangs are quickly socialized into gang life. This young boy knew how to "blood up" at the young age of ten.
© David Grossman/Alamy

Social Process Theories

Social process theories examine the interactions between people and their environment that influence individuals to become involved in criminal or delinquent behaviors. These sociopsychological theories became popular in the 1960s because they provided a mechanism for understanding how environmental factors influence individual decision making. Differential association, containment, social control, and labeling theories are the social process theories that have been the most widely received.

1. *Differential association theory.* According to Edwin H. Sutherland's **differential association theory**, criminals and youthful offenders learn crime from others. Thus, crime, like any other form of behavior, is a product of social interaction. Sutherland began with the notion that criminal behavior is to be expected of those individuals who have internalized a preponderance of definitions favorable to law violations. That is, individuals are taught their basic values, norms, skills, and perceptions of self from others; therefore, it makes sense that they also learn crime from "significant others."[51]

2. *Containment theory.* Walter C. Reckless developed **containment theory** in order to explain why individuals do not commit crime and delinquent acts. He argued that individuals are affected by a variety of forces, some driving them toward—and others restraining them from—crime. As a control theory, which can explain both conforming behavior and deviance, containment theory has two elements: an internal control system and an external control system. Internal containment is made up of self-control, a positive self-concept, ego strength, a well-developed superego, high frustration tolerance, and a high sense of responsibility. External containment represents the buffers in the person's immediate environment that are able to hold him or her within socially acceptable bounds. The assumption is that strong internal containment and reinforcement of external containment provide insulation against delinquent or criminal behavior.[52]

3. *Social control theory.* Travis Hirschi developed another version of control theory that examines the individual's ties to conventional society. In *Causes of Delinquency*, Hirschi outlined **social control theory**, in which he linked delinquent behavior to the bond an individual has with conventional social groups, such as the family and the school. The social bond, according to Hirschi, is made up of four main elements: attachment, commitment, involvement, and belief.[53] See Figure 3–4.

An individual's attachment to conventional others is the first element of the social bond. Sensitivity toward others, argues Hirschi, relates to the ability to internalize norms and to develop a conscience.[54] Attachment to others also includes the ties of affect and respect children have to parents, teachers, and friends. The stronger the attachment to others, the more likely an individual is to take this into consideration when and if he or she is tempted to commit a delinquent act.[55]

Commitment to conventional activities and values is the second element of the bond. An individual is committed to the degree that he or she is willing to invest time, energy, and the self in conventional activities, such as educational goals, property ownership, or reputation building. When a committed individual considers the cost of delinquent behavior, he or she uses common sense and thinks of the risk of losing the investment already made in conventional behavior.[56]

Involvement also protects an individual from delinquent behavior. Because time and energy are limited, involvement in conventional activities leaves no time for delinquent behavior. "The person involved in conventional activities is tied to appointments, deadlines, working hours, plans, and the like," reasoned Hirschi, "so the opportunity to commit deviant acts rarely arises. To the extent that he is engrossed in conventional activities, he cannot even think about deviant acts, let alone act out his inclinations."[57]

The fourth element is belief. Delinquency arises from the absence of effective beliefs that forbid socially unacceptable behavior. Respect for the law and for the social norms of society is an important component of belief. This respect for the values of the law and legal system is derived from intimate relations with other people, especially parents.[58]

4. *Labeling perspective.* Labeling theory contends that society creates deviants by labeling those who are apprehended as "different" from others, when in reality the youths are different only because authorities "tagged" them with a criminal label. Edwin Lemert and Howard Becker are the chief proponents of the view that formal and informal societal reactions to criminal behavior can influence the subsequent attitudes and behaviors of criminals and delinquents.[59]

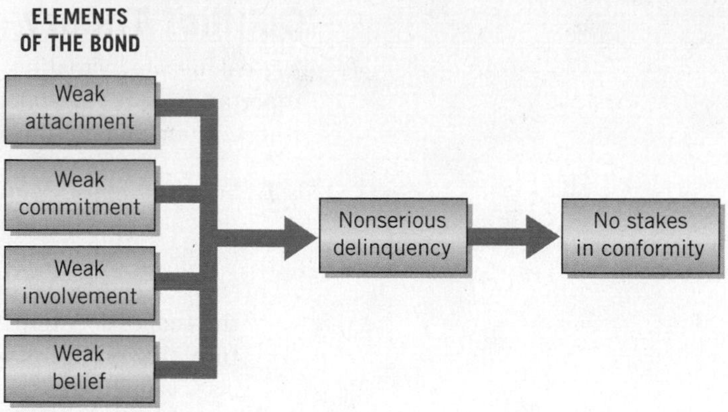

Lemert focused attention on the interaction between social control agents and rule violators and the way certain behavior came to be labeled "criminal" or "deviant." His concept of primary and secondary deviation is regarded as one of the most important insights of this **labeling perspective**. According to Lemert, *primary deviation* refers to the behavior of the individual, and *secondary deviation* is behavior resulting from society's response to that behavior. Lemert contended that society's reaction—use of the "deviant" label—forces a change in the status or role of the individual and, in effect, pressures the person to pursue deviant or criminal behavior.[60] Thus, the social reaction to the criminal is crucial in understanding the progressive commitment of a person to a criminal way of life.

Becker adds that once a person is caught and labeled, that person becomes an outsider and gains a new social status, with consequences for both one's self-image and one's public identity. The person is regarded as a different kind of person, and he or she finds it difficult to regain social acceptance. Hence, society's labeling ultimately forces a juvenile or an adult into a deviant career.[61]

ELEMENTS OF THE BOND

FIGURE 3–4
Elements of Travis Hirschi's Social Bond

Commissioner of Youth Corrections

PREPARATION FOR THE JOB

The title of this person varies from state to state, but this person is expected to have good writing and speaking skills as well as the ability to handle complex managerial decisions. In addition to these personal attributes, this person must be highly regarded in state juvenile corrections, because his or her appointment must come from a person high in state government, sometimes even the governor. It is wise to avoid staying in comfortable positions as individuals begin their juvenile or adult correctional careers. In contrast, young correctional professionals should try to expand their horizons by searching out and accepting new challenges in the workplace.

NATURE OF THE JOB

The director or commissioner of youth corrections is responsible for directing the implementation of the agency's mission and all aspects of youth corrections in that state. This person is charged to perform a number of tasks, including using managerial practices that encourage staff motivation, educating others regarding the agency's mission and practices, presenting budgets to state legislatures, establishing priorities to direct and redirect resources, and promoting and ensuring delivery of staff training programs.

QUALIFICATIONS AND REQUIRED EDUCATION

This person is appointed by some high ranking official in state government. Usually, he or she has had responsible positions in state government before this, perhaps having served a period of time as assistant or associate commissioner. This person almost always has a B.A., many have gone on to earn an M.A., and a few may even have a Ph.D.

JOB OUTLOOK

There are only fifty of these jobs across the nation (one per state), and the commissioner's job is not secure. He or she serves at the pleasure of some high ranking person. If commissioners have problems in one or more of his or her agencies, that could put their job in jeopardy.

EARNINGS OR BENEFITS

Commissioners are well paid. In larger states, some may earn upto or more than $100,000 a state. The salary package is usually supplemented by excellent benefits.

Source: Information gathered by examining state juvenile corrections in a number of states.

Conflict Theory

A great deal of variation exists among conflict theories. Some theories emphasize the importance of socioeconomic class; other theories emphasize power and authority, and others, group and cultural conflict.

1. *Socioeconomic class and Marxist criminology.* Karl Marx, who wrote very little on the subject of crime as the term is defined today, inspired a new school of criminology that is variously defined as "Marxist," "radical," "critical," "left-wing," "socialist," or "new." The **Marxist perspective** views the state and the law itself as ultimate tools of the economic interests of the ownership class. It is capitalism, rather than human nature, that produces egocentric, greedy, and predatory human beings. The ownership class is guilty of the crime of the brutal exploitation of the working class. Conventional crime, according to this perspective, is caused by extreme poverty and economic alienation, products of the dehumanizing and demoralizing capitalist system.

2. *Power and authority relationships.* Ralf Dahrendorf and Austin T. Turk have emphasized the relationships between authorities and their subjects. They contend that power is the critical variable explaining crime. These authors argue that although Marx built his theory on only one form of power (property ownership), a more useful perspective could be constructed by incorporating broader concepts of power.[62]

3. *Group and cultural conflict.* Another dimension of the conflict perspective focuses on group and cultural conflict. Thorsten Sellin and George Vold advocated this approach to the study of crime, the causes of crime, necessary to understand the concept of *conduct norms.* This concept refers to the rules of a group concerning how its members should act under particular conditions. The violation of these rules guiding behavior arouses a group reaction.[63]

Vold views society "as a congeries [an aggregation] of groups held together in a shifting, but dynamic equilibrium of opposing group interests and efforts."[64] He formulated a theory of group conflict that contends that "the whole political process of law making, law breaking, and law enforcement directly reflects deep-seated and fundamental conflicts between interest groups and the more general struggles for the control of the police power of the state."[65]

See Table 3–3 for a comparison of the biological, psychological, and sociological theories.

In sum, when social structural, social process, and social conflict theories are considered separately, a piece of the puzzle of how the environment influences a youth to become involved in crime is missing. Together, they provide a more satisfactory explanation than does each separately for why juveniles become involved in delinquency. This realization led to the development of integrated theory.

Thinking Like a Corrections Professional

You are a drug court judge and a drug user is appearing before you for the fourth time. The offender has more potential than you have seen in a long time. She has finished three years of high school earning high grades, but simply does not seem to be able to successfully complete drug rehabilitation programs. What will be your approach with this offender? What sanctions will you give her?

How Does Integrated Theory Explain Juvenile Crime?

Several integrated theories for delinquent behavior have been developed. Three of the most important are Michael Gottfredson and Travis Hirschi's general theory of crime, Delbert Elliott's integrated social process theory, and Terence P. Thornberry's interactional theory[66]:

1. *Gottfredson and Hirschi's general theory of crime.* In their 1990 publication, *A General Theory of Crime,* Gottfredson and Hirschi define lack of self-control as the common factor underlying problem behaviors.[67] Self-control is the degree to which an individual is "vulnerable to the temptations of the moment."[68] The other pivotal construct in this theory of crime is crime opportunity, which is a function

TABLE 3–3
Comparison of Biological, Psychological, and Sociological Theories

Theory	Proponents	Causes of Crime Identified
Atavistic, or born criminal	Lombroso	The atavistic criminal is a reversion to an earlier evolutionary form.
Developmental	Moffitt	Delinquent behavior proceeds along two developmental paths:
		On one path, early-age delinquents develop a lifelong pattern of delinquency; on the other, the adolescent develops a limited path and desists from delinquency around eighteen years of age.
Psychoanalytic	Freud	Unconscious motivations result from early childhood experiences.
Emotional process and situational factors	Katz	Delinquency becomes an emotional process that is seductive and sensually compelling.
Psychopathic personality	Hare	Lack of affect, impulsiveness, and aggression.
Reinforcement	Wilson and Herrnstein	Several key constitutional and psychological factors.
Social disorganization	Shaw and McKay	Delinquent behavior becomes an alternative mode of socialization through which youths who are part of disorganized communities are attracted to delinquent values and traditions.
Cultural deviance	Miller	The lower class has a distinctive culture of its own, and its local concerns, or values, make lower-class boys more likely to become involved in delinquent behavior.
Strain	Merton	Social structure exerts pressure on those individuals who cannot attain the cultural goal of success to engage in nonconforming behavior.
Delinquency opportunity	Cloward and Ohlin	Lower-class boys seek out illegitimate means to attain middle-class success goals if they are unable to attain them through legitimate means.
Status frustration	Cohen	Lower-class boys are unable to attain the goals of middle-class culture, and, therefore, they become involved in nonutilitarian, malicious, and negative behavior.
Differential association	Sutherland	Criminal behavior is learned by individuals through interaction with others who hold attitudes and definitions favorable to the violation of the law.
Containment	Reckless	Strong inner and reinforced external containment provide insulation against delinquent behavior.
Social control	Hirschi	Delinquent acts result when an individual's bond to society is weak or broken.
Labeling	Lemert and Becker	Society creates deviants by labeling those who are apprehended as different from other juveniles, when in reality, the youths are "different" only because they have been given the label "deviant."
Marxist perspective	Marx	Conventional delinquency and crime are caused by extreme poverty and economic alienation.
General theory of crime	Gottfredson and Hirschi	Lack of self-control is the common factor underlying problem behaviors.
Integrated social process theory	Elliott and colleagues	Integrates the strongest elements of strain, social control, and social learning perspectives into a single paradigm that accounts for delinquent behavior and drug use.
Interactional theory	Thornberry	Associations with delinquent peers and delinquent values make up social delinquency; especially prolonged serious delinquency is learned and reinforced.

of the structural or situational circumstances encountered by the individual. In combination, these two constructs are intended to capture the simultaneous influence of external and internal restraints on behavior.[69] More than two dozen studies have been conducted on general theory, and the vast majority are largely favorable.[70]

2. *Elliott and colleagues' integrated social process theory.* Delbert Elliott and colleagues offer "an explanatory model that expands and synthesizes traditional strain, social control, and social learning perspectives into a single paradigm that accounts for delinquent behavior and drug use."[71] Integrating the strongest features of these theories into a single theoretical model, Elliott and colleagues contend that the experience of living in socially disorganized areas leads youths to develop weak bonds with conventional groups, activities, and norms. High levels of strain, as well as weak bonds with conventional groups, lead some youth to seek out delinquent peer groups. These antisocial peer groups provide both positive reinforcement for delinquent behavior and role models for this behavior. Consequently, Elliott and colleagues theorize, there is a high probability of involvement in delinquent behavior when bonding to delinquent groups is combined with weak bonding to conventional groups.[72] Tests of these proportions are generally supportive of the theory.[73]

3. *Thornberry's interactional theory.* In Thornberry's interactional theory of delinquency, the initial impetus toward delinquency comes from a weakening of the person's bond to conventional society, represented by attachment to parents, commitment to school, and belief in conventional values. Associations with delinquent peers and delinquent values make up the social setting in which delinquency, especially prolonged serious delinquency, is learned and reinforced. These two

---

Evidence-Based Practice
Targeting the Programs That Show Particular Promise

Lipsey et.al. summarize some of the research recognized for about a decade that shows that some popular programs simply do not work. Public and professional favorites such as "Scared Straight," and DARE cost millions of hours in time wasted and dollars lost, even though the programs have a "feel good" aura and a mantel of plausibility about them.

A metanalysis by Lipsey and his colleagues is allowing professionals and practitioners to sharpen their focus on just what works best and plan accordingly. Their findings focus on the risk level of juveniles, therapeutic versus control treatment philosophies, generic programs types and embedded model programs, and amount and quality of service.

Target High-Risk Cases: Their findings make it clear that high risk rather than low risk juveniles should be the focus of attention. Studies indicate that juveniles unlikely to get into trouble anyway will absorb time and funds without significant payback. High-risk juveniles, on the other hand, are well worth the time and cost, and many studies report the important recidivism reductions.

Use Programs That Call on Constructive Personal Development: Analyses of therapeutic programs as opposed to control programs also show considerable differences. Youths who are the subjects of discipline instilling programs, those who are expected to be deterred from crime, and those kept under close surveillance to keep them from bad behavior—or under control types of programs—recidivate more than those who

are on treatment programs. For example, youths who undergo skills development, relationship building, insight, counseling and case management improve significantly more than those under the control programs.

Favor Those Program Types That Have Shown the Largest Effects in Research Studies: Generic types of programs, such as different types of counseling, all show positive gains by juveniles. Group programs, mentoring, mixed methods, family and family crisis programs are successful and do include such "brand name" techniques as Functional Family Therapy and Multisystem Therapy. Cognitive-behavioral therapy, behavioral techniques, and social skills training rate well in the analyses. As might be expected, variations across therapies are found, but the overall impact of the programs is positive.

Implement the Selected Programs Well: The quality and amount of service provided is important. Neither too little nor too much "medicine" must be dispensed for youths to receive maximum benefit without undue costs and, the quality of the programs, although not well reported, can be measured by factors such as dropout rates, staff turnover, and poorly trained staff. These latter factors must be singled out for further attention.

Sources: Adapted and quoted from Mark W. Lipsey, James C. Howell, Marion R. Kelly, Gabielle Chapman, and Darin Carver, "Improving the Effectiveness of Juvenile Justice Programs: A New Perspective on Evidence-Based Practice," *Center for Juvenile Justice Reform: Working Across Systems of Care* (Washington, DC: Georgetown University, December 2010), 22–28.

variables, along with the delinquent behavior itself, form a mutually reinforcing causal loop that leads toward increasing delinquency involvement over time.[74] Moreover, this interactive process develops over the person's life cycle. Thornberry's theory essentially views delinquency as the result of events occurring in a developmental fashion. Delinquency is not viewed as the end product; instead, it leads to the formation of delinquent values, which then contribute to disconnections in social bonds, more attachments to antisocial peers, and further involvement in delinquent behavior. As found in other developmental theories, some variables affect unlawful behavior at certain ages and other factors at other ages.[75]

Best practice programs and their application to juvenile justice have considerable promise in promoting a more effective juvenile justice system. In this chapter, in the Evidence-Based Practice feature, we examine the more promising interventions for reducing aggression and violence.

Why Has Delinquency Across the Life Course Become So Important in Studying the Theories of Juvenile Crime?

Delinquency across the life course (DLC), or life-course criminology, is particularly concerned with documenting and explaining within-individual changes in offending throughout life. Robert J. Sampson and John H. Laub's analysis of the Gluecks' classic longitudinal study of one thousand men has been a major impetus to the life-course perspective.[76] Using life history data drawn from the Gluecks' longitudinal study, Laub and Sampson found that although adult crime is connected to childhood behavior, both incremental and abrupt changes still take place through changes in adult social bonds. The emergence of strong social bonds to work and family among adults deflects early behavior trajectories. Laub and Sampson also argue that the events that trigger the formation of strong adult bonds to work and family commonly occur by chance or luck.[77]

The concept of a **turning point** in the life course is one of the fascinating contributions of Laub and Sampson's research. A turning point involves a gradual or dramatic change and may lead to "a modification, reshaping, or transition from one state, condition, or phase to another."[78] In seeking to unravel the mechanisms that operate at key turning points to shift a risk trajectory to a more adaptive path, Laub and Sampson found that stable employment and a good marriage, or changing roles and environment, can lead to investment of social capital or relations among persons.[79]

Longitudinal studies usually reveal that delinquent careers differ by gender. Male careers usually begin earlier and extend longer into the adult years. Studies of youth gangs reveal that female members are more likely than male members to leave the gang if they have a child. Also, conventional life patterns—particularly marriage, parenting, and work—draw both males and females away from gangs and offending behaviors, but do so more completely and quickly for females.[80]

At least three studies have examined the desistance process among women. Ira Sommers, Deborah R. Baskin, and Jeffrey Fagan found that quality marriages led women to desist from crime, with some variation depending on the class and race of the women being studied.[81] A later study by Sommers and Baskin revealed that the desistance process was quite different for inner-city women of color. These women were more likely to desist as the result of receiving alcohol and drug treatment or because they grew tired or fearful of repeated imprisonments.[82] Finally, as will be discussed in Chapter 4, Peggy C. Giordano and colleagues followed up on a sample of serious adolescent female delinquents and found neither marital attachment nor job stability to be strongly related to female desistance. Instead, desisters underwent a cognitive shift, or transformation, in which they experienced successful "hooks for change." These hooks "facilitated the development of an alternative view of self that was seen as fundamentally incompatible with criminal behavior."[83]

Social Policy in Juvenile Justice: PHDCN LAFANS

The project on human development in Chicago neighborhoods (PHDCN) is an interdisciplinary study of how families, schools, and neighborhoods affect child and adolescent development. It was launched in the mid-1990s with major support from the National Institute of Justice and the John D and Catherine T MacArthur Foundation. PHDCN was led by Felton Earls M.D. at the Harvard University school of Public health and Medical School. Project directors represent a variety of disciplines and major universities.

The project whose data continue to be made available through the University of Michigan's Interuniversity Consortium for Political and Social Research (ICPSR) is remarkable in its scope and design. It combines (1) at longitudinal study of youth, with repeated interviews of more than six thousand youths and their caregivers, along with (2) a neighborhood study that included a survey of almost nine thousand neighborhood residents and systematic observation of levels of social and physical disorder and eighty neighborhoods. Data collection was conducted based on four separate components that focused on a variety of individual and community characteristics.[84]

Early Findings from the PHDCN

Findings from the PHDCNS neighborhood study received widespread attention in both professional and general media. For example, in a widely cited article published in *Science* in 1997 and summarized in a National Institute of Justice *Research Review*, Robert J Sampson, Stephen Raudenbusch, and Felton Earls found that neighborhood social processes had a significant impact on homicide and violence in the community. In particular, homicide and violent victimization rates were found to be lower in neighborhoods where residents shared values, had common expectations that neighborhood would intervene in problem behaviors, and trusted each other. The researchers call this combination of shared values, trust, and an expectation for social intervention "collective efficacy" to control crime and deviance. The level of collective efficacy, in turn, was strongly influenced by neighborhood conditions such as the extent of poverty and the lack of residential stability. Collective efficacy thus seems to be a mediating link between neighborhood conditions and crime and violence. Equally important, among neighborhood with similar conditions, those with greater collective efficacy experience less violence.[85]

Robert J. Sampson, a Harvard University professor, and colleagues developed the concept of collective efficacy as characteristics of the community that they felt would work together to prevent and control crime. Sampson and colleagues contended that the most important influence on neighborhood time is neighbor's willingness to act, when necessary or needed, for one another's benefit, and especially for the benefit of one another's children. Several studies have found that collective efficacy does function ta mediate much of the effect of such community structural variables as hypervigilance poverty, unemployment, single parents, and racial/ethnic heterogeneity.

PHDCN is perhaps the largest interdisciplinary study of the complex influences exerted on human development, ever undertaken. The National Institute of Justice has so far spent $18 billion on the project, and the MacArthur foundation has spent another works $23.6 million. Jeremy Travis, director of the National Institute of Justice from 1994 to 2000, noted, "It is far and away the most important research insight in the past decade. I think it will shape policy for the next generation."[86]

In 2011, PHDCN entered a new phase as part of the Mixed Income Project, a longitudinal study of families and neighborhoods funded by the John D and Catherine T MacArthur Foundation. The aim of the Mixed Income Project is to produce a view of the individual and aggregate dynamics of mixed income housing, including residential mobility, housing change, job loss, and key aspects of physical and mental well-being that occurred during the great recession that began in 2008.[87]

In 2012, Robert J. Sampson, who continues to direct data gathering under the project, published *Great American City and the Enduring Neighborhood Effect*. Sampson concluded that, even in today's complex and highly technological world, "communities still matter because life is decidedly shaped by where you live."[88]

The Los Angeles Family and Neighborhood Survey (LAFANS), which builds on key PHDCN findings, is an ongoing project, began in 2000, that seeks to answer the question of what makes a neighborhood a positive place to live? The survey gathered data on three thousand families and sixty-five Los Angeles neighborhoods in two waves: one between 2000 and 2001, and another between 2006 2008. LAFANS, which is being conducted by the RAND Corporation and the UCLA School of Public health, has resulted in numerous publications, including at least one that shows that members of racial ethnic groups "appear to exhibit negative health risk behaviors when they reside in areas that are disproportionately populated with their co-ethnic peers"[89]

SUMMARY

LEARNING OBJECTIVE 1: Summarize the principles and influences of the classical school of criminology.

The classical school believed that individuals needed to have free will to possess the rationality that is necessary to choose whether to commit criminal behavior or not. The classical school in recent decades has influenced both juvenile and adult justice in perceiving that offenders, especially hard-core ones, have rationality when they commit crime and deserve to be punished for their behaviors.

LEARNING OBJECTIVE 2: Describe biological theories of juvenile crime and delinquency.

A number of early theories relate crime and delinquency to biological factors. More recently, sociobiologists have linked genetic and environmental factors claiming that delinquent behavior, like other behaviors, has both biological and social aspects.

LEARNING OBJECTIVE 3: Describe psychological theories of juvenile crime and delinquency.

Early on, psychoanalytic explanations received great attention, but more recently, a number of psychological factors, including psychopathic factors, sensation seeking, and delinquency and reinforcement theory, have been examined for their contributions in understanding delinquent behavior.

LEARNING OBJECTIVE 4: Describe sociological theories of juvenile crime and delinquency.

The sociological theories of juvenile crime and delinquency can be divided into structural and social process theories. The most

important social structural theories are social disorganization theory, cultural deviance theory, and status frustration theory. Differential association, containment, social control, and labeling theories are the social process theories that have been the most widely received.

LEARNING OBJECTIVE 5: Explain why delinquency across the life course is important in studying theories of juvenile crime.

Delinquency Across the Life Course (DLC) is particularly concerned with documenting and explaining within-in individual changes in offending throughout life. Although research indicates that crime is connected to childhood behavior, the emergence of strong social bonds to work and family among adults defects early behavior trajectories.

LEARNING OBJECTIVE 6: Summarize integrated theories of juvenile crime and delinquency.

The most widely hailed integrated theories are Gottfredson and Hirschi's general theory of crime, Elliott's integrated social process theory, and Thornberry's interactional theory. Each of these theories draws from various theories, typically strain, to generate an integrated theory that captures a larger number of delinquent behaviors.

KEY TERMS

autonomy, p. 58
biological positivism, p. 54
born criminal, p. 55
containment theory, p. 60
cultural deviance theory, p. 58
delinquency across the life course (DLC), p. 65
differential association theory, p. 60
excitement, p. 58
fate, p. 58

felicific calculus, p. 50
free will, p. 50
general deterrence effect p. 53
just deserts p. 52
labeling perspective, p. 61
Marxist perspective, p. 62
positivism, p. 53
psychoanalytic theory, p. 55
rational choice theory, p. 50
reinforcement theory, p. 57

routine activity approach, p. 51
smartness, p. 58
social control theory, p. 60
social disorganization theory, p. 57
sociobiologists, p. 55
sociopath, p. 56
strain theory, p. 58
toughness, p. 58
trouble, p. 58
turning point, p. 65

REVIEW QUESTIONS

1. What is the labeling perspective's definition of why adolescents become delinquent? Do you agree with this interpretation?
2. Which of the three integrated theories makes the most sense to you? What are the advantages of integrated theory? What are its disadvantages?
3. Should poverty exclude an adolescent from responsibility for delinquent behavior? Why or why not?
4. Why have the juvenile courts been so quick to apply the concept of free will and rationality to violent juvenile criminals?
5. To what extent do you believe juveniles are rational in their behavior? What are the implications of your answer for the justice system?

GROUP EXERCISES

1. *Writing to Learn:* Write an essay in class that explains the nature and types of biological positivism. Critique and revise.
2. *Writing to Learn:* Write an essay in class that explains the nature and types of psychological positivism. (Skip the psychoanalytic approach for this particular exercise unless requested by the instructor.) Critique and revise.
3. *Writing to Learn:* Write an essay that explains the nature and types of sociological positivism. Critique and revise.
4. *Class Presentations:* Divide the class into three groups. Ask each group to report on one of the major ideas of structural functionalism, social process, and conflict theories. Let each group defend its ideas against the other approaches as to why their ideas are the strongest.
5. *Group Work:* Divide the class into three groups. Each group should develop one of the three following approaches: the major and minor ideas of Gottfredson and Hirschi's general theory of crime, Elliott's integrated social process theory, and Thornberry's interactional theory. After identifying the components of each theory, have each group pull together all of the ideas of each theory into a schema of the whole theory and present the ideas to the class.

WORKING WITH JUVENILES

You need to communicate that you care for the person and that you are there to help them. They need to know that you care and this will be demonstrated by how you treat them.

NOTES

1. David E. Kalist and Daniel Y. Lee, "First Names and Crime; Does Unpopularity Spell Trouble?" *Social Science Quarterly* 90 (2009), 39–40.
2. Ibid., p. 40. David M. Kennedy, *Deterrence and Crime Prevention: Reconsidering the Prospect of Sanction* (New York: Routledge, 2009).
3. Cesare Bonesana Beccaria, *On Crimes and Punishment*, translated by H. Paolucci (1764), reprinted ed. (Indianapolis, IN: Bobbs-Merrill, 1963).
4. Ysabel Rennie, *The Search for Criminal Man: A Conceptual History of the Dangerous Offender* (Lexington, MA: Lexington Books, 1978), 15.
5. Beccaria, *On Crimes and Punishment*, 179.
6. Rennie, *The Search for Criminal Man*, 22.
7. Edward Cimler and Lee R. Bearch, "Factors Involved in Juvenile Decisions about Crime," *Criminal Justice and Behavior* 8 (September 1981), 275–86.
8. Ronald L. Akers, "Deterrence, Rational Choice, and Social Learning Theory: The Path Not Taken," paper presented at the annual meeting of the American Society of Criminology, Reno, NV, November 1989, 2–3.
9. Lawrence E. Cohen and Marcus Felson, "Social Change and Crime Rate Trends: A Routine Activity Approach," *American Sociological Review* 44 (August 1979), 588–609.
10. Steven F. Messner and Kenneth Tardiff, "The Social Ecology of Urban Homicides: An Application of the 'Routine Activities' Approach," *Criminology* 23 (1985), 241–67.
11. Akers, "Deterrence, Rational Choice, and Social Learning Theory," 12.
12. Akers, however, questions this in his paper, "Deterrence, Rational Choice, and Social Learning Theory," 11.
13. Timothy Brezina, "Delinquent Problem-Solving: An Interpretive Framework," *Journal of Research in Crime and Delinquency* (2000), 3–30.
14. Marvin E. Wolfgang, Terrence P. Thornberry, and Robert M. Figlio, *From Boy to Man, from Delinquency to Crime* (Chicago: University of Chicago Press, 1987).
15. David Matza, *Delinquency and Drift* (New York: Wiley, 1964).
16. Robert Agnew, "Determinism, Indeterminism, and Crime: An Empirical Examination," *Criminology* 33 (1995), 83–109.

17. See David J. Rothman, *Conscience and Convenience: The Asylum and Its Alternatives in Progressive America* (Boston: Little, Brown, 1980), 32.

18. Ibid., 43–60.

19. Cesare Lombroso, Introduction to C. Lombroso-Ferrero, *Criminal Man According to the Classification of Cesare Lombroso* (New York: Putnam, 1911), xiv.

20. Henry Goddard, *Efficiency and Levels of Intelligence* (Princeton, NJ: Princeton University Press, 1920).

21. Edwin Sutherland, "Mental Deficiency and Crime," in *Social Attitudes*, edited by Kimball Young (New York: Henry Holt, 1926).

22. William Sheldon, *Varieties of Delinquent Youth* (New York: Harper & Row, 1949).

23. Ibid.

24. Sheldon Glueck and Eleanor Glueck, *Physique and Delinquency* (New York: Harper & Row, 1956), p. 9.

25. Juan B. Cortes and Florence M. Gatti, *Delinquency and Crime: A Biopsychosocial Approach: Empirical, Theoretical, and Practical Aspects of Criminal Behavior* (New York: Seminar Press, 1972), 18–19.

26. Curt R. Bartol and Anne M. Bartol, *Delinquency and Justice: A Psychosocial Approach*, 2nd ed. (Upper Saddle River, NJ: Prentice Hall, 1998), 89.

27. Sigmund Freud, *An Outline of Psychoanalysis*, translated by James Strachey (1940 reprint, New York: W. W. Norton, 1963).

28. Ibid.

29. Ibid.

30. William Healy, *Twenty-Five Years of Child Guidance Studies from the Institute of Juvenile Research*, Series C, no. 256 (Chicago, IL: Department of Public Welfare, 1914).

31. August Aichhorn, *Wayward Youth* (New York: Viking Press, 1963).

32. Kate Friedlander, *The Psychoanalytic Approach to Juvenile Delinquency* (London: Routledge and Kegan Paul, 1947).

33. Marvin Zuckerman, *Sensation Seeking Beyond the Optimal Level of Arousal* (Hillsdale, NJ: Lawrence Erlbaum, 1979), 10.

34. Ibid.

35. Jack Katz, *Seductions of Crime: Moral and Sensual Attractions in Doing Evil* (New York: Basic Books, 1988).

36. Ibid.

37. Richard L. Jenkins, "Delinquency and a Treatment Philosophy," in *Crime, Law and Corrections*, edited by Ralph Slovenko (Springfield, IL: Charles C Thomas, 1966), 135–36.

38. Hervey M. Cleckley, *The Mask of Sanity*, 3rd ed. (St. Louis, MO: Mosley Company, 1955), 132–37.

39. Robert Hare, "Psychopathy: A Clinical Construct Whose Time Has Come," *Criminal Justice and Behavior* 23 (1996), 25–54.

40. Lee N. Robins, *Deviant Children Grown Up: A Sociological and Psychiatric Study of Sociopathic Personality* (Baltimore, MD: Williams & Wilkins, 1966), 256.

41. Lee N. Robins et al., "The Adult Psychiatric Status of Black Schoolboys," *Archives of General Psychiatry* 24 (1971), 338–45.

42. Rolf Holmqvist, "Psychopathy and Affect Consciousness in Young Criminal Offenders," *Journal of Interpersonal Violence* 23 (February 2008), 209–24.

43. James Q. Wilson and Richard J. Herrnstein, *Crime and Human Nature* (New York: Simon & Schuster, 1985).

44. Ibid.

45. Edgar Z. Friedenberg, "Solving Crime," *Readings: A Journal of Reviews* (March 1986), 21.

46. Clifford R. Shaw and Henry D. McKay, *Juvenile Delinquency and Urban Areas* (Chicago: University of Chicago Press, 1942).

47. Walter B. Miller, "Lower-Class Culture as a Generating Milieu of Gang Delinquency," *Journal of Social Issues* 14 (1958), 9–10.

48. Ibid.

49. Richard A. Cloward and Lloyd E. Ohlin, *Delinquency and Opportunity: A Theory of Delinquency* (New York: Free Press, 1960).

50. Albert K. Cohen, *Delinquent Boys: The Culture of the Gang* (New York: Free Press, 1955).

51. Edwin H. Sutherland, *Principles of Criminology* (Philadelphia: J. B. Lippincott Company, 1947).

52. The principles of containment theory are described in Walter C. Reckless, "A New Theory of Delinquency and Crime," *Federal Probation* 24 (December 1952), 133–38.

53. Travis Hirschi, *Causes of Delinquency* (Berkeley: University of California Press, 1969).

54. Ibid., 18.

55. Ibid., 83.

56. Ibid., 20.

57. Ibid., 22.

58. Ibid., 198.

59. Edwin L. Lemert, *Social Pathology* (New York: McGraw-Hill, 1951); and Howard S. Becker, *Outsiders* (New York: Free Press, 1958).

60. Lemert, *Social Pathology*.

61. Becker, *Outsiders*.

62. Ralf Dahrendorf and Austin T. Turk, *Class and Class Conflict in Industrial Society* (Palo Alto, CA: Stanford University Press, 1959).

63. Thorsten Sellin, *Culture, Conflict, and Crime* (New York: Social Science Research Council, 1938), 28.

64. George B. Vold, *Theoretical Criminology*, 2nd ed., prepared by Thomas J. Bernard (New York: Oxford University Press, 1979), 283.

65. Ibid., 288.

66. Michael G. Gottfredson and Travis Hirschi, *A General Theory of Crime* (Stanford, CA: Stanford University Press, 1990); Delbert S. Elliott, David Huizinga, and Suzanne S. Ageton, *Explaining Delinquency and Drug Use* (Beverley Hills, CA: Sage, 1985); Delbert S. Elliott, Suzanne S. Ageton, and Rachelle J. Canter, "An Integrated Theoretical Perspective on Delinquent Behavior," *Journal of Research in Crime and Delinquency* 16 (1979), 3–27; Terence P. Thornberry, "Toward an Interactional Theory of Delinquency," *Criminology* 25 (1987), 862–91; Terence P. Thornberry

et al., "Testing Interactional Theory: An Examination of Reciprocal Causal Relationships among Family, School and Delinquency," *Journal of Criminal Law and Criminology* 82 (1991), 3–35.

67. Gottfredson and Hirschi, *A General Theory of Crime*.
68. Ibid., 87.
69. Ibid.
70. For a review of these studies, see T. David Evans et al., "The Social Consequences of Self-Control: Testing the General Theory of Crime," *Criminology* 35 (1997), 476–77.
71. Delbert S. Elliott, Suzanne S. Ageton, and Rachelle J. Canter, "An Integrated Theoretical Perspective on Delinquent Behavior," *Journal of Research in Crime & Delinquency* 16 (1979), 862–91.
72. Ibid.
73. Cynthia Chien, "Testing the Effect of the Key Theoretical Variable of Theories of Strain, Social Control and Social Learning on Types of Delinquency," paper presented at the annual meeting of the American Society of Criminology, Baltimore, November 1990.
74. Terence P. Thornberry, "Toward an Interactional Theory of Delinquency," *Criminology* 25 (1987): 886.
75. Donald J. Shoemaker, *Theories of Delinquency: An Examination of Explanations of Delinquent Behavior* (New York: Oxford University Press, 2005), 161–63.
76. Robert J. Sampson and John H. Laub, *Crime in the Making: Pathways and Turning Points Through Life* (Cambridge, MA: Harvard Press, 1993); and John H. Laub and Robert J. Sampson, *Shared Beginnings, Divergent Lives, Delinquent Boys to Age 70* (Cambridge, MA: Harvard Press, 2003).
77. John H. Laub and Robert J. Sampson, "Turning Points in the Life Course: Why Change Matters to the Study of Crime," *Criminology* 31 (August 1993), 309.
78. Ibid., 309.
79. Ibid., 310.

80. J. Bottcher, "Social Practices of Gender: How Gender Relates to Delinquency in the Everyday Lives of High-Risk Youths," *Criminology* 39 (2001), 893–932, 899.
81. Ira Sommers, Deborah R. Baskin, and Jeffrey Fagan, "Getting Out of the Life: Crime Desistance by Female Street Offenders," *Deviant Behavior* 15 (1994), 125–49.
82. Ira Sommers and Deborah R. Baskin, "Situational or Generalized Violence in Drug Dealing Networks," *Journal of Drug Issues* 27 (1997), 833–49.
83. Peggy C. Giordano, Stephen A. Cernkovich, and Jennifer L. Rudolph, "Gender, Crime, and Desistance: Toward a Theory of Cognitive Transformation," *American Journal of Sociology* 107 (January 2002), 990–1064, 1038.
84. Akka Libernan, *Adolescents, Neighborhoods, and Violence: Recent Findings from the Project on Human Development in Chicago Neighborhoods* (Washington, DC: National Institute of Justice), pp. 4–5, from which some of the wording in this section is taken.
85. For more information on collective efficacy, see Robert J. Sampson, "The Embeddedness of Child and Adolescent Development: A Community-Level Perspective on Urban Violence," in *Childhood Violence in the Urban City*, edited by Joan McCord (New York: Cambridge, 1997), 31–77.
86. Robert J. Sampson, et. al., "Neighborhoods and Violent Crime," *Science* 277 (August 1997), 918–24.
87. Adapted from Robert J. Sampson, "Chicago Project ((PHDCN)," http://scholar.harvard.edu/sampson/content/chicago-projecrt-phden-0.
88. Robert J. Sampson, *American City: Chicago and the Enduring Neighborhood Effect* (Chicago: University of Chicago Press, 2012).
89. Renee Frank and Eileen Bjornstrom, "A Tale of Two Cities: Residential Context and Risky Behavior among Adolescents in Los Angeles and Chicago," *Health and Place* 17 (January 2011), 67–77.

4 Gender and Juvenile Justice

LUIS ROMERO/AP Images

Learning Objectives

1. Outline the various explanations for why adolescent females become involved in offending.
2. Describe a feminist theory of delinquency.
3. Identify the relationship between adolescent male and female offending.
4. Describe how gender affects the processing of adolescent females in the juvenile justice system.
5. Identify the relationship between class and delinquency.

Amicus (Latin for friend) is a Minnesota nonprofit organization with forty some years of experience in building positive relationships between juvenile and adult offenders and their communities. This study originated from the following simple idea: Ask the individuals involved with girls throughout the juvenile justice system to share their thoughts on how the system is doing. Women incarcerated in the Shakopee Correctional Facility (Minneapolis) were also asked what could be learned from their experience and lives to inform the work being done with the girls of today.

The Girls' Study included information that was gathered from over 220 individuals through focus groups and targeted interviews of girls, caregivers, professionals, and women prisoners, as well as a review of national and local studies. The girls expressed a deep need to be "listened to and heard," adding that their story does not always get told. They feel that many in the justice system do not communicate directly with them. As one girl in a focus group said when discussing her treatment in the justice system, "Sometimes they make it seem like we have no feelings, like what they say won't hurt us."

Source: Amicus Girls' Study: Paying Attention to Girls in the Juvenile Justice System, (Spring 2010), accessed June 12, 2012 at www.amicususa.org. Preprinted courtesy of Amicus, Minneapolis, MN.

The theories reviewed in Chapter 3 largely reflect social thought from the late 1800s, up through the 1900s, and into the 2000s. Throughout much of that time period, males were considered the primary culprits in committing crime and delinquency. Critics of these early opinions, however, had their doubts because they recognized that different explanations could be applied to why females, delinquents in the lower classes, and members of various racial and ethnic groups got involved in juvenile delinquency. Indeed, as the collection of data and consideration of the social circumstances of different groups involved with delinquency increased, attention shifted. Social observers began calling attention to extreme social circumstances, such as poverty or violent neighborhoods, as possible contributors to delinquency. Other observers noted the possible effects of social values and norms that led to discrimination against females, African Americans, Hispanics, and lower-class youths. Research began in an effort to sort out the basis for the differences among these groups and began to become more nuanced in its observations and thinking. This chapter on causation begins to sort through those issues.

The chapter initially compares the explanations of why males and females become involved in antisocial behaviors and presents a feminist theory of delinquency. The next section considers the various types of female delinquent offending following an examination of how gender affects the processing of the female delinquent. The final two sections investigate the influence of class and race/ethnicity on the handling of male and female youthful offenders and explore how the categories of gender, class, and race are interlocked and influence both delinquent behavior and how this behavior is handled by the juvenile justice system.

Social Context of Delinquency: Gender Roles and Delinquency

To a large degree, understanding of **gender** and gender-based roles are acquired through socialization. Children socialize into pre-existing gender arrangements and construct understanding of themselves and how they relate to others in terms of these frameworks. As Berkeley professor Barrie Thorne noted in her well-known early book on the subject, *Gender Play:*

> Parents dress infant girls in pink and boys in blue, give them gender differentiated names and toys, and expect them to act differently. Teachers frequently give boys more classroom attention than girls. Children pick up the gender stereotypes that pervade books, songs, advertisements, TV programs, and movies. And peer groups steeped in cultural ideas about what it is to be a girl or boy, also perpetuate gender-typed place and interactions. In short, boys and girls are different; they are not born but made that way.[1]

An empirically-based landmark study by the American Association of University women, (AAUW), which included girls of color at all social classes, examined the behavior and treatment of girls in the classroom. The most striking finding in this research was that white girls tended to lose their sense of self-esteem as they advance from elementary school to high school; African American girls, in contrast, were found in maintaining their self-esteem, but too often would become disassociated from school and school work.[2]

Themes found to be unique to the high school age group in the AAUW study and in the girls described in the book *Schoolgirls* by Peggy Orenstein, were: obsessed with physical appearance and popularity based on external characteristics rather than achievement, loss of freedom in later adolescence associated with budding sexuality, close attention to relationships, and intense mother–daughter patterns of communication. Inner-city African American and Latino girls were found to have somewhat unique issues related to life in tough neighborhoods, and the development of a tough exterior was seen as vital for their protection from gangs and violence; and early pregnancy was a reality for many of them. In short, girls' victimization—from sexual harassment, either at school or on the streets to full-blown sexual assault—was a fact of girls' lives and had an important impact on their personalities and later development.[3]

In gender-specific guidelines written for the state of Oregon, P. Patton and M. Morgan suggested that while these statements may not be true of every girl and boy, generally speaking the following can be assumed:

- Girls develop their identity in relationship to other people, whereas boys develop their identity in relation to the world.

- Girls resolve conflict based on relationships, whereas boys resolve conflict based on rules.

- Girls focus on connectedness and interdependence, whereas boys focus on independence and autonomy.

- Girls exhibit relational aggression, whereas boys exhibit overaggression.[4]

Although there has been a recent resurgence in recognizing the importance of biology in determining sex-linked behavior, children in today's society continue to be effectively socialized into **gender roles**. Thorne reminds her readers that children have an active role in society and that the social construction of gender—an active and ongoing process in their lives—is most visible in play. When she observed children in middle school, she could identify gender separation and integration taking place within the classroom, in the lunchroom, and on the playground. Children's active roles in considering and constructing gender could be seen as they formed lives, chose seats, gossiped, teased, and sought access to avoid particular activities. Sociologists Barry Thorne particularly found extensive self-separation by gender on the playground where adults have little control.[5]

In addition to the active and to the social construction of gender roles, there appears to be considerable evidence that girls develop differently than boys. Marty Beyer, a clinical psychologist who has examined adolescent males and females across the nation since 1980, said recently that research has identified different vulnerabilities and protective factors in girls. Girls, for example, have a greater tendency to eat to internalize their experiences and they experience higher rates of anxiety, depression, withdrawal, and eating disorders than do boys. Girls are also more focused on relationship than boys, Beyer claimed.[6]

The Female Delinquent

Female delinquency, like all other social behaviors, takes place in a world where gender still shapes the lives of adolescents in powerful ways. Feminist theory starts with the assumption that juvenile females are positioned in society in ways that produce vulnerability to victimization by males, including abuse and the negative effects of poverty.[7] In addition, the variable of class cannot be ignored in understanding the behavior of juveniles. In all dimensions of their lives, class is important in determining how juveniles perceive themselves, are responded to by others, and are treated by the juvenile justice system. The middle-class male youthful offender typically is treated very differently by the police and court officials than is his lower-class counterpart. Finally, one of the most serious indictments of the juvenile justice system is the mounting evidence of its unfair treatment of African American, Native American, and Hispanic adolescent males and females.

A growing body of research is devoted to the study of the characteristics of delinquent girls.[8] Researchers have identified basic demographic and offense patterns as well as background characteristics such as family dysfunction, trauma, physical abuse, mental health issues, substance abuse, risky sexual behavior, academic problems, and delinquent peers as common features among girls in custody.[9]

Until recently, the study of female delinquency has been largely the study of male delinquency.[10] Things changed, however, in 2003, when the Office of Juvenile Justice and Delinquency Prevention awarded a grant to the North Carolina Research Triangle Institute (RTI) to study female delinquency and its consequences. RTI formed the Girls Study Group with the goal of developing a research foundation that will enable communities to make sound decisions about how best to prevent and reduce delinquency and violence by girls. The work of the Girls Study Group is guided by the following research questions:

- Who is the delinquent girl?
- What are the risks and protective factors associated with girls' delinquency?
- What are the pathways to girls' delinquency?
- What programs can prevent girls from becoming delinquent?
- What are the system responses to girls' delinquency?
- What are the life consequences of girls' delinquency?

The Girls Study Group is currently involved in giving presentations and authoring papers about the issue of female delinquency and promises to be helpful in better understanding the female delinquent in the future.[11]

The profile of at-risk adolescent females that emerges from this and other studies identifies common characteristics, including stories of victimization, unstable family life, school failure, repeated status offenses, and mental health and substance abuse problems.[12] These risk factors are similar to those for boys but different in terms of intensity for girls, except for school failure. Further female gender risk factors singled out by the National Juvenile Justice Networking Forum, a project of the Girls Study Group, are early puberty and physical development, sexual assault, depression and anxiety, mother–daughter conflict, and cross-gender peer influence. For example, girls may be more influenced by romantic partners and boys, especially in the commission of minor delinquent acts.[13] B. Bloom and S. Covington offer a profile of female juvenile offenders in Figure 4–1.

One of the most significant and potentially useful criminological research findings in recent years is the recognition of girls' and women's pathways into delinquency.[14] Researchers generally believe that the first step along females' pathway into the juvenile justice system is victimization. Parents, siblings, or relatives may have sexually abused them at home, and the girls run away.

The second step along females' pathway into the juvenile justice system involves substance abuse. Substance abuse is highly correlated with early childhood sexual victimization, especially among white females. The literature also consistently reports a strong link between childhood abuse and the later development of alcoholism and other drug problems.[15] Significantly, at about the same age as the victimization occurred (usually when the girls were between thirteen and fourteen years old), the girls started using addictive substances.

A third step along females' pathway into the juvenile justice system involves girls acting out at home, in school, in sexual activity,

- She is 13 to 18 years old.
- She has experienced academic failure, truancy, and dropping out.
- She has a history of repeated victimization, especially physical, sexual, and emotional abuse.
- She is from an unstable family background that includes involvement in the criminal justice system, lack of connectedness, and social isolation.
- She has a history of unhealthy dependent relationships, especially with older males.
- She has mental health issues, including a history of substance abuse.
- She is apt to be a member of a community of color.

FIGURE 4–1
The Typical Female Juvenile Offender

in law-violating acts, and in gang involvement. Emotional problems and drugs tend to influence their negative behavior and, as a result, girls do poorly in school, are sometimes suspended or expelled, or drop out and often run away from home. Once caught, the girls come before the juvenile court, or they are referred to the court for their involvement in gangs or delinquent behaviors. Figure 4–2 illustrates the pathways to delinquency.

Why Do Adolescent Females Become Involved in Offending?

One of the research questions frequently raised is whether female delinquency has different explanations than does male delinquency. Little disagreement exists on whether adolescent females experience life differently than adolescent males. Researchers commonly agree that females are more controlled than males, enjoy more social support, are less disposed to crime, and have fewer opportunities to commit certain types of crimes.[16]

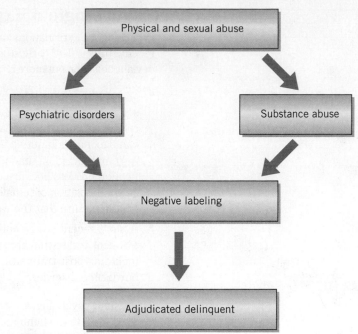

FIGURE 4–2
Pathways to Delinquency

Three different opinions document the approaches to male–female delinquency. One approach focuses on the question of generalizability. Those who support this **gender-neutral** position usually examine social learning, delinquent peer relationships, social bonding, the family, and deterrence and strain.[17] The researchers claim to see no reason to develop theories to account for female and male delinquency and criminality because female delinquents and offenders are pressured into delinquency in the same way as are male delinquents and criminals.[18]

In contrast, the second approach argues that new theories are needed to account for female delinquency and criminality. Eileen Leonard, for example, questions whether common explanations such as differential association, anomie, labeling, subcultural, and Marxist theories can be used to explain the crime patterns of adolescent females and adult women.[19] Meda Chesney-Lind also suggests that existing theories of delinquency are inadequate for explaining female delinquency. Instead, she proposes a **feminist theory of delinquency**, which examines adolescent females' sexual and physical victimization at home and the relationship between these experiences and their crimes.[20] This position argues that the structural categories of gender, class, and race are more helpful than individual or sociopsychological explanations in understanding women's involvement in crime.

In the face of these divergent positions—one seeking to explain away gender gaps and to be gender-neutral and the other focusing on the importance of gender in understanding delinquency and crime—Darrell Steffensmeier and Emilie Allen attempted to put the two approaches together. They contend that there "is no need for gender-specific theories," although they acknowledge that "qualitative studies reveal major general differences in the context and nature of offending."[21] These researchers are developing a third, or "middle-of-the-road," position.

Biological and Constitutional Explanations

More recently, the focus has been on biopsychological vulnerability factors that are related to girls' delinquency. Five general categories are considered: (1) stress and anxiety, (2) attention deficit/hyperactivity disorder and conduct disorder, (3) intellectual deficits, (4) early pubertal maturation, and (5) mental health issues.[22] For example, recently discovered gender-related biological process differences may account for gender differences in stress reactivity, which, in turn, contribute to a heightened vulnerability to behavioral problems with traumatized females.[23]

Psychological Explanations

Psychological explanations of female delinquency also vary between the early and the more recent studies. The early studies addressed the "innate" female nature and its relationship to deviant behavior, but more recent studies focus on psychiatric disorders and female delinquency:

- Gisela Konopka's 1966 study of delinquent females linked a poor home life with a deep sense of loneliness and low self-esteem. Her conception of delinquency relied heavily on the notion of individual pathology, as she concluded that only a female who is "sick" can become delinquent.[24] Konopka identified four key factors contributing to female delinquency: (1) a uniquely dramatic biological onset of puberty, (2) a complex identification process because of a girl's competitiveness with her mother, (3) the changing cultural position of females and the resultant uncertainty and loneliness, and (4) the hostile picture that the world presents to some young females.[25]

- A more recent study, consistent with the other studies, found that along with their physical and sexual abuse, female delinquents tend to exhibit psychopathology, including post-traumatic stress disorder, suicidal behavior, dissociative disorder, and borderline disorder.[26]

In sum, psychological studies of female delinquency shifted in the 1950s from the psychoanalytical to the familial-social, and today to the neuropsychological. As Chapter 3 noted, advances in both the neurological sciences and developmental psychology reflect a much greater understanding of why both male and female delinquents become involved in crime.

Sociological Explanations

Since the late 1970s, numerous studies proceeded from the assumption that sociological processes traditionally related to males could also affect the delinquent involvement of females. General agreement exists among feminists and no feminist literature approaching female delinquency from a sociological perspective offers more promise than literature about biological or psychological causes. Sociological factors focus on blocked opportunity, the women's liberation movement, social bonding, masculinity, power control, and peer group influence to explain much of the gender gap in delinquency.[27]

General Strain Theory (GST)

Males may be more likely to become involved in delinquency than females because males tend to experience strains such as high aspirations but poor schools and a lack of opportunity. They cope with these strains through delinquency. Females, in turn, may experience other strains that may induce other-directed delinquency. For example, GST explains female delinquency by contending that many females experience harsh discipline, parental rejection, peer abuse, negative secondary school experience, homelessness, and a strong need for money.[28]

Blocked Opportunity Theory

The role of blocked or limited opportunity has received considerable attention in the sociological analysis of male delinquency. The usefulness of such variables in studying female delinquency is largely neglected. This is because males are viewed as being concerned with achieving short- and long-term status and economic success, whereas juvenile females are seen as possessing no such aspirations; females are believed to be satisfied to occupy a role that is dependent on males.[29] Several studies have found that such perception of limited opportunity was more strongly related to female delinquency than it was to male delinquency. Both African American and white female delinquents regarded their opportunities less positively than did the male delinquents in studies' samples.[30]

Social Learning Theory

This theory contends that males have higher rates of delinquency than that of females primarily because males tend to be associated with delinquent peers and belong to gangs more often than do females. Some researchers argue that female peer groups are less conducive to delinquency than are mixed-gender or all-male peer groups. However, according to social learning theory, some females tend to associate with others who provide exposure to delinquent models, reinforce delinquent behaviors, and teach identities that are favorable to delinquency. In addition, research studies add that females are inclined to engage in delinquency if they associate with older males or are part of mixed-sex or all-male peer groups.[31]

Social Control Theory

Proponents of social control theory contend that females are less involved in delinquency than are males because **gender-role socialization** results in more social bonds for females than for males.[32] In addition, adolescent females may have less opportunity to engage in delinquent behavior because, in general, young girls are more closely supervised by parents. Adolescent females are also more dependent on others, whereas adolescent males are encouraged to be more independent and achievement-oriented.[33] Those females who are delinquent, according to social control theory, have less parental supervision, are less tied to their homes and families, are weakly bonded to parents and teachers, perform poorly in school, spend less time on homework, are involved in delinquent peer groups, and have less self-control.[34]

Masculinity Hypothesis

Several studies of female delinquents have proposed a **masculinity hypothesis**. Freda Adler contended that if females become more male-like in their roles and acquire more "masculine" traits, in the process, they become more delinquent.[35] Francis Cullen and coworkers found that the more male and female adolescents possessed "male" personality traits, the more likely the girls were to become involved in delinquency, but that the relationship between masculinity and delinquency was stronger for males than for females.[36] William E. Thornton and Jennifer James found a moderate degree of association between masculine self-expectations and delinquency but concluded that males were still more likely to be delinquent than were females, regardless of their degree of masculinity.[37]

Power-Control Theory

John Hagan and colleagues proposed a power-control theory to explain female delinquency.[38] Using a class-based framework and data collected in Toronto, Ontario, the research team contended that as mothers gain power relative to their husbands, usually by employment outside the home, daughters and sons alike are encouraged to be more open to risk taking. Parents in egalitarian families, then, redistribute their control efforts so that daughters are subjected to controls more like those imposed on sons. In contrast, daughters in patriarchal families are taught by their parents to avoid risks.[39] Hagan and colleagues concluded that "patriarchal families will be characterized by large gender differences in common delinquent behavior while egalitarian families will be characterized by smaller gender differences in delinquency."[40] Power-control theory thus concludes that daughters who are freed from patriarchal family relations more frequently become delinquent.[41]

Labeling Theory

Labeling theory focuses on the reaction to delinquency, both the formal reaction by the justice system and the informal reaction by parents, teachers, community residents, and friends. Labeling theorists claim that males are more likely to be labeled as delinquents than are females because of the cultural stereotype that views males as troublemakers and the fact that males engage in more delinquency. Labeling theory does argue that some females are more delinquent than others because they have been informally labeled as delinquents by parents, teachers, and others, and formally labeled by the juvenile justice system.[42]

Interactionist Theory of Delinquency

Karen Heimer reported that delinquency for both females and males occurred through a process of role taking in which youths considered the perspectives of significant others; and among both boys and girls, attitudes favoring deviance encouraged delinquency. She also found that "girls' misbehavior can be controlled by inculcating values and attitudes, whereas more direct controls may be necessary to control a boy's deviance."[43]

Deterrence, Rational Choice, and Routine Activities Theories

Females have a higher level of supervision, more self-control, less time spent in unstructured and unsupervised activities, and less prior delinquency, and these factors make them less vulnerable to delinquency than males. In contrast, females that spend more unstructured and unsupervised time with peers have higher rates of delinquency. This is particularly true of those females who run away from home and spend a lot of time on the streets.[44]

Evaluating Explanations of Female Delinquency

The discussion of female delinquency readily leads to the conclusion that biological explanations are the less predictive factors. Personal maladjustment hypotheses may have some predictive ability in determining the frequency of delinquency in girls, but sociological theories appear to be able to explain female delinquency far more adequately. Some feminists are satisfied with the conclusions of sociological studies that males and females are differentially exposed to or affected by the same criminogenic associations.[45] Strain theory, general theory, social learning theory, social control theory, differential association theory, power-control theory, and labeling theory all have received some support.[46] Other feminists, as the next two sections will show, contend that the unique experiences of females require gender-specific theories. Table 4–1 summarizes the explanations for female delinquency.

TABLE 4–1
Summary of Types of Explanations for Female Delinquency

Types	Explanation
Biological and constitutional explanations	Biopsychological vulnerability factors related to girls' delinquency
Psychological explanations	Focus on psychiatric disorders
Sociological explanations	Focus on social structure and relationships among groups
General strain theory	Females can experience strain, especially in the family and school, conducive to female delinquency.
Blocked opportunity theory	Some evidence has been found that the perception of limited opportunity is more strongly related to female delinquency than it is to male delinquency.
Social learning theory	Some females are more likely than others to become involved in delinquent behavior because of their exposure to delinquent models.
Social control theory	Females who are delinquent have less parental supervision and bonding to the school.
Differential association	Emotional bonds to families are negatively related to the learning of violent definitions for girls but not for boys.
Masculinity hypothesis	Some studies have found that as females become more male-like and acquire more masculine traits, they become more delinquent.
Power-control theory	When daughters are freed from patriarchal family relations, this theory concludes that they become more delinquent.
Labeling theory	Males are more likely to be labeled as delinquent than females, but some females—especially the more delinquent girls—can be informally labeled by parents, the school, and the justice system.
Interactionist theory of delinquency	For both males and females, delinquency occurs through a process of role taking.
Deterrence, rational choice, and routine activities theories	Some females see the costs of crime as low and the rewards as high. They usually spend more unstructured and unsupervised activities with peers.

What Is a Feminist Theory of Delinquency?

The feminist theory of delinquency mentioned earlier argues that girls' victimization and the relationship between that experience and girls' crime are largely ignored. Meda Chesney-Lind, one of the main proponents of this position, states that it has long been understood that a major reason for girls' presence in juvenile court is their parents' insistence on their arrest. Those who study female offending, as well as those who work with female offenders, have discovered that a substantial number are victims of both physical and sexual abuse.[47]

Chesney-Lind developed a number of propositions on the causes of female delinquency. First, girls are often the victims of violence and sexual abuse (estimates are that up to three-quarters of sexual abuse victims are girls); but, unlike those of boys, girls' victimization and their responses to that victimization are shaped by their status as young women. Second, their victimizers (generally male caretakers) have the ability to invoke official agencies of social control to keep daughters or stepdaughters at home and vulnerable. Third, as girls run away from abusive homes characterized by sexual abuse and parental neglect, they are forced into the life of an escaped prisoner. Unable to enroll in school or take a job to support themselves because of fear of detection, female runaways are forced to engage in panhandling, petty theft, and, often, prostitution to survive. Finally, it is no accident that girls on the run from abusive homes or on the streets because of impoverished homes become involved in criminal activities that exploit their sexuality. Apart from their sexuality, these females have little value to trade and feel compelled to utilize their one resource.[48] Figure 4–3 shows Chesney-Lind's four propositions on the feminist theory of delinquency.

What Are the Most Important Dimensions of Female Delinquent Behavior?

The studies of female delinquents have examined several dimensions of delinquent behavior: females' involvement in offenses; their use of drugs and alcohol; their participation in illegal behaviors, including prostitution and violence; their experiences across the life course; and their desistance and persistence as offenders. Gang behavior among female delinquents is addressed in Chapter 13. A feminist theory of delinquency addresses childhood victimization and the ways in which discrimination and oppression, based on a juvenile's race or gender, can shape experiences, options, and identity.

Relationship Between Male and Female Patterns of Adolescent Offending

Early cohort studies provide some evidence of the relationship between male and female patterns of delinquency. Delinquency cohort studies generally include all people born in a particular year in a city or county and follow this group, or cohort, through part or all of their lives. The second Philadelphia cohort study examined all males and females born in 1958 in that city. It found that males were two and a half times more likely than females to become involved in delinquent acts. Law-violating females were much more likely to be one-time offenders and less likely to become chronic offenders.[49] The Columbus cohort study found that males outnumbered females by almost six to one in the delinquent population. The violent cohort consisted of 84.6 percent boys and 15.7 percent girls.[50]

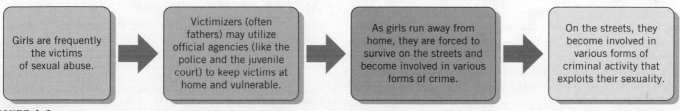

FIGURE 4–3
Chesney-Lind's Four Propositions on the Feminist Theory of Delinquency

Moffitt, Lynam, and Silva's examination of the neuropsychological status of several hundred New Zealand males between the ages of thirteen and eighteen revealed that poor neuropsychological scores "were associated with early onset of delinquency" but were "unrelated to delinquency that began in adolescence."[51] Moffitt's developmental theory views delinquency as proceeding along two developmental paths. On one path, the **early-onset, persistent offenders (life-course persistent [LCP])** develop a lifelong course of delinquency and crime at an early age. On the other path, that of **adolescence-limited (AL) delinquents**, the majority of male delinquents begin offending during the adolescent years and desist from delinquent behaviors around their eighteenth birthday. The early and persistent problems found in members of the LCP group are not found in the AL delinquents.[52]

Female Use of Drugs and Alcohol

Comparative studies reveal a marked decrease in the use of drugs as well as a decrease in gender differences among adolescent drug users during the past decade and a half. An exception to this general trend is that the use of marijuana and ecstasy increased from 2009 to 2011 among both males and females.[53] Data indicate that female high school seniors are slightly more likely than male high school students to smoke cigarettes, although males may be switching to smokeless tobacco, hookah pipes, and snuff instead of cigarettes; on the positive side, cigarette and tobacco use are at their lowest levels for all youths since 1975.[54] Females use alcohol and marijuana at about the same rates as male high school seniors. Male adolescents, conversely, are more likely than female adolescents to be involved in heavy, or binge, drinking.

The primary difference between males and females, according to Patrick Zickler, is that males have greater access to drugs than females but, once given access to drugs, both males and females are equally likely to try the drugs. Presented with the opportunity to use, males tended to use at relatively higher rates than females.[55] The significance of these findings for females is that delinquency may lead to pregnancy, drug-induced dependency of

---

Career Box
Forensic Psychologist Profile

PREPARATION FOR THE JOB

Forensic psychology is the interaction of psychology and the law. Psychologists interested in this line of applied work should have experience working in juvenile correctional facilities, prisons, jails, rehabilitation centers, law firms, police departments, schools, or government agencies. To prepare for their jobs, they should gain experiences working directly with attorneys, defendants, offenders, victims, families, or with residents within the state's corrections or rehabilitation centers.

NATURE OF THE JOB

Forensic psychologists apply the knowledge and scientific methods from the field of psychology in legal settings. They evaluate the mental health of offenders in juvenile and adult corrections, run inmate and youth residents' mental health programs, and provide counseling to victims. Moreover, in the court system, forensic psychologists consult with attorneys to assess individuals' mental health to determine how their mental health relates to the trial. Finally, they consult with law enforcement in order to apprehend criminals. For example, they may create a psychological profile of a suspect to predict their behavior.

QUALIFICATIONS AND REQUIRED EDUCATION

A forensic psychologist will need either a master's or doctoral degree. A master's degree will qualify forensic psychologists for entry level work in places like jails, juvenile facilities, prisons, and mental health centers. The two most advanced programs are a doctorate of philosophy (Ph.D.) and a doctorate of psychology (Ps.D.) in forensic psychology.

JOB OUTLOOK

The number of educational institutions that offer graduate programs in forensic science is relatively small, so entry into a program is competitive. But with the recognition of the importance of psychological factors in behavior and functioning, the outlook is good.

EARNINGS AND BENEFITS

Most forensic psychologists, especially, those with Ph.D or Ps.D earn between $75,000 and $100,000 a year.

Source: In thirty years of court work on capital cases, in working with students who went on to pursue degrees in forensic psychology, and in conversations and interviews with forensic psychologists, I have gleaned the above information.

fetuses in the womb, having to raise children without the presence of the father, fetal alcohol syndrome, malnourished and damaged fetuses, the death of fetuses, and having to drop out of school. Some girls become involved with gangs, theft, and prostitution; experience early deaths from overdoses; and contract hepatitis and HIV/AIDS as a result of their problems. Knowing the paths young women take to drugs may assist in developing prevention strategies. For example, the latest publication of the *Monitoring the Future* study indicates that the nation has experienced a "generation history gap" in people's understanding of the harmful effects of drugs. Society must develop a comprehensive plan to make students aware of the risks of using drugs to reduce the demand side.

Adolescent Females and Prostitution

Silbert and Pines's study found that a high percentage of street prostitutes had been abused sexually as juveniles.[56] Chesney-Lind and Rodriguez's investigation of the backgrounds of adult women in prison underscored the links between victimization as children and later careers as prostitutes.[57] Furthermore, R. J. Phelps and colleagues' survey of 192 female youths in the Wisconsin juvenile justice system revealed that 79 percent of them had been subjected to physical abuse that resulted in some form of injury.[58]

Adolescent Females and Violent Behavior

Since the late 1960s, the media have been quick to identify the violent female criminal, a type not previously supported by research on females and crime.[59] In the late 1980s, the media focused on the rise of violence among juvenile girls when reporting increased arrest trends. Between 1992 and 2003, juvenile females' arrests increased by 6.4 percent, while arrests of adolescent boys decreased by 16.4 percent. While decreases were present across many crimes of violence for both juvenile males and females, the period saw a 7 percent increase in girls' arrests for aggravated assault and a 29.1 percent decrease in boys' arrests for this offense. Similarly, arrests of juvenile girls for simple assaults climbed 40.9 percent, while arrests of juvenile males rose only 4.3 percent.[60]

Brown, Chesney-Lind, and Stein's article, "Patriarchy Matters: Toward a Gendered Theory of Teen Violence and Victimization," challenges this notion of a rise of violence among juvenile females. They claim that self-report data sources reveal that juvenile girls' and boys' violence *decreased* dramatically in the late 1990s. They also cite the findings of the Youth Risk Behavior Survey, the biennial survey of the Centers for Disease Control and Prevention. In this survey, 34.4 percent of girls surveyed in 1991 said that they had been in a physical fight the previous year; by 2001, this figure had dropped to 23.9 percent, a 10.5 percent decrease in girls' fighting. Furthermore, these researchers are skeptical of arrest data reporting rises in violence among young women, because studies of other systems that monitor injury and mortality do not show dramatic increases in violent victimization. Finally, in considering other forms of violence, such as robbery and murder, no data show that girls are becoming more violent. Instead, arrests of juvenile girls for other crimes of violence, including the most lethal, have shown decreases rather than increases.[61]

Brown, Chesney-Lind, and Stein conclude that "someone's behavior has been changing, but it is likely not the behavior of girls, but rather that of police and those who monitor youthful behavior, including the behavior of girls."[62] They believe that three factors are at work in this social construction of crime data on juvenile females' increased rates of violence. The first is *relabeling*, often called *bootstrapping*, of female girls' status offense behavior from noncriminal charges like incorrigibility to assaultive charges. The second factor involves a rediscovery of girls' violence, especially in the arrests of both girls and women for domestic violence. These researchers have found that a closer reading of the available studies reveals that most of these juvenile female assaults are "the result of non-serious, mutual combat situations with parents."[63] The third factor is the *upcriming* of minor forms of youth violence (including juvenile females' physical aggression). Upcriming refers to policies, such as "zero tolerance policies," which have the effect of increasing the severity of criminal penalties associated with particular offenses, such as minor forms of fighting and school bullying.[64]

Gender Inequality and Processing of the Female Delinquent

The underlying theme of this chapter is adolescent females grow up in a culture that facilitates domination and control by males. In this society it is claimed that troublesome adolescent females are seen through the lens of discrimination, exploitation, and oppression. Here are six colloraries:

1. *Adolescent females receive discriminatory treatment because of society's disapproval of sexual activity.* Krohn, Curry, and Nelson—Kilger's analysis of 10,000 police contacts in a Midwestern city over a thirty-year period found that adolescent females who were suspected of status offenses were more likely than their male counterparts to be referred to juvenile court for such offenses during all three decades.[65] Several studies have indicated that juvenile females are treated more harshly than males because of their sexual history.[66] Some studies have found that police officers adopt a more paternistic and harsher attitude toward younger females to deter any further violation or inappropriate sexual behavior.[67]

2. *Offering another perspective, Rosemary C. Sarri concludes that juvenile law has long penalized females.* She claimed that although the law may not be discriminatory on its face, the attitudes and ideologies of juvenile justice practitioners administering it may result in violations of the equal protection clause of the Fourteenth Amendment, by leading them to commit females to longer sentences than males are committed to, under the guise of "protecting" the female juveniles.[68] She added that females have a greater probability of being detained and held for longer periods than males, even though the overwhelming majority of females are charged with status offenses.[69]

3. *Juvenile females, as a number of studies, receive punitive processing through the juvenile justice system.* This results in their staying longer in detention and having longer stays in juvenile institutions than males for similar offenses.[70]

4. *According to another perspective, the oppressive treatment of adolescent females is hidden in the juvenile justice system.* Following the decriminalization of status offenses since 1979, Anne R. Maloney and Carol Foerster reported that many girls appeared in court for criminal type offenses that had previously been classified as status offenses, and they suggested that the juvenile justice officials may have redefined these girls to be eligible for the kinds of protectionist sanctions that have been traditionally applied.[71]

5. *Another expression of the gender bias found in this "hidden justice." is that certain provisions of the Juvenile Justice and Delinquency Prevention Act provide that status offenders found in contempt of court for violating a valid court order may be placed in secure detention facilities, which permits juvenile judges to use their contempt power to confine repeat status offenders.* If a runaway, for example, was ordered by the court to remain at home and she chose to run away again, she might be found in contempt of court—a criminal type of offense. There is reason to believe that juvenile court judges apply their contempt powers more often to female status offenders than their male counterparts.[72]

6. *The early studies in particular found that police officers, intake personnel, and judges supported a sexual double standard.* Female status offenders, as previously indicated, were more likely than their male counterparts to be petitioned to formal court proceedings, to be placed in preadjudicatory detention confinements, and to be confined in juvenile institutions. But at the same time, males who commit delinquent acts frequently receive harsher treatment than their female counterparts.[73]

Figure 4–1 provides a summary of the six collieries of gender bias and the processing of female delinquents.

On balance, some evidence does exist that the discriminatory treatment of female status offenders may be declining since the passage of the Juvenile Justice and Delinquency Prevention Act.[74] No longer do many states send status offenders to training schools with delinquents. But the long tradition of sexism in juvenile justice will be difficult to change. Due process safeguards for female delinquents, as well as for female status offenders, must be established to ensure them greater social justice in the juvenile justice system. The intrusion of extralegal factors into the decision-making process in the juvenile court has led to discrimination against the adolescent female, which must become a relic of the past.

▲ The party has been broken up and several juveniles are arrested. There was alcohol and drugs present, but the parents were out of town.
Thomas Allison/Associated Press

Thinking Like a Correctional Professional

You have been contacted by a member of the governor's committee to bring reform to juvenile justice. The committee wants you to develop a plan to send all institutionalized female delinquents to an out-of-state facility rather than working with them in state as you have done in the past. What is involved in developing such a plan?

Class Oppression

As part of the female delinquent's "multiple marginality," **class oppression** is another form of exploitation experienced by an adolescent female.[75] In a number of ways, serious problems of childhood and adolescence related to poverty set the stage for the young person's entry into homelessness, unemployment, drug use, survival sex and prostitution, and, ultimately, even more serious delinquent and criminal acts. Even adolescents from middle-class homes may be thrust into dire situations for economic survival if they choose to run away from abusive environments.

Traditional theories fail to address the life situations of girls on the economic and political margins, because researchers fail to examine the situations or talk with these girls. For example, nearly all urban females identified by police as gang members have been drawn from low-income groups.[76] Lee Bowker and Malcolm Klein's examination of girls in gangs in Los Angeles revealed the importance of class as well as racism:

> We conclude that the overwhelming impact of racism, sexism, poverty, and limited opportunity structure is likely to be so important in determining the gang membership and juvenile delinquency of women and girls in urban ghettos that personality variables, relations with parents, and problems associated with heterosexual behaviour play a relatively minor role in determining gang membership and juvenile delinquency.[77]

Class becomes important in shaping the lives of adolescent females in a number of ways. Lower-class adolescent females tend to confront higher risks than middle- and upper-class adolescent females. They tend to have more unsatisfactory experiences at school, to lack educational goals beyond high school, to experience higher rates of physical and sexual abuse, to deal with pregnancy and motherhood more frequently, to be involved in higher rates of drug and alcohol dependency, and to lack supportive networks at home.[78] Not all adolescent females at risk end up in the juvenile justice system, but the likelihood of such a placement is greater for lower-class girls.

Prevention of Delinquency

Formerly called the Girls Club of America, Girls Inc. is a nonprofit organization that inspires all girls to be strong, smart, and bold through a network of local organizations in the United States and Canada. Girls Inc. responds to the changing needs of girls and their communities through research-based programs and advocacy that empowers girls to reach their full potential and to understand, assert, and value their rights.

- *Preventing Adolescent Pregnancy.* Seeking to educate girls about the issues of sex and pregnancy, this program is designed to prepare girls to be able to decide when they want to engage in sexual practices.
- *Operation Start.* Aiming to increase the interests and abilities of girls in math, science, and technology, this program specifically seeks to prevent girls who show interest in these areas from adopting an attitude that technology and science are the exclusive arena of males and that females cannot excel in them.
- *Project Board.* Teaching girls about violence and its prevention, this program is designed to help girls resist violence at home and the school. It further shows concrete examples of how to defend themselves.
- *Media Literacy.* Teaching girls to think critically about the images of women presented by the media, this program focuses on issues such as body image and the dysfunctional manner in which the media portrays a female body as a sexual object.
- *Economic Literacy.* Teaching girls how to handle money, this program presents the basic issues such as debt, credit card practices, interest rates, and the value of savings. This program focuses on teaching girls how to plan and control their own economic future.
- *National Scholars.* Making it possible to provide scholarships for deserving young women, Lucille Miller Wright, a long-time supporter of Girls Inc., bequeathed 6.4 million from her estate to the organization to fund scholarships for young women members.

With commitment to provide girls with strong and healthy self-concepts so that they may grow into competent women, Girls Inc. has developed the Girls Bill of Rights.

Gender Across the Life Course

Jean Bottcher, in a study that targeted brothers and sisters of incarcerated teenagers, conceptualized gender as social practices and used these practices is the unit of analysis. Her study revealed social factors that intertwined with delinquent activities, limiting female delinquency while at the same time enabling and rewarding male delinquency, male dominance, differences in routine daily activities, variation in both sexual interest and transition to adulthood, and an ideology that defined both crime as male activity and child care as female activity.[79]

Longitudinal studies usually reveal that delinquent careers differ by gender. Male careers usually begin earlier and extend longer into the adult years. Studies of youth gangs reveal that female members are more likely than male members to leave the gang if they have a child. Also, conventional life patterns—particularly marriage, parenting, and work—draw both males and females away from gangs and offending behaviors, but do so more completely and quickly for females.[80]

Amy V. D'Unger and colleagues' follow-up of the second Philadelphia cohort study found the presence of both LCP and AL delinquents (see Moffitt's classification scheme earlier in the chapter) among the males. There was a higher and lower category for each group. Among the females were comparable AL groups as with the boys, though with lower overall offending levels. The high-rate AL female offenders did share marked similarities with low-rate chronic male offenders. Yet the chronic or persistent category of offenders was less prominent among the females.[81]

Rebecca S. Katz, using waves 1 and 7 of the National Longitudinal Survey of Youth, found that much as in other studies, childhood victimization, sexual discrimination, adult racial discrimination, and domestic violence largely explain women's involvement in crime and deviance. Katz found some support for revised strain theory as an explanation for female involvement in criminal behavior, but she concluded that female crime also may require a unique theoretical model that more directly takes into account female social and economic development in a racist and patriarchal society.[82] Alex R. Piquero, Robert Brane, and Terry D. Moffitt, using data from the Cambridge study of males and from the Dunedin New Zealand birth cohort, found that the vast majority of both males and females never experienced a conviction, and for those who do, the number of convictions is quite small. They also stated that boys, more than girls, tended to become involved in crimes with major by conviction experience and that boys once they are involved, exhibit more variation in conviction activity than do girls; the data further revealed that boys can be separated into the low-, medium-, and high-frequency offender groups, whereas girls could become separated into low- and medium-frequency groups. Finally, their analysis found that "the process of continuity in criminal activity is formed by the end of adolescent similarity for both male and females" and that "there appears to be more similarities than differences across gender in how adolescents and adults patterns of offenses are linked."[83]

▲ A juvenile suspect is arrested by a police officer. His arrest may be dismissed or he could end up in juvenile court and even sent to an institution. A few arrested juveniles are transferred to an adult court.
Radius Images/Almay

In their follow-up of a sample of serious adolescent female delinquents, Peggy C. Giordano and her colleagues developed a theory of cognitive transformation to explain desistance, or the dropping out of committing crime. They found that neither marital attachment nor job stability was strongly related to female desistance. Instead, demisters underwent a **cognitive transformation**. These researchers found that four types of cognitive transformation take place as an integral part of the desistance process: (1) a shift takes place in the actor's openness to change; (2) the individual is exposed to a hook or set of hooks for change; (3) the individual begins to envision and fashion an appealing and conventional "replacement self"; and (4) a transformation takes place in the way the actor views the former deviant lifestyle. These cognitive transformations or shifts not only influence receptivity to one or more hooks of change but also inspire and direct behavior. These hooks "facilitated the development of an alternative view of self that was seen as fundamentally incompatible with criminal behavior."[84]

Social Policy and Juvenile Justice

One other problem is that female offenders represent one of the least—serviced juvenile justice populations. There are only a few effective gender—specific programs nationally. The continuum of programs and services that are required to reduce females' entry into the juvenile justice system must be responsive, both to gender and age and to developmental age.

A gender-responsive policy approach calls for a new vision of the juvenile justice system, one that recognizes the behavioral and social differences between female and male offenders that have specific implications for gender—responsive policy and practice.[85] While gender-responsive policy provides effective interventions that address the intersecting issues of substance abuse, trauma, mental health, and economic oppression, as Bloom and colleagues indicated, a focus on juvenile females' relationships with their family members is paramount as well. (See Table 4–2.)

TABLE 4–2
Gender—Responsive Policy

- Provide effective interventions that address the intersecting issues of substance abuse, trauma, mental health, and economic oppressions.
- Focus on juvenile females' relationships with their family members.
- Provide intensive family-based programs tailored to the needs of adolescent females.
- Provide the opportunities for the development of positive relationships between female offenders and their children.
- Provide community-based services such as family counseling, substance abuse, prevention, and educational services.

Source: B. Bloom, B. Owen and S. W. Covington, "Women offenders and the Gender Effects of Public Policy," *Review of Public Research* 21 (2004), 31–48.

Optimal environment for at-risk females of this age would be intensive, family-based programs tailored to the needs of adolescent females.[86] Another possibility that has merit is a community-based, all-girls school setting anchoring such services as family counseling, substance abuse prevention, specialized educational services (e.g., learning disabilities assessment), and mentoring services. A further gender-specific strategy is offering programs that provide the opportunity for the development of positive relationships between female offenders and their children.[87]

SUMMARY

LEARNING OBJECTIVE 1: Outline the various explanations for why adolescent females become involved in offending.

The focus has been on biopsychological vulnerability factors related to girls' delinquency. In terms of psychological explanations, the early studies addressed the "innate" female nature and its relationship to deviant behavior, but more recently the focus has been on psychiatric disorders and female delinquency. Researchers have also focused on sociological factors such as blocked opportunity, social bonding, masculinity, power control, and peer group influence. Research has discovered that the causal factors identified by these theories can explain much of the gender gap in delinquency.

LEARNING OBJECTIVE 2: Describe a feminist theory of delinquency.

The feminist theory of delinquency argues that girls' victimization, especially physical and sexual abuse, and the relationship between that experience and girls' crime have been continually ignored. In addition, their victimizers have the ability to invoke official agencies of social control to keep girls home and vulnerable. Further, girls on the run from abusive homes become involved in criminal activities that exploit their sexuality and, as a result, bring them to the attention of the juvenile and adult justice systems.

LEARNING OBJECTIVE 3: Identify the relationship between adolescent male and female offending.

Gender still shapes the lives of adolescents in powerful ways. Males are more likely to become involved in delinquent behavior, but female adolescents are also involved in the use of alcohol and drugs, especially alcohol and marijuana, at about the same rates as male high school seniors. Females who become prostitutes are likely to be victimized at home, and the data do not show that girls are becoming more violent.

LEARNING OBJECTIVE 4: Describe how gender affects the processing of adolescent females in the juvenile justice system.

Female offending, like all other social behavior, takes place in a world where gender still shapes the lives of adolescents in powerful ways. Female adolescent offenders have been treated unfairly, particularly those who end up in juvenile institutions. This is so because of society's disapproval of sexual activity; because of the tendency to give females longer sentences than males, under the guise of "protecting" the female juveniles; because of keeping girls longer in detention and juvenile institutions, as compared to males detained for similar offenses; and because the juvenile justice officials sometimes redefine girls to make them eligible for the kinds of protectionist sanctions that have been traditionally applied.

LEARNING OBJECTIVE 5: Identify the relationship between class and delinquency.

The influence of class cannot be ignored in the handling of youthful offenders by police officers and officials of the juvenile justice system. An examination of how the categories of gender, class, and race are interlocked and influence delinquency across the life course will lead to needed insights into the problems female delinquents face in the United States.

KEY TERMS

adolescence-limited (AL) delinquents, p. 80
class oppression, p. 83
cognitive transformation, p. 85

early-onset, persistent offenders (life-course persistent [LCP]), p. 80
feminist theory of delinquency, p. 75

gender roles, p. 73
gender-neutral, p. 75
masculinity hypothesis, p. 77
gender-role socialization, p. 77

REVIEW QUESTIONS

1. How has the social context affected the legal context in terms of female delinquency?
2. How is an understanding of gender learned?
3. Has your experience led to the conclusion that social class matters in the way individuals are perceived and handled in this society?
4. What are the main explanations of female delinquency?
5. What is the feminist theory?

GROUP EXERCISES

1. *Group Work:* All members of the class should look up what is meant by the social definition of reality. Then, probably the next day, form small groups or whatever works best to discuss whether the differences among males, females, blacks, ethnic groups, or social classes are real or are the result of a social definition of reality based on social values.
2. *Writing to Learn:* Write three fairly long paragraphs of about half a page each that describe the biological, psychological, and sociological causes of the behavior of delinquent girls.
3. *Class Presentations:* Break the class up into groups for presentations on gender, social class, and race/ethnicity. Have each group summarize what the book—and outside sources if time permits—states about each. What are the unique problems faced by each social construction?
4. *Group Work:* Have students discuss what the social definition of reality was like in their family, neighborhoods, schools, and communities concerning the behavior of girls, blacks, whites, and social classes. In other words, what were the social realities that everyone grew up with? How about at their current college or university?
5. *Writing to Learn:* Have each member of the class write a paragraph on the area of causation on which they are the weakest and then, in small groups or before the class as a whole, read their answers and revise them on the basis of suggestions made by other students.

WORKING WITH JUVENILES

You have several adolescents on your caseload who cut or mutilate themselves. How will you deal with this?

NOTES

1. Barrie Thorne, *Gender Play and Boys in School* (New Brunswick, NJ: Rutgers University Press, 1993), 2.
2. American Association of University Professor (AAUP), *How Schools Are Shortchanging Girls* (Washington, DC: AAUP Education Foundation, 1992).
3. Peggy Orenstein, *Schoolgirls* (New York: Doubleday, 1994)
4. Marcia Morgan and Pam Patton, "Gender Responsive Programming in the Justice System: Oregon's Guidelines for Effective Programming for Girl," *Federal Probation Journal* (September, 2002).
5. Thorne, *Gender Play and Boys in School,* 57
6. Marty Beyer, "Delinquent Girls: a Developmental Perspective," *Kentucky Children Rights Journal* 9 (Spring, 2001), p. 17.
7. C. S. W. Lederman, G. A. Dakof, M. A. Larreal, and L. Hua, "Characteristics of Adolescent Females in Juvenile Detention," *International Journal of Law and Psychiatry* 27 (2004), 321–27; and M. Zahn, "The Causes of Girls' Delinquency and Their Program Implications," *Family Court Review* 45 (2007), 456–65.
8. Lederman et al., "Characteristics of Adolescent Females in Juvenile Detention."
9. Meda Chesney-Lind has articulated this point in her publications through the years.
10. See http://girlsstudygroup.rti.org.
11. B. Bloom and S. Covington, "Effective Gender Responsive Interpretations in Juvenile Justice: Addressing the Lives of Delinquent Girls," paper presented at the Annual Meeting of the American Society of Criminology, Atlanta, Georgia, 2001. See also B. Bloom. "Gender Responsive Treatment Services in Correctional Settings," in *Inside and Out: Women, Prison, and Therapy*, edited by E. Leeder (London: Haworth Press, 2006). Also published as *Women and Therapy*, Vol. 29, no. 3/4. With B. Bloom, "Creating Gender-Responsive Services in Correctional Settings: Context and Considerations," paper presented at the American Society of Criminology Annual Meeting, Nashville, TN, November 2004.
12. National Juvenile Justice Networking Forum, *Girls Study Group* (Washington, DC: Research Triangle Institute, 2007), accessed http://girlsstrudygroup.rtl.lorg/docs/GSG_NJJNC _June_2007.pdf.
13. Meda Chesney-Lind's feminist theory of delinquency identified these pathways.

14. W. R. Downs, T. Capshew, and B. Rindels, "Relationships Between Adult Men's Alcohol Problems and Their Childhood Experiences of Parental Violence and Psychological Aggression," *Journal of Studies on Alcohol* 65 (2004), 336–45.

15. *Juvenile Female Offenders: A Status of the States Report* (Washington, DC: Office of Juvenile Justice and Delinquency Prevention, 1998).

16. Jody Miller, *One of the Guys: Girls, Gangs, and Gender* (New York: Oxford University Press, 2001), 3–4.

17. Kathleen Daly, "Looking Back, Looking Forward: The Promise of Feminist Transformation," in *The Criminal Justice System and Women: Offenders, Victims, and Workers,* edited by B. R. Price and N. J. Sokoloff (New York: McGraw-Hill, 1995), 447–48.

18. Eileen Leonard, "Theoretical Criminology and Gender," in *The Criminal Justice System and Women: Offender, Victims, and Workers,* 54–70.

19. Meda Chesney-Lind, *The Female Offender: Girls, Women, and Crime* (Thousand Oaks, CA: Sage Publications, 1997).

20. D. Steffensmeier and E. Allen, "Gender and Crime: Toward a Gendered Theory of Female Offending," *Annual Review of Sociology* 22 (1996), 459–87.

21. Diana Fishbein, Shari Miller, Donna Marie Winn, and Gayle Dakof, "Biopsychological Factors, Gender, and Delinquency," in *The Delinquent Girl,* edited by Margaret A. Zahn (Philadelphia: Temple University Press, 2008), 84.

22. Fishbein et al., "Biopsychological Factors, Gender, and Delinquency," 84–106.

23. Gisela Konopka, *The Adolescent Girl in Conflict* (Englewood Cliffs, NJ: Prentice-Hall, 1966).

24. These key factors from Gisela Konopka's *The Adolescent Girl in Conflict* are listed in Peter C. Kratcoski and John E. Kratcoski, "Changing Patterns in the Delinquent Activities of Boys and Girls: A Self-Reported Delinquency Analysis," *Adolescence* 18 (Spring 1975), 83–91.

25. Ossai Miazad, *High Rights,* Brief 10, Washington College of Law, accessed April 17, 2012, at http://www.wel.american .edu//hrbrief/10gender.cfm.

26. Robert Agnew, "The Contribution of 'Mainstream' Theories to the Explanation of Female Delinquency," in *The Delinquent Girl,* 7.

27. Ibid., 9–11.

28. Talcott Parsons, "Age and Sex in the Social Structure of the United States," *American Sociological Review* 7 (October 1942), 604–16; James S. Coleman, *The Adolescent Society* (New York: Free Press, 1961); Ruth Rittenhouse, "A Theory and Comparison of Male and Female Delinquency" (Ph.D. dissertation, University of Michigan, Ann Arbor, 1963).

29. Susan K. Datesman, Frank R. Scarpitti, and Richard M. Stephenson, "Female Delinquency: An Application of Self and Opportunity Theories," *Journal of Research in Crime and Delinquency* 12 (1975), 120; Jeffery O. Segrave and Douglas N. Hastad, "Evaluating Three Models of Delinquency Causation for Males and Females: Strain Theory, Subculture Theory, and Control Theory," *Sociological Focus* 18 (January 1985), 13; Stephen A. Cernkovich and Peggy C.

Giordano, "Delinquency, Opportunity, and Gender," *Journal of Criminal Law and Criminology* 70 (1979), 150.

30. Agnew, "The Contribution of 'Mainstream' Theories," 11–14.

31. Ibid.

32. William E. Thornton Jr., Jennifer James, and William G. Doerner, *Delinquency and Justice* (Glenview, IL: Scott Foresman, 1982), 268.

33. Agnew, "The Contribution of 'Mainstream' Theories," 11–14.

34. Freda Adler, *Sisters in Crime* (New York: McGraw-Hill, 1975).

35. F. T. Cullen, K. M. Golden, and J. B. Cullen, "Sex and Delinquency: A Partial Test of the Masculinity Hypothesis," *Criminology* 15 (1977), 87–104.

36. William E. Thornton and Jennifer James, "Masculinity and Delinquency Revisited," *British Journal of Criminology* 19 (July 1979), 225–41.

37. John Hagan, John Simpson, and A. R. Gillis, "Class in the Household: A Power-Control Theory of Gender and Delinquency," *American Journal of Sociology* 92 (January 1987), 788–816; John Hagan, A. R. Gillis, and John Simpson, "The Class Structure of Gender and Delinquency: Toward a Power-Control Theory of Common Delinquent Behavior," *American Journal of Sociology* 90 (1985) 1151–78.

38. Hagan et al., "Class in the Household," 791–92.

39. Ibid., 793.

40. Ibid., 813–14.

41. Agnew, "The Contribution of 'Mainstream' Theories," 17–18.

42. Karen Heimer, "Gender, Interaction, and Delinquency: Testing a Theory of Differential Social Control," *Social Psychology Quarterly* 59 (1996), 57.

43. Agnew, "The Contribution of 'Mainstream' Theories."

44. Ibid.

45. Peggy C. Giordano and Stephen A. Cernkovich, "Changing Patterns of Female Delinquency," research proposal submitted to the National Institute of Mental Health, February 28, 1979, 24–28.

46. Chesney-Lind, *The Female Offender.*

47. See Clemens Bartollas, *Juvenile Delinquency,* 7th ed. (Boston: Allyn & Bacon, 2006), 211–12.

48. M. Wolfgang, R. M. Figlio, and T. Sellin, *Delinquency in a Birth Cohort* (Chicago: University of Chicago Press, 1972).

49. D. Hamparian, R. Schuster, S. Dinitz, and J. P. Conrad, *The Violent Few: A Study of Dangerous Juveniles* (Lexington, MA: D. C. Heath and Co., 1980).

50. T. E. Moffitt, M. Lynam, and P. A. Silva, *Sex Differences in Antisocial Behavior: Conduct Disorder, Delinquency, and Violence in the Dunedin Longitudinal Study* (Cambridge: Cambridge University Press, 2001).

51. T. E. Moffitt, "Adolescent-Limited and Life-Course Persistent Antisocial Behavior: A Developmental Taxonomy," *Psychological Review* 100 (1993), 674–701.

52. See http://archives.drugabuse.gov/NIDA_notes/nnv5n4/ prevalence.html, accessed May 20, 2012. Please note that the data are not entirely consistent. Recent upturns in the use of certain drugs may be significant or simply a "blip" in the sociocultural patterns of behavior. See L. D. Johnston,

P. M. O'Malley, J. G. Bachman, and J. E. Schulenberg, Between *Monitoring the Future National Results on Adolescent Drug Use: Overview of Key Findings, 2010* (Ann Arbor, MI: Institute on Drug Abuse of the National Institutes of Health, 2011).

53. Johnson, et al., *Monitoring the Future National Results on Adolescent Drug Use.*

54. See http://archives.drugabuse.gov/NIDA_notes/nnv5n4/prevalence.html, accessed May 20, 2012.

55. Mini Silbert and Ayala Pines, "Entrance into Prostitution," *Youth and Society* 13 (1982), p. 476.

56. Cited in Meda Chesney-Lind, "Girls, Crime, and Women's Place: Toward a Feminist Model of Female Delinquency," paper presented at the Annual Meeting of the American Society of Criminology, Montreal, Canada, November 1987, p. 16.

57. Ibid.

58. Federal Bureau of Investigation, *Uniform Crime Reports* (Washington, DC: U.S. Government Printing Office, 2003).

59. L. Brown, M. Chesney-Lind, and N. Stein, *Patriarchy Matters: Toward a Gendered Theory of Teen Violence and Victimization,* Working Paper No. 417 (Wellesley, MA: Center for Research on Women, Wellesley College, 2004), 5.

60. Ibid., 6.

61. Ibid.

62. Ibid., 8.

63. Ibid.

64. Marvin D. Krohn, James P. Curry, and Shirley Nelson-Kilger, "Is Chivalry Dead?" *Criminology* 21 (1983), 417–37.

65. Christy A. Fisher, "Gender, Police Arrests Decisions, and Norms of Chivalry," *Criminology* 21 (1983), 5–28.

66. Jean Sreauss, "To Be Minor and Female: The Legal Rights of Women under Twenty One," *Ms* 1 (1972), 70–5.

67. Rosemary C. Sarri, "Juvenile Law: How It Penalizes Females," in *The Female Offender,* edited by Laura Crites, 67–85 (Lexington, MA: D. C. Heath and Co., 1977).

68. Ibid.

69. Randall G. Shelton and John Horvath, "Processing Offenders in a Juvenile Court: A Comparison of Males and Females, paper presented at the annual meeting of the Western Society of Criminology," Newport Beach, CA. February–March, 1986.

70. Ibid.

71. Ann Rankin Moloney and Carol Forster, "Family Delinquency in a Suburban Court," in *Judge, Lawyer, Victim, Thief: Woman Gender Roles and Criminal Justice,"* edited by Nicole Hahn and Elizabeth/Anne Stanbko (Boston: Northeastern University Press, 1982), 22–54.

72. Donna M. Bishop and Charles E. Fraziwe, "Gender Bias in Juvenile Justice Processing: Implications of the JJDP Act," *Journal of Criminal Law and Criminology* (1992), 132–52.

73. Ibid.

74. Ibid.

75. Chesney-Lind, *The Female Offender.*

76. Lee H. Bowker and Malcolm M. Klein, "Female Participation in Delinquent Gang Activities," *Adolescence* 15 (1992), 509–19.

77. Ibid.

78. J. G. Dryfoos, *Adolescents at Risk: Prevalence and Prevention* (New York: Oxford University Press, 1990).

79. J. Bottcher, "Social Practices of Gender: How Gender Relates to Delinquency in the Everyday Lives of High-Risk Youths," *Criminology* 39 (2001), 899.

80. Ibid., 899.

81. A. V. D'Unger, K. C. Land, and P. L. McCall, "Sex Differences in Age Patterns of Delinquent Criminal Careers: Results from Poisson Latent Class Analysis of the Philadelphia Cohort Study," *Journal of Quantitative Criminology* 18 (2002), 371–73.

82. Rebecca S. Katz, "Evaluating Girls and Women and Desistance in the Context of their Victimization Experiences," *Violence Against Women* 6 (June 2000), 633–60.

83. Alex Piquero, Robert Brame, and Terrie E. Moffitt, "Extending the Study of Continuity and Gender: Differences in the Linkage between Adolescent Oddending," *Journal of Quantitative Criminology* 21 (June 2005), 219–43.

84. Peggy Giordano, Stephen A. Cernkovich, and Jennifer L. Rudolph, "Gender, Crime, and Delinquency: Toward a Theory of Cognitive Transformation," *American Journal of Sociology* 107 (January, 2002), 1038.

85. B. Bloom, B. Owen, and S. W. Covington, "Women offenders and the Gender Effects of Public Policy," *Review of Public Research,* 21 (2004), 31–48.

86. Ibid.

87. Ibid.

ACE STOCK LIMITED/Alamy

Learning Objectives

1. Summarize the history of police–juvenile relationships.
2. Summarize the police's attitudes toward juveniles.
3. Summarize juveniles' attitudes toward the police.
4. Describe police discretion and the factors that influence discretion.
5. Summarize how police process juveniles.
6. Describe the legal rights of arrested juveniles.
7. Describe how police agencies are structured to deal with juvenile crime.
8. Summarize developing trends in how police deal with juveniles.

How does one explain the raw excitement of being a cop? This is an excitement so powerful that it consumes and changes the officer's personality. For the officer all five senses are involved, especially in dangerous situations. They are stirred in a soup of emotions and adrenaline and provide an adrenaline rush that surpasses anything felt before. You are stronger and more agile; your mind functions on a higher level of quickness and alertness. Afterwards, the grass seems greener; the air fresher; food tastes better; and the spouse and children are even more precious. It is an addictive feeling that makes the runner's high in comparison feel like a hangover. Police work gets into the blood and possesses the spirit. You become the job and the job becomes you, until the day you die.[1]

—Veteran police officer

In the chapter-opening quote, the veteran police officer makes a passionate statement about the joys of becoming a police officer. He clearly sees policing more as a calling than as a job or a set of bureaucratically defined duties. He believes that policing demands the very best that a person has to offer. Once it gets into your blood, he warns, it will change your identity and self-image and will stay with you for the rest of your life.

This officer, despite his positive attitude about a police career, has little interest in working with juveniles. With him, as well as with many officers, many problems exist in policing juveniles. Juvenile crimes are viewed as minor, and the arrest of a juvenile is not considered a real arrest. The due process rights accorded to juveniles in recent decades also make the police feel that their crime-fighting hands are tied. Furthermore, police officers are distrusted by many juveniles, some of whom view the police as the enemy. The police, then, must deal with juveniles' hostile attitudes, which can become explosive and violent at a moment's notice. Finally, the nature of juvenile crime is changing; the spread of malls, the explosion of drug use, and the proliferation of gangs have complicated the lives of police officers across the country.

Police officers are faced with juveniles whose misbehaviors range from drinking in parks to murder. At one end of the spectrum are status offenders who have conflicts with their parents, schools, and community but who are not true criminals in either behavior or intent. At the other end are the violent, repetitive offenders. These youths commit murder, aggravated assault, rape, and grand theft; some are in organized crime, and some deal in drugs. Between these extremes are varieties of runaways and mentally ill, dependent, neglected, abused, victimized, and delinquent youths.

The history of police–juvenile relationships in the United States is reviewed in this chapter, followed by juveniles' attitudes toward the police, the cycle of alienation, factors that influence police discretion, the informal and formal dispositions of juvenile offenders, and the changing legal rights of juveniles. The final sections of this chapter consider police organizations and functions as they relate to juveniles, as well as the special challenges that juveniles' drug use, gang involvement, and gun possession bring to community-based policing.

What Is the History of Police–Juvenile Relations?

The earliest Puritan communities in the United States used informal methods of controlling juveniles. Probably the most effective of these informal methods was *socialization*, by which youths were taught the rules of society from the time they were born until the rules became internalized. If a youth violated a law, the family, church, and community stepped in to bring the youth back into line. The family was expected to punish the youth, and if the family failed, church and community elders assumed the task of punishment.

The industrialization and urbanization that began in the late 1700s reduced the effectiveness of informal social controls. As the population increased and cities grew, the traditional tight-knit family and community structures became disorganized and street crime increased. Religious, ethnic, and political violence also increased, leading the society to look for other methods of social control.[2] Police forces were created to help solve the problem.

In the 1830s and 1840s, full-time police forces were established in larger cities, such as Boston, New York, and Philadelphia; by the 1870s, all the major cities had full-time forces, and many of the smaller cities had part-time forces. Social control had moved from the family to police officers walking the beat. The police emerged as a coercive force employed to keep youthful criminals, gangs, ethnic minorities, and immigrants in line.

Police officers had the power to arrest juveniles, but they still used many informal techniques of social control. Some officers undoubtedly were effective in striking up friendships with juveniles and convincing them to mend their ways. In other cases, police reprimanded juveniles verbally or turned them over to their parents or parish priests. Unfortunately, the power of police officers at this time was virtually unlimited; some officers talked abusively to children, roughed them up, or beat them in alleys. The result was that, added to the corruption found in many police departments, considerable tension existed between police officers and the communities they patrolled. Few, if any, efforts to remedy this problem occurred before the 1900s.

In the first three decades of the twentieth century, the Portland, Oregon, New York City, and Washington, D.C., police departments started to address the problem of juvenile crime. Police chiefs began to think in terms of prevention instead of mere control. Policewomen were hired to deal with delinquents and runaway and truant children by patrolling amusement parks, dance halls, and other places where juveniles might be corrupted. The job of these officers was to dissuade the youths from engaging in a life of crime.[3]

The idea of prevention was so popular that 90 percent of the nation's largest cities had instituted some type of juvenile program by 1924.[4] The Police Athletic League was launched in the 1920s to provide children with safe playgrounds, and by the 1930s, most large police departments had either assigned welfare officers to difficult districts, initiated employment bureaus for youthful males, assigned officers to juvenile courts, or set up special squads to deal with juvenile crime.[5] Other innovative actions included instituting relief programs, giving poor children gifts at Christmas, and developing programs whereby police spoke to various groups of youths, such as the Boy Scouts and Campfire Girls.[6]

A major development occurred in the mid-1920s. Until this time, departments had not effectively organized their juvenile crime prevention efforts. Chief August Vollmer of the Berkeley, California, police department is credited with being the first chief to bring together the various segments of a police force to form a youth bureau.[7] The concept spread to other urban areas, and soon youth bureaus, often called *youth aid bureaus*, *juvenile bureaus*, *juvenile control bureaus*, *juvenile divisions*, or *crime prevention bureaus*, were founded throughout major cities in the United States. The police in these bureaus were the forerunners of the modern juvenile officers.

Two developments formalized the increasingly important role of juvenile officers in the United States. In 1955, the Central States Juvenile Officers Association was formed, followed soon after by the International Juvenile Officers Association in 1957. Meetings were held by these and similar groups at regional, national, and international levels. For the first time, the responsibilities, standards, and procedures necessary in juvenile work began to be developed. In addition, the increase in social science research on youths highlighted the necessity of training juvenile officers better, because these officers were expected to help, rather than punish, youthful offenders.

Preventive police work with juveniles continued through the 1960s. Programs were developed to reduce delinquency and to improve the way youths viewed the police. Police officers volunteered to speak to elementary, junior high, and high school students, and some departments developed special programs for these purposes. The Police Athletic League expanded its athletic programs and set up courses in leadership and moral training for youths. Furthermore, some police agencies helped youths find jobs and worked with schools to reduce truancy. Programs to fight drugs and alcohol and to show the consequences of drinking and driving were also developed.

In the 1970s, 1980s, and 1990s, severe budgetary restrictions forced many police departments to reduce their emphasis on juvenile programs. Some dropped their juvenile divisions altogether, whereas others limited their programs to dependent, neglected, and

FIGURE 5–1
Timeline of Police–Juvenile Relations

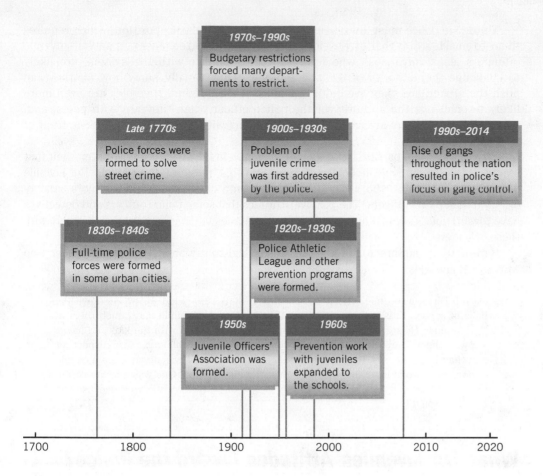

abused children; these programs had commenced in response to the increasingly recognized problems of domestic violence. By the late 1990s and the first decade of the twenty-first century, some police departments were experimenting with community-based or **problem-oriented policing** as well as restorative justice practices.

Beginning in the late 1980s and continuing to the present, youth gangs have developed in nearly every urban and suburban area of the nation, as well as in some rural areas. The problems created by these gangs have resulted in the police being given the responsibilities of identifying and controlling these gangs. Gang divisions were developed in many departments, and other law enforcement emphases were designed to control gangs. Figure 5–1 illustrates the timeline of police–juvenile relations.

Police Attitudes Toward Youth Crime

The police overall have more positive attitudes today toward youthful offenders than in the past, but three occupational determinants of the police work against even more positive attitudes toward youth crime. First, the police see themselves as skilled in their ability to apprehend criminals, but the leniency of juvenile court codes makes them believe that nothing will happen to apprehended youth unless the offense is serious. The police in large cities, especially, think that youth crime is out of control because of the permissiveness of the juvenile justice system.

Second, the dangers inherent in their jobs require the police to be alert to assailants who indicate trouble or danger and, therefore, experienced police officers know that they must be guarded in the police–juvenile encounter because juveniles' unpredictability and resistance makes their arrests difficult. The hard-core offender represents the greatest danger to the police officer. Some gang members, for example, have few qualms about killing police officers. The recent shooting of Michael Brown in Ferguson, Missouri, is a vivid reminder of the dangers of juvenile work.

Third, the police must always defend the authority of their position, which requires them to quash any verbal or physical abuse from either teenagers or adults. Juvenile offenders, especially, those who have had prior contact with the system, are likely to challenge the authority of the police officer. They usually know how far they can push the officer, and they are quite cognizant of their rights. Juveniles are even more likely to challenge the authority of the police officer when they are with peers, and, therefore, new officers are advised to avoid talking with a youthful offender in front of his or her peers.

Patrol officers are particularly reluctant to engage in the juvenile—encounter; their first reaction is to call out juvenile police officers to get this "mess" off their hands. But juvenile officers and detectives who work with juveniles on a day-to-day basis are more service-oriented than patrol officers. The positive attitudes that some police officers and detectives have toward youthful offenders enable them sometimes to develop remarkable report with these offenders.

Here is what the director of a youth facility had to say about one police officer who works with juveniles:

> Darrell Dirks, a juvenile officer, is beautiful. He talks like a kid. He walks down the halls of school. Kids will punch him in the shoulder. He'll smile and punch them in the shoulder. He solves many crimes simply because he talks with the kids and hangs out with them. They will tell him who's doing what. The kids all have more respect for him than I've ever seen for a juvenile police officer. When I was down there a couple of days ago, two kids came in his office just to talk with him. One was a runaway and didn't know what to do, but she went to the police to talk with Darrell because she knew he would help.[8]

What Are Juveniles' Attitudes Toward the Police?

- The subject of juveniles' attitudes toward the police received considerable attention in recent decades. Several studies have reported that juveniles who have had contact with the police have more negative attitudes toward them than those who have not had contact.[9] This seems to be especially true of African American youth whose cultural accepted view of police is independent of their arrest experience.[10]

- Scott H. Decker's 1981 review of literature on attitudes toward the police concluded that youths had more negative attitudes toward the police than did older citizens and that race, the quality of police services, and previous experiences with the police also affected citizens' attitudes.[11]

- Komanduri S. Murty, Julian B. Roebuck, and Joann D. Smith found in a 1990 Atlanta study that "older, married, white-collar, highly educated, and employed respondents reported a more positive image of the police than did their counterparts—younger, single, blue-collar, poorly educated, unemployed/underemployed respondents."[12]

- Michael J. Leiber, Mahesh K. Nalla, and Margaret Farnworth challenged the traditional argument that juveniles' interactions with the police are the primary determinant of their attitudes toward law enforcement officers. Instead, they saw juveniles' attitudes toward authority and social control developing in a larger sociocultural context, and global attitudes toward police affecting youths' assessment of specific police contacts.[13]

- Data from the *Monitoring the Future* survey of high school seniors from the late 1980s through the mid-1990s indicated that high school seniors' attitudes toward the police became more negative during that period across all subsets of the sample. However, the *Monitoring the Future* data for 2007 revealed that when high school seniors were asked their opinions of the police and other law enforcement agencies, 35.8 percent (up from 26.6 percent in 1996) responded either "good" or "very good." If the 30.2 percent of "fair" responses were added to the "good" and "very good"

TABLE 5–1
Attitudes Toward the Police

Favorable Attitudes Toward Police	Less Favorable Attitudes Toward Police
younger children	older children
Caucasians	African Americans
girls	boys
middle- and upper-class youngsters	lower-class youngsters

categories, roughly 61 percent of high school seniors could be considered to have a positive attitude toward law and the police.[14]

- Research continues today into subcultural theory and the relations of juveniles with the police. Terry Nihar and colleagues predictably find that juveniles' attitudes toward the police are positively correlated with the youths' attitudes toward parents and teachers.[15] In a different type of study, Yoland G. Hurst found that rural youths exhibit a more positive attitude toward the police than do urban youths and that whites did not have a significantly more positive view than did African Americans.[16]

- Youthful offenders, as anyone who's worked with this population contest, are the most negative for the police. Many juveniles claimed they had experienced police harassment on a regular basis and police brutality on occasion. They often charged that these police run them off the streets without justification, simply stop and arrest without probable cause, and that the police are quick to put their hands on them.

Summing up, as Leiber and colleagues point out, juveniles' attitudes toward the police are formed in a larger sociocultural context. Most youths appear to have positive attitudes toward the police. Younger juveniles have more positive attitudes than boys, Caucasians are more positive than African Americans, girls are more positive than males, and middle- and upper-class youths tend to be more positive than lower-class ones. The more deeply involved a juvenile is in crime, the more hostile he or she is toward the police. But the findings about the influence of contacts with the police are mixed. Some researchers have found that the more contacts a juvenile has with the police, the more negative he or she feels about the police; others have concluded that for Caucasians youths, positive contacts tend to neutralize the effect of negative contacts.

Finally, a survey of high school seniors revealed that the attitudes of juveniles toward the police today seem to be more positive than they were during the 1980s and 1990s. See Table 5–1.

How Does Police Discretion Affect the Police Response to Juveniles?

Police discretion can be defined as a choice a police officer makes between two or more possible means of handling the situation. Discretion needs to be both professional and personal. Discretion is important, for the police actually act as a court of first incident in initially categorizing a juvenile. The police officer thus becomes a legal and social traffic director who can use his or her wide discretion to deter juveniles from the justice system or involve them in it.

Police discretion has come under attack because many believe the police abuse their broad discretion, but most police contacts with juveniles are impersonal and nonofficial consisting simply of orders to "Get off the corner," "Break it up," or "Go home." Studies generally estimate that only 10 percent to 20 percent of police juvenile encounters become official contacts.[17] In 2004, Stephanie Meyers reporting on data collected from the project on Policing Neighborhoods, a study of police in Indianapolis, Indiana, and St. Petersburg, Florida, found that 84 (13 percent) percent of the 654 juvenile suspects were arrested.[18]

The point can also be made that the juvenile justice system could not function without police discretion. Urban courts, especially, are overloaded; probation officers' caseloads are entirely too high; and many juvenile correctional institutions are jammed to capacity. If police officers were to increase by two or three times, the number of youths they referred to the system, the resulting backlog of cases would be unmanageable.

The police officer's disposition of the juvenile is mainly determined by eleven factors: (1) offense; (2) citizen complainants; (3) gender; (4) race; (5) socioeconomic status; (6) the individual characteristics of the juvenile; (7) police–juvenile interactions; (8) demeanor; (9) police officer's personality; (10) departmental policy; and (11) external pressures.

Offense

The most important factor that influences the disposition of the youthful offender is the seriousness of the offense.[19]

Citizen Complainants

A number of studies have found that the presence of citizens or the complaint of a citizen is an important determining factor in the disposition of an incident involving a youth.[20] If a citizen initiates a complaint, remains present, and wishes the arrest of a juvenile, the likelihood increases that the juvenile will be arrested and processed.[21] If the potential arrest situation results from police patrol, the chances are much greater than the youth will be warned and released.

Gender

Traditionally, girls have been less likely than boys to be arrested and referred to the juvenile court for criminal offenses, but there is some evidence of the erosion of police "chivalry" in the face of youthful female criminality. Yet, as chapter 4 notes, girls are far more likely be referred to the court if they do violate traditional role expectations for them through behavior such as running away from the home, failing to obey parents, or being sexually promiscuous.[22]

Race

Studies differ on the importance of race in determining juvenile disposition. On the one hand, several studies (after results were corrected to account for offense seriousness and prior record) have found that the police are more inclined to arrest minority children; however, several other studies failed to find much evidence of racial bias. It is difficult to appraise the importance of race in the disposition of cases involving juveniles because African Americans and members of other minority groups appear to be involved in serious crimes more often than Caucasians. Nevertheless, it does seem that racial bias makes minority groups special targets of the police.[23]

Socioeconomic Status

Substantiating the effect of class on the disposition of cases involving juveniles is difficult because most studies examine race and social economic status together, but lower-class youngsters, according to many critics of the juvenile justice system, receive different "justice" than middle or upper-class youths. What the critics mean by this is that lower-class youths are dragged into the net of the system for the same offenses for which middle- and upper-class juveniles often are sent home.

Individual Characteristics of the Juvenile

Such individual factors as a prior arrest record, previous offenses, prior police contacts, age, peer relationships, family situation, and the conduct of parents also have a bearing on how the police officer handles each juvenile.[24] A juvenile, who is older and has committed several previous offenses, is likely to be referred to the juvenile court.[25] The family of the juvenile is also an important variable.

TABLE 5–2
Factors That Influence the Disposition of Juvenile Offenders

Individual Factors
Personality characteristics of the juvenile
Personality characteristics of the police officer
Interaction between the police officer and the juvenile

Sociocultural Factors
Citizens' complaints
Gender of the juvenile
Race/ethnicity of the juvenile
Socioeconomic status of the juvenile
The influence of cultural norms in the community and values of the wider society on both
   juveniles and police officers

Organizational Factors
Nature of the offense
Departmental policy

Police–Juvenile Interaction and Demeanor

A number of studies have found that a juvenile's behavior toward a police officer is a significant factor in determining disposition.[26] As would be expected, they show that juveniles who act with disrespect are most likely to be arrested.[27]

Departmental Policy

Police departments vary in their policy on handling misbehaving juveniles. James Q. Wilson found that the more professional police departments had higher numbers of juveniles referred to the juvenile court because they used discretion less often than departments that were not as professional.[28]

External Pressures in the Community

The attitudes of the press and the public, the status of the complainant or victim, and the philosophy and available resources of referral agencies usually influence the disposition of juvenile lawbreakers.[29]

In sum, a sufficient number of studies have been done to provide the outline of an empirical portrait of the policing of juveniles. Of the eleven factors influencing police officers dispositions of juveniles, the seriousness of the effect of the offense and complaints of citizens appear to be more important than the other nine. However, individual factors, department metal policy, and external pressures are also highly influential in determining how police–juvenile encounters are handled. See Table 5–2.

How Do Police Process Juveniles?
Informal Options: On the Streets

Police view youths in the context of their community. This means that officers see how youths interact in their neighborhoods with friends and family and witness the many different ways the youths get along with others. The good beat officer knows who belongs to various peer groups and gangs, who is stable and who is unstable, who is belligerent and who is not; these officers also often know the circumstances of youths' lives. These factors affect

▲ Police officers are required to "know their beats," which includes knowing the people and what is "normal" for their neighborhoods. List some options you might have as a police officer in meeting these youths on your beat.
Constinia Charbonnette

how the **police process** a particular event or incident. For example, some of the following police actions are informal responses to youthful misbehavior, and no permanent record of the incident will be kept, nor will juveniles be held for further actions by the juvenile court:

- Kids clowning around on the sidewalk are simply ignored by a passing officer.
- Police officers suggest that youths take their sidewalk soccer game into a nearby playground or vacant lot if they are bothering people, if someone could get hurt, or if a citizen has complained.
- An officer might talk to a youth bullying others and suggest that the bully change his or her ways.
- Some officers strike up friendships with local youths, sit and talk with them, and sometimes go to their school or sporting events.
- Officers who see youths fighting or stealing something might talk to them about the harm they are causing and how they might get into trouble as a result.
- An officer might write down the juvenile's name and address in a notepad for future reference.

Informal Options: At the Station (Station House Adjustment)

- Youths are taken to the police station where their situation is discussed with them and their parents; the youths are then sent home with their parents.
- In larger departments, youths are sent to a police youth bureau that consists of specially trained officers or other personnel who counsel the youths and their parents but who permit the youths to remain in the community.
- Police officers or youth bureau personnel unofficially refer or direct youths and/or their parents or guardians to anger management classes, vocational training programs, shelters, or counseling programs for alcohol, drug, mental illness, or other problems.
- Police or youth service personnel contact and work with school personnel in getting truant youths back in schools or into special programs. (School personnel may initiate these contacts, and special programs may be set up in cooperation with police departments.)
- Police contact the probation department informally to access probation department programs for a youth in question. (The probation department also handles many cases informally.)
- Police unofficially contact children and youth services to get proper care for dependent and neglected or other children in need of supervision.

Combined Informal and Formal Processing

- A youth is taken into custody or arrested; he or she is then booked, talked to, and released without further action.
- A youth is taken into custody or arrested and booked and then released with the firm warning that any further problems will be dealt with by arrest and prosecution.
- Once a youth is in custody, officers officially notify community agencies such as children and youth services that a youth needs their services and either send the youth to the agency or have the agency pick up the youth.

Thinking Like a Corrections Professional

A police officer describes how she decides on a course of action in an incident involving a juvenile.

Let's take an accident: A juvenile male involved in some form of criminal mischief. He causes a little damage to a house, for example, egging, spray painting. His basic intention was not to cause any major damage, but primarily as a plank.

How would I handle this depends on several factors: how much damage was done, what kind of damage, the juvenile's intent, and how the victim feels. If the damage is minor, and the victim does not want to press charges, but the victim still wants some type of restitution, the juvenile may be asked to come back and clean out the damage and/or pay for the damage him or herself. Along with that is a juvenile's intent and attitude. Was it just a plank in the juvenile and the juvenile's apologetic for, or does he have the attitude that he won't clean it up and does not feel remorseful for the damage? Finally, how much support does the juvenile have at home? Are the parents supportive of the police and the victim, and will they hold the juvenile accountable for his actions? Or is there no support at home? If the attitude of the juvenile is poor and if the juvenile is not to be held accountable for the damage by his parents, then I would most likely have to handle it in a more formal way, with charges.

Formal Processing: At the Station

- The parents of arrested youths are called to the police station and, after booking, have their child released to their care and supervision. The case may end at that point or may be referred to juvenile court for further consideration.

- The youth is taken into custody, booked, fingerprinted, and then referred to juvenile intake, which has both informal and formal options. After evaluation by either the police or the court intake personnel, youths may be placed in secure detention awaiting their preliminary hearing and trial. This secure detention may, in some cities, be in the local jail or a youth detention center.

- Police in states with legislative waiver will, after arresting and booking a youth, automatically waive the youth directly to adult court, which further evaluates the youth.

The further youths are processed into the system, the less discretionary authority the police have. On the street, the amount of discretion a police officer has is considerable; in states with legislative waiver, police discretion is limited, especially as it pertains to violent crimes. In addition, police discretion is governed to a considerable extent by departmental policy.

What Legal Rights Do Juveniles Have with the Police?

Juveniles were at the mercy of the police for much of the twentieth century. Few or no laws protected juveniles in trouble because of the rehabilitative ideal in juvenile justice. Police officers, whose primary mission was to maintain law and order, used whatever tactics seemed appropriate to restore the peace. Friendliness, persuasion, threats, coercion, and force were all used to gain the compliance of juveniles. If these tactics failed, juveniles were taken into juvenile court or, depending on the laws of the state and the seriousness of the crimes, to adult court for prosecution. Few protections were granted to juveniles in the areas of search and seizure, interrogation, fingerprinting, lineups, or other procedures.

In the 1960s, the U.S. Supreme Court's decisions began to change this relationship between the police and juveniles. Although not all police departments have endorsed or adhered to the guidelines laid down by the courts, most departments have made a conscientious effort to abide by the standards of justice and fairness implied by these decisions.[30]

Search and Seizure

The Fourth Amendment to the Constitution of the United States protects citizens from unauthorized **search and seizure**. This amendment states:

> The right of the people to be secure in their persons, houses, papers, and effects, against unreasonable searches and seizures, shall not be violated, and no Warrants shall issue, but upon probable cause, supported by Oath or affirmation, and particularly describing the place to be searched, and the persons or things to be seized.

▲ Private security police face multiple problems with juveniles in the malls including drugs, theft, fights, and behaving in ways that make senior citizens feel uncomfortable. Here a security officer escorts a shoplifter to the security office where his parents will be called.
Kathryn O'Lare

The issue here is the right to privacy. All citizens are guaranteed the right by the Constitution to feel secure in their person and home. Law enforcement officers may not abridge that right without following very strict due process guidelines. In 1961, the Supreme Court decision in *Mapp v. Ohio* affirmed Fourth Amendment rights for adults. This decision stated that evidence gathered in an unreasonable search and seizure—that is, evidence seized without probable cause and without a proper search warrant—was inadmissible in court.[31] This inadmissibility of illegally obtained evidence is referred to as the *exclusionary rule*. In the 1967 *State v. Lowery* case, the Supreme Court applied the Fourth Amendment ban against unreasonable searches and seizures to juveniles:

> Is it not more outrageous for the police to treat children more harshly than adult offenders, especially when such is violative of due process and fair treatment? Can a court countenance a system, where, as here, an adult may suppress evidence with the usual effect of having the charges dropped for lack of proof, and, on the other hand, a juvenile can be institutionalized—lose the most sacred possession a human being has, his freedom—for "rehabilitative" purposes because the Fourth Amendment right is unavailable to him?[32]

Juveniles, therefore, are protected from unreasonable searches and seizures. Juveniles must be presented with a valid search warrant unless they have either waived that right, have consented to having their person or property searched, or have been caught in the act. If these conditions have not been met, courts have overturned rulings against the juveniles. For example, evidence was dismissed in one case when police entered a juvenile's apartment at 5:00 A.M. without a warrant to arrest him.[33] In another case, Houston police discovered marijuana on a youth five hours after he had been stopped for driving a car without lights and a driver's license. Confined to a Texas training school for this drug offense, the youth was ordered released by an appellate court because the search took place too late to be related to the arrest.[34] The least right to privacy is on the street, followed generally by the automobile and school; the greatest right to privacy is in the home.[35]

On the Streets

When a crime is committed in the community, the job of the police officer is to solve the crime and make an arrest. The officer must, however, follow legal rules that guarantee that the alleged offender is treated fairly. How do police proceed?

Consider a police stop as an example: the police officer has the right to stop a youth on the streets and ask questions. Juveniles, however, do not have to stop or answer any questions if they do not want to answer. The officer cannot pat them down, and they may leave if they desire.

A second example is that of the police approaching a youth with a specific and articulable suspicion that the juvenile is armed and possibly dangerous. The law enforcement experience of the police officer, a high-drug-dealing area of town, an obvious bulge in clothing, or the presence of another officer who may have arrested the youth previously and found a weapon on the youth may all lead to reasonable suspicion justifying a pat down. In this case, the officer may do a *Terry* search; that is, pat down the youth's outer clothing in a search for weapons only.[36] Police may not do pat downs as part of their routine stops or in order to find contraband. The pat down is for weapons only. However, in doing the pat down, if the police find an illegal weapon, they may take the weapon and arrest the youth for possessing it; then, they legally may search the youth for other contraband.[37]

A third scenario illustrates another type of concern. A police officer temporarily detains a youth on the street or takes the youth to the station. When is the juvenile actually under arrest? Some jurisdictions consider an arrest as occurring whenever the person stopped does not feel free to leave the presence of the police officer. Indeed, youths in any of the above examples could be taken or asked to come to the police station, be interviewed, and then be allowed to leave; this would be perfectly legal and within the juveniles' rights in some states and jurisdictions. The clearest indicator, of course, is when an offender officially is charged with a crime and given notice to appear at further hearings. A juvenile may, in fact, ask the officer if it is permissible to leave. The options for the police officer here are to release the juvenile immediately, detain the juvenile longer and let him or her go after further questioning and satisfying their concerns, or arrest the youth.

In the Vehicle

Officers cannot pull over youths driving a vehicle and search the vehicle without a reason. The reason can be something simple, like a broken taillight or muffler, but an officer must have an articulable reason to stop the car. The juveniles being nervous or making nervous movements when stopped is not usually sufficient reason to search the car.[38]

Once the car is pulled over, officers may look into it from the outside for anything that is illegal and "in plain view," particularly weapons.[39] If nothing is visible, the officers may not search the car. A 2009 U.S. Supreme Court decision, *Arizona v. Gant*, held that police may search the passenger compartment of an arrested offender's vehicle only if the police reasonably believe that the arrestee might grab something in the passenger compartment at the time of the search or that the vehicle contains evidence relevant to the arrest. But if the officers have information from reliable sources that the youths have contraband, they can search for the contraband. Also, if alcohol or marijuana can be smelled, the officers have a reasonable or articulable suspicion that a crime is occurring and can push their search to the next level, because they now have a reasonable suspicion or probable cause for doing so.

If a weapon or other contraband is visible from outside the car and is within the reach of the juvenile, the officers will ask the youth to get out of the car, and search the areas of the car in view, including the glove compartment, for other weapons and contraband. The police officers can search all areas in the interior of the car that the juvenile could reach into and possibly grab a weapon or attempt to dispose of contraband. Police may not, however, search the trunk of the car without a warrant because the trunk is out of reach of the juvenile.[40] If contraband is found, the police officers can then take the juvenile into custody or make an arrest and take the juvenile to the station; there the youth will be processed either formally or informally.

So, if the police reasonably believe that the above is true or present, it is permissible discrimination. If the above are not present or true, it is impermissible discrimination and not a valid search.

At Home

Police officers may come into a home without a warrant for a number of reasons. First, they may enter a home if a person authorized to let them in gives them permission or invites them in. They may even search a youth's room if they ask permission of the youth's parents, but many police officers still take the precaution of getting a warrant before going to the house. Police may also enter a home without a warrant if they have a reasonable or articulable reason or probable cause to suspect that a crime is being or will be committed. For example, if police are in "hot pursuit," believe that someone will be hurt or killed, or believe that contraband will be disposed of before they can get a warrant, then they may enter a home without a warrant.[41]

Officers may also go into a home if they are standing in the doorway and see illegal substances "in plain view." Now they may enter the house (or dorm room) and conduct a search relevant to only the contraband, as well as to the possibility that weapons may be within reach of the offenders. Any further searches are contingent on getting a warrant.

In the School

Juveniles' use of weapons and drugs is changing the nature of police–student relations in schools. The police are being called on in increasing numbers of communities to enforce drug-free school zone laws. Drug-free zones generally are defined as the school property and the area within a one-thousand-foot radius of the property's boundaries. The police are also called on to enforce the 1990 federal Gun-Free School Zones Act.

The use of dogs to sniff for drugs; the administration of a Breathalyzer test; the installation of hidden video cameras; and the routine searches of students' purses, pockets, school lockers, desks, and vehicles on school grounds are increasing as school officials struggle to control crime in schools. In some cases, school officials conduct their own searches; in other cases, the police are brought in to conduct the searches.[42]

In *New Jersey v. T. L. O.* (1985), the U.S. Supreme Court examined whether the Fourth Amendment right against unreasonable searches and seizures applies to the school setting.[43] The facts of this case are the following: A teacher at Piscataway High School in Middlesex County, New Jersey, discovered on March 7, 1980, that two girls were smoking in a bathroom. He reported this violation of school rules to the principal's office, and the two students were summoned to meet with the assistant vice principal. T. L. O., one of the two, claimed that she had done no wrong, and the assistant principal demanded to see her purse. His examination discovered a pack of cigarettes and cigarette rolling papers, some marijuana, a pipe, a considerable amount of money, a list of students who owed T. L. O. money, and letters implicating her in marijuana dealing. T. L. O. confessed later at the police station to selling drugs on school grounds.[44]

The juvenile court found T. L. O. delinquent and sentenced her to probation for one year. She then appealed her case to the New Jersey Supreme Court on the grounds that the search of her purse was not justified in the circumstances of the case. When the court upheld her appeal, the state appealed to the U.S. Supreme Court, which ruled that school personnel have the right to search lockers, desks, and students as long as they believe that the law or the school rules have been violated. The importance of this case is that the Court defined that the legality of **school searches** need not be based on obtaining a warrant or on having probable cause that a crime has taken place. Instead, the legality of the search depends on its reasonableness, considering the scope of the search, the student's gender and age, and the student's behavior at the time.[45] See Focus on Law 5–1.

Focus on Law 5–1
Search and Seizure in the Wisconsin Schools

The Wisconsin Department of Justice has summarized the Fourth Amendment requirements for search and seizure rules as applicable to Wisconsin schools.* These rules are as follows:

SCHOOL OFFICIALS

- The Fourth Amendment restricts public school officials, but to a lesser degree than the police. The Fourth Amendment does not apply to private or parochial school officials.
- School officials may search students and their belongings if they have reasonable suspicion.
- The police may also search with reasonable suspicion (as opposed to their usual probable cause standard) if they are working at the request of, and in conjunction with, school officials.

CONSENT SEARCHES

- In order for consent to be valid, it must be voluntary and the person giving consent must have the authority to do so.
- Consent does not have to be in writing, but this form is preferable.
- A refusal to consent does not give a school official reasonable suspicion to believe that the student is hiding something.
- It is recommended that the student be advised what a school official is searching for prior to asking for consent to search.
- Consent to search a generalized area is consent to search any items found in that area.

NONCONSENSUAL SEARCHES OF THE STUDENT'S PERSON AND PERSONAL BELONGINGS

- A school official may search a student or his or her belongings if the official has a reasonable suspicion that the area being searched contains contraband or evidence of a violation.
- School officials should balance the intrusion of the search with the severity of the violation involved.
- A school official of the same gender as the student should do any physical search of a student.
- School officials may not strip search students.

LOCKER SEARCHES

- School officials may make random searches of lockers if the school has a written policy on this practice and the policy is widely disseminated to the student body.
- The Wisconsin legislature recently passed Wisconsin Statutes Section 118.325, which codifies the school's right to conduct random searches of lockers.

VEHICLE SEARCHES

- School officials may search a vehicle parked on school premises if they have a reasonable suspicion that the vehicle contains contraband or evidence of a violation.
- School officials may also search a vehicle with the consent of the student.

DRUG-DETECTION CANINES

- Random canine searches on school property are permissible, as they do not constitute a search within the meaning of the Fourth Amendment.
- If a properly trained canine alerts officials to the presence of drugs in an area, this constitutes probable cause to justify a search of the area.

POINT OF ENTRY/EXIT INSPECTIONS

- Random inspection of student items at specific locations is permitted if the school has a clear policy on this practice, clearly marks the area involved, and performs these inspections in a fair and even-handed way.

METAL DETECTORS

- Metal detectors are considered minor intrusions; thus, their use can be justified without reasonable suspicion or consent.
- The wand metal detector is more intrusive than a stationary unit, and its use should be limited to those occasions when the school official has an articulable suspicion.

SURVEILLANCE TECHNOLOGY AND SEARCH ISSUES

- School officials may use visual surveillance in any area where a student does not have a reasonable expectation of privacy.
- School officials should refrain from visual surveillance in areas where it is likely that students could be observed in a partially nude state.
- Audio surveillance is a Fourth Amendment intrusion, and schools should not monitor telephone conversations without the consent of one of the participants in the conversation.

CRITICAL THINKING QUESTION:

What is your evaluation of these search and seizure requirements?[*]

---

*Some of these requirements will vary by state.

Source: For the complete Search and Seizure statement by the Department of Justice for the state of Wisconsin, see http://www.doj.state.wi.us.

School officials' searches of students suspected of violating school rules, especially regarding drugs and guns, have continued to be upheld by the courts since the *T. L. O.* decision. Indeed, of the eighteen cases decided since 1985, state appellate decisions applied the *T. L. O.* decision in fifteen.[46]

School officials, however, do not have unlimited search and seizure rights. The June 2009 Supreme Court decision in *Safford Unified School District v. Redding* placed limitations on strip searches of students. School officials in Safford, Arizona, strip searched a thirteen-year-old girl, forcing her to expose her breasts and pelvic area in a search for two Advils. The court ruled that the search was unreasonable because school officials had not demonstrated that either the power of the drugs and/or their quantity was sufficiently dangerous such as to warrant a search that was intrusive, humiliating, frightening, and embarrassing.[47]

Interrogation and Confession

The Fifth and Fourteenth Amendments to the Constitution address standards of fairness and due process in obtaining confessions. The significant statement in the Fifth Amendment relevant to juvenile interrogations is that no person

> shall be compelled in any criminal case to be a witness against himself, nor be deprived of life, liberty, or property, without due process of law….

Two concerns arise here. First, no one can be "compelled" to testify or incriminate himself or herself. Second, all persons must be afforded due process of law if they might lose their freedom. For the courts, the key issue is whether juveniles are in custody at the time they make any statements to the police.[48] If we look at some of the previous examples of police stops on the streets or brief detainments in the police station, the issue is whether the juvenile feels free to leave. Juveniles who are not in custody, that is, who feel free to leave, can and will have anything incriminating they say held against them; that is, they can and will be arrested and charged and their comments held against them in court.

If juveniles are in custody or arrested, their strongest option is not to say anything or answer any questions until their parents or a lawyer is present. At this point, the now familiar *Miranda* warnings are relevant. A typical *Miranda* warning is:

> You have the right to remain silent. If you give up that right, anything you say can and will be used against you in a court of law. You have the right to an attorney and to have

an attorney present during questioning. If you cannot afford an attorney, one will be provided to you at no cost. During any questioning, you may decide at any time to exercise these rights, not answer any questions, or make any statements.[49]

At this stage of processing, the police have probable cause that the youth is a suspect and has information important to the case. Youths inadvertently can say something that ties them to a crime and results in their prosecution. For this reason, police are required to warn the juvenile against self-incrimination and, if the juvenile requests, make certain that a lawyer is present to discuss with the youth the answers to any questions the police might ask.

For the police to use a confession by a youth in court it must be obtained legally; that is, the youth must have been informed of his or her *Miranda* rights before giving the confession. Otherwise, the confession may not be used as evidence, because the youth's statements are inadmissible under the exclusionary rule.

At what age does a juvenile become capable of intellectually understanding the importance of the *Miranda* rights? Are juveniles under the influence of drugs or alcohol capable of legally waiving their rights? Should youths with mental illness be able to waive their rights? What about youths who do not understand English well?

These issues have been coming before various state courts for a number of years. In one case, the state of California upheld the confessions of two Spanish-speaking youths, one of whom had a mental age of slightly over ten years.[50] A North Carolina court upheld the confession of a twelve-year-old.[51] In another case, a Maryland appeals court upheld the confession of a sixteen-year-old high school dropout with an eighth-grade education.[52]

The questions raised by these court decisions require careful consideration. A study by T. Grisso found that almost all the juveniles questioned by St. Louis police in 1981 had waived their *Miranda* rights. Yet, Grisso questioned whether these juveniles were able to understand the significance of the *Miranda* warnings. Grisso also concluded, after conducting a survey of juveniles, that almost all fourteen-year-olds and one-half of fifteen- and sixteen-year-olds were too young to understand the importance of their *Miranda* rights.[53] In addition, the police must stay within certain standards of fairness in their questioning.

The Supreme Court ruled in *Brown v. Mississippi* (1936) that force may not be used to obtain confessions.[54] In the *Brown* case, police used physical force in extracting an admission of guilt from a suspect. Other confessions have been ruled invalid because the accused was too tired; was questioned too long; or was not permitted to talk to his wife, friends, or lawyer either while being interrogated or until he confessed.[55]

The *Haley v. Ohio* case (1948) is another early example of police **interrogation** excesses.[56] Haley, a fifteen-year-old juvenile, was arrested five days after a robbery and shooting of a store owner. The youth confessed after five hours of interrogation (i.e., formal questioning) by five or six police officers with neither parents nor a lawyer present. During the questioning, the officers showed him alleged confessions of two other youths. The Supreme Court responded by stating:

> The age of the petitioner, the hours when he was grilled, the duration of his quizzing, the fact that he had no friend or counsel to advise him, the callous attitude of the police toward his rights combine to convince us that this was a confession wrung from a child by means which the law should not sanction. Neither man nor child can be allowed to stand condemned by methods which flout constitutional requirements of due process of law.[57]

The *Fare v. Michael C.* decision (1979) applies the "totality of the circumstances" approach to juveniles' interrogations. In this case, sixteen-year-old Michael C. was implicated in a murder that took place during a robbery. The police arrested the youth and brought him to the station. After he was advised of his *Miranda* rights, he asked to see his probation officer. When this request was denied, he proceeded to talk with the police officer, implicating himself in the murder. The Supreme Court ruled that Michael seemed to understand his rights, and even when his request to talk with his probation officer was denied, he still was willing to waive his rights and continue the interrogation.[58]

The states have passed statutes to force the police and the courts to comply with the standards of a constitutional interrogation of juveniles. Among these requirements are that

TIMELINE

1936	1948	1966	1967	1979	1989
Brown v. Mississippi: Confessions cannot be extracted by police violence.	**Haley v. Ohio:** Methods used in obtaining juvenile's confession violated the Due Process Clause of the Fourteenth Amendment.	**Miranda v. Arizona:** This prohibits the use of a confession in court unless the individual was advised of his or her rights before interrogation.	**In re Gault:** This made the right against self-incrimination and the right to counsel applicable to juveniles.	**Fare v. Michael C.:** This applied the "totality of the circumstances" approach to the interrogation of juveniles.	**Commonwealth v. Guyton:** No other minor, not even a relative, can act as an interested adult (acting *in loco parentis*).

FIGURE 5–2
Timeline of Important Police Court Cases on the Police Interrogation of Juveniles

parents or attorneys must be notified and present during questioning and that questioning should take place in an area other than the police station. In *Commonwealth v. Guyton* (1989), a Massachusetts motion appeals judge held that no other minor, not even a relative, can act as an interested adult.[59] Some states require that questioning occur at a juvenile detention facility, at the juvenile court, or at some other neutral place where the juvenile will not be intimidated by the surroundings. Figure 5–2 summarizes important police court cases about interrogation of juveniles, and the Evidence-Based Practice feature highlights a study about interrogation policies and practices.

Evidence-Based Practice
Police Interrogation of Juveniles: An Empirical Study of Policy and Practice

The Supreme Court does not require any special procedural safeguards when police interrogate juveniles and use the adult standard—"knowing, intelligent, and voluntary under the totality of the circumstances"—to gauge the validity of juveniles' waivers of *Miranda* rights. Developmental psychologists, as Chapter 7 will discuss, have questioned whether juveniles possess the cognitive ability and competence necessary to exercise legal rights and have argued that immaturity and vulnerability make juveniles uniquely susceptible to police interrogation tactics. In the more than five decades since the Court decided *Miranda*, there has been almost no empirical research about what actually occurs when police interview criminal suspects and no research about how police routinely interrogate delinquents.

Since 1994, the Minnesota Supreme Court has required the police to record all interrogations of criminal suspects, including juveniles. Barry C. Feld's analysis of these data has begun to fill the empirical void about adolescents' competence in the interrogation room. He analyzed quantitative and qualitative data—interrogation tapes and transcripts, juvenile court filings, police reports, and probation and sentencing reports—of routine police interrogations of fifty-three juveniles, sixteen years of age and older, who had been charged with felony-level offenses and had waived their *Miranda* rights. This study provided the first empirical analyses of the tactics and techniques police use to interrogate juveniles and how youths respond to them.

Males comprised 86 percent of the questioned youth. About two-thirds (65 percent) were sixteen years of age at the time of their questioning. Over half of the youths were charged with crimes against the person—murder, armed robbery, aggravated assault, and criminal sexual conduct. Furthermore, these offenders were criminally experienced: almost half (42 percent) had one or more felony arrests prior to their current felony referrals; nearly two-thirds (62 percent) had prior juvenile court referrals. The majority of juveniles whom police questioned (68 percent) were members of ethnic and racial minority groups.

In the vast majority of cases (89 percent), a single officer conducted the interrogation. Police used the *Miranda* warning process subtly in order to predispose juveniles to waive their rights and talk with the police. Police interrogators used a two-pronged strategy to overcome suspects' resistance and to enable them to admit responsibility. Maximization techniques intimidate suspects and impress on them the futility of denial; in addition, they also provide moral justifications or face-saving alternatives that enable them to confess.

Police may overstate the seriousness of the crime or make exaggerated or false claims about the evidence. Police confront suspects with statements of witnesses or co-defendants, physical evidence, and fingerprints. They most typically (70 percent) refer to witnesses who identified the juvenile. In more than half of the cases (55 percent) in which police confronted suspects with evidence, they referred to statements purposely made by other participants or co-defendants implicating these suspects. Officers sometimes suggest that an admission might garner leniency, while a refusal to confess could result in more punishment.

(continued)

One possibility of reducing interrogation wrongdoing by the police with juveniles is mandatory recording of all interrogations. Despite the value of taping interrogations, the question still remains: Who will review the tape? Despite the burdens and the time involved in going through the tapes, recording is absolutely essential to increase the visibility and reliability of police interrogations.

Another possibility is that the courts should also consider limiting the length of time that police may interrogate suspects, especially juveniles. The fact is that the longer the interview process is, the more likely that a false confession will be made. Most of the interviews in this study were of short duration, less than one or two hours, but lengthy interrogation questioning can pose problems of juveniles falsely implicating themselves.

A third possibility of reducing interrogation surrounding police interrogations of juveniles is concerned with the willingness of police to deceive suspects. There is no way to know, according to Feld, the prevalence of false evidence tactics or false confessions, and there is also no way to know how false evidence affects the ratios of true confessions by guilty people versus false confessions by innocent ones. The unique vulnerability of youth seems to make this practice particularly undesirable.

Source: Barry C. Feld, "Police Interrogation of Juveniles: An Empirical Study of Policy and Practice," *Journal of Criminal Law and Criminology* 97 (Fall 2006), 219–316.

Fingerprinting

The **fingerprinting** of juveniles is a controversial practice. The basic concern of critics is that the juveniles' records will not be destroyed when youths no longer fall under juvenile court jurisdiction. If they are labeled as criminals early in life, social analysts fear, the juveniles will not be able to escape such a label as they mature.

Some states have passed statutes that prohibit the fingerprinting of juveniles without a judge's permission. Many of these states also require that judges control who has access to the fingerprints and further require that the fingerprints be destroyed after the juvenile becomes an adult.[60] In other states, the police control fingerprinting policy. Some police departments follow the courts' suggested guidelines, whereas others routinely fingerprint every juvenile taken into custody.

The most important fingerprinting case to reach the courts to date is *Davis v. Mississippi* (1969).[61] In that case, the U.S. Supreme Court ruled, among other things, that fingerprints taken by the police could not be used as evidence. The youth in question was detained by the police without authorization by a judicial officer, was interrogated at the time he was first fingerprinted, and was fingerprinted again at a later date. The Court ruled that the police should not have detained the youth without authorization by a judicial officer, that the youth was unnecessarily fingerprinted a second time, and that the youth should not have been interrogated at the first detention when he was fingerprinted.[62]

Lineups and Photographs

A **lineup** consists of the police placing a number of suspects in front of witnesses or victims, who then try to identify the person who committed the crime against them. If no one can be identified, the suspects are released to the community. If one of the persons is identified as the perpetrator, the police then proceed with his or her prosecution. The courts have been careful to set standards for the police to follow, because innocent youths could end up labeled as delinquents and confined in an institution.

One important standard is that the offender must have an attorney at the initial identification lineup. This is to ensure that the identification of the offender is not tainted. For example, if a single suspect is shown to a victim with the suggestion by the police that they think "they got the offender," the victim might be pressured to identify the person even though the victim had never seen the accused before. Another concern is the possibility that simply showing a single suspect is "unnecessarily suggestive" and might bias the victim or witness.[63]

In *United States v. Wade* (1967), the Supreme Court ruled that the accused has the right to have counsel present at postindictment lineup procedures.[64] In *Kirby v. Illinois* (1972), the Court went on to say that the defendant's right to counsel at postindictment lineup procedures goes into effect as soon as the complaint or the indictment is issued.[65] In *In re Holley* (1970), a youth who was accused of rape had his conviction reversed by the appellate court because of the lack of counsel during the lineup identification procedure.[66]

TABLE 5–3
Legal Rights of Juveniles

Category	Brief Description of Juvenile Rights with Each Category
Search and Seizure	Juveniles, like adults, are protected from unauthorized search and seizure.
Interrogation Practices	Police must adhere to standards of fairness and due process in obtaining confessions.
Fingerprinting	Police handle the fingerprinting of juveniles in a wide variety of ways; however, there is more consistency in how they destroy the records after their purpose has been served.
Pretrial Identification Practices	The photographing and placing of juveniles in lineups are controversial but are more frequently taking place today than in the past.

Photographs also can play an important part in the identification of offenders. For example, in one case, a rape victim was shown a photograph of one suspect only. She could not identify the offender from the photograph, but then later identified her attacker in a probation office. A California appellate court noted that permitting the identification of offenders on the basis of only one photograph was inappropriate because it could prejudice the victim.[67]

Another problem with photographs is their permanency and potential stigmatizing effect on youths in the community. A youth taken in for questioning who has his or her photograph taken is easily identified. Because photographs are filed and frequently reviewed by police officers, the police examine these photographs whenever something happens in the community. Innocent youths may never be able to escape the stigma of such labeling. For these reasons, some states require that judges give the police written consent to take photographs, that the photographs not be published in the media, and that the photographs be destroyed when the youths become adults. Table 5–3 summarizes our discussion of the legal rights of juveniles.

Social Context of Juvenile Crime: The Police and the Prevention of Juvenile Offenses

Three ways in which police departments are attempting to implement policing in the prevention and deterrence of youth crime are community-based, school-based, and gang-based interventions (see Figure 5–3).

Community-Based Interventions

Community relations are a major focus of police officers who work with juveniles. They must cultivate good relations with school administers and teachers, with the staff of community agencies, with the staff of local youth organizations and youth shelters, with the juvenile court, and with merchants and employees at popular juvenile hangouts. Of course, juvenile police officers also must develop good relations with the parents of youthful offenders as well as with the offenders themselves. The officer who has earned the respect of youth of the

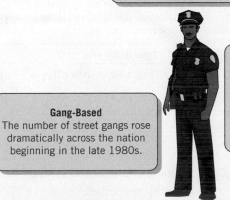

> **Community-Based**
> Community relations are a major focus of police officers who work with juveniles.

> **School-Based**
> Developing effective delinquency prevention programs in schools is one of the most important challenges facing the police today.

> **Gang-Based**
> The number of street gangs rose dramatically across the nation beginning in the late 1980s.

FIGURE 5–3
Three Types of Police Interventions

community will be aware of what is happening in the community and will be more likely called on for assistance by youths in trouble.

One of the important challenges police face today is finding missing children. The AMBER Alert system began in 1996 when Dallas–Fort Worth broadcasters teamed with local police departments to develop an early warning system to assist in finding abducted children, which they called the Dallas AMBER plan. AMBER, which stands for America's Missing: Broadcast Emergency Response, was named in memory of nine-year-old Amber Hagerman, who was kidnapped and brutally murdered while riding her bicycle in Arlington, Texas, in 1996. Other states and communities soon set up their own alert plans and the AMBER network was adopted nationwide.[68]

The police are called on to intercede in a variety of juvenile problems. These include enforcing the curfew ordinances that more and more communities across the nation are passing,[69] enforcing drug laws,[70] preventing hate crimes committed by teenagers against minority groups (Jews, other ethnic groups, and homosexuals),[71] focusing attention on the serious habitual offender, enhancing the quality and relevance of information that is exchanged through active interagency collaboration, and controlling gun-related violence in the youth population.

In many larger cities, police departments formed special juvenile units to address youth crime. A 2000 survey of law enforcement agencies (those with 100 or more sworn officers) reported that a large proportion of these agencies had special units targeting juvenile justice concerns[72] (see Table 5–4).

School-Based Interventions

Developing effective delinquency prevention programs for the schools is one of the most important challenges facing the police today. Community Predelinquent Programs have included courses in high school, junior high school, and elementary school settings that address school safety, community relations, drug and alcohol abuse, city government, court proceedings, bicycle safety, and juvenile delinquency. The Officer Friendly and McGruff "Take a Bite out of Crime" programs were established throughout the nation to develop better relations with younger children.

More recently, popular prevention programs have included Gang Resistance Education and Training (G.R.E.A.T.) and Law Enforcement Education (LRE). Since the G.R.E.A.T. program began in 1991, more than twelve thousand law enforcement officers have been certified as G.R.E.A.T. instructors and close to 6 million students have graduated from the G.R.E.A.T. program.[73] This program is found in all fifty states and in the District of Columbia and is in used in over five hundred communities across the United States. During

---

TABLE 5–4
Special Units Targeting Juvenile Concerns

	Type of Agency	
Type of Special Unit	**Local Police**	**State**
Drug education in schools	70%	30%
Juvenile crime	62	10
Gangs	45	18
Child abuse	46	8
Domestic violence	45	10
Missing children	48	31
Youth outreach	33	6

Source: Office of Juvenile Justice and Delinquency Prevention, *Juvenile Offenders and Victims: 2006 National Report* (Washington, DC: U.S. Government Printing).

1999–2000, the program underwent an extensive program and curriculum review. The original program was expanded to thirteen lessons, placed more emphasis on active learning, and increased teacher involvement. The G.R.E.A.T. program currently consists of a thirteen-week middle school curriculum, an elementary curriculum, a summer program, and family training.

Evaluations were conducted in 1999, 2001, 2004, and another one—of the new curriculum—was scheduled to conclude in 2012. From all of the surveys conducted, the consistent finding was that the G.R.E.A.T. program did not reduce youths' involvement in gangs and delinquent behavior, but it did help them develop positive attitudes and relationships with law enforcement.[74]

LRE is designed to teach students the fundamental principles and skills needed to become responsible citizens in a constitutional democracy. One of the few studies evaluating the LRE program found that these programs, when properly conducted, can reduce tendencies toward delinquent behavior and improve the range of attitudes relating to responsible citizenship, and have found that successful students were also less likely to associate with delinquent peers and to use violence as a means of resolving conflict.[75]

New York City's School Program to Educate and Control Drug Abuse, Project SPECDA, a collaborative effort of the city police department and the board of education, is another highly praised drug prevention program. In this project, a sixteen-session curriculum, with the units split evenly between fifth and sixth grade, imparts basic information about the risk and effects of drug abuse, makes students aware of the social pressures that lead to drug abuse, and teaches acceptable methods for resisting peer pressure to experiment with drugs.[76]

In addition to drug prevention programs, the police respond to incidents ranging from student fights and assaults to drug and weapon possession. Officers also drive by schools during night and weekend patrols to prevent vandalism and burglary to school property, and

Juvenile School Resource Officer (SRO)

PREPARATION FOR THE JOB

In order to prepare for this job a person should first become a police officer because this job is usually for police officers who are designated to a particular school in the area. This job requires that the person can work well with students of all ages and be able to help them in any way that may come across during duty. The person must also be able to work closely with the administration of the school to create effective programs that can help limit criminal behavior.

QUALIFICATION AND EDUCATIONAL REQUIREMENTS

Each department may have different qualifications for an SRO, but most have already been employed in law enforcement before they are sent to be an SRO. Some places require that an SRO has a law enforcement certificate and previous academic experience. Since law enforcement jobs require that a person has a high school diploma or something that is the equivalent so it would be smart to assume that is needed at any location that has SROs. Having an advanced degree could be useful in getting a job as an SRO especially if it is in psychology, or something to do with counseling since this job includes the duties of counseling the students.

DUTIES

Provide protection to school age children ranging from kindergarten through 12th grade. There are three main roles of responsibility for an SRO. First is to fulfill their roles as a law enforcement officer, second is to develop a relationship with the students, and third is to investigate criminal incidents that happen with the students and to refer students to the juvenile authorities when necessary. This job will also include night and weekend events that may happen with the school, so if you are unable to work these times then it is not the job for you. Another part of this job includes being there to counsel the students.

DEMAND FOR SROs

SROs are becoming more needed in our society because of the crimes that are starting to develop more in the school systems. There are school shootings that are beginning to happen at a faster rate, and cyber bullying is also becoming one of the lead problems in the school system. SROs can help to eliminate cyber bullying, and they may be able to help anticipate a school shooting or at least to educate the students on what to do if that situation were to occur.

SALARY

Most SROs are paid the same salary as patrol officers, which was an average of $55,270 in 2012. This number can change according to which department you work for.

Source: "What Is the Job Description of a School Resource Officer" http://work.chron.com/job-description-school-resource-officer-19546.html (accessed October 30, 2014).

the police are responsible for providing security and safety to the schools. In some schools, this requires conducting searches of students as they come into the school, monitoring the halls, doing conflict mediation when necessary, and protecting students as they come to and go home from school. The police are frequently called on to assist the school in searching for weapons and drugs on school property and are charged to enforce drug-free school zone laws and the federal Gun-Free School Zones Act. The police are also expected to enforce school attendance programs in a few school districts across the nation.

The federal Office of Community-Oriented Policing Services (COPS) has awarded almost $715 million to more than 2,900 law enforcement agencies to fund more than 6,300 school resource officers (SROs) through the COPS in School (CIS) program. In addition, COPS has appropriated nearly $21 million to train COPS-funded SROs and school administrators in partnering school or school districts to work more collaboratively through the CIS program. SROs in schools can serve in a variety of ways: they may function not only as law enforcement officers but as problem solvers, LRE educators, and community liaisons; they may teach classes about crime prevention, substance abuse awareness, and gang resistance; they may monitor and assist troubled students through mentoring programs; and they may promote social and personal responsibility by encouraging student participation in community service activities. Moreover, these officers help students develop policies to address delinquent activity and school safety.

Gang-Based Interventions

The number of street gangs rose dramatically across the nation beginning in the late 1980s. The characteristics of these gangs vary widely from one city to another. Some of these gangs are simply groups of adolescents who hang around together and who seldom get into any serious trouble; other gangs engage in extensive drug activity, and some have become involved in violent drive-by shootings in which innocent children have been killed.

Drugs and violence have made gangs a problem for the police. For example, police officers caught a group of Los Angeles Crips conducting a drug sales seminar in St. Louis, Missouri.[77] Once a community becomes aware of the seriousness of its drug problem—usually after a violent gang incident has taken place—pressure is typically put on the police to solve the problem. Police departments have frequently responded to this pressure by setting up one of three types of intervention units to work with gangs.

A **Youth Service Program**, which is one such unit, is formed to deal with a specific gang problem and is not a permanent unit within the department; officers continue to perform their regular duties and are not exclusively concerned with gang problems. The **gang detail** is a second type of unit in which the officers are generally pulled from detective units or juvenile units. The gang detail differs from the Youth Service Program in that its officers are assigned solely to gang problems and do not routinely work on other assignments. The **gang unit** is a third type of unit that is permanent. The members of these permanent units see themselves as specialists who work on gang problems specialists, for example, many gang units will develop extensive intelligent networks with gang members in the community.

Formalizing Police Referral Programs

The police are the first line of contact with law-violating juveniles. They frequently have the discretion to divert a youth or refer him or her to the attention of the juvenile justice system, especially when the juvenile is involved in a minor offense. As repeatedly stated in this text, there is no question that the juvenile who has an early onset of crime behavior and comes to the attention of the justice system is more likely to be involved with the justice system longer and go on to the adult system than the youth who is diverted from the system or begins his or her onset of crime at a later date in adolescence. The police, who must try everything possible to avoid contributing to the ongoing delinquency and later criminality of individuals, can undertake activities such as those shown in Figure 5–4.

Common sense drove police officers and police chiefs to support prevention and referrals to community agencies since the early 1900s, but the programs were locally administered and sporadically implemented. Some larger cities hired youth officers and juvenile specialists, put police officers in schools as truancy officers, and set up counseling services and performed referral functions.

Today, federal, state, and local police departments are beginning to address childhood development and delinquency.

Tom Sanchez, captain of the Hollywood, Florida, Police Department, identifies what police departments must do to effectively set up police referral programs. Department administrators must determine how many at-risk youths require referral; how many services for youths are in existence; which programs meet the police department's standards for inclusion; determine the means and frequency of evaluating the programs; and make certain that the intervention process starts early.[78]

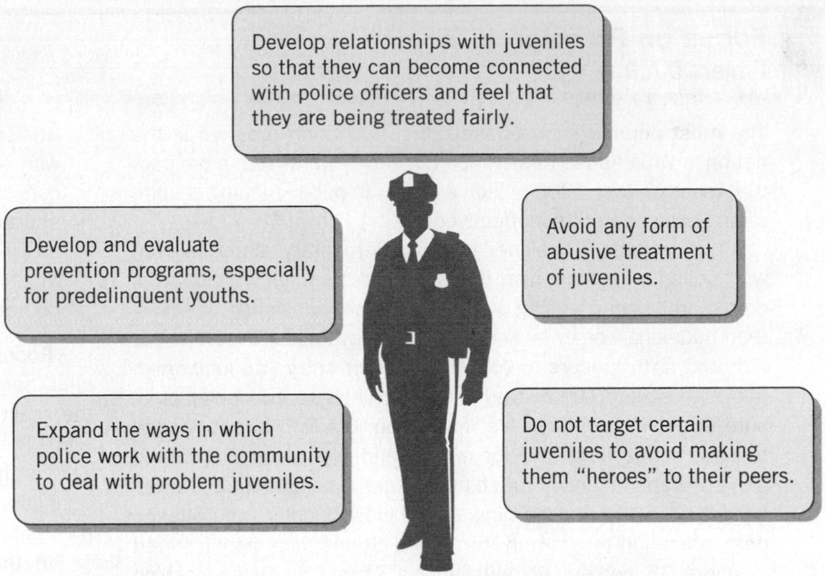

Project SHIELD was founded in 1996 by the Bureau of Justice Assistance and implemented in the Westminster City Police Department in Orange County, California. Two primary goals of this program included, first, to build on the long-standing recognition that police officers do much more than simply control crime through arresting and processing offenders. Officers are often the initial responders to crisis situations involving at-risk youths. The police are the first to recognize community, individual, peer group, school, and family risk factors at homes, on the streets, and in schools. Second, knowing these risk factors enables police to then utilize multidisciplinary teams consisting of community and school representatives to refer youths to the appropriate agencies. Thus, whether youths witness violence or experience neglect, emotional, or sexual abuse; drunken, mentally ill, or addicted parents; or disturbing events on the streets, police can utilize approved and formalized procedures called for by SHIELD to get the youths to appropriate agencies.

The candidates for the program are evaluated by the SHIELD resource officer (SRO) to determine a youth's appropriateness for intervention. Assessment techniques are used to place youths in low-, medium-, or high-risk categories for both delinquency and gang involvement. Different risk assessment tools are used for youths ages 6 to 11 and those 12 to 14 to analyze how youths at different developmental levels are affected by different risk factors. The youths are also analyzed to determine how many protective factors surround them in order to gain as comprehensive a view of the youth's life as possible. All the information gathered by the SROs is then sent to a multidisciplinary Youth and Family Resource Team that meets weekly to determine the appropriate agency referrals. The assignment to a specific program may or may not require parental consent, a potential problem for some youths because abusive parents often strongly oppose the participation of their son or daughter in a program. The Youth and Family Resource Team receives regular reports from the referral agencies on each youth's progress, which allows the team to track and reassess the youths when necessary.[79]

In a 2013 article, Eleda T Broddus and colleagues describe a program that the Baltimore police provide youth—The Baltimore Outward Bound Police Insight Program, a unique one day police–juvenile program, brings officers and middle school students together for a range of team building activities.[80]

Researchers' analysis indicates the program successfully brings officers and youth together in a situation in which they have equal status, share common goals, must cooperate to succeed, and have the support of authority figures. Other key program components are the neutral environment, fun and engaging atmosphere, and open discussion of stereotypes. Outcomes reported by participants include reduced stereotypes of the opposite group and desire for future positive interactions. The researchers recommend that this Police Insight Program model could serve as a stepping stone toward improved relationships between officers and youth in Baltimore and elsewhere.[81]

Develop relationships with juveniles so that they can become connected with police officers and feel that they are being treated fairly.

Develop and evaluate prevention programs, especially for predelinquent youths.

Avoid any form of abusive treatment of juveniles.

Expand the ways in which police work with the community to deal with problem juveniles.

Do not target certain juveniles to avoid making them "heroes" to their peers.

FIGURE 5–4
Police Activities to Combat Delinquency

Focus on Practice 5–2
Project D.A.R.E

The most popular school-based drug education program in the nation is Drug Abuse Resistance Education (D.A.R.E.), a program that receives over $200 million annually in public funding despite strong evidence of its ineffectiveness.

This program is designed to equip elementary school children with skills for resisting peer pressure to experiment with tobacco, drugs, and alcohol. Using a core curriculum consisting of seventeen hour-long weekly lessons, D.A.R.E. pays special attention to fifth and sixth graders to prepare them for entry into junior high and high school, where they are most likely to encounter pressure to use drugs. Since its foundation, D.A.R.E. has expanded to encompass programs for middle and high school students, gang prevention, conflict resolution, parent education, and after-school recreation and learning. As the most popular school-based drug education program in the United States, it is administered in about 75 percent of this nation's school districts, reaching 26 million, and has been adopted in more than fifty countries.

Widely evaluated, the disappointing findings can be summarized in the following way:

- The D.A.R.E. program has some immediate beneficial effects on student knowledge of drugs, social skills, attitudes about drug use, and attitudes toward the police.
- These effects dissipate quickly and are typically gone within one to two years.
- Most importantly, the effects of D.A.R.E. on drug use behavior (measured in numerous ways) are extremely rare and when identified, tend to be small in size and dissipate quickly.

Rosenbaum summarized this collective evidence:

In sum, the results were very disappointing despite high expectations for the program. Across more than

30 studies, the collective evidence from evaluations with reasonably good scientific validity suggests that the core D.A.R.E. program does not prevent drug use in the short-term, nor does it prevent drug use when students are ready to enter high school or college. Students who receive D.A.R.E. are indistinguishable from students who do not participate in the program.

Rosenbaum raises a question that has been widely raised elsewhere: "How can we reconcile this state of knowledge with the reality of worldwide support for D.A.R.E.?" He goes on to say: "The irony for the drug prevention field (and other fields as well) is that a program known to be ineffective receives millions of dollars in support, whereas programs known to be effective or promising are sidelined and remain unfunded."

In the 1990s and early 2000s, dozens of communities dropped the D.A.R.E. program, but the debate whether to continue funding has been waged both nationally and internationally. Proponents of the D.A.R.E. program constitute a strong interest group, and presently are able to maintain federal funding for this delinquent prevention program.

CRITICAL THINKING QUESTION

What explains the popularity of D.A.R.E. when evaluations of this program have been far less than positive?

Source: National Institute of Justice, *The D.A.R.E. Program: A Review of Prevalence, User Satisfaction, and Effectiveness* (Washington, DC: U.S. Department of Justice, 1994); Dennis P. Rosenbaum, "Just Say No to D.A.R.E.," *Criminology & Public Policy* 6 (November 2007), 815–24.

SUMMARY

LEARNING OBJECTIVE 1: Summarize the history of police–juvenile relationships.

In the early 1900s, police became concerned about the problem of juvenile crime. In the 1920s and 1930s, the Police Athletic League and other prevention programs were formed. In the 1950s and 1960s, juvenile police officers associations were formed and became active. In the final decades of the twentieth century, budgetary restrictions forced many departments to restrict juvenile programs, and in the past decade or so, the police have focused on gang control.

LEARNING OBJECTIVE 2: Summarize the Police's Attitudes Toward Juveniles.

The police have more positive attitudes toward juveniles today than in the past, but occupational determinants work against even more positive attitudes toward youth crime. One of the most serious is that e experienced officers are aware that they must be guarded in police-juvenile relationships. The recent negative

mass media coverage of police-juvenile interactions make this even more mandatory.

LEARNING OBJECTIVE 3: Summarize juveniles' attitudes toward the police.

Younger children, whites, girls, and middle- and upper-class youngsters have more favorable attitudes toward the police, while older children, African Americans, boys, and lower-class youngsters have less favorable attitudes toward the police.

LEARNING OBJECTIVE 4: Describe police discretion and the factors that influence discretion.

Police discretion can be defined as the choice between two or more possible means of handling a situation confronting the police officers. The police officer's disposition of the juvenile is largely determined by nine factors: the nature of the offense, citizen complainants, the juvenile's sex, race, socioeconomic status, and other individual characteristics; the nature of the interaction between the police officer and the juvenile; departmental policy; and external pressures in the community.

LEARNING OBJECTIVE 5: Summarize how police process juveniles.

Police view youth in the context of their community. Informal options are available where the youth is taken to the police station and then sent home with the parents. Formal processing is also available where the youth may be referred to juvenile court for further consideration.

LEARNING OBJECTIVE 6: Describe the legal rights of arrested juveniles.

Juveniles have legal rights in terms of search and seizure, interrogation practices, fingerprinting, and pretrial identification practices. With the first two, juveniles have the constitutional rights of adults, but with the latter two, juveniles receive some protection.

LEARNING OBJECTIVE 7: Describe how police agencies are structured to deal with juvenile crime.

Police are attempting to implement juvenile policing in community-based, school-based, and gang-based interventions.

LEARNING OBJECTIVE 8: Summarize developing trends in how police deal with juveniles.

The police continue to support prevention and referrals to community agencies; today, federal, state, and local police departments are getting more organized to address childhood development and delinquency.

KEY TERMS

Police discretion, p. 95
fingerprinting, p. 106
gang detail, p. 110
gang unit, p. 110

interrogation, p. 104
lineup, p. 106
photographs, p. 107
police process, p. 98

problem-oriented policing, p. 93
school searches, p. 102
search and seizure, p. 99
Youth Service Program, p. 110

REVIEW QUESTIONS

1. What could be done to improve police acceptance in the lowest income communities?
2. Should the police be more responsible for intervening in the lives of infants and children?
3. What are the most important legal rights of juveniles?
4. How would you evaluate the police's attempts to prevent and deter delinquency?

GROUP EXERCISES

1. *Group Work:* Many members of the class have experienced contact with police officers (traffic tickets, alcohol or drug queries, or other "events") or know close friends who have. Discuss the nature of those contacts, the attitudes and behaviors of the police, and whether you (usually the women in class) "got off" because you cried. What were the attitudes and feelings after that contact and how do you evaluate those experiences? After small group discussions, "report out" to the class to determine what patterns existed in the observations.

2. *Group Work:* Discuss each of the factors that influence police discretion. Which of those factors are legitimate factors that police should take into consideration and which are not? Should any special circumstances be taken into consideration when examining these factors? All groups should report out to the class as a whole for further discussion.

3. *Writing to Learn Exercise:* Everyone should write for about twenty minutes on the following topics: The nature of police–juvenile relations in the community; and the different ways police can formally or informally process youths upon contact.

4. *Writing to Learn Exercise:* All class members are to write two to three paragraphs on the search and seizure requirements of the police. Critique and revise.

5. *Class Debate:* Split the class into two groups. Charge one group to develop the topic, "Resolved: the police function with juveniles should be limited to order, societal protection, and control of juveniles through legal processing." Charge the other group with the topic, "Resolved: the police should focus on prevention and the referral of juveniles to appropriate community agencies." Give each group sufficient time to develop its arguments and have the groups debate the two topics in class. After one debate, have the groups switch arguments.

WORKING WITH JUVENILES

In working with juveniles, one of the most important attributes is to tell the truth. Many juveniles who have had contact with the police are not used to those in the system telling the truth. So, you want your reputation to be one who will always tell the truth, one who will always be honest.

NOTES

1. Interview contained in Clemens Bartollas and Larry D. Hahn, *Policing in America* (Boston: Allyn & Bacon, 1999), 53.
2. David R. Johnson, *Policing the Urban Underworld: The Impact of Crime on the Development of the American Police, 1800–1887* (Philadelphia: Temple University Press, 1979), 78–89.
3. Robert M. Fogelson, *Big-City Police* (Cambridge, MA: Harvard University Press, 1977), 86–87.
4. Ibid.
5. Ibid.
6. Ibid.
7. Ibid.
8. Interviewed in 2001.
9. L. Thomas Winfree, Jr., and Curt T. Griffiths, "Adolescents' Attitudes Toward the Police: A Survey of High School Students," in *Juvenile Delinquency: Little Brother Grows Up,* edited by Theodore N. Ferdinand (Beverly Hills, CA: Sage Publications, 1977), 79–99.
10. William T. Rusinko, W. Johnson Knowlton, and Carlton A. Hornung, "The Importance of Police Contact in the Formulation of Youths' Attitudes Toward Police," *Journal of Criminal Justice* 6 (Spring 1978), 65.
11. Scott H. Decker, "Citizen Attitudes Toward the Police: A Review of Past Findings and Suggestions for Future Policy," *Journal of Police Science and Administration* 9 (1981), 80–87.
12. Komanduri S. Murty, Julian B. Roebuck, and Joann D. Smith, "The Image of Police in Black Atlanta Communities," *Journal of Police Science and Administration* 17 (1990), 250–57.
13. Michael J. Leiber, Mahesh K. Nalla, and Margaret Farnworth, "Explaining Juveniles' Attitudes Toward the Police," *Justice Quarterly* 15 (March 1998), 151–71.
14. J. G. Bachman, L. D. Johnston, and P. M. O'Malley, *Monitoring the Future: Questionnaire Responses from the Nation's High School Seniors,* 2007 (Ann Arbor, MI: Institute for Social Research). Roughly 13 percent of the youths had no opinion on the question.
15. Terry Nihart et al., "Kids, Cops, Parents and Teachers: Exploring Juvenile Attitudes Toward Authority Figures," *Western Criminology Review* 6 (2005), 79–88.
16. Yolander G. Hurst, "Juvenile Attitudes Toward the Police," *Criminal Justice Review* 32 (2007), 121–41.
17. Stephanie M. Myers, *Police Encounters with Juvenile Suspects: Explaining the Use of Authority and Provision of Support* (Washington, DC: National Institute of Justice, 2004).
18. Stephanie M. Myers, *Police Encounters with Juvenile Suspects,: Explaining the Use of Authority and Provision of Support* (Washington, DC: Institute of Justice, 2004).
19. See Donald J. Black and Albert J. Reiss, Jr., "Police Control of Juveniles," *American Sociological Review* 35 (February 1979), 63–77.
20. Robert M. Terry, "Discrimination in the Handling of Juvenile Offenders by Social Control Agencies," *Journal of Research in Crime and Delinquency* 4 (July 1967), 218–30; Nathan Goldman, *The Differential Selection of Juvenile Offenders for Court Appearances* (New York: National Council on Crime and Delinquency, 1963), 35–47; Black and Reiss, "Police Control of Juveniles"; Irving Piliavin and Scott Briar, "Police Encounters with Juveniles," *American Journal of Sociology* 70 (September 1964), 206–14.
21. Terry, "Discrimination in the Handling of Juvenile Offenders"; Black and Reiss, "Police Control of Juveniles."
22. Gail Armstrong, "Females Under the Law—Protected But Unequal," *Crime and Delinquency* 23 (April 1977), 109–20; Meda Chesney-Lind, "Girls and Status Offenses: Is Juvenile Justice Still Sexist?" *Criminal Justice Abstracts* 20 (March 1988), 144–65; Meda Chesney-Lind and Randall G. Shelden, *Girls: Delinquency and Juvenile Justice* (Pacific Grove, CA: Brooks/Cole, 1992).
23. Philip W. Harris, "Race and Juvenile Justice: Examining the Impact of Structural and Policy Changes on Racial Disproportionality," paper presented at the annual meeting of the American Society of Criminology, Montreal, November 13, 1987.
24. James T. Carey et al., *The Handling of Juveniles from Offense to Disposition* (Washington, DC: Government Printing Office, 1976); A. W. McEachern and Riva Bauzer, "Factors Related to Disposition in Juvenile–Police Contacts," in *Juvenile Gangs in Context,* edited by Malcolm W. Klein (Upper Saddle River, NJ: Prentice Hall, 1967); Ferdinand and Luchterhand, "Inner-City Youths, the Police, the Juvenile Court and Justice," 510–17; Miriam D. Sealock and Sally S. Simpson, "Unraveling Bias in Arrest Decisions: The Role of Juvenile Offender Type-Scripts," *Justice Quarterly* 15 (September 1998), 427–57.
25. Merry Morash, "Establishment of Juvenile Police Record," *Criminology* 22 (February 1984), 97–111.
26. Carl Werthman and Irving Piliavin, "Gang Members and the Police," in *The Police,* edited by David J. Bordua (New York: Wiley, 1967), 56–98.
27. Richard J. Lundman, Richard E. Sykes, and John P. Clark, "Police Control of Juveniles: A Replication," in *Police Behavior: A Sociological Perspective,* edited by Richard J. Lundman (New York: Oxford University Press, 1980), 147–48.
28. James Q. Wilson, "Dilemmas of Police Administration," *Public Administration Review* 28 (September–October 1968), 19.
29. James Q. Wilson, "Dilemmas of Police Administration," *Public Administration Review* 28 (September–October 1968), 19.
30. For a discussion of the Constitution and Supreme Court decisions relevant to the schools, see Reed B. Day, *Legal Issues Surrounding Safe Schools* (Topeka, KS: National Organization on Legal Problems of Education, 1994).
31. *Mapp v. Ohio,* 367 U.S. 643 (1961); Day, *Legal Issues Surrounding Safe Schools,* 25–38.
32. *State v. Lowery,* 230 A. 2d 907 (1967).
33. *In re Two Brothers and a Case of Liquor,* Juvenile Court of the District of Columbia, 1966, reported in *Washington Law Reporter* 95 (1967), 113.

34. *Ciulla v. State*, 434 S.W. 2d 948 (Tex. Civ. App. 1968).

35. For a good general discussion of search and seizure law, see http://law.enotes.com/everyday-law-encyclopedia/search-and-seizure. Among the Supreme Court cases relevant to privacy are *Katz v. U.S.*, 389 U.S. 347, 88 S. Ct. 507. 19 L. Ed. 2d 576 (1967) and *Hester v. U.S.*, 265 I.S. 57, 44 S. Ct. 445, 68 L. Ed. 898 (1924). See also Judge David Demers, "Search and Seizure Outline" (2002), accessed at http://www.judges.com/Demers/page153-179.htm.

36. *Terry v. Ohio*, 392 U.S. 1, 20 L 2d 889, 911 (1968), accessed at http://urban75.org/legal/rights.html.

37. Ibid.

38. For some examples of the use of reasonable suspicion in different types of cases, see Demers, "Search and Seizure Outline."

39. See, for example the plain view doctrine and search and seizure at http://dictionary.law.com/default2.asp?selected=1538 and http://dictionary.law.com/default2.asp?selected=1894.

40. Demers, "Search and Seizure Outline."

41. "Your Rights on Arrest: Legal Advice and Useful Information," accessed at http://www.urban75.org/legal/rights.html.

42. For an extensive discussion of the relevant issues and court decisions related to police in the schools, see Samuel M. Davis, *Rights of Juveniles*, 2d ed. (New York: Clark Boardman Company, 1986), Secs. 3–19 to 3–34.3.

43. *New Jersey v. T. L. O.*, 469 U.S. 325 (1985).

44. Ibid.

45. Ibid.

46. J. M. Sanchez, "Expelling the Fourth Amendment from American Schools: Students' Rights Six Years After T. L. O.," *Education Journal* 21 (1992), 381–413; Day, *Legal Issues Surrounding Safe Schools*, 9–24.

47. *Safford Unified School District v. Redding* (no. 08-479) 557 U.S.—(2009), accessed at http://www.supremecourtus.gov/gp/08-00479gp.pdf.

48. "*Miranda* Warning," accessed at http://en.wikipedia.org/wiki/Miranda_Warning.

49. Ibid. Also, see Findlaw Lawyer Directory at http://criminal.findlaw.com/articles/1387.html for a brief but good discussion of "Police Questioning Prior to Arrest."

50. *People v. Lara*, 62 Cal. Rptr. 586 (1967), cert. denied 392 U.S. 945 (1968).

51. *In re Mellot*, 217 S. E. 2d 745 (C.A.N. Calif., 1975).

52. *In re Dennis P. Fletcher*, 248 A. 2d 364 (Md., 1968), cert. denied 396 U.S. 852 (1969).

53. T. Grisso, *Juveniles' Waiver of Rights: Legal and Psychological Competence* (New York: Plenum Press, 1981).

54. *Brown v. Mississippi*, 297 U.S. 278 (1936).

55. Davis, *Rights of Juveniles*, Sec. 3–45.

56. *Haley v. Ohio*, 332 U.S. 596 (1948).

57. Ibid.

58. *Fare v. Michael C.*, 442 U.S. 23, 99 S. Ct. 2560 (1979).

59. *Commonwealth v. Guyton*, 405 Mass. 497 (1989).

60. Elyce Z. Ferster and Thomas F. Courtless, "The Beginning of Juvenile Justice, Police Practices, and the Juvenile Offender," *Vanderbilt Law Review* 22 (April 1969), 598–601.

61. *Davis v. Mississippi*, 394 U.S. 721 (1969).

62. Ibid.

63. See Davis, *Rights of Juveniles*, Sec. 3–67.

64. *United States v. Wade*, 338 U.S. 218, 87 S. Ct. 1926 (1967).

65. *Kirby v. Illinois*, 406 U.S. 682, 92 S. Ct. 1877 (1972).

66. *In re Holley*, 107 R. I. 615, 268 A. 2d 723 (1970).

67. *In re Carl T.*, 81 Cal. Rptr. 655 (2d C.A., 1969).

68. Office of Justice Programs, *America's Missing Broadcast Emergency Response, Frequency Added Question on AMBER Alert*, accessed at http://www.amberalert-gov/faqa,htm

69. Howard N. Snyder and Melissa Sickmund, *Juvenile Offenders and Victims: 2006 National Report* (Washington, DC: U.S. Department of Justice, Office of Justice Programs, Office of Juvenile Justice and Delinquency Prevention, 2006).

70. Ibid.

71. Mark S. Hamm, *American Skinheads: The Criminology and Control of Hate Crime* (Westport, CT: Praeger, 1993).

72. Snyder and Sickmund, *Juvenile Offenders and Victims*, 2006 National Report.

73. *History of the G.R.E.A.T. Program, 2012*, accessed June 12, 2012, at http://www.great.ca-org/Organizatioln/Histlory.Aspx.

74. F. A. Esbensen and D. W. Osgood, "Gang Resistance Education and Training (G.R.E.A.T.): Results from the National Evaluation," *Journal of Research in Crime and Delinquency* 36 (1999), 194–225; F. A. Esbensen, D. W. T. J. Taylor, D. Peterson, and A. Frenger, "How Great Is G.R.E.A.T.: Results from a Longitudinal Quasi-Experimental Design," *Criminology and Public Policy* 1 (2001), 87–118; J. Ashcroft, D. J. Daniels, and S. V. Hart, *Evaluating G.R.E.A.T.: A School-Based Gang Prevention Program* (Washington, DC: U.S. Department of Justice, 2004).

75. Judith Warrant Little and Frances Haley, *Implementing Effective LRE Programs* (Boulder, CO: Social Science Education Consortium, 1982).

76. William DeJong, *Arresting the Demand for Drugs: Police and School Partnership to Prevent Drug Abuse* (Washington, DC: National Institute of Justice, 1987).

77. Ronald D. Stephens, "School Based Interventions: Safety and Security," in *The Gang Intervention Handbook*, edited by Ron Huff (Beverly Hills, CA: Sage, 1993).

78. Tom Sanchez, "Youth Referral System," *The Police Chief* 71 (September 2004), accessed at http://policechiefmagazine.org/magazine/index.cfm?fuseaction=print_display&article_id=…np.

79. Phelan A. Wyrick, "Law Enforcement Referral of At-Risk Youth: The SHIELD Program," *Juvenile Justice Bulletin* (Washington, DC: U.S. Department of Justice, November 2000).

80. Ellen T. Broddus, Kerry E. Scott, Liane M. Gonsalves, Canada Parrish, Evelyn L. Rhodess, Samuel E. Donavan, and Peter J. Winch, "Building Connections Between Officers and Baltimore Ciry Youth: Key Components of a Police-Youth Teambuilding Program," OJJDP *Journal of Criminal Justice* (Fall 2013), 48-62.

81. Ibid.

6 The Juvenile Court

ZUMA Wire Service/Alamy

Learning Objectives

1. Summarize the development and legal norms of the juvenile court.
2. Describe the social control of the status offender.
3. Explain the structure and key players of the juvenile court.
4. Describe pretrial procedures and decisions of the intake officer.
5. Explain plea bargaining.
6. Summarize the adjudicatory process.
7. Describe the disposition hearing.
8. Describe disposition alternatives.
9. Describe the various sentencing alternatives for juveniles.

Juvenile court judges sometimes have quite challenging decisions. In a case in which I was involved, a twelve-year-old male lived with his father who was charged and convicted of murder. The son was sent to his mother who lived in Indianapolis, Indiana, with a daughter and live-in boyfriend. Up until the son arrived, everything was going smoothly for the family.

It did not go well with the son, who was used to no discipline from a parent. He refused to be home on time for dinner and would not comply with the curfew imposed by his mother. He, refused to clean up after he had prepared his dinner when he arrived home, and did not give his mother or boyfriend proper respect.

One night when he arrived home late, the mother had already gone to bed, the boyfriend did not permit him to prepare his dinner. The next morning, when he got up after breakfast had been eaten by the family and the mother and daughter had left, he made a hostile comment to the boyfriend. With that, the boyfriend told him that he would not have any breakfast. The boyfriend turned his back, and the youth at that point stabbed him fatally with a knife.

The prosecutor wanted the youth transferred to the adult court and given a forty-year sentence in adult prison. The juvenile's public defender wanted the youth retained in the juvenile court. And the judge had to decide what to do. He made the decision to retain the youth in the juvenile system until he was twenty-one years of age. Do you agree?

Source: Personal Experience of the author in this 2002 Indiana case.

The purpose of the court, as expressed in the *Commonwealth v. Fisher* decision in 1905, "is not for the punishment of offenders but for the salvation of children...whose salvation may become the duty of the state."[1] It is this type of statement that resulted in the juvenile court receiving fanatical support from its followers. Ever since the turn of the twentieth century, supporters have argued that the informal setting of the juvenile court, coupled with the fatherly demeanor of the juvenile judge, enables children to be treated, rather than punished, for their problems.[2] The state, the argument goes, rescues these youths from a life of trouble on the streets, rehabilitates them, protects them from placement with adult criminals in correctional facilities, and saves them from a life of crime. According to Judge Leonard P. Edwards, what is implicit in this position is that "children are different from adults, that they have developmental needs which they cannot satisfy without assistance, and that care and supervision are critical to their upbringing." He then argues that "if children were no different from adults, the juvenile court would be unnecessary."[3]

Critics of the juvenile court sharply challenge these idealistic claims. They argue that some cases are far beyond this permissive and rehabilitative approach of the juvenile court, such as the murder cited in the opening quote. Critics also argue that the juvenile court has not succeeded in rehabilitating juvenile offenders, in reducing or even stemming the rise of youth crime, or in bringing justice and compassion to youthful offenders.[4] The juvenile court, they argue, acts in an arbitrary and whimsical fashion. It selects whom it "saves" on the basis of their sex and race, not on the basis of justice. The court harms children by processing them through its system, offering them inadequate programs, and labeling them as they return to the community.[5] Thomas F. Geraghty and Steven A. Drizin, in the introduction to a symposium on the future of the juvenile court, suggest that the future of the juvenile court "is less secure than at any point in its history." They state that part of the problem relates to the perceived seriousness of juvenile crime, and part of the problem is found in a "get-tough" attitude that is affecting the handling of juvenile as well as adult crime.[6]

This chapter describes the changing legal norms of the juvenile court, the social control of status offenders, those who are involved in the processes of the juvenile court, the pretrial procedures of its proceedings, plea bargaining, trial and disposition stages, and the changing sentencing structures of the juvenile court.

How Have Legal Norms Changed?

In the past, **constitutionalists** have argued that the juvenile court was unconstitutional because under its auspices the principles of a fair trial and individual rights were denied. This group primarily was concerned that children appearing before the juvenile court were denied their procedural rights as well as the rights to shelter, protection, and guardianship. The constitutionalists proposed that the procedures of the juvenile court be modified in three ways: (1) by the adoption of separate procedures for dealing with dependent and neglected children and those who are accused of criminal behavior; (2) by the use of informal adjustments to avoid official court actions as frequently as possible; and (3) by the provision of rigorous procedural safeguards and rights for children appearing before the court at the adjudicatory stage.[7]

A series of decisions by the U.S. Supreme Court in the 1960s and early 1970s rapidly accelerated the influence of the constitutionalists on the juvenile court. The five most important cases were *Kent v. United States* (1966), *In re Gault* (1967), *In re Winship* (1970), *McKeiver v. Pennsylvania* (1971), and *Breed v. Jones* (1975). See Figure 6–1 for a timeline of the most important Court decisions concerning juveniles.

Kent v. United States

The first major case was **Kent v. United States**.[8] In this 1966 case, the juvenile court had disregarded all of Kent's due process rights in transferring the case to the adult court. The judge of the juvenile court did not rule on Kent's lawyer's motions. The judge also did not discuss the case with either Kent or Kent's parents, did not present any findings, did not offer any reason for waiving Kent to the adult court, and, in fact, made no reference to the motions filed by Kent's attorney. The judge also apparently ignored reports from juvenile court staff and the Juvenile Probation Section that indicated that Kent's mental condition was deteriorating. Rather, the judge entered an order waiving Kent to the adult court for trial. There, Kent was indicted by a grand jury on eight counts of housebreaking, robbery,

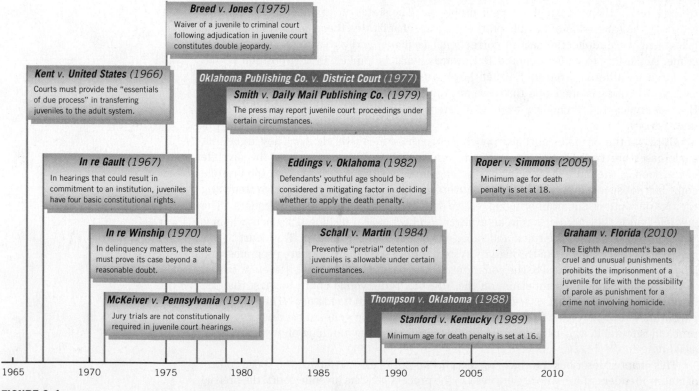

FIGURE 6–1
Timeline of Important Supreme Court Decisions Concerning Juveniles

Source: A series of U.S. Supreme Court decisions made juvenile courts more like criminal courts, but maintained some important differences.

Focus on Law 6–1
Kent v. United States

Morris A. Kent, Jr., a sixteen-year-old living in Washington, D.C., was on juvenile probation when he broke into a house and raped and robbed a woman on September 2, 1961. His fingerprints were found in the woman's apartment, and he was taken into custody by the police on September 5, 1961. He was charged with three counts each of housebreaking and robbery and two counts of rape. Kent apparently admitted not only the offense for which he was taken into custody, but other housebreaking, robbery, and rape offenses as well. He was interrogated by the police into the evening, was taken to the Receiving Home for Juveniles late that evening, and was returned to the police the next day for more questioning. No record exists as to when Kent's mother found out about his detention, but she retained counsel on the second day of Kent's detainment.

The social service director of the juvenile court discussed with Kent's counsel the possibility that Kent's case might be waived to adult court; Kent's counsel opposed the waiver and also arranged for Kent to undergo psychiatric evaluation. Kent's lawyer then filed a motion for a waiver hearing on the juvenile court's jurisdiction and provided a psychiatrist's affidavit certifying that Kent was "a victim of severe psychopathology" and recommending that he be hospitalized for psychiatric observation. The affidavit concluded that Kent could be rehabilitated if provided adequate treatment. Kent's counsel also requested a copy of Kent's social service file for use in his defense.

CRITICAL THINKING QUESTION
What did Supreme Court Justice Fortas mean when he said that "there may be grounds for concern that the child receives the worst of both worlds?" Do you agree with his criticism of the juvenile court?

Source: *Kent v. United States*, 383 U.S. 541, 86 S. Ct. 1045, 16 L. Ed. 2d 84 (1966).

---

and rape, and was sentenced to a total of thirty to ninety years in prison. Focus on Law 6–1 describes the facts of this case.

Kent's counsel initiated a series of appeals that led to review of the case by the U.S. Supreme Court. The counsel argued throughout these appeals that Kent's parents had not been notified in time, that Kent's interrogation and detention were illegal because neither his parents nor his counsel was present, that probable cause for Kent's detention had not been established, that he had not been told of his right to remain silent or of his right to counsel, and that he was fingerprinted illegally.

The Supreme Court agreed that the procedures followed by the juvenile court were inadequate. In addition, the Court ruled that Kent had the right to a transfer hearing in which evidence was presented, that Kent had the right to be present at a waiver hearing, that Kent's attorney had the right to see the social service reports, and that the judge had to state the reasons for the transfer.[9] In this decision, Judge Abe Fortas stated:

There is evidence, in fact, that there may be grounds for concern that the child receives the worst of both worlds; that he gets neither the protection accorded to adults nor the solicitous care and regenerative treatment postulated for children.[10]

In re Gault

In May 1967, the U.S. Supreme Court reversed the conviction of a minor in the case of **In re Gault**.[11] This has been one of the most influential and far-reaching decisions to affect the juvenile court. In this case, the Court overruled the Arizona Supreme Court for its dismissal of a writ of habeas corpus. This writ had sought the release of Gerald Gault, who had been adjudicated to the state industrial school by the Juvenile Court of Gila County, Arizona. Focus on Law 6–2 presents the facts of this case.

In reviewing the decision of the Arizona Supreme Court, which upheld the confinement of Gault, the U.S. Supreme Court considered which of the following rights should apply to juveniles:

1. Right to receive notice of the charges
2. Right to be represented by counsel
3. Right to confront and cross-examine witnesses
4. Right to avoid self-incrimination
5. Right to receive a transcript of the proceedings
6. Right to request appellate review[12]

Focus on Law 6–2
In re Gault

Gerald Gault, a fifteen-year-old Arizona boy, and a friend, Ronald Lewis, were taken into custody on June 8, 1964, on a verbal complaint made by a neighbor. The neighbor had accused the boys of making lewd and indecent remarks to her over the phone. Gault's parents were not notified that he was taken into custody; he was not advised of his right to counsel; he was not advised that he could remain silent; and no notice of charges was made to either Gerald or his parents. In addition, the complainant was not present at either of the hearings. In spite of considerable confusion about whether or not Gerald had made the alleged phone call,

what he had said over the phone, and what he had said to the judge during the course of the two hearings, Judge McGhee committed him to the State Industrial School until he reached the age of twenty-one or until he was discharged by the law.

CRITICAL THINKING QUESTION

What due process rights did this case grant juveniles? What due process rights did juveniles still lack after the decision?

Source: *In re Gault*, 387 U.S. 1, 18 L. Ed. 2d 527, 87 S. Ct. 1428 (1967).

Justice Fortas, in delivering the Court's opinion, recalled other cases that had provided juveniles with due process of law. In both *Haley v. Ohio* (1948) and *Gallegos v. Colorado* (1962), the U.S. Supreme Court had prohibited the use of confessions coerced from juveniles; in *Kent v. United States,* the Court had given the juvenile the right to be represented by counsel.[13] Justice Fortas concluded this review of legal precedent with the sweeping statement that juveniles have those fundamental rights incorporated in the due process clause of the Fourteenth Amendment of the Constitution.

The *In re Gault* decision answered in the affirmative the question of whether a juvenile has the right to due process safeguards during confinement. But the Supreme Court did not rule that juveniles have the right to a transcript of the proceedings or the right to appellate review.

In rejecting the latter two rights, the Court clearly did not want to transform the informal juvenile hearing into an adversarial trial. The cautiousness of this decision was expressed in a footnote that indicated that the decision did not apply to preadjudication or postadjudication treatment of juveniles. Several other important issues were also left unanswered, such as the following:

1. May a judge consider hearsay in juvenile court?
2. Does the exclusionary evidence principle derived from the Fourth Amendment apply?
3. What is the constitutionally required burden of proof necessary to support a finding of delinquency?
4. Is a jury trial required?
5. Does the requirement of a "speedy and public trial" apply in juvenile court?[14]

In re Winship

The Supreme Court ruled in the **In re Winship** case (1970) that juveniles are entitled to proof "beyond a reasonable doubt."[15] The *Winship* case involved a New York boy who was sent to a state training school at the age of twelve for taking $112 from a woman's purse. The commitment was based on a New York statute that permitted juvenile court decisions on the basis of a "preponderance of evidence." The Court reasoned that "preponderance of evidence," a standard much less strict than "beyond a reasonable doubt," is not a sufficient basis for a decision when youths are charged with acts that would be criminal if committed by adults.

The findings in the *Winship* case not only expanded the implications of *In re Gault*, but also reflected other concerns of the U.S. Supreme Court. The Court desired both to protect juveniles at adjudicatory hearings and to maintain the confidentiality, informality, flexibility, and speed of the juvenile process in the prejudicial and postadjudicative states. The Court obviously did not want to bring too much rigidity and impersonality to the juvenile hearing.

McKeiver v. Pennsylvania, In re Terry, and *In re Barbara Burrus*

The Supreme Court heard three cases together: (**McKeiver v. Pennsylvania**, **In re Terry**, and **In re Barbara Burrus**) to determine whether the due process clause of the Fourteenth Amendment (guaranteeing the right to a jury trial) applied to juveniles.[16] The decision, which was issued in *McKeiver v. Pennsylvania* (1971), denied the juveniles the right to have jury trials. Focus on Law 6–3 reveals the facts of these three cases.

The Supreme Court explained its ruling that juveniles do not have the right to a jury trial as follows:

1. Not all rights that are constitutionally assured for adults are to be given to juveniles.

2. If a jury trial is required for juveniles, the juvenile proceedings may become a fully adversarial process, putting an end to what has been the idealistic prospect of an intimate, informal, and protective proceeding.

3. A jury trial is not necessarily a part of every criminal process that is fair and equitable.

4. If the jury trial is injected into the juvenile court system, it could bring with it the traditional delays, the formality, and the clamor of the adversarial system.

5. There is nothing to prevent an individual juvenile judge from using an advisory jury when he or she feels the need. For that matter, there is nothing to prevent individual states from adopting jury trials.[17]

Although a number of states do permit jury trials for juveniles, most states adhere to this constitutional standard set by the Supreme Court. What is significant about this decision is that the Court indicated an unwillingness to apply further procedural safeguards to juvenile proceedings. This especially appears to be true concerning the preadjudicatory and postadjudicatory treatment of juveniles.

Twelve jurisdictions have statutes specifying that a juvenile delinquent has no right to a jury trial at specified stages of the juvenile court hearing process. These jurisdictions are: Colorado, the District of Columbia, Florida, Louisiana, Maine, Montana, Nebraska, New Mexico, North Carolina, Texas, Wisconsin, and Wyoming.

Focus on Law 6–3
Right of a Jury Trial for Juveniles

MCKEIVER V. PENNSYLVANIA

Joseph McKeiver, who was sixteen years of age, was charged with robbery, larceny, and receiving stolen goods, all of which were felonies under Pennsylvania law. Found delinquent at an adjudication hearing, the youth was placed on probation after his request for a jury trial was denied.

IN RE TERRY

Edward Terry, who was fifteen years of age, was charged with assault and battery on a police officer, which were misdemeanors under Pennsylvania law. His counsel requested a jury trial, which was denied, and he was adjudicated a delinquent on the charges.

IN RE BARBARA BURRUS

Barbara Burrus and approximately forty-five other youths, ranging in age from eleven to fifteen years, received juvenile court summonses in Hyde County, North Carolina. The charges arose out of a series of demonstrations in the county in late 1968 by African American adults and children, who were protesting school assignments and a school construction plan. The youths were charged with willfully impeding traffic. The several cases were consolidated into groups for hearing before the district judge, sitting in a juvenile court. A request for a jury trial in each case was denied. Each youth was found delinquent and placed on probation.

CRITICAL THINKING QUESTION

What is the actual difference between "preponderance of the evidence" and "proof beyond a reasonable doubt"? What was the importance of this difference in this case?

Sources: *McKeiver v. Pennsylvania*, 403 U.S. 528 (1971); *In re Terry*, 438 Pa. 339, 265 A. 2d 350 (1970); and *In re Barbara Burrus*, 275 N.C. 517, 169 S.E. 2d 879 (1969).

Thirteen states allow a juvenile delinquent the right to a jury trial only in specified circumstances. These states are: Arkansas, Colorado, Idaho, Illinois, Kansas, Minnesota, Montana, New Mexico, Oklahoma, Rhode Island, Texas, Virginia, and Wyoming.[18]

Breed v. Jones

The **Breed v. Jones** (1975) case was slightly different from the *Kent* case. Jones was taken into custody for committing a robbery and was detained for a hearing in juvenile court. At the juvenile court hearing, the allegations against Jones were found to be true. At the disposition hearing, the court determined that Jones could not be helped by the services of the juvenile court; Jones was waived to adult court, where he was found guilty of robbery.

Jones's lawyer appealed the case, arguing that Jones had been subjected to double jeopardy; that is, this decision had violated the standard used in adult courts that prevents adults from being tried twice for the same crime. The Supreme Court concurred, stating that Jones's hearing in the juvenile court involved evidence being presented at an adjudication hearing and that his trial in adult court constituted double jeopardy.[19] For waiver to adult court to occur legally, according to the Supreme Court, juvenile courts must transfer youths to the adult court jurisdiction before any adjudicatory hearings are held on their cases.

In sum, the *In re Gault* and *In re Winship* decisions have unquestionably effected profound changes in the legal status of the juvenile justice system. The *McKeiver v. Pennsylvania* decision and the more conservative stance of the Supreme Court since 1971, however, have raised some questions about whether or not this ultimate appellate court will be willing to change legal norms much more. These court decisions have, of course, received varying endorsements from juvenile courts across the United States. Some juvenile courts gave procedural rights to juveniles even before the Supreme Court decisions, but others have lagged far behind in implementing these decisions.

How Is the Status Offender Controlled?

Youths can be charged with at least three different categories of offenses:

- Offenders can be charged with a felony or misdemeanor under federal, state, and local statutes.
- Youths are subject to relatively specific statutes applying exclusively to juvenile behavior: truancy, consumption of alcoholic beverages, and running away from home are examples.
- Juveniles can be prosecuted under general omnibus statutes that include such offenses as acting beyond the control of parents, engaging in immoral conduct, and being ungovernable and incorrigible.

Offenses under both the second and third categories are status offenses. The status offense statutes pertaining to behavior for which an adult could not be prosecuted have drawn increasing attention in recent years. Status offenders can be processed through the juvenile justice system along with youths who have committed criminal offenses, or they can be handled separately from felons and misdemeanants. States that pursue the latter course usually refer to status offenders as MINS (minors in need of supervision), CINS (children in need of supervision), PINS (persons in need of supervision), FINS (families in need of supervision), or JINS (juveniles in need of supervision). Some jurisdictions handle these youths in a different court; others will not place them in detention with delinquents or send them to a juvenile correctional institution.

The handling of status offenders has focused on two questions: should status offenders be placed with delinquents in correctional settings, and should the juvenile court retain jurisdiction over status offenders?

Deinstitutionalization of Status Offenders

The **deinstitutionalization of status offenders** (to no longer confine status offenders in secure detention facilities or secure correctional facilities with delinquents) has received increased acceptance in the past couple of decades. What served as the real impetus for a nationwide deinstitutionalization of status offenders was the passage of the 1974 **Juvenile Justice and Delinquency Prevention (JJDP) Act** and its various modifications.[20] As a condition for states to continue receiving federal funding for juvenile justice programs, the JJDP Act required that status offenders be kept separate from delinquents in secure detention and institutionalization. The act also limited the placement of juveniles in adult jail facilities.[21]

The **deinstitutionalization of status offenders (DSO)** provision of the JJDP Act has been successful in encouraging states to amend laws, policies, and practices that led to secure confinement of juveniles who committed no criminal act. This Act gave the juvenile justice system the impetus to no longer confine status offenders in secure detention facilities or secure correctional facilities with delinquents. The DSO core protection of the JJDP Act is premised on the belief that juveniles who exhibit problematic behavior but have not violated the laws are more properly served by social service, mental health, and community agencies and may actually be damaged by placement in secure detention or correctional institutions.[22] Following the adoption of the JJDP Act and its DSO requirement, the Office of Juvenile Justice and Delinquency Prevention (OJJDP) recorded approximately 171,581 violations of the DSO requirement. According to OJJDP's 2006 compliance monitoring reports, the number of DSO violations had dropped to 6,324.[23]

Jurisdiction over Status Offenders

The juvenile court's long-standing jurisdiction over status offenders is an even more volatile issue. Critics present at least four distinct arguments for the removal of status offenders from the jurisdiction of the juvenile court:

- The legal argument states that the lack of clarity of the status offender statutes makes them unconstitutionally vague in their construction; that they often are blatantly discriminatory, especially in regard to gender; and that government bodies have no legitimate interest in many of these proscribed behaviors.

- Although status offenders have not committed a criminal act, they frequently are confined with chronic or hard-core offenders.

- In keeping with the *parens patriae* philosophy of the juvenile court, the procedure of processing and confining the status offender is not in his or her best interests. Some theorists argue that the formal intervention of the juvenile court promotes rather than inhibits unlawful behavior.

- Many charge that status offenders are a special class of youth who must be treated differently from delinquents.[24]

Juvenile court judges, not surprisingly, challenge the movement to strip the court of jurisdiction over status offenders. They charge that status offenders will have no one to provide for them or to protect them if they are removed from the court's jurisdiction. The essence of this position is that other agencies will have to take over if the court relinquishes jurisdiction over these offenders and that few options are presently available for providing status offenders a nurturing environment in lieu of the home.

The states of Maine, New York, and Washington have **decriminalized status offenses**, thus removing from the juvenile court's jurisdiction youthful behavior that would not be a chargeable offense if committed by an adult.[25] However, the status offense legislation in Maine and Washington was partly repealed to give the juvenile courts a degree of jurisdiction, especially over abandoned, runaway, or seriously endangered children.[26] The most broad-based movement to strip the juvenile court of jurisdiction over status offenders took place in New York State, heralded by the passage of the 1985 PINS Adjustment Services Act. Under a new law that became effective on November 1, 2001, the New York State

Legislature passed a bill that raised the PINS eligibility age to eighteen. The intent of this bill was to assist and support families seeking help with troubled older children.[27]

It is unlikely that many more states will remove status offenders from the juvenile court's jurisdiction in the near future. The widespread resistance comes mainly from those who feel that status offenders need the control of the juvenile court over their lives or they will become involved in increasingly destructive behaviors. The fact is that juvenile court personnel do have jurisdiction over the status offender because they have the option of labeling youngsters downward as dependent or neglected youths, upward as delinquent youths, or laterally into private mental health facilities.[28] Thus, even in states that strongly support deinstitutionalization, the juvenile court still can institutionalize status offenders by redefining them as delinquents or as requiring mental health services. A truant may be charged with a minor delinquent offense and be institutionalized in a private facility, or a court may require school attendance as a condition of probation and then define further truancy as a delinquent offense.[29] Abuse, neglect, and delinquency cases must also be dealt with by the juvenile court, and then there are those social welfare cases that cross to the juvenile justice system.

Crossover Youth

Juveniles in the child welfare system often cross into the juvenile justice system. Because these youth are known to both the child welfare system and the juvenile justice system, they are frequently referred to as "crossover youth." Other terms used to describe these youth are "dual-jurisdiction cases," "dual jurisdiction," "dually adjudicated youth," and "cross-system cases."

Evidence-Based Practice
Best Programs in Juvenile Court

In 1997, the federal Adoption and Safe Families Act (ASFA) established the goals of permanence, well-being, and safety for children in foster care with an emphasis on achieving "permanence" for children. In 1999, the Carolina General Assembly incorporated the ASFA standards into Chapter 7B of the North Carolina General Statutes. Child welfare agencies, as well as the courts in North Carolina, use these laws to improve how the state child welfare system responds to allegations and findings of child abuse, neglect, or dependency.

In 1996 and 2001, juvenile court improvement funds were used to conduct studies to identify methods of improving juvenile abuse, neglect, and dependency (A/N/D) proceedings in North Carolina. The 1996 study, conducted by the Research Triangle Institute, identified a number of barriers to achieving timely permanency for children and their families served by North Carolina juvenile courts. They identified the following barriers to achieving permanency:

- A shortage of adoptive homes for children with special needs
- A shortage of child welfare workers to work with parents and children in care
- Parental noncompliance with case plans
- Frequent court continuances
- Lack of supportive services for parents
- High emphasis on reuniting families that should not be reunited
- Too many court hearings for each case
- Poor court orders

A 2001 evaluation of the juvenile Court Improvement Program (CIP), conducted by the Jordan Institute for Families at the University of North Carolina–Chapel Hill, measured the effectiveness and implementation of new local court rules to juvenile CIP districts. The local rules were intended to improve the manner in which the courts process juvenile A/N/D cases. Results of the evaluation reflected that the new rules affected both positive and compelling changes in the way juvenile cases were handled. The study identified:

- Reductions in the number of cases heard by multiple judges
- Reductions in the number of continuances granted
- Reductions in time to achieve critical junctures in juvenile cases (e.g., findings, adjudications, dispositions)
- Reductions in the overall duration of cases
- Reductions in the number of out-of-home placements of children
- Accelerated time to permanency

In 2007, the North Carolina Administrative Office of the Courts selected six judicial districts to implement juvenile case management activities, specialized training, and best practices in juvenile court. Lessons learned from these districts have been used to inform this best practices guide.

What has taken place in North Carolina with cases related to abuse, neglect, and dependency offers the promise of being extended to delinquency cases throughout the nation.

Source: North Carolina Administrative Office of the Courts, *Best Practices for North Carolina's Juvenile Abuse, Neglect, and Dependency Court Improvement Programs* (Raleigh, NC: Court Programs and Management Services Division, 2010), 3–4.

Crossover youth often move back and forth between a child welfare system in which they are looked on as victims, and a juvenile justice system that sees them as offenders. Yet, little integration and coordination take place between the two systems. In fact, in many jurisdictions, a common practice is for child welfare agencies to abruptly close the cases of children who become involved in the juvenile justice system.[30]

Many crossover youth experience co-occurring mental health and drug and alcohol abuse problems, which are often left unscreened and untreated in both systems. These youth frequently do poorly in school and end up being suspended or dropping out. Once in the juvenile justice system, they often continue to penetrate deeper into the system. Youth in the child welfare system who are placed in out-of-home settings are at greater risk of crossing over into the juvenile justice jurisdiction. Child welfare placements in group home settings, especially, have been found to be predictive of future involvement with the juvenile justice system.[31]

Another matter of grave concern to juvenile justice is that the disproportionate number of crossover minority youth is directly related to the disproportionate involvement of minority youth in the welfare system. Research sponsored by the Annie E. Casey Foundation reports that although minority children are not abused more often than other children, they are put into foster care faster, receive fewer services, stay there longer, and are reunited with their families less often than white children.[32]

A question raised continually in this text is: What can be done? Researchers have identified four promising court-related practices in which family and juvenile court programs can work together to address at least some of the difficulties posed by crossover cases:

▲ Juveniles may be brought to juvenile court by their parents, police officers, school counselors, or community helping agencies concerned over the welfare of children.
AL SCHELL/Associated Press

- *Routine screening and assessment*. Routine screening of youth on intake by both dependency and juvenile courts would assist in identifying the strengths and needs of these youth.

- *Case assignment*. Effective case management should include joint prehearing conferences by all parties involved and combined dependency and delinquency hearings, which will help ensure that different agencies coordinate their efforts.

- *Case planning and supervision*. Case managers should work with multidisciplinary teams of professionals with training in dual-jurisdiction matters who have the expertise and tools to develop action plans that meet the specific needs of and build on the individual strengths of crossover youth.

- *Interagency collaboration*. Judges should take the lead in making certain that the child welfare and juvenile justice systems collaborate by contributing financially in providing needed treatment and services.[33]

See the Evidence-Based Practice feature for a discussion of the safety of children in foster care.

What Does the Juvenile Court Look Like Today?

The structure of the juvenile court varies from jurisdiction to jurisdiction. Special and separate juvenile courts in certain urban areas devote their total effort to the legal problems of children. Juveniles in smaller cities and rural areas are often tried by judges of the adult courts. A separate statewide court exists in several states, and only juvenile judges sit on cases in the various districts of those states. In other parts of the country, juvenile offenders are handled exclusively by family court judges who hear both juvenile and domestic relations cases.

More typically, juvenile courts are part of a circuit, district, county, superior, common pleas, probate, or municipal court. This broad-based trial court may be either the highest court of general trial jurisdiction or the lower trial court in which lesser criminal and limited-claim civil matters are heard.

Nationally, juvenile courts today are affected by a movement toward a single trial court, inclusive of all courts in which initial trials take place. For example, in a massive court reorganization in Cook County, Illinois, 208 courts became the circuit courts for Cook

TABLE 6–1
Personnel in Juvenile Court

Personnel Role

Juvenile judge: Most important role is to decide the legal issues that appear before the court.

Referee: Some states use these individuals as primary hearing officers, while disposition, if necessary, is left to the judge.

Defense attorney: Can be an adversarial advocate for the child, a surrogate guardian or parent to child, and an assistant to the court with responsibilities to the children.

Prosecutor: Is expected to protect society, but, at the same time, to ensure that children appearing before the court receive their constitutional rights.

Probation officer: Acts as an intake officer, assesses the needs of children, writes reports, and supervises youth.

Nonjudicial support personnel: These include volunteers, staff from agencies providing services to the court, and paid workers who perform routine administrative functions.

County. The juvenile court of the District of Columbia was absorbed into the new single-trial court for the I District.

A variety of personnel serve the juvenile court (see Table 6–1). These include the judge, who heads up the court; referees, who are assistants to the judge; the defense attorney and the prosecutor, who, respectively, defends the client and tries the case; probation officers, who investigate and supervise cases; and the nonjudicial support personnel, who do everything from providing client services to keeping the court running smoothly. The numbers and qualifications of these persons vary widely from court to court.[34] The juvenile judge and referee have received attention in previous chapters, but the position of the defense attorney is discussed here and the prosecutor and probation officers' positions are described in future chapters.

Juvenile Court Defense Attorney

PREPARATION FOR THE JOB

In order to be a great defense attorney, a person must be great at communication because part of their job is to make complicated legal concepts understandable to minors who may not completely understand what is going on. The person must also be good at critical thinking and reasoning. Some important traits for a juvenile defense attorney are that they have excellent writing, reading, research, speaking, and persuasive skills.

QUALIFICATION AND EDUCATIONAL REQUIREMENTS

To become a juvenile defense attorney there are a lot of rigorous educational requirements. First, aspiring defense attorneys must get a bachelor's degree so that they can be accepted into a law school. They must also take the Law School Admission Test (LSAT) in order to be accepted by a law school. After being in law school, they must get their Juris Doctor (J.D) degree. And finally, they must pass the Multistate Bar Examination (MBE). The qualifications of the state will determine which tests you have to pass. There are some states that require you to pass a test that may be different from other states.

DUTIES

The job of a juvenile defense attorney is to advise their client(s) and the guardians of their client(s) in legal strategies that they should use in court. Their job is to interview and prepare the client(s) for trial. Once in trail it is the defense attorney's job to argue the case in a way that gives the client(s) a fair result. The juvenile defense attorney also must communicate or interact with the judicial clerks, judges, law enforcement officers, law clerks, parents, private investigators, and expert witnesses.

DEMAND FOR

The demand for attorneys is expected to grow 10 percent from the years 2010–2020. Becoming any type of lawyer is a very competitive job.

SALARY

The mean salary of a juvenile defense attorney in 2009 was $129,929. The average hourly wage of a defense attorney is $62.03 as of 2009. The wage can range quite dramatically from $55,270 to $113,240.

Sources: "Child Defense Attorney Job Description," http://www.ehow.com/facts_6835588_child-defense-attorney-job-description.html (accessed October 30, 2014); "Defense Attorney: Duties, Outlook, and Requirements," http://education-portal.com/articles/Defense_Attorney_Duties_Outlook_and_Requirements.html (accessed October 30, 2014).

What Are the Pretrial Procedures of the Juvenile Court?

The jurisdiction of the juvenile court, despite variations among and even within states, generally includes delinquency, neglect, and dependency cases. Children's courts may also deal with cases concerning adoption, termination of parental rights, appointment of guardians for minors, custody, contributing to delinquency or neglect, and nonsupport. The proceedings of the juvenile court can be divided into pretrial procedures and adjudicatory and dispositional hearings.

The pretrial procedures consist of the detention hearing, the intake process, and the transfer procedure. In 2005, 81 percent of delinquency cases were brought before the courts by law enforcement authorities, but there were variations across offense categories. Ninety-one percent of drug law violation cases, 91 percent of property cases, 87 percent of person offense cases, and 61 percent of public order offenses were referred by law enforcement agencies. The remaining cases resulted from complaints by parents, citizens, probation officers, victims, school officials, and others.[35]

The reasons for referring youths to the courts vary. Of the delinquency offenses, police officers brought youths to the juvenile court for property and drug offenses more than for any other category. Of the status offenses, liquor law and curfew violations headed the list for law enforcement officers. Conversely, sources other than law enforcement officers were most likely to refer youths for public order offenses and for status offenses, such as truancy, curfew violations, and ungovernability; the referral of runaways was about equally divided between law enforcement and other sources.

▲ Once juveniles are taken to court by the police, numerous and different types of hearings are used to determine what to do with them next.
Washington & Jefferson College

Detention Hearing

The use of detention has been a problem ever since the founding of the juvenile court. The original purpose of detention was to hold children securely until intake personnel reviewed the case and made a decision. The **detention hearing**, at which the decision to detain is made, must be held within a short period of time after arrest, generally forty-eight to seventy-two hours, excluding weekends and holidays. Those urban courts having intake units on duty twenty-four hours a day for detention hearings frequently act within a few hours.[36]

Detention hearings may occur at three points: (1) when the youth is taken in by the police; (2) during and after the time intake personnel review the case to decide whether to refer the case to juvenile court; and (3) after the adjudicatory hearing. See Focus on Practice 6–4 for some of the problems of detention.

Police, as noted previously, make the first detention decision. Frequently, they must place the youth in a police lockup or local jail while they notify parents and decide what to do with the youth. The police usually exercise the option of simply releasing the youth to his or her parents. If police believe conditions warrant, as they often do with serious offenders and sometimes do with status offenders, they may hold these youths for their protection or for the protection of society. In other words, the police base their decision partly on how they classify the youth.[37]

The second point at which detention may occur is after the police take the youth to the intake personnel of the juvenile court. Intake personnel then review the case to determine whether the youth should be referred to the juvenile court. They, too, often make the decision to release the youth to his or her parents, but the intake personnel may decide that the youth needs to be detained either for his or her own protection or for the protection of society (**preventive detention**), or while awaiting the adjudicatory hearing.

The third point at which a detention hearing may be held is after the adjudicatory hearing. If the youth is adjudicated delinquent, the court may in some circumstances sentence the youth to a detention center, shelter care, or in-home detention for a period of time as punishment. Detention is then used as a *sanction*, in which juveniles serve their "sentence" in detention and are released afterwards. More commonly, the court sentences the youth to a private or public residential facility.

Focus on Practice 6–4
The Dangers of Detention

In a report by the Justice Policy Institute, they list the following dangers of detention.

- Detention can increase recidivism. Congregating delinquent youths together negatively affect their behavior and increases their chances of reoffending. Detention also pulls youth deeper into the juvenile and criminal justice system. Alternatives to detention can curb crime and recidivism better than detention.
- Detention can slow or interrupt the natural process of aging out of delinquency. The point is that most young people age crime of their own and do not need detention.
- Detention has a negative impact on young people's mental health and propensity to self-harm. Detention makes mentally ill youth worse.
- Detention has a negative impact on the education of detained youth. Detained youths with special needs failed to return to school.
- Detention has a negative impact on youth employment. Formally detained youths have reduced success in the labor market.
- Detention is expensive—more expensive than alternatives to detention. That is, detention is not cost-effective.

- The rise of youth detention is borne by youth of color. This is another example of disproportionate minority confinement, a disturbing issue of juvenile justice.

The results of the Northwestern Juvenile Project—a longitudinal study of youth detained at the Cook County Juvenile Temporary Detention Center in Chicago, Illinois, examined the degree of youth's functional impairment as assessed three years after the release from detention. This study found that more than one third of youth were severely impaired in the school/work area; more than: 7 percent were severely impaired at home; more than half (51 percent) of youth were severely impaired in the community; and more than one quarter (25.7 percent) were severely impaired in the substance abuse domain. Only 7 percent of youth of the sample demonstrated no impairment.

CRITICAL THINKING SKILLS

Do you believe these studies overstate the negative impact that detention can have on youth?

Sources: Justice Policy Institute, *The Dangers of Detention: The Impact of Incarcerating Youth in Detention and Other Secure Facilities* (Washington, DC: Justice Policy Institute, 2013); Ken M. Abram, Jeanne J. Washburn, Eric G. Romero, Linda A. Teplin, and Elena D. Bassett, "Functional Impairment in Delinquent Youth," *Juvenile Justice Bulletin* (December 2013).

Youths who are held in detention are assigned to one of four types of placement. The detention home is the most physically restrictive. Shelter care is physically nonrestrictive and is available for those who lack home placements or who require juvenile court intervention. The jail or police lockup is juveniles' most undesirable detention placement and is not recommended for any juvenile. The final option available in many jurisdictions is in-home detention, which restricts a juvenile to his or her home, usually under the supervision of a paraprofessional staff member.

Five states have legislated a hearing on probable cause for detained youths, and appellate courts in other states have moved in the direction of mandating a probable-cause hearing to justify further detention. Georgia and Alaska courts have ruled that a juvenile is entitled to counsel at a detention hearing and to free counsel if indigent. The supreme courts in California and Alaska, as well as a Pennsylvania appellate court, have overturned cases in which no reason or an inadequate reason was stated for continuing detention. Furthermore, courts in the District of Columbia, Maryland, and Nevada have ruled that a youth in detention is entitled to humane care.

Bail for Children

Bail is *not* a form of punishment. Rather, its purpose is to ensure that the defendant will show up at his or her adjudicatory hearing. The court usually determines the amount of bail required at an early intake hearing, which reviews such factors as the youth's behavior, past history, and relationship with parents and school authorities. Once bail is set, the defendants and their families then have to come up with a percentage (usually 10 percent) of the required amount.

The controversies over bail are similar in adult and juvenile justice. The Eighth Amendment to the U.S. Constitution states that bail shall not be excessive, but determining what is excessive is difficult. In addition, the U.S. Supreme Court in *ex parte Crouse* stated that the Bill of Rights did not apply to children. This ruling therefore implied that the states and their courts may do as they please in setting bail. The result is that few can agree whether juveniles may be released on bail, and states and courts vary widely in their practices.

For example, some states prohibit bail altogether; Hawaii, Kentucky, Oregon, and Utah fall into this category. Other states allow bail, but not for juveniles. This practice is based on the assumption that normal juvenile court procedures and due process guarantees are sufficient to protect juveniles and allow their early release. In some of these states, it should be noted, judges occasionally require a juvenile to post a bond. For the most part, however, requirements that juveniles are to be released to their parents as soon as possible are believed to be sufficient protection for juveniles.

Bail for juveniles is permitted in nine states: Arkansas, Colorado, Connecticut, Georgia, Massachusetts, Nebraska, Oklahoma, South Dakota, and West Virginia. Even though few juveniles are released on bail, most juvenile court statutes do limit the time that accused juveniles may be held in custody before their hearings.[38]

The possibility of judges setting excessive bail has led some states to require higher courts to review the bail set by lower courts. In addition, some experts suggest releasing more youths on their own recognizance or under the supervision of third parties. Some recommend that states utilize citation programs; that is, police officers simply issue youths a "ticket," or summons, that requires the youth to appear in court on a certain date. Others suggest that police should require youths to report to the station house for a consultation with officers or members of the police youth bureau. Figure 6–2 outlines the pretrial processes in a juvenile court.

Preventive Detention

The 1984 *Schall v. Martin* decision of the U.S. Supreme Court represents a fundamental change that appears to be taking place in detention practices.[39] The plaintiffs originally filed a lawsuit in federal district court claiming that the New York Family Court Act was unconstitutional because it allowed for the preventive detention of juveniles:

> The District Court struck down the statute as permitting detention without due process and ordered the release of all class members. The Court of Appeals affirmed, holding...the statute is administered not for preventive purposes, but to impose punishment for unadjudicated criminal acts, and that therefore the statute is unconstitutional.[40]

In reversing the decision of the appeals court, Justice William Rehnquist declared that the "preventive detention under the statute serves the legitimate state objective held in common with every state, of protecting both the juvenile and the society from the hazards of pretrial crime."[41] Although the ultimate impact of this decision remains to be felt, there is reason to believe that the Court's ruling may encourage a significant expansion of preventive or secure detention for juveniles.

Preventive detention raises several controversial questions. First, laws are not supposed to be enforced against people unless some sort of overt act has occurred that violates the juvenile or criminal code. To put a youth in preventive detention under the assumption that he or she might commit an offense runs counter to the intent and, supposedly, the practice of the law. Second, preventive detention is experienced by the detainee as *punitive* confinement, regardless of the stated purpose of the practice. Finally, the propriety of incarceration before the determination of guilt and the procedural safeguards that must accompany such a practice are major issues to be considered. Indeed, evaluations of the detention process indicate that the majority of juveniles who are preventively detained are not charged with serious offenses.[42]

In examining the impact of early juvenile court decisions and subsequent court outcomes on youth, Kareem Al Jordan found that early

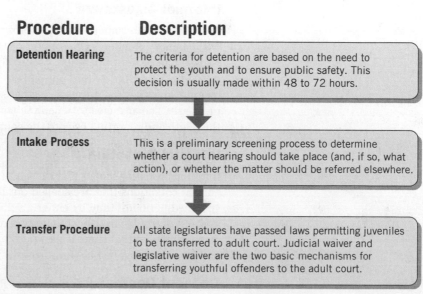

Procedure	Description
Detention Hearing	The criteria for detention are based on the need to protect the youth and to ensure public safety. This decision is usually made within 48 to 72 hours.
Intake Process	This is a preliminary screening process to determine whether a court hearing should take place (and, if so, what action), or whether the matter should be referred elsewhere.
Transfer Procedure	All state legislatures have passed laws permitting juveniles to be transferred to adult court. Judicial waiver and legislative waiver are the two basic mechanisms for transferring youthful offenders to the adult court.

FIGURE 6–2
Pretrial Processes in the Juvenile Court

court decision points can have a negative effect on youth later in the court process. In his study and examination of youth who were adjudicated delinquent in West Virginia, he found that preventive detention increases the probability of out-of-home placement for youth. He also adds that other studies reveal a strong empirical link between preventive detention and sentencing out-of-home placement.[43]

Intake Process

The **intake process** has several purposes: First, it screens cases to determine whether children need the help of the juvenile court. Second, it controls the use of detention, which is discussed later. Third, it reduces the courts' overwhelming caseloads. Fourth, it keeps inappropriate cases (e.g., minor cases) out of the juvenile court. Finally, it directs children to appropriate community agencies.[44]

Some probation departments have intake units, but in many departments, especially smaller ones, juvenile probation officers make intake decisions as part of their duties. When there are intake units, despite the similarity of their functions, they do not operate the same way. Juvenile court organization and available resources vary widely among the states. In addition, few states have attempted to spell out the criteria intake personnel should use to make their decisions. The result is that intake personnel exercise a great deal of discretion in deciding what to do with youths.

The first decision intake personnel must make is whether the case comes under their jurisdiction; for example, staff must determine whether the child or the child's offense falls under the appropriate age or offense category. If not, then the second decision of the staff will be either to dismiss the case or to refer it to an appropriate social agency or the adult court. Third, staff must decide whether the youth before them requires secure detention. Other options are to divert the case to a nonjudicial agency through an informal adjustment, put the youth on informal probation, issue a consent decree, or file a petition.

Case Dismissal

An intake officer reviews the cases of all youths brought to the court's attention. Often this review takes place with the police officer, the youth's parents, and perhaps the prosecutor and the youth's lawyers present. If the particular behavior in question is not an offense under the state's code, the charge will be dismissed. The case also will likely be dismissed if it is too weak to bring before the court, if it is the youth's first offense, if the youth appears genuinely contrite, and if the parents appear concerned about the youth's behavior and promise to get the him or her help. Youths whose cases are dismissed are sent home with their parents.

Informal Adjustment

This alternative, sometimes called *nonjudicial adjustment*, often is used for status and other minor offenders. One option of the intake official is simply to warn the child and release him or her to parents. A more stringent option is to require the youth to pay restitution to the victim. A third option is to refer the youth to local diversion programs, which include youth service bureaus or other social agencies that are qualified to work with their problems. The agencies to which the youth is referred are then responsible for supervising the youth and reporting back to the court.

Informal Probation

Informal probation means that the youth is released back to the community but must accept certain conditions that are spelled out by the court. The youth is usually supervised for a specified period of time by either a volunteer or a probation officer. If the youth is able to stay out of trouble in the community, a report is then sent back to the court, and the case is discontinued at that time. If the youth has difficulty, a petition may be filed with the court, and he or she may be held for further adjudication.

Consent Decree

Consent decrees are intermediate steps between informal handling and probation, and the decrees are used to place the child under the jurisdiction of the court without a finding

Focus on Law 6–5
Informal Sanctions

Informal processing usually is considered when the decision makers (such as the police, intake workers, probation officers, prosecutors, or other screening officers) believe that accountability and rehabilitation can be achieved without intervention from formal courts.

Informal sanctions are voluntary and, therefore, a juvenile cannot be forced to comply with an informal disposition. If a court decides to handle a matter informally (in lieu of formal prosecution), a youthful offender at that time has to agree to comply with one or more sanctions. These sanctions could include voluntary probation supervision, community service, and victim restitution. In some jurisdictions, the youth not only has to agree to sanctions but also has to agree that he or she committed the alleged act.

A case that is informally handled is usually held open pending the successful completion of the informal disposition. After the agreement on sanctions and the completion of this disposition, the charges against the offender are dismissed. But if the offender does not fulfill the court's conditions for informal handling, the case is likely to be reopened and formally prosecuted.

Informal handling has become less common but still occurs in a large number of cases. About half of the delinquency cases are handled informally. Informal handling is more likely to take place in smaller jurisdictions than in larger ones.

CRITICAL THINKING QUESTION

What is your evaluation of informal sanctions? What do you see as their strengths and weaknesses?

Source: Howard N. Snyder and Melissa Sickmund, *Juvenile Offenders and Victims: A National Report* (Washington, DC: Office of Juvenile Justice and Delinquency Prevention, 2006), 159.

---

that the child is delinquent. Generally, a consent decree requires the child to agree to fulfill certain conditions in spite of the fact that he or she has not been found guilty. For informal sanctions, see Focus on Law 6–5.

Petition

The intake officer can choose to file a petition if none of the preceding options is satisfactory. There is some evidence that the broad discretionary power given to intake workers is sometimes abused. For example, Duran Bell, Jr., and Kevin Lang's study of intake in Los Angeles found that some extralegal factors, especially cooperative behavior, are important in reducing the length of detention.[45]

Thinking Like a Correctional Professional

As a local juvenile court judge, you have been assigned the case of William, a thirteen-year-old juvenile so short he can barely see over the bench. On trial for armed robbery, the boy had been accused of threatening a woman with a knife and stealing her purse. Barely a teenager he already had a long history of involvement with the law. At age 11, he was arrested for drug possession and placed on probation, and soon after, he stole a car. At age 12, he was arrested for shoplifting. William is accompanied by his legal guardian, his maternal grandmother. His parents are unavailable because his father abandoned the family years ago and his mother is currently undergoing inpatient treatment at a local drug clinic. At a dispositional hearing, his court appointed attorney tells you of the tough life William has been forced to endure. His grandmother states, although she loves the boy, her advanced age makes it impossible for her to provide the care he needs to stay out of trouble. She says that William is a good boy who has developed a set of bad companions; his current scrape was participated by his friends. A representative of the school system testifies that William has above average intelligence and is actually respectful of teachers. She claims that he has potential but his life circumstances have short-circuited his academic success. William himself shows remorse and appears to be a sensitive youngster who is easily led astray by older youth.

You must now make a decision. You can place William on probation and allow him to live with his grandmother while being monitored by county probation staff. You can place him in a secure facility for up to three years. You can also put him in an intermediate program, such as a community-based facility, which would allow him to attend school during the day while residing in a halfway house and receiving group treatment in the evenings. Although

William appears salvageable, his crime was serious and involved the use of a weapon. If he remains in the community, he may offend again. If he is sent to a correctional facility, he will interact with older, tougher kids. What mode of correctional treatment which you choose?

The Transfer Procedure

Some critics contend that the juvenile court should only work with youths who fall into the dependent/neglected and victimized/abused categories, not with those who violate the criminal code. These latter offenders, some critics believe, should be dealt with by adult courts.[46] They argue that the juvenile court not only has failed in its rehabilitative mission, but is relatively powerless to effect change in more seasoned and hard-core youthful offenders. Thus, the critics insist that offenders who commit felonies should be subject to the same punishments to which adults are subject. The popularity of this position led to an increase in the number of youths transferred to adult courts in the past decade (see Chapter 7 for an expanded discussion and evaluation of transfer to adult court).

Plea Bargaining

Plea bargaining is increasingly emerging as an important issue in juvenile justice. One juvenile probation officer noted, "When I was a juvenile probation officer in a mid-sized urban county in Pennsylvania, many, if not most, of the cases were plea bargained."[47] Although little is known about how often or when it occurs, the increased trends toward "criminalization" of the juvenile court, on the one hand, and the expansion of community-based corrections, on the other, make it likely that plea bargaining will come under increased attention.[48]

A **plea bargain** is a deal made between the prosecutor and the defense attorney. The defense attorney, after consultation with his or her client, agrees that the client will admit to committing a lesser offense if the prosecutor will drop the more serious charges. The client receives a lighter sentence, and the necessity of having an adjudicatory hearing is avoided. The caseload of the court is thereby reduced.[49] Plea bargaining also involves dropping the number of charges a youth faces. For example, a youth is charged with two crimes and agrees to plead to one in exchange for the second charge being dropped. Or plea bargain can be for a lesser sentence for the original charge.

Critics of plea bargaining are concerned with its fairness. Their fear is that juveniles who are innocent of any wrongdoing may plead guilty to a lesser offense for fear that they will receive a harsh sentence if tried and found guilty of the more serious offense. This obviously is unfair to the innocent; even guilty youths may be subjected to inappropriate community referrals or placements if care is not taken to place them wisely. In addition, truly violent and dangerous youths may be able to negotiate a release back into the community when they should in all probability be placed in secure institutions. The problem at this time is that few guidelines exist to help direct prosecutors and defense attorneys in plea bargaining.

What Are Other Stages of Juvenile Court Proceedings?

After the pretrial procedures (discussed earlier in this chapter), the adjudicatory hearing, or the fact-finding stage, and the disposition hearing are the two remaining stages of the juvenile proceedings.

Adjudicatory Hearing

The **adjudicatory hearing** for juveniles is equivalent to the trial in adult court. It is the point at which the judge reviews the charges as described in the petition, hears testimony from the parties involved, and decides whether the youth committed the offense.

Adjudicatory hearings today are a blend of the old and the new. First, the hearings are still somewhat less formal than the adult trial. Second, the hearings have been traditionally

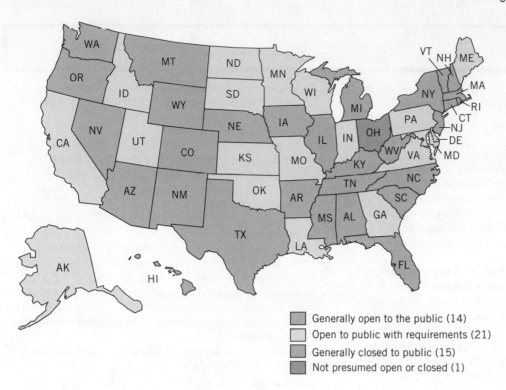

FIGURE 6–3
Confidentiality of Juvenile Proceedings

Generally open to the public (14)
Open to public with requirements (21)
Generally closed to public (15)
Not presumed open or closed (1)

closed in order to protect the juvenile's name and reputation in the community but that has been changing in many jurisdictions in terms of keeping the proceedings closed and of releasing juveniles' names to the public. Figure 6–3 indicates which states have juvenile adjudicatory hearings that are open to the public and which have confidential hearings. Third, a few juvenile courts, because they disagree strongly with the recent Supreme Court decisions, tend to ignore the new standards and operate much as in the past. Little change has occurred in these courts.

On the other side of the ledger, most states now spell out their procedural requirements very carefully. For example, all juveniles now have the right to a hearing, which is likely to be much more formal than in the past. Written petitions are required, and these may be amended if necessary. Hearsay is prohibited, and the case must be proved beyond a reasonable doubt. Youths have the right to protect themselves against self-incrimination, and they may cross-examine witnesses and victims. Attorneys and prosecutors are likely to be present. Finally, some state codes call for a separation of the adjudication and disposition hearings.

If an attorney has not been appointed or retained by the juvenile by this point in time, one will be appointed by the court and, hopefully, the date of the hearing reset to allow the attorney time to talk with the youth, review the case, and prepare the defense. Some courts may assign a public defender to the youth, allow the defender a couple of minutes to read the documents and talk with the youth, and go immediately into the adjudication hearing.

The National Council of Juvenile and Family Court Judges recommends that a script similar to that in Focus on Law 6–6 be used by the judge to ensure that the due process rights of the juvenile are maintained. These due process rights are given to the juvenile as a result of the *Kent, Gault, Winship, Breed v. Jones*, and *McKeiver* cases discussed earlier in the chapter.

If the youth's attorney and the prosecutor have agreed on a plea bargain, the agreement is presented to the judge at this time. If the judge accepts the plea bargain, the judge will issue a predisposition at this time, a process called a *sequential hearing*, and immediately assign a disposition in the case that will likely parallel those the juvenile may already have experienced earlier in his or her career. If the judge rejects the plea bargain, the adjudicatory hearing continues.

Focus on Law 6–6
Legal Rights of the Juvenile

Juvenile Delinquency Court Judge: "I am now going to advise you of your legal rights:"

1. A petition has been filed against you, and it says that you (explain the offense).
2. Do you understand what you are charged with?
3. You have the right against self-incrimination. This means that you do not have to say anything about your part in the charges or even whether you were anywhere near where the charges happened if you do not want to. If you do choose to talk about it, what you say can be used against you. Do you have any question about what this means?
4. You have the opportunity to either admit to the charges if they are true or to deny the charges if they are not true. If you deny the charges, there will be a trial to determine whether or not the charges are true. At the trial, you have the right to:
   • Confront witnesses [who] testify against you, which means your attorney gets to ask them questions to try and show that the charges are not true. Do you have any questions about what this means?
   • Compel witnesses, which means the court can require a person who your attorney thinks can help you show [that] the charges are not true to come to court and tell what they know. However, you are not required to bring any witnesses. Do you have any questions about what this means?
   • You can choose to testify or not to testify at the trial. You can remain silent and not say anything if you want. If you decide not to testify, your choice will not be held against you. Do you have any questions about what this means?
   • If you admit the charges, or if I find you are guilty at the trial, by law I can (explain what dispositions can be imposed). Do you have any questions about what this means?

5. Do you admit or deny the charges? Are the charges true or not true? If the youth denies the charge, proceed to set the trial date and deal with all pretrial issues.
6. If the youth admits the charges:
   • Do you understand that in saying the charges are true, you are giving up your right to a trial, which means you are also giving up your right to confront witness[es], make witness[es] testify for you, and to remain silent about the charges?
   • Has anyone made any threats or promises to you to get you to do this?
   • Have you taken any drugs, medicine, or alcohol within the last twenty-four hours? (If the youth answers yes, the judge must explore further to determine if the drug currently impairs the youth, which would mean [that] the plea should not be accepted.)
   • Are you admitting these charges to benefit yourself and nobody else?
   • At the time you did this, did you know those things were wrong? (If the youth's answers support a plea of admit, the judge should ask the parent, custodian, or [person acting] in loco parentis whether they know of any reason that the judge should not accept the plea.)

If the judge accepts the plea, the judge should call on the youth to explain what happened in detail. If the youth's explanation indicates that he or she is not really admitting to the offense, the judge should consider withdrawing the acceptance of the plea and setting the case for trial.

CRITICAL THINKING QUESTION

How are the juvenile's due process rights protected by such a script? Do you believe that most youthful offenders appearing before the court in an adjudicatory hearing have any understanding of what the script means?

Source: National Council of Juvenile and Family Court Judges, *Juvenile Delinquency Guidelines* (Reno, NV: Author, 2005), Appendix.

The length of the hearings varies throughout the country from a "five-minute children's hour" to a full hour or more, possibly with continuances, if more evidence such as forensic data or social service agency data is needed. During the hearing, the prosecutor will present the facts of the case, the defense will present the youth's side of the story, and the parents will be asked for their input, as will be the probation officer and the victim. In some jurisdictions today, the judge will render a verdict immediately after the conclusion of the trial. More and more jurisdictions, however, are setting a date for a disposition hearing, often within ten days to two weeks after the adjudicatory hearing. The reason for this time frame is to keep all hearings as close to the time the offense was committed as possible in order to have the maximum impact on the juvenile.

In some jurisdictions, it is possible for juveniles to receive a jury trial. Twelve states presently mandate a jury trial for juveniles who request one during their adjudicatory hearings and who face the possibility of institutional confinement. But twenty-three states deny juveniles the right to a jury trial. South Dakota is the only state of the remaining ones that specifies whether juveniles are entitled to jury trial. In that state, a juvenile court order is required for a jury trial to be conducted in juvenile court.[50]

Disposition Hearing

Disposition hearings, which are equivalent to sentencing hearings in adult courts, are of two basic types. The first type, which is used less and less frequently in the United States, occurs at the same time as the adjudicatory hearing. The judge, after hearing the case and discussing it with the youth, the youth's parents, the prosecutor, and the defense attorney, reviews the social service report submitted by a probation officer and decides what disposition would be most effective for the youth.

The second type of disposition hearing occurs following the adjudicatory hearing. This *bifurcated system*, as it is sometimes called, has different evidentiary rules than are used in the single adjudicatory hearing. In the adjudicatory hearing, for example, the standard of "proof beyond a reasonable doubt" requires stringent rules and a limiting of the kinds of information that may be introduced. The dispositional hearing, however, calls for the judge to have as wide a range of information as possible concerning the youth; this often involves information that would be inadmissible or inappropriate in the adjudicatory hearing.[51]

The reason for separating the two hearings is to prevent judges from learning information that is prejudicial to the defendant. In a combined hearing, the judge may discover information that is not relevant to the case but nevertheless biases his or her finding of guilt or innocence. If the judge does not receive this extraneous information until after the finding of guilt, the defendant is protected from being found guilty on the basis of information unrelated to the specific allegation.

Predisposition Report

Another advantage of the bifurcated system is that it gives the probation department time to make a more comprehensive study of the youth's needs and background than is possible when presentencing reports are given at the time of the adjudicatory hearing. This, too, increases the amount of information available to the judge in making a disposition decision.

Predisposition reports are essential to defendants, defense attorneys, prosecutors, probation departments, and judges. California and Maryland Supreme Courts in fact have overturned lower-court decisions because judges have not held dispositional hearings to consider relevant sentencing information.[52] This information is crucial because the reports contain background information on defendants that helps judges make individualized decisions.

The social work perspective has helped shape the way caseworkers and probation officers develop the predisposition reports. Since the 1920s, for example, the court has used psychiatric and psychological information obtained from existing school, social agency, and medical records. If such information is not available but is believed necessary, probation officers may refer juveniles for appropriate medical, psychological, or psychiatric evaluations to determine whether they are mentally ill or restricted. Other information is collected from law enforcement agencies, social service agencies that have dealt with the juvenile previously, the juvenile, and the juvenile's family, friends, and neighbors. The object is to collect any and all information that might be relevant to the case.[53]

The written report, then, contains a description of the referral incident as well as the youth's past conduct, prior contacts with the police and courts, and family environment and relationships. Information on the youth's employment history, school records, interests, and activities is also collected. If police officers have information on special problems of the youth or if his or her special needs are discovered, these, too, are included in the report.

Once the fact finding has been completed, probation officers recommend a course of action to the court. The predisposition report draws up a plan for what the youth needs and how he or she can be helped best. The report is submitted to the judge, who reviews it for the dispositional hearing and usually follows the advice given in the report. The juvenile has the right to be present at this hearing.

Both formal and informal factors influence decision making at the dispositional stage. The most important formal factors are the recommendation of the probation officer and the information contained in the social study investigation, or predisposition report; the seriousness of the delinquent offense; the juvenile's previous contact with the court; and the available options. Although the recommendation of the probation officer is usually followed by the juvenile judge, the seriousness of the delinquent behavior and the previous contacts with the court probably have the greatest impact on judicial decision making at this stage.[54] M. A. Bortner found from his examination of disposition decision making in a large Midwestern county that age, prior referrals, and the detention decision were the most important influences.[55]

The informal factors that sometimes influence judicial decision making include the values and philosophy of the judge, the social and racial background of the youth, the youth's demeanor, the presence or absence of defense counsel, and political repercussions of the alleged delinquent acts. The most disturbing of these informal factors relates to the social and racial background of the youth. Ruth D. Peterson found that racial, ethnic, gender, and age disparities affected the disposition of older adolescents in New York State courts. Although race and ethnicity did not significantly influence disposition decisions in New York City, minority juveniles tended to be stereotyped and to receive harsh treatment outside the city.[56] Figure 6–4 outlines the trial proceedings in a juvenile court.

Judicial Alternatives

The alternatives that are available to different juvenile courts vary significantly. Large urban courts have all or most of the following eleven alternatives at their disposal, but rural courts may have only a few:

1. *Dismissal.* Dismissal is one of the possible dispositions for juveniles. The fact-finding stage may have shown that a juvenile is guilty, but the judge can decide, for a variety of reasons, to dismiss the case.

2. *Restitution.* One very desirable option is restitution, where youths may be required to work off their debt with a few hours each week, but their lives are not seriously interrupted.

3. *Outpatient psychiatric therapy.* Whether in the court clinic, in the community mental health clinic, or with private therapists, outpatient therapy is a treatment-oriented decision and is often reserved for middle-class youths to keep them from being sent to "unfitting" placements.

ADJUDICATORY HEARING

This is the fact-finding stage of the court's proceedings and usually includes the youth's pleas, the presentation of evidence by the prosecution and defense, the cross-examination of witnesses, and the judge's finding.

DISPOSITION HEARING

The traditional purpose is to administer individualized justice and to set in motion the rehabilitation of the delinquent. Accordingly, the judge is not limited by constitutional safeguards as much as he or she was at the adjudication hearing.

JUDICIAL ALTERNATIVES

These alternatives available to juvenile courts vary significantly from one court to another, but most courts have a variety of choices.

RIGHT TO APPEAL

Juveniles do not have a constitutional right to make an appeal of their cases to a higher judiciary, but nearly all states permit the right to appeal by statute.

FIGURE 6–4
Trial Proceedings in the Juvenile Court

4. *Probation.* As the most widely used disposition, probation seems to be a popular decision with delinquents and a good treatment alternative for the court. Probation is sometimes set for a specific length of time, usually a maximum of two years. The judge can direct the probation officer to involve the youth in special programs, such as alternative schools, speech therapy, or learning disability programs.

5. *Foster home placements.* Foster home placements are more restrictive, inasmuch as youths are removed from their natural homes. These placements are used most frequently for status offenders and dependent and eclectic youths.

6. *Day treatment programs.* Day treatment programs are a popular alternative with juveniles because youths who are assigned to these programs return home in the evening, but these programs are few in number and are available in only a few states.

7. *Community-based residential programs.* There are different types of community-based residential programs, such as group homes and halfway houses that are available to many judges. These residential facilities may be located in the youth's community or in a nearby community, but they are not as desirable as community-based treatment programs because youths are taken from their homes to live in these facilities.

8. *Institutionalization in a mental hospital.* Institutionalization may be seen as appropriate for a youth's needs. A psychiatric evaluation is required when this alternative is chosen. After the evaluation, the doctor may recommend that the court initiate proceedings for commitment to a mental hospital.

9. *County or city institution.* Some county or city institutions are available to a few judges across the nation. Placement in these facilities may be deemed appropriate for youth who need more security than can be offered by probation offers but who do not require long-term placement in a state training school.

10. *State or private training school.* The state or private training schools usually are reserved for youths who have committed serious offenses or for whom everything else has failed. In some states, state training schools include minimum-security (forestry camps, farms, and ranches), medium-security, and maximum-security institutions.

11. *Adult facility or youthful offender facility.* In a few states, if a youth has committed serious offenses and is seen as too hard-core for a juvenile correctional institution, he or she is placed in an adult facility or youthful offender facility.

What Right Does the Juvenile Have to Appeal?

Juveniles do not yet have a constitutional right to appeal. Nevertheless, practically all states, following the lead of the U.S. Supreme Court, grant juveniles the right to appeal by statute for some of the following reasons. The Court pointed out in *In re Gault* that juveniles should have the same absolute right as adults have to appeal under the equal protection clause of the Constitution. Since that ruling, most state legislatures have passed laws granting juveniles the right to appeal. In addition, state courts have ruled that statutes granting the right to appeal for juveniles must be applied uniformly to all juveniles; this decision effectively undermines the tradition in some courts of giving judges the discretion to determine which juvenile cases could be appealed. The common practice today is to give juveniles the same rights to appeal as adults are given.[57]

The right to appeal is for the most part limited to juveniles and their parents. States may appeal in some circumstances, but this right is seldom exercised and few such cases have come before the courts. Some variation exists in the types of orders that may be appealed. States generally permit the appeal of "final" orders, although what is final varies from state to state. For example, some states authorize juvenile courts to order juveniles to be confined in secure facilities for a period of time. That is a final order. Nevertheless, certain states permit the youth or his or her parents to appeal that final order. States also vary in how they handle appeals. Most state statutes call for the case to be appealed to an appellate court, but a few states call for a completely new trial. Other common statutory rights of juveniles at appeal are the right to a transcript of the case and the right to counsel.[58]

What Is the Juvenile Sentencing Structure?

Determinate sentencing is a new form of sentencing in juvenile justice and in some jurisdictions is replacing the traditional form of indeterminate sentencing. In addition, increasing numbers of juvenile courts are using a "blended" form of sentencing.

Criticism of the decision making of the juvenile court has increased in the past thirty years. Early on, the criticism focused on the arbitrary nature of the decision making that violated the due process rights of juveniles; more recently, this criticism has been based on the belief that the juvenile court is too "soft" on crime. This latter criticism, especially, has led to a number of procedures that change sentencing and other juvenile procedures.

One of the first efforts at reform was the Juvenile Justice Standards Project, jointly sponsored by the Institute of Judicial Administration and the American Bar Association. Officially launched in 1971 by a national planning committee under the chairmanship of Judge Irving R. Kaufman, comprehensive guidelines for juvenile offenders were designed that would base sentences on the seriousness of the crime rather than on the needs of the youth. The proposed guidelines represented radical philosophical changes and still are used by proponents to attempt to standardize the handling of juvenile lawbreakers.

The belief that disparity in juvenile sentencing must end was one of the fundamental thrusts of the recommended standards. To accomplish this goal, the commission attempted to limit the discretion of juvenile judges and to make them accountable for their decisions, which would then be subject to judicial review. Also important in the standards was the provision that certain court procedures would be open to the public, although the names of juveniles still would remain confidential.

At the beginning of the twenty-first century, juvenile court judges remain quite concerned about these proposed standards. Their basic concern is that these standards attack the underlying philosophy and structure of the juvenile court. Judges also are concerned about how these standards would limit their authority. They see the influence of the hardliners behind this movement toward standardization and feel that the needs of children will be neglected in the long run. They also challenge the idea that it is possible, much less feasible, to treat all children alike.

Nevertheless, the standards are being adopted across the nation. New York State was the first to act on them through the Juvenile Justice Reform Act of 1976, which went into effect on February 1, 1977. The Act orders a determinate sentence of five years for Class A felonies, which include murder, first-degree kidnapping, and first-degree arson. The initial term can be extended by at least one year. The juvenile, according to the Act, should be placed in a residential facility after the first year. Then, if approved by the director of the division, the confined youth can be placed in a nonresidential program for the remainder of the five-year term. But the youth must remain under intensive supervision for the entire five-year term.

In 1977, the state of Washington also created a determinate sentencing system for juveniles in line with the recommendations of the Juvenile Justice Standards Project. Moreover, in the 1980s, a number of states stiffened juvenile court penalties for serious juvenile offenders, either by mandating minimum terms of incarceration (Colorado, Kentucky, and Idaho) or by enacting a comprehensive system of sentencing guidelines (Arizona, Georgia, and Minnesota).[59]

In 1995, the Texas legislature introduced such get-tough changes in the juvenile justice system as lowering the age at which waiver could occur to fourteen for capital, first-degree, and aggravated controlled-substance felony offenses and greatly expanding the determinate sentence statute that was first enacted in 1987. Under determinate sentences, any juvenile, regardless of age, can be sentenced for up to forty years in the Texas Youth Commission, with possible transfer to the Texas Department of Corrections. Finally, prosecutors can choose to pursue determinate sentence proceedings rather than delinquency proceedings, but they first must obtain grand jury approval.[60]

Daniel P. Mears and Samuel H. Field's examination of the determinate sentencing statute for Texas found that increased proceduralization and criminalization of juvenile courts did not eliminate consideration of age, gender, or race/ethnicity in sentencing decisions.[61]

In the 1990s, nearly every state enacted mandatory sentences for violent and repetitive juvenile offenders. The development of graduated, or accountability-based, sanctions was another means in the 1990s that states used to ensure that juveniles who are adjudicated delinquent received an appropriate disposition by the juvenile court. Several states have created a blended sentencing structure for cases involving repeat and serious juvenile offenders. Blended sentences are a mechanism for holding those juveniles accountable for their offenses. This expanded sentencing authority allows criminal and juvenile courts to impose either juvenile or adult sentences, or at times both, in cases involving juveniles.[62]

Delinquency Prevention

In the past twenty years, as we have indicated throughout this text, there has been an increased emphasis on evidence-based practice and treatment aimed at reducing recidivism and at-risk behavior. The most effective of these interventions with juvenile with juvenile offenders are aimed at addressing ecological factors and parenting skill. Ecology refers to the systems that surround youth in everyday life, including perhaps most importantly, the family. Multisystemic therapy, one of the most well-known and widely disseminated programs for at-risk and offender youth, is built on the theoretical assumptions that guardians/caretakers are a significant influence in changing problem behavior in children and adolescents. Other family-based interventions, such as Family Integrated Transitions, and the systems of care strategies of Wraparound Planning also demonstrated evidence of reducing recidivism. Six of the 11 programs listed as model programs in the Blueprint for Violence Prevention initiative at the University of Colorado's Center for the Study and Prevention of Violence are either family-based interventions or involve parenting training and/or parent reunification[63].

Increasingly, juvenile courts are looking to the family to become involved in the juvenile court process. Juvenile courts are creating juvenile drug courts, which often include families in treatment planning, and may also request or order that parents attend parenting classes or other skill building courses. Family group conferencing is increasingly being used as a diversion from formal court proceedings. In this model, families are empowered to make and implement their own decisions through family meetings that are open to all family members and key support personnel.[64]

Social Policy in Juvenile Justice: Toward Excellence in the Juvenile Delinquency Court

The National Council of Juvenile and Family Court Judges has identified the functions of the court and its judges. The council believes that the juvenile court should have exclusive jurisdiction in all matters affecting juveniles and families in delinquency cases, should have the same status as general trial courts, and should have the power and authority to "order, enforce, and review delivery of court ordered services and treatment for children and families."[65]

To overcome the many different forms and practices it has developed over the last one hundred years, the National Council on Juvenile and Family Court Judges made recommendations in 2005 to promote the best practices of the juvenile court and its personnel across the country[66] (see Figure 6–5).

Excellence in Juvenile Courts

Applies to the entire system

- Juvenile justice systems must have adequate staff, facilities, and program resources.

Applies specifically to judges

- Judges should engage in judicial leadership and encourage system collaboration. Status should be the same as other judges and judge should have multiple-year or permanent assignment.
- Judges should make certain that cases are diverted to alternative systems whenever possible and appropriate.
- Judges should make certain that victims have access to services they need.
- Judges should make certain that court dispositions are individualized and that they include graduated sanctions and incentives.
- Judges should ensure that effective post-dispositions are provided to each youth.
- Judges should ensure accountability among courtroom participants.
- Judges should ensure that an adequate information system is available to evaluate performance.
- Judges are responsible to see that all court staff are adequately trained.

Apply to other staff members

- All members of the court team should treat youths, families, crime victims, witnesses, and others with respect, dignity, courtesy, and cultural understanding.
- Youths charged in the delinquency court should have qualified and adequately compensated legal representation.
- Staff should encourage family members to participate in the development and implementation of the youth's intervention plan.

Apply to the court

- Delinquency courts and juvenile abuse courts should have integrated one-family–one-judge case assignments.
- Courts should render timely and just decisions, and trials should conclude without continuances.[78]

FIGURE 6–5
Principles of Excellence

SUMMARY

LEARNING OBJECTIVE 1: Summarize the development and legal norms of the juvenile court.

A number of cases resulted in the development of the juvenile court, ensuring that juveniles would have more constitutional rights accorded to them at the time of judicial proceedings:

- *In re Gault*—This is a U.S. Supreme Court case that brought the process and constitutional procedures into juvenile courts. *In re Kent*—At the time of transfer, juveniles are accorded an evidential hearing.
- *In re Winship*—Supreme Court ruled that juveniles are entitled to proof beyond a reasonable doubt during the adjudication proceedings.
- *McKeiver v. Pennsylvania*—Juveniles are not guaranteed the right to a jury trial.
- *Breed v. Jones*—A juvenile court cannot adjudicate a case and then transfer it over to the criminal court for adult processing on the same offense.

LEARNING OBJECTIVE 2: Describe the social control of the status offender.

There are two major decisions in terms of status offenders: (1) whether to deinstitutionalize them from delinquency youth—the majority of states have complied with the federal mandate to do this; and (2) whether the juvenile court should retain jurisdiction of status offenders—nearly all states have agreed that they should.

LEARNING OBJECTIVE 3: Explain the structure and key players of the juvenile court.

The key players of the juvenile court are the judge, the referee, the defense attorney, the prosecutor, the probation officer, and nonjudicial support personnel.

LEARNING OBJECTIVE 4: Describe pretrial procedures and decisions of the intake officer.

An intake officer reviews all cases brought before the juvenile court. At this point, the charges may be dismissed or the decision made to put a juvenile in detention or send him or her home.

The decision may also be to refer the juvenile to the juvenile court. The juvenile judge may decide to grant the youth an informal adjustment, informal probation, or consent decree or he or she may be required to appear in court for an adjudicatory hearing.

LEARNING OBJECTIVE 5: Explain plea bargaining.

A plea bargain is a deal made between the prosecutor and the defense attorney. The defense attorney, after consultation with his or her client, agrees that the client will admit to committing a lesser offense if the prosecutor will drop the more serious charge.

LEARNING OBJECTIVE 6: Summarize the adjudicatory process.

The adjudicatory hearing for juveniles is equivalent to the trial in adult court. It is the point at which the judge reviews the charges as described in the petition, hears testimony from the parties involved, and decides whether the youth committed the offense.

LEARNING OBJECTIVE 7: Describe the disposition hearing.

Disposition hearings, which are equivalent to sentencing hearings in adult courts, are of two basic types. The first type occurs at the same time as the adjudicatory hearing. The judge decides what disposition would be most effective for the youth. The second type of disposition hearing occurs following the adjudicatory hearing. This *bifurcated system,* as it is sometimes called, has different evidentiary rules than are used in the single adjudicatory hearing.

LEARNING OBJECTIVE 8: Describe the disposition alternatives.

The various alternatives are dismissal, restitution, outpatient psychiatric therapy, probation, foster home placements, day treatment programs, community-based residential programs, institutionalization in a mental hospital, county or city institution, state or private training school, and adult facility or youthful offender facility.

LEARNING OBJECTIVE 9: Describe the various sentencing alternatives for juveniles.

Determinate sentencing is a new form of sentencing in juvenile justice and in some jurisdictions is replacing the traditional form of indeterminate sentencing. In addition, increasing numbers of juvenile courts are using a "blended" form of sentencing.

KEY TERMS

adjudicatory hearing, p. 132
bail, p. 128
Breed v. Jones, p. 122
constitutionalists, p. 118
decriminalized status offenses, p. 123
deinstitutionalization of status
 offenders, p. 123
deinstitutionalization of status
 offenders (DSO), p. 123

detention hearing, p. 127
disposition hearing, p. 135
ex parte Crouse, p. 128
In re Barbara Burrus, p. 121
In re Gault, p. 119
In re Terry, p. 121
In re Winship, p. 120
intake process, p. 130

Juvenile Justice and Delinquency
 Prevention (JJDP) Act, p. 123
Kent v. United States, p. 118
McKeiver v. Pennsylvania, p. 121
plea bargain, p. 132
preventive detention, p. 127
probation officers, p. 126

REVIEW QUESTIONS

1. What is an adjudicatory hearing and what procedures does it follow?
2. What is a disposition hearing and the role of the disposition report in that hearing?
3. What range of dispositions is available to judges in the disposition hearings?
4. What are the basic arguments in favor of and in opposition to the retention of the juvenile court?

5. How did the juvenile court get to where it is today?
6. What is preventive detention? What is your evaluation of this movement in juvenile justice?
7. What role does plea bargaining play in juvenile court proceedings? What is your evaluation of plea bargaining?
8. Do you think the juvenile court should be changed? Why? How?
9. Which of the methods for appointing judges is the best? Why?

GROUP EXERCISES

1. *Writing to Learn Exercise:* Write two or three paragraphs on the nature of adjudicatory hearings today, including the reasons for the way hearings are set up and the nature of predisposition reports. Critique and revise.
2. *Group Work:* Drawing on your personal experience as a youth, "think through" the characteristics of different types of juveniles who might come into the juvenile court. Then,

discuss the judicial alternatives group members would recommend to judges for the juveniles who have engaged in different types of misbehavior.
3. *Writing to Learn Exercise:* Write two paragraphs, one on "Geraghty believes that adult courts are not appropriate places to try juveniles" and another on "how Geraghty believes the juvenile court could guarantee justice for juveniles." Critique and revise.

4. **Group Work:** Spell out in detail the assumptions and procedures of the original juvenile court. Then, each group must go through the cases highlighted in the chapter to develop the due process requirements asked for in the various court decisions.

5. **Writing to Learn Exercise:** Either after completing Exercise 4 or in place of it, have each student identify the court cases most relevant to the juvenile court and write up the due process requirements for juveniles involved in each type of circumstance.

6. **Writing to Learn Exercise:** Write one or two paragraphs identifying and describing the roles of different juvenile court personnel. Critique and revise.

7. **Group Work:** Discuss the pretrial procedures of the juvenile court, including the general process, detention hearings, bail for juveniles, and preventive detention, and the different legal issues found in each.

8. **Group Work:** Discuss the intake process and the different outcomes possible for juveniles processed through the intake process.

WORKING WITH JUVENILES

Working with a juvenile always means that you are an advocate for youth. This goes far beyond representing the juvenile in the court process because whatever way you are involved with the juvenile, you are always advocating for him or her.

NOTES

1. G. Larry Mays, "Transferring Juveniles to Adult Courts: Legal Guidelines and Constraints," paper presented at the annual meeting of the American Society of Criminology, Reno, NV, November 1989, 1.

2. *Commonwealth v. Fisher,* 213 P. 48, 62 A, 198 (1905).

3. Leonard P. Edwards, "The Juvenile Court and the Role of the Juvenile Court Judge," *National Council of Juvenile and Family Court Judges* 43 (1992), 4.

4. Barry Krisberg, *The Juvenile Court: Reclaiming the Vision* (San Francisco: National Council on Crime and Delinquency, 1988); Arnold Binder, "The Juvenile Court: The U.S. Constitution, and When the Twain Shall Meet," *Journal of Criminal Justice* 12 (1982), 355–66; Charles E. Springer, *Justice for Children* (Washington, DC: U.S. Department of Justice, 1986).

5. Barry C. Feld, "The Transformation of the Juvenile Court," *Minnesota Law Review* 75 (February 1991), 711; Barry C. Feld, "The Juvenile Court Meets the Principle of the Offense: Legislative Changes in Juvenile Waiver Statutes," *Journal of Criminal Law and Criminology* 78 (1987), 571–73; Barry C. Feld, "*In re Gault* Revisited: The Right to Counsel in the Juvenile Court," paper presented at the annual meeting of the American Society of Criminology, Montreal, November 1988.

6. Thomas F. Geraghty and Steven A. Drizin, "The Debate over the Future of Juvenile Courts: Can We Reach Consensus," *Journal of Criminal Law and Criminology* 88 (1998), 2–3.

7. Ellen Ryerson, *The Best Laid Plans: America's Juvenile Court Experiment* (New York: Hill and Wang, 1978), 574–75.

8. *Kent v. United States,* 383 U.S. 541, 86 S. Ct. 1045, 16 L. Ed. 2d 84 (1966).

9. Ibid.

10. Ibid.

11. *In re Gault,* 387 U.S. 1, 18 L. Ed. 527, 87 S. Ct. 1428 (1967).

12. Ibid.

13. *Haley v. Ohio,* 332 U.S. 596 (1948); *Gallegos v. Colorado,* 370 U.S. 49, 82 S. Ct. 1209 (1962); *Kent v. United States.*

14. Noah Weinstein, *Supreme Court Decisions and Juvenile Justice* (Reno, NV: National Council of Juvenile Court Judges, 1973).

15. *In re Winship,* 397 U.S. 358, 90 S. Ct. 1968, 25 L. Ed. 2d 368 (1970).

16. *McKeiver v. Pennsylvania,* 403 U.S. 528, 535 (1971). *In re Barbara Burrus,* 275 N.C. 517, 169 S.E. 2d 879 (1969).

17. Ibid.

18. Linda Symanski, "Juvenile Delinquents to a Jury Trial," *NCJJ Snapshot* (Pittsburgh, PA: National Council of Juvenile Justice, 2008).

19. *Breed v. Jones,* 421 U.S. 519, 95 S. Ct. 1779 (1975).

20. U.S. Congress, Senate Committee on the Judiciary, Subcommittee to Investigate Juvenile Delinquency, 1973, *The Juvenile Justice and Delinquency Prevention Act,* S.3148 and S.821. 92d Cong. 2d sess.; 93d Cong. 1st sess.

21. National Council on Juvenile Justice, *National Juvenile Court Case Records 1975–1992* (Pittsburgh, PA: National Center for Juvenile Justice, 1994).

22. Federal Advisory Committee on Juvenile Justice, *Annual Report 2008* (Washington, DC: Office of Juvenile Justice and Delinquency Prevention, 2008), 1.

23. Ibid., 2.

24. Charles W. Thomas, "Are Status Offenders Really So Different?" *Crime and Delinquency* 22 (1976), 440–42.

25. Martin Rouse, "The Diversion of Status Offenders, Criminalization, and the New York Family Court," paper presented at the annual meeting of the American Society of Criminology, Reno, NV, November 1989, 1, 2, 10–11.

26. Thomas, "Are Status Offenders Really So Different?" 438–455.

27. New York State Office of Children and Family Services, *PINS Reform Legislation,* accessed May 3, 2012, at http://www.olcfs.state.ny.us/main/legal/legislation/pins.

28. Bary Feld, *Bad Kids: Race and the Transformation of the Juvenile Court* (New York: Oxford University Press, 1999), 178.

29. Ibid.

30. Federal Advisory Committee on Juvenile Justice, *Federal Advisory Committee on Juvenile Justice: Annual Report 2010* (Washington, DC: U.S. Department of Justice, 2010), 3.

31. T. P. Thornberry, "Co-Occurrence of Problem Behavior Among Adolescents," paper presented at Multi-System Approaches in Child Welfare and Juvenile Justice Wingspread Conference, Milwaukee, WI, May 7–9, 2008.

32. National Resource Center for Family Centered Practice, *Minority Youth and Families Initiative (MYFI)* (Baltimore, MD: Annie E. Casey Foundation, 2005).

33. Federal Advisory Committee on Juvenile Justice, *Federal Advisory Committee on Juvenile Justice,* 5.

34. For a more expansive examination of juvenile court personnel, especially the juvenile court judge, see Ted. H. Rubin, *Behind the Black Robes: Juvenile Court Judges and the Court* (Beverly Hills, CA: Sage Publications, 1985); Ted H. Rubin, "The Juvenile Court Landscape," in *Juvenile Justice: Policies, Programs, and Services,* edited by Albert R. Roberts (Chicago: Dorsey Press, 1989); and Edwards, "The Juvenile Court and the Role of the Juvenile Court Judge."

35. Charles Puzzanchera and Melissa Sickmund, *Juvenile Court Statistics 2005* (Pittsburgh, PA: National Center for Juvenile Justice, 2008), 31.

36. Brenda R. McCarthy, "An Analysis of Detention," *Juvenile and Family Court Journal* 36 (1985), 49–50. For other discussions of detention, see Lydia Rosner, "Juvenile Secure Detention," *Journal of Offender Counseling, Services, and Rehabilitation* 12 (1988), 77–93; and Charles E. Frazier and Donna M. Bishop, "The Pretrial Detention of Juveniles and Its Impact on Case Dispositions," *Journal of Criminal Law and Criminology* 76 (1985), 1132–52.

37. Charles P. Smith, T. Edwin Black, and Fred R. Campbell, *A National Assessment of Case Disposition and Classification in the Juvenile Justice System: Inconsistent Labeling,* Vol. III, Reports of the National Juvenile Justice Assessment Centers (Washington, DC: U.S. Government Printing Office, April 1980), 97.

38. For a discussion of the use of bail for juveniles in Massachusetts, see Alida V. Merlo and William D. Bennett, "Criteria for Juvenile Detention: Who Gets Detained?" paper presented at the annual meeting of the American Society of Criminology, Reno, NV, November 1989.

39. *Schall v. Martin* (1984), *United States Law Review* 52 (47), 4681–96.

40. Ibid., 4681.

41. Ibid.

42. Feld, "Criminalizing Juvenile Justice," 191, 199. See also Deborah A. Lee, "The Constitutionality of Juvenile Preventive Detention: *Schall v. Martin:* Who Is Preventive Detention Protecting?" *New England Law Review* 38 (1987), 13–19.

43. Kareen L. Jordan, "Preventive Detention and Out-of-Home Placement: A Propensity Score Matching and Multilevel Modelling Approach," *OJJDP Journal of Juvenile Justice 1* (Fall 2012), 41–53.

44. See the section on intake in Patrick Griffin and Patricia Torget, *Desktop Guide to Good Juvenile Probation Practice* (Washington, DC: National Center for Juvenile Justice, 2002), 41–48.

45. Duran Bell, Jr., and Kevin Lang, "The Intake Dispositions of Juvenile Offenders," *Journal of Research of Crime and Delinquency* 2, no. 4 (1985), 309–28. See also Randall G. Sheldon and John A. Horvath, "Intake Processing in a Juvenile Court: A Comparison of Legal and Nonlegal Variables," *Juvenile and Family Court Journal* 38 (1987), 13–19.

46. Samuel M. Davis, *Rights of Juveniles: The Juvenile Justice System* (New York: Clark Boardman, 1984). Reprinted with Permission of West, a Thompson Business (St. Paul, MN: Updated March 2003), 4–26, 4–27. See also Barry C. Feld, "The Transformation of the Juvenile Court"; and Feld, "The Juvenile Court Meets the Principle of the Offense."

47. Conversation with this officer in 1990.

48. For an excellent discussion of the "criminalization" of the juvenile court, see Feld, "Criminalizing Juvenile Justice," 141–276.

49. Joyce Dougherty, "Negotiating Justice in the Juvenile Justice System: A Comparison of Adult Plea Bargaining and Juvenile Intake," *Federal Probation* 52 (1988), 72–80.

50. Kathleen Maguire and Ann L. Pastore, *Bureau of Justice Statistics: Sourcebook of Criminal Justice Statistics—1994* (Washington, DC: U.S. Government Printing Office, 1995).

51. Patrick Griffin and Patricia Torbet, eds., *Desktop to Good Juvenile Probation Practice: Mission-Driven, Performance-Based, and Outcome-Focused* (Pittsburgh, PA: National Center for Juvenile Justice, 2002), 64.

52. Ibid.

53. Ibid., 63–71.

54. Terence P. Thornberry, "Sentencing Disparities in the Juvenile Justice System," *Journal of Criminal Law and Criminology* 70 (Summer 1979), 164–71; M. A. Bortner, *Inside a Juvenile Court: The Tarnished Idea of Individualized Justice* (New York: New York University Press, 1982); Lawrence Cohen, "Delinquency Dispositions: An Empirical Analysis of Processing Decisions in Three Juvenile Courts," *Analytic Report* 9 (Washington, DC: U.S. Government Printing Office, 1975), 51.

55. Bortner, *Inside a Juvenile Court.*

56. Ruth D. Peterson, "Youthful Offender Designations and Sentencing in the New York Criminal Courts," *Social Problems* 35 (April 1988), 125–26.

57. Ibid.

58. Ibid., See *Morrissey v. Brewer,* 408 U.S. 471 (1972) and *Gagnon v. Scarpelli,* 411 U.S. 778 (1973).

59. Martin L. Forst, Bruce A. Fisher, and Robert B. Coates, "Indeterminate and Determinate Sentencing of Juvenile Delinquents: A National Survey of Approaches to Commitment and Release Decision-Making," *Juvenile and Family Court Journal* 36 (Summer 1985), 1.

60. Daniel P. Mears and Samuel H. Field, "Theorizing Sanctioning in a Criminalized Juvenile Court," *Criminology* 38 (November 2000), 985–86.

61. Ibid., 983.

62. Barry C. Feld, "Violent Youth and Public Policy: Minnesota Juvenile Justice Task Force and 1994 Legislative Reform," paper presented at the annual meeting of the American Society of Criminology, Miami, FL, 1994, 4. See also Feld, "Violent Youth and Public Policy: A Case Study of Juvenile Justice Law Reform," *Minnesota Law Review* 79 (May 1995), 965–1128. Blended sentences are discussed in greater detail in the next chapter.

63. Sarah Cusworth Walkr, Michael D. Pullmann, and Eric W. Trupin, "Juvenile JUSTICE 101; Addressing Family Support System Needs in Juvenile Court," *OJJDPO Journal of Juvenile Justice* (Dall 2002), 56.

64. Ibid.

65. National Council of Juvenile and Family Court Judges, *Juvenile Delinquency Guidelines: Improving Court Practice in Juvenile Delinquency Cases* (Reno, NV: Summer 1995), 37.

66. Ibid., 16.

Zbigniew Bzdak/MCT/Newscom

Learning Objectives

1. Explain the differences in maturity between juveniles and adults.

2. Explain how transfers to adult court take place as well as the different types of waivers.

3. Summarize blended sentencing and the different blended sentencing models.

4. Describe what an intermediate correctional system for juveniles would be like.

5. Discuss the death penalty for juveniles.

6. Summarize the debate about juveniles receiving a sentence of life without parole.

The body of Shirley Crook was found bound with electric cable and leather straps in the Meramec River in St. Louis County, Missouri, in 1993. Her head was wrapped in duct tape, her ribs were cracked, and she had bruises on her body. The offender had thrown her, still alive, off a bridge, and she drowned.

Christopher Simmons, aged seventeen, was arrested the next day at school and charged with the crime. He was interrogated for three hours without a parent or lawyer present and eventually confessed to the murder. Prior to the crime, Simmons had no previous criminal record.

On June 16, 1994, Christopher Simmons was convicted and sentenced to be executed for the crime.

Mr. Simmons is the product of a dysfunctional family with intergenerational psychiatric disorders and is himself predisposed to mental illness. As a child, he was the victim of severe physical and psychological abuse by his alcoholic stepfather. For example, his stepfather took him to a bar at the age of four and got him drunk to entertain the bar's patrons; his stepfather beat him severely. Mr. Simmons continued to use drugs such as LSD, marijuana, and alcohol as an adolescent and was encouraged to commit crimes by a neighbor. He viewed himself as a helpless victim unable to change. Mr. Simmons exhibited low self-esteem, impulsivity, loneliness, hopelessness, and depression.

On August 26, 2003, the Missouri Supreme Court held that to execute Simmons would violate the Eighth Amendment to the Constitution of the United States and vacated his execution. That decision was appealed to the U.S. Supreme Court and was heard on October 13, 2004.

On March 1, 2005, the U.S. Supreme Court ruled that the execution of juveniles under the age of eighteen was unconstitutional.[1]

The mission of the juvenile court, as previously discussed, is debated hotly today. Proponents contend that its original mission was to deal with all juvenile crime, from minor misbehaviors to assault, robbery, and murder. The rise in violent youth crime during the past decades, however, has increased the public's fear of juvenile crime. In addition, the emergence of a "hard line" since the late 1970s has increased the willingness of others to question the juvenile court's original mission. The result of this get-tough policy is that numerous proposals are being made that increase the chances that juvenile lawbreakers, even very young ones, will be punished with the same severity as are their adult counterparts.

This chapter examines some of the issues involved in ensuring justice for both juveniles and society. Beginning with the issue of immaturity and responsibility, this chapter considers the transfer to adult court, the 2005 *Roper v. Simmons* case that led to the abolishment of the juvenile death penalty, the sentence of a juvenile to a youthful offender system or to an adult prison, and a proposed adult court for juveniles.

Children or Adults?

As noted in Chapter 1, in terms of wrongdoing, the elusive concept of responsibility has its roots in the notions that individuals know right from wrong, have developed a social conscience, feel guilty or remorseful over their actions, are mentally sharp enough to know the rules, do not have any disease that reduces their ability to get along in society, fully understand that their actions are harming others, and are emotionally mature.

None of these criteria is measurable; but, for over a century, the assumption of the juvenile court has been that juveniles are deficient in one or more of them. Proponents of the juvenile court also assume that the court should have jurisdiction over the youths until their deficiencies are corrected and until they have developed the mental and emotional maturity of adults. What fuels the controversy over waiver to adult court is the disagreement over when youths reach this stage.

"Maturity" is a psychological term that is used to indicate when a person responds to the circumstances and environment in an appropriate manner. The fact is that this response is typically learned rather than instinctive and is determined by one's age. Maturity is involved with being aware of the correct time and place to behave and with knowing when to act appropriately, according to the situation and the culture in which a person lives.

In examining the extent to which young people should be held responsible for their criminal activity, Steven J. Morse contends that a "robust" theory of responsibility would result in most youths (in middle to late adolescence) being held responsible for their actions. He claims that there is empirical research to substantiate the position that it is often difficult to distinguish between the moral responsibility of children and young adults. Thus, he reasons, the responsibility of a juvenile should be no less than that of a similarly situated young adult. He does not believe that juveniles' susceptibility to peer pressure justifies differential allocation of responsibility.[2]

Elizabeth Scott and Thomas Grisso, in evaluating the differences between adults and youths, conclude that substantial differences exist between very young juveniles and adults in "moral, cognitive, and social development."[3] Scott and Grisso's developmental evidence does "support the argument of the post-Gault reformers of the 1970s and 1980s that a presumptive diminished responsibility standard be applied to juveniles."[4] They believe that this presumptive diminished responsibility is best applied in juvenile court systems, and they question whether the criminal justice system is able to respond to this developmental reality: "The ability or inclination of the criminal justice system to tailor its response to juvenile crime so as to utilize the lessons of developmental psychology is questionable. The evidence suggests that political pressure functions as a one-way ratchet, in the direction of ever stiffer penalties."[5]

They further question the assumption, proposed by Morse and others, that most juvenile offenders, even those in mid-adolescence, are as cognitively competent as adults are in decision-making capacity. They claim that the cognitive decision-making abilities of adolescents and adults are similar only when nondelinquent juveniles from middle-class backgrounds of above-average intelligence are compared with adults. But when children involved in the justice system, many of whom have emotional problems and learning disabilities that hinder their capacity for understanding, are compared with adults, there is real reason to question the cognitive competence of these youths.[6]

Thomas Grisso and colleagues reported that the abilities associated with competence were assessed among 927 adolescents in juvenile detention facilities and community settings. Adolescents' abilities were compared to those of 466 young adults who were in jails and in the community. Participants compared two standardized measures of abilities relevant for competence to stand trial. They found that youths ages 15 and younger performed more poorly than did young adults, with a greater proportion manifesting a level of impairment consistent with those found incompetent to stand trial. In addition, juveniles tended more often than adults to make choices in terms of plea bargaining that reflected compliance with authority and also psychological immaturity. See Table 7–1.

The fact of the matter is that some youths do commit brutal crimes, and the viciousness of their acts causes one to question the justice of their remaining in the juvenile system. Indeed, the media testify nearly daily to violent youth crime as they describe senseless killings and rapes committed by juveniles. Violent youth crime has contributed to the perception that something is seriously wrong with our society. Those who have been victims of youthful thugs feel especially vulnerable and call for stronger measures to deal with youthful predators.

Examples of savage attacks include the following: On September 24, 2009, four members of a teen gang brutally murdered Derrion Albert, an honor roll student and a bystander to gang violence in Chicago. Videotapes of the beating of Albert with two-by-fours were shown

▲ The formal setting of the adult court differs dramatically from the informal setting of the juvenile court and may be intimidating and scary to juveniles.

David R. Frazier Photolibrary, Inc./Alamy

TABLE 7–1
Arguments for and Against Juveniles' Diminished Responsibility

Juveniles are responsible, especially those in mid-adolescence, because	Juveniles lack adult maturation because
They know right from wrong.	They are substantially different from adults in moral, cognitive, and social development.
They have developed a social conscience.	They are particularly different in cognitive decision making from adults when they have low average intelligence.
They feel guilt or remorse over their actions.	They are different from adults when they have learning disabilities.
They are mentally sharp enough to know the rules.	They also may not understand the language of a *Miranda* warning well enough to make a valid waiver.
They do not have any disease reducing their ability to get along in society.	They often make choices in terms of plea bargaining that reflect compliance with authority as well as psychological immaturity.
They fully understand their actions when they harm others.	
They are emotionally mature.	

across the nation and shocked the conscience of the city of Chicago.[7] In 2011, two young men, one a seventeen-year-old, assaulted a homeless man, and videos of the attacks were posted on *YouTube*. The victim is seen on tape being tackled, punched, pushed, kicked, kneed, and mocked by his assailants.[8]

How Does Transfer to Adult Court Take Place?

Because of concern over violent juvenile offenders and the threat they pose to the community, state legislatures have passed laws permitting juveniles to be transferred or waived to adult court, where they can be tried and punished as adults. Waiver is a very serious issue because it means that a minor child can be sent to an adult prison institution where they will interact with and be influenced by experienced criminals. See Focus on Offenders 7–1 for the relationship between juvenile behavior and a life of crime.

Today, all state legislatures have passed laws permitting juveniles to be transferred to adult court. More than two hundred thousand youths are prosecuted in the adult criminal justice system each year and ten thousand children are held in adult jails and prisons.[9] Juveniles transferred to adult court are the least known group of juvenile offenders, but beginning in 2010, the Bureau of Justice Statistics funded Westat Inc. to conduct a survey of juveniles charged in adult criminal court. It is anticipated that this survey will reveal a valid estimate of how many juveniles are moved into adult courts in the United States, the demographics of these youths, the charges for which they are arraigned, and perhaps what happens after the decision is made to move a juvenile into an adult system.[10]

What is currently known is that transfer is believed to be taking place less frequently than in the past. In 2002, courts had fewer judicial waivers of juveniles to adult court than in 1985, and 2001 had the fewest judicial waivers of juveniles to adult court of any year since 1985.[11] In 2007, juvenile courts are estimated to have waived jurisdiction in about 8,500 cases.[12] The number of cases judicially waived to criminal court in 2009 was 45 percent less than in 1994, the peak year.[13] See Figure 7–1.

States vary widely in the criteria they use in making the waiver decision. Some states focus on the age of the offender, and others consider both age and offense. For example, some states such as Kansas, Vermont (age ten), Georgia, Illinois, and Mississippi[14]

Focus on Offenders 7–1
The Youthful Offender and a Future Life of Crime

One of the areas that has received vast examination is the relationship between juvenile behavior and adult crime. The following findings receive support:

- Adolescent gang involvement contributes to a likelihood of involvement in street crime and arrests in adulthood.
- Some evidence exists that delinquents who become adult offenders are somewhat more likely than other delinquents to have had more seriously offensive delinquent careers.
- The cumulative disadvantages of some delinquents (individual and parental deficits) make gang use, drug involvement, and gang involvement more attractive, leading to dropping out of school and unemployment into their adult years. In turn, these antisocial behaviors continue from childhood delinquency into adult crime.
- Childhood victimization with females, especially sexual victimization, can contribute to adult involvement with drugs and prostitution.

- Being institutionalized as a juvenile seriously compromises adult adjustment, especially for juveniles.
- Some studies have found a relationship among such factors as poor parental supervision, parental rejection, parental criminality, and delinquent siblings and late adult criminality.

CRITICAL THINKING QUESTION

How will these findings impact the field of juvenile justice?

Source: Marvin D. Krohn, Jeffrey T. Ward, Terence P. Thornberry, Alan J. Lizotte, and Rebekah Chu, "The Cascading Effects of Adolescent Gang Involvement Across the Life Course," *Criminology* 49 (November 2011), 991–1025; Nadine Lanctot, Stephen A. Cernkovich, and Peggy C. Giordano, "Delinquent Behavior, Official Delinquency, and Gender: Consequences for Adult Functioning and Well-Being," *Criminology* 45 (2007), 191–222; and Brian Francis, Keith Soohill, and Alex R. Piquerro, "Estimation Issues and Generational Changes in Modeling Criminal Career Length," *Crime and Delinquency* 53 (January 2007), 3–37.

(age thirteen) and others transfer children at very young ages. More states transfer juveniles at fourteen than at any other age; seven states transfer juveniles at either fifteen or sixteen years of age.

The offenses juveniles commit are also important in the waiver decision. Some states permit waiver for any criminal offense, whereas others waive only those offenses specifically mentioned in the state's statutes. Many states permit waiver to the adult court if the juvenile[15] previously has been adjudicated delinquent or has a prior criminal conviction. Depending on the state, three major mechanisms are used to waive juveniles: judicial waiver, prosecutorial discretion, and statutorial exclusion. Table 7–2 reveals that most states have access to multiple ways of imposing adult sanctions on offenders of juvenile age.

Judicial Waiver

Except where state laws mandate that a youth be tried in adult court, someone has to make the decision to waive a youth. **Judicial waiver**, the most widely used transfer mechanism, involves the actual decision-making process that begins when the juvenile is brought to intake. Predictably, the mechanisms used vary by state. For every 1,000 petitioned delinquency cases, about nine are judicially waived to criminal court.[16] In some states, intake personnel, juvenile prosecutors, or judges make the decision based, in part, on the age or offense criteria. In other states, a court other than the juvenile court makes the decision. For example, the prosecutor or judge in the adult court may decide where a juvenile is to be tried.[17] The decision is determined by the requirements of the state and the way the intake officer, prosecutor, or judge interprets the youth's background. Typically, the criteria used include the age and maturity of the child; the child's relationship with parents, school, and community; whether the child is considered dangerous; and whether court officials believe that the child may be helped by juvenile court services. Table 7–3 lists states that exclude certain serious offenses from juvenile court.

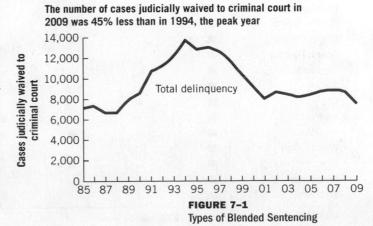

The number of cases judicially waived to criminal court in 2009 was 45% less than in 1994, the peak year

FIGURE 7–1
Types of Blended Sentencing

TABLE 7–2
Most States Have Multiple Ways to Impose Adult Sanctions on Juveniles

State	Judicial waiver			Prosecutorial discretion	Statutory exclusion	Reverse waiver	Once an adult always an adult	Blended sentencing	
	Discretionary	Presumptive	Mandatory					Juvenile	Criminal
Number of states	45	15	15	15	29	24	34	14	18
Alabama	■				■		■		
Alaska	■	■			■			■	
Arizona	■			■	■	■	■		
Arkansas	■			■	■	■		■	■
California	■	■		■	■	■	■		■
Colorado	■	■		■	■	■		■	■
Connecticut			■				■	■	
Delaware	■		■		■	■	■		
Dist. of Columbia	■	■		■			■		
Florida	■			■	■		■		■
Georgia	■		■	■	■		■		
Hawaii	■						■		
Idaho	■				■		■		■
Illinois	■	■	■		■		■	■	■
Indiana	■		■		■		■		
Iowa	■				■	■	■		■
Kansas		■			■		■		
Kentucky	■				■		■		■
Louisiana	■		■	■	■		■		
Maine	■	■					■		
Maryland	■				■	■	■		
Massachusetts					■			■	■
Michigan	■			■			■	■	■
Minnesota	■				■		■	■	
Mississippi	■				■		■		
Missouri	■						■		■
Montana				■	■		■	■	
Nebraska				■		■			■
Nevada	■	■			■	■	■		
New Hampshire	■	■					■		
New Jersey	■	■	■						
New Mexico					■			■	■
New York					■	■			
North Carolina	■		■				■		
North Dakota	■	■			■		■		
Ohio	■		■				■	■	
Oklahoma	■			■	■	■	■		■
Oregon	■				■	■	■		
Pennsylvania	■	■			■	■	■		
Rhode Island	■	■	■				■	■	
South Carolina	■		■		■		■		
South Dakota	■				■	■	■		
Tennessee	■					■	■		
Texas	■						■	■	
Utah	■	■			■		■		
Vermont	■			■	■	■			■
Virginia	■		■	■	■	■	■		■
Washington	■				■	■	■		■
West Virginia	■		■		■	■			■
Wisconsin	■				■		■		■
Wyoming	■			■		■			

Note: Table information is as of the end of the 2009 legislative session.

Source: Patrick Griffin, Sean Addie, Benjamin Adams, and Kathy Finestine, Trying Juveniles as Adults: An Analysis of State Transfer Laws and Reporting (Washington, DC: Juvenile Offenders and Victims, National Report Series Bulletin, September 2011), 3.

TABLE 7–3
Many States Exclude Certain Serious Offenses from Juvenile Court Jurisdiction

State	Any criminal offense	Certain felonies	Capital crimes	Murder	Certain person offenses	Certain property offenses	Certain drug offenses	Certain weapon offenses
Alabama		16	16				16	
Alaska					16	16		
Arizona		15		15	15			
California				14	14			
Delaware		15						
Florida				16	NS	16	16	
Georgia				13	13			
Idaho				14	14	14	14	
Illinois		15		13	15			15
Indiana		16					16	16
Iowa		16					16	16
Louisiana				15	15			
Maryland			14	16	16			16
Massachusetts				14				
Minnesota				16				
Mississippi		13	13					
Montana				17	17	17	17	17
Nevada	16*	NS		NS	16			
New Mexico				15				
New York				13	13	14		14
Oklahoma				13				
Oregon				15	15			
Pennsylvania				NS	15			
South Carolina		16						
South Dakota		16						
Utah		16		16				
Vermont				14	14	14		
Washington				16	16	16		
Wisconsin				10	10			

*In Nevada, the exclusion applies to any juvenile with a previous felony adjudication, regardless of the current offense charged, if the current offense involves the use or threatened use of a firearm.

Note: An entry in the column below an offense category means that there is at least one offense in that category that is excluded from juvenile court jurisdiction. The number indicates the youngest possible age at which a juvenile accused of an offense in that category is subject to exclusion. "NS" means no age restriction is specified for an offense in that category. Table information is as of the end of the 2009 legislative session.

Source: Patrick Griffin, Sean Addie, Benjamin Adams, and Kathy Finestine, Trying Juveniles as Adults: An Analysis of State Transfer Laws and Reporting (Washington, DC: Juvenile Offenders and Victims, National Report Series Bulletin, September 2011), 6.

Prosecutorial Discretion

Prosecutorial discretion occurs in states with **concurrent jurisdiction** statutes. These laws give prosecutors the authority to decide whether to try juveniles in either juvenile or adult court.

Juvenile Court Prosecutor

PREPARATION FOR THE JOB

Preparing for this job would require that a person is competitive by nature because getting into this field requires so much competition. A person also has to be determined because the schooling and the actual career require a lot of hours and dedication. Something to consider while getting an undergraduate is taking other classes that can enhance/broaden a person's outlook.

QUALIFICATION AND EDUCATIONAL REQUIREMENTS

To become a juvenile prosecutor there are a lot of rigorous educational requirements. First, an aspiring prosecuting attorney must get a bachelor's degree so that they can be accepted into a law school. They must also take the Law School Admission Test (LSAT) in order to be accepted by a law school. After being in law school they must get there Juris Doctor (J.D) degree. And finally, they must pass the Multistate Bar Examination (MBE).

DUTIES

In order to become a juvenile prosecuting attorney a person will have to work in a law office that is big enough to have specific areas of law because if a person works in a smaller law office then they may be required to handle more cases than just that particular area. Once the prosecutor has their case they must review the police reports and start to preform research to support their case against the defense. They also may have to preform interviews with witnesses or victims to get more information. The prosecuting attorney must be able to clearly and effectively present their evidence in the courtroom, which usually consists of the prosecution, the defense, the client, and the judge.

DEMAND FOR

The demand for attorneys is expected to rise 10 percent from the years 2010–2020. The competition to become any type of lawyer is very high.

SALARY

As of 2012, the average salary for an attorney was $130,880.

Source: "Prosecuting Attorney: Job Description, Duties, and Requirements." http://educationportal.com/articles/Prosecuting_Attorney_Job_Description _Duties_and_Requirements.html, accessed October 30, 2014.

Statutorial Exclusion

Some states have a **statutorial exclusion** of certain offenses from juvenile court, thereby automatically transferring perpetrators of those offenses to adult court.

Other variations on waiver also exist, some very subtle. One such variation is a state legislature lowering the age over which the juvenile court has jurisdiction. For example, if a state's age of juvenile court jurisdiction is eighteen, the legislature may lower the age to sixteen. This approach focuses entirely on the age of the juvenile and ignores the offenses committed.

Yet other state legislatures have specified that juveniles of specific ages who commit specific crimes are to be tried in adult court. For example, until recently, Indiana statutes stated that any child age ten or older who committed murder would be tried as an adult. This method of legislative waiver focuses as much on the offense as it does on the age of the offender.

Another method of waiver is one in which the statutes simply state that anyone who commits a specific crime may be tried in adult court. No reference is made to the age of the offender. This approach is attractive to those who believe that any youth who violates the law should receive an appropriate punishment.

Thinking like a Correctional Professional

There has been recent break of violent juvenile crime. Even though juvenile violence has decreased dramatically across the nation, there is strong concern among the media, politicians, and policymakers that the juvenile court is too permissive, and one solution being offered is to transfer more juveniles to adult court. You have been delegated by the governor to put together a study whether more juveniles ought to be transferred to adult court. How would you go about this study? What assistance do you need?

Reverse Waiver and Blended Sentencing

In *reverse waiver*, some state laws permit youths who are over the maximum age of jurisdiction to be sent back to the juvenile court if the adult court believes the case is more appropriate for juvenile court jurisdiction. For a reverse waiver, defense counsel and prosecutors attempt to make their case for their desired action. Some evidence and testimony are allowed, and arguments are presented. When each side has had a chance to present its case and to rebut the opponents' arguments, the judge makes the decision.[18]

A *blended sentence* is a sentence imposed by a juvenile court that blends a juvenile disposition and an adult sentence for certain serious youthful offenders. Some states permit juvenile court judges at the disposition hearing in the delinquency court to impose both an adult and a juvenile sentence concurrently. This option may be given to juveniles who have received a direct file, mandatory or a prosecutorial waiver, to the adult court. In these cases, the juvenile is given both sentences but is first given the juvenile disposition. If the juvenile fulfills the requirements of this disposition satisfactorily, the adult disposition is suspended. If the juvenile does not fulfill the conditions of the juvenile disposition, the juvenile is then required to fulfill the conditions of the adult disposition. Connecticut, Kentucky, and Minnesota are among the states adopting this sentencing authority.

In some states, the juvenile may be required to fulfill the juvenile disposition until he or she reaches the age of majority; at this point, the juvenile must begin to fulfill the adult sentence minus the time already spent fulfilling the juvenile disposition. In Texas, the juvenile court may impose a juvenile sanction that extends beyond the extended age of juvenile court jurisdiction, at which time the transfer of the youthful offender to an adult correctional facility is required. Under this form of expanded sentencing authority, the juvenile court judge or jury can impose a sentence of up to 30 years, depending on the seriousness of the offense. Legislation in 1995 added several offenses for which a juvenile may receive a determinate, fixed term of 40 years.[19] See Figure 7–1 for the types of blended sentencing:

Another common way for the adult criminal court to levy juvenile sanctions is through the creation of youthful offender programs. Otherwise known as "intermediate" or "third systems," these systems provide a mechanism that allows states to impose strict, adult sanctions on juveniles or young adults convicted of violent offenses, while maintaining a rehabilitation focus.

Since Colorado enacted the first program of this type, at least eleven other states have followed suit. These youthful offender-type programs are viewed in these states as giving juveniles one last chance before being they are sent to an adult facility.[20] See the discussion later in this chapter on these youthful offender camps.

Changing Criteria for Waiver

In the past, youths were waived to adult court without hearings, without sufficient fact finding on the part of the court, without reasons being given for the waiver, and without the youth having the benefit of an attorney. Critics fought these procedures. Their essential argument was that the decision to waive juveniles to adult court was a serious matter and that youths should be entitled to due process rights. On reviewing two cases in particular, *Kent v. United States* and *Breed v. Jones* (see Chapter 6), the U.S. Supreme Court ruled that traditional juvenile court procedures for waiver were inadequate and that juveniles were guaranteed many of the same due process rights as were adults. Since *Kent* and *Jones*, most states now require that waiver hearings be held before transferring juveniles to adult court. Yet these hearings are not required in all states; some states permit prosecutors to make the waiver decision. In addition, states that provide for mandatory legislative waiver do not have to hold such hearings.

Where juvenile courts are responsible for making the waiver decision, the Supreme Court stated in *Kent* that they must use the following criteria:

1. The seriousness of the alleged offense to the community and whether the protection of the community requires waiver

2. Whether the alleged offense was committed in an aggressive, violent, premeditated, or willful manner

3. Whether the alleged offense was against persons or against property, greater weight being given to offenses against persons, especially if personal injury resulted

4. The prosecutorial merit of the complaint, that is, whether there is evidence on which a grand jury may be expected to return an indictment

5. The desirability of trial and disposition of the entire offense in one court when the juvenile's associates in the alleged offense are adults who will be charged with a crime in the criminal court

6. The sophistication and maturity of the juvenile as determined by consideration of his home, environment, emotional attitude, and pattern of living

7. The record and previous history of the juvenile

8. The prospects for adequate protection of the public and the likelihood of reasonable rehabilitation of the juvenile (if he [or she] is found to have committed the alleged offense) by the use of procedures, services, and facilities currently available to the juvenile court.[21]

What Happens in the Transfer or Waiver Hearing?

Once a prosecutor has decided that a juvenile is beyond the help of the juvenile court and has reviewed the legal sufficiency of the case, the prosecutor files a motion to send the youth to adult court; this motion requires a probable-cause hearing by a juvenile judge. These hearings are required for both a mandatory judicial waiver and a discretionary judicial waiver. The judge begins either hearing by explaining the nature of the hearing and making certain that the youth and his or her parents understand the youth's rights and the consequences of the outcome. All interested parties should be present at this hearing.[22]

In a probable-cause hearing, everything said should be under oath. The prosecutor presents the state's case against the juvenile, affirming the identity of the juvenile and of witnesses and reviewing the affidavit, petition, and jurisdiction requirements—both of the age of the offender and of the geographical region from which the offender comes. The defense attorney then challenges the evidence of the prosecutor and may present witnesses; both the prosecutor and the defense attorney cross-examine the witnesses on the legal facts of the case. Both attorneys then summarize their cases at the conclusion of testimony.[23]

If the judge believes that probable cause has been established, he or she then determines whether the case satisfies the state's legally sufficient requirements for mandatory judicial waiver. If it does, the youth is transferred to criminal court. If probable cause is not established and the prosecutor's motion is denied, the National Council of Juvenile and Family Court Judges recommends the dismissal of the case. Some courts, in practice, refer the youth back to the probation department.[24]

In the judge's review of the case, the youth's dangerousness to self and others, the youth's sophistication and maturity in understanding the nature and consequences of his or her behavior, and the youth's amenability to further treatment are all evaluated. Whether to waive or retain also is based on whether the youth had a history of violent crimes, was a gang member, tested antisocial, had co-offenders, engaged in premeditated offenses, and had experienced trauma in childhood and adolescence. Very important is the availability of alternative treatments, including out-of-state placements. The youth's attorney plays a critical role in helping to evaluate the youth and in presenting alternatives that can benefit the youth. The judge must decide, if the youth is in detention, whether to continue detention or release the youth. The decision the judge finally makes should be based on clear and convincing evidence.[25]

Waiver to Criminal Court

Once the waiver decision is made, the juvenile's case is transferred to the adult court prosecutor. Prosecutors in some states may decide to send the case back to the juvenile court because the case may not meet the standards of legal sufficiency, such as probable cause. The prosecutor may confer with a judge about any legal questions the prosecutor believes the judge might have about the case before making a decision. In some states, the prosecutor takes the case to a grand jury; in other states, the prosecutor sets a date for an arraignment. There, the legal process starts all over again with the same people present, with the result that some juveniles are put on informal or formal probation and others are tried in adult court. The case now usually is tried in front of a jury, and the youth has the potential of receiving the same sentence as an adult.[26]

Evaluation of Waiver

Although waivers are still relatively infrequent and have recently increased slightly in number, they are an important issue in juvenile justice. Significantly, juveniles waived to adult court are not always the most serious and violent offenders. Examinations of waiver have found that little consensus exists today on which criteria should be used in making the waiver decision. Furthermore, although remanded youth are receiving severe penalties, waiver generally does not result in more severe penalties than juvenile offenders would have received in juvenile court. Several states have attempted to develop a process that would identify those juveniles unfit for retention in juvenile court. For example, using such criteria as age, offense, and prior record, Minnesota has codified the transfer procedures to be followed by judges and prosecutors. Given the adult courts' massive caseload and their limited judicial experience with sentencing youths, little evidence exists that adult judges know what to do with juveniles appearing before them. Finally, even when waiver does occur, some evidence exists that waiver may have the effect not of deterring crime by juveniles, but of increasing it.[27] Richard E. Redding summarized the recent Juvenile Justice and Delinquency Prevention Act–funded research on juvenile transfer by saying that transferred juveniles are more likely to offend, that they have a greater likelihood of rearrest, and that the process of transfer is found to increase recidivism.[28]

How Does a Youthful Offender System Work

Juveniles sentenced in adult courts are subject to the same range of dispositions as are adults. Cases may be dismissed or offenders may be found guilty. If found guilty, youths may be released to the care of their parents, placed on probation, fined, ordered to pay restitution, or referred to a social agency qualified to deal with their problem. But a very controversial disposition is the placement of youths in adult correctional facilities.

The crowding, violence, and exploitative relationships found in adult prisons make this disposition extremely questionable. Furthermore, although some states have attempted to develop special institutions for juveniles, even these appear to have the same characteristics as adult prisons. Youths who are placed in them can no better protect themselves than they can in adult facilities. Given the young age of even the most violent of these offenders, society has the task of deciding whether any type of adult institutional placement is appropriate for these youths.

By the year 2000, five states and the District of Columbia held no juveniles in adult prisons under the age of seventeen or younger.[29] Some variations on the practice of confining a juvenile in an adult institution do exist among the states. In some jurisdictions, states have no alternative but to place juveniles in adult institutions if the courts require incarceration. Some states can, under special circumstances, place youths in either juvenile or adult institutions; yet other states can refer juveniles back to juvenile court for their disposition. In some instances, very young juveniles are sent to juvenile facilities but then are transferred to adult institutions when they become of age. Recognizing the dangers and inadequacies of placing juveniles with adults, some jurisdictions have developed special institutions for these younger adult offenders, who are usually sixteen to nineteen years of age.

In a **youthful offender system**, as it has been proposed, programs in these institutions would emphasize work readiness, job training, and work experience. They would also attempt to establish close ties to the community to which the youth would return; employ flexible staff who would act as positive role models; enforce the rules strictly; provide opportunities for decision making, with consequences clearly and fully related to the choices made; provide opportunities to enhance self-esteem; create a continuity of care between the program or treatment sequence and integration into the community to which the youth is returning; and offer supportive services in the community after completion of the program or treatment sequence as long as the youth needs them.[30]

The California Youth Authority has long extended its jurisdiction over youthful offenders to those up to twenty-three years of age. North Carolina was one of the first states to develop youthful offender camps for sixteen- to eighteen-year-old males. In the 1990s, Colorado, New Mexico, and Minnesota also developed transitional, or intermediate, systems between the juvenile and adult systems. The Minnesota Juvenile Justice Task Force recommended the following:

> A more graduated juvenile justice system that establishes a new *transitional component between the juvenile and adult systems* ... [T]his new [Serious Youthful Offender] category will create viable new dispositional options for juvenile court judges facing juveniles who have committed serious or repeat offenses. It will give the juvenile *one last chance* at success in the juvenile system, with the threat of adult sanctions as an incentive not to re-offend.[31]

In 1994, the Minnesota legislature adopted the task force's recommendation but relabeled the category "extended jurisdiction juvenile" (EJJ) to make the label less attractive to delinquent "wannabes." For juveniles who are designated as EJJs, final legislation extended the juvenile court's jurisdiction until age twenty-one. The Department of Corrections was also required to license and regulate regional secure treatment facilities for EJJs.[32]

Intermediate sentencing for youthful offenders that bridges the juvenile and adult systems certainly appears to be a positive means for keeping some juveniles out of adult correctional facilities. It is hoped that the 1994 legislation in Minnesota, as well as the youthful offender systems in Colorado and New Mexico, will encourage the development of such legislation in more states.

The current get-tough mood of society does not seem to be one in which the development of youthful offender systems will be viewed as an attractive option to policy makers in many states. Yet, if the juvenile population explosion occurs in the next two decades, as predicted by some experts, and if increasing numbers of juveniles are referred to the adult systems, perhaps there will be greater receptivity toward an intermediate correctional system for youthful offenders.

What Is Life Like for a Juvenile Sent to Prison?

Adult prisons are a world apart from most training schools. Prisons are much larger, sometimes containing several thousand inmates and covering many acres of ground. Life on the inside is generally austere, crowded, and dangerous, and institutionalized juveniles are particularly subject to sexual victimization and sexual assault. Richard E. Redding concluded from his review of the programming that juveniles receive in adult correctional facilities: "Once incarcerated in adult facilities, juveniles typically receive fewer age-appropriate rehabilitative, medical, mental health and educational services, and are at greater risk of physical and sexual abuse and suicide."[33]

In 2009, state prisons held more than 2,700 juveniles. About 46 percent of these inmates were held in prisons in southern states.[34] Table 7–4 reveals that more than half of inmates younger than age eighteen held in state prisons come from states with a younger age of criminal responsibility. Between 1997 and 2004, the number of inmates under age eighteen fell significantly. However, this decline of the youth proportion of prison population was primarily the result of the large increase in the total prison population during this period.

From 1994 to 2001, almost 3,000 juveniles were committed to the custody of the federal Bureau of Prisons (BOP) for offenses committed when they were under eighteen years of age. Of these, 1,639 were committed to the BOP as delinquents and 1,346 as adults. The vast majority of these juveniles committed as delinquents (about 70 percent) were American Indians.[35] Federal prisons did not report holding any juveniles at mid-year 2007.[36]

In some states, judges opt for the **life without parole sentence** to incarcerate juveniles for the rest of their natural lives. See Focus on Law 7–2 for an Iowa case in which a fifteen-year-old received a life without parole sentence.

TABLE 7–4
State Prisons and Age of Responsibility

State	Inmates*	State	Inmates*	State	Inmates*
U.S. total	2,778	Upper age 17	1,368	Montana	1
		Alabama	118	Nebraska	21
Upper age 15	737	Alaska	7	Nevada	118
Connecticut	332	Arizona	157	New Jersey	21
New York	190	Arkansas	17	New Mexico	3
North Carolina	215	California	0	North Dakota	0
		Colorado	79	Ohio	86
Upper age 16	673	Delaware	28	Oklahoma	19
Georgia	99	Florida	393	Oregon	13
Illinois	106	Hawaii	2	Pennsylvania	61
Louisiana	15	Idaho	0	Rhode Island	1
Massachusetts	8	Indiana	54	South Dakota	1
Michigan	132	Iowa	13	Tennessee	22
Missouri	31	Kansas	5	Utah	6
New Hampshire	0	Kentucky	0	Vermont	4
South Carolina	89	Maine	0	Virginia	16
Texas	156	Maryland	58	Washington	2
Wisconsin	37	Minnesota	13	West Virginia	0
		Mississippi	28	Wyoming	1

*Reported number of inmates younger than age 18 held in custody in state prisons, 2009.

Source: Authors' adaptation of West's Prison Inmates at Midyear 2009—Statistical Tables, *Prison and Jail Inmates at Midyear.*

Source: Patrick Griffin, Sean Addie, Benjamin Adams, and Kathy Finestine, *Trying Juveniles as Adults: An Analysis of State Transfer Laws and Reporting* (Washington, DC: Juvenile Offenders and Victims, National Report Series Bulletin, September 2011).

Providing for the care and special needs of juvenile offenders in adult facilities is proving to be a real problem. The youthful offender may be as young as thirteen and feel overwhelmed by older and more aggressive offenders. Indeed, most juvenile offenders placed in adult prisons are not violent offenders. A gang culture may be present in the prison, in which gang members pressure youthful offenders to become part of their gang, usually to exploit them. Furthermore, with their need to be part of something, youthful offenders tend to be highly impressionable and easily used or manipulated.[37]

The state of Washington has attempted to manage imprisoned youthful offenders more effectively. In 1997, the state enacted Senate Bill 3,900 defining the jurisdiction, custody, and management requirements for juvenile offenders. This legislation requires juvenile offenders to be placed in adult prisons for serious offenses such as aggravated murder. But all necessary measures must be taken to protect youthful offenders, including separating them from adult inmates and placing them in protective custody units.

Female youthful offenders are placed at the Washington Corrections Center for Women (WCCW), and males are confined at the Clallam Bay Corrections Center. A multidisciplinary team was formed in September 1997 in order to meet the challenge of accommodating juveniles in adult prisons. This team has been concerned with providing a safe and secure environment, an environment distant from adult offenders' contact and influences; programs and services similar to those available to the general population; and an educational program offering credit for a high school diploma or GED.[38]

Focus on Law 7–2
You Will Spend the Remainder of Your Natural Life in Prison

In 1994, four Midwestern teenagers decided to take a Ford Bronco belonging to one of their parents and run away to Canada. The Bronco broke down in a neighboring state, and they realized that they would need to steal another car. They stopped a woman, who thought that the Bronco with lights on top was a police vehicle. One of the teenagers approached the woman and pretended to be a police officer. She demanded to see identification. He returned to the Bronco and instructed one of his companions to take the .22 rifle they had brought along and shoot her. The fifteen-year-old youth, who had committed no more serious acts than vandalism, complied. He shot her once, broke the window of her vehicle on the driver's side when she locked the door, and stabbed her thirty-one times.

The four youths called their parents after they left the crime scene. Later that night, one of their parents arrived and took them home. Within a couple of days, all four were arrested and charged with this crime. Tried in the jurisdiction where the crime was committed, the four juveniles were quickly transferred to the adult court.

During the trial of the youth who had committed the stabbing, his defense attorney attempted to explain the youth's ruthless behavior: The jury was informed that he came from a totally inadequate family background. He had been sexually abused by his natural father at the age of two and had been physically assaulted by an adopted father at the age of 15. His mother had been married eight times, and she failed to supply his emotional needs in a number of ways. He also did poorly in school and had failed twice. He had been charged with using marijuana on a couple of occasions but had not been involved in any serious personal or property offenses. He was particularly fearful of the youth who had instructed him to shoot the woman. In summary, the defense attorney claimed that what had taken place that night emerged from the totality of the youth's experiences, frustrations, inadequacies, and unmet needs. The child deserved punishment, the attorney admitted, but not to the extent of spending the rest of his life in prison.

Upon being sentenced to prison for life without parole, the youth admitted that he was fearful of being sexually assaulted. As a small white youth, his fears were not unreasonable. He said that he had made up his mind to be placed in the prison population (with other inmates). He did not want to be locked up twenty-four hours a day for the rest of his life. Whatever it took, he vowed, he would keep the other inmates off him. He was briefly placed in a diagnostic facility. Later, when he was transferred to an adult reformatory, it did not take him long to attack a pressuring inmate with a shank. He was charged with attempted murder and placed in administrative segregation.

CRITICAL THINKING QUESTION:

How much time do you believe this offender should spend in prison for a crime he committed when he was fifteen? If you were this inmate, would you want to be locked up in protective custody or try to make it in the prison population? If you chose the prison population, what would you be willing to do to protect yourself?

Source: One of the authors was involved with this defense as an expert witness.

The Juvenile Death Penalty: Three Decades of Change

The most severe sentence in the adult courts is, of course, the death penalty. Much debate has centered on this issue, and in June 1989, the U.S. Supreme Court ruled that sixteen- and seventeen-year-old juveniles could be executed for their crimes.[39]

This decision generated an outburst of debate. It was applauded by conservatives, who contended that society needs the death penalty for its retributive and deterrent effects on violent crime. Conservatives also believe that juveniles are mollycoddled by the juvenile court and that juveniles who break the law deserve the same punishments as do adults. Liberals, however, decried the decision.[40] Their objections reflect, in part, the disdain that many have for the death penalty in a "civilized" society. These modern progressives also believe that youthful offenders should be rehabilitated because they are young and still in the formative years of their lives.

Victor L. Strieb traces the development of the current debate. The constitutionality of the death penalty was decided in *Gregg v. Georgia* in 1976.[41] In that decision, the U.S. Supreme Court ruled that the death penalty did not violate the Eighth Amendment's prohibition against cruel and unusual punishment. The Court did stipulate that before lower courts handed down the death penalty, the special characteristics of the offender, such as his or her age, as well as the circumstances of the crime, had to be considered.[42] In later decisions, considering statutes in Ohio and other states, the Court ruled that mitigating circumstances had to be considered in any death penalty case. Accordingly, states that have handed down the death penalty without considering mitigating circumstances have had their cases overturned.[43] States that permit the death penalty today, in other words, must statutorily require that mitigating circumstances be considered.

In some ways, the debate over the death penalty for juveniles is a curious one. Strieb points out that historically, few juveniles were ever executed for their crimes. Indeed, even when juveniles were sentenced to death, few, if any, executions were carried out.[44] In the United States, for example, youths under the age of eighteen were executed at the rate of twenty to twenty-seven per decade, or about 1.6 to 2.3 percent of all executions from the 1880s to the 1920s.[45] The peak in the United States occurred in the 1940s, when fifty-three, or 4.1 percent of all those executed, were juveniles.[46]

Of the thirty-eight states that permitted capital punishment, twenty-four allowed it for individuals who were under the age of eighteen when they committed the crime. Fourteen states have never executed juveniles, but Georgia leads all states with forty-one juvenile executions, followed by North Carolina and Ohio, with nineteen each.

In 1982, in the case of *Eddings v. Oklahoma*, the Supreme Court was able to avoid directly addressing the constitutionality of the juvenile death penalty by ruling that "the chronological age of a minor is itself a relevant mitigating factor of great weight."[47] Monty Lee Eddings was sixteen when he shot and killed an Oklahoma State Highway Patrol officer, but his execution sentence was reversed in 1982 because of his age.[48]

In *Wilkins v. Missouri*, sixteen-year-old Heath A. Wilkins of Missouri stabbed Nancy Allen Moore to death on July 27, 1985, as she worked behind the counter of a convenience store. The jury found him guilty of first-degree murder, armed criminal action, and carrying

TABLE 7–5
Juveniles Executed in the United States in the Modern Era (Since January 1, 1973)

Name	Date of Execution	Place of Execution	Race	Age at Crime	Age at Execution
Charles Rumbaugh	9/11/85	Texas	White	17	28
J. Terry Roach	1/10/86	South Carolina	White	17	25
Jay Pinkerton	5/15/86	Texas	White	17	24
Dalton Prejean	5/18/90	Louisiana	Black	17	30
Johnny Garrett	2/11/92	Texas	White	17	28
Curtis Harris	7/1/93	Texas	Black	17	31
Frederick Lashley	7/28/93	Missouri	Black	17	29
Ruben Cantu	8/24/93	Texas	Latino	17	26
Chris Burger	12/7/93	Georgia	White	17	33
Joseph Cannon	4/22/98	Texas	White	17	38
Robert Carter	5/18/98	Texas	Black	17	34
Dwayne Allen Wright	10/14/98	Virginia	Black	17	24
Sean Sellers	2/4/99	Oklahoma	White	16	29
Douglas Christopher Thomas	1/10/00	Virginia	White	17	26
Steven Roach	1/13/00	Virginia	White	17	23
Glen McGinnis	1/25/00	Texas	Black	17	27
Shaka Sankofa (Gary Graham)	6/22/00	Texas	Black	17	36
Gerald Mitchell	10/22/01	Texas	Black	17	33
Napoleon Beazley	5/28/02	Texas	Black	17	25
T.J. Jones	8/8/02	Texas	Black	17	25
Toronto Patterson	8/28/02	Texas	Black	17	24
Scott Allen Hain	4/3/03	Oklahoma	White	17	32

▲ The stress of being a victim or witness testifying in court is often overwhelming. Some require the assistance of their lawyers and court personnel to make it through their testimony.
LOU TOMAN/KRT/Newscom

a concealed weapon. During the sentencing hearing, both the prosecution and Wilkins himself urged the court to apply the death penalty. The aggravating circumstances of the case led the court to decide that the death penalty was appropriate and sentenced Wilkins to die. The Missouri Supreme Court later upheld this decision.[49] Wilkins had not been executed by the time the *Roper v. Simmons* decision was made to eliminate the juvenile death penalty.

In 1988, the U.S. Supreme Court heard the case of *Thompson v. Oklahoma*.[50] Wayne Thompson was fifteen when he was arrested, along with his twenty-seven-year-old half-brother and two other older men, for the shooting and stabbing death of Charles Keene, Thompson's former brother-in-law. The Court ruled by a five-to-three vote that "the Eighth and Fourteenth Amendment[s] prohibit the execution of a person who was under sixteen years of age at the time of his or her offense."[51]

The Supreme Court upheld the constitutionality of the death penalty for juveniles in two 1989 cases. In the case of *Stanford v. Kentucky*, Kevin Stanford, a seventeen-year-old African American youth, repeatedly raped and sodomized his victim during a robbery.[52] He then drove her to a secluded area, where he shot her point blank in the face and in the back of the head. A jury convicted Stanford of first-degree murder, first-degree sodomy, first-degree robbery, and receiving stolen property. Stanford was sentenced to death on September 28, 1989, and was transferred to death row.[53] He was not executed.

The important *Atkins v. Virginia* decision, rendered on June 20, 2002, emphasized very clearly the importance of mental retardation as a mitigating factor to be considered in sentencing juveniles. Atkins was convicted of abduction and armed robbery with a semiautomatic handgun. After the robbery, he drove the victim to a remote location and murdered him. Atkins was convicted of capital murder and sentenced to death. However, he was mentally deficient, and the Supreme Court ruled that mentally retarded juveniles could not be executed for their offenses.[54]

Individuals who were given capital sentences for crimes committed while they were juveniles continued to be executed until 2005. For example, on April 3, 2003, Scott Allen Hain was executed in Oklahoma for a murder he committed at age seventeen. Nevertheless, the juvenile death penalty had many vocal opponents. The human rights organization Amnesty International, the United Nations General Assembly, and other influential organizations continued to opt for the elimination of the juvenile death penalty in the United States. On March 1, 2005, in the case of *Roper v. Simmons* the Supreme Court ruled, in a five-to-four decision, that no juveniles who committed their crimes under the age of eighteen could be executed.[55]

The fact is that the death penalty for juveniles who commit crimes when under age eighteen has been outlawed, but, as Focus on Policy 7–3 points out, juveniles can still die in prison for crimes they have committed.

Evidence-Based Practice
The Lives of Juvenile Lifers: Findings from a National Survey

Life in prison without the possibility of parole (LWOP) gives no chance for fulfillment outside prison walls, no chance for reconciliation with society, no hope. Maturity can lead to that considered reflection which is the foundation for remorse, renewal, and rehabilitation. A young person who knows that he or she has no chance of leaving prison before life's ends has little incentive to become a responsible individual.

Graham v. Florida, *2010*

The United States stands alone worldwide in imposing a life without parole sentence on juveniles. Survey findings from 1,579 individuals around the country who are serving these sentences for crimes committed while juveniles demonstrate extreme racial disparities in the imposition of these punishments, high rates of social economic disadvantage, sentences often imposed without judicial discretion, and counterproductive corrections policies that make efforts at rehabilitation difficult. Highlights of this report include the following:

- Juvenile lifers experienced a high level of exposure to violence in their homes and communities. For example, 79 percent of these individuals reported witnessing violence in their homes and more than half (54.1 percent) witnessed weekly violence in their neighborhoods.
- Juvenile lifers, particularly girls, suffered high rates of abuse. Nearly half (46.9 percent) experienced physical abuse, including 79.5 percent of girls, and 77.3 percent of girls reported a history of sexual abuse. Overall, 20.5 percent of juvenile lifers reported having been victims of sexual abuse.
- Juvenile lifers generally experience significant social and economic disadvantage in their homes and communities. About a third of juvenile lifers (31.5 percent) were raised in public poverty. Juvenile lifers faced significant educational challenges. Fewer than half of these individuals had been attending school at the time of their offense, and the vast majority of juvenile lifers had been suspended or expelled from school at some point in their academic career.
- The racial dynamics of victims and offenders may play a key role in determining which offenders are sentenced to juvenile life without parole. The proportion of African Americans serving these sentences for the killing of a white person (43.4 percent) is nearly twice the rate at which white juveniles are arrested for taking a white person's life (23.2 percent).
- The majority of these sentences are imposed in states in which judges are obligated to sentence individuals without consideration of any factors relating to a juvenile's age or his or her life circumstances. States such as Pennsylvania, which holds the nation's largest population of juvenile lifers, require that youth of any age charged with homicide be tried in adult court and, upon conviction, sentenced to life without the possibility of parole.
- Most (61.9 percent) juvenile lifers are not engaged in programming in prison, but this is generally not due to lack of interest, but because of state or prison policies.
- Many juvenile lifers are engaged in constructive change during their incarceration when they are permitted the opportunity to do so.

CRITICAL THINKING QUESTION

Do actual differences exist between a capital sentence and a sentence of a life without parole? Discuss.

Sources: Robert Barnes, "Supreme Court Restricts Life Without Parole for Juveniles," *Washington Post,* May 2010, accessed May 1, 2012, at http://www.washingtolnpost.com/wp-dyn-content-article-2010/05/17/AR2010051701355.htm; Lilianna Segura, "Will the Supreme Court Toss Life Without Parole for Juveniles?, *The Nation,* March 2012, accessed May 1, 2012, at http://www.thenation.com/blog/166925/2will-supreme-court-toss-life-without-parole- juveniles; and Ashlcy Nellis, *The Lives of Juvenile Lifers: Findings from a National Survey* (Washington, DC: The Sentencing Project, March 2012), 2–4.

Policy for Juvenile Justice

SHOULD JUVENILES BE ALLOWED TO DIE IN PRISON?

Locking up a juvenile for the rest of his or her life for a crime committed while a juvenile may be cruel punishment, but it is not unusual. There are currently 2,390 people in this nation who are serving life sentences (LWOP) for crimes they committed before they turned eighteen. There are seventy-three juveniles who have committed crimes when they were thirteen or fourteen and were given this sentence. Nationally, 59 percent of the juveniles serving life without parole sentences had no prior criminal convictions before being placed in prison for life.

Forty-two states currently allow life without parole for minors. California has 225 inmates serving life sentences for crimes committed as minors. Pennsylvania is estimated to have 360 to 443 inmates serving life without parole for crimes committed as juveniles.

In the wake of the *Roper* decision forbidding the death penalty for juvenile offenders, the next notable Eighth Amendment battleground could be LWOP sentences for juveniles. Proponents of LWOP sound much like those who favored the death penalty for juveniles in the past, and those who would abolish LWOP use many of the same arguments that opponents of the death penalty for juvenile formerly used.

On May 18, 2010, the U.S. Supreme Court ruled, by a 5-to-4 vote, that juveniles may not be sentenced to life in prison without parole for any crime short of homicide. The majority of the courts in this ruling made it clear that youthful offenders must be treated differently from adults even for heinous crimes.

Anthony M. Kennedy, writing for the majority, said states must provide juveniles who receive lengthy sentences a "meaningful" chance at some point to show that they should be released.

The case involved Terrance Jamar Graham, who was convicted of robbery in Jacksonville, Florida, when he was sixteen. He received a short jail term and probation but was arrested again at seventeen for taking part in a home invasion. The judge in the case gave him the sentence of life without the possibility of parole.

Judge Kennedy said there were 129 juveniles in eleven states, including Virginia, who had not committed homicide but were serving sentences of life without parole. The majority of them—77—were in Florida.

In the summer of 2012, the U.S. Supreme Court ruled on *Jackson v. Hobbs* and *Miller v. Alabama,* that juveniles under eighteen when they committed the homicide could not long be sentenced to life without parole.[56] These two cases that were argued back to back. In both cases, fourteen-year-old juveniles were sentenced to life without parole. Jackson was with a couple of colleagues who were robbing a video store when one of them killed the clerk. Miller, in contrast, committed a homicide, beating a man with a bat and setting fire to his trailer.

SUMMARY

LEARNING OBJECTIVE 1: Explain the differences in maturity between juveniles and adults.

Defining when childhood ends and adulthood begins is a worrisome problem; unfortunately, no objective tests are available to help society draw the line. The result is much confusion from state to state over the ways in which youths and adults are defined. The basic issue is one of deciding the elusive concept of responsibility and of defining the relationship between age and mental and emotional maturity.

LEARNING OBJECTIVE 2: Explain how transfer to adult court takes place as well as the different types of waivers.

Juveniles appearing before the juvenile court can be transferred or certified to the adult court. The different types of waivers are judicial waiver, prosecutorial discretion, statutorial exclusion, reverse waiver, and blended sentencing. Proponents of the practice of transfer believe that if juveniles are processed by adult courts, punishment is ensured and society will become safer as a result.

LEARNING OBJECTIVE 3: Summarize blended sentencing and the different blended sentencing models.

A blended sentence is a sentence imposed by a juvenile court that blends a juvenile disposition and an adult sentence for certain serious youthful offenders. Some states permit juvenile court judges at the disposition hearing in the delinquency court to impose both an adult and a juvenile sentence concurrently.

LEARNING OBJECTIVE 4: Describe what an intermediate correctional system for juveniles would be like.

A youthful offender system has been developed in a number of states for young adults, ages sixteen to nineteen. These are transitional, or intermediate systems between the juvenile and adult systems.

LEARNING OBJECTIVE 5: Discuss the death penalty for juveniles.

Up to the *Roper v. Simmons* decision, which outlawed the death penalty for juveniles for crimes committed under the age of eighteen, the most serious consequence for juveniles was the possibility of being sentenced to the death penalty.

LEARNING OBJECTIVE 6: Summarize the debate about juveniles receiving a sentence to life without parole.

Forty-two states presently allow life without parole for minors. About 2,500 people in this nation are currently serving life without parole sentences for crimes they committed before they turned eighteen. On May 18, 2010, the U.S. Supreme Court ruled, by a 5-to-4 vote, that juveniles may not be sentenced to a life in prison without parole for any crime short of homicide. In cases to be decided in the summer of 2012, *Jackson v. Hobbes* and *Miller v. Alabama*, the Supreme Court ruled on the constitutionality of life without parole for juveniles.

KEY TERMS

concurrent jurisdiction, p. 151
judicial waiver, p. 149

life without parole sentence, p. 156
prosecutorial discretion, p. 151

statutorial exclusion, p. 152
youthful offender system, p. 155

REVIEW QUESTIONS

1. At what point are children considered adults by society today? When do different state and local organizations in the United States consider you an adult?
2. What are the main types of waiver to the adult court?
3. Why is waiver such a controversial matter in juvenile justice?

4. What is your stand on the death penalty for juveniles? Do you support it or oppose it? Why?
5. When is treatment in the juvenile system no longer desirable for a juvenile?
6. Should any juvenile be confined for life? If so, who and why?

GROUP EXERCISES

1. *Group Work:* Discuss the different types of waivers found throughout the states and how those waivers work.
2. *Writing to Learn Exercise:* As an alternative to Exercise 1, have all students identify and describe each of the different types of waivers and then critique each others' answers for style and substance.
3. *Group Work:* Discuss the stages, issues, and court decisions involved in the evolution of the juvenile death penalty.

4. *Class Debate:* Divide the class into two groups, one of which is to argue, "Resolved: Juveniles receive sufficient due process, and more juveniles should be sent to community-based corrections for rehabilitation and treatment." The other is to argue "Resolved: Juveniles should be treated as adults, sanctions against them strengthened, and more youths should be sent to the adult court for prosecution and punishment."

WORKING WITH JUVENILES

How do you handle working with serious juvenile offenders who realistically can pose a threat to you? What can you do to protect yourself? What signs are there that a particular juvenile may pose a danger to you?

NOTES

1. Compiled from the International Justice Project, "Juveniles: Christopher Simmons," accessed at http://www.international justiceproject.org/juvCSimmons.cfm; Death Penalty Information Center, "U.S. Supreme Court: *Roper v. Simmons*," accessed May 5, 2006, at http://www.deathpenaltyinfo.org; American Bar Association, "Christopher Simmons," accessed May 5, 2006, at http://www.abanet.org/crimjust/juvjus/simmons.html.

2. Stephen J. Morse, "Immaturity and Responsibility," *Journal of Criminal Law and Criminology* 88 (1998), 19–20. See also Thomas F. Geraghty and Steven A. Drizin, "Foreword—The Debate Over the Future of Juvenile Courts: Can We Reach Consensus?" *Journal of Criminal Law and Criminology* 88 (1998), 6.

3. Elizabeth S. Scott and Thomas Grisso, "The Evolution of Adolescence: A Developmental Perspective on Juvenile Justice Reform," *Journal of Criminology and Criminal Justice* 88 (1998), 137–74.

4. Ibid., 174–75.

5. Ibid., 189.

6. Ibid., 174–75.

7. "Beating Death of Derrion Albert, 16, Caught on Video," *Huffington Post,* accessed at http://huffingtonpost .com/2009/09/27/beating-death-of-derrion_n_30/319.htm. See also "Four Teens Charged in Fatal Beating of Chicago Student," *USA Today,* September 29, 2009, accessed at http://www.usatoday.com/news/nation/2009-09-28-chicago -beating_N.htm.

8. "Police: Suspects Did This for Nothing More Than Their Own Savage Amusement," December 20, 2011, accessed at http://newyork.cbslocal.com/2011/12/202-charged-in-attack-of-nj -homeless-man-after-video-posted-on-youtube.

9. Todd D. Minton, *Jail Inmates at Midyear 2009* (Washington, DC: U.S. Department of Justice, Office of Juvenile Justice and Delinquency Prevention, June 2010).

10. John Kelly, "Justice Initiates New Study of Juveniles Transferred to Adult Court," *Youth Today,* November 2, 2010, accessed April 26, 2012, at http://www.youthtoday.org/view _article.cfm?article_id=4420.

11. Howard N. Snyder and Melissa Sickmund, *Juvenile Offenders and Victims: 2006 National Report* (Washington, DC: U.S. Department of Justice, Office of Justice

Programs, Office of Juvenile Justice and Delinquency Prevention, 2006), 186.

12. Patrick Griffin, Sean Addie, Benjamin Adams, and Kathy Finestine, *Trying Juveniles as Adults: An Analysis of State Transfer Laws and Reporting* (Washington, DC: Juvenile Offenders and Victims, National Report Series, September 2011), 10.

13. Benjamin Adams and Sean Addie, *Delinquency Cases Waived to Criminal Court, 2009* (Washington, DC: U.S. Department of Justice, 2012), 1.

14. For the state of Mississippi, see *OJJDP, Statistical Briefing Book*, accessed at http://ojjdp.ncjrs.org/ojstatbb/structure _process/qa04110.asp?qaDate=2004.

15. Adams and Addie, *Delinquency Cases Waived to Criminal Court, 2009*.

16. Griffin et al., *Trying Juveniles as Adults*.

17. Samuel M. Davis, *Rights of Juveniles: The Juvenile Justice System*, 2d ed. (New York: Clark Boardman, 1986), Section 4-2; see also Melissa Sickmund, *How Juveniles Get to Juvenile Court* (Washington, DC: Juvenile Justice Bulletin, 1994).

18. Davis, *Rights of Juveniles*, 24–26.

19. *Juvenile Justice Reform Initiatives in the States, 1994–1996*, accessed April 30, 2012, at http://wwwl.ojjdp.gov/pubs/reform/ch2_k.html.

20. Ibid.

21. See the National Council of Juvenile and Family Court Judges, *Juvenile Delinquency Guidelines: Improving Court Practice in Juvenile Delinquency Cases* (Reno, NV: Summer 2005), 51.

22. Ibid., 106.

23. Ibid.

24. Ibid., 107.

25. Ibid., 108.

26. Ibid., 110.

27. Griffin et al., *Trying Juveniles as Adults*.

28. Richard E. Redding, "Juvenile Transfer Laws: An Effective Deterrent to Delinquency?" *OJJDP Juvenile Justice Bulletin* (August 2008), 5–6.

29. James Austin, Kelly Dedel Johnson, and Maria Gregoriou, *Juveniles in Adult Prisons and Jails: A National Assessment*, accessed at http://www.ncjrs/gov/pdffiles1/bja/183503pdf.p.x.

30. Donna Martin Hamparian et al., *The Violent Few: A Study of Dangerous Juvenile Offenders* (Lexington, MA: Lexington Books, 1980), 33–34.

31. Quoted in Barry C. Feld, "Violent Youth and Public Policy: Minnesota Juvenile Justice Task Force and 1994 Legislative Reform," paper presented at the annual meeting of the American Society of Criminology, Miami, FL, 1994, 9.

32. Ibid. See also Barry C. Feld, "Violent Youth and Public Policy: A Case Study of Juvenile Justice Law Reform," *Minnesota Law Review* 79 (May 1995), 965–1128.

33. Richard E. Redding, "Juvenile Offenders in Criminal Court and Adult Prison: Legal, Psychological, and Behavioral Outcomes," *Juvenile and Family Court Journal* 50 (1999), 1–20.

34. Griffin et al., *Trying Juveniles as Adults*, 25.

35. Ibid., 117.

36. William Sabol and Heather Couture, *Prison Inmates at Midyear 2007* (Washington, DC: U.S. Department of Justice, Bureau of Justice Statistics, June 2008), 9.

37. Salvador A. Godinez, "Managing Juveniles in Adult Facilities," *Corrections Today* 61 (April 1999), 86–87.

38. Ibid., 133.

39. The decision was rendered in two cases. One was *Stanford v. Kentucky,* No. 87–5765. See Linda Greenhouse, "Death Sentences Against Retarded and Young Upheld," *New York Times,* June 27, 1989, A1, A18.

40. Much of the current section on the development of the death penalty comes from Victor L. Strieb, *Death Penalty for Juveniles* (Bloomington: Indiana University Press, 1987), 21–40.

41. *Gregg v. Georgia,* 48 U.S. 153 (1976).

42. Ibid., 197.

43. Strieb, *Death Penalty for Juveniles,* 22.

44. Ibid., 24–25.

45. Ibid.

46. Ibid.

47. *Eddings v. Oklahoma,* 102 S. Ct. 869 (1982).

48. Ibid.

49. *Stanford v. Kentucky,* 492 U.S. 361 (1989); *Wilkins v. Missouri,* 109 S. Ct. 2969 (1989).

50. *Thompson v. Oklahoma,* 487 U.S. 815 (1988).

51. Ibid.

52. *Stanford v. Kentucky.*

53. Ibid.

54. *Atkins v. Virginia,* 536 U.S. 304 (2002).

55. *Roper v. Simmons* (03-633), 112 SW 3d 397 (2003).

56. *Jackson v. Hobbs,* 10-9647 (2012).

Greatbass.com/Fotolia

Learning Objectives

1. Explain how probation is administered.

2. Explain the functions of probation services.

3. Describe how classifications and risk/needs assessments are used in juvenile probation.

4. Describe the use of restitution programs.

5. Summarize the roles and responsibilities of probation officers.

6. Explain the use of intermediate punishments, including intensive supervision programs.

7. Describe the use of house arrest and electronic monitoring.

8. Explain how probation can be revoked and the rights of probationers.

9. Summarize juvenile probation's effectiveness.

At the final hearing of Attorney General Eric Holder's National Task Force on Children Exposed to Violence in Detroit, officials from the Justice Department and the city of Detroit underscored efforts to keep youth safe and prevent youth violence. At the hearing, Acting Associate General Tony West announced the release of a new Justice Department research bulletin showing that 46 percent of victimized children were known to police, school, and medical authorities.

"While more children are reporting violence to authorities, many continue to endure the pain of victimization in silence," said Acting Associate General West. "Through the work of the Attorney General's task force, we hope to find more ways to identity those children in need and make sure they have access to effective prevention and treatment options."

Composed of twelve leading experts, the task force includes practitioners, child and family advocates, academic experts, and licensed clinicians. Their findings were scheduled to be published in late 2012 as a final report to the attorney general. The report presents policy recommendations and serves as a blueprint for preventing and reducing the negative effects of such violence across the nation.[1]

Youth violence is a serious national concern, and probation officers, who can be called the "workhorses" of the juvenile justice system, have an important role in monitoring and controlling youth misbehavior, including violence. Juvenile probation officers have contact with juveniles from the time they come into the system until they are either released from the jurisdiction of the system or are sent to an institution.

Probation is a correctional service allowing an offender to remain in the community under supervision by an officer of the court. Not only does each state have different requirements for juvenile probation but each county frequently has different expectations. County Juvenile probation has always referred to nonpunitive legal disposition for delinquent youths and has emphasized treatment without incarceration. The probation officer assists offenders in their efforts to meet the conditions of the court. As expressed vividly by the quote in Focus on Offenders 8–1, the basic goal of probation—over and above giving troublesome youths a second chance—is to provide services that will help offenders stay out of trouble with the law. Probation is the most widely used judicial disposition of the juvenile court.

About 300,000 youths are placed on formal probation each year, which amounts to more than 60 percent of all juvenile dispositions. The use of probation has increased significantly since 1993 when around 224,500 adjudicated juveniles were placed on probation.[2]

The word *probation* is used in at least four ways in the juvenile justice system. It can refer to (1) a disposition of the juvenile court in lieu of institutionalization, (2) the status of an adjudicated offender, (3) a subsystem of the juvenile justice system (the term's most common use), and (4) the activities, functions, and services that characterize this subsystem's transactions with the juvenile court, the youthful offender, and the community. The probation process includes the intake phase of the juvenile court's proceedings, preparation of the social investigation for the disposition stage, supervision of probationers, and obtaining or providing services for youths on probation.

Probation is considered a desirable alternative to institutionalization for several reasons: First, it allows offenders to retain their liberty but provides society with some protection against continued disregard for the law. Second, it promotes the rehabilitation of offenders because they can maintain normal community contacts by living at home, attending school, and participating in community activities. Third, it avoids the negative impact of institutional confinement, and furthermore, it costs less than incarceration.

How Is Probation Administered?

Two questions about the organization of the probation services have been debated for some time: Should probation administration be controlled by the judicial or the executive branch of government? Should this control be centralized in a state or in a local administration?

Focus on Offenders 8–1
One Success Story

When asked to recall a success story, a juvenile probation officer told the following:

> One success story I remember is that of a seventeen-year-old black girl who had been arrested on first-degree robbery and prostitution. She had never been referred before. What it came down to was there were two juvenile girls with two adult males who were their boyfriends, and they were in a bar trying to shake down this white guy. The girls got him up to their apartment, and they were going to get it on with him. Then their boyfriends came up and were real mad because he was with their women. The white guy said, "Take anything," and they took some money he had in his car. The robbery charge was dropped, but there was a finding of fact on the prostitution charge. She was placed on supervision until her eighteenth birthday. When I got her, the first thing we did was go out to the hospital's family practice center to have her checked and placed on birth control. But she was already pregnant. The majority of time we spent together was concentrated on job, education, getting ready for the baby, and independent living skills. It wasn't a traditional probation case. We spent a lot of time together, getting ready for her future. Her mother was dead and her father was in the Mental Health Institute. Several older sisters were already on ADC [Aid to Dependent Children], weren't married, and were not models by any means. So I felt like I'm the one she counted on. I took her to the hospital when she had her baby and was with her during delivery. It was a neat experience. She asked me to be the godmother for her baby. She's now very motivated to make something out of herself. She is now nineteen, has her own car, and keeps an apartment fairly well. She has neither gone to school nor worked since before she had the baby. With what she has had to work with, it's amazing she is doing so well.

Source: Interviewed by one of the authors. The interviewee is a probation officer in Waterloo, Iowa.

Locally Administered Probation Department

In those states in which probation is a local responsibility, the state is accountable only for providing financial support, setting standards, and arranging training courses. This locally based approach is used in one-third of the juvenile probation departments in the United States. Those states that have Community Corrections Acts provide financial mechanism in which states legislatures have funded local units to plan, fund, and deliver correctional services.

One of the most persuasive arguments for local administration of probation is that citizens and agencies in the community more readily support programs that are open to their participation and are responsive to local needs and problems. Another supporting argument is that small operations are more flexible, adjust more quickly to change, and are less encumbered by bureaucratic rigidity. Yet three arguments against local administration have won the support of many policy makers: (1) A state administrative probation system can set standards of service, thereby ensuring uniformity of procedures, policies, and services. (2) A large agency can make more effective use of funds and personnel. (3) Greater efficiency in the disposition of resources is possible when all probation officers are state employees.

State or Executive Administered Probation Departments

Assignment of probation to the executive branch on a statewide basis allows for standard policy making, recruitment, training, and personnel management. Coordination with the state department of corrections is also facilitated. The most significant disadvantage is the development of a large probation bureaucracy with echelons of decision makers shuffling memorandums from out-basket to in-basket and having little contact with the real world of the streets. Firm leadership with a grasp of sound management procedures can prevent this dismal prospect.

Combination Approach

Each of these approaches has some support because the administration of juvenile probation varies both among and within states. Juvenile probation is under the control of the juvenile court and is funded by city or county government in fifteen states and the District

TABLE 8–1
Summary of the Organization and Administration of Juvenile Probation

Type	Advantages
Local programs	Citizens and agencies of the community respond to local programs
State or executive administered recruitment, training, and personnel	Allows for uniform standards of policy making, management
Combination approach	Juvenile probation is under juvenile court control but some local programs are state funded.

Type	Disadvantages
Local programs	Jurisdictions are not as well funded as state or combined programs tend to be.
State or executive	Probation system can lack personal appeal and be more bureaucratic in nature.
Combination	Juvenile probation is under juvenile court control but some local programs are state funded.

of Columbia. The other thirty-five states organize administered juvenile probation in a variety of ways; fourteen use a combination of approaches. The best strategy for administration of juvenile probation appears to be placing it under the control of the juvenile court and funding it through local governmental agencies while, at the same time, providing revenue support or staff from the state to those local agencies that meet state standards. Table 8–1 summarizes the various approaches to juvenile probation.

Private contractors have been used in juvenile probation, especially for providing intensive probation and aftercare services. For example, in January 2011, the Nebraska Department of Health and Human Services transferred case management functions in the eastern and southeastern service areas of the state to private contractors (who are known as family permanency specialists) in the juvenile services system as part of Nebraska's "Families Matter" reform. The goal of this reform is to improve the outcomes of child and community safety and also the permanency and well-being of children, youth, and families.[3]

To bring about greater uniformity in administration of local probation, several states offer rewards of either revenue support or manpower to local systems if they comply with state standards. Michigan, for example, assigns state-paid probation officers to work with local probation officers. Usually, though, states make direct payments to local governments to defray part of the costs of probation services. In New York State, for example, a local community that is willing to meet state staffing patterns is reimbursed up to 50 percent of its operating costs for probation services.

Other states, such as California, Nevada, Oregon, and Washington, have developed **probation subsidy programs** that encourage a decreased rate of commitment of offenders by counties to state institutions. The money saved by the state is returned to the counties. California initiated this program after a study indicated that many offenders committed to state correctional institutions could safely remain in the community under good probation supervision. With the closing of the training schools in California in 2010, county probation will assume the type of supervisory responsibility it did with the passing of the original probation subsidy programs.

What Are the Functions of Probation Services?

The four basic functions of juvenile probation are intake, management of caseloads, supervision and investigation, and reports to the court. At the intake stage of the court proceedings, the probation officer decides whether or not to file a petition on a child referred to the court. Supervision, initiated when the judge places a youth on probation, focuses primarily on risk control and crime reduction. The management of a caseload is an important responsibility of a probation officer. Investigation involves compiling a social history or study of a child judged delinquent to assist the judge in choosing the wisest disposition.

Intake

During the intake stage of the court proceedings (which was discussed in Chapter 6), the probation officer carefully screens the referrals to the court. Both the statutes of the state and the office of the state's prosecutor are helpful in determining whether or not any case referred to the court actually falls under its jurisdiction. At **intake**, the probation officer also conducts a preliminary investigation, which includes an interview during which the youth is advised of his or her legal rights. If parents or guardians have not already been contacted, the probation department gets in touch with them to discuss the status of the child and to advise them of their right to have an attorney. The intake probation officer may need to interview the family, witnesses, victims, arresting officers, peers, or neighbors to obtain sufficient information with which to make a sound determination on the necessity of filing a court petition for detention of the child. The probation officer also may need to contact the school and other agencies that have worked with the child. If the youth has been in court before or is already on probation, the intake officer must also familiarize himself or herself with the previous reports.

Casework Management

The probation officer maintains a file on each probationer for whom he or she is responsible. Within this file are the court documents that spell out the requirements of probation, chronological entries of contacts between the officer and the probationer and others whose relationship with the probationer might be sufficient, items of correspondence, and periodic reports made to the courts or to officials of the agency.

Commonly, probation officers divide probationers into several categories, based on their needs or on the risk they pose to the community. Some offenders are placed on minimum supervision status and are required only to mail in a report once a month or even less frequently. Offenders on medium supervision status must visit their probation officers at least once a month. Offenders on maximum or intensive supervision status must see their officers several times a month.

Probation officers' caseloads are so large that maintaining contact with probationers is difficult. Studies in adult probation seeking to link combined size and recidivism in probation go back forty years. Since the late 1970s, five major studies sought to identify the impact of caseloads on recidivism, and three of the five studies found evidence supporting the contention that smaller caseloads were related to lower recidivism rates. More recently, John L. Worrall and colleagues' macro-level analysis of the relationship between probation caseloads and property crime rates in California counties found over a nine-year period that as probation loads increased, so did property crime.[4] It stands to reason that this would also be true in juvenile probation.

Supervision, Investigation, and Surveillance

The length of time a juvenile must spend on probation varies among states. The maximum length in some states is until the juvenile reaches the age of majority, which is usually age sixteen or seventeen. Other states limit juvenile probation to a specific duration. In Illinois, it is limited to five years; in New York, two years; in Washington, D.C., one year; and in California, six months.

Once a youth has been placed on probation, the probation officer is required to provide the best possible **supervision**, which includes surveillance, casework services, and counseling or guidance. Surveillance involves careful monitoring of the minor's adjustment to the community. To accomplish this, the officer must establish personal contact with the minor and must learn whether the youth is attending school or is working each day, whether adequate guidance is being received from parents, and whether the child is obeying the terms of probation. At the same time, the probation officer must determine if the youth is continuing to break the law.

A popular means of probation for some departments has been team probation. Officers are divided into teams, and each team takes responsibility for a caseload and makes decisions on what community resources are needed by clients. New probationers are interviewed by a member of the team, and their needs are plotted on a needs-assessment scale. The members of the teams are usually specialists in "needs subsystems," dealing with such problems as drug abuse, alcoholism, mental illness, or runaway behavior, and the specialist links the probationer with whatever services in the community are necessary.

Concerns for public safety in the 1980s persuaded many probation departments to develop classification systems or to use the Wisconsin system or community assessment centers to place probationers under intensive, medium, or minimum supervision. Under the **Wisconsin system**, a risk/needs assessment is conducted for each probationer at regular intervals. The risk scale was derived from empirical studies that showed certain factors to be good predictors of recidivism—prior arrest record, age at first conviction, the nature of the offense for which the probationer was convicted, school or employment patterns, and so forth. The needs assessment focuses on such indicators as emotional stability, financial management, family relationships, and health. The scores derived from the risk/needs assessment are used to classify probationers by required level of supervision—intensive, medium, or minimum. Reassessment of cases takes place at regular intervals, and the level of supervision may be increased or reduced.[5]

The most widely used risk/needs assessment of human behavior is the Problem Severity Index, a screening tool that gives intake officers and others clues about the types of problems the offenders might have. Once a problem area(s) is identified, the juvenile is assessed using diagnostic tools in an attempt to identify the problem more specifically. Clinicians then can combine various diagnostic measures to develop protocols for treatment. Risk assessment today is used to classify offenders, to predict future behavior for reducing recidivism, and to plan interventions.[6] An examination of risk assessments distinguishes between risk assessments that are developed to *predict* behavior and those developed to enable probation officers to *manage* behavior.[7]

The use of risk/needs assessments in juvenile probation raises the issue of how effective they are in predicting juveniles' behaviors. The fact is that it is very difficult to predict behavior, especially for juveniles. Thus, whatever predictive techniques or classification systems are used in juvenile justice, the results are far less than desirable in forecasting juvenile behavior.[8]

There is also the issue of whether a gendered assessment instrument is needed. One study did a meta-analysis of risk assessment predictive validity with male and female offenders. Considering 20 samples, findings indicate that predictive validity is equivalent for male and female offenders. The findings also reveal that when gender differences are observed in individual studies, they provide evidence for gender biases in juvenile justice decision making and case processing rather than the ineffectiveness of risk assessment instruments with female offenders.[9]

Accountability models for supervising juvenile probationers began to be formulated in the 1980s. For example, Dennis Maloney, Dennis Romig, and Troy Armstrong developed what they called the **balanced approach to juvenile probation**. Its purpose is to protect the community from delinquency, to impose accountability for offenses committed, and to equip juvenile offenders with the required competencies to live productively and responsibly in the community.[10] One of the popular features of this balanced approach is the equal attention it gives to the community, the victim, and the juvenile offender (see Figure 8–1). Juvenile probation departments in Oregon, Texas, and Wisconsin have implemented this accountability model in supervising juvenile probationers.[11]

The formulation of the balanced approach to juvenile probation has led to the development of the **restorative justice model**. This model, as suggested in Chapter 1, gained impetus in the 1970s and 1980s from the victim's movement, from youthful offenders' experiences with reparative sanctions, and from the rise of informal neighborhood

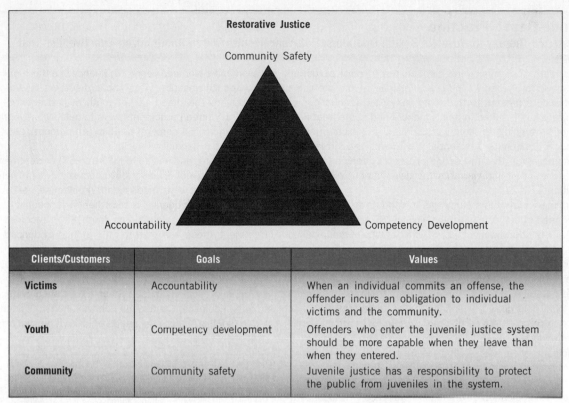

FIGURE 8–1
Graphic Representation of the Balanced Approach Mission

Source: Adapted from D. Maloney, D. Romig, and T. Armstrong, *Juvenile Probation: The Balanced Approach* (Reno, NV: National Council of Juvenile and Family Court Judges, 1998).

programs and dispute resolution programs in the community.[12] The purpose of this integrated, balanced, and restorative justice model is to reconcile "the interests of victims, offenders, and the community through common programs and supervision practices that meet mutual needs."[13]

The Washington State Legislature has been funding evidence-based programs in the Washington State juvenile courts since 1999. The state-funded evidence-based programs are:

- Aggression Replacement Training (ART)
- Coordination of Services (COS)
- Functional Family Therapy (FFT)
- Family Integrated Transitions (FIT)
- Multisystemic Therapy (MST)

See the Evidence-Based Practice feature for an evaluation of the Multisystemic Therapy program.

Reports to the Courts

If a juvenile court uses the bifurcated hearing (separation of adjudicatory and disposition stages), a **social study report** is ordered by the judge when a youth is found delinquent at the fact-finding stage of the court proceedings. Probation officers usually are given up to sixty days to make their **investigation**, but if the court combines the adjudicatory and disposition stages, the social study must be completed before a youth appears in front of the judge. The judge is not supposed to read this social study *until* the child is found to be delinquent.

The social study report details the minor's personal background, family, educational progress, present offense, previous violations of law, and employment. Also included

Evidence-Based Practice
Multisystemic Therapy for Juvenile Sexual Offenders: One-Year Results from a Randomized Effectiveness Trial

Rigorous tests of promising interventions for juvenile offenders have rarely been conducted, in spite of the problems these offenders present to the community. The seriousness of this behavior has resulted in policy makers and some treatment professionals arguing for lifelong placement on sexual offender registries and extended residential treatment. Yet, virtually all stakeholders agree that the scope of sexual offending by juveniles is substantial and warrants the development of effective interventions.

The primary aim of this study was to conduct a rigorous community-based effectiveness trial in which MST adapted for juvenile sexual offenders was compared with the type of group-based services that are typically provided to such offenders. The sexual offender treatment groups were led by seven specially trained probation officers, of whom three held bachelor's degrees and four held master's degrees. Three MA level treatment probation officers also held clinical licenses, and all treatment probation officers had completed a certification course for treating juvenile sexual offenders.

Participants were 127 youths referred by the county state's attorney. Inclusion criteria were (1) judicial order for outpatient sexual offender treatment either as part of postadjudication probation or preadjudication diversion; (2) presence of a local caregiver with whom the juvenile resided; (3) age of juvenile between eleven and seventeen years; (4) fluency in either Spanish or English; and (5) absence of psychotic disorders or serious mental retardation. The mean age of youth at pretreatment was 14.6 years; only three participants were female. Most youth were African American (54 percent) or white (44 percent), and 31 percent of youth had Hispanic ethnicity.

Youth were randomized to MST ($n = 67$) or treatment as usual for juvenile sexual offenders. Outcomes through twelve months postrecruitment were assessed for problem sexual behavior, substance use, delinquency, mental health functioning, and out-of-home placements. Relative to youths who received traditional treatment, those assigned to MST groups evidenced significant reductions in sexual behavior problems, substance abuse, delinquency, externalizing symptoms, and out-of-home placements. These findings suggest that family- and community-based interventions, particularly those with an established evidence base in treating adolescent antisocial behavior, hold considerable promise in meeting the clinical needs of juvenile sexual offenders.

Source: Elizabeth J. Letourneau, Scott W. Henggelder, Charles M. Borduin, Paul A. Schewe, Michael R. McCart, Jason E. Chapman, and Lisa Saldana, "Multisystemic Therapy for Juvenile Sexual Offenders: 1-Year Results from a Randomized Effectiveness Trial," Journal of Family Psychology 23 (February 2009), 89–102.

are a description of the offender's neighborhood; the family's ability to pay court and institutionalization costs; the minor's physical and mental health; the attitude of the family, the police, neighbors, and the community toward the minor; and the attitude of the minor toward the offense in question and toward himself or herself. The social study concludes with the probation officer's diagnoses and treatment plan for the youth. An important part of this treatment plan is the probation officer's recommended course of action. In this report the officer determines whether the juvenile should remain in the community; if so, the conditions of probation are stated.

How Do Probation Officers Do Their Jobs?
Thinking like a Correctional Professional

You accepted a position in the William County Probation Department. You lack experience and you want to be effective in your new job. Your supervisor hands you a casebook and tells you to do the best job you can. She says she is swamped with reports to write and court appearances and cannot spend much time with you. What should you do first, second, and third?

During your first hours after settling in the job, six young man burst in your office. They are very belligerent. They want to know whether you're going to continue the racist actions of your predecessor, filing reports against members of the gang for wearing gang colors. What is the best way to respond to this confrontation?

The probation officer does not have an easy job. He or she is sometimes asked to supervise youths on aftercare as well as those on probation. The officer may be given a large caseload; may be responsible for youths who are on house arrest and are monitored with electronic equipment; or may be charged with intake or secure detention responsibilities. In addition, the probation officer is expected to be a treatment agent as well as an agent of social control.[14]

The juvenile probation officer plays an important role in the justice process, beginning with intake and continuing throughout the period in which a juvenile is under court supervision. Probation officers are involved at four stages of the court process. At *intake*, they screen complaints by deciding to adjust the matter, refer the juvenile to an agency for service, or refer the case to the court for judicial action. During the *predisposition* stage, they participate in release or detention decisions. At the *postadjudication* stage, they assist the court in reaching its dispositional decision. During *postdisposition*, they supervise juveniles placed on probation.

Their general duties are as follows (also see Figure 8–2):

- Provide direct counseling and casework services
- Interview and collect social service data
- Make diagnostic recommendations
- Maintain working relationships with law enforcement agencies
- Use community resources and services
- Direct volunteer case aides
- Write predisposition or social investigation reports
- Work with families of children under supervision
- Provide specialized services, such as group therapy
- Supervise specialized caseloads involving children with special problems
- Make decisions about the revocation of probation and its termination

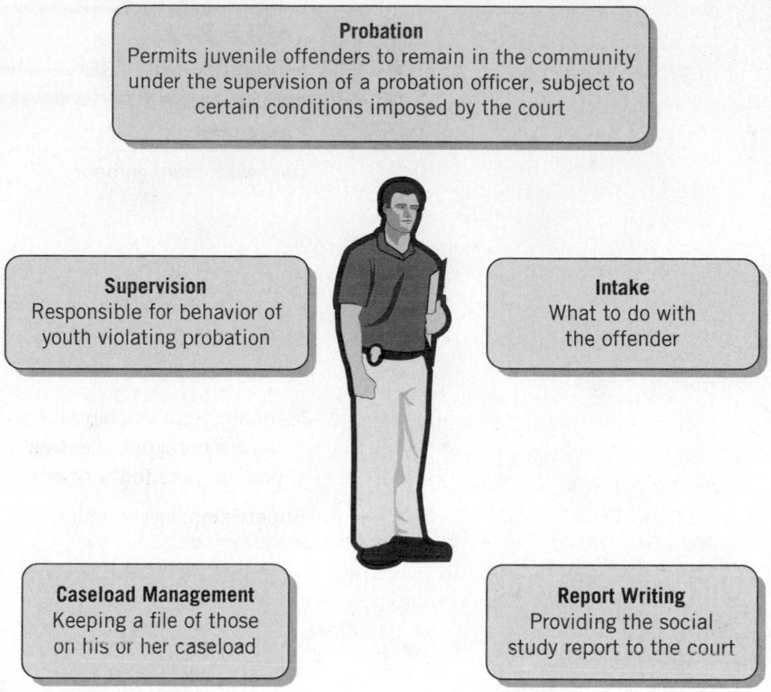

FIGURE 8–2
Duties of the Juvenile Probation Officer

The importance on juvenile probation/parole officers' training on youth recidivism can be seen in a two-part study. In this study, twelve field offices of a state juvenile justice agency took part in a controlled experiment aimed at advancing knowledge on implementing evidence-based practices in juvenile assessment, placement, and treatment planning. Using stratification and random assignment, case managers in four of the offices were assigned to a control/no training condition and case managers in the other eight offices took part in an initial training and two follow-up sessions on research-based supervisory practices. In four of these offices, training was enhanced by the inclusion of peer coaches who provided internal support for practice implementation. The results of 1,518 youth in two follow-up cohorts tracked over 18 months indicate those supervised in the enhanced sites show a pattern of reduced recidivism compared to those in the standard and control sites.[15]

Role Conflict

The nearly opposite roles of law enforcement and treatment create problems for the probation officer. The police and citizens of the community are constantly challenging the treatment role of probation officers, berating them for leaving dangerous and hard-core youths in the community. At the same time, probation officers encounter hostility from probationers because of their law enforcement role. The wide use of urinalysis testing for alcohol and drug use is evidence of this law enforcement role. Probation officers must convince the juvenile judge that they are properly filling both roles and are doling out proper portions of treatment and control.

The roles of probation officers today also are more complex than at any time in the past. The increased knowledge developed in fields that study human behavior demands that probation officers continually upgrade their knowledge and skills about child and adolescent

TABLE 8–2
Categories Depict a Probation Officer

Categories	Duties
Casework management	Maintains a file for each probationer
	Meets with the probationer periodically as assigned by the court
	Ensures that the requirements of the court are met
	Is part of a team to monitor or manage the offender
Maintains relationship with public and private nonprofit agencies to help refer probationers to these programs as needed	Refers probationers to the court when stricter or looser requirements are warranted
Supervision, investigation	Becomes familiar with the history and background of probationers
	Checks with employers and others to confirm what the probationers have told the officer
	Visits the probationer at home, at school, and at work
Presentence investigation	Conducts presentence investigation on probation
	Examines the offense, prior criminal record, and personal and family data
	Compounds and reports to the court information contained during the presentence investigation
	Develops appropriate sentencing and community alternatives
	Formulates specific recommendations to the court

development. In addition, schools and other community agencies that share clients with probation departments are being inundated with the same new knowledge. As these professionals become aware of cutting-edge research about potential causes of problems and their solutions, they too, are scrambling to incorporate the findings into their programs and to seek out those in their communities who can assist them. Probation officers, particularly those in the larger urban departments, often find themselves as the brokers between these organizations and the juvenile court.

Conflicting Pressures

Probation officers not only encounter role dilemmas, they also must satisfy three needs: the juvenile justice system's needs, their own ego needs, and the human needs of the client. That the system comes first is a reality that probation officers face early in their careers. If the juvenile judge wants a youth's social study completed by next Tuesday, it must be done, regardless of the needs and problems of other probationers during that week. Similarly, probation officers know that the system will not tolerate too much adverse publicity; consequently, it is wise for them to be conservative in terms of taking chances on troublesome youths.

Probation officers, too, are human. They have ego needs and want to feel important. They want approval and acceptance from the juvenile judge; from the director of probation

EXHIBIT 8–1
Differences Between Probation and Aftercare

Probation	Aftercare
Often given to defendants instead of detention or institutional time	Is an early release from training school
Sentence set by the court and probation officer provides supervision	Name varies from aftercare to parole depending upon the jurisdiction
Probationers are supervised by a probation officer	The juvenile judge, institutional staff, the parole board or aftercare officers make the decision when youths are placed on aftercare
The administration of probation can be on the local, state, or combined levels	Aftercare is frequently under the jurisdiction of the state
Some probation officers are paid much better than other officers	Youths on aftercare may be supervised by a parole or aftercare officer or a probation officer
The purpose of probation is to use the supervision of probation officers to achieve prosocial behavior from offenders	The function of aftercare is to try to reintegrate youth into society
The conditions of probation are usually the result of a court order	Aftercare conditions may be set by the juvenile judge, the parole board, or aftercare officer.

or court services; from other probation officers; and from clients. Even though interest in others brought many of them to their jobs, few probation officers can function effectively or happily if their own needs are not met. If an adolescent female fails to respect her probation officer, she is not likely to receive much tolerance from that officer. If an adolescent male is constantly arguing with or harassing his officer, he can expect the full weight of justice if he violates his probation terms.

The client, all too often, is considered long after the needs of the system and the officer have been satisfied. If the officer's initial job enthusiasm and involvement have waned and he or she regards the job only as one that demands much, pays little, and offers little opportunity for advancement, his or her clients may indeed be shortchanged. The endless paperwork, the hours spent on the road trying to locate clients, the broken appointments, the intractable and undependable probationers, and the hostility directed toward the probation officer also make it difficult for the officer to maintain close involvement with clients.

A basic problem for the conscientious probation officer is disciplining the violator without alienating him or her. For example, one probation officer, in describing the problems he had working with a boy, lamented the fact that just as he began to get close to him, he would be forced to discipline him: "I can't let him go too far or you'll have to snap him back. And this destroys any kind of relationship.... He just clams up.... Underneath it all, I think he's an angry boy."[16]

But regardless of how effective and committed the probation officer may be, a number of troublesome youths will flagrantly violate their probation terms and will have to be returned to the juvenile court, which may lead to probation revocation. Before punishing a youngster who has violated the terms of his or her probation, the probation officer should make every effort to gain the compliance of the youth. An understanding of the negative impact of institutionalization should compel the probation officer to return a youth to the court only as an extreme last resort.

How About Risk Control and Crime Reduction?

In the 1990s, as juvenile probation continued to face the criticism that it allowed probationers to escape punishment, reduce risk, and increase surveillance models received major emphasis. Restitution and intensive supervision were the most widely used of these short-term behavior control models, but house arrest, and electronic monitoring also gained some attention.

Restitution

Restitution, a disposition that requires offenders to repay their victims or the community for their crime, began to be used widely in probation during the 1970s and 1980s. Indeed, by 1985, formal programs were known to exist in more than four hundred jurisdictions; more than thirty-five states now have statutory authority to order monetary or community service restitution.[17] Part of the reason for the skyrocketing growth of restitution programs is that the Office of Juvenile Justice and Delinquency Prevention (OJJDP) has spent some $30 million promoting the use of restitution in eighty-five juvenile courts across the nation.[18] OJJDP followed this initiative with the National Restitution Training Program in 1983 and the Restitution Education, Specialized Training, and Technical Assistance (RESTTA) Project in 1985. These initiatives are directly responsible for most of the growth of restitution programs.[19]

Three broad types of restitution obligation can be ordered by the juvenile court: straight financial restitution, community service, and direct service to victims. Community service is the most common type, probably because it is the easiest to administer. Direct service is the most rare, largely because of victims' reluctance to have contact with offenders. However, the three program types frequently blend together. For example, a local jurisdiction may organize work crews and even enter into recycling, janitorial, and other service contacts with public or private agencies in order to provide youthful offenders with jobs so that they can pay restitution. The most common goals of restitution programs are holding juveniles accountable, providing reparation to victims, treating and rehabilitating juveniles, and punishing juveniles.[20]

When it comes to making restitution and community service work, probation officers are key players, and in many jurisdictions it is up to a juvenile probation officer to handle some or all of a number of responsibilities:

- Determining eligibility for participation
- Calculating appropriate amounts
- Assessing the offender's ability to pay
- Developing a payment/work schedule
- Monitoring performance
- Closing the case[21]

Juvenile courts have instituted job skills preparation classes to help juveniles with ordered restitution to find and hold jobs. The private and public sectors sometimes provide jobs in which youths required to make restitution can earn money and compensate victims. Juveniles failing to complete their restitution payments may have their probation term extended.

With community work restitution, probationers generally are required to work for a certain number of hours at a private nonprofit or government agency. Sites where the work may be performed include public libraries, parks, nursing homes, animal shelters, community centers, day care centers, youth agencies, YMCAs and YWCAs, and local streets. In large departments, restitution programs provide supervised work crews in which juveniles go to a site and work under the supervision of an adult. For community service in Hennepin County, Minnesota (Minneapolis), see Focus on Practice 8–2.

Intensive Supervision

In the early 1980s, **intensive supervision programs (ISPs)** began to be used in adult probation as a response to the emerging issues of prison crowding, cost escalation, and society's hard-line response to crime. It was called *intensive probation supervision* because it was operated or administered by probation offices, because it involved increased contacts, and because it generally emphasized external controls and surveillance.[22]

Juvenile justice soon followed adult justice, as so frequently happens, in implementing ISPs in juvenile probation. Georgia, New Jersey, Oregon, and Pennsylvania have

Focus on Practice 8–2
Performing Community Service

In Hennepin County, Minnesota (Minneapolis), youthful offenders quickly discover themselves placed by the juvenile judge on a Saturday work squad for a specified amount of community service. First-time offenders usually find that they are sentenced to forty hours. Every Saturday, these youths are required to be at the downtown meeting place at 8:00 A.M. From there, five trucks are sent out with ten youths and two staff members in each truck. The coordinator of the program, who is on the staff of the probation department, then assigns each youth to a specific work detail. These details include:

- Recycling bottles and cans
- Visiting patients at a nursing home
- Doing janitorial work
- Cleaning bus stops
- Planting trees or removing barbed wire fences at a city park
- Working at a park reserve

Source: Information gained during an onsite visit and updated in a phone call to a staff member.

The Recreational Therapist

PREPARATION FOR THE JOB

This person needs to have had some experience in working in corrections and have an understanding and skill in athletics.

Recreational therapist, also referred to as therapeutic recreational specialist, organizes and encourages participation in recreational activities suited to residents' physical capacity, intelligence, level of interest; supervises and coordinates a specialized recreational program area for an institution; plans activities to improve general physical and mental health; maintains records on residents' progress and reactions; teaches academic or recreational skills, orders and maintains supplies and equipment; leads activities in specific skills areas; and may supervise volunteers, explore new sports and games for programs, perhaps arrange special programs involving other institutions, and perform related work as required.

QUALIFICATION AND EDUCATIONAL REQUIREMENTS

A college degree in recreation or related field is required or an equivalent combination of training experience and recreational group work appropriate to the demands of the program. This person needs to have good knowledge of the area in which employees must function; and a working ability to communicate effectively with residents. He or she needs to have the ability to deal with problem behavior; to teach skills to persons with varying abilities; to interview in crisis situations; to use a program approach to accompany particular treatment goals; and to identify individual and group problems.

DEMAND FOR

The market for recreational therapist in juvenile corrections is good. This corrections position might require applicants to move to another state or area.

SALARY

Generally, the salary level ranges from $27,361 to $4,4471. Those at the upper end of the salary range are the ones who have worked for a number of years.

Source: Pay scale from www.payscale.com (July 26, 2009 and materials on occupation from the Home School, Minneapolis, Minnesota, Occupational Handbook, and the US Department of Labor).

experimented with or have instituted statewide ISPs for juveniles.[23] Indeed, by the end of the 1980s, juvenile judges across the nation were commonly placing high-risk offenders on small caseloads and assigning them frequent contact with a probation officer.

For example, the Juvenile Court Judges' Commission in the Commonwealth of Pennsylvania developed such a project in the 1980s because of its concern with increased commitments to training schools.[24] The standard adopted for this project included a caseload size of no more than fifteen, a minimum of three contacts per week with the youth, a minimum of one contact per week with the family or guardian, and a minimum of six months and a maximum of twelve months of intensive services.[25] Thirty-two counties in Pennsylvania had established ISPs with these standards by the end of 1989.[26]

An integrated Social Control model of intensive supervision recently has been developed to address the major causal factors identified in delinquency theory and research. This proposed model integrates the central components of strain, control, and social learning theories (see Figure 8–3). It contends that the combined forces of inadequate socialization,

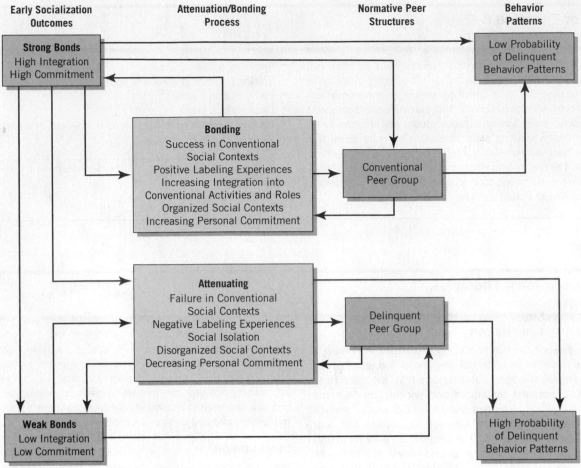

FIGURE 8–3
Integrated Strain–Control Paradigm

Source: Barry Krisberg et al., *Juvenile Intensive Supervision: Planning Guide* (Washington, DC: Office of Juvenile Justice and Delinquency Prevention, 1994), 7.

strains between educational and occupational aspirations and expectations, and social disorganization in the neighborhood lead to weak bonding to conventional values and to activities in the family, school, and community. Weak bonding, in turn, can lead juveniles to delinquent behavior through negative peer influence.[27]

The evaluation of adult ISPs in adult probation has received encouraging results in prevention of recidivism.[28] Two national evaluations of these programs in juvenile probation, however, have discovered that "neither the possible effectiveness nor the possible ineffectiveness of these programs had been carefully examined. As a result, their status in this regard, including their impact on recidivism, was essentially unknown."[29]

House Arrest and Electronic Monitoring

House arrest, or home confinement, is a program of intermediate punishment whereby youths are ordered to remain confined in their own residences during evening hours after curfew and on weekends.[30] Those receiving house arrest may be allowed to leave during the day for doctors' appointments, school, employment, or approved religious services. Electronic monitoring equipment may be used to verify probationers' presence in the residence in which they are required to remain.

Electronic monitoring (EM) was developed when a New Mexico district court judge read a comic strip in which the character Spiderman was tracked by a transmitter affixed to his wrist. At the judge's request, an engineer designed an electronic bracelet to emit a signal picked up by a receiver placed in a home telephone. The design of the bracelet was such that if an offender moved more than 150 feet from his or her home telephone, the transmission

Focus on Technology 8–3
Technocorrections: Electronic Monitoring and GPS Systems in the Community

People generally think of electronic systems as a technological method to keep tabs on offenders in the community. However, use of the technology is expanding into a variety of applications. For example, at Bryan Adams High School in East Dallas, Texas, students who have been chronically truant are now being monitored with a global positioning system (GPS), which tracks their whereabouts 24/7 in an attempt to keep them in school. In Midland, Texas, county officials have started using electronic ankle monitors to track the most chronically truant students.

The use of electronic monitoring to track criminal offenders who are granted community release should also expand as systems become more sophisticated. Some of the services provided by EM systems including the following:

- *Identity verification devices* can recognize different parts of the body to ensure that the reporting person is the offender.
- *Programmed contact devices* call the juvenile probationer at scheduled or random times and use various technologies to determine the identity of the person who answers, such as voice verification or a device worn by the probationer to insert in a verifier box attached to the phone, or a camera for visual verification).
- Another device is the *Tattle Tail*, which can detect alcohol or drug use by the offender. It senses these substances through the pores in perspiration.
- *Ignition interlock devices* are linked to the electronic systems of automobiles. The driver expels deep lung air into the device, and the vehicle will not start if the driver's blood alcohol content is registered above the level deemed unsafe for driving.
- *Victim notification systems* alert the victim when the offender is approaching his or her residence. A transmitter is worn by both the offender and the victim, and the receiver is placed in both residences.

- *Field-monitored devices*, or drive-by units, are used by probation or parole officers or other authorities. They are portable devices that can be handheld or used on a vehicle with a roof-mounted antenna. When within 200 to 800 feet of an offender's ankle or wrist transmitter, the portable device can detect the transmitter's radio signals.
- *Group monitoring units* permit supervisors to monitor several offenders in the same location, in order to verify attendance of multiple offenders in a day reporting program or to monitor offenders confined in a residential setting.
- *Global positioning systems* require the juvenile probationer to wear a transmitter that sends signals to a satellite and back to a computer monitor, pinpointing the offender's whereabouts at all times. *GPS location tracking systems* have receivers that detect satellite signals relating the exact time the signal is sent and the identity of the satellite sending the system. This expensive technology, which is generally used for high-risk offenders, can determine when an offender leaves an area where he or she is supposed to be (inclusion zone) or enters an area where he or she is not allowed to be (exclusion zone) as ordered by a judge.

These and other EM systems should revolutionize community supervision, allowing more people to be placed in probation and intermediate sanctions programs without compromising community safety.

Source: Sam Merton, "For Whom the Bell Tolls," *Dallas Observer,* June 16, 2008, www.dalas.observer.com/2008-06-26/news/for-whom; Secure Trac Systems, Omaha, Nebraska, www./securetrac.com/Services.aspx?-p-EMManagement; and Massachusetts Probation Service, "The Electronic Monitoring Program Fact Sheet," www.mass.gov/courts/probation/elmofactsheet.pdf (all cites accessed May 8, 2012).

---

signal would be broken. Authorities then would know that the offender had left his or her residence.[31] See Focus on Technology 8–3 for a discussion of the various types of electronic monitoring equipment.

More than 150,000 offenders, or approximately 20 percent of those subject to community-based supervision in the United States, are monitored at home.[32] Electronic monitoring equipment is being provided by some twenty private companies. Internationally, about 20 percent of 50,000 offenders in England and Wales who are under pre- or postrelease supervision receive electronic monitoring. In Sweden, about 25 percent of all inmates are placed on electronic monitoring.[33] The use of electronic monitoring in juvenile justice has gradually gained acceptance. For example, according to a November 1988 survey, only eleven juvenile programs used electronic monitoring.[34] Today, electronic monitoring programs are used in juvenile justice programs throughout the United States. These programs have the following goals:

- To increase the number of juveniles safely released into existing home confinement programs.
- To reduce the number of juveniles returned to juvenile detention for violating home confinement restrictions.
- To reduce the number of field contacts required of home confinement officers.

▲ Many probation programs involve youths in community projects to teach them marketable skills and teamwork. These youths are in a program in which they are helping to repaint a classroom of their school. *Washington County Juvenile Probation Services*

- To provide a reasonably safe alternative for lower-risk offenders.
- To provide for early reunification with the juvenile's family.
- To allow the juvenile to return to school.[35]

What Is the Role of Volunteers in Probation?

As mentioned earlier, throughout the second half of the nineteenth century, volunteers were used widely to provide probation services, but they largely disappeared at the beginning of the twentieth century and did not reappear until the late 1950s. Indeed, only four courts were using volunteers in 1961; but today more than two thousand court-sponsored volunteer programs are in operation in this country. The use of volunteers has become one of the most valuable ways to help offenders adjust to community life.

The National Information Center on Volunteers in Court has identified several areas in which volunteers can work effectively with juvenile offenders. A volunteer can provide a one-to-one support relationship for the youth with a trustworthy adult; can function as a child advocate with teachers, employers, and the police; can be a good role model; can set limits and teach prosocial values; can teach skills or academic subjects; and can help the youth to develop a realistic response to the environment.

In addition to these areas of direct contact, volunteers can assist in administrative work. They can help recruit, train, and supervise other volunteers; can serve as consultants to the regular staff; can become advisers to the court, especially in the policy-making area; can develop good public relations with the community; and can contribute money, materials, or facilities.

Volunteers can improve the morale of the regular probation staff, because they are usually positive and enthusiastic about the services they provide. Because many volunteers are professionals (physicians, psychiatrists, psychologists, and dentists), they can provide services that the probation department may not have the financial resources to obtain. Finally, their contributions can reduce the caseload of the regular staff.

Several criticisms have been leveled at volunteer programs: The programs tend to attract a high ratio of middle-class persons, and they often create more work than they return in service. Volunteers cannot handle serious problems and sometimes in fact can harm their clients. Parents may resist the volunteer as an untrained worker. Although inappropriate volunteers clearly can do a great deal of damage, proper screening, training, and supervision can do much to ensure high-quality probation services from volunteers.

What Programs Are Found in Juvenile Probation?

Juvenile probation usually has a number of programs available for probationers. Table 8–3 lists the types of programs to which probation officers can refer youths at the intake stage or later in the juvenile court process. Some jurisdictions, of course, have more of these programs than do others.

Of the programs listed in Table 8–3, the most widely found would be restitution programs, in which youths are assigned to a work crew to fulfill their community service sanctions; volunteer programs in which volunteers are trained to work with probationers; mentoring programs in which youths individually or in a group are assigned mentors, especially to work with them on their school assignments; youth courts or teen courts, in which juveniles themselves are given a voice on what happens to their peers; after-school study programs for youths doing below-average school work; drug or alcohol counseling, conducted individually or in groups; and sex offenders programs for youthful sex offenders. Some programs are established and then disappear when their funding runs out.

TABLE 8–3
Some Programs Utilized by Local Probation Departments

4-H programs	Self-improvement classes	Day schools
Social skills development	Youth courts	Evening care
School-based probation	Teen courts	Community service
Truancy programs	Drug courts	Volunteer work
After-school study programs	Positive peer groups	Big Brothers/Big Sisters
Sports programs	Reintegration programs	Volunteers in probation
After-school counseling	Faith-based initiatives	Drug counseling
Writing a paper	Treatment courts	Sex offender programs
Curfew requirements	Job training	Aggression replacement training
Restorative programs	Alcohol counseling	Runaway programs
Restitution programs	Mentoring programs	

The Safe Houses in Minneapolis and St. Paul, Minnesota, which provide a haven for female prostitutes, constitute one such important probation program. Safe Houses' staff are particularly eager to involve adolescent females who have run away from home and ended up as prostitutes. When adolescent residents of the Safe Houses who were on probation for having committed prostitution were interviewed, they revealed that these facilities and their staff represent a hope for them to escape from street life and the inevitable drug use that accompanies street life.[36] With the downturn of the economy in the early twenty-first century in the United States, these types of programs have become more essential for dealing with increasing numbers of teenage runaways, homeless juveniles, juveniles with mental health issues, and juveniles "strung out" on drugs.

What Are the Rights of Probationers?

The U.S. Supreme Court has ruled on two cases concerning probation revocation: *Mempa v. Rhay*[37] and *Gagnon v. Scarpelli*.[38] The Court held in the *Mempa* case that the Sixth Amendment's right to counsel applies to the sentencing hearing because it is an important step in criminal prosecution. The Court then extended this right to deferred sentencing and probation revocation hearings, and it reversed the decision of the lower courts because Mempa did not have counsel at his revocation hearing.

Gagnon v. Scarpelli involved an offender whose probation was revoked in Wisconsin without a hearing. Scarpelli, who had been sentenced to fifteen years of imprisonment for armed robbery, had his sentence suspended and was placed on probation for seven years. He was given permission to reside in Illinois, where he was subsequently arrested for burglary. His probation at that point was revoked without a hearing. Scarpelli appealed this revocation, claiming that his failure to receive a hearing and to have counsel violated his due process rights. Although the Supreme Court held that the right to counsel should be decided on a case-by-case basis, the Court did indicate that counsel should be provided on request when the probationer denies that he or she committed the violation or when the reasons for the violation are complex.[39]

These two adult cases have influenced what takes place during probation revocation in juvenile court, because in many jurisdictions the juvenile probationer has the

▲ Getting youths outside and engaging them in constructive supervised activities is important to probation departments across the country. These are only some of the many ways youths can engage in community restitution.
Washington County Juvenile Probation Services

same basic rights as an adult. The juvenile has the right to a hearing, the right to five-day notification of the probation revocation hearing, the right to be represented by an attorney, the right to confrontation, and the right to see the reports citing his or her violations.

"Reasonable efforts" is the standard that most juvenile judges adhere to at the probation revocation hearing. According to this standard, the probation officer must show that reasonable efforts have been made to provide different services and programs to the probationer. The standard requires that clear and convincing evidence be presented that the youth's refusal or inability to profit from these services and programs show that he or she cannot be kept in the community.[40]

The Prevention of Delinquency: Is Probation Effective?

Studies evaluating the probation efforts of the 1960s and 1970s indicated that probation was more effective than any other method for rehabilitating youthful offenders. For example, Douglas Lipton and colleagues' work reviewed the studies of adult and juvenile probation and arrived at the following conclusions: (1) evidence exists that a large proportion of offenders now incarcerated could be placed on probation without any change in the recidivism rates; (2) probationers have a significantly lower violation rate than do parolees; and (3) intensive probation supervision (a fifteen-ward caseload) is associated with lower recidivism rates for youths under age eighteen.[41]

But a major problem in evaluating the effectiveness of probation today is that probation has changed so much since these early evaluation studies. The risk reduction programs, such as restitution, intensive supervision, and house arrest, are still in the early stages of evaluation. Evidence suggests that restitution and intensive supervision studies are returning some positive results, but it is much too early to draw any conclusions about the present effectiveness of juvenile probation from these studies.

Two positive possibilities can be used to improve the effectiveness of juvenile probation: (1) to implement as much as possible the successful probation practices in adult probation (see Focus on Practice 8–4) and (2) to examine the juvenile probation

Focus on Practice 8–4
Successful Probation Practices in Adult Probation

- *The use of risk and needs assessments.* Corrections research supports the use of risk and needs assessments when offenders are first placed on probation and periodically thereafter. These assessments provide probation departments with resources to be able to prioritize intensive rehabilitation services.
- *Referral to community-based programs to reduce recidivism.* Offenders are more likely to be successful while on probation when effective treatments and assistance programs are provided. This includes drug treatment and mental health counseling, employment assistance, and anger management. In the current period of fiscal austerity being experienced in the United States, with its high rates of unemployment, jobs are particularly needed.
- *Manageable supervision caseloads.* No national standard is available for how many probationers should be on a probation officer's caseload. Supervision generally is

only effective at reducing recidivism when coupled with treatment-oriented programs.
- *A system of graduated sanctions.* One of the key strategies for effectively intervening and interrupting the cycle of reoffending is to establish a system of graduated sanctions.
- *Program reviews and evaluations.* Certain programs and practices have been found to result in better outcomes and reduce recidivism. Several states, such as Oregon, utilize assessment tools to assess a program's fidelity, a measurement of how well the program or practice is implemented. In addition to measuring programs' fidelity, it is important to collect data on probationer outcomes that can indicate which programs are most effective in rehabilitating offenders.

Source: Mac Taylor, *Achieving Better Outcomes for Adult Probation: Executive Summary* (Sacramento, CA: California Legislative Analyst's Office, May 29, 2009), accessed May 20, 2012, at www.lao.ca.gov/2009/crim/probation/probation_052909.pdf.

practices that are found across the nation and to utilize those that might be helpful to your jurisdiction. For example, in the Department of Juvenile Justice in Florida, juvenile probation officers play a major role throughout the juvenile justice process because they work with youth from the time they are arrested to the time they transition back into the community. The strength of this approach to juvenile probation is that it provides a continuum of contact and services, so that juvenile probation officers continue their supervision of those with whom they have worked in the past, as they are processed through the juvenile justice system.[42]

Social Policy and Juvenile Justice: Communications with Clients

Probation officers who relate well and do an effective job with clients tend to have certain characteristics in common:

1. They are genuine in their relationships with probationers and do not hide behind a professional role; that is, they attempt to avoid barriers that would isolate them from their clients. Furthermore, they try to be honest with their clients and expect the juveniles to be honest in return.

2. They respond to others with respect, kindness, and compassion. Because they are caring people, they are able to listen and reach out to others.

3. They are not gullible or easily hoodwinked by probationers, because they know what life on the streets is like.

4. They are able to encourage others to pursue positive experiences; they also have an uncanny knack of knowing what to say and do when others fail.

5. They have a good understanding of themselves and have a reasonable idea of their own problems, shortcomings, and needs. They know, in addition, their biases, prejudices, and pet peeves.

6. They are very committed to their jobs, for the job to them is much more than a paycheck. Moreover, their enthusiasm does not wane following the first few weeks or months as probation officers.

Probation officers who continually have problems with clients also have certain characteristics in common:

1. They do not keep their word. Either they promise more than they are capable of delivering or they simply fail to follow through on what they have said they would do.

2. They become bored with their jobs, chiefly because they see little meaning in working with youths whom they regard as losers who will always be marginal citizens.

3. They either have unreal expectations for probationers or are inflexible in interpreting the terms of probation.

4. They permit their personality problems to affect their performance on the job, which often results in a lack of warmth, a preoccupation with self, or a sharp, biting response to others. Not surprisingly, these personality traits alienate them from both probationers and other probation staff.

5. They seem to be unable to respond to lower-class youths who do not share their own middle-class values, so they become judgmental and moralistic in dealing with clients.

6. They are unwilling to pay the price of changing their own lives in order to influence or alter the lives of juvenile offenders.

SUMMARY

LEARNING OBJECTIVE 1: Explain how probation is administered.

Probation can be administered locally, state or executive administered, or a combination of both. One popular way is to place juvenile probation under the control of the juvenile court and to fund it through local government agencies.

LEARNING OBJECTIVE 2: Explain the functions of probation services.

Probation is a judicial disposition under which youthful offenders are subject to certain conditions imposed by the juvenile court and are permitted to remain in the community under the supervision of a probation officer.

LEARNING OBJECTIVE 3: Describe how classifications and risk/needs assessments are used in juvenile probation.

Concerns for public safety in the 1980s persuaded many probation departments to develop classification systems or to place probationers under intensive, medium, or minimum supervision. The most widely used risk/needs assessment of human behavior is the Problem Severity Index, a screening tool that gives intake officers and others clues about the types of problems the offenders might have.

LEARNING OBJECTIVE 4: Summarize the roles and responsibilities of probation officers.

Probation officers' many responsibilities include intake, caseload management, supervision and investigation, and report writing.

LEARNING OBJECTIVE 5: Explain the use of intermediate punishment, including intensive supervision programs.

One of the graduated sanctions, or intermediate punishment programs used in juvenile justice is intensive supervision program. Probationers who are placed on intensive probation are required to have increased contacts with their probation officers and other forms of external controls, and surveillance might also be required.

LEARNING OBJECTIVE 6: Describe the use of restitution programs.

Restitution is a disposition of the courts that requires offenders to repay their victims or the community for their crimes. It can be either financial restitution or community service restitution.

LEARNING OBJECTIVE 7: Describe the use of house arrest and electronic monitoring.

House arrest is a program of intermediate sanctions whereby youths are ordered to remain confined in their own residences during evening hours after curfew and on weekends. Electronic monitoring equipment may be used to verify probationers' presence in the residence in which they are required to remain.

LEARNING OBJECTIVE 8: Explain how probation can be revoked and the rights of probationers.

The juvenile has the right to a hearing, the right to five-day notification of the probation revocation hearing, the right to be represented by an attorney, the right to confrontation, and the right to see the reports citing his or her violations.

LEARNING OBJECTIVE 9: Summarize juvenile probation officers' effectiveness.

Early evaluations indicated the effectiveness of juvenile probation, but recent evaluation data are lacking. There is reason to believe that restitution and intensive supervision, as well as risk reduction programs, will reflect their effectiveness. The new methods of crime control are currently being evaluated.

KEY TERMS

balanced approach to juvenile
    probation, p. 170
electronic monitoring (EM), p. 178
house arrest, p. 178
intake, p. 169

intensive supervision programs
    (ISPs), p. 176
investigation, p. 171
probation, p. 166
probation subsidy programs, p. 168

restitution, p. 176
restorative justice model, p. 170
social study report, p. 171
supervision, p. 169
Wisconsin system, p. 170

REVIEW QUESTIONS

1. What do you feel is the most effective way to administer probation?
2. Do you believe that probation and parole should be administered together?
3. How can probation officers establish better relations with probationers?

4. Would you like to be a probation officer? Why or why not? What major problems would you face? How would you attempt to solve them?

GROUP EXERCISES

1. *Group Work:* Discuss what probation is, how it operates, and how it is organized across the nation.

2. *Writing to Learn Exercise:* Write a paragraph identifying and describing the functions of probation. Critique and revise.

3. *Group Work:* Discuss what to do with a youthful offender who commits a violent crime. If he or she is sent to an adult prison, how can this offender be protected? What services does this offender need?

4. *Writing to Learn Exercise:* Write a paragraph on how the courts approach the issues of risk control and crime reduction. Critique and revise.

5. *Writing to Learn Exercise:* Write a paragraph or two on the characteristics of the best behaviors of probation officers. Critique and revise.

WORKING WITH JUVENILES

One of my basic principles in working with juveniles is to take no nonsense. Take no verbal or physical nonsense. This simply means that you are firm what your boundaries are, and they include taking any form of abuse from the juvenile. Remember that physical abuse follows verbal abuse!

NOTES

1. U.S. Department of Justice, Office of Public Affairs, *Attorney General Eric Holder's Task Force on Children Exposed to Violence Holds Final Public Hearing in Detroit,* Tuesday, April 24, 2012.

2. Howard N. Snyder, and Melissa Sickmund, *Juvenile Offenders and Victims: 2006 National Report* (Pittsburgh, PA: National Center for Juvenile Justice, 2006), 174–75.

3. See http://www.partnering4students.org/part-three/tool-d1 .html (accessed May 19, 2012).

4. John L. Worrall, Pamela Schram, Eric Hays, and Matthew Newman, "An Analysis of the Relationships Between Probation Caseloads and Property Crime Rates in California Counties," *Journal of Criminal Justice* 32 (2004), 231–41.

5. Joan Petersilia, *The Influence of Criminal Justice Research* (Santa Monica, CA: Rand, 1987), 72.

6. K. Heilbrun, C. Cottle, and R. Lee, "Risk Assessment for Adolescents," *Juvenile Justice Fact Sheet* (Charlottesville: Institute of Law, Psychiatry, and Public Policy, University of Virginia, 2000).

7. Ibid.

8. C. Cottle, R. Lee, and K. Heilbrun, "The Prediction of Criminal Recidivism in Juveniles: A Meta-Analysis," *Criminal Justice and Behavior* 28, no. 3 (June 2001), 367–94.

9. Craig S. Schwalbe, "A Meta Analysis of Juvenile Justice Risk Assessment Instruments: Predictive Validity by Gender," *Criminal Justice and Behavior* 35 (November 2008), 1367–81.

10. See Dennis Maloney, Dennis Romig, and Troy Armstrong, "The Balanced Approach to Juvenile Probation," *Juvenile and Family Court Journal* 39 (1989), 1–49.

11. Ibid., 10. See also Gordon Bazemore and Mark S. Umbreit, *Balanced and Restorative Justice: Program Summary* (Washington, DC: Office of Juvenile Justice and Delinquency Prevention, 1994).

12. Bazemore and Umbreit, *Balanced and Restorative Justice,* 5.

13. Ibid., 7.

14. See Lori L. Colley, Robert C. Culbertson, and Edward J. Latessa, "Juvenile Probation Officers: A Job Analysis," *Juvenile and Family Court Journal* 38 (1987), 1–12.

15. Douglas W. Young, Jill L. Farrell, and Faye S. Taxman, "Impacts of Juvenile Probation Training Models on Youth Recidivism," *Justice Quarterly* (2013), 1068–89.

16. Robert Emerson, *Judging Delinquents: Context and Process in the Juvenile Court* (Chicago: Aldine, 1969), 253.

17. Anne L. Schneider, "Restitution and Recidivism Rates of Juvenile Offenders: Results from Four Experimental Studies," *Criminology* 24 (1986), 533.

18. William G. Staples, "Restitution as a Sanction in Juvenile Court," *Crime and Delinquency* 32 (April 1986), 177.

19. OJJDP Model Program Guide, *Restitution/Community Service,* accessed at http://www.dsgonline.com/mpg_non_flash/restitution?community?service.htm.

20. Patrick Griffin and Patricia Torbet, eds., *Desktop Guide to Good Juvenile Probation Practice: Mission-Driven, Performance-Based, and Outcome-Focused* (Pittsburgh, PA: National Center for Juvenile Justice, 2002), 85.

21. Ibid., 85–86.

22. Ted Palmer, *The Re-Emergence of Correctional Intervention* (Newbury Park, CA: Sage Publications, 1992), 80.

23. Emily Walker, "The Community Intensive Treatment for Youth Program: A Specialized Community-Based Program for High-Risk Youth in Alabama," *Law and Psychiatry Review* 13 (1989), 175–99.

24. Cecil Marshall and Keith Snyder, "Intensive and Aftercare Probation Services in Pennsylvania," paper presented at

the annual meeting of the American Society of Criminology, Baltimore, MD, November 7, 1990, 3.

25. Bernadette Jones, "Intensive Probation, Philadelphia County, November 1986–February 1989," paper presented at the annual meeting of the American Society of Criminology, Baltimore, MD, November 1990, Appendix, p. 1.

26. Marshall and Snyder, "Intensive and Aftercare Probation Services in Pennsylvania."

27. Barry Krisberg et al., *Juvenile Intensive Supervision: Planning Guide* (Washington, DC: Office of Juvenile Justice and Delinquency Prevention, 1994), 7.

28. For a review of these studies in intensive supervision programs for adults, see Clemens Bartollas and John P. Conrad, *Introduction to Corrections*, 2nd ed. (New York: HarperCollins, 1992).

29. Palmer, *The Re-Emergence of Correctional Intervention*, 82.

30. J. Robert Lilly and Richard A. Ball, "A Brief History of House Arrest and Electronic Monitoring," *Northern Kentucky Law Review* 13 (1987), 343–74.

31. Richard A. Ball, Ronald Huff, and Robert Lilly, *House Arrest and Correctional Policy: Doing Time at Home* (Newbury Park, CA: Sage Publications, 1988), 35–36.

32. Jennifer Lee, "Some States Track Parolees by Satellite," *New York Times*, January 31, 2002, A3.

33. Ralph Gable and Robert Gable, "Electronic Monitoring: Positive Intervention Strategies," *Federal Probation* 69 (2005), 21–25.

34. Joseph B. Vaughn, "A Survey of Juvenile Electronic Monitoring and Home Confinement Programs," *Juvenile and Family Court Journal* 40 (1989), 4–22. For a description of another program, see Michael T. Charles, "The Development of a Juvenile Electronic Monitoring Program," *Federal Probation* 53 (1989), 3–12.

35. Vaughn, "A Survey of Juvenile Electronic Monitoring and Home Confinement Programs."

36. One of the authors and his wife interviewed willing residents of these Safe Houses.

37. *Mempa v. Rhay*, 339 U.S. 128, 2d Cir. 3023 (1968).

38. *Gagnon v. Scarpelli*, 411 U.S. 778 (1973).

39. Ibid.

40. Information gained from an interview with a juvenile probation officer in Iowa.

41. Douglas Lipton et al., *The Effectiveness of Correctional Treatment: A Survey of Evaluation Studies* (New York: Praeger, 1975), 59–61.

42. Florida Department of Juvenile Justice, *Florida Juvenile Justice Probation and Community Intervention*, accessed May 21, 2012, a http://www.djj.state.fl.us/services/probation.

Community-Based Programs

Directphoto.org/Alamy

Learning Objectives

1. Summarize the philosophy and objectives of community-based corrections.
2. Explain how community-based programs are administered.
3. Explain the importance of delinquency prevention.
4. Describe diversion and various diversion programs.
5. Describe residential programs in the community.
6. Evaluate the effectiveness of community-based programs.

From 1969 to 1973, Dr. Jerome Miller was head of the Massachusetts Department of Youth Services, during which time he closed the reform schools in Massachusetts and replaced them with a few small, secure units and a diverse array of community-based services.

Miller creatively and courageously acted to change Massachusetts from large state schools to one of community-based programs. He described and implemented several principles:

1. *Reform the "deep end" first. Eliminate large rural institutions and replace them with small urban-based alternatives for the "worst kids." If the least deserving youth are treated with fairness and decency, the rest of the system will follow.*

2. *Ensure that the funds follow the youth to the community; otherwise the alternatives to institutions will become supplements, increasing costs and capacity and unnecessarily isolating more youth.*

3. *Stay partially connected to the youth. Seek to understand and respect the uniqueness of each person and his or her life story.*

4. *Develop a diversity of alternative responses to youths' behavior, in a meaningful and dynamic process for matching youth and programs.*

5. *Seize the moment. True reform is much more a matter of messy increments through risk taking, creative fund management, and manipulation of personnel rules and staff appointments than master planning and smooth administration.*

6. *Build broad coalitions. Seek support not only from the usual child advocacy and juvenile reform groups, but also rely heavily on groups such as the League of Women Voters.*[1]

This chapter-opening quote describes the late Dr. Jerome Miller's accomplishments in converting Massachusetts' juvenile justice system from one of state-dominated institutions to community-based programs and services. His principles continue to inspire those who are leading the way toward focusing on corrections and are a reminder that community-based programs offer a more effective approach to youth in trouble than long-term institutional care. Today, an impressive array of programs for juvenile offenders exists in communities across the nation. These programs include delinquency prevention, runaway facilities, foster care facilities, diversion, day treatment programs, group homes, and wilderness learning experiences. The ongoing search for solutions to the problem of juvenile crime, the popularity of deinstitutionalization in juvenile justice, and the emphasis in the past 20 years on short-term behavioral control probably best explains why there are so many programs for juvenile offenders. Community-based programs range from those focusing on delinquency prevention and diversion from the juvenile justice system to those designed for short-term residential care; the trend toward evidence-based programming continues to influence these efforts.

What Is the Philosophy Underlying Community-Based Corrections?

Three somewhat diverse philosophies guide community-based programming: (1) reintegration, (2) a continuum of sanctions, and (3) restorative justice and peacemaking.

Reintegration

Community-based programs have rested on a **reintegration philosophy** that assumes that both the offender and the receiving community must be changed. The community is as important as the client and plays a vital role in facilitating the reabsorption of offenders into its life. The task of corrections, according to this philosophy, involves the reconstruction, or construction, of ties between offenders and the community through maintenance of family bonds, employment and education, and placement in the mainstream of social life. Youths should be directed to community resources, and the community should be acquainted with the skills and needs of youthful lawbreakers.

Continuum of Sanctions

Advocates for more effective juvenile justice are increasingly calling for a range of punishment options, providing graduated levels of supervision in the community. Judges are able to exercise discretion by selecting, from a range of sentencing options, the punishment that best fits the circumstances of the offense and the youth. Intermediate sanctions are said to allow juvenile judges to match the severity of punishment with the severity of the crime. Juvenile institutions, then, are treated as backstops, rather than backbones, of the corrections systems.[2]

Providing justice through a **continuum of sanctions**, ranging from diversion programs to being placed in community correctional facilities, is one of the exciting innovations in juvenile corrections today. The intermediate sanctions can be grouped from those less intrusive to offenders to those that are most intrusive. The basic aim behind intermediate sanctions, or alternative sanctions, is to escalate punishments to fit the offense. These sanctions typically are administered by probation departments and include intensive probation (which was examined in Chapter 8), community service, house arrest, and electronic monitoring. But they also involve sentences that are administered independently of probation, such as day treatment programs, drug courts, and residential care. See Figure 9–1.

Less Intrusive to Offenders
Prevention programs
Diversion programs
Probation
Day treatment programs
Community restitution
Drug courts
More Intrusive to Offenders
Intensive probation
House arrest
Electronic monitoring
Residential facilities

FIGURE 9–1
Continuum of Sanctions

Restorative Justice

Restorative justice recently has been coupled with intermediate sanctions. Humanistic in its treatment of offenders, restorative justice has as its focus the welfare of victims in the aftermath of crime. In bringing criminal and victim together to heal the wounds of violation, the campaign for restorative justice advocates alternative methods to incarceration, such as intensive community supervision. The most popular of the restorative strategies are victim–offender conferencing and community restitution. In many states, representatives of the victims' rights movement have been instrumental in setting up programs in which victims/survivors confront their violators.[3]

Other elements are involved in most restorative justice approaches. Restorative justice processes pay attention not only to the harm inflicted on the direct victims of a crime, but also to the ways in which the crime has harmed the offender and the community. The focus, thus, is on victim healing, offender reintegration, and community restoration. This emphasis on victim healing has persuaded some to consider restorative justice to be a victim-centered approach. Yet the emphasis on providing offenders an opportunity to make amends and to increase their awareness of the consequences of their actions has persuaded others to regard restorative justice as offender focused. It is the third emphasis, community restoration that puts victim healing and offender reparation into perspective.

How Are Community-Based Programs Administered?

Comprehensive state-sponsored, locally sponsored, and privately administered programs are the three basic types of organizational structures in community-based programs.

In California, Indiana, Kansas, Michigan, Minnesota, and Oregon, the state sponsors residential and day treatment programs under the **community corrections acts**. The Minnesota Community Corrections Act, which has become a model for other community corrections acts, provides for a state subsidy to any county or group of counties that chooses to develop its own community corrections system. The costs for juvenile offenders who are adjudicated to a training school are charged back to the county, and these costs are subtracted from the county's subsidy. Counties in Minnesota have been understandably reluctant to commit youths to training schools because of the prohibitive costs and therefore have established and encouraged a wide variety of residential and day treatment programs.

▲ Some community-based corrections have as a goal the teaching of skills to youths who may have none. Here a supervisor is working with young men teaching them the basics of cooking.

Washington County Juvenile Leader program

The deinstitutionalization movements in Maryland, Massachusetts, North Dakota, South Dakota, Utah, and a number of other states also has led to the development of a wide network of residential and day treatment programs for youths. In Massachusetts, the Department of Youth Services administers some of these programs, but more often the juvenile court sponsors these programs, or state or local agencies contract for services for those youths from private vendors in the community. Regardless of who administers these community programs, the most innovative and effective ones attempt to provide a continuum of care for youthful offenders.

Private delivery of correctional services to youthful offenders originated in the early days of juvenile justice in this nation. Most of these programs were religious or business backed, but died in the early to mid-1900s. In 1972, the private sector reentered the field of juvenile corrections in an unprecedented manner. Privatization, or placing control of facilities in the hands of the private sector, has expanded significantly in the past few decades. Privately run programs are emerging as a result of budget problems that prevent local or state agencies from supplying the services in an efficient manner. Privatization has become big business and has sparked the interests of investors from all walks of life. Those operating in the private sector receive payment for their programs through federal, state, or local funding, from insurance plans, or from the juvenile's parents.

Federal grants are the basis of the funding of many community programs. SafeFutures is a program funded by the Office of Juvenile Justice and Delinquency Prevention (OJJDP) that appears to be a model worth replicating in communities across the nation. The SafeFutures urban sites are located in Boston, Massachusetts; Contra Costa County, California; Seattle, Washington; and St. Louis, Missouri. The other two sites are Imperial County, California (rural), and Fort Belknap Indian Community, Harlem, Montana (tribal government). SafeFutures seeks to improve the service delivery system by creating a continuum of care that is responsive to the needs of youths and their families at all points along the path toward juvenile reintegration. This coordinated approach of prevention, intervention, and treatment is designed both to serve the juveniles of a community and to encompass the human service and the juvenile justice systems. A national evaluation is being conducted to determine the success of the continuum of services in all six sites.

Project CRAFT (Community Restitution and Apprenticeship-Focused Training program), a vocational training program for high-risk youths, is sponsored by the Home Builders Institute (HBI), the educational arm of the National Association of Home Builders (NAHB). Project CRAFT offers pre-apprenticeship training and job training for adjudicated juveniles referred to the program. It was started in 1994 by HBI in Bismarck, North Dakota; Nashville, Tennessee; and Sabillasville, Maryland. It has been replicated in five sites in Florida (Avon Park, Daytona Beach, Fort Lauderdale, Lantana, and Orlando), in Texas, and in Connecticut.[4] This program works in partnership with private facilities, juvenile judges,

Focus on Treatment 9–1
Project CRAFT

Project CRAFT has been teaching court-involved youth ages fifteen to nineteen marketable construction trade skills that help them find jobs, instill a sense of confidence and excitement about the future, and provide them with a viable career option. Once graduates earn their industry-recognized pre-apprenticeship certification, Project CRAFT staff helps them find jobs, continue their education, or join the military.

Journey-level trade instructors teach the HBI's Pre-Apprenticeship Certificate Training (PACT) curriculum in electric wiring, carpentry, landscaping, facilities maintenance, plumbing, and painting, depending on the program. Some of their accomplishments include the following:

* HBI Project CRAFT Avon Park Youth Academy students have installed solar panels on academy buildings to reduce its carbon footprint.

* Students at HBI Project CRAFT Baltimore have renovated Family League of Baltimore City office space into a state-of-the-art conference room and built a bench for a presiding Baltimore City juvenile judge.

* HBI Project CRAFT Okeechobee Girls Academy is the only juvenile justice residential program in Florida that provides career and technical education to young women.

Source: Home Builders Institute, "Project CRAFT," n.d., accessed May 12, 2012, at http://www.hbi.org/Programs/PreApprenticeship/ProjectCRAFT .aspx.

juvenile justice system personnel, educational agencies, and other human service agencies.[5] Although the initial sample size was small, an early study indicates that most youths, 15 percent, recidivate during their first year after release, 10 percent recidivate in their second year, and 1 percent recidivate in their third year after release; these data compare favorably with an untreated sample with a 50 percent recidivism rate over three years.[6] See Focus on Treatment 9–1.

What Is the Role of Delinquency Prevention?

Delinquency prevention is defined as any attempt to thwart youths' illegal behavior before it occurs. The Juvenile Justice and Delinquency Prevention Act of 1974 and the Juvenile Justice Amendments of 1977, 1980, and 1984 established the prevention of delinquency as a national priority.[7] Anne Newton has identified three levels of delinquency prevention:

* *Primary prevention* is directed at modifying conditions in the physical and social environment at large.

* *Secondary prevention* is directed at early identification and intervention in the lives of individuals or groups in criminogenic circumstances.

* *Tertiary prevention* is directed at the prevention of recidivism (after delinquent acts have been committed and detected).[8]

An example of primary prevention is the 1960s Mobilization for Youth program, which took place in a sixty-seven-block area of Manhattan's Lower East Side in New York City. This project was designed to improve educational and work opportunities for area youth, to make a variety of services available to individuals and families, and to provide assistance in community organization.[9]

A number of primary and secondary prevention programs have been conducted since the beginning of the twentieth century, using neighborhood groups, the family and school environment, youth gangs, and social and mental health agencies as points of intervention.[10] Unfortunately, the results of most of these programs have been disappointing.[11] The Chicago Area Projects, however, is one program that achieved some success in the fifty years or so that it was conducted (see Focus on Policy 9–2). More recently, a number of programs have been developed that promise to be more effective in preventing juvenile crime, including juvenile violence and drug abuse.

Focus on Policy 9–2
The Chicago Area Projects

Clifford Shaw and Henry McKay, the founders of the Chicago Area Projects (CAP) in 1934, were committed to creating community consciousness directed at solving social problems on the local level. The first projects were initiated in three areas: South Chicago, the Near West Side, and the Near North Side. Today, each project area has a committee that operates as an independent unit under the guidance of a board of directors chosen by the local community residents. Twenty such projects have functioned in Chicago, and others have formed throughout the state. In addition, other groups in Illinois have taken the projects as the model for their own delinquency control programs.

The projects have three basic goals: First, they provide a forum for local residents to become acquainted with new scientific perspectives on child rearing, child welfare, and juvenile delinquency. Second, they initiate new channels of communication between local residents and the institutional representatives of the larger community, those influencing the life chances of local youth. Third, they bring adults into contact with local youths, especially those having difficulties with the law.

The philosophy of CAP is based on the belief that instead of quickly turning over youth to the justice system, the community should deal with its own problems and intervene on behalf of its youth. Citizens of the community show up in juvenile court to speak on behalf of the youths; they organize social and recreational programs so that youths can participate in constructive activities. The leaders of the local groups, often individuals who were once in CAP programs, know how to relate to and deal with youths who are having problems at school or with the law.

More than fifty years ago, Saul Alinsky stated, "It's impossible to overemphasize the enormous importance of people doing things for themselves." What is ultimately significant about CAP is that this philosophy was its basic approach to delinquency prevention. CAP advocated grassroots leadership, neighborhood revitalization, the community's role in policing itself, and the importance of community dispute resolution. These same emphases were incorporated into most community crime prevention strategies in the late 1990s.

Source: The description of CAP is largely derived from Harold Finestone, *Victims of Change: Juvenile Delinquents in American Society* (Westport, CT: Greenwood Press, 1976), 125–30.

Promising Prevention Programs

The Blueprint for Violence Prevention, which was developed by the Center for the Study and Prevention of Violence at the University of Colorado–Boulder and supported by the OJJDP, identified eleven model programs as well as twenty-one promising violence prevention and drug-abuse programs that had been demonstrated—through rigorous empirical evaluation—to work.[12] Table 9–1 presents the complete list of models and promising programs the researchers identified; the following discussion briefly describes the eleven model programs:

- *Big Brothers Big Sisters of America (BBBSA)* With a network of more than five hundred local agencies throughout the United States that maintain more than 145,000 one-to-one relationships between youth and volunteer adults, BBBSA is the best known and largest mentoring program in the nation. The program serves youths ages six to eighteen, a significant number of whom are from disadvantaged and single-parent households.[13] An eighteen-month evaluation found that compared with a control group waiting for a match, youths in this mentoring program were 46 percent less likely to start using drugs, 27 percent less likely to start drinking, and 32 percent less likely to hit or assault someone. They also were less likely to skip school and more likely to have improved family relationships.[14]

- *Bully Prevention Program* The primary purpose of the Bully Prevention Program is to restructure the social environment and secondary schools in order to provide fewer opportunities for bullying and to reduce the peer approval and support that reward bullying behavior.[15] In a large sample evaluated in Norway and South Carolina, the Bully Prevention Program has proved effective. For example, children in thirty-nine schools in South Carolina in grades four through six reported that they experienced a 25 percent decrease in bullying by other children.[16]

- *Functional Family Therapy (FFT)* A short-term family-based prevention and intervention program, FFT has been successfully applied in a variety of contexts to treat high-risk youths and their families. Specifically designed to help underserved

TABLE 9–1
Model and Promising Programs and Age Groups of Juveniles Targeted

Blueprints Program	Age Group				
	Pregnancy/ Infancy	Early Childhood	Elementary School	Junior High School	High School
Model Programs					
Big Brothers Big Sisters of America (BBBSA)			X	X	X
Bullying Prevention Program			X	X	
Functional Family Therapy (FFT)				X	X
Incredible Years		X	X		
Life Skills Training (LST)				X	
Midwestern Prevention Project (MPP)				X	
Multidimensional Treatment Foster Care (MTFC)				X	X
Multisystemic Therapy (MST)				X	X
Nurse–Family Partnership	X				
Project Toward No Drug Abuse (Project TND)					X
Promoting Alternative Thinking Strategies (PATHS)			X		
Promising Programs					
Athletes Training and Learning to Avoid Steroids					X
Brief Strategic Family Therapy			X	X	X
CASASTART			X	X	
Fast Track			X		
Good Behavior Game			X		
Guiding Good Choices			X	X	
High/Scope Perry Preschool		X			
Houston Child Development Center	X	X			
I Can Problem Solve		X	X		
Intensive Protective Supervision				X	X
Linking the Interests of Families and Teachers			X		
Preventive Intervention				X	
Preventive Treatment Program			X		
Project Northland				X	
School Transitional Environmental Program				X	X
Seattle Social Development Project			X	X	
Strengthening Families Program: Parents and Children 10–14			X	X	
Student Training through Urban Strategies				X	X
Syracuse Family Development Program	X	X			
Yale Child Welfare Project	X	X			

Source: Sharon Mihalic, et al., *Blueprints for Violence Prevention* (Washington, DC: Office of Juvenile Justice and Delinquency Prevention, 2004), Table 1–1.

and at-risk youth ages eleven to eighteen, this multisystemic clinical program provides twelve one-hour family therapy sessions spread over three months. More difficult cases receive up to twenty-six to thirty hours of therapy.[17] The success of this program has been demonstrated and replicated for more than twenty-five years. Using controlled follow-up periods of one, three, and five years, evaluations have demonstrated significant and long-term reductions in the reoffending of youth, ranging from 25 to 60 percent.[18]

• *Incredible Years: Parent, Teacher, and Child Training Series* The Incredible Years model program has a comprehensive set of curricula designed to promote social competence and to prevent, reduce, and treat conduct problems in children ages two to eight who exhibit or are at risk for conduct problems. In the parent, teacher, and child training programs, trained facilitators use videotaped scenes to encourage problem solving and sharing of ideas.[19] The three series of this program have received positive evaluations as meeting their original goals.[20]

- *Life Skills Training (LST)* LST is a three-year intervention curriculum designed to prevent or reduce the use of "gateway" drugs, such as tobacco, alcohol, and marijuana. The lessons emphasize social resistance skills training to help students identify pressures to use drugs.[21] Using outcomes from more than a dozen studies, evaluators have found LST to reduce tobacco, alcohol, and marijuana use by 50 to 75 percent in intervention students compared to control students.[22]

- *Midwestern Prevention Project (MPP)* MPP includes school normative environment change as one of the components of a comprehensive three- to five-year community-based prevention program that targets gateway use of alcohol, tobacco, and marijuana. The school-based intervention is the central component of the program. The program begins in either sixth or seventh grade and includes ten to thirteen classroom sessions taught by teachers trained in the curriculum.[23] Researchers followed students from eight schools who were randomly assigned to treatment or control groups for three years and found that the program brought net reductions of up to 40 percent in adolescent smoking and marijuana use, with results maintained through high school graduation.[24]

- *Multidimensional Treatment Foster Care (MTFC)* MTFC has been found to be a cost-effective alternative to group or residential treatment, confinement, or hospitalization. This program provides short-term (usually about seven months), highly structured therapeutic care in foster families. Its goal is to decrease negative behaviors, including delinquency, and to increase youths' participation in appropriate prosocial activities, including school, hobbies, and sports.[25] Evaluations of MTFC demonstrated that youths who participated in the program had significantly fewer arrests (an average of 2.6 versus 5.4 offenses) and spent fewer days in lockup than youths placed in other community-based programs.[26]

- *Multisystemic Therapy (MST)* MST provides cost-effective community-based clinical treatment of chronic and violent juvenile offenders who are at high risk of out-of-home placement. The overarching goal of the intervention is to help parents understand and help their children overcome the multiple problems contributing to antisocial behavior. Treatment generally lasts for about four months, which includes about sixty hours of therapist–family contact.[27] Program evaluations have revealed 25 to 70 percent reductions in long-term rates of rearrest and 47 to 64 percent reductions in out-of-home placements. These and other positive results were maintained for nearly four years after treatment ended.[28]

- *Project Toward No Drug Abuse (Project TND)* This project targets high school youth ages fourteen to nineteen who are at risk for drug abuse. Over a four- or five-week period, twelve classroom-based lessons offer students cognitive motivation enhancement activities, information about the social and health consequences of drug use, correction of cognitive misperceptions, help with stress management, training in self-control, and instruction in active listening.[29] At a one-year follow-up, participants in forty-two schools revealed reduced use of cigarettes, alcohol, marijuana, and hard drugs.[30]

- *Promoting Alternative Thinking Strategies (PATHS)* A comprehensive program for promoting social and emotional competencies, PATHS focuses on the understanding, expression, and regulation of emotions. The yearlong curriculum is designed to be used by teachers and counselors within classrooms of children in kindergarten through fifth grade. The basic outcome goals are to provide youths with tools to achieve academically as well as to enhance the classroom atmosphere and the learning process. Evaluations have found positive behavioral changes related to hyperactivity, peer aggression, and conduct problems.[31]

Violent Juvenile and Delinquency Prevention Programs

Spearheaded by the OJJDP, the belief emerged in the 1990s that the most effective strategy for juvenile corrections is to place the thrust of the prevention and diversion emphases on high-risk juveniles who commit violent acts. These are the juveniles who commit the more serious and most frequent delinquent acts and are the youths whom officials are quick to place into the adult system. At the same time that the seriousness of their behaviors has effected changes in juvenile codes across the country, research is beginning to find that these high-risk youths can be impacted by well-equipped and well-implemented prevention and treatment programs.[32]

These programs are based on the assumption that the juvenile justice system does not see most serious offenders until it is too late to effectively intervene.[33] Advocates also presume that in order to reduce the overall level of violence in American society successful intervention in the lives of high-risk youth offenders, who commit about 75 percent of all violent juvenile offenses, is necessary.[34]

The general characteristics of these programs is that they (1) address key areas of risk in youths' lives, (2) seek to strengthen the personal and institutional factors that contribute to the development of a healthy adolescent, (3) provide adequate supervision and support, and (4) offer youths a long-term stay in the community.[35] Importantly, these prevention programs must be integrated with local police, child welfare, social services, school, and family preservation programs. Comprehensive approaches to delinquency prevention and intervention require a strong collaborative effort between the juvenile justice system and other service provision systems, such as health, mental health, child welfare, and education. An important component of a community's comprehensive plan is to develop mechanisms that effectively link these service providers at the program level.[36]

The comprehensive, or multisystemic, aspects of these programs are designed to deal simultaneously with many aspects of youths' lives. The intent is that they are intensive, often involving multiple contacts weekly, or possibly daily, with at risk youth. They build on the strengths of these youths, rather than dwell on their deficiencies. These programs operate mostly, although not exclusively, outside of the formal justice system under a variety of public, nonprofit, or university auspices. Finally, they combine accountability and sanctions with increasingly intensive treatment and rehabilitation services that are achieved through a system of graduated sanctions, in which an integrated approach is employed to stop the penetration of youthful offenders into the system.[37]

In 1996, three communities—Lee and Duval Counties in Florida and San Diego County in California—collaborated with the OJJDP to apply the processes and principles that were described in the *Comprehensive Strategy for Serious, Violent and Chronic Juvenile Offenders*. Initial evaluations of the three pilot projects found that each of the sites has benefited significantly from the comprehensive planning process. Although it was deemed premature to assess any long-term impact on juvenile delinquency, several short-term indicators of success were found.[38] The following are among the pilot programs' accomplishments:

- Enhanced community-wide understanding of prevention services and sanctions options for juveniles
- Expanded networking capacity and better coordination among agencies and service providers
- Institution of performance measurement systems
- Hiring of staff to spearhead the ongoing *Comprehensive Strategy* planning and implementation efforts
- Development of comprehensive five-year strategic action plans.[39]

What Is the Role of Diversion?

In the late 1960s and early 1970s, **diversion programs** sprung up across the nation. *Diversion*, which refers to keeping juveniles outside the formal justice system, can be attempted either through the police and the courts or through agencies outside the juvenile justice system. The main characteristic of diversion initiated by the courts or police is that the justice subsystems retain control over youthful offenders. A youth who fails to respond to such a program usually will be returned to the juvenile court for continued processing within the system.

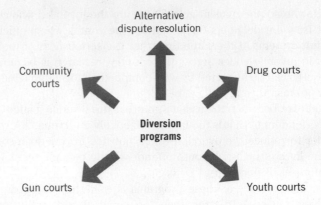

FIGURE 9–2
Diversion Programs

In the 1990s, new forms of diversion developed in the United States and included community courts, alternative dispute resolution, gun courts, youth courts, and drug courts. Youth courts and drug courts are described next in more detail. See Figure 9–2.

Youth Courts

Youth courts, also known as *teen courts, peer courts,* or *student courts,* are juvenile justice programs in which youths are sentenced by their peers. Established and administered in a variety of ways, most youth courts are used as a sentencing option for first-time offenders ages eleven to seventeen who are charged with misdemeanor nonviolent offenses. The offender typically acknowledges his or her guilt and participates in a youth court voluntarily, rather than going through the more formal juvenile justice procedures.[40] See Figure 9–3 for a timeline covering the history of youth courts. In 2005, more than 110,000 youths volunteered to hear more than 115,000 juvenile cases, and more than 20,000 adults volunteered to be facilitators for peer justice in youth court programs. Also, in 2005, there were 1,158

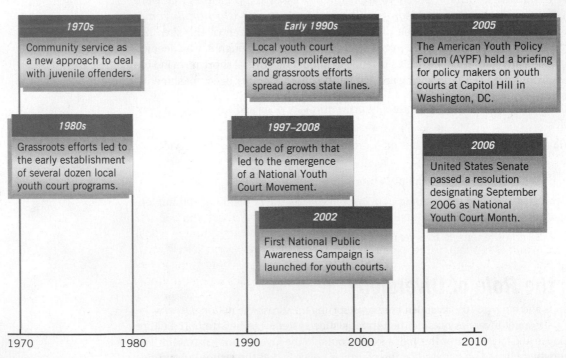

FIGURE 9–3
Timeline of the Development of Youth Courts

Source: Scott B. Peterson and Jill Beres, *Report to the Nation 1993–2008,* published by Scott B. Peterson, 2008.

youth court programs in forty-nine states and the District of Columbia providing restorative justice for youthful offenders.[41]

Four possible case-processing models are used by these courts:

- *Adult judge*. An adult serves as judge and rules on legal terminology and courtroom procedures. Youths serve as attorneys, jurors, clerks, bailiffs, and so forth.
- *Youth judge*. This is similar to the adult judge model, except that a youth serves as the judge.
- *Tribunal*. Youth attorneys present the case to a panel of three youth judges, who decide the appropriate disposition for the defendant. A jury is not used.
- *Peer jury*. This model does not use youth attorneys: the case is presented to a youth jury by a youth or adult. The youth jury then questions the defendant directly.[42]

Youth courts usually handle first-time offenders who are charged with offenses such as theft, misdemeanor assault, disorderly conduct, and possession of alcohol. The majority of these teen courts (87 percent) reported that they rarely or never accepted any juveniles with prior arrest records. The most common disposition used by these courts is community service. Following this disposition in level of use are victim apology letters (86 percent), apology essays (79 percent), teen court jury duty (75 percent), drug/alcohol classes (59 percent), and monetary restitution (34 percent).[43]

The Juvenile Drug Court Movement

By 2007, approximately two thousand juvenile drug courts had opened. The juvenile drug court movement is part of an expanding adult drug court movement that is dedicated to juveniles and that has been stimulated by Title V of the Violent Crime Control and Law Enforcement Act of 1994, an act that authorizes the attorney general to make grants to various agencies to establish drug courts. These agencies include states, state and local courts, units of local government, and Indian tribal governments.[44]

A number of strategies are common to juvenile drug courts compared with traditional juvenile courts:

- Much faster and much more comprehensive intake assessments
- Much greater focus on the functioning of the juvenile and the family throughout the juvenile court system
- Much closer integration of the information obtained during the assessment process as it relates to the juvenile and the family
- Much greater coordination among the court, the treatment community, the school system, and other community agencies in responding to the needs of the juvenile and the court
- Much more active and continuous judicial supervision of the juvenile's case and treatment process
- Increased use of immediate sanctions for noncompliance and incentives for progress for both the juvenile and the family.[45]

In 1998, six states operated juvenile drug courts, with the greatest activity in California and Florida. By January 1, 2008, there were 2,148 drug courts operating throughout the United States; included in this number are 455 juvenile and 301 family courts. Both types of courts are noted here because both frequently share similar types of clients and, indeed, often the same clients. The development of these innovative approaches was motivated by the spike in the crack cocaine epidemic in the late 1980s and the early 1990s and the difficulty regular courts had in handling the resulting increased caseloads. The innovation was also fueled by the increasing numbers of drug cases among juveniles and families.[46] The goals of the juvenile drug courts are to:

- Provide immediate intervention treatment, and structure in the lives of juveniles who use drugs through ongoing, active oversight and monitoring by the drug court judge.

- Improve juveniles' level of functioning in their environment, address problems that may be contributing to their use of drugs, and develop/strengthen their ability to lead crime- and drug-free lives.

- Provide juveniles with skills that will aid them in leading productive crime- and drug-free lives—including skills that relate to their educational development, sense of self-worth, and capacity to develop positive relationships in the community.

- Strengthen families of drug-involved youth by improving their ability to provide structure and guidance to their children.

- Promote accountability of both juvenile offenders and those who provide services to them.[47]

Unfortunately, little research exists today that addresses how successful youth courts are in reducing drug use and criminal recidivism. We may, nevertheless, perhaps learn some lessons from the successes of the adult courts, keeping in mind that extrapolating findings from adult drug courts to juvenile courts is extremely risky. Huddleston et al., summarize adult drug court research by noting that some programs reduce recidivism by 7 to 14 percent and others by up to 35 percent. The programs also are cost-effective because successfully treated offenders remain free from law enforcement activities, judicial case processing, and the victimization that occurs as a result of repeat criminal activity.[48]

A 2013 publication compared juvenile drug courts (JDC) youth with youth receiving standard probation on alcohol and other drug (AOD) and delinquency /criminal reoffending at 3 to 30 months post – exit from the JDC program or probation. This quasi-experimental study tested JDC's effectiveness by examining re-arrests for drug and alcohol and other drug offenses and criminal offenses 30 months post–intervention and into adulthood. Participants included youth who were involved in either JDC (n = 622) or probation only (n = 596) between the years 2003 and 2997. JDC and probation youth did not significantly differ at any of the follow-up time intervals on AOD offending. On the other hand, JGC youth had statistically significant fewer delinquency/criminal offenses than probationers at all follow-up points, with the difference between the groups getting larger with longer follow-up periods.[49]

Juvenile Mental Health Courts (JMHCs)

Juvenile mental health courts (JMHCs) are voluntary diversionary programs, which address the needs of children with mental health needs. These courts rely on cooperation and collaboration among members of a multidisciplinary team working with and for the benefit of youth and their families. Similar to mental health courts for adults, JMHCs have two main goals: first to decrease recidivism; and second, to increase participants' adherence to treatment.[50]

CHCS were introduced in Colorado in 1997, York County Pennsylvania in 1998, in Mahoning County Ohio in 2000, and in Santa Clara County, California in 2001. By early 2012, there were approximately fifty JMHCs in fifteen states, either in operation or in the planning stages. Ohio housed nine, and California, eight. Most of the evaluations of mental health courts focus on those for adults. Preliminary results indicate that they are effective both in reducing recidivism and increasing the use of mental health services. Yet, few outcome studies have evaluated the effectiveness of JMHCs, especially with viable comparison groups using postparticipation recidivism rates.[51]

One of the few courts that has been evaluated is California Santa Clara's County Court for the Individualized Treatment of Adolescents. Researchers found a significant reduction in recidivism during the youths' participation in this program. However, the researchers did not have information on a viable comparison group or on postrelease recidivism patterns. A more recent positive report is on the California Alameda County Juvenile Collaborated Court. But the sample size of thirty-four participants (twenty-nine successful completers) who attended between 2007 and 2009, was quite small. Even more encouraging results are found in an evaluation of the JMHC of Colorado's First Judicial District. There was a reduction in their recidivism while in the program and at least one year following successful completion.[52]

Juvenile Mediation Program

The purpose of the Juvenile Mediation Program is for all involved parties to join together to resolve differences without court involvement. It began in Brooke County, West Virginia, and spread to Hancock, Marshall, Ohio, Tyler, and Wetzel counties. The program works with school-age children and adolescents, ages six to eighteen, and their families or guardians.[53] Status and nonviolent offenders from the aforementioned five counties are eligible to participate in this program. A mediator is used whose responsibilities include determining the sincerity of remorse of the accused juvenile, deciding a fair and just penalty for his or her wrongdoing, and concluding whether any services are necessary. Before proceeding to the mediation hearing, the juvenile must have admitted that he or she is guilty of a crime and signed a waiver of rights. This waiver relinquishes the right to have witnesses or lawyers present.[54]

The program is designed to last no more than ninety days and is terminated under one of the following conditions: (1) successful: juvenile completed the required contractual agreement in ninety days; (2) unsuccessful: juvenile failed to meet the required agreement and is referred to the probation department for formal proceedings; or (3) dismissal: the mediator recommends dismissal prior to disposition. As of September 30, 2000, the rate of successful contract resolutions was 93 percent, or 625 of the first 670 participants. As of July 1, 2001, all 625 juveniles had remained nondelinquent and status offense–free.[55]

Community/Residential Treatment Programs

The three types of community/residential treatment programs discussed next are day treatment programs, group homes, and wilderness programs (Figure 9–4).

How Do Day Treatment Programs Operate?

Day treatment programs, in which youngsters spend each day in the program and return home in the evenings, have been widely used in community-based juvenile corrections. These court-mandated programs are popular because they are more economical than residential placements, do not need to provide living and sleeping quarters, make parental participation easier, require fewer staff members, and are less coercive and punishment oriented.

Nonresidential programs generally serve male juveniles although California has operated two programs for girls and several coeducational ones. Nonresidential programs have been used widely by the California Treatment Project, the New York Division for Youth, and the Florida Division of Youth Services. Nonresidential programs in New York, which are called STAY, are similar to many other nonresidential programs in that they expose youths to a guided-group interaction experience.

Day treatment programs, similar to diversion programs, were used less in the 1980s and early 1990s than they were in the 1970s, but two of the most promising programs—the Associated Marine Institute (AMI) and Project New Pride—continue to thrive. The AMI is described here.

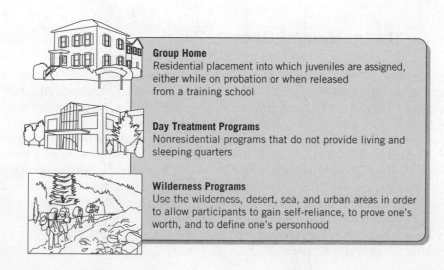

Group Home
Residential placement into which juveniles are assigned, either while on probation or when released from a training school

Day Treatment Programs
Nonresidential programs that do not provide living and sleeping quarters

Wilderness Programs
Use the wilderness, desert, sea, and urban areas in order to allow participants to gain self-reliance, to prove one's worth, and to define one's personhood

FIGURE 9–4
Three Types of Community Programs

Associated Marine Institute

The original Associated Marine Institute (AMI) was a privately operated program funded jointly by state and private donations. It tailored its programs to the geographical strengths of each community, using the ocean, wilderness, rivers, and lakes to stimulate productive behavior in youths referred by the courts or by the Division of Youth Services. Of the forty schools and institutes of the AMI, twenty-five were nonresidential. The fourteen- to eighteen-year-old male and female trainees in the nonresidential programs lived at home or in foster homes.[56]

The Marine Institutes, which constituted most of the schools, set individual goals for the training period in a dozen categories, including diving, ship-handling skills, ocean science, lifesaving, first aid, and such electives as photography and marine maintenance. In a nationally broadcast television program, in which he announced his crime bill, President Bill Clinton said, "These [AMI] programs are giving young people a chance to take their future back, a chance to understand that there is good inside them."[57]

Today, AMI is renamed AMIkids and operates fifty-six programs in eight states. The reorganization and new name reflect the fact that the program now includes many different types of programs across the nation that formerly operated independently. Rather than just operating marine programs, today's AMIkids programs provide probation services including community service, wilderness programs, substance abuse counseling, varied after-school programs, and volunteering their services to veterans, the homeless, senior citizens, shoreline cleanups, and other types of community service supporting President Obama's call for community service.[58]

The Family Centered Treatment (FCT) in Maryland allows youth to remain in their homes and communities. This innovative, family-driven treatment program requires family participation in the development of strategies and goals for success and family adherence to the goals identified. The FCT plan is based on the desires and needs of the family and uses a strength-based model of intervention that engages youth and their families through intensive contract, commitment, and collaboration. The outcomes analyzed included recidivism rates, posttreatment placement rates, and program costs. The findings reveal that FCT provides significant positive behavioral results based on a 2-year follow-up and reduces posttreatment placement. Additionally, cost analysis demonstrates that the FCT model is a cost-effective alternative to residential placement.[59]

Thinking like a Correctional Professional

You are the director of a group home for juveniles and become aware that two of your staff members are having an affair. Both are married, and they are not attempting to hide their affair. You have a small staff of 20, and this affair seems to have an adverse effect upon them. You are an ethical person and oppose this affair. Is there anything you can do? Is there anything you should do?

How Do Group Homes Operate?

The group home, the group residence, and the group foster home are all used in juvenile corrections in this country. The term **group home** generally refers to a single dwelling owned or rented by an organization or agency for the purpose of housing offenders. Although it is not part of an institutional campus, this facility provides care for a group of about four to twelve children, and staff are viewed as house parents or counselors rather than as foster parents. The administrative, supervisory, and service responsibility for the group home rests with the parent agency or organization. Usually indistinguishable from nearby homes or apartments, the group home reaches out to the community for resources and service.

The terms *group residence* or *halfway house* are used in some parts of the country to identify a small facility serving about thirteen to thirty-five youths. It usually houses two or more groups of youths, each with its own child care staff. This residence tends to use agency rather than community services, and its architecture and large size differentiate it from nearby homes and apartments.

Group homes fulfill several purposes in juvenile corrections. First, they provide an alternative to institutionalization. Dependent, neglected, and other noncriminal youths, especially, are referred to them. Second, group homes may be used as short-term residences. The communities in which they are located provide the youths with the resources to deal with such problems as family conflict, school difficulties, and peer interactions. Third, group homes can be used either as a "halfway-in" setting for offenders who are having difficulty keeping to the conditions of probation or as a "halfway-out" setting for juvenile offenders who are returning to the community but do not have adequate home placement.

Group home programs tend to vary from home to home because they have been developed to meet the varying needs of different populations and communities, and standard guidelines do not exist. Consequently, group homes often reflect the personal philosophies of their founders or directors. Intake criteria, length of stay, treatment goals, target population serviced, quantity and quality of staffing, services offered, physical facilities, location in relation to the rest of the city, and house rules are extremely diverse in group homes in this country. This diversity need not be a problem, however, if additional support services are available. One of the most important studies of juvenile justice found a significant reduction in recidivism in Massachusetts when community-based programs had an integrated network of services.[60]

Many group homes are treatment oriented. Group therapy often is used as a treatment modality. These group sessions are largely supportive; they do not probe very deeply, and discussion usually is limited to problems as they arise. Guided Group Interaction (GGI) is probably the most popular treatment method; the members of the group are expected to support, confront, and be honest with one another so that they may be helped in dealing with their own problems. The role of the therapist in GGI is to help the members develop a more positive and prosocial group culture. Some group homes deliberately avoid a comfortable climate, and staff may even try to arouse anxiety. The treatment philosophy behind this is that without a relaxed atmosphere, youths are more likely to become unsettled and thereby more receptive to personality change.

One of the most innovative programs is the House of Umoja (HOU) project, which was founded in 1968 and was officially organized in 1970 as a youth development agency. When she became aware that one of her six sons had joined a gang, Sister Falaka and her husband, David Fattah, took the bold step of inviting the gang to become a part of their family. Sister Falaka saw possible solutions to the violence of gangs in "the strength of the family, tribal concepts, and African value systems." She and her husband created an African-style extended family in which members of the gang could find alternative values to those of their street-life culture. Residents are required to be drug-free and are encouraged to maintain good grades. Since its establishment, three thousand adolescents belonging to seventy-three different street gangs have passed through the HOU doors. The success of the Umoja concept has led to its duplication in Bridgeport, Connecticut, and Portland, Oregon. The principles of this resident program are part of the National Center for Neighborhood Enterprise's highly successful Violence-Free Zone initiative that has been instituted in five cities.[61]

Focus on Offenders 9–3
What Quakerdale Meant to Me

I spent an entire day thinking about what Quakerdale really means to me. I didn't want to just write a bunch of meaningless prose—I wanted to capture the truth of Quakerdale's impact on my life. As I was thinking, [I] realized that I could probably write an entire novel about my experiences there and what it has done for me. Quakerdale taught me tolerance, patience, respect, self-restraint, and communication.

When I was admitted to Quakerdale, I was a lost, hopeless, self-serving seventeen year old. I had recently attempted suicide, run away from home, dropped out of high school, gotten into marijuana, was a self-mutilator, and didn't understand the meaning of "impulse control." Throughout my six months there, I worked intensively with staff and participated whole-heartedly in groups and peer activities, as well as actively "working my program."

I learned patience when dealing with others and when working through my own problems. I learned that sometimes, I will not get what I want or expect, but that it's still okay.

I learned respect. I did not need to learn to respect others so much as to respect myself. I came to realize that my behavior was hurting no one worse than it was hurting me. It was destroying me physically and, especially, emotionally. And I deserved a lot better than that. I opened my eyes to the ways in which I was treating myself. I realized that I would hope to never allow another person to treat me the way I was treating myself. I saw that the worst relationship I had in my life was my relationship with me. For example, I would never dream of murdering someone, but that's exactly what I tried to do to myself. I realized that I could not hope to be happy if I continued my present, self-hating relationship.

If I was to ever learn to love myself, I needed to learn self-restraint. Quakerdale taught me this, as well. Sometimes, it's better to delay gratification for a more permanent, safer sense of gratification. Impulse control is still something that I work on daily, but I think it is obvious from my present life circumstances versus my "pre-Quakerdale" life circumstances that I learned a great deal about self-control. I think that a big part of what helped me learn self-control was Quakerdale's "open door" policy. I had the option to run away, but every day that I chose to remain, I gained more responsibility and privileges. After only four months

at Quakerdale, I was allowed to walk to and from East High School every day by myself. This showed me that staff trusted me, which made me *want* to be trustworthy. I received positive reinforcement for acting and reasoning appropriately, which built up my confidence in myself and [the] staff's ability to help me.

I learned communication. I had family sessions once a week, and I had group [sessions] many times a week. We were always encouraged to hold others accountable, hold ourselves accountable, and be honest. I learned that telling the truth can be much more rewarding than trying to "stay out of trouble" by lying. If I did something wrong or lied to staff, I was positively reinforced if I confessed on my own. I learned that it is my responsibility to be honest, and *others'* responsibility to react to my honesty in an appropriate way. It is not my responsibility to keep everyone happy, especially if it ruins me inside. However, I also learned to "pick my battles."

What it all comes down to is that: before Quakerdale, I was literally taking my life in my hands and not even caring if I dropped it. Since Quakerdale, I have gone on to graduate from Dowling High School with a 3.89 cumulative grade point average, made [the] National Honor Society, received the Aquinas Key, [and] received an Academic medal, and [a] letter in academics. I was accepted to all three colleges to which I applied, and I now attend the University of Minnesota, where I have a cumulative grade point average of 3.48, made the Dean's List second semester, and am majoring in English and taking a minor in psychology. I am by no means completely "cured" of the emotional difficulties that I had before Quakerdale, but I can honestly say that I have learned how to live a wonderful life, despite, and sometimes due to, my trials and difficulties. Thank you, Quakerdale, for helping me grow into the woman I have become [italics included in the original].

CRITICAL THINKING QUESTIONS
Why do you think this program was so successful with this young woman? What would it take for us to have more House of Umoja and Quakerdale programs?

Source: Letter received from Rita Fernau, director of the Quakerdale program, and used with permission of the author.

Yet, innovative programs still are not typical of group homes across the nation. In too many group homes, vacancies are hard to find and many even have long waiting lists. Staff are notoriously underpaid, believe that they have not been properly trained, and have high rates of turnover.[62] Residents also typically have longer stays than they would have in training schools, and this raises real questions about whether group homes are a less punitive placement than juvenile institutions. The evaluations of residential programs further make it difficult to support the conclusion that residential programs in the community result in lower rates of recidivism than do institutional programs. Nevertheless, a convincing case can be made that residential programs are at least as successful as training schools, with far less trauma to youths and usually at less cost to the state. In Focus on Offenders 9–3, a former resident writes a letter to the director of Quakerdale, a residential program for girls, expressing her appreciation for what the program has meant to her life.

Evidence-Based Practice
Tracking the Recidivism Outcomes of a Home-Based Paraprofessional Intervention

Utah Youth Villages Families First Program is an intensive in-home intervention used in the past two decades, helping families with a variety of behavioral and emotional problems. While it was developed within a specific agency in Utah, the intervention is based on the Teaching Family Model that has been tested and applied across the nation as well as internationally.

Families with youth in the juvenile justice system are referred to Families First by the juvenile courts. But before the juvenile courts refer such youth to Families First, they evaluate each youth and family's risk level and unique needs using the evidence-based protective assessment tool. Information gathered about youth and family risk factors focuses the ensuing intervention in several ways. First, this information is used to ensure that services target youth offenders who are at moderate to high risk for recidivism. Second, those responsible for delivering the intervention target the development of a youth's social skills to meet her or his specific needs that initiated this juvenile's involvement with the juvenile court system in the first place. This focus on skill based training has been shown to reduce recidivism compared with general community probation efforts.

Following additional information gathering, a trained Families First paraprofessional family specialist goes in the home of a referred family for an average of 8 to 10 weeks, spreading between six and 10 hours a week with the family over multiple visits during the week. To be hired as Families First Specialist, an applicant needs a bachelor's degree and previous experience working with youth.

Training of Families First Specialist takes place in three stages. The first involves training on policy, procedures, and teaching model in a classroom setting over a two-week period; during this time, training trainees also conducted a few "shadow" visits with other specialists. In the second stage, the new specialist accompanies the supervisor during an eight week intervention. In the third stage, about halfway through the apprentice intervention, specialists receive the first family assignment, with the supervisor accompanying them on at least half of these visits. In addition to in-home observation, new specialists participate in weekly supervision and staff meeting. Over the course of this first year, the amount of direct supervision tapers, and new specialists must pass a formal evaluation after one year. The rigor of this training process is designed to ensure high intervention fidelity within the program.

Throughout a typical in-home intervention, a Families First specialist or his or her supervisor is available to the family 24 hours a day, seven days a week. From crisis intervention and support to online training and coaching for parents and youth, the specialist then spends on an average of 6 to 10 hours with the family weekly—reflecting one unique benefit of paraprofessional based services. In addition to individualized teaching and real-time skill development, these professionals also spend time in relationship-building activities and service to the family. A primary focus of these efforts is addressing the parent/child conflicts and general deficiencies in social skills that first brought the juvenile into the court's purview.

By working on family dynamics within their natural environment, the ultimate aim of the Families First specialist is to alter the instinctive response of parents and juveniles toward each other until the interactions reflect a healthy balance of accountability and warmth. Along with communication skills and bonding activities, the importance of positive reinforcement, effective consequences, continued supervision, and basic household structures are all emphasized as essential to reducing the risk of further recidivism. By cultivating new additional responses and concretely trying those responses to the rewarding behavior of others, the intervention thus seeks to sculpt the home environment into a mutually rewarding parent/child dynamic.

The Family First specialist continues to be available for the next year as a continuing support to the family. The fact is that specialists also conducts four brief evaluations of the juvenile and family during the first year to track long-term success and help families overcome any obstacles that may arise. These periodic check-ins focus on the family's overall stability, new problems, additional needs, or any scale review that may be indicated.

A Kaplan-Meyer survival analysis indicates the Family First group has s significantly lower recidivism rate than the risk-adjusted juvenile court group, based on a one-year follow-up of new misdemeanor or felony charges. This analysis also found that the program reduced self-reported rebelliousness, attitudes favorable to antisocial behavior, and attitudes favorable to drug use, and increased belief in the moral order.

These results indicate that home intervention that relies on paraprofessional teachers can have a measurable impact on recidivism rates, in particular, the results confirm significant reduction in rebellious and antisocial attitude and an increased believe in the moral order following the in-home intervention. Since changes in these attitudes accompany the changes and documented offenses, it can be concluded that the home training of the family played a meaningful role in ensuring reduced recidivism over time.

One of the limitations of this study is that it did not measure the attitudinal change of parents as part of the documented change. Also, although the comparison group was adjusted for level of risk, the comparison group was not matched to take into account other factors that may influence reoffense rates. Taking into account these limitations, these findings are consistent with evidence from other in-home interventions, including significant lower rates of new charges, significant reduction in rearrest with multisystemic therapy, and fewer new arrests with the Family Empowerment Intervention.

CRITICAL THINKING QUESTION

Is this study a reminder that paraprofessionals are under-utilized in the treatment of youthful offenders? How it is possible to persuade paraprofessionals to be involved with such extensive training?

Source: Jacob Z. Hess, Wayne Arner, Elliot Sykes, and Andrew G. Price, "Helping Juvenile Offenders on Their Own Turf": Tracking the Recidivism Outcomes of Home-Based Paraprofessional," *OJJDP: Journal of Juvenile Justice* (Fall 2012), 12–24.

What Are Wilderness Programs?

Outward Bound is the best-known wilderness, or survival program. All of the outdoor **wilderness programs**, whether they take place in the mountains, canoe country, the forest, the sea, or the desert, conclude that the completion of a seemingly impossible task is one of the best means to gain self-reliance, to prove one's worth, and to define oneself as a person.

Outward Bound

Outward Bound programs were first used in England during World War II. The first Outward Bound school in the United States was the Colorado Outward Bound School, which was established in 1962 and accepted its first delinquents in 1964. This program, situated in the Rocky Mountains at an altitude of 8,800 feet, consists of mountain walking, backpacking, high-altitude camping, solo survival, rappelling, and rock climbing. Other Outward Bound programs soon followed in Maine, Minnesota, North Carolina, Oregon, and Texas. A similar program, a Homeward Bound school, was opened in 1970 in Massachusetts. Several community-based wilderness programs that begin and end in the community but include sessions in a nearby wilderness area are also in operation.[63]

Today, Outward Bound has twelve regional schools: Alabama, Baltimore, California, Hurricane Island, New York City, North Carolina, Northwest, Omaha, Philadelphia, Rock Mountain, Thompson Island, and Voyageur. They offer 750 wilderness courses serving adults, teens, and youths. Courses include rock climbing, kayaking, dogsledding, sailing, rappelling, backpacking, and more. Over 10,000 students have participated in wilderness courses. Outward Bound also offers multiyear partnerships with 150 schools across the United States. It encourages over 30,000 students and 4,000 teachers to reach high levels of achievement and to discover their potential.[64]

Substance Abuse Counselor

PREPARATION FOR THE JOB

Counselors help people with personal, family, educational, mental health, and career decisions and problems. The specific duties are dependent upon the individuals they serve and where they work. Substance abuse counselors will counsel persons who are addicted to alcohol or drugs, help them to identify behaviors and problems related to their addictions, and then assist them to change these behaviors. They may create and conduct programs to prevent addictions and work in a variety of settings, such as residential treatment facilities, institutions, or private offices.

QUALIFICATION AND EDUCATIONAL REQUIREMENTS

Forty-eight states and the District of Columbia have some form of counselor license that governs the practice of counseling, which typically requires a master's degree. Candidates may require a master's degree in social work or related field from an accredited school to meet this requirement. Within the graduate program, one will usually have to complete a period of supervised clinical internship experience. Counselors will also have to participate in workshops and personal studies to maintain their certificates and licenses. Candidates frequently may also have supervised clinical experience beyond a master's degree, passed a state exam,

adherence to ethical codes, and standards, and annual continuing education courses. One should check with the state and the place one wishes to work to find out all the requirements.

DEMAND FOR

Overall, employment of counselors is expected to be excellent. Drug courts, residential employment, therapeutic communities, detoxification units, short-term treatment programs, and institutional positions are expected to continue to increase. Demand is expected to be strong because drug offenders are increasing and are being sentto treatment programs, other than jail. Job openings will also occur as counselors retire or leave the profession.

SALARY

The mean annual salary for this position is $34,800. Government employees generally pay a higher wage, followed by hospitals and social service agencies. Residential facilities often pay the lowest wage. The lowest annual salary is $25,310 and the highest annual salary is $44,920.

Source: "Counselors," *Occupational Handbook,* 2008–2009 Edition (Bureau of Labor Statistics: U.S. Department of Labor), accessed 2009.

Social Policy and Juvenile Justice:
Are Community-Based Programs Effective?

Increasing numbers of studies demonstrate empirically that many community-based correctional programs reduce recidivism and are less expensive than confinement. So what more needs to be done? It would appear that improving the effectiveness of community-based corrections ultimately requires breaking down community resistance and obtaining greater citizen involvement in community-based programs, while at the same time developing a broader continuum of services in the community for juveniles who need such services.

To break down community resistance and to obtain greater citizen involvement in community-based programs, departments of juvenile corrections must develop and implement a certain plan of action. A well-developed plan should (1) establish programs and (2) decide who will be placed in community facilities. Unfortunately, no agreement has been reached on how to implement either of these strategies.

Careful planning is obviously necessary to gain greater public support for community-based programs. A department should mount a massive public education effort through the communications media, should seek support for the project from the various sub-communities of the community—ethnic, racial, and special interest groups—and should develop a sophisticated understanding of the decision-making processes in society. But should this be done before or after a program has been initiated in the community?

Advocates of keeping the community informed as soon as a site for a program is chosen claim that to do otherwise is dishonest. Opponents of this approach argue that advance information will permit the community to mobilize resistance against the proposed community program. They claim that the community is more likely to accept an already established and successful program than one that exists only on the drawing board.

Widespread controversy also exists over the selection of youths to be placed in community-based programs. One approach is conservative: if the wrong youth is put in the wrong place at the wrong time and commits a serious or violent crime, such as rape or murder, the adverse publicity may destroy the best-planned and implemented program. Therefore, to preserve the viability of community-based programs, only juveniles most likely to be helped should be kept in the community. The opposite approach argues that all but the hard-core recidivist should be retained in the community, for it is there that the youth's problems began in the first place. Advocates of this position believe that institutionalization will only make more serious criminals out of confined youths. Some of these supporters even propose leaving many of the hard-core or difficult-to-handle youths in the community.

Finally, improving the continuum of services for juveniles in a community usually requires a strong deinstitutionalization emphasis. The programs that have this integration of services are more likely to have positive effects on youthful offenders assigned to them. Another advantage of these continuum-of-service programs is that they are not as likely to experience the fragmentation and duplication of services that are found so frequently in other programs in the juvenile justice system.

SUMMARY

LEARNING OBJECTIVE 1: Summarize the philosophy and objectives of community-based corrections.

The three philosophies that are guiding community-based programming are reintegration, the necessity for a continuum of sanctions, and restorative justice and peacemaking.

LEARNING OBJECTIVE 2: Explain how community-based programs are administered.

The three types of organizational structures in community-based programs are comprehensive state-sponsored, locally sponsored, and privately administered programs.

LEARNING OBJECTIVE 3: Explain the importance of delinquency prevention.

The importance of delinquency prevention is that it attempts to thwart youths' behavior before it becomes delinquent. Many promising delinquency programs exists

LEARNING OBJECTIVE 4: Describe diversion and various diversion programs.

Diversion programs aim to keep juveniles outside the formal justice system. One of the most celebrated of these diversionary programs is youth courts. Another type is juvenile drug courts.

LEARNING OBJECTIVE 5: Describe residential programs in the community.

Three common types of community/residential treatment programs are day treatment programs, group homes, and wilderness programs.

LEARNING OBJECTIVE 6: Evaluate the effectiveness of community-based programs.

- The effectiveness of community-based programs is controversial. Even in studies that have found lower recidivism rates for youths left in the community, the criticism is often made that juveniles who were more likely to succeed were selected for the experimental group and that the authorities altered the results by giving the experimentals more chances than the controls before returning them to the juvenile court. Even though it is difficult to substantiate the widespread conclusion that community-based programs lower the recidivism rate, a good case can be made for the assumption that community-based corrections programs are at least as successful as institutional confinement is, with far less trauma to youngsters and less cost to the state.

- Community-based programs continue to face several challenges, especially those posed by the reduction of federal funding and the public's preference for getting tough on youth crime. Yet the cost effectiveness of these programs, as opposed to the prohibitive expense of long-term institutions, should continue to lead to an increased use of alternative programs in the community.

KEY TERMS

community corrections acts, p. 189
continuum of sanctions, p. 189
day treatment programs, p. 199

delinquency prevention, p. 191
diversion programs, p. 195
group home, p. 200

reintegration philosophy, p. 188
restorative justice, p. 189
wilderness programs, p. 204

REVIEW QUESTIONS

1. Why have delinquency prevention programs generally been so ineffective?
2. Why is the widening criticism of many of the delinquency prevention programs a serious indictment?
3. Of the programs discussed in this chapter, which do you feel is the best for helping offenders reintegrate into the community?
4. What specific strategies can departments of juvenile corrections pursue to enlist greater support from the community for community programs?

5. What are the main types of residential and nonresidential programs for juvenile delinquents?
6. How effective are community-based corrections? What is the essential link in increasing the effectiveness of community-based corrections?

GROUP EXERCISES

1. *Group Work:* First, identify Ann Newton's three levels of delinquency prevention. Then develop the specific kinds of variables identified by Newton's three types of delinquency.
2. *Group Work:* Describe all of the different programs implemented in community-based corrections. Which of Newton's levels does each program represent and why?

3. *Writing to Learn Exercise:* Write approximately two paragraphs that identify the different model prevention programs and their rates of success—with the textbook closed. Critique and revise after reviewing the rates of success of each of the programs as cited in the text.

WORKING WITH JUVENILES

One of your counselors (you are her supervisor) recently lost her husband, and she is having difficulty handling it. She says that she wants to come back to work and has been a good employee for the past seven years. However, she has been off for three months and it does not appear that she is anywhere near being ready to return to work. It is a real problem getting others to cover her paperwork and other duties. What are you going to do? How much longer will you give her?

NOTES

1. Joseph Heinz, Theresa Wise, and Clemens Bartollas, *Successful Management of Juvenile Residential Facilities: A Performance-Based Approach* (Alexandria, VA: American Correctional Association, 2010), 35–36.

2. Patricia M. Harris, Rebecca D. Petersen, and Samantha Rapoza, "Between Probation and Revocation: A Study of Intermediate Sanctions Decision-Making," *Journal of Criminal Justice* 29 (2001), 308.

3. Ibid., 175.

4. For more information on Project Craft in Florida and Connecticut, visit the Project Craft website at http://www.hbi.org/page.cfm?pageID=129.

5. Robin Hamilton and Kay McKinney, "Job Training for Juveniles: Project CRAFT," *OJJDP Fact Sheet* (Washington, DC: Office of Juvenile Justice and Delinquency Prevention, 1999), 1.

6. Steve V. Gies, *Aftercare Services* (Washington, DC: Office of Juvenile Justice and Delinquency Prevention, September 2003), 18–20, accessed at http://www.ncjrs.gov/pdffiles1/ojjdp/201800.pdf.

7. For an expanded treatment of delinquency prevention, see Clemens Bartollas, *Juvenile Delinquency*, 8th ed. (Englewood Cliffs, NJ: Pearson, 2011).

8. Anne M. Newton, "Prevention of Crime and Delinquency," *Criminal Justice Abstracts* (June 1978), 4.

9. Marylyn Bibb, "Gang-Related Services of Mobilization for Youth," in *Juvenile Gangs in Context: Theory, Research, and Action*, edited by Malcolm W. Klein (Upper Saddle River, NJ: Prentice Hall, 1967), 175–82.

10. For a description of the various prevention programs, see Bartollas, *Juvenile Delinquency*, 521–51.

11. For a review of these studies examining the effectiveness of prevention programs, see ibid., 524.

12. Sharon Mihalic et al., *Successful Implementation: Lessons from Blueprints* (Washington, DC: Office of Juvenile Justice and Delinquency Prevention, 2004), 1.

13. Sharon Mihalic et al., *Blueprints for Violence Prevention* (Washington, DC: Office of Juvenile Justice and Delinquency Prevention, 2004), 55.

14. D. E. McGill, S. Mihalic, and J. K. Grotpeter, "Big Brothers Big Sisters of America," in *Blueprints for Violence Prevention: Book 2*, edited by D. S. Elliott (Boulder: University of Colorado, Institute of Behavioral Science, Center for the Study and Prevention of Violence, 1997).

15. Mihalic et al., *Blueprints for Violence Prevention*, 30–31.

16. M. A. Pentz, S. Mihalic, and J. K. Grotpeter, "The Midwestern Prevention Project," in *Blueprints for Violence Prevention: Book 1*, edited by D. S. Elliott (Boulder: University of Colorado, Institute of Behavioral Science, Center for the Study and Prevention of Violence, 1997).

17. Mihalic et al., *Blueprints for Violence Prevention*, 26–27.

18. J. E. Alexander et al., "Functional Family Therapy," in *Blueprints for Violence Prevention: Juvenile Justice Bulletin*, edited by D. S. Elliott (Boulder: University of Colorado, Institute of Behavioral Science, Center for the Study and Prevention of Violence, 2000).

19. Mihalic et al., *Blueprints for Violence Prevention*, 22–23.

20. C. Webster-Stratton et al., "The Incredible Years: Parents, Teachers and Child Training Series," in *Blueprints for Violence Prevention: Book 11*, edited by D. S. Elliott (Boulder: University of Colorado, Institute of Behavioral Science, Center for the Study and Prevention of Violence, 2001).

21. Mihalic et al., *Blueprints for Violence Prevention*, 47.

22. G. Botvin, S. Mihalic, and J. K. Grotpeter, "Life Skills Training," in *Blueprints for Violence Prevention: Book 5*, edited by D. S. Elliott (Boulder: University of Colorado, Institute of Behavioral Science, Center for the Study and Prevention of Violence, 1998).

23. Mihalic et al., *Blueprints for Violence Prevention*, 31–33.

24. Pentz et al., "The Midwestern Prevention Project."

25. Mihalic et al., *Blueprints for Violence Prevention*, 56–58.

26. P. Chamberlain and S. Mihalic, "Multidimensional Treatment Foster Care," in *Blueprints for Violence Prevention: Book 8*, edited by D. S. Elliott (Boulder: University of Colorado, Institute of Behavioral Science, Center for the Study and Prevention of Violence, 1998).

27. Mihalic et al., *Blueprints for Violence Prevention*, 27–28.

28. S. W. Henggeler et al., "Multisystemic Therapy," in *Blueprints for Violence Prevention: Book 6*, edited by D. S. Elliott (Boulder: University of Colorado, Institute of Behavioral Science, Center for the Study and Prevention of Violence, 2001).

29. Mihalic et al., *Blueprints for Violence Prevention*, 47–48.

30. Ibid., 48.

31. Ibid., 46.

32. James C. Howell, ed., *Guide for Implementing the Comprehensive Strategy for Serious, Violent, and Chronic Juvenile Offenders* (Washington, DC: Office of Juvenile Justice and Delinquency Prevention, 1995), 10.

33. Ibid., 3.

34. Ibid., 5.

35. Ibid.

36. Ibid., 9–10.

37. Ibid., 11.

38. Kathleen Coolbaugh and Cynthia J. Hansel, "The Comprehensive Strategy: Lessons Learned from the Pilot Sites," *Juvenile Justice Bulletin* (2000), 1.

39. Ibid., 10.

40. Scott B. Peterson and Jill Beres, *The First Report to the Nation on Youth Courts and Teen Courts* (published by Scott B. Peterson, 2008).

41. Ibid.

42. Ibid.

43. T. M. Godwin, *Peer Justice and Youth Empowerment: An Implementation Guide for Teen Court Programs* (Lexington, KY: American Probation and Parole Association, 1998). For a recent study of a youth court, see Brenda Vose and Kelly Vannan, "A Jury of Your Peers: Recidivism Among

Teen Court Participants," *OJJDP Journal of Juvenile Justice 3, 97–109/*

44. Marilyn Roberts, Jennifer Brophy, and Caroline Cooper, *The Juvenile Drug Court Movement* (Washington, DC: Office of the Juvenile Justice and Delinquency Prevention, 1997), 1.

45. Ibid., 1–2.

46. C. West Huddleston III, Douglas B. Barlowe, and Rachel Casebolt, *Painting the Current Picture: A National Report on Drug Courts and Other Problem Solving Court Programs in the United States* (Washington, DC: Bureau of Justice Statistics, 2008), 1–16.

47. *Juvenile Drug Courts: Strategies in Procedure* (Washington, DC: Bureau of Justice Statistics, March 2003). Accessed at http://www.ncjrs.gov/pdffiles1/bja/191866.pdf.

48. Huddleston et al., *Painting the Current Picture*.

49. Audrey Hickert, Erin Becker, Moises, and Kristina Moleni, Impact of Juvenile Drug Courts on Drug Use and Criminal Behavior," *OJJDP Journal of Juvenile Justice* 3 (Fall 2013), 60–77.

50. Donna M. Heretick and Joseph A. Russell, "The Impact of Juvenile Mental Health Court on Recidivism Among Youth," *OJJDP Journal of Juvenile Health* 3 (Fall 2013), 1–14. See also Ashley M. Maywarm and Jill D. Sharkey, "Mental Health Outcomes of a Community-Based Delinquency Intervention *OJJDP Journal of Juvenile Justice* 3 (Fall 2013).

51. Ibid.

52. Ibid.

53. Robert R. Smith and Victor S. Lombardo, "Evaluation Report of the Juvenile Mediation Program," *Corrections and Compendium* 26 (October 2001), 1.

54. Ibid., 2.

55. Ibid. For a more recent study, see Alicia Summers, Steve Wood, and Jesse Russell, "Assessing Efficiency and Workload Implications of the King County Mediation Project," *OJJDP Journal of Juvenile Justice* 1 (2011), 48–59.

56. Information on the Associated Marine Institute was supplied in a 1995 phone conversation with Magie Valdés.

57. Unpublished mimeographed statement circulated by AMI, n.d.

58. For additional information on AMIkids, see Jasmine Ouhrt, "New Name, Same Mission: AMI Lakeland Is Now AMIkids," accessed at http://www.theledger.com/article/20090725/NEWS/907255003?Title=New-Name-Same-Mission-AMI-Lakeland-Is-Now-AMIKids. Also see Links on AMIkids on Facebook at http://www.facebook.com/posted.php?id=108818992527.

59. Melonie Sullivan, Lori Snyder Bennear, Karen F. Honess, William E. Pointer, Jr., and Timothy Wood, "Family Centered Treatment—An Alternative to Residential Placements for Adjudicated Youth: Outcomes and Cost-Effectiveness," *OJJDP Journal of Juvenile Justice* 2 (Fall 2012), 25–40.

60. B. Krisberg, J. Austin, and P. Steele, *Unlocking Juvenile Corrections* (San Francisco: National Council on Crime and Delinquency, 1991).

61. For the House of Umoja, see http://www.volunteersolutions.org/volunteerway/org/1236595.

62. One of the authors has had a number of former students who were employed in group homes, and they consistently make these criticisms.

63. Joshua L. Miner and Joe Boldt, *Outward Bound USA: Learning Through Experience* (New York: Morrow, 1981).

64. For Outward Bound USA, see http://www.outwardbound.org.

10 Juvenile Institutionalization

Lisa F. Young/Fotolia

Learning Objectives

1. Describe the purpose and operation of short-term confinement facilities, including jails, detention centers, and shelter care facilities.

2. Describe the purpose and operation of various long-term juvenile correctional facilities, including boot camps, reception and diagnostic centers, and ranches/forestry camps.

3. Describe the goals, programs, and operation of training schools.

4. Summarize the rights of juveniles who are institutionalized.

5. Summarize the factors that should be taken into consideration when implementing a confinement policy for juveniles.

The conditions under which juveniles are housed in institutional care have met with harsh criticism. California juvenile facilities, according to a recent report, are failing the state's children. The children have little chance of leaving improved, the report says, and some are worse off than when they arrived.[1] In March 2007, responding to the reports of sexual abuse of youths at Texas Youth Commission institutions, Texas Governor Rick Perry placed the Texas Youth Commission under conservatorship to guide reform of the agency. A report documents the violence, sexual abuse, and lack of accountability in the juvenile facilities of the state.[2] The Connecticut Juvenile Training School has been a headache for state authorities since its opening in 2001. The high-security perimeter fence, thick steel doors, and small cells with slits for windows make it feel more like a prison than a rehabilitation center for juveniles. The problems increased in 2010 as Connecticut raised the maximum age for juvenile offenders from fifteen to seventeen years old, moving many of the 250 to 300 sixteen- and seventeen-year-olds who previously went to adult prisons each year to juvenile facilities.[3]

The U.S. Department of Justice has filed lawsuits against juvenile facilities in eleven states as a result of supervision that is either abusive or negligent. In addition, the Associated Press contacted each state agency that oversees juvenile correctional centers and asked for information on the numbers of allegations and confirmed cases of physical, sexual, and emotional abuse by state members from January 2004 through 2007. According to this survey, more than thirteen thousand claims of abuse were identified in these facilities during this time period—a disturbing number given that the total population of detained youth was about forty-six thousand at the time the states were surveyed.[4]

The juvenile justice system often is accused of being too lenient, yet youths who are believed to be dangerous or who show little sign of mending their ways frequently find themselves locked up behind walls. The facilities in which these youths are placed are divided into two general categories: temporary-care facilities and correctional facilities. Jails, detention centers, and shelters are temporary-care facilities; boot camps, reception and diagnostic centers, ranches/forestry camps, and training schools are long-term correctional facilities. The primary differences between these two categories of facilities are the absence of correctional programs and the shorter lengths of stay in temporary-care facilities. Temporary-care facilities frequently house both males and females in the same general location, whereas correctional facilities often separate them. Juveniles waived to the adult court can also be sentenced to adult prisons, or they can be transferred to mental health placements. This chapter focuses on the training school because of the length of time it holds youths and because of the special role it has played in juvenile justice. See Focus on Policy 10–1.

What Types of Short-Term Confinement Are Used for Juveniles?

Juvenile offenders are placed in jails, detention centers, and shelter care facilities for short-term confinement.

Jails, as suggested in an earlier chapter, were one of the reasons that motivated reformers to establish houses of refuge. It was commonly agreed that the jails were no place for a juvenile. Overcrowded conditions and idleness fostered a lawless society, one in which the juvenile was frequently a sexual victim. Juveniles also had alarming rates of suicide in jails.

Still, partly because so few alternatives were available, large numbers of juveniles continued to be confined in county jails and police lockups. Estimates vary, but about 100,000 youths were locked up in jails each year during the 1970s.[5]

The numbers appeared to decline in the 1980s and 1990s, chiefly because of the Juvenile Justice and Delinquency Prevention Act (JJDPA) of 1974. This Act provided restrictive criteria governing the confinement of juveniles in adult facilities. Congress amended the

Focus on Policy 10–1
Good News in Juvenile Corrections

In the midst of the bad news about juvenile institutionalization, there is good news from California. In the past decade, California has closed eight of its eleven juvenile facilities and successfully turned the responsibility for its nonviolent offenders over to the counties. Governor Jerry Brown also wants to complete the transformation by phasing out the three remaining state facilities that hold a thousand serious offenders. The state realized that it needed to develop different facilities for managing violent young offenders. Spending on the system has dropped by almost half, from nearly $500 million to about $245 million, and the state has cut its juvenile population from about ten thousand in the mid-1990s to about a thousand today. Some critics are concerned that without a state juvenile system to hold violent offenders prosecutors may try more young people as adults, but the state can prevent this by monitoring and penalizing counties that overprosecute juveniles, and by allowing for extended custody in local facilities for those juveniles who have committed more serious crimes.

The Department of Corrections and Rehabilitation's Division of Juvenile Facilities, the former California Youth Authority, is still under a consent decree due to abusive conditions, systemic mismanagement, and ineffectual services (*Farrell v. Cate*, 2004). The closure of the state juvenile facilities would eliminate the state's obligation under the *Farrell* litigation, resulting in a potential $5 million budget reallocation to assist counties with the realignment and reduce the state's current deficit.

CRITICAL THINKING QUESTION

Is this good news? Is this something that would help reform the operation of juvenile institutions?

Source: Catherine McCracken and Selena Teji, *An Update: Closing California's Division of Juvenile Facilities: An Analysis of County Institutional Capacity* (Sacramento: Center on Juvenile and Criminal Justice, October 2010), accessed at http://www.cjcj.org.

JJDPA in 1980, requiring participating states to remove all juveniles from adult jails and lockups by the end of 1985 if they wanted to receive federal funding for juvenile justice. The 1985 deadline was extended to 1988 and then again was amended in 1989 because so few states had achieved full compliance.[6] Over the years, the number of youths in adult jails has been dramatically reduced. At the same time, with an increasing number of states sending juveniles to adult court, the percentages of youths in adult jails is increasing.

According to data published in 2006, an estimated 6,159 youth younger than age eighteen were held in adult jails on June 30, 2004. These inmates accounted for 1 percent of the total jail population, as in 2003. In 2004, 87 percent of the jail inmates younger than eighteen were held as adults; this proportion was greater than the 80 percent in 2000 and the 76 percent in 1994.[7] Figure 10–1 contains the data related to the confinement of juveniles in adult jails.

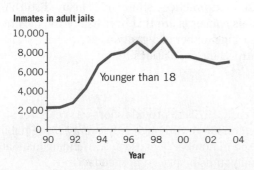

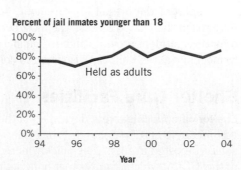

FIGURE 10–1
Juveniles in Adult Jails by Year and Percentage

- Between 1990 and 1999, while the adult jail inmate population increased 48%, the jail inmate population under age 18 increased more than 300%.
- Between 1999 and 2004, the adult jail inmate population increased 19%, while the jail inmate population under age 18 decreased 25%.
- The number of jail inmates younger than 18 held as adults was 6,159 in 2004—up 21% from 1994.
- The number of jail inmates younger than 18 held as juveniles in 2004 was 924—down 42% from 1994.

▲ The Palm Beach Regional Juvenile Detention Center is operated by the Division of Juvenile Justice3 and detains youths whiile they are awaiting their court appearances or placements in a commitment facility. There are twenty-one detention facilities divided into three regions throughout the state of Florida.

Kathryn O'Lare

Several reasons exist why removal of juveniles from jail continues to remain a distant goal. First, juveniles who are transferred to adult court and are waiting criminal trials make up an increasingly large category of youths confined in jail. Second, many states continue to resist full compliance with the JJDPA jail-removal mandate. The claim is frequently made that the states lack the necessary resources and alternatives to implement the jail-removal mandate.[8] Third, the belief is widely held that separating juveniles from adult inmates is sufficient to protect the juveniles against the harmful effects of jail confinement.

What is hopeful is that a number of states have taken a strong stand against the jailing of juveniles. California and Utah have made it unlawful to jail a youthful offender.[9] Illinois, Missouri, North Carolina, Tennessee, and Virginia enacted legislation in the 1980s, either prohibiting the jailing of minors or restricting the number of admissions.[10]

Detention Centers

Established at the end of the nineteenth century as an alternative to jail for juveniles, **detention centers**, also called *juvenile halls*, are intended to be temporary holding centers. The court administers the majority of juvenile detention centers, although state agencies, city or county governments, welfare departments, and juvenile courts also manage these facilities. The state governments of Connecticut, Delaware, Vermont, and Puerto Rico assume responsibility for administering juvenile detention centers. Georgia, Maryland, Massachusetts, New Hampshire, and Rhode Island operate regional detention facilities.

The traditional detention center has sparked many horror stories, and on more than one occasion, former residents have described to the authors the toxic environment of these facilities. Fortunately, detention in the United States has experienced marked improvement in the past two decades. A nationwide movement to develop standards for detention and more innovative detention programs has provided the impetus to improve detention practices in the United States.

Attention homes were initiated in Boulder, Colorado, and have spread to other jurisdictions. Their stated purpose is to give juveniles *attention* rather than *detention*. These facilities have no fences, locked doors, or other physical restraints. They also provide more extensive programming and encourage more interaction among residents and staff. Home detention, as previously discussed, is a nonresidential approach to confinement. It was first used in St. Louis, Missouri; Newport News and Norfolk, Virginia; and Washington, D.C., and is now being used throughout the nation.

In spite of the overall improvement, detention practices still exhibit many disturbing features in the United States. The most serious concerns are that over half of the facilities offer no treatment program and that an increasing number of detention centers have turned to mechanical restraints and isolation to control their populations.[11]

Shelter Care Facilities

Shelter care facilities were developed in the early 1970s to provide short-term care for status offenders and for dependent or neglected children. Although only twenty-three public shelters existed in 1975, they quickly increased in number because of the funding mandate of the JJDPA, which requires that noncriminal youths be placed in such facilities.

The length of stay in these nonsecure facilities with no locked doors varies from overnight to a few days. Occasionally, a juvenile must stay several weeks because of difficulty in scheduling court-required family therapy sessions or because of hearing delays in the juvenile court. Delinquent youths may be placed in shelter care facilities if the county has no detention center and the juvenile judge is reluctant to detain the youth in the county jail, or if a judge decides to reward a delinquent youth's positive behavior in detention by transferring him or her to the more open shelter care. Shelter care facilities do permit residents to enjoy home visits on weekends and field trips into the community during the week.

TABLE 10–1
Short- and Long-Term Confinement Facilities for Juveniles

Training schools tend to be state facilities, detention centers tend to be local facilities, and group homes tend to be private facilities

Facility operation	Total	Detention center	Shelter	Reception/ diagnostic center	Group home	Ranch/wilderness camp	Training school	Residential treatment center
Number of facilities	2,111	705	137	72	528	68	188	763
Operations profile								
All facilities	100%	100%	100%	100%	100%	100%	100%	100%
Public	51	87	35	69	18	47	91	34
State	21	20	3	57	10	9	80	18
Local	30	67	32	13	9	38	11	15
Private	49	13	65	31	82	53	9	66
Facility profile								
All facilities	100%	33%	6%	3%	25%	3%	9%	36%
Public	100	57	4	5	9	3	16	24
State	100	33	1	9	12	1	34	32
Local	100	74	7	1	7	4	3	18
Private	100	9	9	2	42	3	2	49

Facility type

- Detention centers, reception/diagnostic centers, and training schools were more likely to be public facilities than private facilities; however, a substantial proportion of reception/diagnostic centers were private.
- Most shelters were private facilities, as were group homes and residential treatment centers.
- Detention centers made up the largest proportion of all local facilities and approximately half of all public facilities.
- Training schools constituted 32% of all state facilities.
- Group homes accounted for 40% of all private facilities.

Note: Counts (and row percentages) may sum to more than the total number of facilities because facilities could select more than one facility type category.

Source: Author's analysis of *Juvenile Residential Facility Census 2008* [machine-readable data file]; Sarah Hockenberry, Melissa Sickmund, and Anthony Sladky, *Juvenile Residential Facility Census, 2010: Selected Findings* (Washington, DC: U.S. Department of Justice; 2013), 3.

The openness of these settings, not surprisingly, creates problems with runaways and makes it difficult to control use of contraband drugs among residents. Another problem for staff is that these facilities have their share of disciplinary problems among residents, who often have difficulty controlling their attitudes and actions. See Table 10–1 for numbers on the different types of short-term confinement facilities for juveniles just discussed and the long-term facilities discussed next.

What Types of Long-Term Confinement Are Used for Juveniles?

Boot camps, reception and diagnostic centers, ranches and forestry camps, and training schools are the main forms of long-term juvenile correctional institutions (see Table 10–2). Juveniles also may be transferred to mental health placements or sentenced to youthful offender facilities and adult prisons.

Boot Camps

Boot camps received increased attention in juvenile justice in the late 1980s and 1990s. Emphasizing military discipline, physical training, and regimented activity for periods that typically range from 30 to 120 days, the intent of these programs is to shock youthful offenders to prevent them from committing further crimes. Boot camp programs generally are

TABLE 10–2
Types of Juvenile Placements

Type	Goals	Characteristics
Boot Camps	Shock treatment	Short term and emphasizes military discipline
Reception and Diagnostic Center	Evaluation and placement	Used to evaluate juveniles for possible placement in other facilities
Forestry Camps and Ranches	Minimum security	Involves informal contact with staff, and a less secure placement than training schools
Public and Private Training Schools	Longer and more secure stays	Larger physical facilities, longer terms of stay, and sometimes violent residential life institutional placement

designed for offenders who have failed with lesser sanctions such as probation. The Orleans Parish program, established in 1985, was the first boot camp for juveniles in the country.

This program accepts anyone who is sentenced by the juvenile judge, but most programs generally exclude sex offenders, armed robbers, and violent offenders.[12]

The rationale for juvenile boot camps is consistent with the juvenile justice system's historical emphasis on rehabilitation, usually incorporating explicit assumptions about the needs of delinquent youths and providing counseling and aftercare programs necessary to address these needs.[13] All of the programs employ military customs and courtesies, including uniformed drill instructors, a platoon structure, and summary punishment of participants, including group punishment under some circumstances. Although there are differences in emphasis, juvenile boot camp programs generally have discovered that they must tailor their environment to participants' maturity levels.[14]

Boot camps for juveniles are generally reserved for midrange offenders; those who have failed with lesser sanctions such as probation but who are not yet hardened delinquents. The shock aspect of the boot camp experience includes incarceration as suggested by the environment within which the program takes place.[15] Only a few programs limit themselves to youths who are nonviolent, have committed their first serious offense, or are being confined for the first time.[16]

Three programs—located in Cleveland, Denver, and Mobile—were funded through the OJJDP, which launched a three-site study of boot camps for youthful offenders in 1991. The program guidelines of these three experimental programs identified six key components to maximize their effectiveness: education and job training and placement, community service, substance abuse counseling and treatment, health and mental health care, individualized and continuous case management, and intensive aftercare services. A 1994 evaluation of the three sites found that the sites were unable to implement the program guidelines fully. Each program "experienced considerable instability and staff turnover" and was unable to "implement and sustain stable, well-developed aftercare services."[17]

Boot camps for juveniles include some type of work detail; most allocate more than half the day to educational and counseling activities, and most include some form of drug and alcohol counseling. In addition, most of the boot camp programs assign graduates to a period of intensive community supervision.[18]

A fair assessment may be that the quality of boot camps depends largely on how much they tailor their programs to participants' maturity levels and how effective they are in implementing and sustaining effective aftercare services. Doris McKenzie and colleagues completed a study of twenty-six juvenile boot camps, comparing them with traditional facilities (the experiences of 2,668 juveniles in twenty-six boot camps were compared to 1,848 juveniles in twenty-two traditional facilities).[19] They found that overall, juveniles in boot camps perceived their environments as more positive or therapeutic, less hostile or danger-ous, and more structured than how juveniles in traditional facilities perceived their environ-ments. Moreover, this study revealed that, over time, youths in boot camps became less antisocial and less depressed than did youths in traditional facilities.[20]

Almost all other follow-ups on juvenile boot camps have found recidivism rates of boot camps to be slightly higher or about the same as those of traditional juvenile facilities.[21] Charges of abuse in boot camps have taken place in almost all states with boot camps. In a 2007 federal report that examined the cases of 10 adolescents who died while at programs in six states, it was found that there was "significant evidence of ineffective management" and "reckless or negligent operating practices." The report revealed evidence that teenag-ers were forced to eat their own vomit, were starved, and were required to wallow for hours in their own excrement.[22]

The disappointing recidivism results, combined with the charges of abuse, have prompted Arizona, Florida, Georgia, Maryland, and South Dakota to shut down or reevalu-ate the "get tough with juveniles" approach popularized in the early 1990s. Arizona removed fifty juveniles. Maryland shut down one boot camp and suspended the military regimens at its other two facilities after reports of systematic assaults. The charges of abuse in Maryland led to the ouster of the state's top five juvenile justice officials.[23] In March 2006, Florida closed all of its boot camps after charges of abuse and the beating to death of a juvenile by boot camp staff.

Panaceas die hard in juvenile corrections, and this highly publicized approach of the past two decades will likely continue to be used in some states across the nation. The recent criticisms and disappointing recidivism data surrounding boot camps will probably result in fewer new programs being established and more scrutiny of existing programs.

Reception and Diagnostic Centers

The purpose of **reception and diagnostic centers**, which are both publicly and privately administered, is to determine which treatment plan suits and which training school is the best placement for each adjudicated juvenile. See Focus on Practice 10–2.

A few of the larger states have reception and diagnostic centers, but for most states, this diagnostic process takes place in one of the training schools. Although staff are more concerned about short-term diagnosis than long-term treatment, youths frequently receive

Focus on Practice 10–2
Indiana Implements a Faith- and Character-Based Housing Program

During the 2005 session, the Indiana General Assembly passed a new law, House Bill 1429 Transitional Dormitories that permits the Indiana Department of Correction (IDOC) to operate faith-based transitional dormitories at any facility operated by the agency. Before the bill was signed into law, IDOC began develop-ing curricula for pilot programs, named Purposeful Living Units Serve (PLUS), at three facilities, one of which was a juvenile one—the Plainfield Juvenile Correctional Facility. Since the open-ing of the three pilot sites, this program has expanded to sixteen facilities. The PLUS program is available at female and male facilities, juvenile and adult facilities, and at all security levels.

The Juvenile PLUS program takes sixteen weeks to complete. In addition to their appropriate treatment program, those in the PLUS program participate in additional programming from a faith- or character-based perspective. The PLUS curriculum focuses on helping students integrate the core values of respect, respon-sibility, honesty, tolerance, and compassion into the education they are already receiving. PLUS program staff members, along with volunteer members, assist the students in this reflection process.

The following topics are used with juvenile participants from a faith or character perspective: religious/cultural diversity, commu-nity service projects, mentoring from a community volunteer, and victim impact/restorative justice. The major goals of PLUS are:

• Better behavior which is measured by fewer conduct reports
• Better adjustment as measured by fewer grievances
• Restitution in the form of community service
• Smoother transition back to home
• Reduced recidivism rates

CRITICAL THINKING QUESTION

What are the advantages and disadvantages of using faith or character-based juvenile facilities in juvenile corrections?

Source: Stephen T. Hall, "Indiana Implements a Faith- and Character-Based Housing Program," *Corrections Today* (March 2008), 62–67.

more attention during this period than at any other time during their confinement. A psy-chiatrist usually will evaluate the youth and will see him or her several times if the youth is confined for a violent crime. A clinical psychologist, or a person with skills in administer-ing psychological tests, frequently will subject the youth to a battery of tests to determine intelligence, attitudes, maturity, and emotional problems. A social worker, meanwhile, com-pletes a case study of each youth. Equipped with background material from the court, which sometimes takes a week or two to arrive at the reception center, the social worker primarily investigates the youth's family background. Academic staff identify any learning problems and determine the proper school placement. Physical and dental examinations also are fre-quently administered. Finally, cottage or dormitory supervisors evaluate the youth's institu-tional adjustment and peer relationships. A case conference on each resident is held once all the reports have been prepared, the needs and attitudes of the youth are summarized, and recommendations are made as to the best cottage or institutional placement.

Although previously staff had evaluated residents over a period of four to six weeks, this process has been condensed today to an average length of stay of thirty-four days.[24] The youth is then transferred to the approved institutional placement, and the diagnostic report goes with him or her. It is not uncommon for this report to receive little attention, so the youth often must repeat a similar process in the admitting institution.

Ranches and Forestry Camps

Ranches and forestry camps are minimum-security institutional placements that are nor-mally reserved for youths who have committed minor offenses or who have been committed to the department of youth services or private corrections for the first time.

In these camps, residents typically do conservation work in a state park, cutting grass and weeds, cleaning up, and doing general maintenance. Treatment programs generally consist of individual contacts with social workers and the child care staff, group therapy, and an occasional home visit. Residents may be taken to nearby towns on a regular or weekly basis to make purchases and to attend community events.

These facilities generally have a minimum amount of security, and only about 20 percent have one or more confinement features other than locked sleeping rooms. They contrast with detention homes and long-term secure facilities, roughly 90 percent of which have one or more confinement features beyond locked sleeping rooms. Unlike in the past, when ranches and camps tended to be populated by white youths, today's ranch and camp resi-dents are 76 percent minority offenders; 12 percent of the residents are female. Also, in keeping with today's concerns, it is important to note that 68 percent of secure facilities screen incoming youth on their first day for suicide risk.[25]

The Hennepin County Home School, one of the most innovative juvenile institutions in the nation, combines features of camps and ranches. Except for a fourteen-bed security unit, it is an open facility, located in a beautiful 160-acre wooded site approximately sev-enteen miles from downtown Minneapolis. The 164-bed facility is coeducational and holds youths who range in age from thirteen to seventeen, with an average age of fifteen. The school receives no status offenders; instead, the population is made up of those who have committed a variety of property and personal offenses. The typical resident has had at least five prior court involvements, and far more than half the residents have been involved in some type of out-of-home placement before their commitment to the Hennepin County Home School.[26]

The institution comprises three juvenile male offender cottages, two juvenile sex offender cottages, one cottage for female offenders, and one Beta cottage for short-term restitution offenders. The residents remain in the Beta program for three to eight weeks and in other cottages for as long as a year. Each resident of the juvenile sex offender cottages would have received an indeterminate sentence, while residents of the other cottages would have received a determinate sentence. The institution's sophisticated treatment program uses such modalities as an educational program that focuses on those with learning dis-abilities, family therapy, transactional analysis, behavior modification, and reality therapy. Horseback riding and canoeing are favorite recreational activities.[27]

Residents are typically more positive about a placement at a forestry camp or ranch than about placement in a training school. They like the more relaxed security, the more frequent community contacts, the shorter stays, and the better relations with staff. Yet some youths cannot handle these settings. They may be too homesick or too victimized by peers, so they repeatedly run away until they are transferred to more secure facilities.

Training Schools

In 2010, there were a total of 2,111 juvenile facilities, holding 66,322 offenders. There were 1,074 public facilities, holding 46,677 juvenile offenders, and 1,037 private facilities, holding 18,645 offenders.[28] Table 10–3 lists the numbers of juveniles detained and in custody in each state.

Eighteen percent of facilities reported that the number of residents they held on the 2010 census date put them at or over the capacity of their standard beds or that they relied on some makeshift beds. The largest facilities were the most likely to be crowded. Overall, the juvenile offender custody population dropped 18 percent from 2008 to 2010. In fact, forty-three states held fewer juvenile offenders in 2010 than in 2008.[29]

The 2006 report, *Safety and Welfare Plan: Implementing Reform in California* reveals the skyrocketing average cost of juvenile institutional care and the average length of stay in months. California spends $115,129 per year to institutionalize a resident, which is greater than the cost in five other states for which data were available (see Figure 10–2). California's length of stay, in 2004, was 25.9 months, which was nearly three times as long as the average of the nineteen states that participated in a nationwide survey (see Figure 10–3). Note that California is one of only six states that have an extended age of jurisdiction that goes beyond the age of twenty. California's length of stay for a juvenile offender goes up to twenty-four years of age, and this has contributed to the lengthy stay for those sentenced to juvenile facilities in California.[30]

California, Illinois, Michigan, New York, and Ohio each has several **training schools**. Smaller states have one training school for boys and another for girls, and Massachusetts and Vermont have no training schools. Although coeducational institutions gained some acceptance in the 1970s and North Carolina even converted all of its training schools into coeducational facilities, that trend seems to have passed.

Organizational Goals and Security Levels

Organizational goals vary among training schools. David Street, Robert D. Vinter, and Charles Perrow's classic study of several public and private training schools identified three basic organizational goals: obedience/conformity, reeducation/development, and treatment. They found that staff in obedience/conformity institutions kept residents under surveillance and emphasized rules. They were also punitive with residents and did not become involved with them. Although staff in reeducation/development institutions demanded conformity, hard work, and intellectual growth, they were more willing to give additional rewards for conformity to positive behavior and to develop closer relationships with residents. Staff in treatment-oriented training schools were much more involved with residents as they worked with, helped, and permitted residents to become more emotionally involved with them.[31]

The philosophy of *parens patriae* has encouraged administrators at training schools to claim rehabilitation as their official goal, but the overall objective for most training schools is to provide a safe, secure, and humane environment. The actual goal depends on the security level of the training school. States that have only one training school for boys and one for girls must enforce all security levels in the one facility, but states with several training schools have the option of developing minimum-, medium-, and maximum-security institutions.

Security features and size vary by the types of facilities. More than 38 percent of facilities reported that at least some of the time residents are locked in their sleeping rooms. Seventy-six percent of public facilities and 62 percent of state facilities reported that they locked residents in sleeping rooms. Few private facilities locked residents in sleeping rooms (5 percent). Among facilities that locked youth in sleeping rooms, most did this at night (85 percent) or when a youth was out of control (77 percent).[32]

TABLE 10-3
Juveniles Detained and in Custody in Each State, 2010

On October 27, 2010, 51% of juvenile facilities were publicly operated; they held 70% of juvenile offenders.

State	Juvenile facilities			Juvenile offenders		
	Total	Public	Private	Total	Public	Private
U.S. total	2,111	1,074	1,037	66,322	46,677	19,645
Alabama	49	13	36	1,059	504	555
Alaska	19	8	11	274	216	58
Arizona	33	15	18	1,398	947	451
Arkansas	33	11	22	748	260	488
California	202	109	93	10,908	9,781	1,127
Colorado	44	13	31	1,367	819	548
Connecticut	10	4	6	286	216	70
Delaware	7	6	1	208	195	13
Dist. of Columbia	9	2	7	250	196	54
Florida	97	34	63	4,526	1,565	2,961
Georgia	33	25	8	2,055	1,694	361
Hawaii	5	3	2	86	79	7
Idaho	20	14	6	477	411	66
Illinois	40	27	13	2,161	1,949	212
Indiana	70	34	36	1,968	1,275	693
Iowa	63	14	49	989	298	691
Kansas	34	16	18	889	695	194
Kentucky	33	28	5	851	806	45
Louisiana	34	17	17	1,087	837	250
Maine	4	2	2	185	181	4
Maryland	30	14	16	892	702	190
Massachusetts	52	19	33	694	261	433
Michigan	62	30	32	1,793	939	854
Minnesota	54	22	32	955	585	370
Mississippi	16	13	3	243	211	32
Missouri	64	60	4	1,237	1,168	69
Montana	13	8	5	153	130	23
Nebraska	12	5	7	680	412	268
Nevada	22	13	9	875	676	199
New Hampshire	7	2	5	130	64	66
New Jersey	39	34	5	1,209	1,178	31
New Mexico	21	15	6	504	458	46
New York	126	31	95	2,356	1,005	1,351
North Carolina	41	24	17	824	577	247
North Dakota	13	4	9	193	76	117
Ohio	77	63	14	2,683	2,508	175
Oklahoma	35	15	20	698	460	238
Oregon	44	23	21	1,267	1,009	258
Pennsylvania	131	29	102	4,403	1,012	3,391
Rhode Island	11	1	10	292	144	148
South Carolina	21	8	13	864	556	308
South Dakota	21	8	13	426	228	198
Tennessee	38	26	12	884	675	209
Texas	97	82	15	4,916	4,451	465
Utah	28	16	12	637	383	254
Vermont	3	1	2	26	13	13
Virginia	52	49	3	1,759	1,709	50
Washington	34	31	3	1,182	1,134	48
West Virginia	26	11	15	467	341	126
Wisconsin	66	20	46	1,077	583	494
Wyoming	16	2	14	231	105	126

Notes: "State" is the state where the facility is located. Offenders sent to out-of-state facilities are counted in the state where the facility is located, not the state where they committed their offense. Data collected from six facilities in Puerto Rico and the Virgin Islands, and 19 tribal facilities are not included.

Source: Authors' analysis of *Juvenile Residential Facility Census 2010* [machine-readable data file].

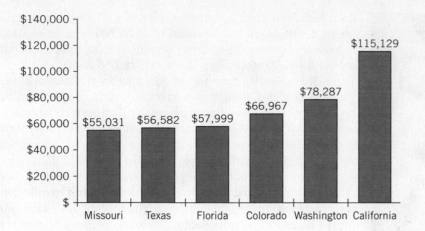

FIGURE 10–2
Comparison of Cost per Youth
per Year in Some States

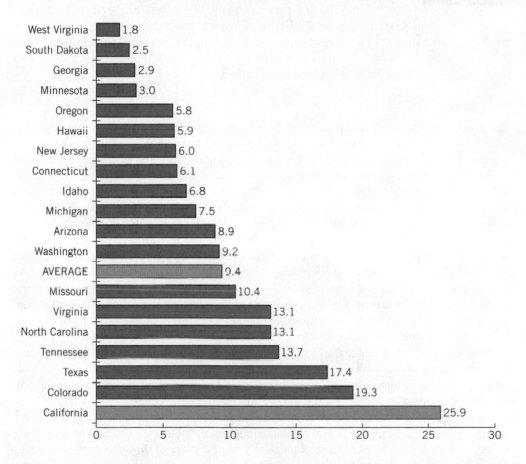

FIGURE 10–3
Average Length of Stay in Months
for Males, 2004

The Lighthouse Youth Center at Paint Creek in southern Ohio is one of the most widely hailed minimum-security institutions in the nation. This privately operated facility has the capacity to hold thirty-three residents but generally has a population of twenty-six or twenty-seven. Juveniles who have committed serious offenses from the southern counties of the state are typically committed to this facility. The facility features a comprehensive and integrated therapeutic approach that emphasizes accountability, social learning, and positive peer culture. The center also includes a school where youth can receive a high school diploma or GED. It has a choir and a choir director, a horticulture program, a pottery program, and a family therapy program and also offers intensive aftercare services to those residents returning to the community.[33]

The physical design of medium- and maximum-security training schools varies from fortress-like facilities with individual cells to open dormitories with little privacy to the homelike atmosphere of small cottages. Maximum-security training schools usually have one or two

▲ Security is a must for correctional facilities. This facility has three layers of security at just the entrance. The first layer consists of a metal detector, the second has a revolving door that can lock, and the third is a door that must be electronically opened by a staff member. Inside are more locked doors throughout the facility.
© Spaces Images/Alamy

fairly high fences and sometimes even a wall. The interiors in maximum-security schools are characterized by bleak hallways, locked doors, and individual cells covered by heavy screens or bars; the youths' daily lives are constrained by rules (see Focus on Practice 10–3).

Medium-security training schools usually are designed as dormitories or cottages. Similar to maximum-security institutions, medium-security training schools usually have the perimeter security of a six- or seven-foot-high fence. The atmosphere in medium-security institutions is more relaxed, and residents can move around more freely than they can in maximum-security training schools.

Institutional security is the primary emphasis in medium- and maximum-security training schools. Administrators' jobs typically depend on their success in preventing runaways. The account of a runaway incident from a maximum-security facility, for example, may receive statewide media coverage. If a runaway commits a violent crime, then even more pressure is placed on institutional administrators and their staff. Fortunately, the federal courts' recent involvement in juvenile institutions has eliminated some of the past abuses that sometimes took place to punish those who attempted to run away and those who actually did but were caught and returned.

Programs

The programs in medium- and maximum-security training schools are much more adequate than those in jails or detention homes and more varied than those in camps and ranches. Most of the larger training schools have a full-time nurse on duty and a physician who visits one or more days a week. Such services as the removal of tattoos are sometimes made available if residents desire them.

Most medium- and maximum-security training schools provide educational programs for residents. These may be accredited by the state for granting high school diplomas, and most offer classes to prepare for a GED test. In addition to the regular academic courses, training schools usually offer basic skills classes consisting of a review of the necessary techniques for reading, writing, and arithmetic; some programs have laboratories and programmed instruction as well. Classes are usually small, and pupils are permitted to progress according to their own rate of learning. The Indiana Boys School is an example of one training school that focuses on the learning disabilities of residents, because Indiana correctional officials believe that learning disabilities are closely linked to delinquent behavior.

Well-equipped male training schools offer vocational training in automobile repair, printing, welding, carpentry, woodworking, barbering, machine shop skills, drafting, and food service. Training schools for girls generally are more limited and offer training programs in sewing, food service, secretarial skills, and beauty care.

As a rule, this vocational training does not help residents secure jobs after release for several reasons: they have difficulty gaining admission to the necessary labor unions; they lack the necessary credentials, such as a high school education; or they simply choose not to pursue the skills they learned. Yet some residents leave the institution and acquire excellent jobs with their acquired skills.

Recreation has always been popular in training schools. Some staff emphasize it because they believe that a tired youth is a well-behaved one or, in the words of one recreation leader, "If we wear them out during the day, they won't fool around at night." Other staff advocate a heavy dosage of recreation because they believe that teaching residents a competitive sport builds self-respect and self-confidence. Still other staff know that juveniles like to play, and recreation is simply a good way for them to entertain themselves and to work off excessive energy. Male residents can compete in softball, volleyball, flag football, basketball, and sometimes even boxing. Cottages usually compete against one another, and the institution may even have a team that competes with other institutions or with teams in the surrounding community. Nonathletic recreational activities include movies, building model cars, painting, decorating the cottages (especially at Christmas), and playing ping-pong, pool, checkers, and chess. Female residents also have recreational possibilities

Focus on Practice 10–3
Rules of Youth Conduct

1. You will not be allowed to fight with peers or staff.
2. You will follow the direct orders of staff.
3. You will treat others with courtesy by avoiding the use of profanity, disrespectful language, or physical gestures.
4. You will avoid sexually inappropriate language or gestures toward staff and other youth.
5. You will avoid horseplay, rowdy-rough play, body punching, shadow boxing, verbal taunting, running, [and] wrestling, which could lead to more serious behavior.
6. You will avoid destroying, defacing, or altering state property or the property of others.
7. You will avoid the use of and/or passing of any form of tobacco, alcohol, and drugs.
8. You will avoid the use of and/or possession of contraband.
9. You will avoid leaving trash on tables, chairs, or floors by placing it in proper receptacles.
10. You will maintain personal grooming, hygiene, and clothing at all times throughout the institution. Appropriate dress includes shirttails in pants, pants zipped and uncuffed (not pegged), belt fastened, shoes tied, and socks on.
11. You will refrain from borrowing, lending, buying, trading, betting, selling, and gambling with peers, staff, or visitors.
12. You will play radios only in acceptable areas and at acceptable times.
13. You will not enter any office or restricted areas without staff permission.
14. You will avoid interfering with staff members' duties.
15. You will report any injury or any change in a medical condition to a staff member immediately.
16. You will not steal.
17. You will adhere to all movement instructions.
18. You will not spit.
19. You will not use any phone without staff supervision.
20. You will not use the restroom without permission.

CRITICAL THINKING QUESTION

Do you believe all these rules are necessary? What rules would you substitute? How would you feel if restricted by these rules?

Source: The Ohio Department of Youth Services, Training Institution, Central Ohio, 1990.

---

such as softball, volleyball, and basketball. In addition to the nonathletic recreational activities that the boys have access to, girls perform in talent shows or dramatic productions, and occasionally, they have dances with boys from nearby training schools.

Religious instruction and services are always provided in state training schools. Larger training schools usually have a full-time Protestant chaplain and a part- or full-time Roman Catholic chaplain. Smaller training schools contract for the services of clergy from a nearby community. Religious services generally include Sunday mass and morning worship, confession, baptism, instruction for church membership, choir, and the participation of community groups. Yet, few residents have much interest in organized religion, and they are usually quite resistant to compulsory attendance at these religious services.

The most widely used treatment modalities are transactional analysis, reality therapy, psychotherapy, behavior modification, guided group interaction, positive peer culture, and drug and alcohol treatment. The errors-in-thinking modality, models to deactivate gangs, and law enforcement education are new forms of treatment recently implemented in a number of private and public training schools across the nation (see Chapter 11 for an examination of these modalities).

Volunteers are an important adjunct to institutional programs, and an institution that has an active volunteer program can greatly enrich the stay of its residents. Some states have better developed volunteer programs than others and have volunteer coordinators in their major institutions. Confined offenders frequently are receptive to services rendered by unpaid volunteers who do not represent authority figures, but who can present the needs of youth and become their advocates in the community. Among the many services that volunteers provide for institutionalized youths are the following:

1. Education—tutoring and supplying books
2. Entertainment—arranging choral programs and other means of entertainment provided by community groups
3. Chaperones—escorting selected youths to community events
4. Counseling—providing one-to-one contact with offenders
5. Family service—contacting and reassuring parents on the progress of their children

6. Financial aid—providing money for youths' canteen accounts

7. Gifts—supplying Christmas and birthday remembrances

8. Job-finding—assisting youths in locating community jobs while they wait to be released or in securing permanent jobs after release

9. Letter writing—helping youths to correspond with family and friends

10. Recreation—playing basketball, softball, and other sports with residents

Finally, prerelease programs are a desired component of institutional activities. These programs typically occur more in minimum- than in medium- or maximum-security facilities. In some training schools, residents are transferred to another cottage or to another location to begin a formal program of community reintegration, including exposure to experiences designed to prepare them for a full return to the community. Techniques of interviewing for a job, instruction in reading the help-wanted section of a newspaper, and assistance in money management are important elements of these programs.

Home furloughs, afternoon trips off campus, and permission to work in the community are typical of the privileges given to residents of prerelease cottages or to those who are just a step or two away from release. Home furloughs are probably the most widely used. Some staff believe that reintegrating youths gradually to the community after a long absence of perhaps several years will help ease the shock of release. Home visits also provide opportunities for residents to interview for jobs and visit with family members. Some training schools allow trips off campus for several hours with parents. This enables parents and children to spend time together away from the institution and possibly to shop for clothing or to eat in a restaurant. Community jobs generally are reserved for those youths who are only two or three months from release and who need financial resources before they return to community living. Staff members are very careful in choosing the residents who are permitted to work in the community. Prerelease programs usually have a positive impact on residents, but home visits, especially, result in a high percentage of runaways.

Social Control of Institutional Residents

Until the last ten years or so, most training schools still employed cottage parents. These individuals often were a retired couple who were attracted to this work because of their interest in young people. Cottage parents sometimes provided a strong parental model for the youth placed in their care. The cottage parents system was continued so long simply because institutional administrators felt that cottage parents created more of a homelike atmosphere for confined delinquents than did staff members who worked eight-hour shifts and lived in the nearby community. But the appearance of increasingly difficult-to-handle delinquents and efforts to develop more efficient institutional management techniques resulted in the replacement of cottage parents with staff members who are commonly called *youth supervisors, youth leaders, cottage supervisors, group supervisors*, or *group-care workers*.

The emerging nature of this role has left a number of questions unanswered: How much of a homelike atmosphere should these supervisors establish in the cottages? How involved should they become with residents? Are they to be only custodial agents, or do they also have treatment responsibilities? What are they to do if residents refuse to cooperate? What personal fulfillment can they expect to achieve in their jobs? Although encumbered by these and other questions, the role of youth supervisor is well established in juvenile correctional settings in this country. For increased control of residents, see Focus on Technology 10–4.

The youth supervisors wake residents in the morning, see to it that their charges wash and dress for breakfast, supervise the serving of breakfast in the cottage or escort residents to a central dining facility, and conduct a brief room inspection. They also ensure that those youths enrolled in the academic and vocational programs go to school and that those who work on the grounds, in the kitchen, or in the community go to their jobs. In medium- and maximum-security training schools, residents are usually escorted to their particular assignments, but on many honor farms, and in conservation camps and ranches, they are permitted movement without staff supervision.[34] A number of recommendations for the management of a juvenile facility are listed in Focus on Policy 10–5.

Focus on Technology 10–4
Technocorrections

Compared with only a few years ago, institutional correctional technologies are not only better and more reliable today, but they are also cheaper. Technology provides innovations that offer substantial savings in staffing and operations costs. A few of the more intriguing technological developments are listed below. These are obviously more widely used in adult corrections, but they appear to be the wave of the future in juvenile corrections as well.

- *Ground-penetrating radar.* Ground-penetrating radar (GPR) is able to locate tunnels inmates use to escape. GPR works almost like an old-fashioned Geiger counter, but rather than detecting metal, the system detects changes in ground composition, including voids such as those created by a tunnel.
- *Heartbeat monitoring.* Now it is possible to prevent escapes by monitoring inmates' heartbeats! The Advanced Vehicle Interrogation and Notification system (AVIAN) works by identifying the shock wave generated by the beating heart, which couples to any surface the body touches. The system takes in all of the frequencies of movement, such as the expansion and contraction of an engine or rain hitting the roof, and determines if there is a pattern similar to a human heartbeat.
- *Nonlethal electrified fences.* Nonlethal electrified containment fences stop inmates without causing severe harm or death. If an inmate tries to climb or cut through the perimeter fence, he or she will receive a nonlethal jolt of electricity, which causes temporary immobilization. At the same time, the system both initiates an alarm to staff that an escape attempt has occurred and identifies its location.
- *Backscatter imaging system for concealed weapons.* This system utilizes a backscatter imager to detect weapons and contraband. The primary advantage of this device over current walk-through portals is that it can detect nonmetallic as well as metallic weapons. It uses low-power X-rays equal to about five minutes of exposure to the sun at sea level. Although these X-rays penetrate clothing, they do not penetrate the body.
- *Body-scanning screening system.* This is a stationary screening system to detect nonmetallic weapons and contraband in the lower body cavities. It uses simplified magnetic resonance images (MRI) as a noninvasive alternative to X-ray and physical body-cavity searches. The stationary screening system makes use of first-generation medical MRI.
- *Transmitter wristbands.* These wristbands broadcast a unique serial number via radio-frequency every two seconds so that antennas throughout the prison can pick up the signals and pass the data via a local area network to a central monitoring station computer. The wristbands can sound an alert when an inmate gets close to the perimeter fence or when a prisoner does not return from a furlough on time; they can even tag gang members and notify guards when rivals come into contact with each other.
- *Personal health status monitor.* The personal health status monitor uses acoustics to track the heartbeat and respiration of a person in a cell. More advanced health status monitors are now being developed that can monitor five or more vital signs at once, and based on the combination findings, can produce an assessment of the inmate's state of health.

This more advanced version of the personal health status monitor may take another decade to develop, but the current version may already help save lives that would otherwise be lost to suicide.

- *All-in-one drug detection spray.* Drug detection sprays can determine whether someone possesses marijuana, methamphetamines, heroin, or cocaine. A specially made piece of paper is wiped on a surface; when sprayed with one of the aerosol sprays, it changes color within fifteen seconds if as little as four to twenty micrograms of the drug is present. A new detection device is now being developed that uses a single spray that will test for all drugs at once. The test paper will turn different colors depending on which drugs the spray contacts, and several positive results will be possible with a single use of the spray.
- *Radar vital signs monitor/radar flashlight.* The handheld radar flashlight can detect the respiration of a human in a cell from behind a 20-centimeter hollow-core concrete wall or an eight-inch-thick cinder block wall. It instantly gives the user a bar-graph readout that is viewed on the apparatus itself. Other miniature radar detectors give users heartbeat and respiration readings. The equipment is expected to be a useful tool in searches for people who are hiding, because the only thing that successfully blocks its functioning is a wall made of metal or conductive material.
- *Personal alarm location system.* It is now possible for prison employees to carry a tiny transmitter linking them with a computer in a central control room. In an emergency, they can hit an alarm button and transmit a signal to the computer that automatically records whose distress button has been pushed. An architectural map of the facility appears onscreen, showing the exact location of the staff member in need of assistance.
- *Under-vehicle surveillance system.* An under-vehicle surveillance system utilizes a drive-over camera that records a video image of the license plate and the underside of any vehicle entering or leaving the secure perimeter of the prison. This system allows prison staff to check each vehicle for possible escape attempts and keeps a digital recording of every vehicle that enters or exits the prison.
- *Biometric recognition.* A new biometric system, the facial-recognition system, utilizes facial recognition by matching more than two hundred individual points on the human face with a digitally stored image. The system is currently used to control access to buildings and rooms inside buildings, and it will become more and more common in the near future.

Sources: Jeff Goodale, Dave Menzel, and Glen Hodgson, "High-Tech Prisons: Latest Technologies Drive Cost Savings and Staff Efficiencies," *Corrections Today* 67 (July 2005), 78; John Ward, "Jump-Starting Projects to Automatic Correctional Processes," *Corrections Today* 66 (2006), 82–83; John Ward, "Security and Technology: The Human Side," *Corrections Today* 66 (2004), 8; Frank Lu and Laurence Wolfe, "Automated Record Tracking (SWMART) Application," *Corrections Today* 66 (2004), 78–81; Gary Burdett and Mike Rutford, "Technology Improves Security and Reduces Staff in Two Illinois Prisons," *Corrections Today* 65 (2003), 109–10; and Tony Fabelo, "Technocorrections: The Promises, the Uncertain Threats," in *Sentencing & Corrections: Issues for the 21st Century Series*, no. 5 (Washington, DC: National Institute of Corrections, May 2000).

Cottage parents typically remain in the cottage to prepare lunch and to take care of other cottage tasks, but youth supervisors are generally assigned duties that keep them occupied until they pick up their residents for lunch. These duties may include school patrol, inspection of the rooms of residents on restriction, and outside patrol of the recreation field.

Residents are met at the academic area and escorted back to the cottage for lunch, after which they are returned to school or to other assigned duties. The afternoon shift of supervisors picks up the youths in school and brings them back at the end of the day. If the institution has an active group program and youth supervisors are involved, they usually hold several group meetings a week after school. Guided group interaction, positive peer culture, and transactional analysis are the most popular group modalities used in these sessions. Time generally is structured after school because many administrators believe that problems arise when youths have a great deal of free time, but in some institutions the period from the end of school until the evening meal is a free one.

After the evening meal, especially during warmer weather, residents are permitted to engage in outside recreational activities. They may participate in organized activities or may choose to throw a football, shoot a basketball, pitch a softball, or talk with a friend. Staff must at this time be particularly alert, because runaway attempts often take place during these outside activities. Following a shower and a little television, residents are usually sent to their rooms and lights are out around 10 P.M.

The night shift, normally consisting of one person, takes over at 11 or 11:30 P.M. This person's job basically is to make certain that youths do not escape from the cottage during the night and to be available if a problem such as an illness or escape attempt occurs. The youth supervisor generally spends the greater part of the eight-hour shift sitting at a desk in the staff office and responding to a periodic phone check on cottage security.

As part of their daily tasks, youth supervisors also intervene in conflicts among residents, respond to emergency situations, search residents and residents' living quarters, orient new residents, advise residents concerning personal or institutional progress, and assign tasks to residents and monitor their performance.

Thinking like a Correctional Professional

You' have been contacted the governor's office about the feasibility of developing a faith- and character-based juvenile facility in your state. The governor would like to have a faith-based facility for males as well as for females. How would you approach this issue? What in your opinion would be the advantages and disadvantages of such facilities?

Differences Between Public and Private Training Schools

A little more than half (53 percent) of juvenile facilities holding offenders in 2008 were private, but public facilities held over two-thirds (69 percent) of the juvenile offenders. Compared with public facilities, private facilities hold a smaller share of delinquents and a larger share of status offenders.[35] Table 10–3 compares the various types of juvenile custody facilities and shows how the numbers and profiles of these facilities have changed. Public facilities hold more than three-quarters of those confined for homicide, robbery, aggravated assault, weapons possession, and technical violations of probation or aftercare. Nevertheless, as noted in the *2006 Juvenile Offenders in Correctional Facilities*, "public and private facilities had fairly similar offense profiles in 2003."[36]

David Shichor and Clemens Bartollas's examination of the patterns of public and private juvenile placements in one of the larger probation departments in southern California, however, revealed that few offense differences existed between juveniles sent to public and private facilities. Although juveniles placed in private facilities had more personal problems and those in public institutions were somewhat more delinquent, placements in private facilities included delinquents with serious offenses.[37]

Second, privately administered training schools are probably better known to the public than are state facilities because of their public solicitation of funds. Boys' Town in Nebraska and Glen Mills School in Pennsylvania (near Philadelphia) are two private institutions that are well-known to the public.[38] Private training schools also have

The Superintendent of a Training School

PREPARATION FOR THE JOB

The superintendent is expected to have college degree with a background in criminology, sociology, social work, public administration, or some related field. More and more, it is advantageous for superintendents to have a master's degree. As part of their preparation for the job, the superintendent is required to have sound understanding of all aspects of institutional life including both direct and indirect services. This means that superintendents must be exposed to both the treatment and custodial aspects of administration.

QUALIFICATION AND EDUCATIONAL REQUIREMENTS

The superintendent is ultimately responsible for everything that takes place within the facility. The superintendent typically delegates responsibility for custodial services and/or program services to assistants. The superintendent's job responsibility encompasses establishment of policy, planning, civil suits, institutional moderating, staff development, and fiscal management. The effective treatment of youth will not occur until the facility has developed and maintained a positive prosocial culture sponge that is safe, supportive, and nurturing. It's a difficult goal to achieve but administrators must make it a priority. Building a positive culture is about leadership which is having the persistence to communicate often what the facility stands for, and what is and is not acceptable behavior.

DEMAND FOR

There are limited jobs in juvenile corrections for superintendents. Sometimes, they are recruited from outside the agency, even from another state, but other times they are promoted from within the institution. There is a high turnover in terms of this position, especially in private facilities.

SALARY

Salaries of prison wardens vary from one state to the other; wardens tend to be very well paid in most states and the job usually comes with a number of perks. For example, in California, the Federal Bureau of Prisons, and a number of other states, wardens make more than a $100,000 a year. However, superintendents in juvenile facilities make less than prison wardens, and their salaries are usually in the $60–$80,000 range for state facilities and less for private facilities.

Source: Clemens Bartollas, *Becoming a Prison Warden: Striving for Excellence* (Maryland: American Correctional Association, 2004).

---

avoided most of the scathing critiques faced by public training schools during the past two decades.

Third, proponents of private training schools claim that they are more effective than public training schools because they have a limited intake policy that allows them to choose whom they want to admit; they have more professional staff; they have better staff–client ratios; they are smaller; and they are more flexible and innovative.

Gaylene Styve Armstrong and Doris Layton MacKenzie examined forty-eight residential juvenile correctional facilities in nineteen states (sixteen private and thirty-two public facilities). Using both self-report surveys and data from facility records, they found that private facilities had a more extensive admission process, had a higher percentage of juvenile delinquents incarcerated for property offenses, were smaller, and held a higher percentage of males than female offenders. Yet they found that there were no significant differences between private and public juvenile facilities in terms of the quality of their environments.[39]

The advantage of private over public rehabilitation programs may have been more true in the past than in the present. The increased use of interstate compact of children has resulted in some private schools taking as many children as they can get. Indeed, some private institutions exploit the inadequate licensing procedures of the states to warehouse youths as cheaply as possible and thereby reap good profits.[40] It is also true that private training schools are smaller than public ones, but even so, half of the private institutions hold one hundred or more children; these are still too large to effectively rehabilitate juveniles. It is probably accurate to say that private institutions offer greater flexibility of programs because they are relatively free from political processes and bureaucratic inertia. Yet, Bartollas and Shichor's comparison of the attitudes of staff and residents at a state training school for adolescent males in the Midwest and at a private facility in the same state found that the enforcement of excessive rules in the private placement created a rigid cottage structure and living environment.[41] Moreover, Shichor and Bartollas found that private placements in southern California do not always provide the services of professional treatment personnel that they purport to provide.[42] Perhaps the old adage is true after all: the best institutions are private ones and the worst institutions are also private ones.

Juvenile Victimization

Institutionalization is a painful process for most youthful offenders, though it is clearly more painful for some than for others. Juvenile victimization is one of the most troubling aspects of juvenile institutionalization.

Many studies of training schools for boys reflect an inmate society in which the strong take advantage of the weak:

- In their study of the State Industrial School for Boys in Golden, Colorado, Gordon E. Barker and W. Thomas Adams found two types of residential leaders: one held power through brute force and the other ruled through charisma. According to these researchers, residents were involved in an unending battle for dominance and control.[43]

- Howard W. Polsky studied a cottage in a residential treatment center in New York. The staff in Cottage Six were unable to keep residential leaders from exploiting peers. The social hierarchy the researchers identified in this cottage had a pecking order; those at the bottom of the status hierarchy found life so debilitating that most of them ended up in mental hospitals.[44]

- Sethard Fisher studied a small training school in California and identified victimization and patronage as two of the major behaviors taking place. He defined **victimization** as "a predatory practice whereby inmates of superior strength and knowledge of inmate lore prey on weaker and less knowledgeable inmates."[45] *Patronage* referred to youths' building of "protective and ingratiating relationships with others more advantageously situated on the prestige ladder." Fisher also saw victimization as being made up of physical attack, agitation, and exploitation.[46]

- Clemens Bartollas, Stuart J. Miller, and Simon Dinitz's *Juvenile Victimization: The Institutional Paradox* examined the culture that end-of-the-line delinquents established in a maximum-security institution in Columbus, Ohio (TICO). In this training school, dominant youths exploited submissive ones in every possible way. Ninety percent of the one hundred fifty residents were involved in this exploitation matrix; 19 percent were exploiters who were never themselves exploited, 34 percent were exploiters and victims at different times, 21 percent were occasionally victims and never exploiters, and 17 percent were chronic victims. Ten percent of the residents were neither victims nor exploiters.[47]

- In a fifteen-year follow-up evaluation of this training school, Miller, Bartollas, and Dinitz found that the negative youth culture described in the 1976 study still thrived and that the strong still victimized the weak. Staff members were more disillusioned than they were at the time of the first study. They also were more fearful of victimization from residents.[48]

- Martin Forst, Jeffrey Fagan, and T. Scott Vivona, relying on data collected in both juvenile facilities and adult correctional facilities, found that 1.7 percent of youth in training schools reported having been sexually attacked while in the facility and 8.6 percent (five times as many) of juveniles in adult correctional facilities reported such victimization while incarcerated during the previous twelve months.[49]

- Following the passage and signing of the Prison Rape Elimination Act of 2003, three major government-sponsored research effectors have provided additional insights about the conditions and scope of sexual victimization of confined juveniles. The first drew on a nationally representative sample of 7,073 youths held in 203 facilities and found that 3.6 percent (1 in every 28) of juveniles in residential facilities reported having been sexually victimized at least one time.[50] A second study based on the administrative records data collected by the Bureau of Justice Statistics as part of the PREA-mandated study of sexual violence incidence and prevalence in U.S. correctional institutions found that in 2004, the rate of sexual victimization reported by authorities in juvenile institutions was more than 5 percent of confined juveniles.[51] The third study was conducted in twelve facilities during 2007 that were located in six states and included nine male facilities, one female facility, and two coeducational facilities. According to the study, 19.7 percent of responding youth reported at least one incident of sexual victimization during the previous twelve months of confinement.[52]

See the Evidence-Based Practice feature for more about sexual victimization in juvenile facilities.

In sum, although many exceptions to the lawless environment described in these studies exist, an environment in which the strong take advantage of the weak, the fact is that the quality of life for male residents in too many training schools is extremely problematic. Even more troubling are the high rates of staff involvement in the sexual victimization of residents.

What About Facilities for Females?

The **social roles** in training schools for girls are generally based on a family or **kinship social structure**:

- Rose Giallombardo's examination of three training schools for girls in various parts of the United States found that aggressive girls tended to adopt the male sexual roles ("butches") and put pressure on new residents to adopt the female sexual roles ("fems").[53]

- Christopher M. Sieverdes and Bartollas's study of six Southeastern coeducational training schools also revealed the presence of the family social structure in the girls' cottages. This study further divided the seven social roles found in these living units into aggressive, manipulative, and passive roles.[54]

- Alice Propper examined three coeducational and four girls' training schools scattered through the East, Midwest, and South, five of which were public and two of which were private Catholic facilities. In contrast to previously held assumptions, she found little overlap between pseudo-family roles and homosexual behavior; participation in homosexuality and make-believe families was just as prevalent in coeducational as in single-sex institutions, and homosexuality was as prevalent in treatment—as in custody-oriented facilities.[55]

Evidence-Based Practice
Sexual Victimization in Juvenile Facilities

In a 2010 report, *Sexual Victimization in Juvenile Facilities*, the Bureau of Justice Statistics (BJS) conducted the first nationally representative survey of sexual abuse in residential juvenile facilities. This BJS study surveyed 26,550 adjudicated youth held in state-operated and large local or privately operated juvenile facilities; overall 91 percent of the youth in these facilities were male and 9 percent were female. It was found that an estimated 12 percent of youth in state facilities and large nonstate facilities (representing 3,220 youth nationwide) reported one or more incidents of sexual victimization by another youth or facility staff member in the previous months or since admission.

- About 2 percent of youth (700 nationwide) reported an incident involving a peer and, alarmingly, 10.3 percent (2,730) reported an incident involving facility staff.
- About 4.3 percent of youth (1,150) reported having sex or other sexual activity with facility staff as a result of some type of force, 6.4 percent of youth (1,710) reported contact with facility staff without force or threat.
- Approximately 95 percent of all youth reporting staff sexual misconduct said they had been victimized by female staff. In 2008, 42 percent of staff in state juvenile facilities were female.
- Rates of sexual victimization varied among youth: 9.1 percent of females and 2.0 percent of males reported unwanted sexual activity with other youth.

- Youth with a sexual orientation other than heterosexual reported significantly higher rates of sexual victimization by another youth (12.5 percent) compared to heterosexual youth (1.3 percent).
- Youth who had experienced any prior sexual assault were more than twice as likely to report sexual victimization in the current facility (24.1 percent), compared to those with no sexual assault history (10.1 percent).
- Among youth victimized by another youth, 20 percent said they had been physically injured, and 5 percent reported they had sought medical attention for their injuries.
- Among youth victimized by staff, 5 percent reported a physical injury, and fewer than 1 percent had sought medical attention.

CRITICAL THINKING QUESTION

If a juvenile facility must be safe for residents, then this BJS report, as well as other recent ones, is a serious indictment of this nation's policy of juvenile institutionalization. How can juveniles be better protected from each other as well as from exploitative staff?

Source: Allen J. Beck, Paige M. Harrison, and Paul Guerino, *Sexual Victimization in Juvenile Facilities Reported by Youth, 2008–2009* (Washington, DC: U.S. Government Printing Office, Bureau of Justice Statistics, 2010), 1.

In sum, similar to institutions for adolescent males, those for adolescent females also provide an environment in which strong girls take advantage of weaker ones and where aggression is the dominant force in the living environment.

Racial Differences in Juvenile Justice Processing

When racial/class gender disparities do occur, they take place at any stage of processing within the conviction and incarceration rates with respect to their population base. A serious issue, of course, is whether this disproportionate representation in the juvenile justice system is due to a pattern of racist decision making.

Janet L. Lauritsen, in examining what is known about racial and ethnic differences in juvenile offending, offers the following conclusions, which have wide support in the literature:

- Rates of juvenile homicide are higher for minorities than for white youthful offenders. Variations do exist in rates of lethal violence among minority groups.

- Official data suggest disproportionate involvement in nonlethal violence on the part of African American youth. When arrest data are restricted to specific forms of nonlethal violence, African American youth appear to be disproportionately involved in robbery, aggravated assault, and rape.

- Juvenile property crime data show that African American youths are slightly more involved than white youths, although the level of disproportionate involvement varies by type of property crime.

- Arrest data show that white youths are disproportionately involved in alcohol offenses, and that American Indian youths are slightly more likely than African American or Asian youths to be arrested for these crimes.

- African American youths are disproportionately arrested for drug abuse violations and drug use, but data from juveniles on their own drug use and selling do not confirm the differences between African American and white youths suggested by the arrest data. Indeed, white youths are somewhat more likely to report using marijuana (ever and in the past thirty days), selling any drugs, and selling marijuana.

- The arrest data for weapons violations indicate that African American youths are disproportionately likely to be arrested for weapon violations.[56]

Lauritsen contends that the empirical evidence suggests that the relationship between race and ethnicity and juvenile involvement in delinquency is complex and contingent on the type of offense. Although the most commonly occurring crimes exhibited few group differences, the less frequent and serious crimes of violence showed generally higher levels of African American and Latino youth involvements.[57]

Donna Bishop, in what will likely become a definitive article on race and ethnicity in juvenile justice, concludes that minority overrepresentation is attributable to inequities in the juvenile justice process rather than the incidence, seriousness, and persistence of their offending. Minorities are overrepresented among youths held in secure detention, petitioned to juvenile court, and adjudicated delinquent. Among those who are adjudicated delinquent, minorities are more often committed to the "deep end" of the justice system. When confined, they are more likely to be housed in large public institutions rather than privately run, specialized treatment facilities or group homes. Furthermore, at "the end of the line," prosecutors and judges are quicker to relinquish jurisdiction over minorities, transferring them to criminal court for prosecution and punishment as adults.[58]

Carl E. Pope and William H. Feyerherm's highly regarded assessment of the issue of discrimination against minorities reveals that two-thirds of the studies they reviewed found "both direct and indirect race effects or a mixed pattern [being present at some stages and not at others]."[59] They add that selection bias can take place at any stage and that small racial differences may accumulate and become more pronounced as minority youth are processed into the juvenile justice system.[60]

The Coalition for Juvenile Justice (the former National Coalition of State Juvenile Justice Advisory Groups) brought national attention to this problem of **disproportionate minority confinement** in their 1988 annual report to Congress. In that same year, Congress responded to this evidence of disproportionate confinement of minority juveniles in secure facilities by amending the Juvenile Justice and Delinquency Prevention Act (JJDPA) of 1974 by mandating that states participating in the Formula Grants Program must address efforts to reduce the proportion of the youth detained or confined in secure detention facilities, secure correctional facilities, jails, and lockups who are members of minority groups if such proportion exceeds the proportion such groups represent in the general population.[61]

During the 1992 reauthorization of the JJDPA, Congress substantially strengthened the effort to address disproportionate confinement of minority youth in secure facilities. Disproportionate minority confinement was elevated to the status of a "core requirement" alongside deinstitutionalization of status offenders, removal of juveniles from adult jails and lockups, and separation of youthful offenders from adults in secure institutions.[62]

The JJDPA was reauthorized in late 2002 and took effect in October 2003. The first three mandates, for the most part, stayed the same. The fourth mandate was changed from disproportionate minority confinement to **disproportionate minority contact**. The focus is currently on efforts to reduce minority contact with the system. Programs geared to delinquency prevention, as well as a multipronged approach to DMC, are encouraged.[63]

Prior to 2002, the JJDPA required states to assess their level of disproportionate minority confinement (DMC) by using a statistic dividing the proportion of a given minority group of youths who were detained or confined in a state's secure detention facilities, secure correctional facilities, jails, and lockups by the proportion that group represented in the general population. If this DMC Index was significantly greater than 1.0, the state was required to develop and implement a plan to reduce the disproportionality.[64]

However, it was soon evident that problems existed in interpreting the DMC Index. First, comparing one jurisdiction's index to another was difficult. The value of the DMC

Evidence-Based Practice
Disproportionate Minority Confinement/Contact

The disproportionate minority confinement/contact (DMC) directive was designed to ensure that youthful offenders, regardless of their race or position in the social structure, receive equitable treatment within the juvenile justice system. Recently Michael Leiber and his associates examined the impact of the DMC on the processing of juvenile offenders within a state juvenile justice system. They chose Iowa for their study because it is one of the states that was selected to serve as a model for the implementation of strategies to reduce DMC. Their research focused on the extent that race influences decision makers and whether the implementation of the DMC effort would result in the reduction or elimination of a race effect on decision-making outcomes. After controlling for a wide array of variables, they found that African Americans were more likely than whites to be referred at intake for further proceedings both before and after the implementation of the DMC initiative. The relative influence of race on intake decision making did not change following the implementation of the DMC initiative.

In some instances the researchers found that the DMC created an effect in opposition to what was intended. During the decade prior to the implementation of the DMC mandate, white adolescents who committed property offenses were less likely than African Americans to be referred to juvenile court for further proceedings. However, during the decade after the implementation of the DMC mandate, whites who committed property offenses were more likely than African Americans to be referred to juvenile court for further proceedings. While this change can be viewed as a movement toward equality, it was actually an overcorrection. Rather than helping African American youths it penalized white offenders.

Decision making was influenced by gender and family household structure. African American males were more likely than their white males to receive a court referral, and this racial disadvantage remained in the post-DMC period. After DMC was in place, African Americans who came from single-parent households were more likely to be referred to juvenile court than those who resided in two-parent households, although this was not the case for whites. Stated differently, after the DMC mandate, the effects of race became more covert and indirect, operating through family structure. One might conclude that this result reflects decision makers' reliance on stereotypes involving assessments of the African American single-parent family as dysfunctional and less able than either the white single-parent household or the African American two-parent household to supervise and socialize children effectively. In sum, there was little to no evidence that the DMC legislation impacted decision makers to rely less on race and more on legal and extralegal considerations at intake. The DMC initiative, to some extent, may have reduced the influence of being African American on the judicial decision-making process, but not quite in the manner anticipated.

Source: Michael Leiber, Donna Bishop, Mitchell Chamlin, "Juvenile Justice Decision-Making Before and After the Implementation of the Disproportionate Minority Contact (DMC) Mandate," *Justice Quarterly* 28, no. 3 (2011), 460–92.

Index was related in part to the proportion of minority youths in the general population. Those communities with low minority proportions could have very high DMC Indexes, in contrast with communities with high proportions. Another problem, even more critical, was that the index provided limited guidance on where to look for the source(s) of disparity. Was disparity introduced at all stages of the system? Or did it accumulate from beginning to end? Or was it introduced only at the earliest stage and then remained through the end stages?[65]

Measuring the disparity at each decision point gives a better understanding of where disparity is introduced and/or magnified in the handling of cases by the juvenile justice system. To address problems with the DMC Index, the Office of Juvenile Justice and Delinquency Prevention developed a tool, called the **DMC Relative Rate Index**, to measure the level of disparity at each decision point.[66]

In sum, the disproportionate numbers of minority youths confined in long-term training facilities, as well as the disproportionate numbers of these youths processed through the juvenile justice system, is a serious issue. Hopefully, the recent federal intervention will, in the long run, result in the reduction of minority representation in long-term institutional care.

Although the DMC initiative was begun with great promise, the following Evidence-Based Practice feature shows that achieving racial justice can often be a difficult path.

Do Institutionalized Youths Have Rights?

The rights of juveniles are a major issue in juvenile justice. The Children's Rights Movement, as system, challenges whether institutionalized youths have sufficient legal protection. It argues that confined juveniles ought to receive three basic rights: the right to treatment, the right not to be treated, and the right to be free from cruel and unusual punishment. The rights of confined offenders have been examined by the federal courts and the Civil Rights of Institutionalized Persons Act.

Right to Treatment

Several court rulings have found that a juvenile committed to a training school has a right to treatment. In the Illinois' *White v. Reid* (1954) case, the court ruled that juveniles could not be held in institutions that did not provide for their rehabilitation.[67] In a Rhode Island case, the *Inmates of the Boys' Training School v. Affleck* (1972) decision also stated that juveniles have a right to treatment because rehabilitation is the true purpose of the juvenile court.[68] In *Nelson v. Heyne* (1974), Indiana's Seventh Circuit agreed with the district court that inmates of the Indiana Boys' School have a right to rehabilitative treatment.[69]

Moreover, in the 1973 *Morales v. Turman* decision, the U.S. District Court for the Eastern District of Texas held that a number of criteria had to be followed by the state of Texas in order to ensure that proper treatment would be provided to confined juveniles. These criteria included minimum standards for assessing and testing children committed to the state; minimum standards for assessing educational skills and handicaps and for providing programs aimed at advancing a child's education; minimum standards for delivering vocational education and medical and psychiatric care; and minimum standards for providing a humane institutional environment.[70] This finding was overruled by the Fifth Circuit Appeals Court on the grounds that a three-judge court should have been convened to hear the case. On *certiorari* to the U.S. Supreme Court, the Court reversed the court of appeals and remanded the case. What may affect future considerations of confined juveniles' right to treatment is whether the order of the district court can withstand the assault against it.

Right of Access from the Courts and to Refuse Treatment

Juveniles committed to training school have a constitutional right of access to the courts. They can petition the juvenile court for relief from earlier judicial decisions. Institutionalized juveniles also have a right to refuse treatment. In addition, treatment should be voluntary and should not be related to the length of institutional confinement. The standards of the Institute of Judicial Administration of the American Bar Association (IJA-ABA), for example, propose that children may voluntarily refuse services except in three cases: "services juveniles are legally obliged to accept (as school attendance), services required to prevent clear harm to physical health, and services mandated by the court as a condition to a nonresidential disposition."[71]

Right to Be Free from Cruel and Unusual Punishment

Some courts have applied the Eighth Amendment, barring cruel and unusual punishment, to juvenile institutions to forbid the use of corporal punishment in any form, the use of Thorazine and other medications for the purpose of control, and the use of extended periods of solitary confinement.[72] The *Pena v. New York State Division for Youth* (1976) decision held that the use of isolation, hand restraints, and tranquilizing drugs at Goshen Annex Center was punitive and antitherapeutic and, therefore, violated the Eighth Amendment.[73] In the case of *Inmates of the Boys' Training School v. Affleck*, the court also condemned such practices as solitary confinement and strip cells, and it established minimum standards for youths confined at the training school.[74] In the *Morales v. Turman* decision in Texas, the court found instances of physical brutality and abuse, including staff-administered beatings and tear gassings, homosexual assaults, excessive use of solitary confinement, and the lack of clinical services.[75] In *Morgan v. Sproat*, a 1977 Mississippi case, the court found that youths were confined in padded cells with no windows or furnishings and only flush holes for toilets and were denied access to all programs or services except a Bible.[76] Finally, in *State v. Werner*, the court found that residents were locked in solitary confinement; were beaten, kicked, slapped, and sprayed with mace by staff; were required to scrub floors with a toothbrush; and were forced to stand or sit for prolonged periods without changing position.[77] In each of these cases, the courts condemned these cruel practices.

CRIPA and Juvenile Correctional Facilities

As of November 1997, the Civil Rights Division had investigated three hundred institutions under the Civil Rights of Institutionalized Persons Act (CRIPA). Of these, seventy-three institutions, or about 25 percent, were juvenile detention and correctional facilities.

Social Policy and Juvenile Justice
Recommendations for Juvenile Facility Management

- *Pursue excellence in the facility.* Successful administrators set high standards. They not only expect excellence, they demand it.
- *A meaningful institutional program requires a carefully thought-out plan of action or strategy.* Administrators must determine where they want to go (their vision) and understand how they are going to get there (implementing the vision).
- *Management should be proactive.* An anticipatory and preventive approach is fundamental in maintaining institutional control.
- *Professionalism should be held up as a goal to all staff.* Staff development and training are important steps in staff seeing themselves as professionals.
- *Cleanliness and orderliness of the facility are absolute necessities.* Cleanliness shows that the staff are in control.
- *The institutional environment must be safe for youths and staff.* If an institution is not a safe environment, little positive can be accomplished.
- *Both residents and staff must be treated with dignity and respect.* The norm for staff is that they treat residents as they would want their own sons or daughters to be treated.
- *Good programming by committed staff must be available for those youths who want to make positive changes in their lives.*

Treatment programs must be delivered effectively to those interested residents, especially those with additions and anger management.
- *An effective system of accountability for both staff and youths is necessary.* Sufficient consequences are required for inappropriate behavior, especially when rules are broken.
- *The services that are promised must be delivered to youths when they are scheduled to be delivered.* It is important for the system to be predictable and trusted to do what was promised.
- *Facilities, as much as possible, should have the following characteristics.* They should be as close as possible to juveniles' families; offer smaller, personalized services; be family-friendly; and be managed in a caring manner.
- *The administrator must be a model of integrity in every way, both inside and outside the facility.*
- *Accreditation is an important process in a juvenile residential facility offering humane confinement and mission effectiveness.*

Source: Joseph Heinz, Theresa Wise, and Clemens Bartollas, *Successful Management of Juvenile Residential Facilities: A Performance-Based Approach* (Alexandria, VA: American Correctional Association, 2010), 43–44.

FIGURE 10–4
The Three Major Rights of Juveniles

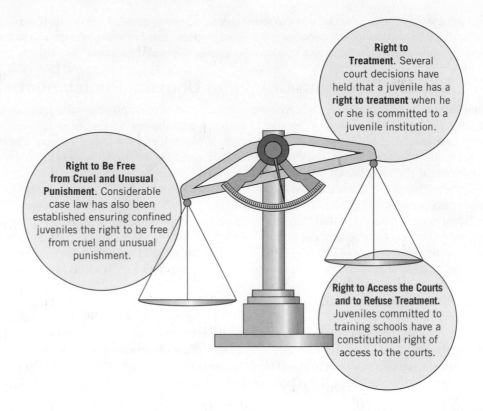

The Civil Rights Division is monitoring conditions in thirty-four juvenile correctional facilities through consent decrees in Kentucky, New Jersey, and Puerto Rico. The consent decree filed in Kentucky covers all thirteen juvenile facilities in the state; the decree in New Jersey is for one facility, and in Puerto Rico, for twenty facilities.[78]

Figure 10–4 illustrates the three major rights of juveniles.

SUMMARY

LEARNING OBJECTIVE 1: Describe the purpose and operation of short-term confinement facilities including jails, detention centers, and shelter care facilities.

More than seven thousand juveniles continue to be placed in the problematic settings of adult jails. Detention centers that are temporary holding centers for juveniles vary from the traditional detention centers to model facilities for youth. Shelter care facilities are more open settings in which youths in trouble, often status offenders, are placed for a short period of time

LEARNING OBJECTIVE 2: Describe the purpose and operation of various long-term correctional facilities, including boot camps, reception and diagnostic centers, and ranches/forestry camps.

Boot camps were widely regarded in the early 1990s, and supporters often viewed them as a panacea for juvenile corrections. More recently, high recidivism rates, as well as charges of abuse, have persuaded some states, including Arizona, Florida, Georgia, Maryland, and South Dakota, to shut these programs down or to reevaluate them. Reception and diagnostic centers found in larger states are used to determine the best treatment plan for delinquents

adjudicated to long-term institutional care. Ranches and forestry camps are minimum-security institutional placements that are normally reserved for youths who have committed minor offenses.

LEARNING OBJECTIVE 3: Describe the goals, programs, and operation of training schools.

Disagreements on social policy for training schools range from arguing for an increase in the number of these facilities to arguing for closing all training schools. There are those who believe that with proper staff–resident ratios and improved programs, these facilities can provide well for juveniles in trouble. Others assert that training schools are violent, inhumane, and damaging to all children. Some believe that these facilities should be located in the community, and still others recommend isolating them in rural areas. Beyond these disagreements is the reality that the number of youthful offenders confined in residential facilities increased 27 percent between 1991 and 2006. Private training schools were usually reserved for status offenders, while delinquents were adjudicated to public training schools; but the offense backgrounds of those placed in private and public training schools are quite similar now.

LEARNING OBJECTIVE 4: Summarize the rights of juveniles who are institutionalized.

Juveniles have three basic rights: the right to treatment, the right too refuse treatment,, and the right to be free from cruel and unusual punishments. The rights of confined offenders have been examined by the federal courts and the Civil Rights of Institutionalized Persons Act (CRIPA).

LEARNING OBJECTIVE 5: Summarize the factors that should be taken into consideration when implementing a confinement policy for juveniles.

- If at all possible, youths should be kept in their home communities.

- If confinement is necessary, the detention home or training school (jails should never be used for children) should be in or very near the home community.

- The facilities should remain small, with detention home populations not exceeding thirty and training school populations not exceeding fifty.

- The facilities should be pleasantly furnished and security features provided only after adequate staffing, programming, and a satisfactory, safe physical plan have been developed. If such facilities are absolutely necessary, they should be completely committed to full use of community resources and, wherever possible, should integrate residents into community programs.

KEY TERMS

attention homes, p. 212
boot camps, p. 213
detention centers, p. 212
disproportionate minority contact, p. 228
DMC relative rate index, p. 230

jails, p. 210
kinship social structure, p. 227
ranches and forestry camps, p. 216
reception and diagnostic centers, p. 215
shelter care facilities, p. 212

social roles, p. 227
training schools, p. 217
victimization, p. 226

REVIEW QUESTIONS

1. How would you describe the social structure of residents in training schools?
2. Why are training schools damaging to some youths?
3. How can training schools be improved?
4. What are the major shocks a juvenile faces upon release to the community?

5. On the basis of everything you have read and heard about boot camps, would you recommend their continued use? Why or why not?

GROUP EXERCISES

1. *Group Work:* Identify the different types of short-term care facilities, their characteristics, and their clientele.
2. *Group Work:* Identify the different types of long-term care facilities, their characteristics, and their clientele.
3. *Writing to Learn Exercise:* Write a paragraph on each of the following: the characteristics of short- and long-term confinement facilities, their goals, and the types of programs likely to be found in each.

4. *Group Work:* Discuss the characteristics of both private and public juvenile facilities. How is the life of residents structured in these facilities?
5. *Writing to Learn Exercise:* Each student is to write a paragraph on the social organization of inmates in cottages and the roles inmates play in that structure. Critique and revise.
6. *Group Work:* Discuss the legal rights of youths in juvenile facilities.

WORKING WITH JUVENILES

You are sitting in your office, and you received a phone call indicating a resident's mother has died. You need to call him in your office and tell him about his mother. How will you do this? What will you say to him? What will you say if he can or cannot attend the funeral?

NOTES

1. Christopher Murray, Chris Baird, Ned Loughran, Fred Mills, and John Platt, *Safety and Welfare Plan: Implementing Reform in California* (Sacramento: California Department of Corrections and Rehabilitation, Division of Juvenile Justice, 2006).

2. David W. Springer, *Transforming Juvenile Justice in Texas: A Framework for Action* (Austin, TX: Blue Ribbon Task Force Report, 2007).
3. "Juvenile School Would Grow," *Hartford Courant,* February 10, 2008; Alison Leigh Cowan, "New Connecticut Law May

Save a Troubled Prison for Juveniles," *New York Times,* July 30, 2007; Christine Smart, "Juvenile Injustice," *CJ News Junkie,* July 19, 2006; and Nan Schnitzler, "Connecticut Juvenile Training School to Close," *New England Psychologist,* October 2005.

4. "Abuse Claims Plague Juvenile Detention," *Star Bulletin* 63 (March 3, 2008).

5. According to Rosemary C. Sari, the number of youths confined in jail each year during the 1970s ranged from 90,000 (Children's Defense fund) to 100,000 (Fund to National Council on Crime and Delinquency). See Sari, "Gender Issues in Juvenile Justice," *Crime and Delinquency* 29 (1983), 390.

6. Howard N. Snyder and Melissa Sickmund, *Juvenile Offenders and Victims: A National Report* (Pittsburgh: National Center for Juvenile Justice, 1995), 72.

7. Ibid., 236.

8. Charles E. Frazier and Donna M. Bishop, "Jailing Juveniles in Florida: The Dynamics of Compliance to a Sluggish Federal Referral Initiative," paper presented at the annual meeting of the American Society of Criminology, Baltimore, MD, November 1990, 4.

9. Ira M. Schwartz, Linda Harris, and Laurie Levi, "The Jailing of Juveniles in Minnesota: A Case Study," *Crime and Delinquency* 34 (1988), 146; David Steinhart, "California's Legislature Ends the Jailing of Children: The Story of a Policy Reversal," *Crime and Delinquency* 34 (1988), 169–70.

10. David Steinhart and Barry Krisberg, "Children in Jail," *State Legislature* 13 (1987), 12–16.

11. Dale G. Parent et al., *Conditions of Confinement: Juvenile Detention and Corrections Facilities* (Washington, DC: Office of Juvenile Justice and Delinquency Prevention, 1994), 180–81. For other criticisms of detention practices, see Ira M. Schwartz and William H. Barton, eds., *Reforming Juvenile Detention: No More Hidden Closets* (Columbus: Ohio State University Press, 1994).

12. Roberta C. Cronin, *Boot Camps for Adult and Juvenile Offenders: Overview and Update*, Final Summary Report (Washington, DC: National Institute of Justice, 1994), 37. See also Mark Jones and Steven Cuvelier, "Are Boot Camp Graduates Better Probation Risks?" paper presented at the annual meeting of the American Society of Criminology, New Orleans, LA, November 1992; and Thomas W. Waldron, "Boot Camps Offer Second Chance to Young Felons," *Corrections Today* 52 (1990), 144–69.

13. Jean Bottcher, "Evaluating the Youth Authority's Boot Camp: The First Five Months," paper delivered to Western Society of Criminology, Monterey, CA, February 1993; Institute for Criminological Research and American Institute for Research, *Boot Camp for Juvenile Offenders: Constructive Intervention and Early Support—Implementation Evaluation Final Report* (New Brunswick, NJ: Rutgers University Press, 1992).

14. Cronin, *Boot Camps for Adults and Juvenile Offenders.*

15. Anthony W. Salerno, "Boot Camps: A Critique and a Proposed Alternative," *Journal of Offender Rehabilitation* 20 (1994), 149.

16. Ibid., 37.

17. Michael Peters et al., *Boot Camps for Juvenile Offenders: Program Summary* (Washington, DC: Office of Juvenile Justice and Delinquency Prevention, 1997), 3, 35.

18. Ibid.

19. Doris Layton MacKenzie et al., "The Impact of Boot Camps on Traditional Institutions of Juvenile Residents: Perceptions, Adjustment, and Change," *Journal of Research in Crime and Delinquency* 38 (August 2000), 279–313.

20. Ibid., 279.

21. Brent Zaehringer, "Juvenile Boot Camps: Cost and Effectiveness vs. Residential Facilities," Koch Crime Institute White Paper Report, accessed at http://www.hrf.uni-koeln.de/sitenew/content/e/filejuvbootcamps.pdf.

22. For this report, see Diana Jean Schemo, "Report Recounts Horrors of Youth Boot Camps," *New York Times,* December 11, 2007, accessed September 20, 2012, at http://www.nytimes.com/2007/10/11/washington/11report.htm.

23. Marks, "States Fall Out of (Tough) Love with Boot Camps," *Christian Science Monitor,* December 27, 1999, 1.

24. For the classification system in California, the most highly developed in the nation, see Murray et al., *Safety and Welfare Plan*, 12–18.

25. For the most recent data on ranches and camps, see Snyder and Sickmund, *Juvenile Offenders and Victims: 2006 National Report*, 208, 221–27; Sickmund, "Juvenile Residential Facility Census, 2002: Selected Findings."

26. A basic description of this program is included in a brochure developed by the Hennepin County Home School (n.d.). See also the website of the Hennepin County Home School.

27. One of the authors has interviewed Teresa Wise and other administrators of the Hennepin County Home School and was given this information. See also http://www.co.hennepin.mn.us/portal/site/HCInternet/menuitem.14c0cacfe630405b258caf10b1466498/?vgnextoid=393ebe2f09b7c010VgnVCM1000000f094689RCRD.

28. Sarah Hockenberry, Melissa Sickmund, and Anthony Sladky, *Juvenile Residential Facility Census, 2010: Selected Findings* (Washington, DC: U.S. Department of Justice, Juvenile Offenders and Victims: National Report Series Bulletin, July 2013), 2.

29. Ibid., 6.

30. Murray et al., *Safety and Welfare Plan*, 2.

31. David Street, Robert D. Vinter, and Charles Perrow, *Organizations for Treatment: A Comparative Study of Institutions* (New York: Free Press, 1966).

32. Hockenberry et al., *Juvenile Residential Facility Census, 2008*, 4.

33. "Youth Center at Paint Creek Provides Opportunities," *Lighthouse Views,* Winter 2008, 1.

34. Experiences of one of the authors in several juvenile institutional systems have revealed these activities of youth supervision.

35. Snyder and Sickmund, *Juvenile Offenders and Victims: 2006 National Report*, 197.

36. Ibid.

37. David Shichor and Clemens Bartollas, "Private and Public Juvenile Placements: Is There a Difference?" *Crime and Delinquency* 36 (April 1990), 286–99.

38. Glen Mills School, for example, was featured in Bill Howard, "Florida Tries to Clone Preppy Glen Mills," *Youth Today: The Newspaper on Youth Work* 5 (July–August 1996), 1, 12, 13.

39. Gaylene Styve Armstrong and Doris Layton MacKenzie, "Private versus Public Juvenile Correctional Facilities: Do Differences in Environmental Quality Exist?" *Crime and Delinquency* 49 (October 2003), 542–63.

40. Shichor and Bartollas, "Private and Public Juvenile Placements."

41. Clemens Bartollas and David Shichor, "Juvenile Privatization: The Expected and the Unexpected," paper presented at the annual meeting of the American Society of Criminology, Baltimore, MD, November 1990.

42. Shichor and Bartollas, "Private and Public Juvenile Placements," 286–99.

43. Gordon E. Barker and W. Thomas Adams, "The Social Structure of a Correctional Institution," *Journal of Criminal Law, Criminology and Police Science* 49 (1959), 417–99.

44. Howard W. Polsky, *Cottage Six: The Social System of Delinquent Boys in Residential Treatment* (New York: Russel Sage Foundation), 69–88.

45. Sethard Fisher, "Social Organization in a Correction Residence," *Pacific Sociological Review* 5 (Fall 1961), 89.

46. Ibid., 89–90.

47. Clemens Bartollas, Stuart J. Miller, and Simon Dinitz, *Juvenile Victimization: The Institutional Paradox* (New York: Sage Publications, 1976), 131–50.

48. Stuart J. Miller, Clemens Bartollas, and Simon Dinitz, *Juvenile Victimization Revisited: A Fifteen-Year Follow-Up at TICO* (unpublished manuscript).

49. Martin Forst, Jeffrey Fagan, and T. Scott Vivona, "Youth in Prisons and Training Schools: Perceptions and Consequences of the Treatment–Custody Dichotomy," *Juvenile and Family Court Journal* 40 (1989), 1–14.

50. Andrea Sedlack, "Sexual Assault of Youth in Residential Placement," presentation at Bureau of Justice Statistics Workshop, Washington, DC, January 18, 2005.

51. Allen J. Beck and Timothy A. Hughes, *Sexual Violence Reported by Correctional Authorities 2004* (Washington, DC: Bureau of Justice Statistics, 2005).

52. Cited by Richard Tewksbury, "What We Know About Sexual Violence in Juvenile Corrections," paper presented at the 2007 Winter Conference, Grapevine, TX.

53. Rose Giallombardo, *The Social World of Imprisoned Girls: A Comparative Study of Institutions for Juvenile Delinquents* (New York: Wiley, 1974).

54. Christopher M. Sieverdes and Clemens Bartollas, "Social Roles, Sex, and Racial Differences," *Deviant Behavior* 5 (1982), 203–18.

55. Alice Propper, *Prison Homosexuality: Myth and Reality* (Lexington, MA: D. C. Heath, 1981).

56. Janet L. Lauritsen, "Racial and Ethnic Differences in Judicial Offending," in *Our Children, Their Children: Confronting Racial and Ethnic Differences in American Juvenile Justice,* edited by Darrell F. Hawkins and Kimberly Kempf-Leonard (Chicago: University of Chicago Press, 2005), 91–95.

57. Ibid., 99.

58. Donna M. Bishop, "The Role of Race and Ethnicity in Juvenile Justice Processing," in *Our Children,* 23. See also *Federal Advisory Committee on Juvenile Justice: Annual Report 2010* (Washington, DC: U.S. Government Printing Office, 2010).

59. Carl E. Pope and William H. Feyerherm, "Minority Status and Juvenile Justice Processing: An Assessment of the Research Literature," *Criminal Justice Abstract* (June 1990), 333–34. See also Donna Bishop and Charles E. Frazier, "The Influence of Race in Juvenile Justice Processing," *Journal of Research in Crime and Delinquency* 25 (August 1988), 242.

60. Pope and Feyerherm, "Minority Status and Juvenile Justice Processing."

61. Donna Hamparian and Michael J. Leiber, *Disproportionate Confinement of Minority Juveniles in Secure Facilities: 1996 National Report* (Champaign, IL: Community Research Associates, 1997), 1.

62. Ibid.

63. Howard N. Snyder and Melissa Sickmun, *Juvenile Offenders and Victims: 2006 National Report* (Washington, DC: National Center for Juvenile Justice and Office of Juvenile Justice and Delinquency Prevention, 2006), 189.

64. Ibid.

65. Ibid, 190.

66. Ibid.

67. *White v. Reid*, 125 F. Supp. 647 (D.D.C. 1954).

68. *Inmates of the Boys' Training School v. Affleck*, 346 F. Supp. 1354 (D.R.I. 1972).

69. *Nelson v. Heyne*, 355 F. Supp. 451 (N.D. Ind. 1972).

70. *Morales v. Turman*, 364 F. Supp. 166 (E.D. Tex. 1973).

71. H. Swanger, "Juvenile Institutional Litigation," *Clearinghouse Review* 11 (1977), 22.

72. See *Lollis v. N.Y. State Department of Social Services*, 322 F. Supp. 473 (S.D.N.Y. 1970) and N. N. Kittie, *The Right to Be Different: Deviance and Enforced Therapy* (Baltimore: Johns Hopkins University Press, 1971), for more information on this subject.

73. *Pena v. New York State Division for Youth*, 419 F. Supp. 203 (S.D.N.Y. 1976).

74. *Inmates of the Boys' Training School v. Affleck.*

75. *Morales v. Turman.*

76. *Morgan v. Sproat*, 432 F. Supp. 1130 (S.D. Miss. 1977).

77. *State v. Werner*, 242 S.E.2d 907 (W. Va. 1978).

78. Patricia Puritz and Mary Ann Scali, *Beyond the Walls: Improving Conditions of Confinement for Youth in Custody Report* (Washington, DC: Office of Juvenile Justice and Delinquency Prevention, 1998), 4–7.

ZUMA Press/Newscom

Learning Objectives

1. Describe the goals of aftercare.
2. Decide who is responsible for releasing youths from training school.
3. Summarize why so many youths fail on aftercare.
4. Describe the role of the aftercare officer.
5. Describe means by which aftercare can be improved.

Marco, a nineteen-year-old Latino, was incarcerated for being the "trigger man" on a drive-by shooting. As he neared the end of his sentence, Marco vowed that he was finished with gang violence, telling me: "I'm not putting in any more work, though... no more drive-bys." He did intend to sell drugs when he was back in the community, but he had thought carefully about how to reduce the risk. He said that he would not take a lot of risk and would not be a visible dealer out on the street corner. Instead, he planned to make his deals with a pager; with a pager, he said, "You know who is calling you, and you can arrange to meet in a safe place." He also said that he would not carry the drugs in plastic baggies, because "baggies are used to prove intent to sell/ deliver," which would carry a longer, more severe sentence.[1]

Release is the prime goal for a confined youth. The days, weeks, months, and sometimes years spent in confinement are occupied by thoughts and fantasies of release or even escape. For many youths, the thoughts and desires of release become all-consuming passions and govern every action of theirs. Youths who have been intractable become compliant, the weak feign strength, the ill pretend health, and the worst become the best. Every action becomes a show for the benefit of those who can expedite release—the staff, social workers, teachers, chaplains, and others.

An estimated one hundred thousand youthful offenders are released each year from secure correctional institutions, including jails, juvenile facilities, and adult prisons. Many juveniles who leave these facilities have multiple risk factors and are struggling with co-occurring mental health and alcohol and drug issues and also have difficulty succeeding in school.[2] These problems, all too typically, are not sufficiently addressed in residential facilities. Specifically, researchers found shortcomings in substance abuse, mental health, and education programs provided to juveniles held in residential services.[3] In addition, some juveniles may be exposed to violence and trauma that leave them even more troubled when they are released to the community.[4]

These problems are further compounded when unprepared juveniles are sent back to surroundings that may have contributed to their delinquent acts in the first place—communities that have high rates of poverty and crime, poorly performing schools, and few community health and social services. Crossover youth are particularly vulnerable to future difficulties because they frequently come from abusive or neglectful families. To successfully rejoin their families and communities, these youths need aftercare services that can assist them in developing the skills and protective factors they need to resist further risky and unlawful behavior and, ultimately, to avoid return to custody.[5]

Despite this need, many state and local juvenile justice and child welfare systems fail to focus on or provide aftercare or reentry programs for juvenile offenders. Much of the current work in juvenile justice is focused on the front-end issue of confinement, rather than on the back end of reentry. As a result, little is known about the effective reentry of juveniles.[6]

This chapter explores juvenile aftercare, the final episode in the correctional endeavor. Beginning with a definition and a discussion of the release process and considering it from the perspectives of resident, staff, and society, the chapter reviews the problems and the opportunities facing the youth on aftercare status, the aftercare officer, and society once a youth is released. General operational problems are considered, and, finally, the issue of improving aftercare is discussed.

What Is Aftercare and What Are Its Objectives?

Aftercare can be defined as "as reiterative services that prepare out-of-home placed juveniles for reentry into the community by establishing the necessary collaborative arrangements with the community to ensure the delivery of prescribed services and supervision."[7] The term *aftercare* is a misnomer because aftercare involves much more than "after an offender is released." It ideally begins at or after sentencing and continues through confinement and a youth's release to the community. It requires a seamless set of systems across formal and informal social control networks and a continuum of community services to prevent the reoccurrence of delinquent behaviors. Public–private partnerships are often involved in expanding the capacity of youth services.[8]

A major concern in juvenile justice in the past forty years has been the development of a workable philosophy and concept of aftercare. A number of objectives for juvenile aftercare, or **parole**, have been developed through the years:

1. Release residents from confinement at the most favorable time for community adjustment.
2. Prepare youths for their successful reintegration into the community on completion of aftercare.
3. Reduce the crimes committed by released juveniles.
4. Reduce the violent acts committed by released offenders.
5. Increase community confidence in parole.
6. Alleviate overcrowding of training schools.
7. Monitor youthful offenders as they refrain from abusing or trafficking drugs.
8. Discourage the return of youths to street gangs

The achievement of these objectives requires extensive planning and research. For example, to determine the most favorable time for release requires far more knowledge than is presently available. Many new and innovative techniques for prediction can be developed; research must enable releasing authorities to compare the costs of leaving juveniles in institutions with the possible harm to society if they are released.

Planning must clearly take place in each institution. Such planning is necessary if the functions of the various community agencies are to be articulated with institutional services. Evaluation procedures must be developed to assist institutions and agencies to determine their success. Realistic goals and objectives must be spelled out. Thus, the necessary guidelines for implementing a more effective aftercare policy can be formulated so that the number of arbitrary, whimsical, and idiosyncratic aftercare revocations by individual aftercare officers can be reduced.

Who Is Responsible for Releasing Youths from Training Schools?

Juveniles released from training school are placed on aftercare or parole status. The bases on which they are released from these schools vary, and so do those individuals responsible for making the release decision. In forty-four states the authority for making this decision for juveniles rests with the executive branch of state governments. In four states the decision is made by probation or parole officers, and in three states other board agencies make the decision.[9] In Illinois and several other states, juvenile judges have the authority to remove juveniles from training schools.

At present, some controversy exists about who should make the aftercare decision. Some believe that staff who work with the residents know them best and are, therefore, the best judges of when they should be released. The staff see their charges daily, work with them in therapy, interact with them informally, and observe their interaction with peers. The twenty-four-hour living experience should, according to the proponents of institutional decision making, make the institution and its staff outstanding experts on the progress and character of their youths. Such experience, it is believed, will enable institutional officials to know better than anyone the optimum time for release.

This argument has been countered by another: the institutional officials and staff are prone to overreact to residents' inability to get along in the institution. If offenders can stay out of institutional problems and can remain on the good side of the staff members, or if they reach a certain age, or if the institution becomes overcrowded, they are deemed ready for release. But if a youth has a personality conflict with a particular staff member or fights to protect himself or herself, he or she may not be able to get out. According to this view, staff members sometimes are prejudiced or opposed ideologically to what the youth believes. The accusation also is made that staff members occasionally release troublemakers just to get them out of the institution.

Many believe that the decision to release residents should be made by independent agencies and boards that are not swayed by what happens in institutions. One major advantage of setting up independent agencies and boards is that no longer would release be based on factors irrelevant to a resident's ability to get along in the community. Release would be decided impartially, regardless of whether or not a few rules were violated or a resident did talk back to staff from time to time.

Institutional staff members, however, believe that those independent agencies and boards are too far removed from institutions to know what is going on within them. Staff members further believe that autonomous boards are unrealistic and uninformed about the problems that staff members and other officials face in working with difficult and troublesome youths. They also believe that important aspects of various cases are ignored by independent boards, resulting in inappropriate decisions at times. Moreover, staff members believe that the establishment of these boards downgrades their own professional competence and introduces an unnecessary complication. See Table 11–1 for arguments concerning the release decision for youths released from training school.

Some question whether any method is effective in assessing when to release an institutionalized youth. For example, a study of 16,779 juveniles in Florida released from confinement programs to the community found that no consistent relationship existed between length of confinement and recidivism. The length of confinement, this 2008 study found, was only significant for youths released from high-risk facilities and male offenders.[10]

States that use determinate or mandatory sentencing for juveniles usually have determined the time of institutional release when the youth is committed to training school. A variation of this approach is for the length of confinement to be determined within the department responsible for institutional care, using such guidelines as offense severity, previous offense history, and, perhaps, other criteria. For example, in the late 1980s, the Ohio Department of Youth Services established an Office of Release Review in order to provide a structured, centralized, objective release decision-making process. The goal of this office was to set a length of institutional stay for each juvenile felony offender proportionate to the severity of his or her offenses and the impact on the victims. A parole hearing officer scored each youth using a specialized worksheet. In most cases, the score established the length of stay unless overriding conditions were present, as determined by an administrative committee within the office.[11] Today, Ohio and other states are moving toward a decision tree or logical analysis framework to broaden the number of youthful risk and need factors that can be considered in making the release decision.[12]

In Minnesota, the release of a juvenile from a training school has been until recently the responsibility of a juvenile aftercare hearing officer who used a scale incorporating the severity of the offense history. For example, a youthful offender who committed

---

TABLE 11–1
Controversy About Training School Release Decisions

Decision Makers	Support For	Arguments Against
Support for institutional staff	Are the best judge for when youths are ready for release	Make inappropriate decisions, based on factors, unreleased to community adjustment
Independent agencies	Decisions are not based on irrelevant factors.	These boards are too far removed from institutions to know what is going on within them.
Determinate or mandatory sentencing	Guidelines of offense severity, previous offense history	Personal factors pertinent to a juvenile's case are not considered.

FIGURE 11–1
Projected Institution Length of Stay
in Months

Severity Level	Most Serious Current Offense*	Delinquent History Factors			
		0	1	2	3
I	Violation of Probation Contempt of Court Prostitution Assault—4th & 5th Degree Driving Under Influence of Alcohol Negligent Fires Burglary—3rd & 4th Degree Damage to Property—$2,500 or less Forgery—$2,500 or less Possession of Controlled Substance Receiving Stolen Goods—$2,500 or less Theft—$2,500 or less Unauthorized Use of Motor Vehicle Dangerous Weapons (not including firearms) Trespass All Other Misdemeanors and Gross Misdemeanors	4–3	5–3	6–4	7–5
II	Assault—2nd & 3rd Degree Burglary—2nd Degree Damage to Property—Over $2,500 Forgery—Over $2,500 False Imprisonment Receiving Stolen Goods—$2,500 Felony Possession/Sale of Controlled Substance Theft from Person Theft—Over $2,500 Arson—3rd Degree Criminal Sexual Conduct—3rd & 4th Degree Simple Robbery Terroristic Threats Criminal Vehicular Homicide Dangerous Weapons—Firearms	6–3	7–4	8–5	9–6
III	Burglary—1st Degree Criminal Negligence Resulting in Death Aggravated Robbery Arson—1st & 2nd Degree Criminal Sexual Conduct—1st & 2nd Degree Kidnapping Manslaughter Assault—1st Degree	10–6	11–7	12–8	13–9
IV	Murder (all degrees)**	**	**	**	

*Commitment offenses not specifically listed shall be placed on the grid at the discretion of the hearing officer at the time of the initial institution review.
**Murder shall be dealt with on an individual basis.

first-degree burglary would have a severity level of 3. If his or her delinquent history factors equaled 3, this offender would normally be paroled somewhere between the ninth and thirteenth months. This scale, consistent with other sentencing structures for juveniles in Minnesota was based on the justice model.[13] Minnesota, too, is reworking the state's procedures for release.

Early release from training school due to overcrowding conditions has complicated this decision-making process. In six states, a parole board appointed by the governor considers early release for institutionalized juveniles. This is not done as frequently as in adult corrections, especially because youths are serving much shorter sentences in juvenile institutions than would be true in adult corrections.

This impasse on decision making for institutional release will not be easily resolved. Institutional officials and staff deserve the wide criticisms they have received. Little evidence exists that juvenile parole boards have been sharply criticized in recent years. The recent move in juvenile justice to use formalized and structured instruments to make release decisions also has its share of problems. Unless researchers can predict with some accuracy the risks and needs of youths before release to facilitate the success of those released on aftercare or parole, this approach becomes extremely questionable.

Assessment of Those on Aftercare

One of the means of assessing juveniles on aftercare is the Level of Service Inventory-Revised (ISI-R). The Level of Service Inventory–Revised™ (LSI-R™) is a quantitative survey of offender attributes and their situations relevant to level of supervision and treatment decisions. The LSI was developed in the late 1970s in Canada through a collaboration of probation officers, correctional managers, practitioners, and researchers. It is designed for ages 16 and older, and helps predict parole outcome, success in correctional halfway houses, institutional misconducts, and recidivism.

The LSI–R Manual explains the use of the LSI–R as well as summarizes research studies on its reliability and validity. The LSI–R can be used by probation and parole officers and correctional workers in detention facilities, jails, and correctional halfway houses to assist in the allocation of resources, to help make decisions about probation and placement, to make appropriate security level classifications, and to assess treatment progress.

Forms

The LSI-R QuikScore

The LSI-R QuikScore™ form is professional-completed and includes the necessary elements for scoring the instrument. The QuikScore™ forms contain special aids that make scoring of the test very quick and efficient, while minimizing potential for key errors.

Scales

- Criminal History
- Education/Employment
- Financial
- Family/Marital
- Accommodation
- Leisure/Recreation
- Companions
- Alcohol/Drug Problems
- Emotional/Personal
- Attitudes/Orientation[14]

The **LSI-R:SV** is a screening instrument ideal for use when a complete LSI-R™ assessment may not be feasible, due to time constraints or insufficient staff resources. The LSI-R:SV consists of eight items selected from the full LSI-R. It provides a brief summary of dynamic risk areas that may require further assessment and possible intervention. Research with the LSI–R:SV shows it is predictive of a variety of outcomes important to offender management. Among probation samples, the LSI–R:SV scores predicted violent recidivism and violations while under community supervision. Among incarcerated offenders, scores have predicted success in correctional halfway houses and institutional misconduct.[15]

Characteristics of Those on Aftercare

Unlike adult corrections, in which an article, *Probation and Parole in the United States,* reveals each year the characteristics of adults on probation and parole, the listing of the characteristics on aftercare lacks up-to-date data.[16]

Howard N. Snyder has contributed to our understanding more of the portrait of juveniles returning to the community. He reported that nearly one hundred thousand juvenile offenders are released annually from juvenile facilities. These youths have spent a considerable proportion of their adolescent years in custody. Most are male, minority, and nonviolent offenders. About half live in single-parent families and about one-fourth have a sibling. In addition, about one-fourth have a father who has been incarcerated. Most have not completed eighth grade, which can be compared to one-fourth of similarly aged youth across the nation. The prevalence of the presence of a learning disability is higher than that in the general adolescent population. Excluding alcohol, two-thirds indicate regular drug use. Two-thirds of youths adjudicated to training school have a mental health disorder, with the rate for females being higher. The majority of females leaving a correctional facility have a history of physical or sexual abuse. Finally, a majority of these juveniles will be returning home to an impoverished family and neighborhood.[17]

In a more recent 2010 study, authors Laura S. Abrams and Susan M. Snyder reported that the vast majority of this population is made up of older (81 percent) members of an ethnic minority group (36.6 percent non-Hispanic white, 39.4 percent African American, and 19.8 percent Hispanic). The majority came from single-parent homes (56 percent) or did not live with a parent (26 percent) prior to confinement and approximately one out of eleven were parents themselves.[18] See Table 11–2 for the characteristics of youths returning to the community.

Risk Control and Crime Reduction

The current emphasis in aftercare, as in juvenile probation, is on short-term behavior control. Consequently, we can assume that, even if more states adopt determinate sentencing statutes for juveniles, the likelihood is that mandatory aftercare services will continue to

---

TABLE 11–2
Empirical Portrait of Youths Returning to the Community

Size of Returnees	About one hundred thousand per year
Gender	Mostly male. The majority of females have a history of physical or sexual abuse
Race/Ethnicity	Mostly minority
Offense Background	Most are nonviolent offenders
Age	Mostly older
Family Background	About half live in single-parent households, one-fourth have a father who has been incarcerated, and about 10 percent are parents themselves
Educational Background	Most have not completed eighth grade and have high rates of learning disabilities
Mental Health	Two-thirds of youth have a mental health disorder
Previous Custodial Experience	Most have spent the majority of their adolescence in custody
Economic Background	The majority will be returning home to an impoverished family and neighborhood

Source: Howard Snyder, "An Empirical Portrait of the Youth Re-entry Population," *Youth Violence and Juvenile Justice* (2004), 39–55; and Laura S. Abrams and Susan M. Snyder, "Youth Offender Re-entry: Models for Intervention and Directions for Future Inquiry," *Children and Youth Services Review* 12 (December 2010), 1787–95.

be provided for those released from public and private placements; indeed, some cities and states are beginning to use the terms *aftercare probation* or *probation aftercare* to emphasize the necessity of planning early for the release of juveniles. These efforts are directed, for the most part, to **intensive supervision programs**. Nevertheless, these in-house detention and electronic monitoring programs still have not received the attention that they have in adult probation. Juvenile aftercare also emphasizes drug and alcohol urinalysis (sometimes called *drug drops*) and turned toward "boot camp" programs in the 1980s and 1990s as a means of releasing juveniles early from training school.

Intensive Aftercare Supervision

Intensive aftercare supervision (IAS) can be conceived as operating "in the context of decision making and planning for the *early release* of juveniles from secure confinement" and as "imposing higher levels of supervision on youth(s) being released after serving a *full* institutional term."[19] In terms of intensive aftercare supervision, three populations of juveniles can be targeted: all parolees, medium- to low-risk parolees, and high-risk parolees.[20]

More than eighty intensive aftercare supervision programs were active across the United States in the 1980s and 1990s. The most noteworthy of these intensive programs were those in the thirty counties of Pennsylvania; the Lifeskills '95 program, which was the Violent Juvenile Offender Research and Development Program in Boston, Memphis, Newark, and Detroit; the Skillman Intensive Aftercare Project; the Michigan Nokomis Challenge program; the PARJO program in New York; and the Office of Juvenile Justice and Delinquency Prevention (OJJDP) IAP project.

One recent concern has been to develop an integrated theoretical framework for guiding intensive supervision of chronic juvenile offenders. The Intensive Aftercare Program (IAP) model is a combination of social control, strain, and social learning theories, and it focuses on the reintegrative process. Its basic assumptions are that serious and chronic delinquency is related to weak controls produced by social disorganization, inadequate socialization, and strain; that strain is produced by social disorganization independent of weak controls; and that peer group influences intervene as a social force between youths with weak bonds and/or strain on one hand and delinquent behaviors on the other.[21]

The IAP project has been implemented in four pilot programs: Colorado (Arapahoe and Jefferson counties), Nevada (Clark County), New Jersey (Camden and Essex counties), and Virginia (Norfolk County). The participation of New Jersey counties ended in 1997, but the other programs carried through on preparing high-risk offenders for progressively increased responsibility and freedom in the community. The well-developed transition components that begin shortly after a youth is adjudicated to an institution and continue through the early months of community adjustments are particularly strict about these programs. The results of the first five years of implementation (1995–2000) reveal a dramatically improved level of communication and coordination between institutional and aftercare staff as well as the ability to involve parolees in community services almost immediately after institutional release.[22]

Intervention Programs

Intervention strategies, such as counseling, behavioral programs, probation, restitution, employment, and academic and vocational programs, seek to prevent delinquency by changing youthful offenders' behavior. Successful treatment approaches appear to have a number of characteristics in common:

- They target specific dynamic and criminogenic characteristics. Research indicates that dynamic criminological factors include attitudes, cognitions, behavior regarding education, peers, employment, authority, substance abuse, and interpersonal relationships.[23]

- They implement a plan, which is strictly adhered to, by trained personnel. Programs must have therapeutic integrity, which means that they must be delivered according to a specific plan and design.

- They require staff and offenders to make frequent contact. Frequent and quality interaction between service providers and offenders is essential for effective intervention.

- They use cognitive and behavioral treatments. A widely observed program evaluation finding is that the most effective intervention programs use structured, focused treatment based on behavioral, skill-oriented, and multimodal methods rather than less structured, less focused approaches.

- They target offenders with the highest risk of recidivism. Several programs have found that the treatment for delinquent behavior is most effective when it is provided to juveniles with the highest risk of recidivism.[24]

What Are the Downsides of the Current Reentry Process?

The juvenile justice system gives some attention to the juvenile's preparation for return to the community. Home visits, especially in private facilities, are frequently made available to juveniles before their release. In Minnesota and other states, parole, or aftercare, officers will visit institutionalized juveniles to help them plan for their community reintegration. Home placements and usually school or job assignments must also be finalized in most jurisdictions before the juvenile is released.

Yet, as with adult corrections, few training schools place much emphasis on prerelease programs that attempt to prepare residents for community experiences. Those that do typically include information and instruction on such matters as job opportunities and employment aids; the importance of being on time; motor vehicle driver training; legal problems and contacts; basic financial management; personal health practices and proper diet; perspectives on family responsibilities; human relations; and the dangers of alcohol, drugs, and cigarettes.

Nor are many juveniles provided the opportunity to work in the community before their release. Private facilities appear to be more concerned than public institutions about juveniles having a work experience prior to their release, but the obstacles to such programs include the security risks involved, the lack of staff to locate jobs and supervise residents, and the inability of residents to handle jobs constructively for more than a short period of time. In juvenile facilities providing such programs, residents leave the facility in the morning, usually with lunch and enough money for transportation, and return at the end of the work day. Some residents are provided transportation to and from work; others depend on public transportation.

Furthermore, in contrast to the number of halfway-in placements for juvenile probationers, relatively few halfway-out houses exist for juvenile parolees. The negative response that juveniles frequently had to such placements in the past apparently has discouraged this movement in juvenile corrections. What has taken the place of halfway-out facilities for juveniles are independent-living placements. Although such placements usually are made for juveniles who lack adequate placements with families or relatives, they do not offer a gradual transition to release that halfway-out residential facilities would permit.

It can be argued that juveniles who have been confined for only a few months in training school do not need **reentry programs** as much as do adults who may have spent years within prison walls. Some adults experience an unexpected jolt when released suddenly and without preparation. They may feel disoriented and confused by the transition from controlled living to life in free society. In contrast, this disorientation and confusion appears much less frequently with the released juveniles. In addition to the much shorter period of confinement, the openness of many training schools permits juveniles to move back and forth between the institution and the community.

Yet a convincing case can be made that juveniles need more of these reentry programs than they usually experience. Confined juveniles often have distorted ideas of what awaits them in the community. They anticipate that long-standing problems with family member will no longer exist. As one aptly put it, "I'm more mature now; I can handle my mom." They also believe that their school adjustment will go more smoothly than it usually does.

Moreover, juveniles typically underestimate the difficulty of returning to the same community and peer relationships. Finally, nearly all juveniles entering the job market dramatically overestimate how much they will earn and what standard of living they will be able to maintain with that income.

What Is the "Continuum of Care" and How Does It Work?

One of the major challenges of aftercare services rests in the need for transition and reentry programs for youths committed to juvenile institutions. Those who had worked in institutions in the past were aware that once a youth was released, staff were prohibited from having contact with the youth. Staff members were sometimes reprimanded if they responded in any way to a released youth seeking contact and advice.

At the same time, the need to connect institutional and aftercare services has long been recognized. A few programs across the nation attempted to provide a continuum between institutional and aftercare services. More recently, an increasing number of jurisdictions are providing what we can call a *continuum of care* model. See Focus on Practice 11–1.

In sum, while the recidivism rates of these and other "continuum of care" models may not be impressive, they clearly provide services that youths need and desire. The reality is that services in the best institutional–community aftercare models cannot begin to match those factors, discussed in the following section, influencing many youths to continue with delinquent behaviors. Still, for some youths these aftercare services make the difference in helping them to desist from delinquency.

Focus on Practice 11–1
Examples of a Continuum of Care Model

- This *continuum of care* model is found in the Intensive Aftercare Program (IAP) model developed by the OJJDP. This model includes six intertwined phases: assessment, case planning, institutional treatment, prerelease, transition, and community reintegration. The follow-up evaluation of the three IAP sites found no differences between IAP and controls on measures of recidivism and in the severity of their offenses. It was found that some indicators of positive impact were lower numbers of misconduct reports during confinement and decreased length of institutionalization for IAP program participants.[25]

- A six weeks, transition services (TLP) for incarcerated youth in a public correctional institution for felony-level juvenile offenders in the Midwest focused on independent living skills. In this specific program, youths spend the night in the TLP cottage but are released to the community during the day to attend work or school. Gradually, they spend more time over the weekends in their home settings. Case managers work closely with youth to work out their daily schedules and plans for release. Participants in this program viewed the transitional living program as having many benefits, especially independent-living skills training, but it appeared to have no positive effect on reducing recidivism rates.[26]

- The Thomas O'Farrell Youth Center (TOYC) is located in Woodstock, Maryland, and is operated by the North American Family Institute under contract with the Maryland Department of Juvenile Justice. Youths spend on average eight months in this residential facility, followed by nine months

in the specialized aftercare component. Once youths have completed phase 1, in which they demonstrate a number of competencies, they enter the aftercare component. During this phase, each TOYC resident receives postrelease services from two aftercare workers; youths are contacted at least twelve days per month for six months. An evaluation of the TOYC program showed promising results; the first fifty-six TOYC graduates had no further court referrals in the year following their release.[27]

- The Bethesda Day Treatment Center in West Milton, Pennsylvania, is a private nonprofit corporation. The center, consisting of several facilities in eighteen Pennsylvania counties, offers an array of intervention options. The center also includes an intensive aftercare component designed to reintegrate residents released from institutional placement. This component uses a needs assessment to determine youths' clinical needs, and once these needs have been determined, aftercare staff refer the youths to the appropriate agencies. A preliminary evaluation revealed a low recidivism rate in the first year after discharge, but this low rate must be view cautiously because of the small sample size ($n = 5$).[28]

Sources: Steve V. Gies, "Aftercare Services," *OJJDP: Juvenile Justice Bulletin* (Washington, DC: U.S. Department of Justice, 2003); Richard G. Wiebush et al., *Implementation and Outcome Evaluation of the Intensive Aftercare Program: Final Report* (Washington, DC: National Council on Crime and Delinquency, 2005); Laura S. Abrams, Sarah K. S. Shannon, and Cindy Sangalong, "Transition Services for Incarcerated Youth: A Mixed Methods Evaluation Study," *Children and Youth Services Review* 30 (2008), 522–35.

Community Experience

In spite of the various institutional and parole programs, many youths do get into trouble after release. The reasons for the failure of aftercare range from organizational factors to the lack of support in the community, and to the personal traits of youths themselves. Organizational factors include the extreme fragmentation encountered in the system, the dubious and even destructive nature of institutional life, and sometimes arbitrary decision making by aftercare officers. The lack of support systems in the community, including the inability to get a job, the stigma associated with being a "bad" person, and the lack of mentors to guide and encourage the youths, also makes it easy to return to crime. Finally, personal factors include an appetite for drugs and alcohol; an inability to walk away from gang involvement; and conflict with parole officers, school authorities, and parents.

Peer groups have considerable impact. Most youths go back to their old group within a day or so of their return, and groups are usually ready to accept them. This return to an old group is particularly true if youths belonged to a gang before their institutional commitment. If the old groups no longer exist, youths then seek new ones. If the family has moved, the problem of influence of antisocial peers is solved by a slowly decreasing rate of interaction with the old groups and the gradual establishment of new friends in the new area.

Parolees face major, sometimes monumental, problems in returning to school and getting jobs. Aftercare officers look upon school attendance and jobs as signs that the youths are performing successfully. Yet many of the youths who did not do well in school before their incarceration do not find it any easier after their return. They usually were behind their classmates when they entered the training schools and are still behind when they come out. Their classmates have changed, principals are leery of accepting these labeled youths, teachers remember them unfavorably, and the training schools have failed to change their attitudes toward academic courses.

The job situation is not any better. Training school programs are often either of a make-work type or otherwise irrelevant to actual jobs available in the home community. In some other cases the training schools prepare the youths for jobs that are available in the area where the training school is located but not in the youths' home communities. The youths may be able to do odd jobs, but their immaturity, lack of desire for a job, and inexperience preclude them from looking for anything more substantial.

These factors, then, provide the matrix within which the youths must operate. What leads them to become delinquent again? For some time it has been known that younger parolees are more likely to fail than older parolees; that persons who were involved in crime for longer periods of time are more likely to fail than individuals with short records; that those who begin early are more likely to continue; that individuals more heavily involved in crime are more likely to fail than those not so heavily involved; that persons frequently confined are more likely to fail than those who have not been confined; and that crimes-against-property offenders fail more than violent offenders. Some attributes, however, seem to separate recidivists and nonrecidivists:

- Recidivists have more difficulty adjusting to their prosocial peers than do nonrecidivists.
- They are more likely than nonrecidivists to be in groups to which it is difficult to adjust.
- They are more likely than nonrecidivists to maintain interaction with older groups that have a history of delinquency.
- They receive less effective antidelinquent teaching than do nonrecidivists.[29]

What Are the Main Responsibilities of Aftercare Officers?

Parole or aftercare officers have much in common with probation officers. Both perform duties that are investigatory and regulatory. They face similar role conflicts and frustrations. Both cope with excessive caseloads, both lack community resources, and both may be

EXHIBIT 11–1
Powelton Aftercare In Philadelphia

A nonprofit organization, Powelton, was created in Philadelphia, Pennsylvania, in December 2001 to provide aftercare services to males and to females, aged eleven to twenty. Clients arrived at Powelton after spending time in private residential facilities, and this program handled about 90 percent of aftercare cases in Philadelphia. Youths spent a maximum of six months in the program and came from over thirty facilities. Its mission emphasized rehabilitation of youth, and had twenty-one primary objectives for its clients, including building positive relationships, going back to school, and finding employment. Its staff included a program director, a senior supervisor, four social works youth supervisors, twenty-five aftercare workers, a part-time substance abuse counselor, a part-time job developer, a GED teacher, as well as support staff.

Aftercare services were mandatory for youth leaving the residential facility, and like all programs in Philadelphia, Powelton had to demonstrate equal commitment to the three prongs of the Balance and Restorative Justice Model: offender accountability, competency development, and community safety. Staff members had an average caseload of 22 clients.

The services youth received while at Powerton were designed to meet individual needs through the development of an Individual Service Plan (ISP) before the point of release. Services included: job preparation and development; recreational activity activities, GED preparation; assistance with completion of community service hours; and other individualized services such as connecting the youth to substance abuse, family, or vocational programming; assisting clients with getting their birth certificates or other forms of identification; providing youth with financial aid forms for college; or helping them get enrolled for entrance exams.

Aftercare workers operated as partners with juvenile probation officers roughly splitting supervisory and supportive tasks. Probation officers (PO) were responsible for most supervisory tasks, such as drug screening, ensuring school attendance, and payment of restitution. Aftercare officers also carried on some supervisory task, making sure those with community service hours received opportunities to complete them and conducting more regular school attendance checks. While probation officer frequently provided their clients with list of jobs opening, aftercare workers were more likely to take young people to job fairs and retail centers to help complete job applications. Because aftercare workers were required to have more frequent contacts with their clients three times a week during the initial period after release, they often had more information about clients and families than probation officers. However, the PO was ultimately responsible for reporting back to the judge about the status of the case and only the PO could determine when the client had violated probation. Aftercare workers were rarely addressed in court to provide details of the case. The power imbalance between probation officers and aftercare workers meant that the provision of aftercare services was dependent upon the degree of by-in by the PO. If a particular PO felt aftercare was a waste of time or was unnecessary for a particular client, she could send explicit or implied messages to the client that a failure to participate would not result in any formal consequences.

CRITICAL THINKING QUESTION

How has this case study expanded your idea about what an aftercare or juvenile parole officer does? Does this two-tier system make a lot of sense to you? Is it something that ought to be implemented elsewhere?

inadequately trained. In fact, in many states, the same officer provides both probation and parole services. In separated departments, state-administered parole services usually pay officers somewhat better than to county-funded probation services. Parole officers also tend to be older and more experienced in the juvenile justice system than probation officers. The youths placed on aftercare require supportive counseling, delivery of certain services, and supervision. But frequently they receive only supervision, because the caseloads tend to be high for each officer. Across jurisdictions, juvenile aftercare may be delivered by aftercare officers (sometimes in private, contracted aftercare programs, juvenile probation officers, or some combination of the two). In contrast to adult parole, aftercare typically combines supervision with support or treatment services or strategies. See Exhibit 11–1 for a case study of a nonprofit aftercare organization in Philadelphia, Powelton, which demonstrates some of the services provided on aftercare.

Supervision

Aftercare officers, more so than probation officers, are looked on even more often as law enforcement figures because they can return offenders to institutional confinement. The director of court services for a large Midwestern probation department compares juveniles on probation and those on aftercare:

The main difference between the child on probation and the child on aftercare is that the child who has been further in the system and who has already received some sort of primary treatment has identified his or her sets of problems. Staff also are aware of these problems, and so we will more carefully scrutinize them. We are also a little more leery about those further in the system because they are more aware how to manage the system to their advantage. But they don't necessarily pose more danger either to the officer or to the community because those early in the system may be unaware of the impact or the consequences of their actions.[30]

To understand the resentment toward some aftercare officers, it is necessary to examine some of the rules to which youths are subject. A Pennsylvania county uses the rules set down in Focus on Practice 11–2, modified according to each parolee's needs. These rules are read by the juvenile, who then signs the statement, "I, the undersigned, have received a copy, read and understood the aforementioned rules and agree to abide by them." The rules are neither hard to agree to nor hard to break, for many of them are not relevant to anything in the lifestyle of offenders. Enforcement of the rules drives youths even farther from genuine communication with officers. Lack of enforcement of a formal set of rules, however, gives juveniles the impression that they are free to do as they wish, and aftercare officers are left in a bind.

Some youths on release to the community will skip school, talk back to parents, get involved in minor traffic violations, or violate curfew. Most aftercare officers realize that many nondelinquent youths behave in the same manner, but one would not consider confining them for such behaviors. Revocation generally is based on the attitudes of the youths. For example, an expression of hostility toward the officers sometimes results in recommitment, even if the offenses and behavior are insignificant. The likelihood of revocation is increased as the severity of behavior increases. The commission of misdemeanors, the continuation of drug use, and a pattern of delinquency suggest that more serious offenses may follow. Aftercare officers may decide at this point that for the protection of both the youth and the community, revocation is necessary. Finally, if felonies are committed, little doubt exists in the minds of most officers that the youth should return to the institution.

Focus on Practice 11–2
Aftercare Rules of One Pennsylvania County

COUNTY JUVENILE PROBATION/SUPERVISION REGULATIONS

Child's name: _____   Docket # _____

Current Charge(s): _____   Probation Officer: _____

Hearing Date: _____   Probation

Officer Phone: _____

You have been placed under the Supervision of the County Juvenile Court. You are expected to obey the conditions placed upon you. Should you have any questions regarding these conditions, it is your responsibility to contact your probation officer for clarification. A violation of these conditions may result in your reappearing before Juvenile Court.

Probation/Supervision Period: _____

While under Court Supervision, I will abide by the following conditions regarding community protection, offender accountability and competency development.

COMMUNITY PROTECTION CONDITIONS

1. I will obey all Federal, State and Local laws.
2. I will give my probation officer prior notice of any changes of address, phone number, education or employment.
3. I will adhere to the following curfew: _____
4. After curfew hours, I will be in the company of a parent or guardian, any exceptions, I will have prior approval of the Probation Office.
5. I will not leave the County without the permission of the Probation Office.
6. I will report to my Probation Officer as directed and permit a PO to visit my residence.

    Where: _____   **When:** _____

    I will give my Probation Officer prior notice for any reasons I cannot meet this requirement.
7. I will not use or carry a firearm in my possession without the express permission of my Probation Officer.
8. _____
9. _____
10. _____
11. _____

CRITICAL THINKING QUESTION

Do you believe that these are reasonable rules for a juvenile on aftercare status? If you were an aftercare officer, would you add to these rules?

Officers who take a supervisory stance in relation to youths and their behaviors some-times consider any violation of the rules as sufficient grounds for revocation. In the past, they simply picked up such offenders and took them back to paroling institutions, ignoring due process. The stepping over of an arbitrary line by the youths was sufficient to warrant taking them into custody. The line often was ill or vaguely defined, and the youths had no idea whether their behavior was within acceptable limits. In addition, since they seldom see the officers, the youths would usually count on getting away with anything they tried, but often the parole officer would suddenly appear and the youth would be sent back to the training school. Revocation depended on chance, the attitude of the youth, and the personal whim of the aftercare officer.

One study of the Kentucky Department of Juvenile Justice's Juvenile Intensive Supervision Team Program, which focused primarily on gang violence among inner-city youth, found that officers perceived rehabilitation as the least important function of their program, behind the functions of ensuring community safety, deterrence through sanc-tioning infractions, and detecting violations through monitoring. Technical violations, not surprisingly, were the most frequently committed violation and weighed heavily in revoca-tion decisions. Other factors given weight included seriousness of prior and current offenses as well as substance abuse.[31]

Some of the problems faced by youths on aftercare status are possibly different from the problems faced by juvenile probationers. Youths who are confined face the shock of complete isolation from their communities. They are exposed to many degrading experi-ences, are sometimes "messed over" by staff and residents, learn behavior that allows them to survive, are not permitted to practice the decision making they would have to practice in the community, and are stigmatized by their stay in the institution. The world they left is changing, and perhaps so are they. Consequently, when youths are ready for release, they are not necessarily ready to reenter the community. As the concept of aftercare changes, how-ever, more and more aftercare officers and training schools are increasingly giving youths prerelease counseling and are allowing home visits to ease their return to normal life.

The Juvenile Aftercare or Parole Officer

PREPARATION FOR THE JOB

Some parole officers work inside correctional facilities, preparing reports for outside boards. They assess offenders before and during confinement, support families with youths' community adjustment, and inform youths what job prospects or school reg-istrations they must have if released. Some officers supervise halfway houses with small groups of boys living together to share experiences and lend each other support.

Officers visit their clients regularly to evaluate their progress. If offenders violate the rules, officers may recommend that af-tercare will be revoked. Aftercare officers can be employed by state parole boards, county probation departments, or by private corporations. Drug therapists, psychiatrists, and social workers often help with juveniles' supervision.

Work may be stressful, for they are under pressure at all times to present parolees positively to their communities. Case works are usually heavy. Officers often work more than 40 hours a week, sometimes making night and weekend appointments with parolees who are at school or at work.

QUALIFICATION AND EDUCATIONAL REQUIREMENTS

A bachelor's degree in sociology, psychology, criminology, or social work is usually preferred. In addition, many agencies require one or two years of work experience in correctional institutions or other social agencies, or master's degree in so-ciology, social work, or psychology. Applicants must generally take written, oral, psychological, and physical examinations. In most states, parole officers must pass training program and be certified.

DEMAND FOR

Employment of aftercare officers is expected to grow for the next several years. Juvenile correctional institutions continue to have a large number of detained youth.

SALARY

Earnings vary depending on location and experience of the applicant. The main salary for a parole officer is around $40,000 a year. The lowest 10 percent earned less than $26,000 and the highest 10 percent more than $46,000. Supervisors and direc-tors often earn much more.

Source: See career as a patrol officer in the American Correctional Associa-tion, American Federation of State County and Municipal Employees and National Council on Crime and Delinquency.

Revocation of Aftercare

The revocation of aftercare is the early termination of a youth's aftercare program, which usually takes place after one or more program violations. Several outcomes are possible when a youthful offender's aftercare is terminated. The youth can be returned to training school. A less severe option is to shift the youth to a different graduated outcome sanction. For example, a youth who is on regular supervision status can be shifted to an intensive supervision caseload. Or an offender may be placed on home confinement, coupled with electronic monitoring.

Aftercare revocation for juveniles is not as clear-cut as parole revocation for adults. Indeed, the U.S. Supreme Court has not yet ruled how juvenile aftercare revocation actions should be conducted. This sometimes has led to prejudicial, whimsical, arbitrary, and irrational actions on the part of the aftercare officers. But the court decisions in *Mempa v. Rhay* (1967), *People ex rel. v. Warden Greenhaven* (1971), *Murray v. Page* (1970), *Morrissey v. Brewer* (1972), and *Gagnon v. Scarpelli* (1973) have been applied to juveniles.[32] The U.S. Supreme Court in the *Mempa* case stated that state probationers have the right to a hearing and counsel when accused of probation violations. In *People v. Greenhaven*, it was stated that inmates are permitted to have counsel at revocation hearings. But the case that set the rationale for the requirement of due process was *Murray v. Page*:

> Therefore, while a prisoner does not have a constitutional right to parole, once paroled, he cannot be deprived of his freedom by means inconsistent with due process. The minimal right of the parolee to be informed of the charges and the nature of the evidence against him and to appear to be heard at the revocation hearing is inviolate. Statutory deprivation of this right is manifestly inconsistent with due process and is unconstitutional; nor can such a right be lost by the subjective determination of the executive that the case for revocation is "clear."[33]

In the 1972 *Morrissey v. Brewer* decision, the Supreme Court first ruled on parole revocation procedures.[34] Morrissey had been paroled from the Iowa State Penitentiary. Seven months after his release, his parole was revoked for a technical violation, and he was returned to prison. In a related case, Brewer was returned to prison on a technical parole violation. Both prisoners petitioned for habeas corpus on the grounds that they had been denied due process law and returned to prison without opportunities to defend themselves at an open hearing. The two cases were consolidated for appeal and eventually reached the Supreme Court.

In his opinion, Chief Justice Warren Burger laid down the essential elements of due process for parole revocation. The first requirement was a hearing before an "uninvolved" hearing officer, who might be another parole officer or an "independent decision maker," who would determine whether there was reasonable cause to believe that a parole violation had taken place. If so, the parolee might be returned to prison, subject to a full revocation hearing before the parole board. Due process in such a proceeding was outlined as follows:

> Our task is limited to deciding the minimum requirement(s) of due process. They include (a) written notice of the claimed violation of parole; (b) disclosure to the parolee of evidence against him; (c) opportunity to be heard in person and to present witnesses and documentary evidence; (d) the right to confront and cross-examine adverse witnesses (unless the hearing officer specifically finds good cause for not allowing confrontation); (e) a "neutral and detached" hearing body such as a traditional parole board, members of which need not be judicial officers or lawyers; and (f) a written statement by the fact finders as to the evidence relied on and reasons to revoking parole.[35]

Gagnon v. Scarpelli involved an offender, Scarpelli, whose probation was revoked in Wisconsin without a hearing. Scarpelli had been sentenced to fifteen years in prison for armed robbery in Wisconsin, but his sentence was suspended and he was placed on probation for seven years. He was given permission to reside in Illinois, where he was later arrested for burglary. His probation was then revoked without a hearing. This case was appealed on the grounds that probation revocation without a hearing and counsel violated Scarpelli's due process rights.

The Supreme Court held that the right to counsel should be decided on a case-by-case basis and that considerable latitude must be given to the responsible agency in making

---

TABLE 11–3
Revocation of Aftercare

Case	Decision
Mempa v. Rhay (1967)	State probationers have the right to a hearing and counsel when accused of probation violations.
People ex rel. v. Warden Green-Haven	Inmates are permitted to have counsel at (1971) revocation hearings.
Murray v. Page (1970)	Once paroled, ex-offender cannot be deprived of freedom by means inconsistent with due process.
Morrissey v. Brewer (1972)	Requirement was a hearing before an "uninvolved" hearing officer who would decide if a parole violation had taken place.
Gagnon v. Scarpelli (1973)	Counsel should be provided on a case-by-case basis and considerable latitude should be provided in making the decision. The significance of this case was also that it equated probation with parole in terms of a revocation hearing.

---

the decision. The Court did indicate that counsel should be provided on request when the probationer claims that he or she did not commit the violation and when the reasons for the violation are complex or otherwise difficult to present. The significance of this case is that it equated probation with parole in terms of a revocation hearing. Although the Court did not rule that all probationers and parolees have a right to be represented by counsel in revocation hearings, it did say that the counsel should be provided when the probationer or parolee makes a good case for contesting the allegations. Table 11–3 summarizes the legal cases involved in the revocation of aftercare.

What Are Interstate Compacts?

It becomes apparent to some juveniles with dysfunctional families that a home placement with a relative in another jurisdiction would probably increase the likelihood of their successful reintegration to society. They would then need to persuade their aftercare officers of the feasibility of such placement. Or an institutional social worker or aftercare officer might come to this same conclusion, and if the youth agrees with such a placement, an **interstate compact**, if needed, would be initiated with the appropriate authorities in this other jurisdiction.

Basically, the compact is an agreement among the states to deal with both the mobility of youths and the need to keep them under supervision. The compact recognizes four basic areas in which the need for cooperation is evident:

1. Cooperative supervision of delinquent juveniles on probation or parole
2. The return, from one state to another, of delinquent juveniles who have escaped or absconded
3. The return, from one state to another, of nondelinquent juveniles who have run away from home
4. Additional measures for the protection of juveniles and of the public, which one or more of the party states may find desirable to undertake cooperatively[36]

Interstate compacts are also drawn up when youths are wanted for crimes in several states at the same time. In addition, youths facing possible arrest, adjudication, sentencing, confinement, or aftercare supervision sometimes flee to another state to escape being held fully accountable for their offenses. The problems for the jurisdictions involved can become quite complicated. For example, an offender may have arrest warrants against him or her in several states at once, several states may wish to prosecute the youth at the same time, or one state may be attempting to rehabilitate him or her while other states are requesting transfer for prosecution. As a result of the implementation of interstate compacts, parents, police, judges, probation officers, and institutional officials can, by going through the appropriate procedures, facilitate the return or supervision of wanted youths.

If a juvenile is to be sent to another state for treatment or rehabilitation, the states within the compact can enter into supplementary agreements that stipulate the rates to be paid for the care, treatment, and custody of out-of-state delinquent youths; that specify that the referring state shall at all times retain jurisdiction over these juveniles; and that ensure that the state receiving the youths into one of its institutions shall be the sole agent for the referring state.

Thinking like a Correctional Professional

As a supervisor of the aftercare unit, you are aware that there are several offenders on the caseloads of your officers who are providing continual problems. At a recent conference, one of your colleagues, a supervisor in another office, recommends that you do what you can to send these problematic offenders to other states on interstate compacts, to find reasons to violate their parole, or to drop them from parole. As a professional, what is your assessment of getting rid of your troublemakers? What are its advantages and disadvantages? Is this any different than the school suspending troublemakers the first few days, sometimes for the entire year?

How Can Aftercare Be Improved?

Aftercare programs too frequently are either underdeveloped or nonexistent. In many jurisdictions, the primary program is one in which probation or aftercare officers see their clients periodically but have few services to offer them. Many youths are required to do no more than send in monthly written reports to the parole officer or to report for a weekly "drug drop" (urinalysis).

The challenge to improving aftercare is even greater today because of the demise of traditional treatment approaches in so many training schools across the nation. As a result, juveniles released from training schools are even less prepared for community living than they were in the past.

The desire to lower recidivism has led to a number of experiments based on the assumption either that the institutions are not doing their job or that conditions in the community prevent parolees from staying out of trouble. The most widely used program provides intensive supervision to high-risk youthful offenders, but, as previously discussed, these programs have had mixed results in terms of reducing recidivism.

Lifeskills '95, one of the more promising aftercare programs, is geared to chronic, high-risk juvenile offenders and is designed to assist these offenders when released from secure confinement. This program begins with a thirteen-week reintegration treatment program that attempts to improve offenders' basic socialization skills, to stop their use or abuse of drugs, and to provide them with employment and/or an educational opportunity. An evaluation of 125 experimentals and 125 controls released to either San Bernardino or Riverside County from a secure California youth authority facility found that Lifeskills '95 was successful in reducing recidivism rates during the period of program participation.[37]

"Aftercare for the Incarcerated through Mentoring" (AIM) is a juvenile reentry program based in Indiana. AIM incorporates the principles of the IAP model and focuses primarily on connecting incarcerated youth and adult mentors. This program seeks to steer juveniles toward productive and successful futures by fostering healthy positive relationships with effective role models.[38] AIM has been carefully evaluated with results reflecting dramatic differences in the likelihood of reincarnation—four years after release, juveniles participating in AIM were 63 percent less likely to have returned to a correctional facility than those who did not participate in the program.[39]

David M. Altschuler, Troy L. Armstrong, and Doris L. MacKenzie recommended the following reforms and changes to improve the effectiveness of aftercare services:

- Community-based aftercare is one part of a reintegrative corrections continuum that must be preceded by parallel services in the corrections facility and must include careful preparations for the aftercare to follow.

- Aftercare is frequently funded and staffed at levels far below what is required to provide truly intensive supervision and enhanced service delivery.

- Intensive aftercare, in contrast to "standard" aftercare, requires close attention via formal assessment procedures to determine which offenders are in need of a level of intervention that includes both highly intrusive supervision and enhanced treatment-related services. See also the Evidence-Based Practice feature below.

- It is clear that a reduction in caseload size and intensification of level of contacts are widely accepted operational principles for intensive aftercare programming.[40]

The 2010 Federal Advisory Committee on Juvenile Justice (FACJJ) made the following recommendations to the president and Congress:

- "The FACJJ recommends that the President and Congress prioritize the importance of reentry in all areas of juvenile justice programming, including solicitation efforts, policy development, and program monitoring. Effective reentry planning should begin upon system entry and should directly involve youth, appropriate family members, positive peer supports, and an array of community assets (such as mentoring) to ensure that effective connections are in place upon a juvenile's exit from confinement."

- "FACJJ recommends that the President and Congress provide funding for the OJJDP Administrator to use to create training and technical assistance content focused on the development of comprehensive reentry tools and approaches consistent with national models to ensure effective implementation and evaluation in state and local jurisdictions."

- "FACJJ recommends that the President and Congress strongly emphasize that states develop effective community-based reentry services that use a system-of-care model and provide funding and training specific to mental health and substance abuse services for youth and families."

- "FACJJ recommends that the President and Congress strongly encourage states to design, develop, and implement reentry approaches that ensure the successful transition of juvenile offenders in secure facilities and crossover youth to adulthood. Such approaches should address education, life skills, work readiness, and community integration."[41]

Evidence-Based Practice
Missouri's Comprehensive Strategy

Missouri has developed a continuum of graduated sanctions and services that sets a high standard for other states to follow. Guided by the Comprehensive Strategy for Serious, Violent, and Chronic Juvenile Offenders, Missouri has created a structured decision-making model that uses a risk and needs assessment and a classification matrix. See Figure 11–2.

The Missouri system has three tools:

- An actuarial risk assessment tool, completed before court adjudication, that classifies youth into three categories—high, moderate, or low—based on their probability of reoffending

- A classification matrix that recommends sanctions and service interventions that seem to be appropriate to the youth risk level and most serious adjudicated offense

- A needs assessment instrument that recommends services that will reduce the likelihood of a juvenile's reoffending by reducing risk factors linked to recidivism

In more recent reforms, Missouri's Division of Youth Services now serves youthful offenders who cannot be maintained in community settings in small, dormitory-style rehabilitative facilities close to their homes. These facilities focus on (1) individualized and group treatment with a clear treatment model; (2) supervision, not correctional coercion; (3) skill building; (4) family partnership and involvement during confinement; and (5) aftercare.

Only 9 percent of juveniles discharged from the Division of Youth Services were sentenced to adult prison within three years of release, and just 15 percent were reincarcerated within two years of release.

Sources: Mark W. Lipsey, James C. Howell, Marion R. Kelly, Gabrielle Chapman, and Darin Carver, Improving the Effectiveness of Juvenile Justice Programs: A New Perspective on Evidence-Based Practice (Washington, DC: Georgetown University, 2010), 44–46; and Annie E. Casey Foundation, The Missouri Model: Reinventing the Practice of Rehabilitation of Youthful Offenders: Summary Report (Baltimore: The Annie E. Casey Foundation, 2010), accessed at http://www.aecf.org/KnowledgeCenter/~/media/Pubs/Initiatives/Juvenile%20Detention%20Alternatives%20Initiative/MOModel/MO_Summary_webfinal.pdf.

Offense Severity	Group 1 Offenses	Group 2 Offenses	Group 3 Offenses
Risk Level	Status Offenses Municipal Ordinances/ Infractions	Class A, B, & C Misdemeanors/ Class C & D Felonies	A & B Felonies
Low Risk	A) Warn & Counsel B) Restitution C) Community Service D) Court Fees & Assessments E) Supervision	A) Warn & Counsel B) Restitution C) Community Service D+) Court Fees & Assessments E) Supervision	B+) Restitution C+) Community Service D+) Court Fees & Assessments E) Supervision F) Day Treatment G) Intensive Supervision H) Court Residential Placement I) Commitment to DYS
Moderate Risk	A) Warn & Counsel B) Restitution C) Community Service D) Court Fees & Assessments E) Supervision	A) Warn & Counsel B) Restitution C+) Community Service D+) Court Fees & Assessments E) Supervision F) Day Treatment	B+) Restitution C+) Community Service D+) Court Fees & Assessments E) Supervision F) Day Treatment G) Intensive Supervision H) Court Residential Placement I) Commitment to DYS
High Risk	A) Warn & Counsel B) Restitution C) Community Service D) Court Fees & Assessments E) Supervision	B+) Restitution C+) Community Service D+) Court Fees & Assessments E) Supervision F) Day Treatment G) Intensive Supervision H) Court Residential Placement I) Commitment to DYS	H) Court Residential Placement I) Commitment to DYS

† Mandatory certification hearings are required by statute for all Class A Felonies. In the event the juvenies not certified, the juvenile officer should refer to this column of the matrix for classification purposes.
+ This symbol indicates options that should never be used as a sole option for youths who score in that cell, but only in conjunction with other options.

FIGURE 11–2
Missouri Risk and Offense Case Classification Matrix

Source: Annie E. Casey Foundation, *The Missouri Model: Reinventing the Practice of Rehabilitating Youthful Offenders: Summary Report* (Baltimore, MD: Annie E. Casey Foundation, 2010).

Social Policy and Juvenile Justice

Public policy makers are now paying more attention to reentry issues than ever before. On April 9, 2008, the Second Chance Act was signed into law; in 2009, over $28 million dollars were awarded to nonprofit organizations and governments to provide services to reentering ex-offenders. In 2010, over $82 million were appropriated with 5 million of those funds, directed toward projects that encourage reintegration of juveniles into the community. This focus on juvenile as a special reentry population demonstrates the importance of providing effective services. To improve aftercare services, a promising approach is proactive caregiving where workers view their clients and time differently than ritualistic adaptations.

Workers using a proactive caregiver approach are also more likely to minimize social distance from their clients, often using their own experience of growing up in urban neighborhoods as a way to connect with youth and parents. Home visits conducted by these workers are often longer, relaxed, and informal than ritualistic workers. Proactive caregiving often involves taking on the role of big Brothers/Big Sisters. Engagement is a key to proactive caregiving. Proactive caregiving also involves persistence. They tend to be workers who have strong social bonds and attachments to the community. They believe in the challenge and value of their work as a duty that extends the hours of 9–5. These workers see their jobs as a way to give back to the community, instead of just a source of income.

Source: Christopher P. Dunn and Jamie J. Fader, "These Are Kids' Lives!" Dilemmas and Adaptations of Juvenile Aftercare Workers," *Justice Quarterly* 30 (2011), 802–04.

SUMMARY

LEARNING OBJECTIVE 1: Describe the goals of aftercare.

Aftercare, or parole, is one part of the corrections continuum, which has traditionally been the least developed segment of juvenile corrections. Aftercare can be defined as reiterative services that prepare out-of-home placed juveniles for reentry into the community.

LEARNING OBJECTIVE 2: Decide who is responsible for releasing youths from training school.

In forty-four states the authority for making this decision rests with the executive branch of state government. Probation or parole officers make the decision in four states, and in three states other board agencies make the decision. In Illinois and several other states, juvenile judges have the authority to remove juveniles from training school. However, there is controversy who should make this aftercare decision.

LEARNING OBJECTIVE 3: Summarize why so many youths fail on aftercare.

Fragmentation and lack of coordination pervade this relatively unknown phase of the treatment of juvenile offenders. Most states have neither developed comprehensive guidelines for coordinating agencies that work with released youths nor implemented a comprehensive plan for overseeing the administration of parole. Once youths have been released from institutions, community forces often negate the effect of any positive programs in which the youths participated.

LEARNING OBJECTIVE 4: Describe the role of the aftercare officer.

Aftercare officers, much like probation officers, have paperwork to do, supervise offenders, and, when necessary, may initiate the revocation process to return juveniles to an institution. Juvenile aftercare, probably even more than juvenile probation, holds to a risk control and crime reduction approach.

LEARNING OBJECTIVE 5: Describe means by which aftercare can be improved.

As a number of programs have done, it is reasonable to assume that if juveniles were provided with comprehensive and integrated complements to institutional programs, their chances of failure while on aftercare would be far less. This continuum of care, from institution to community, is essential to improve aftercare and to contribute to the reduction of recidivism.

KEY TERMS

aftercare, p. 237
intensive supervision programs, p. 243
interstate compact, p. 251

parole, p. 238
reentry programs, p. 244

REVIEW QUESTIONS

1. What are the major shocks a juvenile faces upon release to the community?
2. What is the purpose of aftercare?
3. What programs appear to have the most promise for juvenile aftercare?
4. How might community factors interfere with a youth's chances of success on aftercare?
5. Using the information in the chapter, draw up a set of rules that juveniles on aftercare would consider reasonable and that would contribute to reducing recidivism.

GROUP EXERCISES

1. *Writing to Learn Exercise:* In one or two paragraphs, describe the different methods states use to release youths from training schools. What are the issues involved in the different types of aftercare release decisions? Critique and revise.
2. *Writing to Learn Exercise:* Write two paragraphs describing determinate and indeterminate types of aftercare release. Critique and revise.
3. *Group Work:* Describe what is meant by risk control and crime reduction in aftercare. Then describe each of the types of intensive aftercare supervision and their treatment goals as described in the chapter.
4. *Writing to Learn Exercise:* Discuss the due process rights of juveniles on aftercare. Critique and revise.

WORKING WITH JUVENILES

New aftercare workers can get into a cycle in which they come to their jobs all idealistic, and then they feel let down by their clients. And so they react, going from being treatment-oriented to punishment-oriented. With this shift frequently goes their engagement and enthusiasm in their jobs. The challenge is not to let clients' failure affect their enthusiasm for their jobs, so that they can remain proactive and caregiving.

NOTES

1. Michelle, Inderbitzin, "Lessons from a Juvenile Training School: Survival and Growth,' *Journal of Adolescent Research* 21 (2006), 19.

2. *Federal Advisory Committee on Juvenile Justice: Annual Report 2010* (Washington, DC: U.S. Department of Justice, Office of Justice Programs, Office of Juvenile Justice and Delinquency Prevention, 2010), 31.

3. A. J. Sedlak and K. S. McPherson, *Youth's Needs and Services: Findings from the Survey of Youth in Residential Placement: Bulletin* (Washington, DC: U.S. Department of Justice, Office of Justice Programs, Office of Juvenile Justice and Delinquency Prevention, 2010).

4. See the research in Chapter 10 on juvenile victimization.

5. *Federal Advisory Committee on Juvenile Justice: Annual Report 2010.*

6. Ibid.

7. David M. Altschuler and Troy L. Armstrong, "Reintegrating High-Risk Juvenile Offenders into Communities: Experiences and Prospects," *Corrections Management Quarterly* 5 (2001), 79–95.

8. Steve V. Gies, "Aftercare Services," *OJJDP: Juvenile Justice Bulletin* (Washington, DC: U.S. Department of Justice, 2003), 1.

9. Hunter Hurst IV and Patricia McFall Torbet, *Organization and Administration of Juvenile Services: Probation, Aftercare, and State Institutions for Delinquent Youth* (Pittsburgh, PA: National Center for Juvenile Justice, 1993).

10. Kristin Parsons Winokur et al., "Juvenile Recidivism and Length of Stay," *Journal of Criminal Justice* 36 (2008), 126–37.

11. *Mission Statement, Office of Release Review* (Columbus, OH: Department of Youth Services, n.d.), 1.

12. For civil action taken against the state of Ohio, see S.H. et. al., vs. Tom Stickrath, "Joint Plan for Reforming Release Authority Pursuant to Stipulation for Injunctive Relief" (Doc. 118, para. 32). United States District Court Southern District of Ohio Eastern Division, 4/3/2008. http://www .childrenslawky.org/index/files/92_draft_notice.pdf. To examine some of the principles and processes involved with decision tree analysis see, Danida, M. "Logical Analysis Framework: A Flexible Tool for Participatory Development" (Asiatisk Plads, DK-1448 Copenhagen K. Denmark; Technical Advisory Service, February 1996).

13. Materials received from the department.

14. Don Andrews and James Bonta, LSI–R™ Level of Service Inventory–Revised.

15. Don Andrews, and James Bonta, software developed by Allvest Information Services, Inc.

16. Laura M. Maruschak and Thomas P. Bonczar, *Probation and Parole in the United States, 2012* (Washington, DC: Bureau of Justice Bulletin, 2013).

17. Howard N. Snyder, "An Empirical Portrait of the Youth reentry Population," *Youth Violence and Youth Justice* 2 (January 2004), 39–55.

18. Laura S. Abrams and Susan M. Snyder, "Youth Offender Reentry: Models for Intervention and Directions for Future Inquiry," *Children and Youth Services Review* 32 (December 2010), 1787–95.

19. David M. Altschuler and Troy L. Armstrong, "Intensive Aftercare for the High-Risk Juvenile Parolee: Issues and Approaches in Reintegration and Community Supervision," in *Intensive Interventions with High-Risk Youths: Promising Approaches in Juvenile Probation and Parole*, edited by Troy Armstrong (Monsey, NY: Criminal Justice Press, 1991), 49–50.

20. Ibid., 50.

21. Gies, "Aftercare Services."

22. Ibid.

23. L. W. Sherman et al., *Preventing Crime: What Works, What Doesn't, What's Promising.* Report to the U.S. Congress (Washington, DC: U.S. Department of Justice, 1997).

24. Gies, "Aftercare Services."

25. Richard G. Wiebush et al., *Implementation and Outcome Evaluation of the Intensive Aftercare Program: Final Report* (Washington, DC: National Council on Crime and Delinquency, 2005).

26. Laura S. Abrams, Sarah K. S. Shannon, and Cindy Sangalong, "Transition Services for Incarcerated Youth: A Mixed Methods Evaluation Study," *Children and Youth Services Review* 30 (2008), 522–35.

27. Gies, "Aftercare Services."

28. Ibid.

29. Richard G. Wiebush, Betsie McNulty, and Thao Le, *Implementation of the Intensive Community-Based Aftercare Program* (Washington, DC: Office of Juvenile Justice and Delinquency Prevention, 2000).

30. David M. Altschuler, Troy L. Armstrong, and Doris L. MacKenzie, "Reintegration, Supervised Release, and

Intensive Aftercare," *Juvenile Justice Bulletin* (Rockville, MD: Juvenile Justice Clearinghouse, 1999), 8–9.

31. Nathan C. Lowe et al., "Understanding the Decision to Pursue Revocation of Intensive Supervision: A Descriptive Survey of Juvenile Probation and Aftercare Officers," *Journal of Offender Rehabilitation* 46 (2008), 155.

32. *Mempa v Rhay*, 389 U.S. 128 (1967); *People ex rel. v. Warden Greenhaven*, 318 N.Y.S.2d 449 (1971); *Murray v. Page*, 429 F.2d 1359 (10th Cir. 1970); *Morrissey v. Brewer*, 408 U.S. 471 (1972); *Gagnon v. Scarpelli*, 411 U.S. 778 (1973).

33. *Murray v. Page*, 429 F.2d 1359 (10th Cir. 1970).

34. *Morrissey v. Brewer*, 408 U.S. 471 (1972).

35. Ibid.

36. Purdon's Pennsylvania Statutes Annotated 62 PS. Paragraph 731, 1968, 82.

37. Don A. Josi and Dale K. Sechrest, "A Pragmatic Approach to Parole Aftercare: Evaluation of a Community Reintegration Program for High-Risk Youthful Offenders," *Justice Quarterly* 16 (March 1995), 51–80.

38. *Federal Advisory Committee on Juvenile Justice: Annual Report 2010*, 35.

39. G. R. Jarjoura, *Mentoring as a Critical Tool for Effective Juvenile Reentry.* Written testimony submitted to the Congressional Briefing on youth reentry from Out-of-Home Placement to the Community, November 16, 2009.

40. Altschuler et al., "Reintegration, Supervised Release, and Intensive Aftercare," 11, 15.

41. *Federal Advisory Committee on Juvenile Justice (FACJJO, 36).*

12 Treatment Technologies

Mangostock/Shutterstock

Learning Objectives

1. Summarize the different viewpoints concerning treatment in juvenile justice.
2. Describe the treatment modalities used most frequently in juvenile justice.
3. Evaluate the juvenile justice treatment modalities.
4. Identify suggestions for improving treatment in juvenile justice agencies.

The story of one Cece Miller shows that given the proper help and offenders can turn their lives around and actually become a corrections professional. This heartwarming story reveals a positive impact juvenile and adult corrections can have on offenders' lives and also shows that a career in corrections can be open to anyone with the proper skills and motivation.

Cece Miller had a love of dogs that led her to work in one of the largest animal shelters in South Carolina. In 2007, she found herself in the federal secure female facility at Hazelton, West Virginia. Shortly after arriving at the prison, and with the support of her correctional counselor, Miller started training to become a dog handler at this facility. Within months, she was trading her first dog, Solomon, who eventually went to a young girl who needed a canine companion. Miller became a senior trainer in the present program where she was responsible for ensuring the dogs receive effective, safe training. She mentored all other inmate dog trainers, and remained in that role until she was released in 2010.[1]

Three weeks after her release from prison, the Society for the Prevention of Cruelty to Animals hired Miller as a dog trainer; she built a training program and began to learn more about dogs breeds, diseases, and medications. She volunteered for the paws4 people organization, a nonprofit pet therapy organization that recruits, trains, certifies, and places therapy teams in more than 150 sites in Delaware, Maryland, Pennsylvania, and New Jersey. Miller led a mentoring program for ex-offenders who wish to continue the dog training services after release. Subsequently, she was elected to the board of trust of directors, earned a master's degree, and in 2013, became a full-time employee at paws4 people. Three years after her release, Cece Miller returned to prison as a director of paws4prison program and the PAWS Training Academy. Paws4prisons is a service dog training program dedicated to helping adolescent children with disabilities and veterans suffering from posttraumatic stress disorder. "It is difficult being on this side," says Miller of her return to Hazelton. "But I understand what they are going through. I can be empathetic but also authoritative." Cece Miller provides inmates with the academic and skills training necessary to train service dogs. In addition, she teaches inmates leadership skills, responsibility, and teamwork. "We don't just train a dog—we train a person at the same time."[2]

Miller admits she does not know what she would've done had she not been introduced to dog training while she was an inmate with the Federal Bureau of Prisons. She credits the program at Hazelton with changing her life—she found a career and found herself. Miller believes the program made her a better mother to her children and helped mend her relationship with her own mother. Now when she visits prisons she brings her positive message of change in service for both dogs and people.[3]

J uvenile offenders are confronted and almost overwhelmed by the various methods used to treat, save, rehabilitate, remodel, remake, or otherwise "recycle" them. Juvenile corrections, far more than adult corrections, have as their guiding premise the rehabilitation of youths before they become hardened criminals. To that end, researchers from every discipline have looked for the key that will modify the behavior of youthful offenders.

Punishment was believed to be the answer for a long period of time. But in the 1700s, the founding fathers of our country substituted a religious orientation as the proper approach to working with wayward children. By the second half of the nineteenth century, this moral and religious emphasis slowly gave way to firm discipline and rigorous work training. The study of the character and mental condition of individual lawbreakers was the accepted treatment during the first four decades of the twentieth century. Sociology began to dominate treatment efforts in the 1950s and 1960s with the use of predelinquency community programs, detached workers (social workers whose jobs are on the streets with juvenile gangs), group interaction, job training, and community reorganization. Indeed, during this period, a new idea sprang up nearly every day, each one heralded as the panacea for youth crime. In the 1970s, as discussed in the next section, correctional treatment was bombarded with criticism from all sides and still has not fully regained its former popularity.

Approaches to treatment range from individual to group methods. This chapter presents a general discussion of treatment in juvenile justice, describes and evaluates the treatment modalities that are most popular today, and emphasizes that many treatments have evidence supporting them.

Where Is Treatment Today?

Correctional treatment has experienced several stages since the mid-twentieth century: (1) The "rehabilitation is not appropriate" stage, (2) the "nothing works" stage, (3) the "some treatments work" stage, and (4) the "numerous programs and innovations work" stage.

"Rehabilitation Is Not Appropriate" Stage

Under the leadership of psychiatrists who were well established in juvenile and adult corrections by the 1920s, a medical model was implemented in correctional institutions throughout the nation. However, by the end of the 1960s, the medical model had largely been discredited in American corrections. Critics argued persuasively that rehabilitation's assumptions conflict with basic human values, that rehabilitation philosophy does not work, and that rehabilitation is a disaster in practice.

The "Nothing Works" Stage

Correctional treatment came under increased empirical criticism in the late 1960s and early 1970s. In 1966, reporting on the results of one hundred empirical evaluations of treatment, Walter C. Bailey concluded that there seemed to be little evidence that correctional treatment was effective.[4] Then, in 1974, the late Robert Martinson startled both correctional personnel and the public with the pronouncement that "with few and isolated exceptions, the rehabilitative efforts that have been reported so far have had no appreciable effect on recidivism."[5] The media quickly simplified Martinson's statement to the idea that "nothing works" in correctional treatment. In 1975, Douglas Lipton, Robert Martinson, and Judith Wilks published *The Effectiveness of Correctional Treatment*, which critically evaluated the effectiveness of correctional treatment programs.[6] In that same year, Martinson announced on *60 Minutes* that "there [was] no evidence that correctional rehabilitation reduces recidivism."[7] A spirited debate on the "nothing works" thesis continued to rage from the late 1970s up through the turn of the century.

The "Some Treatments Work" Stage

Ted Palmer, a correctional researcher in California, challenged Lipton and his colleagues' research by tabulating eighty-two studies mentioned in the book and showing that thirty-nine of them, or 48 percent, had positive or partly positive results on recidivism.[8] Palmer used Martinson's own words to reject the "nothing works" thesis:

> These programs seem to work best when they are new, when their subjects are amenable to treatment in the first place, and when the counselors are not only trained people, but "good people" as well.[9]

Paul Gendreau and Robert Ross reviewed the literature published between 1973 and 1978 and found that 86 percent of the ninety-five intervention programs studied reported success.[10] According to Gendreau and Ross, this success rate was "convincing evidence that some treatment programs, when they are applied with integrity by competent practitioners in appropriate target populations, can be effective in preventing crime or reducing recidivism."[11] In the late 1970s, Martinson conceded that "contrary to [his] previous position, some treatment programs *do* have an appreciable effect on recidivism. Some programs are indeed beneficial."[12] But, despite Martinson's recantation of his "nothing works" thesis and Palmer's and Gendreau and Ross's defense of correctional treatment, the general mood regarding offender rehabilitation in the late 1970s and early 1980s was one of pessimism and discouragement.

In the late 1980s, Gendreau and Ross reviewed the offender rehabilitation literature for the period between 1981 and 1987 and again found that the number and variety of successful reported attempts at reducing delinquent behavior contradicted the "nothing works" hypothesis.[13] Moreover, the rehabilitative evidence in the 1980s grew at a much higher rate than it did during the 1970s and suggested several strategies for developing more effective programs.[14]

Several meta-analyses have evaluated the effectiveness of correctional treatment. The statistical tool of meta-analysis has been developed to enable reviewers to combine findings from different experiments. Meta-analysis undertakes the "aggregation and side-by-side analysis of large numbers of experimental studies."[15] One of the advantages of meta-analysis is that it can "incorporate adjustments for the fact that studies vary considerably in the degree of rigor of their experimental design." Thus, taking all of these meta-analyses together, the net effect of treatment is an average reduction in recidivism rates of between 10 and 12 percent.[16] See the Evidence-Based Practice feature.

Evidence-Based Practice
Using Meta-Analysis

The statistical tool of meta-analysis has been developed to enable reviewers to combine findings from different experiments. In meta-analysis, compatible information and data are extracted and pooled. When analyzed, the group data from several different studies provide a more powerful and valid indicator of relationships than is provided by a single study. These more sophisticated techniques have allowed correctional experts to examine some of the most important issues involving the effectiveness of correctional treatment.

Lipsey's comprehensive 2009 analysis of the effects of delinquency interventions consisted of 548 studies that spanned the period from 1958 to 2002. These studies represented all of the intervention research that could be located through an extensive search for published and unpublished reports of research. An overall finding of Lipsey's meta-analysis is that some interventions show relatively large positive effects on the juveniles who participate. What do these programs look like?

- *Risk factors.* One would assume that correctional treatment would be most effective with low-risk, nondangerous offenders. However, meta-analyses does not support this conclusion. Considerable research has found that programs targeting offenders who are higher risk are more effective in reducing recidivism than those that target lower risk offenders; this is referred to as the "risk principle."
- *Program completion.* One would assume that the rehabilitation programs most successful in retaining clients would work the best. And they do. Bernadette Pellisier and colleagues investigated nineteen programs and found that dropouts were, not surprisingly, the least likely to succeed, and that dropouts from treatment were more likely to be women and those who enter treatment with lower levels of motivation. Inmates who were disciplinary discharges from treatment were always more likely to be young, have a history of violence, and have been diagnosed as having an antisocial personality.
- *Voluntariness.* One would assume that inmates who volunteer for treatment would be more successful than those who were coerced into rehabilitation programs. However,

a meta-analysis in the United States showed that this is not always the case. Overall, the evidence suggests that coerced clients do at least as well as those who voluntarily enter programs. When Michael L. Pendergast and colleagues examined the psychological functioning and social functioning between those who voluntarily or involuntarily entered the treatment program of a facility in California, they found that regardless of voluntary or involuntary admission status, treatment participants exhibited significant change during treatment on most measures of psychosocial functioning. Significant change was more often observed on measures of psychological than social functioning.
- *Amount and quality of service.* The quality of the program implementation was an important feature related to the magnitude of the effects.

In sum, while Martinson widely rumored review casts doubt on the effectiveness of correctional treatment, more recent reviews have found that programs can be highly effective under particular circumstances and with specific populations, especially for those residents who complete the programs. In the midst of these hopeful possibilities for treatment, there are at least two deterrents today that discourage the wider use of institutional programs: (1) overcrowded facilities, filled with violence, racial conflict, and sometimes gangs require that the focus be on security and institutional survival; and (2) the "no-frills" institutional emphasis found in adult corrections and in some part in juvenile corrections cuts back on program and treatment as much as constitutionally is permitted.

Sources: See Mark W. Lipsey, James C. Howell, Marion R. Kelly, Gabrielle Chapman, and Darin Carver, *Improving the Effectiveness of Juvenile Justice Programs: A New Perspective on Evidence-Based Programs* (Washington, DC: Center for Juvenile Justice Reform, Georgetown University, 2010), 22; Bernadette Pellisier, Scott D. Camp, and Mark Motivans, "Staying in Treatment: How Much Difference Is There from Person to Person," *Psychology of Addictive Behavior* 17 (2003), 134, 141; and Michael L. Pendergast, David Farabee, Jerome Cortier, and Susan Henkin, "Involuntary Treatment Within a Prison Setting—Impact on Psychosocial Change During Treatment," *Criminal Justice and Behavior* 29 (2002), 5, 26.

> ### TABLE 12–1
> #### Responses to Treatment Today
>
> Treatment has received several responses in the late twentieth century to the present:
>
> - *"Rehabilitation is not appropriate" stage:* Critics charged that rehabilitative philosophy was in conflict with basic human values, did not work, and was a disaster in practice.
> - *"Nothing works" stage:* The research conducted by Robert Martinson and his colleagues was hailed by critics of treatment as evidence that "nothing works."
> - *"Some treatment works" stage:* A number of studies found positive effects from conducting treatment.
> - *"Numerous programs and innovations work" stage:* Much greater support is now found for treatment, but supporters do argue from their analysis of treatment studies that programs with multiple modalities must be used, the intensity of contact must be increased in most programs, and greater attention must be given to offenders' needs and characteristics so that they can be matched with particular programs.

The "Numerous Programs and Innovations Work" Stage

Today, arguing that rehabilitation has staged a comeback is easy. More empirical support for the various treatment modalities, such as drug treatment, cognitive therapy, and therapeutic communities (TCs), exists than in the past. And several promising innovations are increasingly being used:

- *Risk/needs assessments:* This refers to the attempt to offer treatment-relevant information when residents are classified into a new facility.
- *Responsivity principle:* This maintains that programs should consider offenders' situations as well as characteristics that may become barriers to success in a correctional program.
- *Best practice principle:* Principle that states what is done should be based on previous research and successful programming.

In a 2007 article, Mark W. Lipsey and Francis T. Cullen, two highly respected scholars, state this position, as well as the challenges for correctional treatment, clearly:

> The mean recidivism effects found in studies of rehabilitation treatment, by comparison [to supervision and sanctions] are consistently positive and relatively large. There is, however, considerable variability in those effects associated with the type of treatment, how well it is implemented, and the nature of the offenders to whom it is applied. The specific sources of that variability have not been well explored, but some principles for effective treatment have emerged. The rehabilitation treatments generally found effective in research do not characterize current correctional practice and bridging the gap between research and practice remains a significant challenge.[17]

Proponents of intervention's new direction or emphasis largely agreed on the following principles for working with serious offenders: (1) programs with multiple modalities must be used; (2) intensity of contact must be increased in most programs; and (3) greater attention must be paid to offenders' needs and characteristics so that they can be matched with particular program elements.[18] Table 12–1 summarizes the various responses to treatment.

How Are Youthful Offenders Classified?

Throughout the twentieth century, classification was considered the first step of treatment in juvenile correction. Psychiatric evaluations and psychological workups of juvenile delinquents were being conducted in child guidance clinics by the second decade of the

TABLE 12–2	
Risk Assessments Instruments	

Assessment Tool	Purpose of Assessment
YLS/CMI (Youth Level of Service/Case Management Inventory)	This is the youth version of the widely used adult assessment—the Level of Service Inventory Revisited (LSI-R). This instrument is based on three principles of case management: • "Risk principle"—Services should reflect level of risk present. • "Need principle"—Services should be matched with the delinquent needs of the youth. • "Responsivity"—Decisions about interventions should consider other characteristics of the youth and his or her circumstances that may affect responses to the interventions.
J-RAT (Juvenile Risk Assessment Tool)	This is intended for the initial assessment of male juvenile sexual offenders. As of October 2007, the Stetson School in Florida, which treats sexually reactive children, was using the J-RAT Version 3.
YASI (Youth Assessment and Screening Instrument)	This is a method for placing youths in categories that correspond to their likelihood of future arrests and violent offenses. It is being used in New York, Illinois, Washington, Virginia, and Mississippi. It assesses risk, needs, and protective factors and helps develop case plans for youths.
SAVRY (Structured Assessment of Violence Risk in Youth)	With its emphasis on dynamic factors, SAVRY is useful in intervention planning and ongoing progress monitoring, including the formulation of clinical treatment plans, conditions of community supervision, or release/discharge.
MAYSI-2	The MAYSI-2 is a paper-and-pencil self-report inventory of fifty-two Yes/No questions designed to assist juvenile justice facilities in identifying youths ages twelve to seventeen who may have special mental health needs.
PCL-YV (Psychopathy Checklist–Youth Version by Robert Hare)	This is a twenty-item assessment of psychopathic traits in male and female offenders ages twelve to eighteen. It is adapted from the *Hare Psychopathy Checklist Revisited (PCL-R)*, the most widely used measure of psychopathy in adults.

Sources: Data accessed at http://www.stetsonschool.org/Clinical_Materials/Assessment_Tools/IM-RAT-V3.pdf; http://www.hare.org/scales/pclyv.html; http://www.djj.virginia.gov/Initiatives/YASI.aspx; and http://www.stoeltingco.com/stoelting/2294/1467/1497/Psychological/Structured-Assessment-of-Violence-Risk-in-Youth-SAVRY.

twentieth century. A number of reception and diagnostic centers were built in the 1930s and 1940s so that delinquents could be assigned to programs compatible with their psychological, educational, and vocational needs. Classifying youths in terms of their personality dynamics, worldview, and behavior were the three most popular schemes in the 1960s and 1970s. But in the past two decades, classification systems for treatment purposes in juvenile corrections have lost much of their former popularity.

Increasingly popular today are the various risks/needs assessments that are administered to youths as part of pre- and postadjudication case planning. These include the YLS/CMI, J-RAT, YASI, SAVRY, MAYSI-2, and PCL-YV, as discussed in Table 12–2.

Some of these assessment tools are more developed than others, and some are more frequently used in juvenile justice agencies than others. Still, the number of these assessment tools, as well as others, testifies to the importance of needs and assessment as a means of classifying offenders in the juvenile justice system today.

What Are the Main Treatment Modalities?

This section presents a selection of therapeutic methods—both individual and group—that have been used nationally in juvenile correctional facilities and identifies some of their more salient features.

Individual-Level Treatment Programs

The number of different individual techniques includes insight therapy, behavior therapy, and cognitive-behavior therapy. These are reviewed below.

Insight-Based Therapy

It is common for training schools today to employ **insight-based therapy** techniques for the treatment of mental and emotional disorders. There are many different types of insight-based therapy techniques, but in general the therapist utilizes insight, persuasion, suggestion, reinsurance, and instructions so that residents can see themselves and their problems more realistically and can develop a desire to cope effectively with their fears and problems (see Focus on Treatment 12–1).

Psychiatrists, clinical psychologists, and psychiatric social workers have used various forms of insight-based therapies in training schools since the early twentieth century. Residents are encouraged to talk about past conflicts that cause them to express emotional problems through aggressive or antisocial behavior. The insight that residents gain from this therapy supposedly helps resolve the conflicts and unconscious needs that drove them to crime. As a final step, the resident becomes responsible for his or her own behavior.

Insight-based therapy techniques have some fundamental limitations in a training school context. Residents usually do not see themselves as having emotional problems and are reluctant to share their inner thoughts with their therapists. There are also staffing problems. Professional mental health staff make up a small part of agencies' staffs, yet they are expected to provide a wide range of mental health services.

Behavior Therapy

A second form of individual treatment, behavior therapy, rests on the assumption that desirable behaviors are rewarded immediately and will therefore systematically increase, and undesirable behaviors that are not rewarded or punished will diminish and eventually be extinguished. Behavior therapy uses positive and negative reinforcement to encourage desirable and extinguish undesirable behavior. **Behavior modification** is the principal behavior therapy technique and is still practiced informally in a great many training schools. It works like this: residents receive additional privileges as they become more accepting of the institutional rules and procedures and as they exhibit more positive attitudes.

Focus on Treatment 12–1
Insight-Based Therapies

Type	Treatment Goal	Qualifications of Therapist	Length of Treatment Period	Response from Offenders
Psychotherapy	Lead inmates to insight	Psychiatrist, psychologist, social worker	Long-term	Will examine individual problems with therapist
Transactional analysis	Lead inmates to insight	Psychiatrist, psychologist, trained nonprofessional, staff	Usually several months	Will examine individual problems in a group context and will learn a new approach to interpersonal relationships
Reality therapy	Help inmates to obtain basic needs	Psychiatrist, psychologist, trained nonprofessional, staff	Short period of time	Will learn to cope with reality, model responsible behavior, and determine right from wrong

Cognitive-Behavior Therapy (CBT)

Cognitive-behavior therapy (CBT) for offenders is based on the assumption that the foundations for criminal behavior are dysfunctional patterns of thinking. The intent is that by altering routine misinterpretations of life events, offenders can modify antisocial aspects of their personality and consequent behavior. The goal of these interventions is to identify cognitive deficits linked to delinquency. These cognitive deficits are expressed in a concrete thinking style that impinges on the ability to appreciate the feelings and thoughts of others, impairments leading to self-defeating behavior, impulsivity, egocentricity, inability to reason critically, peer interpersonal problem-solving skills, and a preoccupation with self.[19] See Focus on Programs 12–2.

▲ The resident receives advice that it will be necessary for him to have a positive program to shorten institutional stay.
© ZUMA Wire Service/Alamy

CBT in offender treatment targets the thoughts, choices, attitudes, and meaning systems that are associated with antisocial behavior as well as deviant lifestyle. It generally uses a training approach to teach new skills in areas where offenders showed deficits, such as generating alternative solutions, rather than reacting on first impulse; interpersonal problems awareness; opening up and listening to other perspectives; evaluating consequences; resisting; soliciting feedback; taking the person's well-being into account; and deciding on the most beneficial course of action.[20]

The CBT therapists act as teachers, and lessons are usually taught to groups in classroom settings. The lessons may include group exercises involving role-play, rehearsal, homework assignments, and intensive feedback and generally follow detailed lesson plans and structured curriculum.[21] People taking part in CBT learn specific skills that can be used to solve the problems they confront all the time as well as skills they can use to achieve the legitimate goals and objectives. CBT first concentrates on developing skills to recognize unrealistic or distorted thinking when it happens, and then works toward changing that thinking or belief to modify or eliminate problematic behavior.[22]

The most widely adopted of the cognitive-behavioral interventions is the **Cognitive Thinking Skill Program (CTSP)** developed by Robert Ross and Elizabeth Fabiano, which is now a core program in the Canadian correctional system and has been implemented in the United States, New Zealand, Australia, and some European countries.[23]

CTSP was developed through a systematic review of all published correctional programs that were associated with reduced criminal recidivism. The researchers identified one hundred evaluations of effective programs and discovered that they all were designed to target offenders' thinking. Rigid thinking could be minimized by teaching participants creative thinking skills and providing them with prosocial alternatives to use when reporting or responding to interpersonal problems. Core components of CTSP are that teaching offender techniques of self-control could improve social adjustments.[24]

A review of the literature leads to the conclusion that combining elements of cognition and behavior approaches are found in the principle of self-reinforcement. This concept says that behavior and cognitive changes reinforce each other. When cognitive changes lead to changes in behavior, what takes place is a sense of well-being that strengthens its change in thought and, as a result, further strengthens behavioral changes. This self-reinforcing feedback process is a key of the CBT approach and provides a basis for helping offenders understand the cognitive-behavior process.[25]

Cognitive-Behavior Therapy Effectiveness

A considerable amount of research indicates that CBT approaches have positive effects with offenders[26]:

* A meta-analysis of sixty-nine studies covering both behavior and cognitive-behavioral problems determined that the cognitive-behavior programs are more effective in reducing rates of recidivism than behavior programs. The mean reduction was about 39 percent for treated offenders.[27]

* Other meta-analyses of correctional treatment concluded that cognitive-behavioral methods constituted critical aspects of effective correctional treatment.[28]

- Another study determined that the most effective interventions are those employed by cognitive-behavioral techniques to improve cognitive function.[29]

- There is strong evidence that positive results are more likely to take place among certain subgroups. For example, CTSP seems to be more effective with offenders over age twenty-five and with property offenders.[30]

See Figure 12–1 for the recidivism effect associated with skill-building programs.

Group Programs

In addition to therapies at the individual level, most training schools maintain group counseling programs. The most popular of these programs are drug and alcohol treatment programs, guided group interaction, positive peer culture, drug and alcohol treatment programs, and intervention with juvenile sex offenders.

Guided Group Interaction

Guided group interaction (GGI) is probably the most widely used treatment modality. It has been used in at least eleven states: Florida, Georgia, Illinois, Kentucky, Maryland, Michigan, Minnesota, New Hampshire, New Jersey, South Dakota, and West Virginia. Since the 1950s, when this modality was first used, it has been based on the assumption that youths could confront their peers and force them to face the reality of their behavior more effectively than could staff.

The GGI approach is characterized by a nonauthoritarian atmosphere, intensity of interaction, group homogeneity, and an emphasis on group structure. The most important characteristic is the nonauthoritarian atmosphere. Residents in many residential GGI programs, for example, are given considerable say in when a group member will be released, granted a home furlough, or approved for off-campus visits; in how a group will be punished; and in whether the outside door will be locked or left open at night.

Giving residents responsibility for decision making, of course, is a different approach to child care from that followed in most correctional settings. The adult leader constantly refers the decision making back to the group. When informed by a youth that a group member planned to run away, for example, one staff member retorted: "So what do you want me to do? He's your buddy; he's part of your group. You can talk to him if you have to; but it's up to all of you to help one another."[31]

FIGURE 12–1
Mean recidivism effects for the generic program types within the skill building category

Source: Mark W. Lipsey, James C. Howell, Marion R. Kelly, Gabrielle Chapman, Darin Carver, *Improving the Effectiveness of Juvenile Justice Programs,* Center for Juvenile Justice, © 2010.

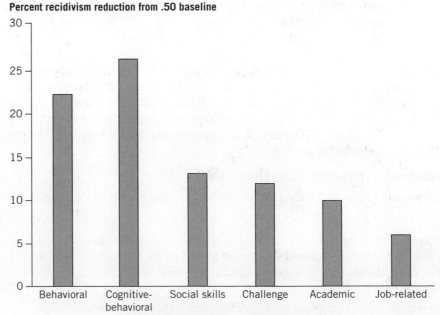

Percent recidivism reduction from .50 baseline

Mean Recidivism Effects for Skill-Building Programs

A great strength of GGI is its determination to circumvent the values of the delinquent-peer subculture. This modality, in urging residents to be honest and open with one another, attempts to move group participants toward a more positive, prosocial stance. Another advantage is that it represents a comprehensive strategy for dealing with troubled youth. In effect, it is a total system for mitigating the impact of a delinquent subculture. A third advantage is that GGI seems to have gained acceptance on the state level. Also important is the fact that GGI can be led by line staff, thereby increasing staff involvement in the treatment process. A final advantage is that responsibility is given to offenders; thus, in interacting with peers, offenders become aware of their problems and are directed toward resolutions.

A major problem in using GGI is the shortage of trained group leaders. Also, since this approach to group work lacks a single spokesman, a number of versions and designs of the basic principles have emerged. As a consequence, no clear and consistent philosophy guides the process of working with offenders in groups. The emphasis of GGI on peer group norms and values further tends to slight the importance of individualism. Extreme care must be taken to ensure that peer-group norms established and monitored by institutional staff do not repress the youthful offenders' needs for self-identity and autonomy. Finally, peer-group norms created by GGI may not always be transferable to the actual life situations that will be encountered upon release.

Although the research findings on GGI have been mixed, the general picture that emerges is that a GGI experience in a nonresidential program is at least as effective as and much less costly than confinement in a state facility and that a GGI experience in an institutional program seems to have a more positive impact on less delinquent youngsters.[32]

Positive Peer Culture

The concept of **positive peer culture (PPC)** generated considerable excitement in juvenile corrections, especially in the 1970s. Developed by Harry Vorrath and associates as an outgrowth of GGI, PPC has been implemented in all of the juvenile state institutions in Michigan, Missouri, and West Virginia.[33]

Vorrath believes that PPC "is a total system for building positive youth subcultures."[34] The main philosophy of PPC is to "turn around" the negative peer culture and to mobilize the power of the peer group in a positive way. PPC does this by teaching group members to care for one another; caring is defined as wanting what is best for a person. Vorrath believes that once caring becomes "fashionable" and is accepted by the group, "hurting goes out of style."[35]

PPC involves the same stages as in GGI, but it places more emphasis on positive behavior. Group members learn to speak of positive behaviors as "great," "intelligent," "independent," "improving," and "winning." In contrast, negative behaviors are described as "childish," "unintelligent," "helpless," "destructive," "copping out," and "losing."

PPC is developed through ninety-minute meetings five times per week. Characterized by trust and openness, PPC focuses on the direct and immediate problems of the lawbreaking youth. Believing that groups function most effectively when they are homogeneous, leaders try to include youths who are similar in age, sex, maturity, and delinquency sophistication. Coeducational groups are believed to be counterproductive.

Vorrath believes that the group has to be involved in decision-making processes, such as whether to give a youth a home visit or when to release a resident. Although he acknowledges that institutional staff ultimately must make these decisions, he states that the recommendations initially should come from the group members. The group, in discussing the possibility of releasing a member, concerns itself with both the member's present problems and those he or she will experience once back in the community.

In sum, although Vorrath believes that the basic assumptions of these youths can be changed, few people change many of their background assumptions over the period of a lifetime—much less when they are stripped of their freedom and are in therapy. For this modality to be properly evaluated, more research is needed. But its present successes should remind both followers and critics that PPC remains one of the most promising ways to treat, change, correct, and rehabilitate juvenile offenders.

▲ A dangerous development with the Internet is the "sexploitation" of young boys and girls by sexual predators online. This young girl could well be in extreme danger since her parents apparently did not monitor her online activities.

Valeriy Velikov/Shutterstock

Drug and Alcohol Abuse Interventions

Drug and alcohol abuse by juveniles, as well as their involvement in drug trafficking in the community, constitutes a serious social problem today. A director of guidance in a training school acknowledged the seriousness of the problem when he said, "Rarely do we get a boy who doesn't have some history of drug or alcohol abuse in his background."[36]

Drug and alcohol abuse interventions increasingly are being developed in community-based and institutional settings to assist those who need help with such problems. These groups are being conducted in training schools in at least three ways: First, institutionalized juveniles assessed to have a problem with alcohol and/or drugs are placed in a separate cottage or in a chemical abuse group. Specialized staff are hired to work in these cottages or lead these groups. Second, in other training schools, the social worker or another cottage staff member conducts ongoing drug and alcohol abuse groups. Third, outside groups, such as Alcoholics Anonymous (AA) or Narcotics Anonymous (NA), come into the institution and hold sessions for interested residents.

Considering the extensiveness of the problem of drug use and trafficking among juvenile offenders, there are still too few programs being offered in juvenile placements. The programs that are offered tend to be relatively unsophisticated and lack adequate theoretical design, treatment integrity, and evaluation follow-up.

Treatment studies done on prison populations have found that when drug programs are well integrated and their effective program elements are implemented carefully, these programs:

- Reduce relapse.
- Reduce criminality.
- Reduce inmate misconduct.
- Reduce mental illness.
- Reduce behavioral disorders.
- Increase the level of the inmates' stake in societal norms.
- Increase levels of education and employment upon returning to the community.
- Improve health and mental health symptoms and conditions.
- Improve relationships.[37]

Unquestionably, development of effective alcohol and drug abuse programs represents one of the most important challenges of juvenile justice today.

Thinking like a Correctional Professional

You are the chairperson of a congressional meeting that's been asked to evaluate the role of treatment in juvenile correctional institutions. how will you do this? Do you think that your committee will consider the following questions:?

- In view of the high recidisim rates of institutional releasees, does this mean that treatment has been ineffective?
- What do you feel needs to be done to make institututional treatment more effective?

What other questions do you think you will consider/? What will your final recommendation be?

Social Worker Profile

PREPARATION FOR THE JOB

Budding social workers should gain experience volunteering in group homes, afterschool programs, and working in the community with at-risk kids.

NATURE OF THE JOB

Social casework, organizational processing of residence, services to residents, and maintenance of community contacts are the main duties of the social worker. Social workers are expected to make use of the principles of social casework in their therapeutic intervention with residents, the purpose of which is to determine the kind of help they need. Social workers guide residents through the institutional process, up to representing them at the periodic reviews before administrative board, and ultimately recommending each client for release (unless they had been given a mandatory sentence). Social workers write frequent evaluation reports on each residents' progress, copies of which are usually sent to the social workers' supervisor, the central office of the youth commission, or department of corrections, and to the youth aftercare officer. Furthermore, the social worker is expected to do all the presentence paperwork when the institutional release procedure has determined that the youth is ready to leave the institution. There is a wide range of community contact responsibilities, which might include determining why parents have not written and encouraging them to visit, reporting on the medical conditions of any hospitalized family member, informing

residents should death occur in the family, contacting aftercare officers about a resident's special concerns, and counseling parents when conflict seems to be present in the home.

QUALIFICATIONS AND REQUIRED EDUCATION

An undergraduate degree in sociology, social work, or criminology is required in most juvenile institutional settings. Many correctional systems also require the applicant to pass an intelligence and aptitude test. To be promoted to social work supervisor frequently requires a master's degree in social work, criminology, or sociology.

JOB OUTLOOK

The job outlook continues to be good for institutional social workers for both state and private institutions.

EARNINGS AND BENEFITS

Ordinarily, social workers in state institutions receive a higher salary than do social workers in private institutions. In some jurisdictions, social workers in private and county facilities make considerably higher salary than do those in state facilities. The average salary in state facilities ranges from $25,000 to $50,000.

Source: Based on Bartollas' four years experience in severing as a social worker and a social work supervisor in a maximum-security juvenile facility as well as institutional social workers interviewed in recent years.

Why Is Treatment Effectiveness So Difficult to Attain?

The increased amount of evidence of best programs in juvenile justice is an indication that there is support for effective treatment in juvenile justice. Unfortunately, the frequent criticism that offender rehabilitation is defective in theory and a disaster in practice is true in too many programs. Program designs have often given little consideration to what a particular program can realistically accomplish with a particular group of offenders and have frequently relied on a single cure for a variety of complex problems. In addition, programs generally have lacked integrity, because they have not delivered the services they claimed with sufficient strength to accomplish the goals of treatment. Furthermore, the research on offender rehabilitation has generally been inadequate, with many projects and reports on rehabilitation almost totally lacking in well-developed research designs.[38]

To improve the quality of institutional treatment even further, three basic steps appear to be necessary: (1) more programs must include the ingredients of effective interventions; (2) more programs must be based on better program design, ensure higher program integrity, and be evaluated by more rigorous research methods; and (3) research must provide more information on what works for whom and in what context.

Ingredients of Effective Programs

Effective programs usually have a number of ingredients in common. They usually are set up by an inspired individual or group of individuals, have developed a unified-team approach among staff, have a transmittable philosophy of life, trust offenders with decision-making responsibilities, help offenders develop needed skills, are regarded as unique and different by offenders, and provide an integrated treatment model.[39]

The Inspired Leader Who Means Business

The inspired individual or group of individuals who is seriously dedicated to setting up a program has been found time after time to be one of the chief ingredients of effective programs. In Outward Bound, Kurt Hahn was able to generate enthusiasm and support among those who contacted him.[40] Sister Falaka Fattah and her husband set up the House of Umoja in Philadelphia, which is committed to dealing with the gang problem in that urban community.[41] The inspiration of Clifford Shaw continues to influence the Chicago Area Projects long after his death.

Unified Treatment Team

A program is more likely to have an impact on offenders if the treatment team is unified. In a unified treatment team, all staff members become treatment agents as they design the program, develop short- and long-range goals for the program, and involve themselves with offenders.

Philosophy of Life That Is Transmittable

Effective programs also generate a sense of mission or purpose among offenders by transmitting a philosophy of life. Martin Groder has noted, "It's not that the guy has to adopt the philosophy of the program, but he's got to learn it well enough to integrate it with his own life experience and come out with his own version."[42] Clemens Bartollas, Stuart J. Miller, and Simon Dinitz reported that having a mission or purpose in life is one characteristic of hard-core offenders who are later successful in the community.[43]

Involvement of Offenders in the Decision-Making Process

Effective programs also frequently provide decision-making responsibilities for juvenile offenders. Although many correctional interventions treat these offenders as helpless children incapable of making decisions for themselves, the more noteworthy programs encourage decision making and then make participants responsible for their choices. The more offenders are permitted to make choices concerning what happens to them, the more likely they are to be involved in a treatment program and to seek to benefit from it.

Skill Development

Effective programs include **skill development**, which helps offenders learn new tasks that prepare them for adjustment in the community. These skills range from educational and vocational to interpersonal and problem-solving skills. Such abilities make offenders believe that they can accomplish something or that they have acquired important insights about themselves or about life.

Uniqueness

The most distinguishing characteristic of effective interventions is sometimes their uniqueness. That is, the components of these programs that make them different from other correctional interventions are sometimes the most important factors in grabbing the attention of youthful offenders and getting them involved in these interventions.

Integrated Treatment Model

The states of Colorado, Texas, and Washington have developed integrated treatment models, and California is in the process of developing such a model. These programs based their treatment philosophy and intervention on cognitive-behavioral treatment. The **integrated treatment model** provides the central guiding vision that unites screening, assessment, case planning, treatment, transition, and aftercare. These concepts are used across all parts of the juvenile correctional system, including the core treatment program, special treatment programs, work, education, recreation, mental health, and parole. All staff members, including administrators, treatment providers, support staff, and line staff, receive training in the model. This not only helps structure the environment to promote success in changing behavior but also creates a common treatment vocabulary for all parts of the agency. Another advantage of this integrated model is that it provides adequate community follow-up in order for offenders to sustain positive changes in their lives.[44]

Strategy for Improving the Effectiveness of Correctional Programs

Improving program effectiveness requires that program designs be based on theoretical premises, that programs be implemented with integrity, and that programs be evaluated with rigorous research methods.

Program Design

The theoretical premises, or constructs, of programs must be examined in order to determine whether they are appropriate for particular groups of offenders. The processes by which any set of interventions will change antisocial behavior must also be examined in order to determine whether the treatment has sufficient strength to produce the desired behavior or attitudinal change. Finally, the theoretical constructs must be meshed with the setting in which treatment takes place to ensure that programs are implemented in appropriate settings.[45]

Program Implementation

Juvenile offenders must be placed in the right program at the optimal time for them to benefit from treatment. Effective interventions must actually deliver the services they claim to deliver, with sufficient strength to accomplish the goals of treatment. In addition, program integrity requires that personnel be equipped to deliver the specified services; thus, treatment personnel must have some degree of expertise in what they are doing, must have sufficient training to do it, and must receive adequate supervision. Finally, it must be possible to modify interventions according to changing interests and needs of offenders.[46]

Program Evaluation

The Panel on Research on Rehabilitative Techniques concluded after nearly two years of examining offender rehabilitation that "the research methodology that has been brought to bear on the problem of finding ways to rehabilitate criminal offenders has been generally so inadequate that only a relatively few studies warrant any unequivocal interpretations."[47] Sample sizes must be large enough to measure subtle effects, such as changes in interactions. True randomized experiments must be conducted whenever feasible because they permit some certainty about causal relationships. Researchers need to identify the common elements of effective programs and to determine how these elements affect success with particular groups of offenders. In addition, researchers need to determine how effective programs can be replicated in other settings. Finally, more empirical work must be done on measuring the outcomes of correctional treatment.[48]

What Works for Whom and in What Context?

Correctional treatment must discover what works for which offenders in what context. In other words, correctional treatment could work if amenable offenders were offered appropriate treatments by matched workers in environments conducive to producing positive effects.[49]

To match individual offenders with the treatments most likely to benefit them will be no easy task. Only through well-planned and soundly executed research will the necessary information be gained. The Panel on Research of Rehabilitative Techniques recommends the use of the "template-matching technique."[50] This technique creates a set of descriptors, or a *template*, of the kinds of people who are most likely to benefit from a particular treatment according to the theory or basic assumptions underlying it.[51] Because of the scarcity of treatment resources, matching programs to those offenders most likely to profit from them is only sensible. See Table 12–3 Treatment Technologies.

TABLE 12–3
Treatment Technologies

Type	Treatment Goal	Qualifications of Therapist	Length of Treatment	Frequency of Treatment	Expected Offender Response
Individual or group psychotherapy	Lead youths to insight	Psychiatrist, psychologist, psychiatric social worker	Frequently extensive or long term	Several times per week if possible	Will examine individual problems with therapist
Transactional analysis	Lead youths to insight	Psychiatrist, psychologist, trained nonprofessional staff	Usually several months	Once or more per week	Will examine individual problems in a group context and will learn a new approach to interpersonal relationships
Reality therapy	Help youths to fulfill basic needs	Psychiatrist, psychologist, trained nonprofessional staff	Short period of time	Once or more per week	To learn reality, responsible behavior, and right from wrong
Behavior modification	Help youths to react positively	Anyone who can assume role of therapist	Usually long term	Continuous rather than interwoven with nontreatment	To continue their reinforced, positive behavior
Guided group interaction	Develop prosocial norms and values	Anyone trained in GGI	Several months	Four or five times per week	Will become responsible for others in the group
Positive peer culture	Develop prosocial norms and values	Anyone trained in PPC	Several months	Four or five times per week	Will genuinely care for other group members
Drug and alcohol abuse programs	Help youths to overcome addiction	Anyone who has understanding of problem	Extensive or long term	Once or more per week	Will gain skills and knowledge to overcome substance abuse
Errors in thinking approach	Insight into individual behavior	Psychiatrist, psychologist, psychiatric social worker	Extensive or long term	Once or more per week	To learn responsible and prosocial behavior
Skill development programs	Personal empowerment	Anyone who can assume role of staff member	Short or long term	Daily	Will gain skills and knowledge to pursue positive behavior

Palmer's approach is somewhat different in determining what works for which offenders in what contexts. He suggests that effective intervention for each offender must take seriously skill deficits, external pressures and disadvantages, and internal difficulties:

1. *Skill/Capacity Deficits:* Various, often major, developmental challenges—frequently including life and social skills deficits in such areas as educational and vocational abilities

2. *External Pressures/Disadvantages:* Major environmental pressures and/or major social disadvantages, including comparatively limited or reduced family, community, and other supports or social assistance

3. *Internal Difficulties:* Long-standing or situational feelings, attitudes, and defenses; ambivalence regarding change; particular motivations, desires, and personal and interpersonal commitments[52]

SUMMARY

LEARNING OBJECTIVE 1: Summarize the different viewpoints concerning treatment in juvenile justice.

(1) The "rehabilitation is not appropriate" stage, (2) the "nothing works" stage, (3) the "some treatments work" stage, and (4) the "numerous programs and innovations work" stage.

LEARNING OBJECTIVE 2: Describe the treatment modalities used most frequently in juvenile justice.

This chapter discusses and evaluates the basic treatment modalities in juvenile justice.

These therapies can be grouped under individual-level treatment programs (insight-based therapy, behavior therapy, and cognitive-behavior therapy) and group therapy (guided group interaction, positive peer culture, drug and alcohol treatment, and intervention with juvenile sex offenders).

LEARNING OBJECTIVE 3: Evaluate the juvenile justice treatment modalities.

It can be argued that we may have expected too much from correctional treatment. Long-term training schools are among the least promising places for treatment to take place. But even in community-based programs, the lack of resources or overworked staff, clients' histories of failure, and drug and alcohol addictions result in far more failures than successes. The danger, however, is to expect too little from correctional treatment. The gathering evidence of best programs is a reminder that treatment technologies are improving and promise to have more positive outcomes and lower rates of recidivism in the future.

LEARNING OBJECTIVE 4: Identify suggestions for improving treatment in juvenile justice agencies.

The future effectiveness of correctional treatment in juvenile justice may be contingent on three conditions:

1. Funding research so that more effective technologies can be developed.
2. Identifying what works for which group of offenders so that youthful offenders interested in treatment can be given the interventions most compatible with their needs and interests.
3. Creating more humane environments, where residents are treated with dignity and respect, so that environmental conditions will not negatively interfere with the treatment process.

KEY TERMS

behavior modification, p. 264

cognitive-behavior therapy (CBT), p. 265

Cognitive Thinking Skill Program (CTSP), p. 265

drug and alcohol abuse interventions, p. 268

guided group interaction (GGI), p. 266

insight-based therapy, p. 264

integrated treatment model, p. 270

positive peer culture (PPC), p. 267

psychotherapy, p. 264

reality therapy, p. 264

skill development program, p. 270

transactional analysis (TA), p. 264

REVIEW QUESTIONS

1. Do you agree that no treatment is effective for juvenile offenders?
2. If you were superintendent of a training school, which treatment methods would you use? Why? What treatment technologies would you use in a residential program for juvenile probationers?
3. What type of staff member would be effective in carrying out the treatment method you chose in Question 2? Why?
4. Would you hire ex-offenders to work in your community-based or institutional facility? Why or why not?
5. Do you feel that the goals of PPC are realistic?
6. How would you treat youths who do not respond to the rules of your prescribed treatment method?

GROUP EXERCISES

1. **Group Work:** Discuss the stages through which the U.S. correctional system has gone in utilizing the idea of rehabilitation in correctional facilities.
2. **Writing to Learn Exercise:** Write a paragraph each on reality therapy and behavioral modification, indicating how each varies from the others. Critique and revise.
3. **Writing to Learn Exercise:** Write a paragraph describing positive peer culture and its goals and processes. Then, write a second paragraph to describe the cognitive-behavior, or the thinking errors, approach and cognitive-behavior therapy interventions.
4. **Class Presentations:** Groups of three or four each are to research and analyze a different therapeutic modality and then report their findings to the class during the next session.
5. **Group Work:** Discuss what has to happen for treatment modalities to work.
   - **Research Center:** Check out the Cybrary and MySearchLab for even more resources.

WORKING WITH A JUVENILE

The role of the treatment agent is to do what she or he can do for each juvenile on his or her caseload. Some juveniles may not be ready to exit or walk away from crime. The treatment agent can still provide treatment that is of help to the juvenile's life.

NOTES

1. PAWS Training Academy, http://pawstrainingcenters.com/paws-training-academy/about/faculty/instructors/cece-miller/ (accessed August 2014).
2. Federal Bureau of Prisons press release, "Coce Miller Finds Purpose in Training Dogs and Helping People," April 17, 2014, http://www.legistrom.com/stormfeed/view_rss/402972/organizations/95552.html (accessed August 2014).
3. paws4 people, http://paws4people.org/cece-miller/ (accessed August 2014).
4. Walter C. Bailey, "Correctional Outcome: An Evaluation of 100 Reports," *Journal of Criminal Law, Criminology, and Police Science* 57 (June 1966), 153–60.
5. Robert Martinson, "What Works?—Questions and Answers About Prison Reform," *Public Interest* 35 (Spring 1974), 22–54.
6. Douglas Lipton, Robert Martinson, and Judith Wilks, *The Effectiveness of Correctional Treatment* (New York: Praeger, 1975).
7. CBS Television Network. Excerpted from *60 Minutes* segment, "It Doesn't Work" (August 24, 1975).
8. Ted Palmer, "Martinson Revisited," *Journal of Research in Crime and Delinquency* 12 (July 1975), 133–52.
9. Ibid., 137.
10. Paul Gendreau and Robert Ross, "Effective Correctional Treatment: Bibliotherapy for Cynics," *Crime and Delinquency* 27 (October 1979), 463–89.
11. Robert R. Ross and Paul Gendreau, eds., *Effective Correctional Treatment* (Toronto: Butterworth, 1980), viii.
12. Robert Martinson, "New Findings, New Views: A Note of Caution Regarding Sentencing Reform," *Hofstra Law Review* 7 (Winter 1979), 244.
13. Paul Gendreau and Robert R. Ross, "Revivification of Rehabilitative Evidence," *Justice Quarterly* 4 (September 1987), 349–407.
14. Ibid. For a review of the meta-analyses of correctional treatment in the 1980s, see Ted Palmer, *The Re-Emergence of Correctional Intervention* (Newbury Park, CA: Sage Publications, 1992), 50–76.
15. James McGuire and Philip Priestley, "Reviewing 'What Works': Past, Present, and Future," in *What Works: Reducing Reoffending—Guidelines from Research and Practice*, edited by James McGuire (New York: Wiley, 1995), 7–8.
16. Ibid.
17. Mark W. Lipsey and Frances T. Cullen, "The Effectiveness of Correctional Rehabilitation: A Review of Systematic Reviews," *American Review of Law and Social Science* 3 (2007), 297–320.
18. Ibid., 4.
19. Gerald G. Gaes, Timothy J. Flanagan, Lawrence L. Motiuk, and Lynn Steward, "Adult Correctional Treatment," in *Crime and Justice, 26th Edition: Prisons*, edited by Michael Tonry and Joan Petersilia (Chicago: University of Chicago Press, 1999), 374–75.
20. Harvey Milkman and Kenneth Wanberg, *Cognitive-Behavior Treatment: A Review and Discussion for Correctional Professionals* (Washington, DC: National Institute of Corrections, 2007), 5.
21. Ibid.
22. Sesha Kentineni and Jeremy Braithwaite, "The Effect of a Cognitive-Behavioral Program for At-Risk Youth: Changes in Attitudes, Social Skills, Family and Community and Peer Relationships," *Victims and Offenders* 6 (2011), 93–116.
23. Patricia van Voorhis, Lis M. Spruance, P. Neal Richey, Shelley Johnson Listwan, and Renita Seebrook, "The Georgia Cognitive skills experiment: A replication of Reasoning and Rehabilitation," *Criminal Justice and Behavior* 31 (2004), 282–305.
24. Ibid.
25. Ibid.
26. Ibid.
27. Frank S. Pearson, Douglas S. Lipton, Charles M. Cleland, and Dorline S. Yee, "The Effects of Behavioral/Cognitive-Behavioral Programs on Recidivism," *Crime and Delinquency* 48 (2002), 476–96.
28. Milkman and Wanberg, *Cognitive-Behavior Treatment*, xix.
29. Ibid.
30. Pearson et al., "The Effects of Behavioral/Cognitive-Behavioral Programs on Recidivism."
31. Interview with Harry Vorrath quoted in Oliver J. Keller, Jr., and Benedict S. Alper, *Halfway Houses: Community Centered Correction and Treatment* (Lexington, MA: D. C. Heath, 1970), 55.
32. Ibid.
33. These materials are adapted from Harry H. Vorrath and Larry K. Brendtro, *Positive Peer Culture* (Chicago: Aldine, 1974).
34. Ibid.
35. Ibid.
36. Interviewed in 1986 in a Midwestern training school.
37. See the Federal Bureau of Prisons, *Substance Abuse Treatment*, accessed May 18, 2012, at http://www.bop.gov/inmate_programs_substance.jsp.
38. Lee Sechrest, Susan O. White, and Elizabeth D. Brown, eds., *The Rehabilitation of Criminal Offenders* (Washington, DC: National Academy of Sciences, 1979); Susan Martin, Lee Sechrest, and Robin Redner, eds., *Rehabilitation of*

Criminal Offenders: Directions for Research (Washington, DC: National Academy of Sciences, 1981).

39. These elements of effective programs are suggested by the work of Martin Groder and of Alden D. Miller, Lloyd E. Ohlin, and Robert B. Coates. See "Dr. Martin Groder: An Angry Resignation," *Corrections Magazine* 1 (July–August 1975), 3; and Alden D. Miller, Lloyd E. Ohlin, and Robert B. Coates, *A Theory of Social Reform: Correctional Change Processes in Two States* (Cambridge, MA: Ballinger, 1977).

40. Joshua L. Miner and Joe Boldt, *Outward Bound USA: Learning Through Experience in Adventure-Based Education* (New York: William Morrow, 1981).

41. Robert L. Woodson, *A Summons to Life: Mediating Structure and the Prevention of Youth Crime* (Cambridge, MA: Ballinger, 1981).

42. Groder, "Dr. Martin Groder," 33.

43. Clemens Bartollas, Stuart J. Miller, and Simon Dinitz, "Boys Who Profit: The Limits of Institutional Success," in *Reform in Corrections: Problems and Issues*, edited by Harry E. Allen and Nancy J. Beran (New York: Praeger, 1977), 18–19.

44. Christopher Murray et al., *Safety and Welfare Plan: Implementing Reform in California* (Sacramento, CA: Safety and Welfare Planning Team, 2006), 42.

45. Sechrest et al., eds., *The Rehabilitation of Criminal Offenders*, 35–37.

46. For the development of these various aspects of intervention, see Palmer, *The Re-Emergence of Correctional Intervention*, 151–57.

47. Sechrest et al., eds., *The Rehabilitation of Criminal Offenders*, 3–4.

48. Martin et al., eds., *Rehabilitation of Criminal Offenders*, 6.

49. Sechrest et al., eds., *The Rehabilitation of Criminal Offenders*, 45.

50. The template-matching technique was originally proposed in D. Bem and D. Funder, "Predicting More of the People More of the Time: Assessing the Personality of Situations," *Psychological Review* 85 (1978), 485–501.

51. Martin et al., *Rehabilitation of Criminal Offenders*, 82.

52. Palmer, *The Re-Emergence of Correctional Intervention*, 113.

Stockbroker/Glow Images

Learning Objectives

1. Outline the development of gangs in the United States.
2. Describe the behaviors and activities of gangs.
3. Identify the primary types of gangs.
4. Identify the seven stages of emergent gang development.
5. Summarize efforts to prevent and control gangs.

The road to success is a hard one. It begins in the family unit. It is in the family that parents plant the seeds for a young person to succeed. This young person is taught morals and ethics and learns behavior patterns.

By the age of seven or eight, this young person has learned whether he will be loved, whether his needs will be met, and how fair life is. What he thinks will have an effect on his behavior. If he feels he is on the short end of the stick, he may wake up angry as hell in the morning. He will seek elsewhere to have his needs met. He is not in a good place to compete with peer pressure.

It is not long before he is in gangs, doing drugs, and hurting people. It is also not long before he is serving time in the "joint." When he comes out, it is even harder to achieve success. It is a lot easier to go back to crime than to stay away from it.

For those of us who are determined not to go back to a life of crime, we may make it. It takes determination. It takes the opportunity to stand on your own feet. It takes support from others. It takes luck. But we are never out of the woods because it is real easy to go back.

What I am saying is that if we want to deal with youth crime, adult crime, and street gangs, we must go back to the family unit, must improve our schools, must make our neighborhoods more desirable, and must [provide] other alternatives to gangs and drugs.

—Fred "Bobby" Gore[1]

In the chapter-opening quote, Fred "Bobby" Gore explains why the social context is important to understanding youth crime and street gangs. Gore became one of the most influential leaders of the Conservative Vice Lords gang, the largest division of the Vice Lord Nation. That was thirty years ago. Until recent years, he was the program director of the SAFER Foundation, a community integration program for ex-offenders. He retired and in the spring of 2014 he died, but he continued to be a positive force against youths becoming involved in gangs.

Beginning in 1988 and continuing through the early 1990s, an upsurge in youth gangs suddenly occurred throughout the United States. Some of these youth gangs used the names of the national **urban gangs**, such as the Bloods and Crips from Los Angeles or the Gangster Disciples, Vice Lords, or Latin Kings from Chicago. Other gangs made up their own names, based on neighborhoods or images they wanted to depict to other peers and the community. By the mid-1990s, nearly every city, many suburban areas, and even some rural areas across the United States experienced the reality of youths who have banded together to form a youth gang.

The good news is that from 1996 to 2003, the estimated numbers of youth gangs and youth gang members in the United States decreased, as did the number of jurisdictions reporting gang problems. Then, however, the numbers steadily increased to 28,100 gangs with 731,000 gang members by 2009. More than one-third of the jurisdictions in the *National Youth Gang Survey* experienced gang problems in 2001, which is the highest annual estimate since before 2000 (see Figure 13–1). Overall, an estimated 3,500 jurisdictions served by city (population of 2,500 or more) and county law enforcement agencies were experiencing gang problems in 2009.[2]

The continuing bad news is that too many juveniles, especially at-risk youths, are involved in gangs; that gang involvement is likely to lead to further involvement in delinquency and drug use; that gang involvement increases the likelihood of the carrying and use of weapons; and that gang involvement increases the probability of going on to adult crime and of spending time in prison.[3]

How Have Gangs Evolved in the United States?

Youth gangs may have existed as early as the American Revolution.[4] Some researchers have suggested that they first emerged in the Southwest following the Mexican Revolution in 1813.[5] In the early 1800s, youth gangs seemed to have spread in New England, with the

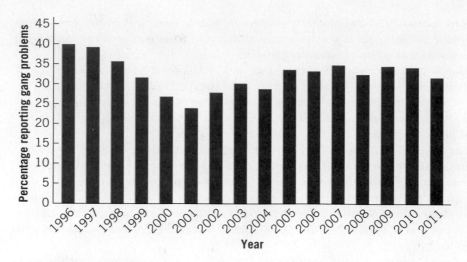

shift from an agrarian to an industrial society. Youth gangs began to flourish in Chicago, New York, and other large cities in the nineteenth century as immigration and population shifts reached record levels.

Youth gangs were primarily Irish, Jewish, and Italian, but this changed in the twentieth century.

Gangs and Play Activity: The 1920s Through the 1940s

A pioneering work on youth gangs was Frederick Thrasher's *The Gang: A Study of 1,313 Gangs in Chicago*.[6] Thrasher viewed these gangs as a normal part of growing up in ethnic neighborhoods. He found that youths who went to school together and played together in the neighborhood naturally developed a strong sense of identity leading to their forming close-knit groups. Evolving from these neighborhood play groups, Thrasher found, they bonded together without any particular purpose or goal. These transitory social groups typically had fewer than thirty members. The youth gangs studied by Thrasher were usually organized in three concentric circles: a core made up of a leader and lieutenants, the rank-and-file membership, and a few youths who drifted in and out of the gang. Each gang was different, but what was universally expected was the protection of turf.[7]

West Side Story Era: The 1950s

Youth gangs became established in Boston, New York, and Philadelphia from the late 1940s through the 1950s. These youth gangs spent time "hanging out" and partying together; when deemed necessary, they fought other gangs. The musical later made into a movie, presented two 1950s New York youth gangs dancing, singing, and battling over turf. It focused on the Sharks, recent immigrants from Puerto Rico, defending their neighborhood ethnic boundaries.

These urban gangs of the 1950s were not the lethal weapons they have become in recent decades, but they were capable of violent behavior. In 1960–1961, one of the authors was hired to work with a white gang in Newark, New Jersey. This job became available because his predecessor, who had been on the job for two weeks, had a knife held to his chest, cutting his shirt and drawing a little blood. Warned that bad things would happen if he did not quit, he chose to resign.

The gangs of the 1950s attracted considerable attention among researchers and policy makers. Millions of dollars in federal, state, and local money were spent on projects and programs designed to prevent and control gang behavior. One of the most widely funded efforts was the detached workers' program. This program sent professional workers into the community to work with gang youths, but this effort proved to have little or no positive effect on reducing their rates of delinquent activities. Indeed, one of the most consistent findings of these detached workers' programs was that workers' efforts ended up increasing the size of the youth gang, as well as the commitment of participants.[8]

Development of the Modern Gang: The 1960s

The 1960s are known as a decade of rapidly changing social and political climates. The development of **supergangs** in Chicago and Los Angeles, the involvement of gangs in social betterment programs, and their participation in political activism were the most significant changes in youth gangs during the 1960s.

The major supergangs developed when neighborhood gangs became larger and more powerful than other gangs in surrounding neighborhoods, and they forced the small groups to become part of their gang organization. Eventually, a few gangs controlled the entire city of Chicago. During this decade, three African American supergangs, the Vice Lords, the Blackstone Rangers, and the Disciples, either had their beginnings or developed into supergangs. See Focus on Offenders 13–1 for a discussion about the development of these Chicago supergangs. In the 1960s, the Crips, an African American supergang, began as a small clique in a section of Los Angeles.[9] It was not long before the Bloods, another African American supergang in Los Angeles, arose to challenge the Crips.

During the late 1960s, the Vice Lords and the Blackstone Rangers, two of Chicago's supergangs, became involved in programs of community betterment. Their social action involvement began in the summer of 1967 when the Vice Lord leaders attended meetings at Western Electric and Sears and Roebuck. Operation Bootstrap, which resulted from these meetings, formed committees for education, recreation, and law, order, and justice. A grant from the Rockefeller Foundation in February 1967 enabled the Vice Lords to fund a host of economic and social ventures. The Vice Lords also worked with Jesse Jackson on Operation Breadbasket and, in the summer of 1969, joined with the Coalition for United Community Action to protest the lack of African American employees on construction sites in African American neighborhoods.

The supergangs in Chicago became involved in political activism when they joined together to work against the reelection of Mayor Richard Daley's Democratic machine. This activism

▲ Youth gang members represent the gang by demonstrating gang signals that are recognized by other gang members and that distinguish it from other gangs.
Steve Skjold/Alamy

Focus on Offenders 13–1
Origins of the Chicago "Supergangs"

THE VICE LORD NATION

In the late 1950s, Edward "Peppilow" Perry was a fifteen-year-old youth who was sent to the St. Charles reformatory for boys. He persuaded Leonard Calloway, Maurice Miller, and four others to form a new gang when they got out. They played with names. It was Calloway who thought of lords, and vice came to mind. He looked both words up in the dictionary and found vice to mean "having a tight hold." He knew he had it. They would be called "Vice Lords."

It was not until 1964 that the name "Conservative Vice Lords" became well known. Maurice Miller was a conservative type, and he wanted *conservative* added to the name. They did that for him, ending up with Conservative Vice Lords.

As the Conservative Vice Lords grew in number and power, they began to take over other youth gangs in their neighborhood and in surrounding neighborhoods. One of the reasons for the success of this gang's development is that while it was annexing groups to the Conservative Vice Lords, this gang allowed other groups to retain their own identity and to become part of the Vice Lord Nation.

For example, Willie Lloyd became a member of the Vice Lords in the mid-1960s and was put in charge of the Peewees, a junior division of the Conservative Vice Lords. But when the Peewees evolved into another youth gang, Willie was not selected as an officer, nor was his suggested group name accepted. He was able to persuade two friends at that point to begin a new youth gang, which they called the "Unknown Conservative Vice Lords." This new gang, in spite of the opposition it initially received from established Vice Lord groups, eventually was accepted as a major division of the Vice Lord Nation.

Alfonso Alford became chief of the Lords in the mid-1960s. Tired of humbugging, he began to search for meaning in a world where fighting was the only honor known. Too old to go back to school and with few jobs available, Al suggested the Lords try to open a business, moving toward construction rather than destruction. The Lords just shook their heads. It just didn't sound right. They enjoyed the partying, the drinking, and the fights. But Al kept insisting that together they could make it happen. They had to try.

Between 1965 and 1967, the Lords stopped the gang wars. They opened businesses and ran community programs for the hungry, the unemployed, the homeless, and the young with nothing to do. They reached out to show the people on the streets that there was a thing called hope. For a moment in time they made a difference, but the forces working against them do not remember the moment. They are all dead now. All but Bobby Gore, who continues to have hope and to fight for his brothers and sisters on the streets.

As the decade came to an end, the Vice Lords had twenty-nine branches. In addition to the Conservatives, the largest groups included the Unknown, Four Corner Hustlers, Mafia Insane, 21st Street Executioners, Travelers, and Maniac Vice Lords, but they were still all Lords.

BLACKSTONE RANGERS

Jeff Fort was a scrawny young man who lived in Woodlawn on the west side of Chicago. He and a few friends began to steal hubcaps and groceries, dividing the proceeds among themselves. As others were attracted to this group, they came to be named the Blackstone Rangers. Fort selected twenty-one leaders, giving them responsibility and power. They became known as the Main 21, and their major role was to enforce the rules of the Blackstone Rangers.

The Reverend John Fry, minister of the First Presbyterian Church in Chicago, permitted this gang to hold its meetings in the gymnasium of the church. The meetings captured the emotions of a religious revival. The Blackstones filled the gym, and the Main 21 were seated in a semicircle across the stage at the end of the gym.

Jeff Fort appeared out of nowhere, going to the microphone and podium. He raised his fist, jerking it back hard, with power they all knew him to have. He yelled, "Blackstone," and together the thunderous roar resounded back, "Blackstone."

Fort whipped the Blackstones into a frenzy. In a deep, booming voice that sent static flying across the gym, he demanded, "Stones run it!" Thousands of bodies extended their right fists like banners hammering the winds and responded, "Stones run it!" Over and over the thunder filled the gym, "Blackstones, Blackstones, Blackstones."

The Stones soon spread beyond their neighborhoods throughout Chicago. It was not long before they were known as America's most powerful gang. Some drug sales took place in the 1960s, but gang arrests were typically for crimes ranging from resisting arrest to armed robbery and murder.

THE DISCIPLES

David Barksdale was a self-directed leader who defied anyone; he was accustomed to reaching out and taking what he wanted.

During his frequent trips as a teenager to the Illinois Youth Commission, he recruited youths from the south, west, and east sides, organizing a domain that was to extend his field of influence beyond that of just the south side. The movement spread.

He was stocky at age fifteen, standing about 5′ 10″ tall. He was stoic, quiet, and always serious, with a charisma that instilled fear and awe at the same time. Well-mannered with few words, he dressed to perfection, looking fine with processed hair. But above all else he was an excellent boxer, one of the very best.

It was Barksdale's boxing skill that led to the development of the Disciples gang. Champ Harris was the nineteen-year-old leader of the Devil Disciples, which had a membership of about four hundred youths. Champ's girlfriend, Linda Samuels, was pursued by Barksdale, and Champ challenged his rival to a boxing match. By the time Harris hit the floor, he had lost his girlfriend and control over his gang.

Barksdale surrounded himself with leaders he could trust. They fought the Egyptian Cobras, led by Charlie Adkins, and the Supreme Gangsters, led by Martin Givens and Larry Hoover. Barksdale looked around for the small, unknown groups just coming up and recruited them easily most of the time; at other times they had little choice, if any.

With Barksdale on the run a couple of years later, Robert Allen, known to most as Old Timer, assumed responsibility for the leadership of the Devil Disciples. He made the decision to offer Larry Hoover an opportunity to coexist with him as leader of this gang. They would coexist together in one land, two kings ruling one nation, each with equal power. David Barksdale would be king of the Devil Disciples, and Larry would be king of the Gangster Disciples. They were allies, six thousand strong.

In the early 1970s, David Barksdale was wounded and then died a couple of years later. His side of the kingdom was taken over by Jerome Freeman and became known as the Black Disciples. Imprisoned Larry Hoover used the magic of the name "Gangster Disciple" to become a legend and to build one of the largest gang organizations in the United States. Known as the King and Chairman of the Board, he is the head of the vast Gangster Disciples nation.

Source: Linda Dippold Bartollas researched and wrote this material. She was assisted by Nehemiah Russell and Samuel Dillon.

---

brought increased strain to their relationship with the Democratic Party organization. With Daley's reelection, gangs in Chicago began to experience what they perceived as harassment from the police. As soon as he began a new term, Daley announced a crackdown on gang violence, and State's Attorney Edward Hanrahan followed his lead by appraising the gang situation as the most serious crime problem in Chicago. The courts complied with this crackdown on gangs by increasing dramatically the number of gang members sent to prison in Illinois.

Expansion, Violence, and Criminal Operations: The 1970s, 1980s, and 1990s

A number of changes took place with gangs in the last three decades of the twentieth century. Among the most important were that gangs became increasingly made up of adults; that street gangs became responsible for a large portion of urban crime, including violent crime; that urban gangs grew in the 1970s and expanded dramatically throughout the nation in the late 1980s and early 1990s; and that crack cocaine hit the streets in the mid-1980s.

What became evident by the late 1960s was that juveniles were not leaving the urban gangs to which they belonged when they became adults. One of the major reasons for this was that these gangs supplied certain needs that were not being met in other social groups or traditional rites of passage into adulthood. Another reason was that the increased imprisonment of gang members fostered the development of prison gangs that kept their allegiance to these gangs while in prison and subsequent to being released from prison. This pattern remains true today—more than half of all gang members are over the age of 18.[10]

In the 1970s and 1980s, urban gangs became responsible for a major portion of muggings, robberies, extortions, and drug-trafficking operations in the United States. With leadership increasingly assumed by adults, gangs were more intent on making money from crime. With legal weapons more readily available than in the past, gangs became much more violent.

The mid-1980s were a turning point for many ghetto-based gangs, for crack cocaine had hit the streets. These urban street gangs competed with each other for the drug trade. Several Los Angeles gangs established direct connections to major Colombian smugglers, which ensured a continuous supply of top-quality cocaine. In some Chicago neighborhoods, heavily armed teams sold drugs openly on the street corners, using gang "peewees" (youngsters) as police lookouts.

The Present

The number of gangs, as well as membership in these gangs, began to decline in the mid-1990s, with the exception to this decline being the recent growth of such ethnic gangs, such as MS-13. At the same time, federal law enforcement has had success in breaking up such urban gangs as the Gangster Disciples and the El Rukns. The street gang traditionally has been a cultural by-product in the United States, but gang-like structures are now being reported in numerous cities worldwide. Cities in Asia/Pacific nations reporting gangs are Beijing, Hong Kong, Melbourne, Papua, New Guinea, and Tokyo. European cities with gangs include Berlin, Frankfurt, London, Madrid, Manchester, and Zurich. There have also been indications that gang activity is taking place in Canada, Russia, and South America.[11] See Figure 13–2 for a timeline on the development of gangs.

Nature and Extent of Gang Activity

The Highlights of the 2012 National Youth Gang Survey estimated that the United States has 30,700 gangs and 850,000 gang members. The 2012 survey's finding is the lowest point in nearly a decade. The decline from 2011 to 2012 can be almost solely attributed to the drop in smaller cities where gang prevalence has dropped nearly 10 percent since 2010.[12]

1920s–1940s	1940s–1950s	1960s
Gangs were largely transitory social groups in Chicago and elsewhere, and gang membership was a type of rite of passage.	**Teenage gangs** became established in Boston, New York, and Philadelphia. Members hung out together, partied together, and gangs fought each other over "turf."	**Drugs began** to influence gang activity, "supergangs" in Chicago and Los Angeles emerged, and some Chicago gangs became involved in social betterment programs.

1970s–1988	1989–1999	2000–present
Leadership of gangs was assumed by adults, street gangs became involved in more unlawful behaviors and drug trafficking, and gangs became increasingly more violent.	**The number of** youth gangs exploded across the United States.	**Gang membership** and the number of gangs have begun to slightly decline, with some ethnic gangs skyrocketing in numbers. Gangs have spread worldwide.

FIGURE 13–2
Timeline: Development of Gangs in the Twentieth and Early Twenty-First Centuries

EXHIBIT 13–1
Gang Scholars

Pioneers	Contributors
Frederick Thrasher	Thrasher's 1927 study was one of the first to define youth gangs, and his examination of more than a thousand gangs in Chicago identifies the role that gangs played in these youths' lives.
Martin Sanchez Jankowski	His study of thirty-seven gangs in both New York and Los Angeles over a decade provides much of an understanding of how urban poor become involved in urban gangs.
Walter B. Miller	Beginning with his analysis of the Mid-city Project in Boston in the early 1960s to his Death in 2004, Miller became one of the giants with his analysis of growth and changes in gangs. He died before his monumental gang study of twenty-one street gangs was published.
Joan Moore	Moore's studied both Mexican American male and females. In the barrios of Los Angeles. her study of female gangs is one of the most important of the twentieth century. It reveals the evolution of female gangs as well as their greater involvement in criminal activity.
James Diego Vigil	He has examined the self-identity and survival of Mexican-American gang members as they deal with life in the barrio.
James F Short, Jr.	Beginning with his research on Chicago gang members in the 1950s, Short has continued to study gangs and our understanding of gangs.
Irving Spergel	Long is a contributor to our understanding of Chicago gangs, Spergel is especially well-known for his role in the Comprehensive Community-Wide Approach to Gang Prevention, Intervention, and Suppression Program.

Knowledge of the gang world requires an examination of the definition of gangs and the profile of gang members, as well as an understanding of gangs' intimidation of the school environment, of the structuring and leadership of street gangs, of emerging gangs in small communities across the nation, of the racial and ethnic background of gang members, and of female delinquent gangs. Exhibit 13–1 lists a number of the individuals who have been pioneers in helping us understand youth gangs.

Definition of Gangs

Considerable disagreement exists about what parameters define a gang, but the US Department of Justice defines a gang by the following criteria:

1. An association or three or more members;
2. Whose members collectively identify themselves by adopting a group identity which they use to create an atmosphere of fear or intimidation frequently by employing one or more of the following: a common name, slogan, identifying sign, symbol, tattoo or other physical marking, style or color of clothing, hairstyle, hand sign or graffiti';
3. The association's purpose in part is to engage in criminal activity and it uses violence or intimidation to further its criminal objectives;
4. Its members engage in criminal activity or acts of juvenile delinquency, which if committed by adults would be adult crimes;
5. With reference to enhance or preserve the association's power, reputation, or economic resources;
6. The association may also possess some of the following characteristics:
   a. The members employ rules for joining and operating within the association;
   b. The members meet on a recurring basis;
   c. The association provides physical protection to its members from other criminals and gangs;
   d. The association seeks to exercise control over particular location or region, or it may simply defend its perceived interest against rivals; and
   e. The association has an identifiable structure.[13]

Profiles of Gang Members

Gang profiles have at least three important dimensions: age of gang members, size of the gang, and attraction of the gang.

Age of Gang Members

The smaller the community, the more likely it is that its gang members will be juveniles. Sample surveys of urban street gang members indicate that 14 to 30 percent of adolescents join gangs at some point.[14] Nonetheless, the percentage of gang members who are juveniles has decreased over time. In 1996, 50 percent of all gang members were reported to be age eighteen years or older, but by 2001, the number had grown to 67 percent. Juvenile gang members make up 70 percent of all gang members in small communities—a statistic that steadily declines as community size increases.[15]

Juveniles become involved in gangs as young as eight years of age, running errands and carrying weapons or messages. They are recruited as lookouts and street vendors and join an age-appropriate junior division of the gang. Gangs use younger and small members to deal cocaine out of cramped "rock houses," which are steel-reinforced fortresses. Gangs have long known that youngsters are invaluable because their age protects them against the harsher realities of the adult criminal justice system.[16]

Size of the Gang

Gangs vary in size depending on whether they are traditional or specialty gangs in urban areas or emerging gangs in small cities or communities. Large and enduring traditional (territorial) gangs in urban areas average about one hundred fifty members, whereas drug-trafficking gangs average about twenty-five members. Some urban gangs (for example, the supergangs of Chicago) have thousands of members, but gangs in emerging areas usually number fewer than twenty-five or so members.[17]

Attraction of the Gang

Why do young people join gangs? Willie Lloyd, legendary leader of a gang called the Almighty Unknown Vice Lords, explained why he became involved in gangs:

> I grew up on the streets of Chicago. When I was growing up, the Lords had a big impact on me. I never saw it as a gang but a cohesive unifying principle by which a person could organize his life. Even as a kid of nine, I was intrigued by the Lords when I first saw them outside of the Central Park Theatre. It was the first time I've ever witnessed so many black people moving so harmoniously together. They were motored by the same sense of purpose and they were all wore similar dress and insignia. They were over a hundred guys, all in black, with capes and umbrellas. To my young eyes, it was the most beautiful expression I had ever seen. They all seem so fearless, so proud, so much in control of their lives. Though I didn't know anyone of them at the time, I fell in love with all of them. In retrospect, I made up my mind the first time I saw the Vice Lords to be a Vice Lord.[18]

Mike Carlie, in his national overview of youth gangs, expanded on the question of why gangs form and what gangs offer to those who join them (see Table 13–1).

Theories of Gang Formation

The classical theories about the origins of youth gangs and gang delinquency date from research done in 1950s and formulated by Herbert A. Bloch and Arthur Niederhoffer, Richard Cloward and Lloyd Ohlin, Albert K. Cohen, Walter B. Miller, and Lewis Yablonsky:

• Bloch and Niederhoffer's theory was based on the idea that joining a gang is part of the experience that male adolescents need to grow up to adulthood, so the basic function of the gang is to provide a substitute for the formalized puberty rites that are found in other societies.[19]

- Cloward and Ohlin's theory used the notion that lower-class boys interact with and gain support from other alienated individuals and that these youngsters pursue illegitimate means to achieve the success they cannot gain through legitimate means.[20]
- Cohen's theory stated that gang delinquency represents the subcultural collective solution to the problems that face lower-class boys of acquiring status when they find themselves evaluated according to middle-class values and the schools.[21]
- Miller held that there is a definite lower-class culture and that gang behavior is an expression of that culture; he saw gang leadership as based mainly on smartness and toughness and viewed the gang as very cohesive and highly conforming to delinquent norms.[22]
- Yablonsky suggested that violent delinquent gangs arise out of certain conditions, which are found in urban slums, that encourage the development of the sociopathic personality in adolescence, and such sociopathic individuals become the core leadership of these gangs.[23]

More recently, **underclass theory** has been widely used to explain the origins of gangs.[24] In the midst of big-city ghettos and barrios filled with poverty and deprivation, it

TABLE 13–1
Attraction of Gangs

Why Gangs Form	What Gangs Offer	Why Youths Join
Social discrimination or rejection	Acceptance	To avoid being discriminated against and to seek acceptance and a sense of belonging
Absence of a family and its unconditional love, positive adult role models, and proper discipline	Surrogate family	To be in a family and to have unconditional love, positive adult role models, and discipline
Feelings of powerlessness	Power	To overcome their powerlessness
Abuse, fear, and lack of security	Security	To reduce their feelings of fear and to feel secure
Economic deprivation	Means of earning money	To gain economically
School failure and delinquency	Alternative to school	To vent their frustration
Low self-esteem	Opportunities to build high self-esteem	To acquire high self-esteem
Lack of acceptable rites of passage into adulthood	Rite of passage to adulthood	To accomplish their passage from childhood to adulthood
Lack of legitimate free-time activities	Activity	To keep from being bored
Pathological needs	Setting in which to act out aggression	To vent their anger
Influence of migrating gang members	Any of the aforementioned	To get any of the aforementioned
Mass media portrayals of gangs and gang members	Any of the aforementioned	To get any of the aforementioned
Choice to follow in others' footsteps	Any of the aforementioned	To follow tradition and to gain acceptance
Ability to join	Any of the aforementioned	To get any of the aforementioned

Source: Adapted from Michael Carlie, *Into the Abyss: A Personal Journey into the World of Street Gangs.* http://people.missouristate.edu/MichaelCarlie/what_i_learned_about/gangs/whyform/why_gangs_form.htm#top. Reprinted with permission from Michael K. Carlie.

TABLE 13–2
Theories of Why Juveniles Join Gangs

Type of Theory	Proponents	Brief Description
Normal Part of Growing Up	Block and Niederhoffer	Joining the gang is part of the experience adolescents need to grow up to adulthood.
Strain Theory	Cloward and Ohlin	Youngsters pursue gangs to achieve the success they cannot achieve through legitimate means.
Subcultural Affiliation and Strain Theory	Cohen	Gang delinquency represents a subcultural and collective solution to the problems racing lower-class boys.
Subcultural Affiliation	Miller	There is a definite lower-class culture and gang behavior is an expression of that culture.
Social Disorganization	Yablonsky	Violent delinquent gangs arise out of certain conditions, which are found in urban slums.
Underclass Theory	Fagan and others	Excluded from participation in labor market occupations, members of the underclass are attracted to other economic alternatives, such as gangs.

is argued gangs are a normal response to an abnormal social setting.[25] Part of the underclass plight according to Jeffery Fagan is being permanently excluded from participating in mainstream labor market occupations, so members of the underclass are forced to rely on other economic alternatives, such as low-paying temporary jobs, part-time jobs, some form of welfare, or involvement in drug trafficking, prostitution, muggings, and extortions.[26] Martin Sánchez Jankowski contended that gang violence and the defiant attitudes of young men are connected with a competitive struggle in poor communities and, being a product of their environment, they adopt a "Hobbesian view of life in which violence is an integral part of the state of nature."[27] Table 13–2 summarizes the theories of why juveniles join gangs.

What Is Important to Know About Urban Street Gangs?

Important features of urban street gangs include their types, organizational features, participation in drug trafficking, their behavior in school, and the degree of law-violating behaviors for juveniles involved in these groups. Juveniles may be a minority in urban street gangs, but they have certain role expectations (usually drug "runners" and lookouts for crack houses) and frequently remain in the gang even after they become adults.

Types of Urban Gangs

Detroit urban gangs, according to Carl S. Taylor, can be classified as scavenger, territorial, and corporate. **Scavenger gangs** lack goals, purpose, and consistent leadership and prey on those unable to defend themselves. **Territorial gangs** define an area as belonging exclusively to them and attempt to defend this space from outsiders. They become the controllers of the streets and defend their territory to protect their narcotics business. Organized or **corporate gangs**, which Taylor views as organized crime groups, have as their main purpose the participation in illegal money-making ventures, especially the trafficking of **crack** cocaine. Different divisions of the gang handle sales, distribution, marketing, and enforcement.[28]

TABLE 13–3
Types of Urban Gangs

Scavenger gangs: Prey on those unable to defend themselves.

Territorial gangs: Defend an area in which they claim ownership.

Corporate gangs: Organized crime groups whose main purpose is participation in illegal money-making ventures.

Hedonistic gangs: Basic purpose is to get high and have a good time.

Instrumental gangs: Focus is on economic gain.

Predatory gangs: Commit a variety of crimes, use and sell cocaine, and purchase more sophisticated weapons to achieve their purposes.

Type 1 gangs: Involved in minor delinquent activities and drug use.

Type 2 gangs: Heavily involved in several types of drug sales.

Type 3 gangs: Little involvement in drug sales but more involvement in both serious and nonserious offenses.

Type 4 gangs: Extensively involved in drug use, drug sales, and serious and nonserious offenses.

C. Ronald Huff's examination of gangs in Cleveland and Columbus, Ohio, identified informal hedonistic gangs, instrumental gangs, and predatory gangs. The basic concerns of informal **hedonistic gangs** were to get high (usually on alcohol, marijuana, or other drugs) and to have a good time. These gangs were more involved in property crimes than in violent personal crimes. The main focus of **instrumental gangs** was economic gain, and they committed a large number of property crimes. Most of these gang members used drugs, including crack cocaine; some members also sold drugs, but doing so was not an organized gang activity. **Predatory gangs** committed robberies, street muggings, and other crimes of opportunity. Members of these gangs were likely to use crack cocaine and to sell drugs to finance the purchase of more sophisticated weapons.[29]

Fagan identified four types of gangs in his analysis of the crime–drug relationships in three cities. Type 1 gangs were involved in a few delinquent activities and only alcohol and marijuana use. These gangs had low involvement in drug sales and appeared to be social gangs. Type 2 gangs were heavily involved in several kinds of drug sales, primarily to support their own drug habits. They were also heavily involved in vandalism. Type 3 gangs had the highest levels of member participation, including extensive involvement in both serious and nonserious offenses. Another feature of this type was less involvement in both drug sales and the use of such substances as cocaine, heroin, PCP, and amphetamines. Type 4 gangs were extensively involved in both serious drug use and serious and nonserious offenses and had higher rates of drug sales. This cohesive and organized type, according to Fagan, "is probably at the highest risk for becoming a more formal criminal organization."[30] Table 13–3 summarizes the types of urban gangs.

Organizational Features of Urban Gangs

Jankowski, who spent more than ten years studying thirty-seven gangs in Los Angeles, New York, and Boston, suggested that the most important organizational features of urban gangs are leadership, recruitment, initiation rites, and migration patterns.[31]

Leadership

Jankowski observed three varieties of **gang leadership**:

1. The *vertical/hierarchical* structure divides leadership hierarchically into several different levels. Power and authority are related to one's position in the line of command.

2. The *horizontal/commission* structure consists of several officeholders who share about equal authority over members. The leaders share the duties as well as the power and authority.

3. The *influential* structure assigns no written duties or titles to the leadership positions. This type of system has two to four members who are regarded as the leaders of the gang. The authority of the influential leaders is derived from charisma.[32]

The most conspicuous example of the vertical/hierarchical type of leadership is found in the Gangster Disciples, the Vice Lords, the Black Disciples, and the El Rukns, whose leaders have become legends. The Bloods and the Crips, the most notorious Los Angeles gangs, are representative of the horizontal/commission type. In a real sense, they are not gangs at all but confederations of hundreds of subgroups, or sets. Sets are established along neighborhood lines, and most sets have twenty to thirty members. The emerging youth gangs across the nation, described later in this chapter, would be examples of influential type of leadership structure.[33]

Recruitment

Gangs regularly go on recruiting parties, and the recruitment of young members, or soldiers, is easy because the life of a gang member looks glamorous. If a prospective member is not receptive, then coercion or threats can be made concerning the consequences of not joining.

Methods of Initiation

The **methods of initiation** into some gangs include some or all of the following:

- A new member may be *blessed-in* to a gang. Those who are blessed-in to a gang usually have older brothers, fathers, mothers, or other relatives who are already in the gang.

Cottage Residential Staff Members

PREPARATION FOR THE JOB

Nonprofessional staff, who have more contact with institutional residents than any other staff member, is another job in a juvenile facility. Although placing a husband and wife in charge of a cottage has traditionally been the most popular policy in training schools, both private and state, the trend today is to employ nonprofessional staff to work eight hour shifts and to live in the community. The latter are referred to by different titles: youth leader, youth supervisor, youth counselor, group supervisor, cottage supervisor, cottage counselor, or correctional officer-but whatever the title, the main task is to provide 24 hour care of residents and to maintain a secure cottage.

The cottage, or youth leaders, wake the youths the morning, see to it that they dress and wash over breakfast, supervise the serving of breakfast, and conduct a brief room inspection. Next, they make sure that those students enrolled in academic and vocational programs go to school and that those who work in the kitchen, on the ground, or in the community arrive at their jobs. In the more secure training schools, youths are escorted to their particular assignments, but in many minimum-security facilities, they are permitted movement without staff supervision.

The youth leader is a key figure in the handling of confined youths. On one hand, some youths become very close to the cottage leader, and a few of them even regard him or her as father or mother figures. Many youths stay in touch with their favorite youth counselor following their release; some even return to the institution to visit. Cottage parents and youth leaders who are interested and very much involved in the charges' lives are the ones who receive a warm response from residents. Some of the staff become remarkable treatment agents and have a permanent impact on youths.

QUALIFICATION AND EDUCATIONAL REQUIREMENTS

The requirement is typically that an applicant only has a high school diploma. It is also seen as desirable for the applicant to have some experience working with youth.

DEMAND FOR

With the high turnover in youth counselors, whatever this position may be called, especially in private institutions, there are always jobs available. It is desirable for the college graduate who wants to make a career in juvenile justice to take this entry-level position. In private institutions, especially the pay may be low and working conditions may be marginal, but it is still a good way to begin your career.

SALARY

There is a world of difference between working in a state institution and a private facility in terms of pay. Those in private institutions may take one half and with substantially less fringe benefits than the salary package of those in state institutions. In many states, these positions in state institutions begin in the high $30,000s to low $40,000s.

- A new male member more typically must be *jumped-in*, or fight other members. He may have to fight a specified number of gang members for a set period of time and demonstrate that he is able to take a beating and fight back. Or he may have to stand in the middle of a circle and fight his way out, or run between lines of gang members as they administer a beating. Under such circumstances, he is expected to stay on his feet from one end of the line to the other. Recently, there has been a movement away from jumped-in initiations in urban gangs, unless there is some question about the initiate's courage.[34]

- A female often is initiated into male-dominated gangs by providing sexual services for one or more gang members.

- A new member in some gangs has been expected to play Russian roulette. Russian roulette involves loading a pistol's cylinder with one bullet, spinning the cylinder, closing it, then pointing the gun to one's head and pulling the trigger. If the player wins, he's in the gang. If he loses, well …

- A new member is often expected to participate in illegal acts, such as committing thefts or larcenies.

- A new member frequently is expected to assist in trafficking drugs.

- A new member in some gangs is expected to participate in "walk-up" or "drive-by" shootings.

- A new member is sometimes expected to commit a gang-assigned murder. Completing the procedure has sometimes been called a *blood-in*, but is rarely part of initiation rites today.[35]

Migration

A final organizational feature of urban gangs is **migration**. Gang migration can occur in the establishment of satellite gangs in another location, in the relocation of gang members with their families, and in the expansion of drug markets. Cheryl L. Maxson, Malcolm W. Klein, and Lea C. Cunningham surveyed law enforcement agencies in more than 1,100 cities nationwide. Of these, 713 reported some gang migration. The most frequent pattern of gang migration was the relocation of gang members with their families (39 percent); the next most common pattern was the expansion of drug markets (20 percent). But their survey failed to offer much support for gangs attempting to establish satellites in other communities across the nation.[36] Indeed, most jurisdictions surveyed for the *National Youth Gang Survey of 2007* indicated that either no or a very small percentage of the gang members with whom they were familiar were migrants to their area. The primary reasons for migration were social reasons (e.g., as mentioned, their family moved), rather than illicit purposes.[37]

Drug Trafficking and Gangs

Beginning in the mid-1980s, street gangs with origins in the urban centers of Los Angeles, Chicago, New York, Miami, and Detroit became criminal entrepreneurs in supplying drugs, especially crack cocaine, to urban communities. They had begun by the late 1980s and early 1990s to develop intrastate and interstate networks to expand their illegal drug market sales.

The Crips and Bloods of Los Angeles have been the most active in **drug trafficking** nationwide. In a 1988 report, the Drug Enforcement Administration claimed that Los Angeles street gangs were identified with drug sales in forty-six states.[38] The Miami Boys of South Florida, the Jamaican Posses of New York and Florida, and the Vice Lords and Gangster Disciples in Chicago are also among the street gangs that have entered the field on the largest scale.[39]

The depth of gang involvement in drugs is documented in the *1997 National Youth Gang Survey*. Respondents to the survey estimate, on the average, that 42 percent of the drug sales across jurisdictions are conducted by gangs. Gangs are responsible for 43 percent of drug sales in suburbs, 35 percent in rural areas, 31 percent in small cities, but 49 percent in large cities.[40]

TABLE 13–4
Organizational Features of Urban Gangs

Features of Urban Gangs	Types
Leadership	
Vertical/hierarchical structure	Divides leadership hierarchically into several different structures.
Horizontal/commission structure	Consists of several officeholders who share about equal authority over members.
Influential structure	Assigns no written duties or titles to the leadership position.
Recruitment	
Friendly	Appeal can be made to join because of the glamor or advantages of gang membership ("we will have your back").
Coercive	Pressure and threats are made. Prospective members are warned about the consequences of failure to join.
Methods of Initiation	
"Blessed-in"	Usually comes because siblings or other relatives are already in the gang.
"Jumped-in"	Must fight other members.
Females' initiation into male-dominated gangs	Must provide sexual services for one or more gang members.
Must participate in illegal acts	These include trafficking drugs or even participating in "walk-up" or "drive-by" shootings.
Migration	
Relocation of gang members with their families	This is the most frequent form of migration.
Expansion of drug markets	Second most common pattern.
Urban gangs' attempt to establish satellite gangs in other communities	Little evidence for this.

When ranking gangs according to their involvement in drug sales at low, moderate, or high levels, data indicate that more than half (53 percent) of gang members were reported to be involved at the low level of drug sales, 18 percent at the moderate level, and 29 percent at the high level.[41] The highest proportion of youth gangs involved in drug sales was in large cities, and the lowest was in small cities. Larger cities apparently have more opportunities for the individual entrepreneur. Table 13–4 summarizes the organizational features of urban gangs.

Gangs in School

Urban schools have become fertile soil for the violence of youth gangs. The percentage of high school students who reported the presence of street gangs at school varied by the type of school and whether the school was public or private. Urban schools had a significantly larger percentage of students who reported the presence of gangs at school than did suburban or rural schools. Indeed, more than twice as many students in urban schools compared with students in rural schools reported the presence of gangs. This same pattern was true of public schools, but it was less true of private schools. Figure 13–3 shows the percentage of students ages twelve through eighteen who reported the presence of street gangs at school in 2007 and again in 2009.[42]

Gangs perpetrate school violence in a number of ways. Gang members are likely to bring concealed weapons into the school. They are constantly recruiting new members, and nongang youths who refuse to join may be assaulted. Also, when more than one gang

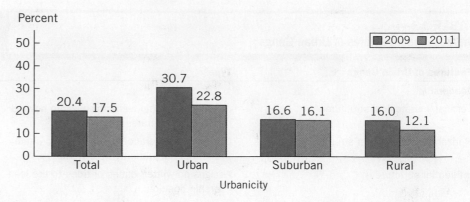

FIGURE 13–3

Percentage of Students Ages Twelve to Eighteen Who Reported That Gangs Were Present at School During the School Year, by Urbanicity, 2009 and 2011

Source: Bureau of Justice Statistics, *School Crime Supplement (SCS) to the National Crime Victimization Survey, 2007 and 2009* (Washington, DC: U.S. Department of Justice, 2011).

is present in a school, conflict among them takes place on a regular basis. Furthermore, conflict among rival gangs in different schools perpetrates violence.

Youths involved in gangs also are known to be disruptive in the classroom, to do poorly in their academic work, to intimidate nongang youth on the way to and from school, to frequently be absent, to be suspended or even expelled from school, and to drop out of school. When an urban high school has a large percentage of gang youths, the culture of that school tends to be chaotic, out of control, and dangerous. A visitor to a typical urban high school is likely to feel very uncomfortable.

Law-Violating Behaviors and Gang Activities

Despite the fluidity and diversity of gang roles and affiliations, experts commonly agree that core members are involved in more serious delinquent acts than are situational or fringe members.

Studies in Aurora, Colorado; Broward County, Florida; and Cleveland, Ohio, found some major differences between the behavior of gang members and that of at-risk youths.[43] Individual gang members in these studies reported that they had stolen more cars, that they had participated in more drive-by shootings, that they were far more likely to own guns, that they owned guns of larger caliber, and that they were more involved in selling drugs as compared to the sample of at-risk youths.[44] Of those youths selling drugs, "gang members reported doing so more frequently, having fewer customers, making more money from the sales, and relying more on out-of-state suppliers than nongang youths who sold drugs." This study added that "both gang members and at-risk youths reported that gangs do not control drug trafficking in their communities."[45]

In Rochester, gang members, who made up 30 percent of the sample, self-reported committing 68 percent of all adolescent violent offenses, which was about seven times as many serious and violent acts as committed by nongang youths.[46] In Seattle, gang members, who made up 15 percent of the sample, self-reported committing 85 percent of adolescent robberies.[47] In Denver, gang members, who made up 14 percent of the sample, self-reported committing 89 percent of all serious violent adolescent offenses. Gang members committed about three times as many serious and violent offenses as did nongang youth.[48]

These Rochester, Denver, and Seattle studies showed that the influence of gang membership on levels of youth violence is greater than the influence of other delinquent peers.[49] Youths commit more serious and violent acts while they belong to a gang than they do after they leave the gang.[50] In addition, the effects of gang membership on a propensity toward violence seem to be long lasting. In all three sites, even though gang members' offense rates dropped after leaving the gang, they still remained fairly high.[51]

The overall number of youth gang homicides has declined since the late 1990s and through 2003. The rate has since remained relatively stable with rates spiking up in some isolated cities and down in others. The *National Youth Gang Survey* analysis documents

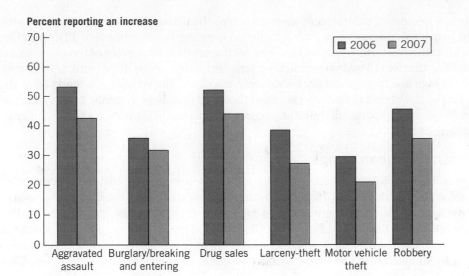

Percent reporting an increase

■ 2006   ■ 2007

FIGURE 13–4
Changes in Reported Gang Related
Crime, 2006–2007

that larger cities and suburban counties are more likely than smaller cities and rural areas to experience gang homicides. One in ten larger cities reports ten or more gang homicides, and one in five larger cities reports from three to nine. A significant majority of smaller cities and rural counties have no gang-related homicides, a distinction that is not found in larger cities and suburban counties.[52] See Figure 13–4.

A final dimension of law-violating behaviors of urban street gangs is an examination of the extent to which they are becoming **organized crime groups**. Scott H. Decker, Tim Bynum, and Deborah Weisel interviewed members of African American and Hispanic gangs in San Diego and Chicago and found that only the Gangster Disciples in Chicago are assuming the attributes of organized crime groups.[53] Several commentaries have spelled out the organizational features of the Gangster Disciples, including a chairman of the board, two boards of directors (one for the streets and one for prisons), governors who control drug trafficking on the streets, regents who supply the drugs, area coordinators who collect revenues from drug-selling spots, enforcers who punish those who violate the rules, and "shorties" who staff drug-selling spots and execute drug deals.[54]

It can be argued that aspects of organized crime groups are found in such drug-trafficking gangs as the Bloods and Crips of Los Angeles, the Miami Boys of South Florida, and the Jamaican Posses of New York and Florida. Beginning in the mid-1980s, these street gangs appeared to become criminal entrepreneurs in supplying illicit drugs. In a brief period of several years, many of these street gangs developed intrastate and interstate networks for the purpose of expanding their illegal drug market sales. As mentioned above, the Crips and Bloods of Los Angeles have been the most active in drug trafficking across the United States.[55] A study by the U.S. Congress concluded that during the latter part of the 1980s the Crips and Bloods controlled 30 percent of the crack cocaine market across the nation.[56]

Racial and Ethnic Gangs

Hispanic/Latino, African American, Asian, and Caucasian constitute the main types of racial and ethnic gangs in the United States. Hispanic/Latino and African American gangs are generally more numerous and have more members than other racial and ethnic gangs.

Hispanic/Latino Gangs

Hispanic/Latino gangs are divided into Mexican American or Chicano, Cuban, Puerto Rican, Dominican, Jamaican, and Central American members. According to the 2005 National Gang

▲ Leaders of gangs command considerable respect in their "hoods." The result is that a member of another gang—or even his own gang—may seek to gain status by killing this man. Indeed, the word on the streets is that this individual is still a target even after serving time in prison.
Constinia Charbonnette

PEOPLE

FOLKS

FIGURE 13–5
Gang Tattoos

Threat Assessment, enforcement agencies across the nation reported that the most prominent Hispanic/Latino gangs in their jurisdiction were the Los Surenos (Sur 13), Latin Kings, MS-13, 18th Street, Nortenos, and La Raza, with more than 50 percent of reporting agencies indicating that Sur 13 was present in their jurisdiction and nearly 40 percent reporting moderate to high Sur 13 gang activity.[57] Currently, the MS-13 Hispanic gang is found throughout the nation and claims to have one hundred thousand members. Hispanic Latino gang members frequently dress distinctly, display colors, communicate through graffiti, use monikers, and bear tattoos.

African American Gangs

African Americans have received more attention in this chapter than any other racial or ethnic group because most of the ghetto-based drug-trafficking gangs that have established networks across the nation are African American. For example, the Bloods and Crips from Los Angeles, the People and Folks from Chicago, and the Detroit gangs are all mostly African American. African American gangs usually identify themselves by wearing certain colors in addition to other identifiers, such as the common hand signs shown in Figure 13–5.

Asian Gangs

California has various types of Asian gangs, including Chinese, Vietnamese, Filipino, Japanese, and Korean groups. The Chinese gangs, especially, have spread to many major cities in the state, and some of the other Asian gangs also are active outside of California. Asian gangs tend to be more organized and have more identifiable leadership than is true of other street gangs. Ko-Lin Chin's examination of Chinese gangs found them involved in some of the worst gang-related violence as well as heroin trafficking, but unlike other ethnic groups, Chinese gangs are closely tied to the social and economic life of their rapidly developing economically robust communities.[58] A study of Vietnamese youth gangs in Southern California found that these youths experience much marginality but attained the American dream by robbing Vietnamese families of large amounts of cash that such families keep at home.

Caucasian Gangs

Until the closing decades of the twentieth century, most gangs were made up of Caucasian youths. Today, according to Reiner, Caucasian adolescents make up about 10 percent of the gang population in the United States.[59] In the 1990s, the West Coast saw a consolidation of lower and middle-class Caucasian youth into groups who referred to themselves as *stoners*. These groups frequently abused drugs and alcohol and listened to heavy metal rock music, and some members practiced Satanism, which includes grave robbing, desecration of human remains, and sacrifice of animals. Stoner groups can be identified by their mode of dress: colored T-shirts with decals of their rock music heroes or bands, Levis, and tennis shoes. The emerging Caucasian gangs across the nation have used many of the symbols of the stoner gangs, especially the heavy metal rock music, but they are not likely to call attention to themselves with their dress, may refer to themselves as neo-Nazi skinheads, and are involved in a variety of hate crimes in addition to drug trafficking.[60]

Thinking like a Correctional Professional

You have been appointed chairperson of a task force on gang violence, and you have the charge to reduce the gang problems in your state. How would you tackle this problem? Whom would you approach for assistance? What information do you need to pursue this task?

Gang Behavior Among Female Adolescents

Traditional sociologists once considered the female gang almost a contradiction in terms. However, research in recent decades has brought an increased awareness of adolescent girls joining gangs:

- A few studies have identified female gangs in Philadelphia and New York. Some of the gangs are extremely violent.[61]

- A number of studies have found that adolescent females are connected to adolescent male gangs. The planning is done by the males, who usually exclude the females. But the female gang members would participate in violent crimes and drug-related gang activities.[62]

- Loyalty to the gang rivaled loyalty to the family, and most friends came from within the gang. The gang, according to John C. Quicker, offered "warmth, friends, loyalty, and socialization" as it insulated its members from the harsh environment of the barrio.[63]

- Finn-Aage Esbensen, Elizabeth Piper Deschenes, and L. Thomas Winfree, Jr., found from their analysis of the Denver Youth Survey that girl gang participants committed a wide variety of offenses and at only a slightly lower frequency than did boys involved in gangs.[64] Carl S. Taylor found in Detroit that women frequently were represented in drug-trafficking gangs.[65] Beth Bjerregaard and Carolyn Smith found that involvement in gangs for both females and males was associated with increased levels of delinquency and substance abuse.[66] Joan Moore and John Hagedorn's 2001 summary of the research on female gangs reports that delinquency rates of female gang members are lower than those of male gang members but higher than those of nongang females and males. Female gang members are likely to be involved in property crimes and status offenses, but they commit fewer violent crimes than do their male counterparts. Female gang members are also heavily involved in drug dealing.[67]

- Esbensen and colleagues' findings also failed to support the notion that girls involved in gangs were mere sex objects and ancillary members. This study also showed that girls aged out of gangs before boys and that girls received more emotional fulfillment from their involvement with gang activity.[68]

- Jody Miller, in several articles and in her 2001 book, *One of the Guys*, has contributed to what is known about gender dynamics in gangs.[69] From research conducted in St. Louis, Missouri, and Columbus, Ohio, Miller found that a female in a mixed-gender gang, an environment that supports gender hierarchies and the exploitation of young women, must learn to negotiate to survive in the gang milieu.[70] Gang involvement does expose young women to risks of victimization. Young women can choose to be "one of the guys" and expose themselves to higher risks of being arrested, injured, or even killed in conflicts with rival gangs. Or they can use gender to decrease their risk of being harmed by not participating in "masculine" activities such as fighting and committing crime. However, females who opt out of violence and crime are often viewed as lesser members and may expose themselves to greater risks of victimization within their gangs.[71]

In sum, most studies have found that girl gangs still serve as adjuncts to boy gangs. Yet an increasing number of important studies show that female gangs provide girls with the necessary skills to survive in their harsh communities while allowing them a temporary escape from the dismal future awaiting them.[72] What these studies reveal is that girls join gangs for the same basic reasons that boys do—and share with boys in their neighborhood the hopelessness and powerlessness of the urban underclass.[73]

What Are Emergent Street Gangs?

In the late 1980s and early 1990s, gangs began to appear in most communities of this nation. In G. David Curry and colleagues' 1992 survey of law enforcement departments in the seventy-nine largest U.S. cities, 91 percent of respondents reported the presence of gang problems. These researchers estimated that there were 4,881 gangs with 249,324 gang members; forty cities reported a total of 7,205 gang members. Twenty-seven cities reported that there were eighty-three independent female gangs. Significantly, these cities with emerging gangs reported that juveniles made up 90 percent of the gang membership.[74]

Emergent gangs have been examined in Denver, Colorado; Kansas City, Missouri; Rochester, New York; and Seattle, Washington. These studies generally found that gang members were involved in levels of delinquent activity that were much greater than those of nongang youth, that the participation in gangs increased each year from the late 1980s to the early 1990s, and that these emerging gangs brought new levels of violence to a community.[75] Seven stages of gang development could be identified at the time:[76]

Stage 1: Gang leaders are aware of the ripe drug markets outside the major urban areas throughout the nation. They are also aware that crack cocaine in these new markets would bring a higher price than it does in the saturated urban areas. A plan is developed—which varies little from one drug-trafficking urban gang to another—for a gang member to go to a city without gangs. When he arrives, either by plane or auto, he goes to a low-income minority neighborhood and recruits several juveniles to sell crack cocaine. As part of his sales pitch, this ghetto-based gang member assures these juveniles that the mother gang intends to develop a connection, or satellite, in their community. The recruited juveniles are promised a percentage of the money they make from the drug sales. The adult gang member agrees to return on a regular basis to supply more drugs, to pick up the money, and to check on operations. It is not long before a second and sometimes a third representative of urban-based gang arrives to recruit youths to sell crack cocaine.

Stage 2: By stage 2, the adult gang member has told the youths selling drugs enough about the gang that they are able to identify with it. They can wear the proper clothing, can represent the gang signs, and can come together as a group. But their basic activity remains that of selling crack cocaine. One Midwestern youth claimed that he was making $40,000 a month selling crack cocaine for the Almighty Unknown Vice Lords when he was arrested and institutionalized. Competition between these youths who claim to be part of the rival street gangs inevitably results in conflict and sometimes violence. Fights are likely to break out during school functions, at athletic events, and in parks. Weapons may be discharged at this time. Police also become aware that increasing numbers of weapons are being brought into the community.

Stage 3: The organization of the gangs develops during stage 3. Gang membership increases as more youths are brought into the core group. Leadership of the gang is usually assumed by a member of the initial core group, as well as by young adult members of the community. Gang members become more visible at school and at school functions, usually by the colors or clothing they wear and by the gang signs they represent. It is not long before a sizable number of "wannabes" are considering themselves gang members. The process of initiation begins at this time, and pressure is placed especially on African American males to join a gang. White youths also frequently are accepted as part of these developing gangs.

Stage 4: The competition between rival gangs erupts in open conflict in school, at school dances, at athletic events, and in shopping centers. Drugs also are increasingly sold in the school environment. White gangs often appear at this time, but African American gangs are more likely to wear their colors and to demonstrate gang affiliation.

Stage 5: Drugs are openly sold in the school, on street corners, and in shopping centers. Extortion of students and victimization of both teachers and students occurs widely in the public schools. Moreover, the gangs are led by adults who remain in the community, and the organizational structure and numbers of gang members show a significant increase.

Stage 6: The gangs are clearly in control in minority neighborhoods, in the school, at school events, and in shopping centers. The criminal operations of the rival gangs also become more varied during stage 6, including robberies, burglaries, aggravated assaults, and rapes. Citizens' fear of gangs dramatically increases, and the police express the inability to control drug trafficking and violence.

Stage 7: The final stage is characterized by the deterioration of the city as a result of gang control. Citizens move out of the city, stay away from shopping centers, and keep their children home from school. See Figure 13–6.

FIGURE 13–6
Stages of Emerging Gangs

Focus on Offender 13–2
Institutionalized Juvenile Who Went Home and Killed

One of the authors was doing a research project comparing a state and a private facility when he was approached by staff members who inquired whether he would like to talk to all the gang kids. Word quickly got around that this coauthor knew Willie Lloyd, the leader of the Unknown Vice Lords, and so all the gang youths wanted to talk to him, especially the Vice Lords. One young man came into the office to talk when this researcher was interviewing staff youth leaders. They were having a good talk, when suddenly the gang youth announced that he had to go home and kill the Crip who had recently killed his nephew.

He would be released the next week and planned to take care of business.

The researcher tried to talk him out of it, with a variety of reasoning ploys. Nothing worked. He went home the next week, and was soon involved in the killing of a Crip on a drive-by shooting. He is presently doing life without parole for this crime.

CRITICAL THINKING QUESTION

If you were in place of this researcher, what would you have said to this young man?

The Toxicity of Gang Involvement

Youths involved in emergent gangs are sounding more and more like those who are members of urban gangs. Both talk about justice. Justice means that honor is revenged. "I feel that what we did that night wasn't enough. Justice, to me, would have been killing seven or eight of them. Even though only one guy shot my brother, there were three guys there."[77]

Both talk about how gang "bangin'" becomes a way of showing that a youth is "bad." "Shootin' guns and stabbin' people" is how a gang youth shows heart and courage, and killing to many gang youths "ain't nothing." The violence of this substitute family makes a youth feel powerful and connected to something worthwhile. To youths who must deal with hopelessness in so many areas of their lives, the fear of dying makes them feel alive.

Beyond gang youths attempting to make sense of their social world is the reality that gangs are destructive to their members. First, gang youths become involved in dangerous, even deadly, games. As one former gang leader put it, "I've gone to more gang funerals than I can even count."[78] Second, although joining a gang may be a normal rite of passage for a youth, gangs minister poorly to such basic adolescent needs as preparation for marriage and employment and learning to adapt to the adult world. Third, juvenile males who join gangs for protection are exposed to dangers that most nongang juveniles are able to avoid. Fourth, gang youth frequently are victimized by both juvenile and adult members of street gangs.[79] Adolescent females who often are exploited sexually by male gang members are an apt example of how gangs victimize younger members. Finally, although joining a gang may provide status and esteem in the present, it also increases the likelihood of incarceration in juvenile and adult facilities.[80] See Focus on the Offender 13–2.

Juveniles who belong to urban street gangs or emerging youth gangs are involved in more serious delinquent acts than are youths who do not belong to gangs. The influence of gang participation on violent behavior has been documented by a number of studies. The studies of gangs in Rochester, New York; Denver, Colorado; and Pittsburgh, Pennsylvania, all found that gang youths committed more violent behaviors than did nongang delinquents and that youths commit more serious and more violent acts when they are gang members than they do after leaving the gang.[81] James C. Howell's examination of youth gang homicides found that the recent growth in youth gang homicides has been driven by increased access to firearms. Yet it appears that gang-related homicides are generally not about drugs but are personal, vendetta-like, and motivated primarily by self-protection.[82]

What Can Communities Do to Prevent and Control Youth Gangs?

Communities across the United States have had a tendency to deny that they have gangs even when gang youths are causing serious problems at schools and in the neighborhoods. When an incident takes place, such as the killing of an innocent victim or a shootout, and one or more youths are killed, communities tend to substitute repression for denial. The problem is turned over to the police with the directive to make gangs invisible. Gang units are sometimes established in police departments to focus on getting rid of the gang problem and very often turn to repressive measures that are of little long-term significance.

Attorney General Eric Holder has recently pushed for more innovation- and evidence-based programs in combating the violence of youths and youth gangs. He has urged communities to find out what does work, using the programs that are successful as well as going "outside the box" to solve problems. High Point, North Carolina, has been cited as using a model developed by David Kennedy to target the most violent offenders for prosecution, then going to lower-level drug offenders and saying, "This is what will happen to you if you don't get your act straight." The young drug dealers are shown videotapes of them dealing drugs and informed that indictments are being prepared for them unless they change their ways. Job training and mentoring are provided to those who are willing to make the adjustments needed in their lives. As a result, Holder reports, the violent crime rate in High Point dropped 57 percent.[83]

Another example of a successful program is the Summer Night Lights Program in Los Angeles. The city, with the cooperation of community leaders and organizations, keeps the lights on in potentially dangerous parks at night and offers recreational, artistic, and educational programs for youths. Gang violence has decreased in the targeted areas by 40 percent.[84] These programs illustrate some of the principles developed below.

What Does Not Work and What Might Work Very Well?

Irving Spergel and colleagues' 1989 survey of forty-five cities with gang problems identified five strategies of intervention: (1) community organization, including community mobilization and networking; (2) social intervention, focusing on individual behavioral and value change; (3) opportunity provision, emphasizing the improvement of basic education, training, and job opportunities for youth; (4) suppression, focusing on arrest, incarceration, monitoring, and supervision of gang members; and (5) organizational development and change, or the creation of special organizational units as well as procedures.[85]

In examining the implementation of these strategies, Spergel and colleagues found that suppression (44 percent) was most frequently used, followed by social intervention (31.5 percent), organizational development (10.9 percent), community organization

---

EXHIBIT 13-2
Father Grey Boyle, S. J.–A Man with a Vision

One of the most remarkable and influential people who has ever worked on gang intervention is Father Greg, as he is known. He was born in Los Angeles, one of eight children, and after graduation from high school in Los Angeles, he decided to become a Jesuit and was ordained in this order in 1984.

While he was a priest in a small congregation at Dolores Mission Church, Father Greg and he local community developed positive alternatives to gang membership, including establishing a daycare program and an elementary school and finding legitimate employment for youth.

In 1982, as a response to civil unrest in Los Angeles, Father Greg launched the first business, Homeboy Bakery. One of its purposes was to enable rival gang members to work side-by-side. The success of the bakery laid the groundwork for the other businesses that followed.

Father Greg is a nationally renowned speaker, and in 2005, was a featured speaker at the White House conference on youth at the personal invitation of Mrs. George Bush. In addition to all the committees serves on, he has received much

recognition and many awards, including the California Peace Prize, on behalf of Homewood Homeboy industries and for his work with former gang members. In 2008, he received the Civic Medal of Honor from the Los Angeles Chamber of Commerce. In 1910, he published Tattoos on the Heart: the Power of Boundless Compassion, retelling his 20 some years in the barrios of Los Angeles.

Father Greg, like many others across the nation, is attempting to make a difference by giving gang youth hope in providing a means of support for them to leave the gang.

CRITICAL THINKING QUESTION
What type of person would it take to be this committed to working with gangs? Do you believe there are others who also are similarly committed and effective in working with gangs?

Source: Carol Ann Morrow, "Jesuit Greg Boyle, Gang Priest," Anthony Mission, http://www.americacatholic.org/Messenger/Aug1999/feature 1.asp (accessed, July 18, 2012).

Evidence-Based Practice
Planning and Implementing the Comprehensive Gang Model

With funding that the U.S. Department of Justice provided in March 1993, Spergel began implementing the initial version of the comprehensive Gang Model in the Little Village neighborhood of Chicago, a low-income and working-class community that is about 90 percent Mexican American.

Called the Gang Violence Reduction Program, the project lasted five years. The program focused on providing services to individual gang members, rather than to the gangs as groups. It targeted mainly older members (ages seventeen to twenty-four) of two of the area's most violent Hispanic gangs, the Latin Kings and the Two Six. The program actually targeted more than two hundred of the "shoot-ers," the most influential members or leaders of the two gangs. As a group, these two gangs accounted for about 75 percent of felony gang violence in the Little Village community—including twelve homicides in each of the two years before the start of the project.

The primary goal of the project was to reduce the extremely high level of gang violence among youth who were actively involved in the two gangs. Outreach youth workers—nearly all of whom were former members of the two target gangs—attempted to prevent and control gang conflicts and to persuade gang youth to leave the gang as soon as possible. Outreach activities included a balance of services, such as brief family and individual counseling and referrals for services, crisis intervention, and surveillance and suppression activities.

The process evaluation of the Gang Violence Reduction Program revealed that it was implemented very well. Spergel, in examining the effects of the Little Village project on the approximately two hundred hard-core gang youth during the five years, found the following results:

- Self-reports of criminal involvement revealed that the program reduced serious violent property crimes, as well as the frequency of various types of offenses including robbery, gang intimidation, and drive-by shootings.
- The program was more effective with older, more violent gang offenders than with younger, less violent offenders.
- Active gang involvement was reduced among project youth, mostly for older members, and this change was associated with less criminal activity.
- Most youth in both targeted gangs improved their educational and employment rates during the program period.
- Employment was seen to be associated with a general reduction in youth's criminal activity, particularly in regard to reductions in drug dealing.
- Program youth had significantly fewer total violent crime and drug arrests.
- The project had no significant effect on total arrests, property arrests, or other minor crime arrests.
- Gang violence was on the upswing during the project period of 1992–1997, but the increase in homicides and other serious violent gang crimes was lower among the Latin Kings and Two Six compared with other Latino and African American gangs in the area, which is one of the deadliest gang-violent areas of the city.

Source: Best Practices to Address Community Gang Problems: OJJDP's Comprehensive Gang Model (Washington, DC: Office of Justice Programs, Office of Juvenile Justice and Delinquency Prevention, 2012), 37–38, Appendix A.

(8.9 percent), and opportunity provision (4.8 percent). Community organization was more likely to be used with gang programs in emerging gang cities, whereas social intervention and opportunity provision tended to be primarily the strategies of programs in cities with chronic gang problems. But in only seventeen of the forty-five cities was there any evidence of improvement in the gang situation.[86]

Spergel and colleagues, in developing a model for predicting general effectiveness in dealing with gang problems, stated:

> A final set of analyses across all cities indicate that the primary strategies of community organization and provision of opportunity along with maximum participation by key community actors is predictive of successful efforts at reducing the gang problems.[87]

What this research by Spergel and colleagues has demonstrated is that only an integrated, multidimensional, community-oriented effort is likely to have any long-term effect in preventing and controlling gangs in the United States. This gang prevention and control model must have several components: (1) the community must take responsibility for developing and implementing this model; (2) this structural model must take seriously the hopelessness arising from the unmet needs of underclass children; (3) prevention programs, especially in the first six years of school, must receive a major emphasis; (4) those who support this model must coordinate all of the gang intervention efforts taking place in a community; and (5) sufficient financial resources must be available for implementing the model. See the Evidence-Based Practice feature.

SUMMARY

LEARNING OBJECTIVE 1: Outline the development of gangs in the United States.

Gangs started out in the 1920s as transitory groups; gangs in the 1950s in urban areas in the east became groups of youth fighting each other and protecting "turf"; the supergangs developed in Los Angeles and Chicago in the 1960s; the 1970s, 1980s, and 1990s were the decades when urban gangs were taken over by adults, accompanied by drug trafficking and violence; and the 2000s to the present have seen a decrease in some gangs and but the growth of ethnic gangs. Much is the same and much is new about youth gangs.

LEARNING OBJECTIVE 2: Describe the behaviors and activities of gangs.

Adolescents who find that their needs are not met in social contacts with family members, teachers, and leaders and participation in churches, school activities, and community organizations are more likely to be attracted to street gangs and youth gangs. These gangs become quasi-families offering acceptance, status, and esteem. Most gang activity consists of simply "hanging out," but some focus also takes place on committing unlawful acts. What is new is the widespread use of gun violence, particularly involving automatic and semiautomatic handguns; the juvenile drug trafficking that takes place now much more than in the past; and the frequency with which youth gangs become street gangs with adults as leaders. Juveniles are often in the minority in these urban street gangs. Gangs have thrived because of the poverty in urban neighborhoods. The hopelessness of these environments makes drug trafficking attractive and gang membership desirable even with the high possibility of being injured, killed, or imprisoned.

LEARNING OBJECTIVE 3: Identify the primary types of gangs.

Scavenger gangs: Prey on those unable to defend themselves.

Territorial gangs: Defend an area in which they claim ownership.

Corporate gangs: Organized crime groups whose main purpose is participation in illegal money-making ventures.

Hedonistic gangs: Basic purpose is to get high and have a good time.

Instrumental gangs: Focus is on economic gain.

Predatory gangs: Commit a variety of crimes, use and sell cocaine, and purchase more sophisticated weapons to achieve their purposes.

Type 1 gangs: Involved in minor delinquent activities and drug use.

Type 2 gangs: Heavily involved in several types of drug sales.

Type 3 gangs: Little involvement in drug sales but more involvement in both serious and nonserious offenses.

Type 4 gangs: Extensively involved in drug use, drug sales, and serious and nonserious offenses.

LEARNING OBJECTIVE 4: Identify the seven stages of emergent gang development.

The seven stages of emergent gang development are (1) implementation; (2) expansion and conflict; (3) organization and consolidation; (4) gang intimidation and community reaction; (5) expansion of drug markets; (6) gang takeover; and (7) community deterioration.

LEARNING OBJECTIVE 5: Summarize efforts to prevent and control gangs.

The number of gang members, as well as the number of youth gangs, decreased from the late 1990s to the present. Youth gangs remain a problem throughout the United States; even small towns and rural areas often must contend with the presence of youth gangs. Grassroots community groups seem to make the most sense in reducing the spread of gangs, but gang reduction actually depends on providing at-risk children with more positive options than they have today.

KEY TERMS

corporate gangs, p. 285
crack, p. 285
drug trafficking, p. 288
emergent gangs, p. 293
gang leadership, p. 286
hedonistic gangs, p. 286

instrumental gangs, p. 286
methods of initiation, p. 287
migration, p. 288
organized crime groups, p. 291
predatory gangs, p. 286

scavenger gangs, p. 285
supergangs, p. 279
territorial gangs, p. 285
underclass theory, p. 284
urban gangs, p. 277

REVIEW QUESTIONS

1. Why are adolescents likely to become involved in youth gangs?
2. How have youth gangs changed throughout the years?
3. If you had the opportunity to teach a class of high school students, most of whom were in youth gangs, what would you say to them?

4. Why is community participation the most effective means of gang prevention and control?
5. Why do you believe gang participation and membership decreased in the final years of the twentieth century?

GROUP EXERCISES

1. *Class Presentation:* Have class groups use the Internet to look up the different ethnic group gangs in the United States such as the Jamaican Posse and Chinese and Vietnamese gangs. Have each group choose one of the ethnic group gangs and report to class on the gang's itinerary, age of members, numbers, and modes of operation.

2. *Group Work:* Discuss the different types of urban gangs as described by researchers. Identify the different classifications described.

3. *Writing to Learn Exercise:* Write a paragraph or two describing the organizational features of urban gangs. Critique and revise.

4. *Writing to Learn Exercise:* Discuss in two paragraphs the different toxic effects of gangs on the community and the school. Critique and revise.

5. *Group Work:* Discuss the seven stages involved in the development of emergent street gangs.

- **Research Center:** Check out the Cybrary and MySearchLab for even more resources.

WORKING WITH JUVENILES

You are a social worker in a training school. One of the residents in your cottage comes to you and says he cannot protect himself against stronger youths, many of whom have been part of gangs in the community. He reports that staff in the cottage tell him to be a man and not to let anyone take advantage of him. He says he cannot stand up to these predatory peers and that he is fearful of sexual assault. What would you say to him? What would you do?

NOTES

1. Interviewed in 1995.

2. Arlen Egley, Jr., and James C. Howell, *Highlights of the 2009 National Youth Gang Survey* (Washington, DC: Office of Juvenile Justice and Delinquency Prevention, 2011).

3. See the section on law-violating behaviors of juveniles for studies supporting these conclusions.

4. Luc Sante, *Low Life: Lures and Snares of Old New York* (New York: Vintage Books, 1991).

5. Robert Redfield, *Folk Culture of Yucatan* (Chicago: University of Chicago Press, 1941).

6. Frederick Thrasher, *The Gang: A Study of 1,313 Gangs in Chicago* (Chicago: University of Chicago Press, 1927).

7. Ibid.

8. See Walter B. Miller, "The Impact of a Total Community Delinquency Control Project," *Social Problems* 10 (Fall 1962), 168–91.

9. John C. Quicker and Akil S. Batani-Khalfani, "Clique Succession Among South Los Angeles Street Gangs, the Case of the Crips," paper presented at the annual meeting of the American Society of Criminology, Reno, NV, November 1989.

10. National Youth Gang Center, *National Youth Gang Survey Analysis 2007* (Washington, DC: Office of Juvenile Justice and Delinquency Prevention, National Youth Gang Center, 2007), at http://www.jjr.com/nygc/nygsa.

11. For an excellent review of the history of gangs, see James C. Howell, *Gangs in America's Communities* (Los Angeles: Sage, 2012).

12. Arlen Egley, Jr., James C. Howell, and Meena Harris, "Highlights of the 2012 National Youth Gang Survey "*Juvenile Justice Fact Sheet* (Washington, DC: U.S. Department of Justice, December 2014), 1.

13. U.S. Department of Justice, *About Violent Gangs,* http://www.justice.gov/criminal/ocgs/gangs (accessed, July 15, 2012).

14. James C. Howell, *OJJDP Fact Sheet* (Washington, DC: Office of Juvenile Justice and Delinquency Prevention, 1997). For an update, see James C. Howell, *Gangs in America's Communities* (Los Angeles, CA: Sage, 2012).

15. See Arlen Egley, Jr., James C. Howell, and Aline K. Major, *National Youth Gang Survey, 1999–2001* (Washington, DC: Office of Juvenile Justice and Delinquency Prevention, 2006), 18. For an update, see Howell, *Gangs in America's Communities*.

16. For the role behavior of juveniles in gangs, see Mike Carlie, *Into the Abyss: A Personal Journal into the World of Street Gangs,* at http://people.missouristate.edu/MichaelCarlie.

17. James C. Howell, "Youth Gangs: An Overview," *Juvenile Justice Bulletin* (Washington, DC: Office of Justice Programs, Office of Juvenile Justice and Delinquency Prevention, 1998). See also Scott H. Decker and B. Van Winkle, *Life in the Gang: Family, Friends, and Violence* (New York: Cambridge University Press, 1996).

18. Interviewed in 1982 at the Iowa State Penitentiary in Ft. Madison, Iowa.

19. H. A. Bloch and A. Niederhoffer, *The Gang: A Study in Adolescent Behavior* (New York: Philosophical Library, 1958).

20. Richard A. Cloward and Lloyd E. Ohlin, *Delinquency and Opportunity: A Theory of Delinquent Gangs* (New York: Free Press, 1960).

21. Albert K. Cohen, *Delinquent Boys: The Culture of the Gang* (Glencoe, IL: Free Press, 1955).

22. Walter B. Miller, "Lower-Class Culture as a Generating Milieu of Gang Delinquency," *Journal of Social Issues* 14 (1958), 5–19.

23. Lewis Yablonsky, *The Violent Gang* (New York: Macmillan, 1962).

24. See William Julius Wilson, *The Truly Disadvantaged: The Inner City, the Underclass, and Public Policy* (Chicago: University of Chicago Press, 1987).

25. G. David Curry and Irving A. Spergel, "Gang Homicide, Delinquency, and Community," *Criminology* (1988), 381–405.

26. J. E. Fagan, "Gangs, Drugs, and Neighborhood Change," in *Gangs in America*, edited by C. Ronald Huff (Newbury Park, CA: Sage Publications, 1990), 39–74.

27. Martin Sánchez Jankowski, *Island in the Streets: Gangs and American Urban Society* (Berkeley: University of California Press, 1991), 138.

28. Carl S. Taylor, *Dangerous Society* (East Lansing: Michigan State University Press, 1990), 4–7.

29. C. Ronald Huff, "Youth Gangs and Public Policy," *Crime and Delinquency* 35 (October 1989), 528–29.

30. Jeffrey Fagan, "The Social Organization of Drug Use and Drug Dealing Among Urban Gangs," *Criminology* 27 (1989), 633–64.

31. Jankowski, *Islands in the Streets*, 5.

32. Ibid., 64–67.

33. Joan Moore, Diego Vigil, and Robert Garcia, "Residence and Territoriality in Chicago Gangs," *Social Problems* 31 (December 1985), 182–94.

34. Conversations with urban gang chiefs in 1996.

35. Carlie, *Into the Abyss*.

36. Cheryl L. Maxson, Malcolm W. Klein, and Lea C. Cunningham, "Street Gangs and Drug Sales," report to the National Institute of Justice (1993).

37. National Youth Gang Center, *National Youth Gang Survey Analysis 2007*.

38. Drug Enforcement Administration, *Crack Cocaine Availability and Trafficking in the United States* (Washington, DC: U.S. Department of Justice, 1988).

39. Shay Bilchik, *1997 National Youth Gang Survey* (Washington, DC: Office of Juvenile Justice and Delinquency Prevention, December 1999), 25.

40. Ibid., 24.

41. Ibid., 40.

42. Arlen Egley, Jr., and Aline K. Major, *Highlights of the 2002 National Youth Gang Surveys* (Washington, DC: U.S. Government Printing Office), 1.

43. See C. Ronald Huff, *Criminal Behavior of Gang Members and At-Risk Youths: Research Preview* (Washington, DC: National Institute of Research, 1998), 1.

44. Ibid., 1–2.

45. Ibid., 1.

46. Terence P. Thornberry, "Membership in Youth Gangs and Involvement in Serious and Violent Offending," in *Serious and Violent Juvenile Offenders: Risk Factors and Successful Intervention*, edited by R. Loeber and D. P. Farrington (Thousand Oaks, CA: Sage Publications, 1998), 147–66.

47. Sara R. Battin-Pearson et al., "Gang Membership, Delinquent Peers, and Delinquent Behavior," *Juvenile Justice Bulletin* (Washington, DC: Office of Justice Programs, Office of Juvenile Justice and Delinquency Prevention, 1998).

48. David Huizinga, "Gangs and the Volume of Crime," paper presented at the annual meeting of the Western Society of Criminology, Honolulu, HI, 1997.

49. Sara R. Battin et al., "The Contribution of Gang Membership to Delinquency: Beyond Delinquent Friends," *Criminology* 36 (February 1998), 93–115.

50. Finn—Aage Esbensen and Dena Carson, "Who Are the Gangsters?: An Examination of the Age, Race/Ethnicity. Sex and Immigration, Status of Self-Reported Gang Members In a Seven City Study of American Youth," *Journal of Contemporary Criminal Justice* 28 (2012), 462–78.

51. Howell, "Youth Gangs."

52. National Institute for Intergovernmental Research, *National Youth Gang Survey Analysis* (2009), at http://www.iir.com/nygc/nygsa/measuring_the_extent_of_gang_problem.htm.

53. Scott H. Decker, Tim Bynum, and Deborah Weisel, "A Tale of Two Cities: Gangs as Organized Crime Groups," *Justice Quarterly* 15 (September 1998), 395–425.

54. James McCormick, "The 'Disciples' of Drugs and Death," *Newsweek* (February 5, 1996), 56–59.

55. For an excellent examination of the Bloods and Crips and other California gangs, see Howell, *Gangs in America's Communities*.

56. U.S. General Accounting Office, *Nontraditional Organized Crime* (Washington, DC: U.S. Government Printing Office, 1989).

57. Robert Walker, "Maria Salvatrucha MS-14 or US," at http://www.gangsorus.com/mariasalvatrucha13.html.

58. James Diego Vigil and Steve Chong Yun, "Vietnamese Youth Gangs in Southern California," in *Gangs in America*, 146–62.

59. Reiner, *Gangs, Violence, and Crime in Los Angeles*.

60. See Pete Simi, Lowell Smith, and Ann M. S. Reiner, "From Punk Kids to Public Enemy Number One," *Deviant Behavior* 29 (2009), 753–74.

61. Freda Adler, *Sisters in Crime: The Rise of the New Female Criminal* (New York: McGraw-Hill, 1975); W. B. Miller, "The Molls," *Society* 11 (1973), 32–35; E. Ackley and B. Fliegel, "A Social Work Approach to Street Corner Girls," *Social Work* 5 (1960), 29–31; Peggy C. Giordano, "Girls, Guys and Gangs: The Changing Social Context of Female Delinquency," *Journal of Criminal Law and Criminology* 69 (1978), 130.

62. Lee Bowker and Malcolm W. Klein, "Female Participation in Delinquent Gang Motivation," *Adolescence* 15 (1980), 509–19; John C. Quicker, *Home Girls: Characterizing Chicano Gangs* (San Pedro, CA: International University Press, 1983).

63. Quicker, *Home Girls*.

64. Finn-Agee Esbensen, Elizabeth Piper Deschenes, and L. Thomas Winfee, Jr., "Differences Between Gang Girls and Gang Boys: Results from a Multi-Site Survey," *Youth and Society* 31 (1999), 27–53.

65. Carl S. Taylor, *Girls, Gangs, Women and Drugs* (East Lansing: Michigan State University Press, 1993), 48.

66. Beth Bjerregaard and Carolyn Smith, "Gender Differences in Gang Participation, Delinquency, and Substance Abuse," *Journal of Quantitative Criminology* 9 (1993), 347–48.

67. Joan Moore and John Hagedorn, "Female Gangs: A Focus on Research," *Juvenile Justice Bulletin* (Washington, DC: Office of Juvenile Justice and Delinquency Prevention, 2001).

68. Finn-Aage Esbensen, Elizabeth Piper Deschenes, and L. Thomas Winfree Jr., "Differences Between Gang Girls and Gang Boys: Results from a Multi-Site Survey," paper presented at the Annual Meeting of the Academy of Criminal Justice Sciences in Albuquerque, NM, 1998, 20–21.

69. Jody Miller, "Gender and Victimization Risk Among Young Women in Gangs," *Journal of Research in Crime and Delinquency* 35 (November 1998), 429–53; Jody Miller and Rod K. Brunson, "Gender Dynamics in Youth Gangs: A Comparison of Males' and Females' Accounts," *Justice Quarterly* 17 (September 2000), 420–47; Jody Miller and Scott Decker, "Young Women and Gang Violence: Gender, Street Offending, and Violent Victimization in Gangs," *Justice Quarterly* 18 (March 2001), 115–39; Jody Miller, *One of the Guys: Girls, Gangs, and Gender* (New York: Oxford University Press, 2001).

70. Miller and Brunson, "Gender Dynamics in Youth Gangs," 443–45.

71. Miller, "Gender and Victimization Risk Among Young Women in Gangs";

72. Karen Joe and Meda Chesney-Lind, "Just Every Mother's Angel: An Analysis of Gender and Ethnic Variations in Youth Gang Membership," paper presented at the annual meeting of the American Society of Criminology, Phoenix, AZ, November 1993, 9.

73. Ibid.

74. G. David Curry, Robert J. Fox, Richard A. Ball, and Darryl Stone, "National Assessment of Law Enforcement Anti-Gang Information Resources," report to the U.S. Department of Justice, National Institute of Justice (1993).

75. For a review of gang research, including that of emergent gangs, see James C. Howell, "Recent Gang Research: Program and Policy Implications," *Crime and Delinquency* 40 (October 1994), 491–515. For the study in Denver, see Finn-Aage Esbensen and David Huizinga, "Gangs, Drugs, and Delinquency in a Survey of Urban Youth," *Criminology* 31 (1993), 565–89. For the study in Kansas City, Missouri, and Seattle, Washington, see Mark S. Fleisher, "Youth Gangs and Social Networks: Observations from a Long-Term Ethnographic Study," paper presented at the annual meeting of the American Society of Criminology, Miami, FL, November 1994. For the study in Rochester, New York, see Terence P. Thornberry et al., "The Role of Juvenile Gangs in Facilitating Delinquent Behavior," *Journal of Research in Crime and Delinquency* 30 (1993), 55–87.

76. These stages were developed as a result of one of the authors' examination of these emerging gangs.

77. Howell, "Recent Gang Research."

78. Ibid.

79. One of the authors interviewed gang members in 1996.

80. For example, see Felix Padilla's *The Gang as an Ethnic Enterprise* (New Brunswick, NJ: Rutgers University Press, 1992) for the way the youths who traffick drugs for the gang are victimized. For a discussion of the destructiveness of gangs to their members, see James F. Short, Jr., "Gangs, Neighborhood, and Youth Crime," *Criminal Justice Research Bulletin* 3 (1990), 3.

81. Thornberry, "Membership in Youth Gangs and Involvement in Serious and Violent Offending," 147–66.

82. James C. Howell, "Youth Gang Homicides: A Literature Review," *Crime and Delinquency* 45 (April 1999), 208–41.

83. Attorney General Eric Holder, *Remarks Prepared for the White House Conference on Gang Violence Prevention and Crime Control* (Washington, DC: The White House, August 24, 2009), http://www.usdoj.gov/ag/speeches/ag-speech-090824.html.

84. Ibid.

85. I. A. Spergel et al., *Survey of Youth Gang Problems and Programs in 45 Cities and 6 Sites.* Tech. Report No. 2, National Youth Gang Suppression and Intervention Project (Chicago: University of Chicago, School of Social Service Administration, 1989), 211.

86. Ibid., 212.

87. Ibid., 211.

14 Special Juvenile Offender Populations*

Simone van den Berg/Shutterstock

*Casady Myers assisted in the research and development of this chapter.

Learning Objectives

1. Describe the different types of drug users, drug traffickers, and the relationship of drug use and delinquency, and treatment.

2. Describe the juvenile sex offender, focusing on backgrounds, offenses, treatment possibilities, and typical life course.

3. Describe the juvenile gang delinquent, both in urban gangs and in emerging gangs in the community, examining their negative behaviors, motivation for becoming involved in gangs, treatment possibilities, and typical life course.

4. Describe the violent offender, focusing on his or her background, relationships with peers, delinquent history, treatment possibilities, and typical life course.

5. Describe the mentally ill juvenile, with typical backgrounds, degrees of mental disorder, treatment possibilities, and delinquent history.

6. Describe the crossover youth, relating his or her background in the foster care of mental health system, his or her involvement in delinquent offenses, treatment possibilities, and typical life course.

7. Describe the juvenile who is homeless, presenting his or her background, behaviors, contacts with the justice system, treatment possibilities, and typical life course.

A 2011 report by the Office of Juvenile Justice and Delinquency Prevention (OJJDP) draws attention to the fact that research has consistently found that substance abuse among adolescents is linked to serious juvenile offending.[1] That finding was additionally supported by research from the ongoing OJJDP-sponsored Pathways to Desistance Study. The Pathway study is a large collaborative, multidisciplinary project that is currently following 1,354 serious juvenile offenders (both male and female) ages fourteen to eighteen for seven years after their adjudication as delinquent. The study is exploring factors that lead juveniles who have committed serious offenses to continue offending or to desist from offending. Some of these factors include individual maturation, life changes, drug use, and involvement with the criminal justice system. A significant major finding of the study to date is that substance abuse treatment reduces both the use of illegal substances and criminal offending. The adolescent offenders profiled in the Pathway to Desistance Study initially self-reported very high levels of substance use and substance abuse problems. The use of illegal substances was linked to other illegal activities that were also engaged in by the study participants. As such, substance abuse was found to be a strong, prevalent predictor of offending. The presence of a drug or alcohol disorder and the level of substance use were both shown to be strongly and independently related to the level of self-reported offending and the number of arrests. "The good news," say researchers involved in the study, "is that treatment appears to reduce both substance abuse and offending." According to these authors, "Youth whose treatment lasted for at least 90 days and included significant family involvement showed significant reductions in alcohol use, marijuana use, and offending over the following six months.[2]

In addition to the news cited in the chapter-opening vignette, other good news comes from findings that substance abuse among adolescents had dropped dramatically since the late 1970s.[3] The bad news is that drug use has significantly increased among high-risk youths and is becoming commonly linked to juvenile lawbreaking. More juveniles are selling drugs than ever before in the history of this nation. Furthermore, the spread of AIDS within populations of intravenous drug users and their sex partners adds to the gravity of the substance abuse problem.

Besides the juvenile drug user, this chapter examines a number of juvenile offenders who are grouped into the following three categories: **special offense youths**—youthful offenders who have substance abuse histories, the juvenile sex offender, the juvenile gang youth, and the youthful violent offenders; **special needs youths**—youths with chronic mental health issues; and **special population residents**—the crossover youth and the homeless youth. Some of whom have received previous attention—the gang delinquent, the violent offender, and the crossover youth—and some deserve attention because of their behaviors or the problems they present to the social orders in which they are a part. Their characteristics, behaviors, treatment possibilities, and the likelihood of their paths in the future are examined.

Special Offense Youthful Offenders

Special offense youthful offenders are linked together because of their prior criminal/deviant behavior issues. Some are substance abuse offenders, some are sex offenders, some are gang delinquents, and some are violent offenders. These offenders engage in multiple-offense patterns, so that a violent offender may have been involved in two or more behavior issues, such as violent gang behavior, violence during drug transactions, or violence during a sex crime.

The Drug Delinquent

Adolescent drug use becomes abuse only when the user becomes dysfunctional (e.g., is unable to attend or perform in school or to maintain family and social relationships; exhibits dangerous, reckless, or aggressive behavior; or endangers his or her health). The

Focus on Offenders 14–1
They Call Me Spacey

I started using drugs when I was eight years old. It makes you feel like you can beat anything that comes along. I thought, "Wow, this is great!" When I was nine, someone asked me if I wanted to take some acid. I figured, sure, why not? This was really great because I could sit around and watch the walls melt. My English teacher deteriorated in her chair one time at school. As the years went by, I started to peddle a lot of speed and acid. Pretty soon, I was drug-dependent. I needed speed in the morning, and I had to take speed in school to make it through the day. I got to the point that I couldn't handle speed anymore. I was too juiced up. Now I regret doing so many drugs because I can't remember simple things that I should remember, like talking with someone over the phone the night before. I became spacey; in fact, people have called me spacey for two years now.

Source: Interviewed by one of the authors.

drug-dependent compulsive user's life generally revolves around obtaining, maintaining, and using a supply of drugs.[4] See Focus on Offender 14–1 for the story of one adolescent whose drug use was out of control.

Drug Use Among Adolescents

Society tends to focus on juveniles' use of harder drugs, although alcohol remains the drug of choice for most adolescents. Drug use among adolescents was extremely high during the late 1960s into the 1970s, reaching epidemic proportions. Overall rates of illicit drug use appeared to peak sometime around 1979 and then leveled off, but even with the leveling off that took place, rates of illegal drug among juveniles remained high for some time. Then, in 2001, there was a significant downturn in drug use levels.[5] According to the 2010 *Mentoring the Future* study, overall illicit drug use by youths continued to decline until 2008, after which increased use of some drugs began to occur.[6]

According to the *2010 National Survey on Drug Use and Health*, an estimated 22.6 million adolescents ages twelve or older were current illicit drug users, which means they had used an illegal drug during the month prior to the survey interview. Illicit drugs include marijuana/hashish, cocaine (including crack), MDMA (Ecstasy), methamphetamine, heroin, hallucinogens, inhalants, and prescription-type psychotherapeutic drugs.[7] The survey documented increases in the specific categories of prescription drugs, marijuana, Ecstasy, and methamphetamine. The increasing use of illegal drugs was driven by a significant increase in current use of marijuana (from 5.8 to 6.9 percent). See Figure 14–1.

FIGURE 14–1
Users of an Illicit Drug in the Past Month in 2010

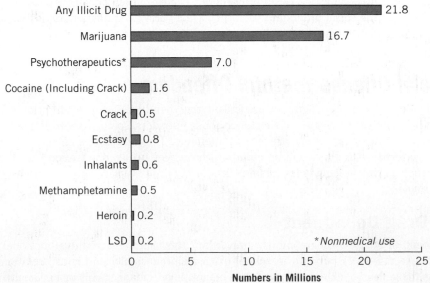

Number of Past-Month Users, Aged 12 or Older (Millions)

- Any Illicit Drug: 21.8
- Marijuana: 16.7
- Psychotherapeutics*: 7.0
- Cocaine (Including Crack): 1.6
- Crack: 0.5
- Ecstasy: 0.8
- Inhalants: 0.6
- Methamphetamine: 0.5
- Heroin: 0.2
- LSD: 0.2

*Nonmedical use

Numbers in Millions

TABLE 14–1
Percentages of High School Students Reporting Drug Use, 2010

Student Drug Use	Eighth Grade	Tenth Grade	Twelfth Grade
Past-month use	9.5%	18.5%	23.8%
Past-year use	16.0	30.2	38.3
Lifetime use	21.4	37.0	48.2

Source: Adapted from Lloyd D. Johnston, Patrick M. O'Malley, Jerald G. Bachman, and John E. Schulenberg, *Monitoring the Future: National Results on Adolescent Drug Use* (Washington, DC: National Institutes of Health, 2010), Tables 5, 6, and 7.

Table 14–1 lists the 2010 percentage of students reporting drug use in the past month, in the past year, and over their lifetime.

What Are the Main Types of Drugs?

The licit and illicit drugs that are used by adolescents, in decreasing order of frequency, are alcohol, tobacco, marijuana, cocaine, methamphetamine, inhalants, sedatives, stimulants (amphetamines and hallucinogens), and heroin. The licit drugs are permitted for users age eighteen and older (for tobacco) and twenty-one and older (for alcohol). The illicit drugs are forbidden by law. Drugs that are an exception to this pattern are those prescribed by a physician, or marijuana in jurisdictions that permit the use of this drug.

What Is the Relationship Between Drug Use and Delinquency?

One of the important issues in the juvenile delinquency/juvenile justice field is whether drugs cause delinquency or delinquency leads to drug use, or whether the use of other drugs precedes both delinquency and the onset of drug use.[8] Research has found that delinquency tends to precede the use of drugs.[9] Other research proposes that what might appear to be a causal association is actually a product of shared antecedents.[10] A common factor may underlay both the frequency and type of drug use.[11] Furthermore, a number of researchers have found that substance abuse is just one of an interrelated and overlapping group of adolescent problem behaviors, including delinquency, teen pregnancy, school failure, and dropping out of school.[12] According to this position, substance abuse is one of the problem behaviors developed by adolescents during their early life course. See Table 14–2.

Consensus is increasing on three findings that explain the onset and continuing use of illicit drugs:

- First, widespread agreement exists that a sequential pattern of involvement in drug use takes place during adolescence.[13] Denise B. Kandel and colleagues, using cross-sectional research and longitudinal data, proposed a developmental model for drug use involvement. This model suggests that alcohol use follows a pattern of minor delinquency and exposure to friends and parents who drink. The use of marijuana follows participation in minor delinquency and adoption of beliefs and values that are consistent with those held by peers but are opposed to parental standards. Finally, an adolescent's use of marijuana proceeds to other illicit drugs if relationships with parents are poor and the youth experiences an increased exposure to peers who use a variety of illegal drugs.[14]

- Second, a number of risk factors seem to be related to delinquency and drug use. Preperinatal risk factors consist of in-the-womb difficulties, minor physical abnormalities, and brain damage. Early developmental risk factors are found in the family environment, including a family history of alcoholism, family conflict, and poor family management

▲ These signs began appearing on streets near schools about a generation ago when drugs and violence became more frequent near schools. Are the signs effective in your experience?
© Andre Babiak/Alamy

TABLE 14–2
Drug Use by Decreasing Order of Frequency

Type of Drug	Description
Alcohol and Tobacco	Both are considered licit drugs because their use by juveniles is prohibited. Their wide use is considered a serious social problem.
Marijuana	The most frequently used illicit drug, marijuana is known by a variety of street names and is usually smoked.
Cocaine	Snorting (inhaling) is the most common method of using cocaine, but freebasing (smoking) cocaine has gained some popularity.
Methamphetamine	This highly addicted stimulant can be injected, smoked, or snorted. This is one of the many so-called club drugs.
Inhalants	With these drugs, youths need to inhale the vapors to receive the high they seek.
Sedatives	The common factor of sedatives is that they are taken orally and depress the nervous system, inducing a drowsy condition.
Ecstasy	Sometimes called a club drug, Ecstasy can be ingested orally, is sometimes snorted, and is occasionally smoked.
Hallucinogens	LSD was used in the 1960s and 1970s, but PCP, a nervous system excitant, has been more recently used by adolescents.
Anabolic Steroids	It is believed that steroids can produce an effect on muscle size; the 100 different types can be taken orally, injected intramuscularly, or rubbed on the skin in the form of creams or gels.

practices. Other risk factors are related to early antisocial behavior and academic failure. Community risk factors include living in disorganized neighborhoods. According to J. David Hawkins, Richard E. Catalano, and Devon D. Brewer, the more of these risk factors a child has, the more likely he or she will become involved in drug abuse.[15]

- Finally, youths who use hard drugs are more likely to engage in chronic delinquent behavior.[16] Delbert Elliott and David Huizinga found that nearly 50 percent of serious youthful offenders were also multiple-drug users. Eighty-two percent of these offenders reported use, beyond experimentation, of at least one illicit drug.[17] David M. Altschuler and Paul J. Brounstein's examination of drug use and drug trafficking among inner-city adolescent males in Washington, D.C., found that the use and sale of drugs affected the frequency and seriousness of delinquent behavior. The heaviest users were significantly more likely than nonusers to commit property offenses; those who trafficked in drugs were significantly more likely to commit crimes against people than were youths who did not sell drugs; and juveniles who both used and sold drugs were the most likely to commit offenses against property and persons.[18]

What Are the Different Types of Drug and Alcohol Users?

As indicated by the statistics in this chapter, drug use is pervasive and increasing among some young people, especially those involved in antisocial behaviors. One group of juveniles includes experimental users; these youths are curious about drugs and occasionally use the drugs to test their effects. Another group consists of social or recreational users who occasionally take drugs to socialize with friends. In a third group are youths who spend considerable time and money obtaining drugs, and these substances play an important role in the users' lives. Despite heavy and regular use, however, adolescents in this group are still functional and able to meet social and academic responsibilities. The lives of juveniles in a fourth group are dominated by drugs, and the process of securing and using drugs interferes with their everyday functioning. These four groups fit into two clusters: (1) social or recreational users and (2) those whose lives are dominated by drugs—**addicts**. Some of these users are plagued by internal demons.

Social or Recreational Users

Adolescents generally prefer substances that are not too costly. Beer and marijuana meet this criterion better than hard drugs do. Availability and potency are also important in drug use, for these substances are likely to be used as a means to other ends, especially for achieving excitement. For example, marijuana, alcohol, and other drugs used at football games, rock concerts, parties, outings, dances, and similar activities provide additional excitement already inherent in such activities or, in some cases, produce excitement when it seems to be lacking. In addition to excitement, experience-enhancing substances serve the purpose of exploration. They enable the youth to experience new social orbits, mating relations, and unfamiliar places. Narcotic substances are further used to escape or retreat from the external world into a private inner self.

The fact is that drug and alcohol use among American adolescents is increasing, with no good news on the horizon. Alcohol use is continuing to rise among *all* American adolescents, rich as well as poor, non-offenders as well as offenders. It constitutes a serious social problem that currently is attracting national attention. More bad news is that the use of marijuana has experienced a major increase among American adolescents in the past decade.[19]

Addicts

Too many adolescents' lives are dominated by drugs. Many of these drug-dependent youths need speed in the morning, and they require speed in school to make it through the day. Others become intoxicated several evenings a week and may even drink at school. Still others use so much marijuana that they become known to their peers as *pot heads*. Even sadder, other youths, especially high-risk females, become addicted to crack cocaine. These girls are likely to be unable to give up this addiction even when they become pregnant. Further, drug-dependent youths typically are multiple-drug users.

The factors that place a youth at **high risk** for later substance abuse include the following:

1. *Early initiation:* use of any substance by the age of ten or twelve
2. *School problems:* low expectation that school will be a positive experience, low grades, disruptive behavior in school, and truancy
3. *Family problems:* lack of parental support and guidance
4. *Peer influences:* relationships with peers who use substances, and an inability to resist their influences
5. *Personality:* nonconformism, rebellion, or a strong sense of independence[20]

Those who work with juvenile offenders argue that rarely is a youth institutionalized or placed on probation who does not have some history of alcohol or narcotic abuse.[21] As one director of guidance noted, "We only have one or two youths a year admitted to this institution who don't have a problem with substance abuse."[22]

The use of drugs, especially on a daily basis, increases the likelihood that a youth will be arrested and referred to the juvenile justice system. Other short-term consequences are vulnerability to other drugs, loss of interest in school, and impaired psychological functioning. Long-term consequences include respiratory problems, drug dependence, chronic depression and fatigue, and social and financial problems. A long-term risk of taking intravenous drugs today is exposure to AIDS.[23]

What About Drug-Trafficking Juveniles?

Some evidence exists that adolescents sell drugs as frequently as, or even more frequently than, drug-trafficking gangs do.[24] Some adolescents also sell drugs independently of any gang affiliation, particularly in suburban settings.

Personal interview data add to this portrait of juveniles involved in drug trafficking. In urban settings, juveniles are members of drug-trafficking gangs, and as part of their membership responsibilities, are supposed to assist in selling drugs. These youths, who can be as young as eleven or twelve, may be given a firearm and told to stand watch at a crack house. If anyone tries to enter who is not supposed to be there, they are told to shoot and kill. As these youths get a little older, they are given the job of what is usually called a *mule*, delivering drugs to specific locations. Older juveniles are placed on street corners where they sell drugs, usually crack cocaine, to regular customers and people driving by.

In the cities and in settings made up of what in Chapter 13 is called *emerging gangs*, those juveniles selling crack cocaine may be working for someone from an urban setting who may or may not be a representative of an organized gang in that setting. They usually get a percentage of the profits from the sale of these drugs. Interviewees have reported that this is up to 10 percent and that they make a fair amount of money selling drugs. They like to talk about how much money they have made selling drugs throughout the years; a couple of the stories in the *Voices* address this issue.

Typically, those who made considerable amounts of money from selling drugs have trafficked in other drugs besides crack cocaine. Those juveniles selling marijuana sometimes make a lot of money. They are able to purchase several cars and have a closet full of expensive clothing. They also buy all kinds of presents for their girlfriends, and always have money to purchase "toys" and any entertainment they want for themselves.

In *Voices*, the stories of youth who spent their lives trafficking drugs and had authority over others who were trafficking drugs are reviewed. In this account, the tragic consequences of drug trafficking, both to those who traffic in drugs and to those who get caught up in this victim and addict cycle of buying drugs, are revealed. Juveniles, especially those who sell drugs, are inevitably caught by the police, quickly processed by the courts, and sent to prison. Sometimes, they end up in training school first, but at other times they are sent directly to prison.

What Explains the Onset of Drug Use?

A number of theories have attempted to explain the onset and escalation of juveniles' drug use:

- *Cognitive-affective theories.* A number of theories have focused on how perceptions about the costs and benefits of drug use contribute to juveniles' decisions to experiment with these substances. Hence, the decision to use substances rests in substance-specific expectations and perceptions held by adolescents.[25]

- *Addictive personality theory.* Another theory for the onset and continued use of drugs is that the typical addict has an addiction-prone personality and suffers from some deep-rooted personality disorder.

- *Stress relief theory.* The desire to get high, which is seen as a way to relieve stress, depression, or the boredom of everyday life, is common in adolescent peer culture.

- *Social learning theory.* Some argue that drug use begins and continues chiefly because juveniles or adults have contact with peers who use drugs. Peers then provide role models, as well as social support, for drug use. Of course, once peers persuade a person to begin using drugs, a pattern of use can be established that may lead eventually to addiction and continued use.[26]

- *Social control theory.* Travis Hirschi's social control theory and Hawkins and Weiss's social development model both assume that emotional attachment to peers who use substances is a primary cause of substance abuse. Unlike social learning theories, however, these two approaches pay specific attention to weak conventional bonds to society and to the institutions and individuals who might otherwise discourage deviant behavior.

- *Social disorganization theory.* This theory explains the onset and escalation of adolescents' drug use by claiming that a bleak economic environment for certain disenfranchised groups has created a generation of young adults in urban inner cities who regularly experience doubt, hopelessness, and uncertainty.

FIGURE 14–2
Explanations for the Onset of Drug Abuse
Source: Adapted from Lloyd D. Johnston, Patrick M. O'Malley, Jerald G. Bachman, and John E. Schulenberg, *Monitoring the Future: National Results on Adolescent Drug Use* (Washington, DC: National Institutes of Health 2010), Tables 1, 3, and 7.

Types of Explanation Description

Cognitive-Affective Theories—These theories relate to how the perceptions about the costs and benefits of drug use contribute to adolescents decision to experiment with these substances.

Addictive-Personality Theory—The typical addict has an addiction prone personality and suffers from deep-rooted personality disorder or emotional problems.

Stress Relief Theory—The desire to get high as a means to relieve stress, depression, or boredom of everyday life is common in adolescent culture.

Social Learning Theory—This theory postulates that an adolescent's involvement in substance abuse begins with observation and imitation of substance specific behaviors, continues with social reinforcement, and cultivates in a juvenile's expectation of positive social and physiological consequences from continued drug use.

Social Control Theories—Emotional attachment to peers who use substances is a primary causes of substance use.

Social Disorganization Theory—The bleak economic environment has resulted in those situated in these settings to experience doubt, hopelessness, and uncertainty, and, as a result, they seek relief in drugs.

Integrated Theories—Elliott and colleagues use strain, social control, and social teaming theories to form a perspective that accounts for delinquent behavior and drug use.

- *Integrated theories.* Elliott and colleagues offer a model that expands traditional strain, social, and social learning theories into a single perspective that accounts for delinquent behavior and drug use.[27] See Figure 14-2.

Solutions to the Drug Problem

Prevention programs, treatment programs, strict enforcement, and harm reduction are all possible means of controlling drug use among adolescents.

Prevention Programs

The 1990s saw dramatic developments in drug prevention programs. The Center for the Study and Prevention of Violence at the University of Colorado began an initiative called Blueprints for Violence Prevention, in which researchers evaluated 600 programs designed to prevent violence and drug abuse and to treat youths with problem behavior.[28] The investigators were able to identify eleven model programs and twenty-one promising programs. Effective programs need to incorporate early childhood and family interventions, school-based interventions, and comprehensive community-wide efforts. The important dimension of drug prevention intervention is use of a multidimensional approach that centers on the family, school, and community.

Treatment Programs

Treatment for drug abusers takes place in psychiatric and hospitals settings for youngsters whose parents can afford it or have the needed insurance benefits. Other youths, particularly those substance abusers who have committed minor forms of delinquency, receive treatment in privately administered placements, which vary tremendously in the quality of program design and implementation. Substance-abusing youths with multiple typical problems may be more malleable than adult offenders, but there is little evidence that the majority of substance abuse programs are any more successful than those for adult substance abusers. For an exception, see the Evidence-Based Practice feature.

Strict Enforcement

The "war on drugs" has not been won with juveniles anymore that it has with adults. A disastrous consequence of the strict enforcement policies that accompany this "war" is the increasing number of minority youths who, having been involved in using or selling crack cocaine, have been brought into the justice system for extended periods of time. Strict enforcement, however, has seemed to make a difference in several ways:

- The destruction of overseas drug-producing crops has no doubt had some impact on the availability of drugs in the United States, raising prices and making some drugs harder to find.

- Heavy penalties associated with the sale of illicit drugs seem to have been somewhat effective in deterring both juvenile and adult offenders.

Harm Reduction

Harm reduction is an approach designed to reduce the harm done by drug use and by the severe penalties resulting from drug use and sales. A number of harm reduction strategies have been employed:

- Programs in which health professionals administer drugs to addicts as part of a treatment and detoxification regimen

- Drug treatment facilities that are available for those drug addicts who desire treatment

- Needle exchange programs that are intended to slow the transmission of HIV and that provide educational resources about how HIV is contracted and spread

---

Evidence-Based Practice
Are Drug Courts Effective?

Drug courts are currently being established throughout the nation and the initial evaluations have been favorable. A number of evidence-based evaluations conducted in Miami, Philadelphia, and Las Vegas reveal that adult drug courts can produce comparatively lower rates of recidivism. Using a nationally representative sample (including all drug courts that had been in operation for at least one year and had at least forty program graduates), the National Institute of Justice and the Drug Court Program Office found that within one year 16 percent of drug court graduates had been arrested and charged with a serious offense (84 percent success rate), and within two years, 28 percent had been arrested and charged with a serious offense (73 percent success rate). The programs seem to work best for high-risk offenders who might normally have been sent to prison.

Although general research findings are that drug courts can reduce recidivism and promote other positive outcomes such as cost savings, several factors affect a drug court program's success: proper assessment and treatment, the role assumed by the judge, and the nature of offender's interactions with the judge. Other variable influences include drug use trends, staff turnover, and resource allocation.

There is reason to believe that juvenile drug courts will work as effectively as adult drug courts. A quasi-experimental 2010 study of juvenile drug courts compared 1,120 youths in juvenile drug courts in multiple jurisdictions with 1,120 youth not in juvenile drug court, but who participated in adolescent outpatient treatment. The juvenile drug courts appeared to do a better job (compared to treatment alone) of helping youth reduce symptoms of their emotional problems and reduce their substance use as measured six months post-intake.

Other findings of this study included the following:

- Using evidence-based treatment matters.
- Juvenile drug court proceedings were less likely than youth in treatment-only to begin treatment within two weeks of intake, which is significant because it has been found that initiation of treatment within two weeks is a major protective factor against relapse and recidivism.
- Contrary to concerns about net widening, juvenile drug courts are one of several ways of getting significantly impaired youths into treatment and reliably achieving positive outcomes.
- Law enforcement's targeting of drug dealers has had some success in getting those dealers off the streets.
- The policing of the sale of tobacco products, especially cigarettes at convenience stores and other places, has made it more difficult for minors to purchase or obtain tobacco products.

CRITICAL THINKING QUESTION

Why is it important that drug courts, both adults and juveniles, appear to be effective? What types of youthful offenders do you believe juvenile drug courts would be more effective with?

Sources: Douglas B. Marlowe, "Evidence-Based Policies and Practices for Drug-Involved Offenders," *Prison Journal* 9 (2011), 27–47; Michael W. Finigan, Shannon M. Carey, and Anton Cox, "Impact of a Mature Drug Court over 10 Years of Operation: Recidivism and Costs," *NPC Research, Inc.*, 2007; National Institute of Justice, "Do Drug Courts Work? Findings from Drug Court Research," at http://nij.gov/nij/topics/courts/drug-courts/work.htm (accessed February 20, 2012); Michelle L. Dennis, Michelle K. White, and Melissa L. Ives, "Individual Characteristics and Needs Associated with Adolescents and Young Adults in Addiction in Treatment." *Children and Family Lives* 9 (2009), 45–72.

Juvenile Sex Offenders

Juvenile sex offenders are defined as adolescents ranging from ages thirteen to seventeen who take part in sexual behaviors that are considered illegal according to the law.[29] Adolescents who have been convicted of being a sex offenders are more likely to have offended someone their own age or younger, but there are cases of adults being sexually abused by adolescents that are sixteen or seventeen.[30] The National Center on Sexual Behavior of Youth also says that "approximately one-third of sexual offenses against children are committed by teenagers."[31]

Violent sex crimes often shape the public's perception of sex offenders and sex offending. The view that immediately comes to mind is that of an adult male who by force, guile, or cunning persuades a young person to perform sexual acts deemed inappropriate or illegal by society.[32] This image of adult offenders is assumed to be true of all youthful sex offenders.

Juvenile sex offender's characteristics, based on the available research, are a history of severe family problems, separated from parents, placement away from home, been a victim of sexual, emotional, and physical abuse, socially awkward, academic and behavioral problems (attention deficit disorder and learning disabilities), poor peer relations, social isolation, poor impulse control, lower IQs, and psychopathology. It is important to remember that this list is not a list of characteristics for ALL juvenile sex offenders, but rather it just shows a general trend of characteristics that may appear in juveniles who are sex offenders.[33]

Much juvenile sexual behavior is concealed in the confines of family, community, and school and remains hidden. Even if it is discovered, children, parents, and teachers may be confused as to what really happened and are often ashamed or embarrassed by their own behavior and by that of their own children, relations, and family friends. Many victims will not report sexual victimization because they believe they deserved

---

EXHIBIT 14–1
Youth Who Commit Sex Offenses Are Still Young People in Development

WHY DO YOUTH COMMIT SEX OFFENSES?

- Youth tend to be present-oriented and are unable to fully understand and appreciate the future consequences of their actions.[34]
- Youth are more likely than adults to make emotional, rather than rational, decisions.[35]
- Youth are more prone to risk-taking and inappropriate sexual behavior, which many outgrow.[36] What some might be quick to label "deviant" behavior may actually be normative, if inappropriate, sexual expression and exploitation.

DO YOUTH WHO COMMIT SEXUAL OFFENSES HAVE HIGH RATES OF RECIDIVISM?

- Youth who commit sex offenses will likely not commit another.
- Studies have found the recidivism rates for youth who commit sex offenses to be between four and seven percent.[37]
- This research shows that their behavior is more likely caused by temporary factors tied to their stage of development than by permanent traits.[38]

DO YOUTH WHO COMMIT SEX OFFENSES REPRESENT A SPECIAL GROUP?

- Youth who commit sex offenses cannot be defined by any single motivator or life circumstance, because they

tend to have more in common with youth who commit other types of offenses than with adults who commit sex offenses.
- Research has found that if youth who have committed sexual crimes reoffend, their next offense will most likely be non-sexual.[39]
- Youth who commit sex offenses cannot, in most cases, be considered pedophiles.

DO YOUTH WHO COMMIT SEX OFFENSES RESPOND WELL TO TREATMENT?

- Youths are immensely receptive to treatment.
- Too many treatments focus on the wrong thing, such as reducing deviant sexual desire, rather than addressing the many influences that lead youth to commit sexual offenses.[40]
- The most effective treatments instead focus on a youth's environment, including his or her family, peer groups, and school, and how these might impact his or her behavior.[41]
- Family- and community-based interventions, including multisystemic therapy, have been shown to effectively reduce problem sexual behavior and delinquency.[42]

what happened, feel guilty, do not want to get others in trouble, or somehow believe that what happened was normal. Yet, the victims often end up psychologically distraught and damaged; sleeplessness, anxiety, depression, sexual dysfunction, and suicide can result. Damaged emotions and fear destroy their ability to form lasting relationships, and many victims' marriages are filled with violence or do not last. The cost to individuals and society often is perpetuated because many imprisoned adolescent and adult sex offenders report having been abused as youths. The cost of a sex offense early in life often extends into adulthood.

Are all sex offenders alike? No. Their relationships with their victims and their personal motives vary widely, making them a diverse lot. The offending behaviors range from non-contact offenses such as voyeurism and exhibitionism to contact offenses such as touching and fondling to sexual penetration with body parts or foreign objects. Most sex offenders also commit nonsexual offenses at rates similar to those of other juvenile offenders. For example, children who experience neglect and physical abuse and who witness family violence are more likely to commit sexual offenses than those who do not, although at an only modestly higher rate.[43] Also, sex offenders who have had prior consensual sexual experiences have higher rates of offending than those without such experiences.

According to C. Veneziano, juvenile sex offenders take part in all sexual acts (35 percent vaginal or anal penetration, 14 percent oral-genital contact, 17.9 percent both). This means that two-thirds of the sexual offenders have done one or both forms of sexual behaviors. Some characteristics of victims that Veneziano found were that there were twice as many female victims as male victims [females = 70 percent, but when the victim was a younger child the males tended to be the victims more (males = 63 percent)]. Adolescent male rapist tended to choose a victim that was relatively the same age. Veneziano also found that "sibling offenders were more likely to have assaulted younger children than non-sibling offenders."[44] (See Table 14–3.)

Recidivism

Juvenile sex offenders have been found to have extremely low recidivism rates; in fact, most studies find that juvenile sexual offenders are more likely to commit a nonsexual offense then a sexual offense.[45] For example, Veneziano found that juvenile recidivism rate was around 10 to 15 percent while nonsexual offenses were 16 percent or higher.[46] Another example is with both the NJJN (2007) and the NCSBY (2003), which document that recidivism for juvenile sex offenders is 5 to 14 percent, while nonsexual offenses was 8 to 58 percent.[47]

Examples of studies showing low recidivism rates:

- A 2000 study by the Texas Youth Commission of 72 young offenders who were released from state correctional facilities for sexual offenses (their incarceration suggests the judges considered these youth as posing a greater risk) found a re-arrest rate of 4.2 percent for a sexual offense.

- A 2000 study of 96 juvenile sexual offenders in Philadelphia showed a 3 percent sexual re-offense rate.

TABLE 14–3
Offenses and Relationships

Adolescent male exploiters	
Victims under age of 12	Greater than 60%
Victims under age of 9	63%
Victims under age of 6	40%
Relation to Victims	
Blood Relation	38.8%
Immediate Family members	46%

Source: Veneziano, C. (2014). "Juvenile Sex Offenders," in *Encyclopedia of Adolescence* (New York, NY: Springer), 1527–1533.

Sex Offender Therapist Profile

PREPARATION FOR THE JOB

This person needs to have considerable experience in working in corrections, with typical offenders as well as sex offenders. He or she should have received training that helps this therapist be part of a treatment team that works with sexual offenders in the community or institutional contexts.

NURTURE OF THE JOB

Treatment begins with comprehensive assessment that includes psychological tests, clinical interviews, and other techniques designed to define treatment goals and strategies for each offender. As part of their treatment approach, therapists have the goals of helping offenders learn to reduce and manage risk, providing information to help the department and its community partners monitor and manage offenders more effectively, and evaluating and improving treatment.

QUALIFICATIONS AND REQUIRED EDUCATION

At least an undergraduate degree in social work, criminology, and psychology, and a master's degree in one of these fields would be advisable. A volunteer experience in working with sex offenders, as part of the undergraduate education, would prepare this person even more for working with these offenders. These jobs are not for the faint in heart.

JOB OUTLOOK

With the increasing numbers of adult and juvenile sex offenders being sent to the justice system, there will likely be an increase in community and institutional programs. Accordingly, for the individual who is properly trained and equipped to work with these offenders, the job outlook is excellent.

EARNINGS AND BENEFITS

The salaries for sex offenders therapists can range from $60,000 to $70,000. This depends on the training and education as well as the jurisdiction.

Source: The nature of the job section is indebted to "Sex Offender Treatment in Prison," www.doc.wa.gov/community/sexoffenders/prisontreatment.asp, (March 12, 2012).

How Do We Treat Sex Offenders?

The treatment goals of many programs for sex offenders include breaking the sex offense cycle. Youths are encouraged to assume responsibility for their abusive behavior and to increase their positive and constructive behaviors in both thinking and relations to others. These goals are designed to prevent further sexual misconduct and the emergence of psychosexual problems and, conversely, to help youths develop appropriate relationships with peers of their own age. Therapists attempt to achieve these goals through individual, group, and family interventions.

One of the biggest questions that seems to be asked in this line of research is whether or not these juveniles have been sexually abused in their life and if maybe that has something to do with why they become a sexual offender. According to Veneziano, 40 to 70 percent of juvenile sex offenders have been sexually abused, but that she knows other studies that suggest much higher rates of sexual victimization on the offenders; and according to National Juvenile Justice Network, the range of juvenile sex offenders that have been sexually abused themselves is more around 20 to 55 percent but they also state that 80 percent were victimized when they were children, and 25 to 50 percent have been physically abused.[48]

The Gang Delinquent

The juvenile gang member is part of a street gang in an urban community, is part of an emerging gang in smaller community, is part of a juvenile gang in a juvenile facility, or is part of a prison gang in an adult facility. The juvenile's role in each of these gangs changes somewhat significantly.

Juvenile as a Member of a Street Gang

Studies reveal that juveniles make up a small proportion of the membership of adult gangs. At one time, adult gangs would have several age groups, including a Peewee group (made up of younger children and youths), a junior group (made up of adolescents and those being prepared for adult gang membership), and the adult gang. This age appropriate differentiation no longer seems to be present today.

Juveniles who are admitted to adult gangs perform several tasks for the adult gang. They run errands, carry weapons, or messages. They are recruited as lookouts and street vendors. Gangs use younger members to deal crack cocaine out of camped "rock houses," which are often steel reinforced fortresses. Adult gangs have further used juveniles to commit violent crimes because it has been felt that their age protects them against the harsh realities of the adult criminal justice system.

These juveniles frequently come to the attention of the juvenile system and are sent to juvenile institutions. Upon arriving at adulthood, these youths are often encouraged to remain with the adult gang and do so. Their life course may then become one of gang involvement selling drugs; imprisonment, perhaps for long periods; and even early death.

Juveniles as a Member of an Emerging Gang

As discussed in the last chapter, beginning in the late 1980s and early 1990s, juveniles in small communities across the nation became involved in gang-like organizations. These gangs had various origins:

1. Sometimes, they were started when a gang member from an urban community came to a community and persuaded youth, usually minority ones, to sell drugs, frequently advising them that they could consider himself or herself a Crip, Blood, Vice Lord, or so forth. It would not be long before they were joined by other youths selling drugs for a different gang affiliation. From this origin, gangs would develop, competing with each other and resulting in conflict and violence.

2. These emerging gangs were sometimes initiated when families from urban communities would move to a smaller community and the youths from these families would start a gang. They would use what they remembered about what gang involvement involved. They would use the name of the gang that they knew from the urban community.

3. They sometimes could trace their origins to youths in one of the communities deciding that they wanted to be part of a gang. They would make up their own names, often the name of a section of the town or a street name. They would make up rules and make decisions on what they wanted their gang to be.[49]

Whatever their origins, there is similarity in their life course. They come to the attention of the juvenile justice system and are labeled as gang members, commit a crime, and are sent to the state's training school where they spend a few months. It is not long after their release that they are returned for another institutional stint. Some youths leave gang involvement, but many go on to the adult system.

The Juvenile Female

In a few urban communities, juvenile females join older women in a female gang. They may engage in behavior that is violent, sometimes even sadistic. However, most females in urban communities either join a gang made up of males or a satellite to a male gang. If they join a male-oriented gang, as with the duties of male females, they may be sexed into the gang and be expected to perform sexual functions for adult members. If they join a gang as a satellite of a male gang, their primary role is to provide assistance to the male gang members—carrying weapons, drugs, and sometimes even involving themselves in gang battles or gang "hits."[50]

The juvenile females in an emerging gang generally go along with the males, performing whatever tasks they are delegated to do. They carry weapons, drugs, and may even be involved in drug trafficking behaviors. They may or may not be expected to perform sexual functions. There are no firm data, but it would appear that they are likely to continue their adult involvement as they become adults. Other adult-related activity, such as raising children, tends to reduce the attractiveness of gang behaviors.

The Juvenile Gang Member in Training Schools or Adult Prisons

In some training schools, especially in the southwest, gangs control the peer culture and make it very difficult for staff to generate a positive peer culture. If there are more than one gang represented in this facility, then conflict and violent will ensue. Whether there is one gang or several, there is an active re-recruitment policy among the non-gang affiliated residents.

In adult prisons, it is a different story. The juvenile has been transferred to adult court and has been sent to prison. For all but a few, the youth arriving at an adult prison is a frightening experience. If a juvenile has belonged to a street gang in an urban community, he or she will likely be accepted by this gang. This juvenile may not be exploited by the older gang members and may in fact be protected by more exploitative inmates. If a juvenile has not belonged to a gang in the community which is represented in that prison, this juvenile may be faced with the proposal of joining the gang and receive protection or be faced with widespread sexual exploitation by other inmates. Receiving protection, however, does not mean that the juvenile will be "sold" out as a prostitute or be subjected to widespread sexual victimization by members of this gang.

Career Outcomes for Juvenile Gang Members in Street Gangs or Emerging Gangs

As indicated in the gang chapters, these gang youths are involved in more crime-related behaviors, including violence. They may be shot and killed, shoot or kill someone and receive a long prison sentence, or become addicted to drugs and go in and out of prison, perhaps for the rest of their lives.

The Violent Juvenile

In examining juvenile violence, several topics merit examination: the reduced rates of juvenile homicide, the types of juveniles who kill, and chronic offenders and their relationship to juvenile violence.

Reduced Rates of Juvenile Violence

In the mid-1990s, several scholars predicted that juvenile crime would rise to new heights by 2010. Albert J Blumstein, James Alan Fox, and John J Dilulio, Jr., based their predictions on the recruitment of young people into the market to sell crack cocaine, as well as juveniles carrying a gun.[51] Dilulio predicted that "the large population of seven to ten year-old boys now growing up fatherless, godless, and jobless, and surrounded by deviant, delinquent, and criminal adults, will give rise to a new and more vicious group of predatory street criminals that the nation has ever known."[52] He added that "We must therefore be prepared to contain the nation's explosion force and limit its damage."[53] In another book published at this time it was argued that a new generation of juvenile criminals was emerging that would be far worse than those in the present. In referring to this new generation of juvenile criminals as superpredators, they said that today's bad boys are far worse than yesterday and tomorrow will be far worse than today.[54]

The fact is that they were wrong! In explaining the dramatically reduced rate of juvenile homicides between 1993 and extending to the present, Cook and Laub are among those arguing that a more limited availability of guns to juveniles has been one of the major factors that has continued to depress rather than escalate juvenile homicides in United States.[55]

As indicated in Figure 14–3, the juvenile violent crime index has been decreasing in the past thirty years, as follows:

- The juvenile Violent Crime Index arrest rate increased in the mid-2000s, and then declined through 2012 to its lowest level since at least 1980. The rate in 2012 was 38 percent below its 1980 level and 63 percent below the peak year of 1994.

- In 2012, there were 182 arrests for Violent Crime Index offenses for every 100,000 youth between ten and seventeen years of age.

- If each of these arrests involved a different juvenile (which is unlikely), then no more than one in every 544 persons, ages ten to seventeen, was arrested for a Violent Crime Index offense in 2012, or less than one-fifth of 1 percent of all juveniles ages ten to seventeen living in the United States.[56]

FIGURE 14–3

Source: Adapted from Puzzanchera, C. (2013). *Juvenile Arrests 2011* (Washington, DC: Office of Juvenile Justice and Delinquency Prevention, 2013).

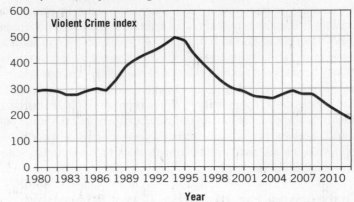

Arrests per 100,000 juveniles ages 10–17, 1980–2012

Types of Juvenile Violence

Juveniles who kill their parents are school shooters, or who kill because of their involvement in gang and drugs are three types of juveniles who commit violent acts. The first two are discussed here because juveniles who kill because of gang and drug involvement have already been discussed.

Why Children Kill Their Parents

Cathy Spatz Wisdom's studies of violence have identified four types of violent offenders:

1. One group had arrests for violence, but no history of child abuse and neglect or Post-Traumatic Stress Disorder (PTSD).

2. One group with documented cases of child abuse and neglect who become violent without developing PTSD.

3. One group with documented cases of child abuse and neglect, engage in violence early in life have developed PTSD, and subsequently have been arrested for violence.

4. One group has histories of child abuse and neglect, engage in violence early in life, and subsequently develop PTSD.[57]

Approximately 300 parents are killed each year by their children. Kathleen M. Heide has contended that killing a parent is frequently an act of desperation—the only way out of the family situation of the abuse they can no longer ignore. Her research revealed that there are three types of youth who kill their parents: (1) the severely abused child who is pushed beyond his or her limits, (2) the severely mentally ill child, and (3) the dangerously antisocial child. According to Heide's research, the severely abused child is the most frequently encountered type of offender.

She found that the characteristics of the severely abused child who killed one or both parents are:

• They have not been previously violent.

• They are abused.

• Their parents are most likely substance abusers.

• They are isolated.

• They kill only when they feel there is no one to help him. They block out the murder, not revel in it.

• They see no other choice.

• They are sorry for what they did.

School Shooters

On December 14, 2012, thirty-year-old Adam Lanza fatally shot twenty young children and six adults staff members at the Sandy Hook Elementary School in the small town of

Newtown, Connecticut. Before his killing rampage, Lanza had gone to his Newtown home and shot his fifty-two-year-old mother, Nancy, to death. The weapons used in the school shooting, two pistols and a semi-automatic assault rifle, belonged to his mother and had been stolen from her house. Lanza committed suicide by shooting himself in the head as first respondents arrived. He was later identified as an awkward kid who wore the same clothing almost every day (green shirt and khaki pants). He liked tinkering with computers and enjoyed playing violent video games.

Prior to the Newtown shooting, the two most deadly school shootings had taken place on April 16, 2007, at Virginia Tech in which thirty people were killed and a Columbia High School on April 20, 1999, in which thirteen people died.

Schools have been settings for horrific shootings that have shocked the nation. Experts offer explanations for school shootings ranging from "merely an aberration," to a lack of intense control in children today, to the breakdown of the family, to the abundance of guns in the hands of young people, and too much violence on television. Whatever their cause, school killings have focused attention on violence in school settings.

The Chronic Offender

The chronic offender, as previously mentioned, is known by many labels: serious defendant, violent offender, hard-core delinquent, or career delinquent. Nevertheless, whatever the label, the predominant characteristic of the issue is their commitment to crime and their involvement in one crime after another, often very serious crimes against persons and property. Chronic offenders often expect to engage in criminal career currently several years, if not for the rest of their lives.

How numerous are chronic offenders? In *Delinquency in a Birth Cohort*, Wolfgang, Figlio, and Sellin have provided the most authoritative answer to this question. These researchers studied all the boys born in Philadelphia in 1945 who continued to live there from their tenth to their eighteenth birthday. Of the nearly ten thousand making up the cohort, 35 percent had incurred one or more police contacts. Tracing the boys through school and police records, these researchers became aware that this delinquent group could be divided into single offenders, multiple offenders, and chronic offenders. Although approximately half of those who committed a single offense later became involved in the second, only 6.3 percent committed more than five violations. Wolfgang and his associates found that 627 chronic offenders were responsible for half of all offenses and two out of every three serious offenses committed in Philadelphia.[58]

Similarly, Wolfgang et al. found that whites were much more likely than nonwhites to be chronic offenders and that lower-class boys were more likely than middle-class boys to be chronic offenders. Data also revealed that group of chronic offenders made more residential moves, had lower IQ scores, including greater percentage of mentally restricted youth, and had less education than either single or multiple offenders.[59]

Thus, these studies present a picture of a few youths committing half or more of all juvenile offenses and an even higher percentage of the violent juvenile offenses in the community. Lower-class boys are much more responsible for violent youth crime in the nation. For an example of chronic offenders, see Focus on Offenders 14–2.

Special Needs Youthful Offenders

Special needs youthful offenders include a variety of people with a particular mental or physical condition that requires that they either be separated from the general institutional population and/or receive unique treatment tailored to their particular circumstance. Residents with a high degree of mental health issues, including depression, anxiety, some psychosis, and suicidal tendencies, as well as those with mental limitations or physical disabilities would be included in this group.

Mentally Ill Juveniles/Emotionally Disturbed Delinquents

According to Desai and colleague, 65 percent of youths in the juvenile justice system have a diagnosable psychiatric or substance abuse disorder, and 75 percent of respondents with

Focus on Offenders 14–2

In Indiana, in the 1960s, there were two juveniles who began to rob "mom and pop" stores, and they were certainly chronic offenders. They would take their shotguns and rob the terrified person behind the cash register. After a few successes, they decided to not only rob the store and its customers, but to rape any attractive women who happened to be unfortunately shopping there. The victim was threatened with a shotgun, while the other youthful predator would rape her.

What finally took place is that following the rape, the other youth put the shotgun up the victim's vagina and discharged it. She was instantly killed. They were arrested shortly thereafter.

The two juveniles were kept in the juvenile system, which would not happen today because they would be transferred to the adult court to stand trial. It was decided to keep one in an Indiana training school and send the other to an Ohio facility. The second one ended up in the facility where I worked, and we had some interactions. He was really cold. Not only did he lack guilt, but he wanted to let everyone know how bad he was. He was what you could call a cold-blooded murderer.

He certainly was evil and probably was consumed by evil. I have no idea what happened to him when he was released several years later. There is an excellent likelihood that he went home and killed someone, perhaps torturing this person in the process.

Source: Personal experience of one of the authors.

---

one disorder met diagnostic criteria for two or more disorders.[60] This can be compared to Hammond, who found that as many as 70 percent of juveniles have a mental disorder, while 66 percent suffer from dual disorders. Hammond also said that one in five juveniles suffer severely from a mental illness to the point where the juvenile is unable to function as a young adult and unable to become a responsible adult.[61]

Hammond states that an emotional disorder is when a child no longer has the ability to function because he or she is impaired by anxiety or depression. She says that there is an estimate that one in 33 children and one in eight adolescents are affected by depression. It has also been shown that juvenile offenders tend to have a higher rate of depression than other youths. When it comes to behavioral disorders like attention deficit hyperactivity disorder, boys are two to three times more likely to be affected than girls. Thirty to 50 percent of juveniles in detention centers are diagnosed with disruptive behavior disorder.[62]

Mental Health Screening and Assessment

Detention facilities are supposed to perform a health screening on all juveniles that come in, and it should be performed within an hour of admission so that they are able to determine any mental conditions and/or drug/alcohol use.[63] Hammond reported that youths who do get screened right away are more likely to have their problems identified and treated.[64] Desai and colleagues (2006) found that in 1998 only 71 percent of juvenile detention centers reported providing screening tests to their incoming juveniles to see if they were at risk for mental health problems, had any specific needs, or if they needed any services.[65] The OJJDP also decided that detention centers should strive to perform a more in-depth screening after the juvenile had been there for seven days, and in 1998 only 56 percent of the facilities reported doing this in-depth screening. Also in 1998, 61 percent of the facilities had a psychiatrist available, while 70 percent also had another mental health professional available.[66]

According to Desai and colleagues there are not many studies on medications used in juvenile facilities, but they were able to discover that it is not uncommon for medications to be used especially if the juvenile has a prediagnosed health disorder. They found out that the 40 to 50 percent of the small facilities, juveniles were on some sort of psychotropic medication (males = 54 percent; females = 72 percent).[67]

In 2002, a national panel of experts was convened to respond to the lack of best practice standards for assessing mental health needs in the juvenile justice system. They recommended five standards for mental health assessment in this population: (1) perform a valid and reliable mental health screen within 24 hours of admission; (2) perform a more extensive assessment by a mental health professional as soon as possible to determine service needs; (3) use multiple sources of information (e.g., medical records, family reports) to determine needs;

(4) screen detainees before their release into the community; and (5) repeat screens on a regular basis while detainees are in custody, to identify emergent problems.[68]

Treatment

There are two different types of detention centers that should be discussed according to Desai and colleagues. One is a preventive detention and the other is a therapeutic detention. A preventive detention holds offenders in secure location for three reasons: (1) the offender may pose a threat to others, (2) the offender may be a flight risk, or (3) officials fear they will not show up to court. A preventive detention handles all of the juvenile's basic needs like education and health problems, but their main job is to hold the offender until the courts decide where they should go next.[69]

Desai and colleagues also discuss how a therapeutic detention facility is similar and different from the preventive detention facilities. A therapeutic detention facility does all the same things as a preventive facility, but they go a few steps farther. They add supportive and therapeutic care like counseling for the juveniles. Desai and colleagues found that there are three problems with the therapeutic detention: (1) The juveniles stay in the facility is too short for there to be an impact, (2) availability of these services are so limited that juveniles could be inappropriately placed, and (3) lack of effectiveness in data.[70]

Even though there may be criticism to the therapeutic detention facilities, the institutions who run these facilities came up with a list to counteract the criticism:

> (1) It is a setting where a wide range of behavior control strategies are available, unlike many community settings such as foster homes or schools; (2) though lengths of stay are short, treatment begun in such settings may steer the momentum in a positive direction; (3) compared with large community programs such as those funded by child welfare agencies, the staff-to-child ratio can be smaller, allowing more personalized attention; and (4) as a community-based resource to court services, such facilities can promote continuity of care by providing links to other community social and mental health care services.[71]

Foster Care/Crossover Juveniles

Crossover juveniles are defined as children and youth who are known to both the child welfare and the juvenile justice systems.[72] According to Perin, there are three established definitions that concern crossover juveniles. The first is crossover youth: any youths who have experienced maltreatment and engaged in delinquency. The second is dually-involved youth: a subgroup of crossover youths who are simultaneously receiving services, at any level, from both the child welfare and the juvenile justice systems. The third is dually-adjudicated youth: subgroup of dually-involved youths, encompassing only those youths who are concurrently adjudicated by both the child welfare and the juvenile justice system.[73]

According to Weimann, foster care youths are more likely to be effected by homelessness, poverty, compromised health, unemployment, and incarcerations after they leave foster care. Some of the statistics from this article are "54 percent earn a high school diploma; 2 percent earn a bachelor's degree or higher; 84 percent become parents too soon; 51 percent are unemployed; 30 percent have no health insurance; 25 percent experience homelessness; and 30 percent receive public assistance."[74]

Ryan and Herz further add that approximately 47 percent of delinquents are associated with at least one substantiated report of maltreatment. Some key factors for this is whether or not the delinquent is living in a group home, has placement instability, and has weak social bonds. This leads my paper into crossover juveniles who are more likely to be housed in group homes and ranches/camps.[75]

Oberst contributes that a third of former foster care youth and a half of crossover youth experience extreme poverty in adulthood, and crossover youth are 1.5 times more likely to receive welfare.[76] Weimann stated that health is often ignored in foster homes and that in 2006 alone California had 65 deaths occur in the foster system.[77] According to Goldstein's recent 2012 article, "the exact number of crossover juveniles is unknown, but that there is an estimate of 9 to 29 percent of child welfare youth in the juvenile system."[78] Goldstein notes that these youth have problems like education difficulties, mental health issues, and

> **TABLE 14–4**
> **Characteristics of Crossover Youth**
>
> - Crossover youth are on average six months younger than non-crossover youth in the delinquency system.
> - A high proportion of crossover youth are girls compared to the proportion of girls in general
> - delinquency populations.
> - African American youth are overrepresented in crossover cases from dependency to delinquency.
> - The child welfare system and the characteristics associated with crossover youth significantly contribute to disproportionate minority contact (DMC) in the juvenile justice system.
> - Crossover youth are more likely to be arrested for a violent or threat-related offense than other youth in the delinquency system.
> - Crossover youth are just as likely to have their cases dismissed as other youth; however, a disproportionate number of Caucasian and Asian youth are more likely than African American and Hispanic youth to have their cases dismissed.
> - Crossover youth are more likely than other youth to be given restrictive placements as first-time offenders—either in group homes or juvenile camps.

Source: Ryan, J., and Herz, D. (2008). *Crossover Youth and Juvenile Justice Processing in Los Angeles County.* Administrative Office of the Courts. Received from http://www.courts.ca.gov.

sometimes sexual assault. He further found that over 55 percent of these juveniles move from group homes and foster care placements three or more times during their lifetimes.[79]

A lot of the studies that have been done on crossover juveniles were done in places like Los Angeles or San Diego. In Table 14–4, Ryan and Herz came up with a list of key characteristics, as above.

Ryan and Herz found that there were 69,009 youths who entered the justice system in Los Angeles from 2002 to 2005. Out of those youths, 4,811 had child welfare cases open. When Ryan and Herz compared the welfare youth to the non-welfare youth, they found the following information: the youth were twice as likely to be African American (46 percent crossover, 21 percent not), they were more likely to be female (37 percent crossover, 24 percent not), and they were more likely to be associated with violence (22 percent crossover, 16 percent not). Female arrests increased 72 percent between the years 1983 and 2002, while the males only increased 30 percent.[80]

When looking at outcomes to juvenile cases, the results in Ryan and Herz study showed that 66 percent received home probation, 16 percent group homes, and 18 percent ranches and camps, but of those the crossover children would be the least likely to get home probation. Crossover youths also have a higher recidivism rate than non-crossover juveniles (Wiemann, n.d). Crossover youth also experience negative outcomes twice as often as other youths (Oberst, 2011). See Table 14–5 for comparison between crossover and non-crossover youth.

Other information about crossover youths is that they cost three times more public service dollars than youth that are in the foster care system alone.[81] According to Oberst, these crossover youths "should be targeted with housing support, education, employment services, and mentoring, if the county and the state are to avoid a lifetime of public dependency by this highly vulnerable population. Better education and mental health treatment are two ways evidence suggests that crossover youth can achieve a better overall performance."[82]

Treatment

According to Adams's 2014 research, there is a practical model that should be put into place to try to help these youth. His model plans to "infuse into this work values and standards; evidence-based practices, policies, and procedures; and quality assurance processes." This process will start right when a youth has crossed over from one to the others so that the people working for these facilities are better able to help the youth. This will also give the

TABLE 14-5
Crossover Juveniles Compared to Regular Juveniles

Have at least one referral in which criminal mischief is the most serious allegation	
Regular juveniles	42%
Crossover	62%
Have at least one referral in which assault is the most serious allegation	
Regular juveniles	20%
Crossover	40%
Adoption as a means of resolving the case	
Regular juveniles	25.3%
Crossover	3.8%

Source: Feyerherm, W., and Johnson, S. (2012). *Juvenile Justice and Child Welfare: Estimates of the Crossover Between Oregon's Systems.* Report for the Youth Development Council. Retrieved from http://www.ode.state.or.us.

workers a better chance to work with the families in decision making to try to maximize the services they can provide to try to prevent crossovers from happening.[83]

Adams lists a number of goals for this model and the interim outcome measures for each site below:

Goals

1. "A reduction in the number of youth placed in out-of-home care

2. A reduction in the use of congregate care

3. A reduction in the disproportionate representation of children of color

4. A reduction in the number of youth becoming dually-adjudicated"

Interim Outcome Measures

1. "A reduction in the number of youth re-entering child welfare from juvenile justice placements

2. A reduction in the penetration of juvenile justice by foster youth

3. A reduction in the use of out-of-home placements

4. A reduction in the use of congregate care as a placement

5. A reduction in the use of pre-adjudication detention

6. A reduction in the rate of recidivism

7. An increase in the use of interagency information sharing

8. An increase in the inclusion of family voice in decision making

9. An increase in youth and parent satisfaction with the process

10. An increase in the use of joint assessment"

Hopefully these new types of systems are taken seriously and are implemented in many different communities.

Homeless Youth

In the (McKinney-Vento Homeless Assistance Act – Title X, Part C of the Elementary and Secondary Education Act – Sec 725), the term "homeless children and youth"

1. A. means individuals who lack a fixed, regular, and adequate nighttime residence, and B. includes children and youths who are sharing the housing of other persons due to loss of housing, economic hardship, or similar reason; are living in motels, hotels, trailer parks, or camping grounds due to the lack of alternative

accommodations; are living in emergency or transitional shelters; are abandoned in hospitals; or are awaiting foster care placement;

2. children and youths who have a primary nighttime residence that is a public or private place not designed for or ordinarily used as a regular sleeping accommodation for human beings;

3. children and youths who are living in cars, parks, public spaces, abandoned buildings, substandard housing, bus or train stations, or in cars, parks, public spaces, abandoned buildings, substandard housing, bus or train stations, or similar settings; and

4. migratory children who qualify as homeless for the purposes of this subtitle because the children are living in circumstances described in clauses 1 through 3.[84]

Being homeless is one of the most disruptive events that can happen to an adolescent's life. This group potentially represents one of the most high risk groups. In one study it was found that factors predicting homelessness in young adulthood were poor quality of family relationship, problems adjusting in school, and the experience of victimization.[85] Another study found that lack of peer support, depression, and substance-abuse predict trauma-related anger among runaway youth.[86]

A theme frequently found in the literature is related to the association between homelessness and victimization. What is associated with increased physical victimization of homeless youth is running away at an early age, running away more often, deviant peer associations, and not having a family member in one's network. Associated why increased sexual victimization are being female, gay, lesbian or bisexual, and having an unkempt physical appearance, having friends who trade sex and panhandling.[87] Post-Traumatic Stress Disorder is associated with alcohol addiction, greater transience, mania, and lower self-efficacy among homeless youth.[88] Slensick and colleagues reported that being victims of abuse in childhood made it twice as likely to experience verbal abuse and physical violence in their relationships.[89]

Toro, Dworsky, and Fowler (2007) found that youthful offenders are likely to experience homelessness disproportionately. For example, in a large youth shelter in New York, 30 percent of youth served had been arrested or incarcerated previously.[90] In addition, because their homelessness forces them to spend more time than their housed peers in public spaces, homeless youth are more likely to have contact with the juvenile justice system for offenses such as loitering, camping, and panhandling.[91] Their offenses are generally non-violent but recurring, likely as a result of their lack of stable homes and frequent moves.

Bernstein and Foster also found that 60 percent of homeless youth had been fined for "quality-of-life offenses," such as panhandling, sleeping or camping in public, and loitering. Most homeless youth cannot afford to pay the fines, which results in the issuance of a warrant for their arrest. Some homeless youth engage in illegal activities in exchange for shelter or food. For example, some youth resort to survival sex, prostitution, or selling drugs in exchange for a place to stay or as a means to earn money to pay for food or shelter.[92] Moreover, many youth experience homelessness on their own, without a parent or guardian to help guide their behavior and negotiate with law enforcement if they become involved in the justice system.[93]

Two groups of homeless youth are the delinquent "throwaway youth" and homeless youth who use drugs. "Throwaway youth" are those who have been forced to leave their parental homes without alternative care arranged and are prevented from returning home.[94]

Treatment

Opening Doors: Federal Strategic Plan to Prevent and End Homelessness sets the goal of ending homelessness for youth (along with families and children) in ten years. While all the objectives in the Plan would affect youth in particular ways, one objective specifically addresses the needs of youth:

> Advance Health and Housing Stability for Youth Aging Out of Systems such as Foster Care and Juvenile Justice

Every year, approximately 30,000 youth age out of foster care and 20,000 to 25,000 age out of the juvenile justice system. Most have limited options for housing, income, and family or other social support. An improved discharge planning connects youth to education, housing, health and behavioral health support; income support and health insurance coverage will improve re-entry back into the community. A targeted outreach to identify the most vulnerable youth experiencing homelessness and improved access to stable health care, housing, and housing support are also critical strategies in ending and preventing homelessness among youth.

Thinking like a Correctional Professional

The governor in your state has become keenly concerned about the expanding problem of homeless youth. He has appointed you as the chairperson of a task force on homelessness among juveniles. He expects positive policy recommendations in your report. How would you handle this assignment? Who would be on your committee?

SUMMARY

LEARNING OBJECTIVE 1: Describe the different types of drug users, drug traffickers, and the relationship between drug use and delinquency, and treatment.

Drug and alcohol abuse is a problem behavior for many juveniles in the United States. Drug use appears to have increased considerably since the late 1970s, but today appears to be declining. The bad news is that high-risk children are becoming increasingly involved in substance abuse. Although the use of crack cocaine may be declining across the nation, it remains the drug of choice for disadvantaged youth. There are three types of drug users: social or recreational users, addicts, and drug trafficking juveniles. It is the latter two groups that most frequently come to the attention of the juvenile justice system. The main theoretical explanations are cognitive-affective theories, addictive personality theory, stress relief theory, social learning theory, social control theory, social disorganization theory, and integrated theories. Solutions to the drug problem include prevention programs, treatment programs, strict enforcement, and harm reduction.

LEARNING OBJECTIVE 2: Describe the juvenile sex offenders, focusing on backgrounds, offenses, and treatment possibilities.

Juvenile sex offenders are defined as adolescents ranging from ages thirteen to seventeen who take part in sexual behaviors that are considered illegal according to the law. Adolescents convicted of being a sex offender are more likely to have offended someone their own age or younger, but there are cases of adults being sexually abused by adolescents who are ages sixteen or seventeen. Usually coming from families with histories of severe family problems, juvenile sex offenders tend to have been victimized in terms of abuse in the home, have behavior and learning problems at school, have poor impulse control, and sometimes have lower IQs. Interestingly, juvenile sex offenders have extremely low recidivism rate. The treatment goals of any programs for sex offenders include breaking the sex offense cycle. Youths are encouraged to assume responsibility for their abusive behaviors and to increase their positive and constructive behaviors and thinking and relationships to others.

LEARNING OBJECTIVE 3: Describe the juvenile gang delinquents, examining their negative behaviors, motivation for becoming involved in gangs, treatment possibilities, and life course.

The juvenile gang member is part of a street gang in an urban community, is part of an emerging gang in a smaller community, or is part of a juvenile gang in the juvenile facility or part of the prison getting an adult facility. The juvenile's role in each of these gangs changes somewhat significantly. Juvenile gangs have both male and female members, and are involved in a variety of negative behaviors—from staff to homicide and the various behaviors between. Explanations vary for why they joined a gang, but usually they want to be part of something greater than themselves. Treatment has not been effective with juvenile gang members, but when it is effective, it is community-oriented.

LEARNING OBJECTIVE 4: Describe the violent offenders, focusing on their backgrounds, relationships, delinquent history, treatment possibilities, and typical life course.

For the past two decades, it has been an attempt to reduce the rate of violent juveniles. There are three types of juvenile violent offenders: those who killed their parents, high-risk school shooters, and chronic offenders. About 300 parents each year are killed by their children, and it is typically a severely abused child who kills one or both parents. Schools have been settings for horrific shootings that have shocked the nation. Experts offer explanations for school shootings which range from "merely an aberration," to a lack of intense control in children today, to the breakdown of the family, to the abundance of guns in the hands of young people, and too much violence on television. Whatever their cause, school killings have focused attention on violence in school settings. Chronic offenders have the characteristic of committing one crime after the other, often serious crimes against persons and property. They may engage in such behaviors for the rest of their lives.

LEARNING OBJECTIVE 5: Describe the mentally ill juvenile, degrees of mental disorder, and treatment possibilities.

Upwards of two-thirds of youthful offenders in the juvenile justice system have a psychiatric or substance abuse disorder. This means that they no longer have the ability to function as a responsible young adult. There are a variety ways for mental health screening and assessment, and screening can be helpful in providing treatment. Much needs to be done in the future to provide adequately for the needs of these children.

LEARNING OBJECTIVE 6: Describe the crossover youth, relating his or her background in the foster care or mental health system, his or her involvement in delinquent offenses, and treatment.

Crossover juveniles are defined as children and youth who are known to both the child welfare and the juvenile justice system. Studies show that crossover children are the least likely to get home probation. Crossover youth also have a higher recidivism rate than non-crossover youths. Crossover juveniles moreover experiences negative outcomes twice as often as other youths. Better education and mental health treatment are two ways evidence suggests that crossover youth can achieve a better overall performance.

LEARNING OBJECTIVE 7: Describe the juvenile who is homeless, presenting his or her background, behaviors, contact with the justice system, and treatment possibilities.

Being homeless is one of the most disruptive events that happen in an adolescent's life. This group potentially represents one of the most high-risk groups. Studies predicting homelessness suggest that poor quality of family relationship, problems adjusting to school, and the experience of victimization contribute to homelessness. Two groups of homeless youth are the delinquent "throwaway youth" and homeless youth who use alcohol and drugs. "Throwaway youth" are those who have been forced to leave their parental homes without alternative care arranged and are prevented from returning to home.

KEY TERMS

addicts, p. 307

high risk, p. 307

special offense youths, p. 303

special needs youths, p. 303

special population residents, p. 303

REVIEW QUESTIONS

1. What explains the popularity of drug use in the United States?
2. "Just say no" is a common saying when it comes to drugs. Will that approach work? Why or why not? Under what conditions will it work or not work? If a friend you know is a user, what can you say to him or her? Would you turn in a friend if you believed you could help this person? Where would you go for help?
3. What do you think is the relationship between drug use and delinquency?
4. Why do college students drink as much as they do? How is their drinking related to the subject matter of this chapter?

GROUP EXERCISES

1. *Group Work:* Without looking in the text, list and describe as many drugs as possible and their effects. After about five to ten minutes, review the drugs noted in the text and fill in the gaps.
2. *Group Work:* Think back to your days in junior high and high school. What are your best recollections of the amount of drug use by students in school (include alcohol), why students did it, and the effect of the drugs? Which drug categories noted in the text did the various students fall into?
3. *Group Work:* Read through three or four of the stories in *Voices* about people who were involved in drugs. What reasons do the addicts give for getting involved with drugs?
4. *Group Work:* Go online and look up the characteristics of addiction. During the next class period, discuss with other members of your group what addiction is and how it takes over the lives of individuals.
   - Research Center: Check out the Cybrary and MySearchLab for even more resources.

WORKING WITH JUVENILES

1. Of the population cited in this chapter, which group would be the most difficult in which to work?
2. Which group do you believe you could be most effective with?

NOTES

1. Jeff Slowkowski, *Highlights from Pathways to Desistance, A Longitudinal Study of Serious Adolescent Behavior* (Washington, DC: Office of Juvenile Justice and Delinquency Prevention, 2011).
2. Ibid.
3. Results from *The 2010 National Survey on Drug Use and Health: National Findings* (Rockville, MD: Substance Abuse and Mental Health Services Administration, 2012).
4. Howard Abadinsky, *Drug Use and Abuse: A Comprehensive Introduction,* 6th ed. (Belmont, CA: Thomson Learning, 2008).
5. *Juveniles and Drugs* (Washington, DC: Office of National Drug Control Policy, 2004).
6. Lloyd D. Johnson et al., *Monitoring the Future: National Results on Adolescent Drug Use. Overview of Key Findings, 2010* (Bethesda, MD: National Institute on Drug Use, 2011).

7. Office of National Drug Control Policy, *2009 National Survey on Drug Use and Health Highlights Fact Sheet* (Washington, DC: Office of National Drug Control Policy, 2010), 1.

8. David M. Altschuler and Paul J. Brounstein, "Patterns of Drug Use: Drug Trafficking and Other Delinquency Among Inner-City Adolescent Males in Washington, DC," *Criminology* 29 (1991), 590.

9. Lloyd D. Johnson et al., "Drugs and Delinquency: A Search for Causal Connections," in *Longitudinal Research on Drug Use: Empirical Finds and Methodological Issues*, edited by Denis B. Kandel, Ronald C. Kessler, and Rebecca Z. Margulies (Washington DC: Hemisphere, 1978), 137–56.

10. Altschuler and Brounstein, "Patterns of Drug Use."

11. Marc Le Blanc and Nathalie Kaspy, "Trajectories of Delinquency and Problem Behavior: Comparison of Social and Personal Control Characteristics of Adjudicated Boys on Synchronous and Nonsynchronous Paths," *Journal of Quantitative Criminology* 14 (1998), 181–214.

12. Richard Jessor and Shirley L. Jessor, *Problem Behavior and Psychosocial Development: A Longitudinal Study of Youth* (New York: Academic Press, 1977).

13. U.S. Bureau of Justice Statistics, *Drugs, Crime, and the Justice System* (Washington, DC: U.S. Government Printing Office, 1993), 23.

14. Kandel et al., eds., *Longitudinal Research on Drug Use.*

15. J. David Hawkins, Richard F. Catalano, and Devon D. Brewer, "Preventing Serious, Violent, and Chronic Juvenile Offending," in *A Sourcebook: Serious, Violent and Chronic Juvenile Offenders*, edited by James C. Howell et al. (Thousand Oaks, CA: Sage Publications, 1995), 48–49.

16. Delbert S. Elliott, David Huizinga, and Suzanne S. Ageton, *Explaining Delinquency and Drug Use* (Beverly Hills, CA: Sage Publications, 1985).

17. Delbert S. Elliott and D. Huizinga, "The Relationship Between Delinquent Behavior and ADM Problem Behaviors," paper prepared for the ADAMHA/OJJDP State of the Art Research Conference on Juvenile Offenders with Serious Drug/Alcohol and Mental Health Problems, Bethesda, MD, April 17–18, 1984.

18. Altschuler and Brounstein, "Patterns of Drug Use," 587.

19. See the statistics on the rise of marijuana use earlier in this chapter.

20. Joy G. Dryfoos, *Adolescents at Risk: Prevalence and Prevention* (New York: Oxford University Press, 1990), 54.

21. A statement made to one of the authors by several training school staff in the early 1990s.

22. Interviewed during the early 1990s.

23. Dryfoos, *Adolescents at Risk*, 48.

24. Malcolm Klein, Cheryl Maxson, and Lea C. Cunningham, "Crack, Street Gangs, and Violence," *Criminology* 29 (November 1991), 623–50.

25. David B. Henry and Kimberly Kobus, "Early Adolescent Social Networks and Substance Use," *Journal of Early Adolescence* 27 (2007), 346–62.

26. For the positive relationship between peers and drug use, see Thomas J. Dishion and Rolf Loeber, "Adolescent Marijuana and Alcohol Use: The Role of Parents and Peers Revisited," *American Journal of Drug and Alcohol Abuse* 11 (1985), 11–25.

27. Elliott et al., *Explaining Delinquency and Drug Use.*

28. Sharon Mihalic, Katherine Irwin, Abigail Fagan, Diane Ballard, and Delbert Elliott, *Blueprint for Violence Prevention, Book 5* (Boulder: University of Colorado, Institute of Behavioral Sciences, Center for the Study and Prevention of Violence, 1998).

29. NCSBY (2003). *What Research Shows About Adolescent Sex Offenders.* Retrieved from http://www.dshs.wa.gov.

30. Ibid.

31. Ibid.

32. Ibid.

33. NCSBY. *What Research Shows About Adolescent Sex Offenders*; Veneziano, C. (2014). "Juvenile Sex Offenders," in *Encyclopedia of Adolescence* (New York, NY: Springer), 1527–1533.

34. Pittman, "Raised on the Registry: The Irreparable Harm of Placing Children on Sexy Offender Registries in the US," *Human rights Watch* (2013), p. 26.

35. Ibid.

36. Ibid.

37. Ibid., p. 30.

38. Michael Caldwell, "Sexual Offense: Adjudication and Sexual Recidivism Among Juvenile Offenders," *Sexual Abuse* (2007), 6.

39. Ashley K. Christiansen and John P. Vincent, "Characterization and Prediction of Sexual and Nonsexual Recidivism Among Adjudicated Juvenile Sex Offenders," *Behavioral Sciences and the Law* 31 (2013), 523.

40. Elizabeth J. Letourneau and Borduin, "The Effective Treatment of Juveniles Who Sexually Offend: An ethical Imperative," *Ethics and Behavior* 18 (2008), 290.

41. Elizabeth J. Letourneau, et al., "Two-Year Follow-Up of a Randomized Effectiveness Trial Evaluating MST for Juveniles Who Sexually Offend," *Journal of family Psychology* 27 (2013), 299.

42. Ibid., p. 983; "National Juvenile Justice Network," *Youth Who Commit Sex Offenses: Research Update* (Washington, DC: National Juvenile Justice Network, October 2014).

43. See the following websites: http://www.casapalmera.com/articles/how-20-prominent-people-died-as-a-result-of-drug-use; http://www.nytimes.com/2008/02/07/nyregion/07ledger.html; http://artsbeat.blogs.nytimes.com/2009/10/01/doctor-reveals-details-of-michael-jacksons-autopsy-report.

44. Veneziano, "Juvenile Sex Offenders,"

45. Veneziano, "Juvenile Sex Offenders"; NJJN, 2007; and NCSBY, *What Research Shows About Adolescent Sex Offenders.*

46. Ibid.

47. NJJN (2007); and the NCSBY, *What Research Shows About Adolescent Sex Offenders.*

48. Veneziano, "Juvenile Sex Offenders."

49. Research done on the origins of emerging gangs by one of the authors.

50. See the research studies cited in the previous chapter on gangs.

51. James Allen Fox, *Trends in Juvenile Violence: A Report to the United States Attorney General on Current and Future Rates of Juvenile Offending. Prepared for the Bureau of Juvenile Statistics* (March 1996), executive summary, p. 19.

52. John J. DiIulio, Jr., "Assessing Ideas: Tougher Law Enforcement Is Driving Down Urban Crime," *Policy Review* (Fall 1995), p. 15.

53. Ibid.
54. William J. Bennett, John J. Dulilio, Jr., and John P. Walter, *Body Count, Moral Poverty, and How to Win America's War Against Crime and Drugs* (New York: Simon and Scvhuster, 1996).
55. Cited in Philip J. Cook, "The Epidemic of Youth Gun Violence," *Perspectives on Crime and Justice, 1997–1998* (Washington, DC: The National Institute of Justice, 1998), 110–111.
56. Adapted from Puzzanchera, C. (2013). *Juvenile Arrests 2011* (Washington, DC: Office of Juvenile Justice and Delinquency Prevention); Sedlak, A., McPherson, K., and Basena, M. (2013), Nature and Risk of Victimization. *Office of Juvenile Justice and Delinquency Prevention Bulletin*, 1–13. Retrieved from www.ojjdp.gov.
57. Cathy Spatz Widom, "Varieties of Violent Behaviors: 2013 Sutherland Address," *Criminology* 52 (August 2014), 321–322.
58. Marvin E. Woolfgang, Robert M. Figlio, and Thorstein Sellin, *Delinquency in a Birth Cohort* (Chicago: University of Chicago Press, 1972).
59. Ibid, p. 30.
60. Desai, R., Goulet, J., Robbins, J., Chapman, J., Migdole, S., and Hoge, M. (2006). Mental Health Care in Juvenile Detention Facilities: A Review. *Journal of the American Academy of Psychiatry and the Law Online*, 34:2:204–214. Retrieved from www.jaapl.org.
61. Hammond, S. (2007). *Mental Health Needs of Juvenile Offenders*. National Conference of State Legislatures, 4–9. Retrieved from http://www.ncsl.org.
62. Ibid.
63. Desai et al., 2006.
64. Hammond, 2007.
65. Desa, 2006, i.
66. Ibid.
67. conditions and/or drug/alcohol use. Hammond reported that youths who do get screened right
68. Desai et al., 2006, p. 6.
69. Ibid.
70. Ibid.
71. Ibid.
72. Adams, J. (program director) (2014). Practice Model. *Center for Juvenile Justice Reform*. Retrieved from http://cjjr.georgetown.edu; Perin, 2012; Goldstein, B. (2012). "Crossover Youth: The Intersection of Child Welfare & Juvenile Justice," *Juvenile Justice Information Exchange*. Retrieved from http://jjie.org; Feyerherm, W., and Johnson, S. (2012). *Juvenile Justice and Child Welfare: Estimates of the Crossover Between Oregon's Systems*. Report for the Youth Development Council. Retrieved from http://www.ode.state.or.us; Oberst, L. (2011). "Youth Involved in Both Foster Care and Juvenile Struggle At Unexpected Rate, LA Study Finds," *Juvenile Justice Information Exchange*. Retrieved from http://jjie.org; Ryan, J. and Herz, D. (2008). "Crossover Youth and Juvenile Justice Processing in Los Angeles County." *Administrative Office of the Courts*. Received from http://www.courts.ca.gov.
73. Perin, 2012.
74. Wiemann, n.d.
75. Ryan and Herz (2008). "Crossover Youth and Juvenile Justice Processing in Los Angeles County."
76. Oberst, (2011). "Youth Involved in Both Foster Care and Juvenile Struggle At Unexpected Rate, LA Study Finds."
77. Sedlak, A., McPherson, K., and Basena, M. (2013), Nature and Risk of Victimization. *Office of Juvenile Justice and Delinquency Prevention Bulletin*, 1–13. Retrieved from www.ojjdp.gov. Wiemann, J. (n.d.). All Foster Care Is Not Created Equal. *Startling Statistics*. Retrieved from http://angelsfoster.org.
78. Goldstein (2012). "Crossover Youth: The Intersection of Child Welfare & Juvenile Justice."
79. Ibid.
80. Ryan and Herz (2008). "Crossover Youth and Juvenile Justice Processing in Los Angeles County."
81. Oberst, (2011). Youth Involved in Both Foster Care and Juvenile Struggle At Unexpected Rate, LA Study Finds. *Juvenile Justice Information Exchange*. Retrieved from http://jjie.org.
82. Ibid.
83. Adams (program director) (2014). "Practice Model."
84. McKinney-Vento Homeless Assistance Act—Title X, Part C of the Elementary and Secondary Education Act.
85. M. B. Van den Bree, K. Shelton, A. Moss, H. Thomas, and P. J. Taylor, "A Longitudinal Population-Based Study of Factors in adolescence Predicting Homelessness in Young Adulthood, *Journal of Adolescent Health* 45 (2009), 571–78.
86. M. D. McCarthy and S. J. Thompson, "Predictors of Trauma-Related Symptoms among Runaway Adolescents," *Journal of Loss and Trauma* 15 (2010), 212–27.
87. K. A. Tyler and M. R. Beal, "The High Risk Environment of Homeless Young Adults: Consequences of Physical and Sexual Victimization," *Violence and Victims* 25 (2019), 101–16.
88. K. Bender, K. Ferguson, S. Thompson, C. Komlo, and d. Pollio, "Factors Associated with Trauma and Post-Traumatic Stress Disorder Among Homeless Youth in Three U.S. Cities: The Importance of Transience," *Journal of Traumatic Stress* 23 (2010), 161–168.
89. N. Slesnick, G. Eredem, and J. Collins, "Prevalence of Intimate Partner Violence Reported by Homeless in Columbia, Ohio," *Journal of Interpersonal Violence* 25 (1579–1593).
90. P.A. Toro, A. Dworsky, and P. J. Fowler, "*Homeless Youth in the U.S.: Recent Research Findings and Intervention Approaches*." Paper presented at the 2007 National Symposium on homelessnesxs Research, wasshington, d.C., 2007.
91. Sedlak, A., McPherson, K., and Basena, M. (2013), Nature and Risk of Victimization. *Office of Juvenile Justice and Delinquency Prevention Bulletin*, 1–13. Retrieved from www.ojjdp.gov.
92. N. Bernstein and L. K. Foster, "*Vocies from the Streets: A Survey of Homeless Youth* by their Peers," California Research Bureau, March 2008.
93. National Center for Homeless Education, 2011.
94. K. L. Montgomery, S. Thompson, and A. N. Barzzyk, "Individual and Relationship Factors Associated with Delinquency Among Throwaway Adolescents," *Children and Youth Services Review* 33 (2011), 1127–33.

© Jeff Greenberg/Alamy

Learning Objectives

1. Describe how juveniles experience victimization.
2. Explain what professionalism is and the need for it.
3. Identify why juvenile corrections is a promising career.
4. Describe the various career options in juvenile corrections.
5. Articulate why an internship in juvenile justice makes sense to the student who is interested in juvenile corrections.
6. Describe the changing face of juvenile justice.
7. Describe what juvenile justice will look like in years to come.

As discussed in Chapter 6, the idea of a juvenile court, separate in proceedings from adult criminal courts, had its beginnings in Chicago in 1899. The juvenile court ideal, which inspired juvenile justice system workers in this country for over 100 years, was, however, disgraced by the actions of a corrupt Pennsylvania judge in the early 2000s. In 2009, former Luzene County (Pennsylvania) juvenile judge Mark Ciavarella, 61, was convicted by a federal jury of racketeering and conspiracy of accepting cash payments totaling nearly $1 million to place juvenile offenders in privately owned detention facilities. Following Ciavarella's conviction, the Pennsylvania Supreme Court quickly dismissed thousands of juvenile court convictions that he had issued, saying that Ciavarella had run his courtroom with "complete disregard for the constitutional rights of juveniles: who came before him, including the right to legal counsel and the right to intelligently enter a plea.[1]

The long-standing mission of juvenile justice is to correct youthful offenders so that they will neither return to the juvenile justice system nor continue on into the life of an adult criminal. Indeed, the opposite often appears to be true, for once trouble-making youths are processed through the correctional system, the chances of their returning are increased, not reduced. Juvenile corrections often breed rather than reform offenders. And there are cases, such as the above, when officials of the juvenile justice system become involved in corruption and abuse of youths.

Yet the mood of this book has not been negative, because we have repeatedly seen that the committed professional can have an exciting and fulfilling career and can make a difference in youths lives, that well-developed programs which receive adequate funding and are executed well do have positive results, and that jurisdictions committed to juvenile justice reform provide more promising programming than those not committed to reform.

This chapter discusses the victimization of juveniles, how professionalism has impacted juvenile justice, why juvenile corrections is a promising career, the various career options in juvenile corrections, why an internship makes sense to someone who wants to work in juvenile justice, and gazes into the crystal ball to see what the future of juvenile justice might look like.

The Context of Juvenile Victimization

Victimization surveys indicate that children too frequently are the targets of crime. In many countries throughout the world, attention to the plight of children is increasing the focus on the victimization of youths in dysfunctional families, in schools, in neighborhoods, and on the streets, by terrorist groups looking for child soldiers, and by authorities. Emotionally damaged as a result of neglect and abuse, these children are often unable to relate to adults and peers, to perform in school, and to make realistic plans for the future. Many of these juveniles are imprisoned as adults.

The Family and the Victimization of Children

As an indication of the extent of maltreatment of children, an estimated 3.3 million referrals involving the maltreatment of approximately 6 million children were made to child protective services during the 2009 fiscal year, and of that number, one-quarter were found to be victims.[2]

The demographics of child maltreatment show that younger children make up the largest percentage of victims. Just over 33 percent of all victims of maltreatment were younger than three years of age, an additional 23.3 percent were ages four to seven, and 18.8 percent were ages eight to eleven. Victimization was split almost evenly between the sexes: 51.1 percent of the victims were girls and 48.2 percent were males. Less than one-half of all victims were white (44 percent), one-fifth (22.3 percent) were African Americans, and one-fifth (20.7 percent) were Hispanic.[3]

The problem of parental maltreatment of children is divided into several different categories. The Children's Bureau reports that in 2009, 78.3 percent of reported maltreatment stemmed from neglect, 17.8 percent from physical abuse, 9.5 percent from sexual abuse, and less than 7.6 percent from emotional maltreatment.[4] Homicide is the most serious form of victimization of children. An estimated 1,770 children died in 2009 due to child abuse or neglect.[5]

The School and Victimization

In the past, the major problems faced by teachers and administrators in the nation's school systems were those of juveniles running the halls, leaving class without permission, writing graffiti on the walls, and occasionally fighting. Today's students, however, are likely to experience the same problems in the schools as they do on the streets. Drugs, alcohol, suicide, rape, robbery, assault, arson, and bomb threats have combined with knives and guns to change the

---

TABLE 15–1
Indicators of School Crime and Safety

Violent deaths at school

- Of the 31 students, staff, and nonstudent school-associated violent deaths occurring from July 1, 2010, through July 30, 2011, there were 11 homicides and 3 suicides of school aged children (5 to 18) at school.

- During the school year 2010–2011, there were 1,396 homicides among school youth ages five to eighteen. During the 2011 calendar year, there were 1,456 suicides of youth age five to eighteen.

Nonfatal school victimization

- In 2011, students ages twelve to eighteen were victims of 1,246,000 nonfatal crimes at school, including thefts and violent crimes.

- In 2011, more students ages twelve to thirteen were victims in major cases of theft at school than away from school.

Nonfatal teacher victimization

- A greater percentage of secondary school teachers (8 percent) reported being threatened by injury, by students than elementary school teachers (7 percent). However, greater percentage of elementary school teachers (6 percent) reported having been physically attacked than secondary school teachers (2 percent).

School environment

- In 1909–2000, 85 percent of public schools reported one or more incidents of crime that had taken place at public schools, amounting to an estimated 1.9 million crimes.

- During the 2009–2010 school year, 16 percent of public schools reported that bullying occurred among students on a daily or weekly basis. In 2009, 23 percent of students ages twelve to eighteen reported having been bullied at school during the academic year.

- In 2011, 18 percent of students ages twelve to eighteen reported that street gangs were operating in their school. During 2011, 19 percent of public schools and only 2 percent of private schools reported the presence of gangs.

- In 2011, 26 percent of students in grades 9 to 12 reported someone had offered, sold, or given them illegal drugs on school property in the past 12 months. This had decreased from 32 percent in 1995.

- In 2011, 9 percent of students, ages 12 to 18, reported that someone at school had used hate-related words against them, more than one third (28 percent) reported seeing related graffiti at school. This had decreased from 12 percent in 2001, and was far lower than 36 percent who reported seeing a related graffiti at school in 1999.

- In 2011, 18 percent of males reported carrying a weapon on school property compared to 2 percent of females.

- In 2011, 33 percent of students reported that they had been involved in physical fight over the previous 12 months and, 12 were involved in a fight on school property.

Source: Simone Roberts, Jijun Zhang, and Jennifer Truman, *Indicators of School Crime and Safety 2012* (Washington, DC: US Department of Education of Justice; US Government Printing Office, 2013).

Critical Thinking Question
If violence in public schools is declining, why do so many teachers feel unsafe in the school setting? What can be done to make public schools safer?

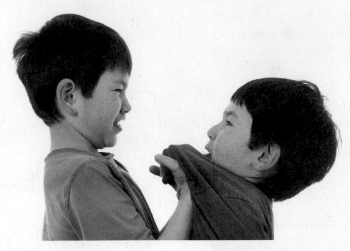

▲ Younger and weaker children are sometimes taken advantage of by older and stronger children.
Keith Publicover/Shutterstock

Critical Thinking Question
Look through the data, think through your own experiences in schools in your home community, and draw some conclusions about how safe the schools you went to were.

atmosphere of schools and to generate fear on the part of parents, who worry about their children's safety. A 2011 report on school crime and **school safety** by the Bureau of Justice Statistics and the National Center for Education Statistics titled *Indicators of School Crime and Safety: 2011* report found the following[6]:

This report helps put the amount of crime in schools into perspective. Males are more likely to be victims of theft than are females, but males and females are the victims of violence about equally. Students in the higher grades are more likely to be victims of violence than are younger youths, and Hispanic students are less likely than whites to be victims of theft. Somewhat predictably, students from urban schools are exposed to greater amounts of victimization than those in rural schools; and suburban schools have the highest number of victimizations.[7]

Death in the Schools

Death in the schools is a rarity. For example, from July 1, 2009, through June 30, 2010, seventeen homicides and one suicide occurred of school-age youth (ages five through eighteen) at school. During the 2008–2009 school year, as previously suggested, 1,579 homicides occurred among school-age youth ages five to eighteen, while during the 2008 calendar year, 1,344 suicides of youth ages five to eighteen took place. Combining these figures translates into about one homicide or suicide of school-age youth at school per 2.7 million students enrolled during the 2009–2010 school year.[8] The small number of child deaths that takes place in the schools as opposed to those occurring in the community is considerable.[9] Unfortunately, the few acts of murder that do happen dramatically color our perception of the safety of schools.

Bullying

Bullying by individuals and groups as a major problem burst onto the scene in the 1990s because of its apparent connection with school shootings by bullying victims. Traditional **bullying** is direct, face-to-face, and physical in nature and occurs when a stronger, more aggressive child hits, pushes, slaps, or beats other children with the intent to produce bodily injury and pain. A second bullying technique is verbal and consists of youths teasing, calling their targets names, and making fun of their victims' families, clothes, faces, and friends, usually with untrue statements, in order to affect the victims' thinking, feeling, and acting. Closely related to verbal abuse is the third technique of emotional or psychological abuse, which generates fear, distress, or anxiety in a weaker child.[10] Although much bullying consists of all three types of victimization, the consequences of bullying may have different effects on different types of children. A common theme running through bullying is the desire to exercise power and to feel superior over victims (see Exhibit 15–1).[11]

The vast majority of adults is uninvolved and uninformed about the online social networks used by children and thus has no real ability to understand or intervene when children are bullied. Children, as might be expected, are more likely to tell their friends than their parents when contacted by a bully and may feel victimized on many separate occasions when other youths place unwanted messages, photos, or videos online again and again. The result is a perceived lack of balance of power on the part of the victim and some youths. Although research is as yet inconclusive on the roles that gender and age play in the bully/victim interactions, some observers suggest that bullied females are likely to become emotionally upset, whereas males tend to deny bullying's effects on them. These observations, however, need much more research because they may simply reflect gender stereotyping.

Studies show that students are able to discount cyberbullying more than traditional bullying. Nonetheless, severe and prolonged bullying does result in embarrassment, stress, depression, and loneliness; if youths are unable to resolve these issues, the pressures on them build, eventually resulting in low self-worth, low confidence in their social competence, and an increase in self-blame for their victimization.[12] The results are a "loss of face, reputation damage, public humiliation, damage to self-esteem, impact on schoolwork and rejection."[13]

EXHIBIT 15–1
Nine Adolescents Charged After Suicide of Classmate

In 2010, a prosecutor brought charges against nine juveniles at South Hadley High School in western Massachusetts who subjected a classmate to relentless taunting and physical threats. This bullying, according to the prosecutor, led the freshman, Phoebe Prince, to hang herself from a stairwell at her home following school. In this case, two boys and four girls, ages sixteen to eighteen, face a variety of felony charges including statutory rape, violation of civil rights with bodily injury, harassment, stalking, and disturbing a school assembly. Prince's family had recently moved to the United States from Ireland. Investigators found that the abuse took place in the school library, the lunchroom, and the hallways. Phoebe went to school officials, but she told a friend that no action was taken. This pattern of abuse included text messages, Facebook postings, threats, and efforts to corner Phoebe, whose actions were described as fearful, distraught, and panicked. She endured three months of it and then hanged herself.

CRITICAL THINKING QUESTION

Why do you think that school administrators did nothing about this ongoing abuse? Do you think that this lack of response is a typical response of school administrators? How frequently do you believe that students' lives are made miserable by bullies at school? What punishment do you believe that bullies in this case should receive?

Sources: Carlin DeGuerin Miller, "Phoebe Prince's Final Days: Bullied Girl Suffered 'Intolerable' Abuse Before Suicide, Say Court Documents," accessed February 13, 2012, at http://www.cbsnews.com/8301-504083_162-20002132-504083.html; Helen Kennedy, "Phoebe Prince, South Hadley High School 'New Girl,' Driven to Suicide by Teenage Cyber Bullies," *Daily News,* March 29, 2010; and Erik Eckholm and Katie Zezima, "9 Teenagers Are Charged After Suicide of Classmate," *The New York Times*, March 30, 2010, A14.

An inability to retaliate keeps the victim feeling helpless, and the result for some victims is an increase in thinking about suicide and suicide attempts.[14] Others move from their homes, neighborhoods, towns, and schools to escape their victimization.

Brothels and the Streets

A hidden side of U.S. culture is child prostitution. The sexual and physical abuse of children outside of their homes is no less devastating than that by parents and relatives. Children coming home from school are picked up on the streets, kidnapped from their driveways and front yards, lured out of malls, and enticed by pimps who prowl bus stations and train terminals. Yet others are recruited from the Internet, by cell phone, by youths who know of vulnerable "candidates," and on Facebook and MySpace. Some children are smuggled into the United States from other countries for purposes of prostitution and almost all girls are kept captive by illegal drugs that make them into addicts. Ninety percent of the children brought into the United States for prostitution are female and 10 percent are male.[15]

Although estimates vary, in 2010, the United States was estimated by some to have three hundred thousand child prostitutes, although the United Nations estimates that the United States has six hundred thousand.[16] These numbers are qualified by the fact that no central clearinghouses for the statistics on child prostitutes exist, by the fact that the numbers likely include youths who have been hidden away by pimps and enslaved for several years, and by statements that the United States has one hundred thousand children who are "at risk" for being turned into sex slaves. Regardless of the actual numbers, the trauma experienced by these juveniles is real and severe; some children are forced to service hundreds of clients a year.

On occasion, some children ages two and three are used as prostitutes and in the pornography industry, and some who are even younger, are occasionally discovered. As children's ages increase, researchers find that the numbers of children exploited also increase, with the ages of six and seven appearing all too frequently. The average age for a girl to become involved in prostitution is around thirteen or fourteen. Unfortunately, that age is slowly lowering because males who use prostitutes, generally males ranging in age from their twenties through their sixties, are tending to prefer younger and younger girls because of the possibility of contracting HIV/AIDS.[17]

▲ Lured to the mall after several months of contact on the Internet, this young girl could be in extreme danger.

Andy Cross/The Denver Post/Getty Images

Mass Media and Delinquent Behavior

Part of the challenge of being the parent today is dealing effectively with the influence that the mass media have on children. For our purposes, the term, *mass media* refers to the Internet, radio, television, commercial motion pictures, videos, CD music, and the press (newspapers, journals, and magazines).

Violent TV Programs and Movies

Most people today watch a lot of television, and many seem to depend on media programming for the understanding of the surrounding world. Consequently, criminologists have shown considerable interest in assessing the relationship between delinquent behavior and the exposure to violence shown on television. Researchers in the area of delinquency generally conclude that TV violence is most likely to negatively impact the behavior of those children who are already predisposed toward violence and that it seems to have much less influence on young people who are not so predisposed.[18]

Violent Video Games

Video games involving violent scenarios, such as "Halo 2," "Grand Theft Auto," and "Asheron Call 2," are the focus of considerable controversy today. Some people accuse video game makers of promoting values that support violence. Not surprising, the software industry, with this annual 28 billion in sales paid by nation's thrust for action, claims that their games are offered only for entertainment purposes.

In August 2005, members of the American Psychological Association (APA) adopted a resolution calling for less violence in video and computer games marketed to children. One APA panelist, Kevin M Kleffer, reported research shows that playing violent video games tends to make children more aggressive and less prone to helping behaviors.[19] Create A Anderson, one of the pioneers of research in this area, adds, "There really isn't any room for doubt that aggressive games leads to aggressive behavior."[20]

Internet-Initiated Crimes

Internet access is easily available to nearly everyone in the United States today, but the Web has become a new carrier for innovative forms of cybercrime. One source of Internet-initiated crime is the supremacists and hate groups that target young people through the Web. In like manner, youthful perpetrators of violent crime are sometimes influenced by information collected or contacts made on the Internet, and child sexual abuse, where initial contacts are made through the Web, now accounts for up to 4 percent for all arrests for serial assaults against juveniles.

Gangsta Rap

Gangsta rap is a form of hip-hop music that some believe negatively influence young people by devaluing human life, the family, religious institutions, the school, and the justice system. Gangster rap, pioneered by Ice-T and other rappers, influenced by Scholly D's hard core rap portrays the lifestyles of inner-city gang members, and its lyrics relates stories of violence-filled lives. Girls played a prominent part of the lyrics and are frequently depicted as a means for attaining manhood and status.

Brown University professor Teresa Rose's 2006 book, *Hip-Hop Wars* claims that hip-hop is in crisis, because its lyrics are becoming increasingly saturated with the involving thugs, pimps, black gangsters, and 'hos. She raises a number of important questions about hip-hop: Does hip-hop cause violence, or does it merely reflects a violent ghetto culture? Is hip-hop sexist, or are its disattractors merely anti-sex? Does the betrayal of black culture in hip-hop undermine social understanding and social advancement? Rose calls for more accurate reflection in the music of a richer cultural sphere, including anger, politics, and sex than the urgent images sound and video provide.[21]

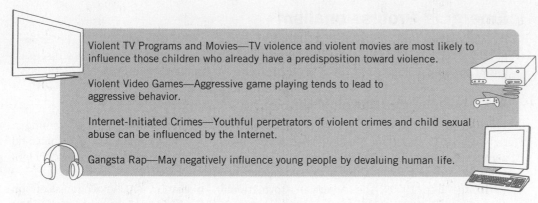

Violent TV Programs and Movies—TV violence and violent movies are most likely to influence those children who already have a predisposition toward violence.

Violent Video Games—Aggressive game playing tends to lead to aggressive behavior.

Internet-Initiated Crimes—Youthful perpetrators of violent crimes and child sexual abuse can be influenced by the Internet.

Gangsta Rap—May negatively influence young people by devaluing human life.

FIGURE 15–1
Mass Media and Delinquent Behavior

In summary, today's parents must face the reality of their children's minds being bombarded with extensive disturbing stimuli. Violence permeates movies and TV screens, video games are no less violent, and the most popular ones among teenagers are probably the most violent. Supremacists and hate groups are targeting young people through their websites. The Internet offers opportunities for this sexual abuse of vulnerable adolescent males and females. Finally, gangsta rap is filled with violence, appears to devalue human life, and contains lyrics promoting homophobia, misogyny, racism, and materialism. Figure 15–1 summarizes the types of media and how they can influence adolescent behavior.

Professionalism in Juvenile Justice

Corrections professionals rather than following a script or providing minimum service, undertake a specialized set of tasks and complete them, believing passionately in what they do, do not compromise their standards or values, and care about clients even if they happen to be juvenile offenders. Correctional professionals, as is true of other types of professionals, are experts at their work. They see their commitment to the organization, as having the objective of obtaining the higher standards of excellence. Becoming a corrections professional means:

- To see yourself as a person of integrity and to live at integrity level. One definition of integrity is to do the right thing when no one is looking.

- To treat youthful offenders with dignity and respect. As one corrections professional put it, treat residents as you would want your father or brother to be treated in a correctional context.[22]

- To model positive behaviors. One way this can be done is to adhere to the ethical principles set forth by the American Correctional Association.

- To be a person committed to a learning model and to be open to new ways of doing things. Such a person seeks to learn throughout his or her career and is always willing to pursue all the training opportunities available.

- To believe that it is possible to make a difference. Believe that you can have an impact and are not limited by what others have done.

- To keep your personal stuff from getting into the way. Do not let your personal problems or issues keep you from doing an effective job.

- To maintain a clean institution; cleanliness and orderliness of the facility are absolute necessities in correctional leadership.

- To remember the importance of accountability, attention to detail, and following the schedule.

- To refuse to accept unethical behavior from fellow staff members.

- To stay positive and do what is possible to create a workplace that is safe, healthy, and free of harassment in any form.

Emerging Professionalism

Professionalism brought corrections into the modern age and will guide it into the future.

However, reaching this standard did not occur overnight. In this section, we discuss a few of the steps taken in the past to reach the current standards of juvenile corrections.

Staff Training and Development

The Federal Bureau of Prisons and a number of states began to emphasize staff training in the early 1970s. It was not long before state corrections training academies were established across the nation. Having developed in adult corrections, soon staff training and development was found in juvenile correctional agencies.

In the late 1970s, the American Correctional Association (ACA) Commission on Accreditation established its training standards, which had wide influence on the field of corrections. One of its standards was to require 120 hours for preservice and 40 hours for annual in-service training. An advantage of staff training is that it ensures uniformity in administration. Staff training was one of the most important impetuses toward professionalism of American juvenile corrections.

Implementing Gender and Racial Integration

The acceptance of women in juvenile corrections took a long time, but not quite as long as it did in adult corrections. It was not until midway through the twentieth century that women were widely accepted in positions of correctional leadership. Since that time, women have been directors of probation, superintendents of training schools, and an increasing number have been wardens of men's prisons, even maximum-security ones. Racial integration in adult corrections also took place in the twentieth century, as it became apparent that with the growing racial influx of inmates and residents in institutional and community-based corrections, a racial balance must also be found with staff. Gender and racial integration in juvenile corrections actually took place before adult corrections and has been implemented at least as much, if not more so, in the juvenile justice system.

Emphasis on Ethics and Integrity

Both corrections and law enforcement agencies realized in the late twentieth century that an emphasis on **i**ntegrity was critically important in being recognized as professional entities. Persons of integrity demonstrate over a period of time that they are honest. They also show that there are no contradictions between what they say and what they do. Thus, "standing tall" is not something that can be earned in a day or a week. It occurs over a substantial period of time during which this integrity is tested on a regular basis. The credibility and honesty of these people are reflected in everything they say and do. As with adult corrections, the same emphasis on integrity took place in the juvenile system and has affected all that takes place with youthful offenders.

Corrections staff with integrity seem to have the ability to maintain their composure, regardless of the circumstances taking place around them. No matter how volatile an incident may be or how much they are upset by the behavior of other staff members or inmates, they are able to keep their cool. This calmness is reassuring to others because they know that even in the worst conditions, you can count on these people to keep their wits about them and stay focused on what has to be done to resolve the situation.

What Remains to Be Done?

Unquestionably, juvenile corrections have come a long way toward professionalism, but there is still a ways to go to accomplish this mission of professionalism.

- Correctional organizations must develop greater clarity about their purpose: why the organization exists—its mission; why it is needed to support the purpose and mission; what should be the future direction of the organization.

- The growing trend toward getting accreditation must continue in both community-based and institutional facilities.

- There needs to be a nationally applicable set of principles and philosophy on what is acceptable behavior toward residents in community-based programs and correctional institutions. Accreditation provides the broad map of what is expected in correctional care, but the subtle things expected from staff need further clarity and explanation.

- The quality of juvenile institutions has improved compared to those in the past, but there seems to be a movement in juvenile corrections in some states to make training schools into juvenile prisons. This is a movement that must be discouraged.

- The level of professionalism is very much affected by the ability to recruit the right staff and, once they are recruited, to explain the principles and behaviors that are expected of them.

- Rehabilitative programs for those who desire them must be based on the most effective design, delivery of services, and follow-up in the community.

- The residential staff's inclination to a culture that sanctions abuse and mistreatment of youths must be eradicated. One way that this can be done is to videotape any disciplinary interaction between correctional staff and residents and to remind officers that charges will be brought in court if they violate the rights of residents.

- The use of restraints in institutional settings must be carefully supervised, because of the possibility of abusive treatment of difficult-to-handle residents.

- The salaries of correctional personnel in the community and institutional contexts need to be revised periodically. The salaries of these staff in some jurisdictions are still far too low. One advantage of increased salaries is that college-educated applicants will be attracted to these positions in higher numbers.

- Administrative correctional staff must be willing to step forth when colleagues are out of line. This may come to the point of termination if that should be necessary.

- Private correctional care, which has always played and still plays an important role, can pose a problem because too frequently privately run institutions pay inadequate salaries to staff, have poorly constructed corrections facilities, and fail to provide needed services for inmates. Private companies, if they intend to be in the corrections business, must maintain the standards of county and state corrections.

Careers in Juvenile Corrections

A career in corrections is a meaningful one in which you can have a positive impact on the lives of others and make a difference in your community.

There are many jobs in juvenile justice and juvenile corrections where opportunities for advancement are great. The jobs in corrections vary from community programs to those in institutions, from juvenile to adult corrections, from privately administered agencies to state and federal agencies. Most states and the federal jurisdiction offer a good salary package for working in corrections. The health insurance and pension plans are further inducements for corrections employment. There is an encouraging movement of professionalism in the field. With a combination of academic study and employment experience, a corrections professional today can commit himself or herself to a long-term contribution to corrections that focuses on providing the highest quality service to others in the workplace, both colleagues and clients.

A career in corrections, although demanding and challenging, can be extremely rewarding and an ideal fit for those wanting to make society safer. Furthermore, the trend toward new generation jails and direct supervision gives correctional officers more involvement with inmates and more control over the populations they supervise, which translates into enhanced professionalism and greater job satisfaction. Once considered "just a guard," as professionalism in this career continues to be recognized and expected, so do opportunities to make a difference. Because most inmates will be released, the impact correctional officers have on those serving their time is significant.

Those who are interested in working with juveniles can work in police departments, in the courts, in community-based corrections, and short- and long-care juvenile correctional facilities. There are career boxes in the chapters for these jobs, but a brief outline would include the following:

Employment in Police Department

* Juvenile unit in a police department,
* School resource officer,
* To be part of a gang detail responsible for gang surveillance,
* And to make presentations in the school setting on D.A.R.E. or G.R.E.A.T.

Jobs in the Courts

* To be a juvenile judge,
* To be a juvenile court referee,
* To be a defense attorney, usually a public defender,
* And to be a prosecutor to those who intervene with juveniles as part of the court process.

Community-Based Corrections

* Probation officer
* Aftercare officer
* Drug court counselor
* Community Correctional Treatment Specialist
* Residential counselor
* Director of court services (chief probation officer)
* Director of residential facility
* Detention worker

Juvenile Correctional Institution

* Social worker
* Clinical psychologist
* Psychiatrist
* Forensic psychologist
* Recreational therapist
* Youth counselor (custodial staff)
* Custodial supervisor
* Assistant superintendent
* Superintendent
* High school teachers
* Vocational teachers
* High school principal
* Chaplain

Internships in Juvenile Corrections

Internships are an excellent way to discover if a specific area of criminal justice is a good fit for you.[23]An internship is an opportunity to receive supervised, practical, on-the-job training in a specific area. Many correctional agencies and institutions offer internships, usually without pay, for those interested in learning about a specific area of employment while acquiring skills that make them more employable in that area. Often, individuals who complete an internship with a specific agency or institution might be hired after their formal education is complete. Or, conversely, the intern or the department may find that the fit is not good, and both are spared a difficult situation.

Locating Internship Opportunities

Although internships may be advertised, they are usually not advertised the way job listings are posted. You need a strategy to know where to find these opportunities. Resources are available that compile tens of thousands of internship sites along with general information about them. Princeton Review's, *The Internship Bible*, claims to offer "100,000 opportunities to launch your career," and *Peterson's Internships* provides almost 50,000 paid and unpaid internships.[24] A quick Internet search for internships in corrections will also provide a wealth of resources, such as the American Correctional Association (ACA), which offers many student internship opportunities, as well as a number of state correctional agencies.

School-Related Internships

Many, if not most, schools have relationships with agencies that provide internships. Some programs are formally structured, with internships taking the format of actual courses for which the student receives credit. Other programs offer rather informal or unstructured internship opportunities where students receive no credit but are afforded an invaluable "inside look" at a career they are considering. Some school-coordinated internships are optional, most likely providing elective credits, whereas other internships are required. An example of this is a criminal justice program that requires students to complete 115 hours of interning at a social service agency, the primary purpose being to learn about resources available to criminal justice practitioners.

Credit Versus Compensation

Some interns receive college credit and some actually get paid. And some are fortunate enough to get both. In some instances it can be the student's choice. Be clear what a particular internship offers and realize that interns are seldom afforded the opportunity to negotiate placement terms.

Start Early and Stay Organized

Internships, especially in the criminal justice field, require that you begin your search well before you are actually interested in beginning. The best internships require long-range planning, sometimes at least a year or more in advance. Many agencies require some sort of background check, so give yourself plenty of lead time when exploring internship options.

Because many people will be looking for a limited number of internships, keep a file of contacts, just as you should as part of your job-seeking strategy, so you have a ready networking list to use now and in the future. In addition to the obvious benefits of internships, the process of seeking such an experience is great, too, because of the similarities to job seeking. It is all about developing a strategy to achieve what you want...and part of that strategy is to recognize the necessary time constraints.

Making the Most of the Experience

Whether a survey or practical internship, for credit or not, you want to make the most of the experience. Not only do you want to gain as much information as possible, but you want to take full advantage of the networking opportunities to develop contacts that may serve your future job-search efforts. You will be meeting people actively engaged in the profession of interest, many of whom may be potential points of contact when you are ready to seek employment. Furthermore, if you participate in an internship long enough, some individuals will likely readily allow you to list them as a reference. You may even find a mentor, someone who will be supportive of and helpful to you throughout your job-seeking efforts, or even your career.

It is generally helpful, when embarking on a new experience, to know a little of what to expect. A criminal justice internship is:

Critical Thinking Question
Recognizing that an internship provides many opportunities to network, how would you go about taking full advantage of this?

- An opportunity to get real exposure to a variety of agencies in the local criminal justice community
- A chance to meet professionals in the field who can advocate for your future employment
- An opportunity to explore a specific profession prior to committing yourself to it in a full-time capacity
- An appointment as a representative and ambassador of your academic institution
- A privilege
- An opportunity to broaden your educational experience with some real practical experience
- A huge responsibility—the vast majority of which falls upon the student
- Unpaid (usually)
- To be set up far in advance of starting, usually five to ten weeks before the internship semester begins
- To be completed by individuals who have declared criminal justice as their major and are of junior or senior standing
- To be granted at the complete and mutual discretion of the internship coordinator and the participating agency
- For students who have demonstrated adequate academic performance, and are in good academic standing with the department, any faculty committees, and the college/university

A criminal justice internship is not:

- To be taken for granted
- A filler because you can't find a class that you like
- Something to do because you can't think of anything else to do
- A "fast-track" to guaranteed post-graduation employment
- A blow-off course
- A right as a student (see "privilege" above)
- Required
- A guaranteed "A"—students are assessed as stringently as in most other courses in the department
- To be done at an agency or business where you already work or have worked in the past
- For students who have any type of criminal history in their past (or present)—this would include outstanding traffic violations and other minor infractions that have turned into warrants

Some may think the worst thing to have happen with an internship is to select one that doesn't produce the anticipated results, whether that is a good grade, a strong letter of recommendation, or a solid job offer. Wrong. The worst thing is to leave on a bad note—one that could haunt you during your future job-seeking efforts.

The Changing Face of Juvenile Justice

In addition to professionalism, the greater use of technology, the expanding use of restorative justice, the ever-increasing use of evidence-based principles, and an emphasis on reentry are affecting the face of juvenile justice in the United States.

Increased Use of Technology

Rather than relying on traditional methods of security and control, the correctional system is now entering a new phase of **technocorrections**, which involves using technology rather than personnel to monitor probation, aftercare, and institutional populations. Today, **technology-driven security** is designed to maintain security both in the community and in the institutions. Examples include the use of motion detectors at the perimeters of institutions that transmit movement to a centralized command center for immediate response; infrared image detectors that use handheld devices no bigger than a flashlight; and better and stronger physical barriers that make escape nearly impossible.[25]

Technical experts are now identifying numerous areas in both community-based and secure settings in which correctional management can be aided by information technology (IT), including reception and commitment, sentence and time accounting, classification, caseload management, security, discipline, housing-bed management, medical treatment, grievances, programs, scheduling, investigations/gang management, property, trust accounting, visitation, release and discharge, and community supervision. Because IT can be applied in so many areas within community and institutional settings, administrators have begun to take advantage of the potential offered by these new technologies.

▲ Security cameras are symbols of our times. Schools, buses, hospitals, and streets are being wired for constant surveillance in an attempt to maintain order in a constantly changing and complex society.
Panotthorn Phuhual/123RF

The Dangers of Technocorrections

Although technocorrections holds the promise of providing greater security and control, it also brings with it a unique set of problems. The danger is that increasingly technology-driven corrections will provide a sterile and isolated environment for inmates, in which contact with staff is greatly reduced or even nonexistent. Correctional institutions, it is true, will be more secure, in both external and internal security, but they may also be less humane, and it is hard to imagine that this environment will not have an adverse effect on prisoners as they return to the community. Technology can also provide a false sense of security in both community-based and institutional settings. For example, knowing where someone is does not mean that it is possible to know what that person is doing.

Ever-Expanding Use of Restorative Justice

The expansion of restorative justice, as discussed in several chapters of this text, is one of the most exciting movements in corrections today. Restorative justice has recently been coupled with intermediate sanctions. From the grassroots level to state and local headquarters, restorative justice is rapidly gaining momentum within the United States. Victim–offender conferencing (sometimes called mediation) is the oldest and most widely used expression of restorative justice, with more than 1,300 programs in eighteen countries.[26] While stressing accountability for offenses committed, restorative strategies operate with the goal of repairing injuries to victims and to communities in which crimes have taken place. Whether these conferences occur before, during, or after adjudication, they promote education and transformation within a context of respect and healing. These models are neither mutually exclusive nor complete in themselves. They can be combined or adapted depending on the special situation at hand.[27]

Evidence-Based Practice
Ten Evidence-Based Principles

- *Principle 1: Target Criminogenic Needs.* Good programs target factors related to offending that can be changed.
- *Principle 2: Target Through Assessment of Risk and Need and Target Programs to High-Risk Offenders.* Risk assessment provides a measure of the risk principle, which states that higher risk offenders are likely to reoffend if not treated, and that low-risk offenders are not likely to reoffend even without treatment. The Level of Service Inventory–Revised (LSI-R) provides insight into which youthful offenders should receive the highest priority for treatment, regardless of their specific problem areas.
- *Principle 3: Base Design and Implementation on a Proven Theoretical Model.* Effective programs work within the context of a proven (evidence-based) theory of criminal behavior. Proven theories include social learning and cognitive-behavioral theories.
- *Principle 4: Use a Cognitive-Behavioral Approach.* Thinking and behavior are linked: youthful offenders behave like offenders because they think like them; changing thinking is the first step toward changing behavior. Effective programs attempt to alter the cognitions, values, attitudes, and expectations of an offender that maintain antisocial behavior. They emphasize problem solving, decision making, reasoning, self-control, and behavior modification, through role playing, graduated practice, and behavioral rehearsal.
- *Principle 5: Disrupt the Delinquency Network.* Effective programs provide a structure that disrupts the delinquency network by enabling offenders to place themselves in situations (around people and places) where prosocial activities dominate. Effective programs also help offenders to understand the consequences of maintaining friendships with criminals. Role playing can help them practice building new prosocial friendships.
- *Principle 6: Provide Intensive Services.* Effective programs offer services that occupy 40 to 70 percent of the youthful offender's time while in the program and last three to nine months. The actual length of the program needs to be driven by the specific behavioral objectives of the program and specific needs of the individual inmate.
- *Principle 7: Match Offender's Personality and Learning Style with Appropriate Program Settings and Approaches.* This is known as the "responsivity" principle. There are important interrelations between the learning and personality style of the youth and their settings or situations.
- *Principle 8: Include a Relapse Prevention Component.* Relapse prevention should be offered, both in training school and in the community, when possible, and should include (1) rehearsal of alternative prosocial responses, (2) practicing prosocial behaviors by rewarding improved competencies in increasingly difficult situations, (3) training family and friends to provide reinforcement for prosocial behavior, and (4) providing booster sessions to youthful offenders following the formal phase of treatment.
- *Principle 9: Integrate with Community-Based Services.* Effective programs refer youths to other programs with good track records.
- *Principle 10: Reinforce Integrity of Services.* Effective programs continually monitor program development, organizational structure, staff development and training, and other core organizational processes. An important part of this effective offender intervention treatment approach is program evaluation.

Source: Lawrence W. Sherman, David P. Farrington, and Brandon Welsh, *Understanding and Implementing Correctional Options That Work* (Harrisburg: Pennsylvania Department of Corrections, 2003).

Greater Use of Evidence-Based Principles and Rehabilitative Approaches

Evidence-based practice principles are used increasingly in juvenile justice today. Professionals contend that programs that follow these principles have a better chance of succeeding than those that do not. Consider the ten principles described in the Evidence-Based Practice feature.

Emphasis on Reentry

The high rates of recidivism of juveniles being released from training school has been one of the stimulators for an increased emphasis on reentry. The importance of a continuum of services for youth being released from an institution to the community has gained support, as have aftercare services for these youth.

What Will Juvenile Justice Look Like by the End of the Twenty-First Century?

Much will remain the same in juvenile justice in the years to come, but there will also be much that is different:

- The U.S. Census Bureau estimates that the population of juveniles under the age of eighteen will increase 14 percent between 2000 and 2025—about one-half of 1 percent per year. By 2050, it is estimated that the juvenile population will be 36 percent larger than it was in 2000.[28] Given this population growth of juveniles in the years to come, it is likely that juvenile justice will have greater demands placed on it.

- Many members of this increased population of juveniles will come from impoverished homes headed by single mothers. In 2012, African American and Hispanic juveniles were more than three times as likely to live in poverty as were non-Hispanic white juveniles. Since juvenile poverty appears to be associated with juvenile crime, it is likely that minority juveniles will continue to be the focus of social control in American society.[29]

- With this increased population of poor juveniles, the rate of juvenile violence, including homicide, may again grow, as it did in the late 1980s and early 1990s.

- The widespread feeling today that more troubled teenagers exist now than in the past will be even more pronounced in the next twenty years. Adolescent psychiatry will be more frequently called on to treat youths who experience problems in early childhood, but it will be the children of the haves who will benefit the most, as their wealthy parents place their children in private hospitals and treatment centers.

- The *Roper v. Simmons* decision reveals that the debate about the death penalty for juveniles under the age of eighteen has been resolved at least for now, and it is unlikely that any changes will take place in the near future.[30]

- The Roper and *Graham v. Florida* decision may be the first two of one or more decisions determining the fate of the life-without-parole sentence for juveniles.

- The trilogy of gangs, drugs, and guns will continue to be a social problem. Youth gangs are increasingly becoming a minority problem, and this trend is likely to increase in the decades to come.

- The drug choices of juveniles may well change in the future, but there is no evidence that drug use will be less of a problem than it presently is. There is currently a widespread movement among juveniles away from the use of crack cocaine to the use of methamphetamine.

- Cigarette smoking among adolescents will likely continue to decrease.

- Juveniles will continue to drink alcohol, and there is no reason to believe that the use of alcohol will be less of a problem than it is at present.

- The issue of gun control will remain a serious problem facing the juvenile justice system.

- The current tendency to create uniformity and reduce discretion in juvenile sentencing procedures is likely to continue.

- The deinstitutionalization movement is likely to continue and even expand, given the high costs of institutionalization and the successful outcomes of many community-based correctional programs.

- Drug courts, teen courts, and gun courts for juveniles will likely continue to increase.

- The use of restorative justice will continue to spread throughout the United States.

- The use of private programs will continue to be an important part of the landscape of juvenile corrections.

- State legislatures will become increasingly involved in passing laws related to the social control of juveniles.

- A structural change that will likely be implemented in those states that do not have it is the removal of serious crimes from the jurisdiction of the juvenile court. What will probably be developed is an increased number of mechanisms for the direct referral of juvenile crimes to the adult court.

▲ Teaching children in the home and at school how to be responsible citizens is a never-ending challenge to all societies. The first lessons must begin in homes by parents and other caregivers. Children need this care and direction for them to be successful in their own lives.
Washington County Juvenile Probation Services

▲ Some schools across the nation are trying seriously to bring the excitement of learning to their students. These young men demonstrate the enthusiasm that ideally should be found in every classroom.
Chris Hondros/Getty Images

- Disproportionate minority confinement, in spite of the efforts of the Juvenile Justice and Delinquency Prevention Act will remain a problem, and juvenile institutions will become even more sought out as dumping grounds for poor and minority children.
- The number of juveniles in adult prisons will probably not greatly decrease. Wardens and their staff will view the protection of these youngsters as one of their most difficult management problems.
- The dissatisfaction with the juvenile justice system will probably continue. Those who want to eliminate the juvenile justice system and the juvenile court will be more vocal and will receive much greater support.
- Yet it remains unlikely that this nation will give up, any time in the near future, on the more-than-a-century-long experiment with a separate system for juveniles.

One of the underlying themes of this text is that working in the juvenile justice system is an exciting job and a fulfilling career. We hope that the student shares our enthusiasm and aspirations about the possibility of creating a better day for youngsters in our society.

If we care for children, we will increase our efforts to diminish the negative effects of the hard-line and punitive approaches to youth.

If we care for children, we will see to it that our ideas are presented forcefully and clearly to policy makers.

And if we care for children, we will not wait until the system finally works; instead, we will reach out and help those youths seeking to find themselves.

SUMMARY

LEARNING OBJECTIVE 1: Describe how juveniles experience victimization.

The family, the socioeconomic structure, the neighborhood, the school, and the media are all influential in both the lawful and illegal behaviors of juveniles. Juveniles are more likely to be victimized than any other age group, and juvenile victims are vulnerable to the exploitation of others.

LEARNING OBJECTIVE 2: Explain what professionalism is and the need for it.

Professionalism in juvenile justice is an approach that maintains the importance of integrity, that sees the importance of treating juveniles with dignity and respect that believes it is possible to make a difference, and that strives to create a workplace that is safe, healthy, and free of harassment in any form. As the number of professionals in juvenile justice increases, what takes place in agencies and institutions will reflect the principles just listed and other principles of professionalism. From the treatment of youth in the community and institutions, to the acceptance of standards and accreditation, to the ever-increasing use of evidence-based corrections, professionalism has affected every aspect of juvenile justice administration and operations.

LEARNING OBJECTIVE 3: Identify why juvenile corrections is a promising career.

In juvenile corrections it as possible the difference in offenders. The opportunities for advancement are great. In most jurisdictions, juvenile corrections jobs offer a good salary package, including salary, health insurance, and pension plan. Juvenile corrections further encourages the development of professionalism.

LEARNING OBJECTIVE 4: Define what jobs are available in juvenile corrections in terms of working with youthful offenders?

Careers in working with juveniles can be pursued in police work, in the juvenile courts, in community-based corrections, and in working in correctional institutions. Those who work in such positions repeatedly say that it is possible to have a meaningful job experience and to make a difference in the lives of young people.

LEARNING OBJECTIVE 5: Explain why an internship in juvenile justice makes sense to the student who is interested in juvenile corrections.

A corrections internship is an excellent way to accomplish several goals: It helps you to decide if juvenile corrections is a good career choice for you and provides hands-on experience on the job. It enables you to become known by those who work in the agency, which might be helpful when a job search is pursued, and it makes it possible to create a positive impression on your resume. The internship can be particularly helpful for the networking experience it provides. While internships vary from granting college credit to no credit, total compensation to no compensation, from the length of time—a summer, one semester, two semesters, or even longer—they put all provide a positive experience to the student.

LEARNING OBJECTIVE 6: Describe the changing face of juvenile justice.

The changing face of juvenile justice involves an increased use of technology, an expanding use of restorative justice, greater use of evidence-based practices and principles, and an emphasis on reentry.

LEARNING OBJECTIVE 7: Describe what juvenile justice will look like in the years to come.

In the years to come, juvenile justice may have an increased juvenile base, whose members will be impoverished and from minority groups headed by single mothers; the rates of violence among juveniles may increase again, so there are likely to be more troubled juveniles in the juvenile justice system; the trilogy of gangs, drugs, and guns will likely to continue to be a problem; drug courts, teen courts, and gun courts are likely to increase in number; and disproportionate minority confinement will remain a problem. Finally, while dissatisfaction will remain with the juvenile justice system, the movement to eliminate this system for juveniles will probably experience no greater in support than it does now.

KEY TERMS

Bullying, p. 330
professionalism, p. 334

school safety, p. 330
technocorrections, p. 339

technology-driven security, p. 339

REVIEW QUESTIONS

1. What are the benefits of various technologies? What are their disadvantages? Which technologies do you believe are the most acceptable?
2. What are some strategies you could use to increase the use of evidence-based juvenile programs?
3. What are some methods you could use in your local communities to address the issues of hope, healing, honor, and habilitation?
4. What would you like the juvenile justice system to look like by 2040?
5. After reading this book, what types of education and training should professionals in juvenile justice receive to prepare them for jobs in the system?

GROUP EXERCISES

1. *Writing to Learn Exercise:* Write a few paragraphs identifying various technological innovations in the community and how the innovations work. Critique and revise.
2. *Group Work:* Describe the new types of technology that can be used in secure institutions. Continue discussions after referring to the chapter.
3. *Writing to Learn Exercise:* Write an essay describing what restorative justice is, which sections of the criminal justice system are using it, and how. Critique and revise.
4. *Writing to Learn Exercise:* Write a paragraph or two that reviews the empirical evidence as to which programs do and do not work. Critique and revise.
5. *Writing to Learn Exercise:* Write two paragraphs on what the nature of the juvenile problem will look like in the year 2020 and beyond. Critique and revise.
6. *Large Group Work:* Discuss what appear to be the most important aspects of professional training needed for the future. How do the authors believe that the juvenile system should be modified in the future?

WORKING WITH JUVENILES

How would professionalism be expressed in your work with youthful offenders? Which tenet of professionalism do you think is most frequently violated in working with these offenders? Why?

NOTES

1. Details for this story come from Michael Rubiinkam, "To Plead Guilty of Racketeering in Kickbay Case," *AOL News*, February 18, 2011.
2. Children's Bureau, *Child Maltreatment 2009* (Washington, DC: U.S. Department of Health and Human Services, 2010), viii.
3. Ibid., 22.
4. Ibid., 23.
5. Ibid., 54.
6. All of the data above are excerpted or quoted from Simone Robers, Jijun Zhang, Jennifer Truman, and Thomas D. Snyder, *Indicators of School Crime and Safety, 2011* (NCES 2012-002/NCJ 236021) (Washington, DC: Bureau of Justice Statistics, National Center for Education Statistics, 2012), iii–vii, accessed at http://nces.ed.gov/pubs2012/2012002.pdf.
7. Ibid., 97.
8. Ibid., 6.
9. Ibid.
10. D. P. Farrington, "Understanding and Preventing Bullying," in *Crime and Justice: A Review of Research*, Vol. 17, edited by M. Tonray (Chicago: University of Chicago Press, 1993), 381–458, cited in U.S. Department of Education, National Center for Education Statistics, *Are America's Schools Safe? Students Speak Out: 1999 School Crime Supplement* (NCES 2002–331), by Lynn A. Addington et al., *Project Officer: Kathryn A. Chandler* (Washington, DC: U.S. Department of Education, 2002), 55.
11. Some observers do not distinguish between verbal and emotional abuse.
12. David Perry, Ernest Hodges, and Susan Egan, "Determinants of Chronic Victimization by Peers: A Review and a New Model of Family Influence," in *Peer Harassment in School: The Plight of the Vulnerable and Victimized* (New York: Guilford, 2001), 73–104. Thanks to Alexis Geeza of Washington and Jefferson College for pulling together much of the research in this section on bullying.
13. Barbara Speers, Phillip Slee, Larry Owens, and Bruce Johnson, "Behind the Scenes and Screens: Insights into the Human Dimension of Covert and Cyberbullying," *Zeitschrift fur Psychologie/Journal of Psychology* 217, no. 4 (2012), 189–96.
14. Anat Brunstein Klomek, Andre Sourander, and Madelyn Gould, "The Association of Suicide and Bullying in Childhood to Young Adulthood: A Review of Cross-Sectional and Longitudinal Research Findings," *Canadian Journal of Psychiatry* 55, no. 5 (2010), 282–88; Perry et al., "Determinants of Chronic Victimization."
15. Polaris Project, accessed at http://www.polarisproject.org/human-trafficking/overview accessed 05/06/2012; BellaOnline: The Voice of Women, "Human Trafficking in America," accessed May 5, 2012, at http://www.bellaonline.com/articles/art175483.asp. A number of children, usually smuggled in from Mexico, are used as laborers and janitors in homes, stores, agricultural enterprises, and businesses in need of cheap labor; these are often brutal experiences. A rather large number of children smuggled into the United States are brought in by well-off parents who are too impatient to wait for legal adoptions to take place. Many children smuggled out of a country end up in international sex pedophile organizations.
16. Change Starts with One, Child Prostitution: A Global Epidemic," accessed May 6, 2012, at http://changestartswithone.wordpress.com/02/07/2012/child-prostitution-a-global-epidemic; U.S. Department of Justice OJP Bureau of Justice Statistics, "The Human Trafficking Project: USDOJ Releases Trafficking Victim Statistics for the U.S.," accessed May 6, 2012, at http://www.traffickingproject.org01/2009/usdoj-releases-trafficking-victim.html.
17. BellaOnline "Human Trafficking," 1. For a good overview of the problem, see International Crisis Aid, "Sex Trafficking in the United States," accessed August 22, 2012, at http://www.crisisaid.org/ICAPDF/Trafficking/traffickstats.pdf.
18. This is the general consensus of the vast amount of research done on this topic.
19. "Experts Debate Effects of Violence Video Games," September 26, 2005, http://homepage.mac.com/iajukes/blogwavestudio/LH20050626175144/LHA2005092622.
20. Ibid.
21. Tricia Rose, *Hip Hop Wars: What We Talk About When We Talk About Hip Hop and Why It Matters* (Jackson, TN: Basic Civitas Books, 2008).
22. Frank Wood, former warden and commissioner of corrections in Minnesota, used to say this all the time. See Clemens Bartollas, Becoming a Model Warden (Landan, Maryland: American Correctional Association, 2004).
23. This section was adapted from Harr and Hess, The authors appreciate their willingness to let us use their material.
24. Princeton Review, *The Internship Bible*, 10th ed. (Princeton, NJ: Princeton University Press, 2005).
25. Debbie Mchaffey, "Security and Technology: The Human Side," *Corrections Today* 13 (January–February 2004), 30.
26. M. Coates, R. Coates, and B. Vos, "The Impact of Victim–Offender Mediation: Two Decades of Research," *Federal Probation* 65 (2001), 29–36.
27. Katherine van Wormer and Clemens Bartollas, *Women and the Criminal Justice System,* 4th ed. (Boston: Allyn & Bacon, 2013.
28. Howard N. Snyder and Melissa Sickmund, *Juvenile Offenders and Victims: 2006 National Report* (Washington, DC: National Center for Juvenile Justice, 2006), 2.
29. Ibid., 7.
30. *Roper v. Simmons* (No. 03-633) 543 U.S. 551, 161 L.Ed. 2d 1, 125 S.Ct. 1183 (2005).

Addict A person who builds up a tolerance to any kind of drug and finds it necessary to keep taking the drug or experience discomfort from withdrawal. Gradually, more and more of the drug must be taken to reduce the withdrawal effects.

Adjudicatory Hearing This hearing for juveniles is equivalent to a trial in adult courts. This is the point when the judge reviews the charges as described in the petition, hears the testimony from the parties involved, and decides whether the youth committed the offense.

Adolescence-Limited Delinquents Individuals who only engage in delinquent behavior during youth and desist from deviant activities around their eighteenth birthday.

Adult Sex Offender An adult male who by force, guile, or cunning persuades a young person to perform sexual acts deemed inappropriate or illegal by society.

Aftercare With the formation of the juvenile court, this became another term for parole.

Aftercare officers Juvenile equivalent of adult parole officers.

Age of onset The age at which a juvenile began law-violating behaviors.

Amphetamine See Methamphetamine.

Anabolic Steroids Synthetic testosterone obtained by prescription and often used by athletes and body builders to increase body size and male characteristics.

Antisocial Personality Disorder Child engages in lying, intimidation of others, aggression toward others, ignoring rules and regulations, abuse relationships with those around him or her, and shows no regrets about the harm he or she causes.

Attention Homes Facilities designed to give attention to the delinquent, not detention. Locked doors, fences, and/or physical restraints are absent.

Autonomy The desire for personal independence is an important concern for lower-class persons because they feel controlled so much of the time.

Bail A security given for the release of a juvenile awaiting hearing. It is not a form of punishment. The purpose of bail is to ensure that the defendant will show up at his or her adjudicatory hearing.

Balanced and Restorative Justice Model A traditional New Zealand approach to juvenile offending. This "balanced" system ensures resources are allocated equally among efforts to ensure accountability to crime victims, to increase competency in offenders, and to enhance community safety.

Balanced Approach to Juvenile Probation The goal of this approach is to protect the community from delinquency, to impose accountability for offenses committed, and to equip juvenile offenders with the required competencies to live productively and responsibly in the community.

Behavior Modification A theory that applies learning theory to problems of human behavior.

Biological Positivism Approach that argues crime is the result of biological differences among people that can be discovered through rigorous scientific measurement.

Bullying A stronger, more aggressive child inducing fear, distress, or harm in a weaker child through physical, verbal, or psychological intimidation.

Capital Punishment The death penalty.

Child Abuse The act of engaging in physical, sexual, verbal, or emotional assaults or neglect of a child.

Chronic Offenders A repeat offender or serious delinquent. Predominant characteristics of these youths are their commitment to crime and their involvement in one crime after another. Chronic offenders may include prostitutes and gang members.

Class Oppression A form of exploitation experienced by some adolescents in which socioeconomic conditions have a direct impact on a youth's criminal behavior are imposed on them that denies lower class youths the ability to live normal lives.

Cocaine (Drug Abuse) A stimulant drug used for thousands of years with some legitimate medical use but today is used illegally to help users feel euphoric and mentally alert to sounds, sight, and touch; different users experience extremely variable effects with some users experiencing negative effects such as anxiety and restlessness; a very powerful addictive drug.

Cognitive-Behavioral Interventions Interventions used to identify the errors characteristic of youthful offenders' thinking by changing their thought patterns and thinking.

Cognitive Transformation Theory that the way an individual thinks and views the world plays an integral part in his or her desisting from crime. As a delinquent begins to change his or her personal beliefs and openness to change, the individual is less likely to engage in criminal acts.

Cohort Studies   A research methodology in which researchers usually identify every juvenile born in a certain time frame in a particular city and then follow those juveniles for many years to track behavioral patterns.

Commitment   A sentence to confinement in a facility for juveniles.

Common Law   Unwritten laws that emerge over time in societies to solve problems.

Community Correction Acts   Residential and day treatment programs are developed under these acts. The Minnesota Community Correction Act has become a model for others because it provides a state subsidy to any county or group of counties that chooses to develop its own community corrections system.

Concurrent Jurisdiction   The right of both juvenile and adult courts to try juveniles for crime. Prosecutors decide which court to try juveniles in.

Conduct Disorder   Often a result of child abuse, this mental problem results in a child who has difficulty following rules, gets into fights, bullies others, sets fires, steals, and is aggressive to or brutalizes animals.

Conduct Norms   The rules of a group that dictate how its members should act under particular conditions.

Constitutionalists   A group that argues that the juvenile court is unconstitutional because under its auspices the principles of a fair trial and individual rights are denied to juveniles.

Containment Theory   Walter Reckless's theory that explains crimes as being the result of internal factors such as poor self-concept and external factors such as weak family, peer and group controls.

Continuum of Care Model   Provided by a number of jurisdictions, this model provides a continuum between institutions and aftercare services to maintain a nurturing environment for youthful offenders.

Continuum of Sanctions   The system of programs, services, and facilities designed to provide escalating punishment as the severity of a youth's criminal behavior increases.

Corporal Punishment   Punishments that involves violence, whipping, and branding; any punishment of the body.

Cottage System   Juvenile facilities that are placed outside of a city and consist of a series of cottages in which youths live in small numbers. The rationale is that youths in rural areas will be reformed when exposed to the rural values.

Crack   A processed crystalline form of cocaine that can be smoked.

Crime Control Model   This model assumes that offenders have free will and should be punished with harsh penalties, such as long prison sentences, to protect society.

Criminal Opportunity Theory   Philip Cook's theory that criminals tend to be selective in choosing a crime target and are most attracted to targets that appear to offer a high payoff with little effort or risk of legal consequence.

Criminal Recidivism   The act of a youth engaging in further or more severe criminal behavior after already being punished for prior delinquent activity.

Cultural Deviance Theory   Walter Miller's theory that the lower-class culture is characterized by a set of focal concerns, or values, that command widespread attention and a high degree of emotional involvement.

Cyclothyme   One of the two body types in Ernst Kretschmer's body type theory. The cyclothyme individual is soft skinned and lacks muscle, and is less likely to engage in criminal behavior than the counterpart schizothyme body type.

Dangerous Poor   In the midto late 1800s and early 1900s, those coming from a poor background were blamed for crime. Many appeared dangerous because they came from different cultural, ethnic, and religious backgrounds.

Day Treatment Programs   Treatment programs in which youngsters participate during the day and return home in the evenings.

Decriminalizing Status Offenders   Removing from the juvenile court's jurisdiction youthful behavior that would not be a chargeable offense if committed by an adult.

Deinstitutionalization of status offenders (DSO)   The removal of youths from secure confinement and the placement of all qualified youths in community programs rather than in institutions.

Deinstitutionalization of Status Offenders   To no longer confine status offenders in secure detention facilities or secure correctional facilities with delinquents.

Delinquency Prevention   Any attempt to thwart youths' illegal behavior before it occurs.

Dependent and Neglected Children   These children are young, live in dysfunctional families, and lack the love and the consistent behavior models required to grow up as socially functional adults.

Desistance from Crime   The termination of delinquency, strongly related to the maturation process, as juveniles either come to desire a conventional lifestyle or do not desire continuing unlawful activities.

Detention   Being held in a short-term facility designed specifically for juveniles or, occasionally, in a local jail until a police department, probation officer or judge decides on what to do with them.

Detention Center   Juvenile hall; intended to be a temporary holding center.

Detention Hearing   Hearing at which a decision to detain is made. The hearing must be held within a short period of time after taking the juvenile into custody, generally forty-eight to seventy-two hours, excluding weekends and holidays.

Determinate Parole   The length of supervision is clearly specified; often related to the period of commitment specified by the juvenile court and is proportionate to the youth's offense.

Deterministic View   The deterministic view states that individuals cannot help committing criminal or delinquent acts because they are controlled either by internal factors (biological or psychological imbalances) or by external factors (poverty, learning crime from others, strain, or societal labeling).

Deviant Sexual Arousal   Frequent and Inappropriate thoughts about rape and sexual fantasies.

Differential Association Theory   Edwin H. Sutherland's theory that criminals and youthful offenders learn crime from others in intimate personal groups.

Diminished Responsibility   The belief that youths are less responsible for their actions than adults due to sociobiological circumstances that prevent a juvenile from fully understanding his or her actions.

Police Discretion   The choice between two or more possible legal means of handling a situation confronting a police officer, prosecutor, probation officer, judge, or other law enforcement official.

Disposition Hearing   Hearing that is equivalent to sentencing in adult courts and is of two basic types. The first may occur at the same time as the adjudicatory hearing and the second occurs at a considerably later date.

Disproportionate Minority Confinement (DMC)   An issue in which individuals belonging to minorities are involved within the justice system at a higher proportion than are whites.

Diversion Programs   Programs that sprouted across the nation in the late 1960s and early 1970s in an effort to keep juveniles outside the formal justice system.

Dopamine (Drug Addiction)   A major neurotransmitter within the brain that regulates movement, emotion, cognition, motivation, and feelings of pleasure. Some drugs mimic dopamine and some drugs result in a flooding of the brain with dopamine, thereby producing pleasure.

Drug and Alcohol Abuse Interventions   These interventions are increasingly developing in community-based and institutional settings to assist those who need help with their drug/alcohol addiction problems.

Ecstasy (MDMA)   Has properties of both stimulants and hallucinations and some users report both time and space distortions; a tablet may contain any of a number of other drugs. Neurotoxicity includes increasing levels of serotonin and dopamine, both neurotransmitters. Hhas adverse long-term effects on higher thought processes.

Electronic Monitoring   Electronic anklets and bracelets are used to verify probationers' presence in the residence in which they are confined.

Emerging Youth Gangs   Gangs developing in smaller towns and villages, sometimes as a result of urban street gangs' efforts to expand their drug markets.

Emotionally Disturbed Offender   A type of youth whose emotional problems severely interfere with his or her everyday life such that he or she ends up in the justice system.

Escalation of Offenses   An increase in the number and severity of crimes committed by an individual.

Excitement   The quest for excitement leads juveniles to the widespread use of alcohol and drugs or engaging in sex and gambling.

Experimental Drug User   Someone who tries different drugs to experience their effects; may lead to addiction.

Family Conferences   Meetings in which a facilitator, the offender, their families, and a community representative participate; held to solve the offender's problems in the community.

Family Therapy   Therapy aimed at treating the entire family. This has become a widely used method when dealing with a youthful offender's socially unacceptable behavior.

Fate   Lower-class individuals feel that their lives are subject to a set of forces over which they have little or no control.

Felicific Calculus   Human beings are presumed to be creatures governed by their desires to gain pleasure and avoid pain.

Feminist Theory of Delinquency   A theory proposed by Meda Chesney-Lind which states that female delinquency is explained by the relationship between the female's crimes and her sexual and physical victimization.

Fingerprinting   Taking a person's fingerprint for possible identification.

Forestry Camps   Minimum-security institutional camps. Residents engage in conservation work in state parks.

Free Will   Human beings are viewed as rational creatures who, being free to choose their actions, can be held responsible for their behavior.

Gang Deactivation   Removing youths from gang involvements.

Gang Detail   Officers of the traditional police unit assigned to gang problems.

Gang Unit   Units established to work solely on gang problems and that develop extensive intelligence networks with gang members in the community.

Gender-Neutral Position   An approach to explaining male–female delinquency that focuses on social learning, delinquent peer relationships, social bonding, the family, and deterrence and strain rather than gender differences. Advocates of this approach explain that females engage with the criminal world using the same methods as males.

Group Home   A single dwelling owned or rented by an organization or agency for the purpose of housing offenders.

Guardian ad litem   A lawyer who is appointed by the court to take care of youths who need help, especially in neglect, dependency, and abuse cases, but also occasionally in delinquency cases.

Guardianship Councils (Brazil)   Five-member groups of local citizens that protect juveniles assigned to them by judges and make recommendations for youth placement in hospitals, with parents, in shelter foster homes, or treatment.

Guided Group Interaction (GGI)   The most widely used treatment modality in juvenile corrections. The modality is based on the assumption that youths can confront their peers and force them to face the reality of their behavior more effectively than staff can.

Heroin   Highly addictive drug that, when laced with fentanyl, has the potential to cause death within hours. Serious health hazards accompany use. Withdrawal occurs soon after the drug is taken and withdrawal symptoms are severe.

High (Drug Addiction)   a feeling of euphoria or excitement as a result of taking a drug.

House Arrest   Home confinement is a program of intermediate punishment whereby youths are ordered to remain confined in their own residences during evening hours, after curfew, and on weekends.

Houses of Refuge   Facilities created for all children in the early 1800s when citizens became concerned about the inhumane living conditions in jails and prisons.

Illicit drug   Any compound defined by law to be illegal for any category of people; includes prescription drugs used for any purpose other than that for which they were prescribed.

Infancy   From birth to approximately two years of age.

Inhalants   Substances that produce a loss of sensation, and even unconsciousness. Irreversible effects include hearing loss, limb spasms, central nervous system or brain damage, or bone marrow damage. Sniffing high concentrations of inhalants may result in death from heart failure or suffocation (inhalants displace oxygen in the lungs).

Insight-Based Therapy   A therapy model employed by training schools to treat mental and emotional disorders. The therapist uses insight, persuasion, suggestion, reassurance, and instructions to provide residents with a realistic view of their problems and can establish a desire to cope in a healthy and effective manner.

Intake   The point at which a probation officer conducts a preliminary investigation that includes an interview during which a youth is advised of his or her legal rights and the officer decides on the next step for the youth.

Intake Process   When probation officers evaluate whether a juvenile offender needs help from the juvenile court; the intake process controls detention, reduces caseloads, and keeps minor cases out of juvenile court.

Intensive Supervision Program (ISP)   Juveniles are placed in small caseloads and receive frequent contacts (up to five or six a day) from their aftercare officers.

Interpersonal Maturity Level (I-Level) Classification System   Developed by J. Grant and M. Grant in the late 1950s, an I-Level classification assumes that personality development follows a normal sequence and attempts to identify the developmental stage of offenders by focusing on their perception of themselves, others, and the world.

Interrogation   Occurs when an individual is formally questioned by the police.

Interstate Compact   An agreement among certain states to deal with both the mobility of youths and the need to keep them under supervision. Interstate compacts may be drawn up when youths are wanted for several crimes in several states at the same time or when a state has a specialized treatment program appropriate to specific offenders.

Investigation   Background check of a the juvenile. Probation officers are usually given up to sixty days to do background checks on a juvenile, but if the court combines the adjudicatory and disposition stages, the social study must be completed before the youth appears in front of a judge.

Jails A local institution for individuals being held for trial or for short-term confinements for sentences of a year of less.

jati A Hindu caste or distinctive social group of which there are thousands throughout India; a special characteristic is often the exclusive occupation of its male members (such as barber or potter).

Judicial Waiver The most widely used transfer mechanism for moving a juvenile case to adult court. This involves the actual decision-making process that begins when the juvenile is brought to intake.

Just Desserts A concept promoted by David Fogel, who believes that the punishment given to juvenile and adult offenders must be proportionate to the seriousness of the offense.

Justice Model A punishment model promoted by David Fogel, who believes that both juvenile and adult offenders are volitional and responsible human beings and deserve to be punished proportionately to the seriousness of their offenses if they violate the law.

Juvenile Court Officer Usually a probation officer.

Juvenile Court Statistics First published in 1929, the purpose of this publication was threefold: to furnish an index of the nature and extent of the problems brought before courts with juvenile jurisdiction, to show the nature and extent of services given by these courts in such a way that significant trends could be identified, and to show the extent to which service given by courts has been effective in correcting social problems.

Juvenile Justice and Delinquency Prevention Act (JJDP) Main policy changes brought about by the act include (1) status offenders must be separated from delinquents in secure detention and (2) institutionalization facilities for adults that hold juveniles may not receive federal funding.

Labeling Perspective Labeling theory contends that society creates the deviant by labeling some juveniles as "different" from others.

Law-Related Education (LRE) An educational program designed to promote the development of character that leads to healthy behaviors. LRE is designed to teach students the fundamental principles and skills needed to become responsible citizens in a constitutional democracy.

Least-Restrictive Approach The "go soft" approach to minor offenders found guilty of a crime. This first became

popular in the 1960s and called for keeping juveniles from penetrating any further than necessary into the system.

Life without Parole Sentence Sentencing used to incarcerate juveniles for the rest of their natural lives.

Lineup Situation in which a number of people, including a suspect, are lined up in front of witnesses or victims who try to identify the person who committed a crime against them.

Mandatory Sentencing Sentences that impose specific sanctions for specific actions regardless of mitigating factors.

Marijuana Leaves from the cannabis plant are used to achieve "highs"; its use is correlated with anxiety and other mental problems, particularly in very young users. Research is mixed on its effects on brain and health, but it is known to increase heart rate; contains many carcinogens. Prolonged use may reduce I.Q.

Marxist Perspective Perspective that views the state and the law itself as ultimate tools of the economic interests of the ownership class.

Masculinity Hypothesis A hypothesis suggesting that as females become more malelike in their social roles and became more masculine as a result they also become more delinquent.

Medical Model The first treatment model to develop from the *parens patriae* philosophy, which argues that youth crime is caused by factors that can be identified, isolated, and treated as in the case of a disease.

Medicalization of Deviance Attributing deviancy to medical causes and treating deviancy as a disease instead of delinquent behavior.

Mental Health Placements Keeping juveniles with mental illnesses out of institutions in the justice system and placing them in mental health systems instead.

Methamphetamine A major addictive stimulant; long-term use can lead to mood disturbances, violent behavior, anxiety, confusion, insomnia, and severe dental problems.

Minor A defendant under the age specified as an adult for legal purposes.

Miranda Rights Established by the 1966 Supreme Court case *Miranda v. Arizona*, these rights must be read by law enforcement officers to individuals prior to arrest. The Miranda rights fully explain the rights the arrested individual is entitled to throughout the justice system and prevents the individual from unknowingly giving up his or her rights or incriminating his or herself.

Missouri Plan Adopted by a dozen states, this plan involves a commission being appointed to nominate candidates for judicial vacancies; an elected official, generally the governor, makes judicial appointments from the list submitted by the commission, and nonpartisan and uncontested elections are held to give incumbent judges an opportunity to run on their records.

Naive Offenders   These types of offenders can be divided into three groups of adolescents: youths who are mentally deficient, those who simply are unaware that they are violating the law, and those who are naïve risk-takers.

National Council of Juvenile and Family Court Judges   Located in Reno, Nevada, this organization has done a great deal to upgrade the juvenile court judiciary. It has sponsored research and continuing legal education efforts.

National Crime Victimization Survey   Analysis of data from this survey is done by the U.S. Bureau of the Census to determine as accurately as possible the extent of crime in the United States by interviewing victims.

Neonatal   From birth to approximately one month after birth.

Nerve Synapses   Spaces between the neurons of the brain and central nervous systems that must be crossed for messages to be sent.

Neurons   Specialized cells of the brain and central nervous system that carry messages throughout the body.

Neurotransmitters   Chemicals that carry messages between the neurons through the nerve synapses.

Objective Research   A method of research that uses quantitative data and is acquired through collecting numerical and statistical data.

Official Statistics   Three main sources of official or governmental statistics pertaining to juvenile delinquency are uniform crime reports, juvenile court statistics, and national victimization studies; any other data collected by governmental as opposed to private agencies.

Oppositional Defiant Disorder   Excessive refusal to cooperate with others; characterized by being angry, swearing, and deliberately hassling others and is a problem if these behaviors last longer than six months. Some of these behavioral symptoms are normal for the "terrible twos" and some teenagers.

Panchayats   Based on traditional Indian methods of working with troublesome youths in the community, the Panchayat is reemerging in Indian society. These are quasi-governmental organizations supported by the government and run by elected elders of the community.

Parens Patriae   A philosophical basis of the treatment model that emerged in the United States with the founding of the juvenile court. The philosophy of the juvenile court is that the state has the right to guardianship over a child found under adverse social/individual conditions that encourage development of crime or other problems. This philosophy has been challenged by due process philosophy since its founding.

Parole   The period of time after institutional release when offenders are still under control of the courts or state.

Perinatal   Any time from roughly one month prior to birth until one month after birth.

Petition   An indictment.

Petitioner   A prosecutor.

Photographs   Pictures taken of offenders for identification and law enforcement files.

Plea Bargain   A deal made between the prosecutor and the defense attorney to reduce charges so the juvenile will receive a lesser sentence.

Positive Peer Culture (PPC)   Developed by Harry Vorrath, PPC is a total system for building positive youth subcultures. Its main philosophy is to turn around the negative peer culture and to mobilize the power of the peer group in a positive way.

Positivism   The dominant philosophical perspective of juvenile justice that argues that human behavior is determined and that the causes of crime can be discovered through rigorous scientific measurement.

Postindustrial Society   Countries moving away from industrial and factory production to a service, communications, and financially based economy.

Predictor Items   These items, based on relevant offender backgrounds, are used to determine whether offenders will remain law abiding or get into trouble after release.

Prescription Drugs (Drug Addiction)   Drugs prescribed for a specific reason to a specific person. Use of the drug for any other purpose by that person or by others for any reason is illegal.

Presumptive Minimum   Involves the assumption that aftercare should terminate after the youthful offender completes a commonly accepted minimum period of time on supervised release.

Preventive Detention   Confinement that is proactive, not punitive, for a specific offense.

Probation   A judicial disposition under which youthful offenders are subject to certain conditions imposed by the juvenile court and are permitted to remain in the community under the supervision of a probation officer.

Probation Subsidy Program   Used in states such as California, Nevada, Oregon, and Washington, these programs encourage a decreased rate of commitment of offenders by counties to state institutions by reimbursing the communities for confining youths locally.

Problem-Oriented Policing   A policy police departments are currently turning to in which police respond to the circumstances that create juvenile problems rather than to the incidents themselves.

Proportionality   The practice that all sanctions must be proportioned according to the seriousness criminal act. A punishment must not be excessive in nature when compared to the crime the individual committed.

Prosecutorial Discretion   The right of a prosecutor to determine whether juveniles are to be tried in adult or juvenile court.

Psychoanalysis   Developed by Sigmund Freud, this therapy helps patients understand their internal emotional states.

Psychotherapy   Therapy based on Freudian psychoanalysis. It is based on the concepts of id, ego, and superego and the oral, anal, and phallic stages of psychosexual development used to understand youths' emotional development.

Qualitative Research   Research data that is based on verbal descriptions and characteristics rather than quantitative data.

Quay Classification System   This system evaluates delinquents in terms of their behavior rather than their worldview and is based on five personality types: inadequate-immature, neurotic-conflicted, unsocialized aggressive or psychopathic, socialized or subcultural delinquent, and subcultural-immature delinquents.

Ranches   Privately or publicly administered minimum-security institutional placements that are normally reserved for youths who have committed minor offenses, who have been committed to the department of youth services or private corrections, or who have been released from confinement in a facility. Widely used in California, these tend to hold primarily white youths.

Rational Choice Theory   An extension of the deterrence doctrine found in the classical school that focuses on the rational calculation of payoffs and costs before delinquent acts are committed.

Rave Culture   An outgrowth of music and drug use in the 1960, today's rave culture builds on the use of psychedelic and other drugs, electronic music, and dancing through the night, sometimes with tens of thousands of youths involved.

Reality Therapy   William Glasser and G. L. Harrington assume that irresponsible behavior arises when a person is unable to fulfill his or her basic needs. According to this approach, the basic human needs are relatedness and respect, and one satisfies these needs by doing what is realistic, responsible, and right.

Reception and Diagnostic Centers   Run by both private and public administrations, these centers provide evaluation for youths to determine which treatment plans or facilities would serve the juvenile in the best way possible based on characteristics and needs for the youth.

Reentry Programs   After being confined within facilities, when they are released, juveniles may feel disoriented and confused by the transition from controlled living into free society; reentry programs are used to help them reenter society.

Referee   In some jurisdictions this individual takes the role of a judge in the juvenile court.

Reformatories   Also known as training schools or industrial schools. Developed in the mid-nineteenth century, reformatories were similar to houses of refuge but also provided schooling half of the day as well as harsh industrial labor for juveniles.

Reinforcement Theory   The theory that behavior is governed by its consequent rewards and punishments as reflected in the history of the individual.

Reintegration Philosophy   Philosophy that assumes both the offender and the receiving community must be brought together in formal programs.

Reliability   One of the two goals of data collection. Reliability is achieved when researchers can produce the same results using the same instruments numerous times. Reliability goes hand in hand with validity to provide accurate data.

Repeat Offender   Individuals who commit criminal behavior even after being charged with previous crimes.

Representing   Secret handshakes, hand signs, and colors used by gang members to identify the gangs to which they belong.

Respondent   A defense attorney.

Restitution   A disposition that requires offenders to pay back their victims or the community for their crime. This began to be used widely in probation during the 1970s and 1980s.

Restorative Justice Model   The purpose of this model is to reconcile the interests of victims, offenders, and the community through common programs and supervision practices that meet mutual needs.

Risk/Needs Assessment   Tests and evaluations that are used to assess an offender's psychiatric and psychological complications. The results of these assessments are used to find which treatment programs will best suit the offender. Popular risk/needs assessments include the YLS/CMI, J-RAT, YASI, SARY, and MAYSI-2.

Routine Activity Approach   This approach links the dramatic increase in crime rates since 1960 to changes in the routine activity structure of U.S. society and to a corresponding increase in target suitability and decrease in the presence of "guardians."

Schizothyme   One of the two body types in Ernst Kretschmer's body type theory. The schizothyme individual is strong and muscular, and is more likely to engage in criminal behavior than the counterpart cyclothyme body type.

School Safety   Drugs, alcohol, suicide, rape, robbery, assault, arson, and bomb threats combine with knives and guns to change the atmosphere of schools and generate fear in parents about student's safety today.

School Searches   Courts have ruled that schools do not need to obtain a warrant or have probable cause that a crime took place to conduct a search of students or their belongings. The legality of the search depends on its reasonableness, the scope of the search, the student's gender and age, and the student's behavior at the time.

Search and Seizure   U.S. citizens are protected by the Fourth Amendment to the Constitution against being searched without probable cause and without a proper search warrant.

Self-Report Studies   Studies used to measure hidden youth crime. Their purpose is to obtain a fuller and more accurate picture of the amount of crime by asking youths what offenses they have committed.

Sensation Seeking   The behavior of an individual who takes extreme risks and engages in new and novel activities. Many youths who take part in sensation seeking turn to delinquent behavior to fulfill these desires.

Sex-Role Socialization   The social phenomenon in which a youth learning his or her sex m Females tend to be supervised by parental figures more than males are, resulting in these gender roles causing females to be less delinquent than males.

Sexual Assault Cycle   Sex offenders are believed to engage in a cycle of emotional and thinking processes that lead them to sex offending, punishment, depression, and sex offending again, which must be broken if offenders are to be helped with their problems.

Situational Offenders   Those who do not normally look upon themselves as committed to youth crime. They drift in and out of crime because of boredom, group pressure, financial need, and the opportunity to commit crime.

Skill Development Programs   Programs that help offenders learn new skills such as reading and interpersonal communication that prepare them for adjustment in the community.

Smartness   A value among the lower class that involves the desire to outsmart, outfox, con, and dupe others.

Social Control Theory   A theory by Travis Hirschi that linked delinquent behavior to the bonds individuals have with conventional social groups such as the family and school.

Social Disorganization Theory   A theory by Clifford R. Shaw and Henry D. McKay that views crime as resulting from the breakdown of social control by the traditional primary groups such as family and the neighborhood because of the social disorganization of the community.

Social Roles   Found in training schools for boys; the roles are classified as aggressive, manipulative, passive, and other roles.

Social Services Act (SoL; Sweden)   This act was passed in 1982 because of the inadequacy of prisons. The act emphasized a social welfare system in which offenders and officials cooperated in finding the best treatment for a child.

Social Study Report   This report is ordered by a judge in a bifurcated hearing when a youth is found delinquent at the fact-finding stage of court proceedings.

Sociobiologists   Researchers who investigate the relationship between antisocial behavior and biological factors and the environment, through studies including, but not limited to, twins, adoption, intelligence, chromosomal activity, and chemical imbalances in the body.

Sociopath   A sociopath or psychopath is a person with a lack of affect, ability to empathize, and who commits crimes in a coldhearted unemotional manner; normally not diagnosed before age 17; some authors distinguish between the two.

Specialization of Offenses   The tendency to repeat one type of crime.

Status Offender   A legal description applied to juveniles who commit acts that are law violations only for juveniles, not adults.

Statutorial Exclusion   Some state legislatures automatically mandate that the perpetrators of specific offenses be tried in adult court.

Statutory law   Laws passed by legislatures that are written down and that police and courts enforce.

Strain Theory   Robert K. Merton's theory that cultural goals and the means to achieve these goals must be reasonably well integrated if a culture is to be stable and smooth running.

Street Gang Members   Any youths who join gangs.

Supervision   Once a youth has been placed on probation, the probation officer is required to provide the best supervision, including surveillance, casework services, and counseling or guidance, available. This also involves careful monitoring of the minor's adjustment to the community.

Synergistic Effect (Drugs) When the combined effect of more than one drug is greater than the sum of the drugs taken together, a multiplier effect occurs.

Taking into Custody Arresting a suspect.

Teenage Prostitution A form of chronic sexual offending in which females are more involved than males.

Tolerance (Drug Addiction) Occurs when a person needs to use more and more of a drug to produce the same effects as already experienced with a smaller amount of the same drug.

Toughness The ideal personality trait in the eyes of lower-class males; the "tough guy" is hard, fearless, undemonstrative, and a good fighter.

Traditional Cultures Cultures that still use internalized and long-standing folkways and mores.

Training Schools Public and private schools that are used to confine youths for long periods of time.

Transactional Analysis (TA) Method that focuses on interpreting and evaluating interpersonal relationships and tries to teach youthful lawbreakers to relate to others in an "adult," mature way instead of as a "parent" or a "child."

Transfer Process Process used to move juveniles who violate criminal codes from the juvenile justice system to the adult justice system to be tried in adult criminal court.

Transition to Adult Crime Occurs when groups of youthful offenders continue to commit offenses into their adult years.

Treatment Model Including the medical model, a model based on the belief that the basic mission of juvenile justice is to rehabilitate youthful offenders. It proposes that juveniles should be treated by specialists for those factors that caused them to commit offenses.

Underclass Theory An explanation for the origin of gangs, this theory states that gangs are a normal response to the abnormal social setting in which underclass (impoverished) youths are exposed to the point that delinquent behavior may be the only means of gaining economic success.

***Uniform Crime Reports* (UCR)** Compiled from police statistics by the FBI. The FBI classifies crimes into Part I and Part II offenses based on their seriousness.

Urban Gangs Gangs found in urban areas that are capable of extremely violent behavior.

Validity One of the two goals of data collection. Validity is achieved when researchers are studying what they believe they are studying. Validity goes hand in hand with reliability to provide accurate data.

Victimization The exploitation of youths not able to protect themselves by predatory peers.

Waiver Hearing A hearing held to decide whether an offender should be sent to adult court.

Welfare Model In Canada, a model that focuses on treating, curing, and helping offenders.

Wilderness Programs Wilderness or survival programs are similar to ranches. Two of the best known are Outward Bound and VisionQuest.

Wisconsin System Under this system, a risk/needs assessment is conducted for each probationer at regular intervals to see what level of supervision to place him or her under.

Youthful Offender System (YOS; United States) Proposed for young adults (sixteen to nineteen years old). Programs in these institutions emphasize work readiness, job training, and work experience.

Arizona v. Gant, **556 U.S. 332 (2009)**—The U.S. Supreme Court ruled that police may search the passenger compartment of a vehicle incident to a recent occupant's arrest only if it is reasonable to believe that the arrestee might access the vehicle at the time of the search or that the vehicle contains evidence of the offense of arrest.

Atkins v. Virginia, **536 U.S. 304 (2002)**—The Supreme Court ruled that juveniles who are mentally retarded cannot be executed for their offenses.

Breed v. Jones, **421 U.S. 519, 95 S. Ct. 1779 (1975)**—The Supreme Court ruled that Jones's hearing in the juvenile court was an adjudicatory hearing and that his trial in adult court constituted double jeopardy.

Brown v. Mississippi, **297 U.S. 278 (1936)**—The Supreme Court ruled that force may not be used to obtain confessions.

Ciulla v. State, **434 S.W. 2d 948 (Tex. Civ. App. 1968)**—A youth confined to a Texas training school after police found marijuana in his car was ordered released by an appellate court because the search took place too late to be related to the arrest.

Commonwealth v. Fisher, **213 P. 48, 62 A. 198 (1905)**—The Court ruled that the juvenile court "is not for the punishment of offenders but for the salvation of children...whose salvation may become the duty of the state."

Commonwealth v. Guyton, **405 Mass. 497 (1989)**—A Massachusetts motion appeals judge held that no other minor, not even a relative, can act as an interested adult in a juvenile's initial hearings.

Davis v. Mississippi, **394 U.S. 721 (1969)**—The Supreme Court ruled, among other things, that fingerprints taken by the police at the youth's initial interrogation could not be used as evidence against him in this case. The Court also ruled that the police should not have detained the youth without authorization by a judicial officer, that the youth was unnecessarily fingerprinted a second time, and that the youth should not have been interrogated at the first detention when he was fingerprinted.

Eddings v. Oklahoma, **102 S. Ct. 869 (1982)**—The Supreme Court was able to avoid directly addressing the constitutionality of the juvenile death penalty by ruling that "the chronological age of a minor is itself a relevant mitigating factor of great weight."

Ex parte Crouse **CASES OF THE SUPREME COURT OF PENNSYLVANIA. EASTERN DISTRICT-DECEMBER TERM, 1838 (Philadelphia, January 5, 1839)**—The Pennsylvania Supreme Court formalized the idea of *parens patriae*, meaning that the court could serve as a guardian in the absence of a responsible parent. *Ex parte Crouse* also dictated that, unlike adults, juveniles were not protected by the Bill of Rights found in the Constitution.

Fare v. Michael C., **442 U.S. 23, 99 S. Ct. 2560 (1979)**—The Supreme Court ruled that Michael seemed to understand his rights and that even when his request to talk with his probation officer was denied, he still was willing to waive his rights and continue the interrogation.

Farrell v. Cate **(Super. Ct. Alameda County, 2004, No. RG03079344)**—A complaint made towards the California Youth Authority (CYA), regarding the conditions within their facilities, resulted in the signing of a consent decree in which expressed that the program needed to provide effective treatments, programs, services, and care for juveniles; in order to correct behavior within their system.

Gagnon v. Scarpelli, **411 U.S. 778 (1973)**—The Supreme Court held that the right to counsel should be decided on a case-by-case basis. The Court did indicate that counsel should be provided on request when the probationer denies that he or she committed the violation or when the reasons for the violation are complex.

Gallegos v. Colorado, **370 U.S. 49, 82 S. Ct. 1209 (1962)**—The U.S. Supreme Court had prohibited the use of confessions coerced from juveniles. —A defendant who was held five days without seeing a lawyer, parent or other amenable adult, including his mother, signed a written confession that he had assaulted an elderly man five days before the victim died and prior to the defendant's being seen by a judge. The Supreme Court ruled the confession was obtained in violation of due process, and the judgment sustaining his conviction was reversed.

Graham v. Florida, **08-7412 982 So. 2d 43 (2010)**—The U.S. Supreme Court ruled that individuals under the age of eighteen could not be sentenced to life without the possibility of parole for nonhomicide offenses.

Gregg v. Georgia, **48 U.S. 153 (1976)**—The U.S. Supreme Court ruled that the death penalty did not violate the Eighth Amendment's prohibition against cruel and unusual punishment.

Haley v. Ohio, 332 U.S. 596 (1948)—The Supreme Court ruled that neither an adult nor a child can be interrogated without counsel present or the requirements of the due process of the law fulfilled.

Inmates of the Boys' Training School v. Affleck, 346 F. Supp. 1354 (D.R.I. 1972)—The Court ruled that juveniles have a right to treatment because rehabilitation is the true purpose of the juvenile court.

In re Barbara Burrus, 403 U.S. 528, 91 S.Ct. 1976, 29 L.Ed.2d 647 (1967)—The Supreme Court ruled that juveniles do not have a constitutional right to a jury trial. Some states do permit jury trials for juveniles.

In re Gault, 387 U.S. 1,18,1,18 L.Ws.2d 527, 87 S.Ct.1428 (1967)—The U.S. Supreme Court ruled that juveniles have the right to due process safeguards during confinement; these rights include receiving notice of the charges, the right to be represented by counsel, the right to confront and cross-examine witnesses, and the right to avoid self-incrimination.

In re Holley R.I. 615; 268 A.2d 723; 1970 R.I—The court's decision was that "the presence of [defendant's] counsel is necessary to preserve[his] basic right to a fair trial as affected by his right meaningfully to crossexamine the witnesses against him and to have effective assistance of counsel at the trial itself." ——Also, that a lineup is a critical stage of a prosecution and denial of the right of counsel at a lineup renders the identification made at that time inadmissible."

In re Terry, 438 pa., 339, 265 A.2d 350 (1970)—The Supreme Court ruled that juveniles do not have a constitutional right to a jury trial. Some states do permit jury trials for juveniles.

In re Winship, 357 U.S. 358, 90 S.Ct. 1968, 25 L. Ed. 2d 368 (1970)—The Supreme Court ruled that juveniles are entitled to proof "beyond a reasonable doubt." The preponderance of evidence standard was thrown out when youths committed acts for which adults would be charged with a criminal offense.

Jackson v. State, 359 Ark. 87, 194 S.W.3d 757 (2004) (10-9647) (2012)—Ruled along side *Miller v. Alabama*, the Supreme Court ruled that a mandatory sentence imposing life imprisonment without the possibility of parole for juveniles is unconstitutional.

Kent v. United States, 383 U.S. 541, 86 S.Ct. 1045, 16 L. Ed. 2d 84 (1966)—The Court ruled that Kent had the right to a transfer hearing in which evidence was presented, that Kent had the right to be present at a waiver hearing, that Kent's attorney had the right to see the social service reports, and that the judge had to state the reasons for the transfer.

Kirby v. Illinois, 406 U.S. 682, 92 S.Ct. 1877 (1972)—Following the *United States v. Wade* decision, the Court went on to say that the defendant's right to counsel at postindictment lineup procedures goes into effect as soon as the complaint or the indictment is issued.

Mapp v. Ohio, 367 U.S. 643 (1961)—The Supreme Court affirmed Fourth Amendment rights for adults. The decision stated that evidence gathered in an unreasonable search and seizure was inadmissible in court.

McKeiver v. Pennsylvania, 403 U.S. 528 (1971)—The decision denied the right of juveniles to have jury trials.

Mempa v. Rhay, 389 U.S. 128 (1968)—The Court upheld that the Sixth Amendment's right to counsel applies to the sentencing hearing because it is an important step in criminal prosecution.

Miller v. Alabama, (10–9646) (2012)—The Court ruled that a mandatory sentence imposing life imprisonment without the possibility of parole for juveniles is unconstitutional.

Morales v. Turman, 364 F. Supp. 166 (E.D. Tex. 1973)—The U.S. District Court for the Eastern District of Texas held that a number of criteria had to be followed by the state of Texas in order to ensure that proper treatment would be provided to confined juveniles.

Morgan v. Sproat, 432 F. Supp. 1130 (S.D. Miss. 1977)—The Court condemned the cruel practices of confining youths to padded cells with no windows or furnishings, and only flush holes for toilets, and denying access to rehabilitation programs or services.

Morrissey v. Brewer 408 U.S. 471 (1972)—The Court ruled that a hearing must be provided to determine the facts for a parole violation.

Murray v. Page 429 F.2d 1359 (1970)—The court stated that once a prisoner is paroled he cannot be deprived of his freedom by means inconsistent with due process. The minimal right of the parolee to be informed of the charges and the nature of the evidence against him and to appear and to be heard at the revocation hearing is inviolate.

Nelson v. Heyne, 355 F. Supp. 451 (N.D. Ind. 1972)—Indiana's Seventh Circuit agreed with the district court that inmates of the Indiana Boys' School have a right to rehabilitative treatment.

New Jersey v. T. L. O, 469 U.S. 325 (1985)—The U.S. Supreme Court held that the Fourth Amendment right against unreasonable searches and seizures does not apply to the school setting. School searches do not have to be based on a search warrant or probable cause; the search, however, must be reasonable.

Pena v. New York State Division for Youth, **419 F. Supp. 203 (S.D.N.Y. 1976)**—The Court held that the use of isolation, hand restraints, and tranquilizing drugs at Gosheen Annex Center was punitive and antitherapeutic and, therefore, violated the Eighth Amendment.

People v. Lara, **62 Cal. Rptr. 586 (1967), cert. denied 392 U.S. 945 (1968)**—The state of California upheld the confession of two Spanish-speaking youths, one of whom had a mental age of slightly over ten years.

Roper v. Simmons, **543 U.S. 551 (2005) 112 S.W. 3td.397**—In 2005 the Supreme Court ruled, in a four-to-five decision, that no juveniles who committed their crimes under the age of eighteen could be executed.

Safford Unified School District v. Redding, **557 U.S. (2009)**—The SupremeCourt ruled that schools do not have unlimited search and seizure rights. The June 2009 Supreme Court decision in *Safford Unified School District v. Redding* placed limitations on strip searches of students. School officials in Safford, Arizona, strip searched a thirteen-year-old girl, forcing her to expose her breasts and pelvic area in a search for two Advil. The court ruled that the search was unreasonable because school officials had not demonstrated that either the power of the drugs and or their quantity was sufficiently dangerous so as to warrant a search that was intrusive, humiliating, frightening, and embarrassing.

Schall v. Martin, **467 U.S. 253 (1984)**—The Supreme Court held that preventive detention upholds a legitimate interest of the state.

Stanford v. Kentucky, **492 U.S. 361 (1989)**—The Supreme Court upheld the constitutionality of the death penalty for juveniles under the age of eighteen but older than sixteen.

State v. Lowery, **230 A.2d 907 (1967)**—The Supreme Court applied the Fourth Amendment ban against unreasonable searches and seizures to juveniles.

State v. Werner, **242 S.E.2d 907 (W. Va. 1978)**—The Court condemned as cruel practices the locking of residents by staff in solitary confinement; beating, kicking, slapping, and spraying them with mace; requiring them to scrub floors with a toothbrush; and forcing residents to stand or sit for prolonged periods without changing position.

Terry v. Ohio **392 U.S. 1, 20 L.2d 889, 911 (1968)**—Police having a specific and articulable suspicion that a juvenile is armed and possibly dangerous, the youth's presence in a high-drug-dealing area of town, an obvious bulge in clothing, or the presence of another officer who may have arrested the youth previously and found a weapon on the youth may all lead to the reasonable suspicion justifying a pat down. An officer may do a *Terry* search, that is, patting down the youth's outer clothing, in a search for weapons only.

Thompson v. Oklahoma, **487 U.S. 815 (1988)**—The Court ruled by a five-to-three vote that "the Eighth and Fourteenth Amendment[s] prohibit the execution of a person who was under sixteen years of age at the time of his or her offense."

United States v. Wade, **338 U.S. 218, 87 S.Ct. 1926 (1967)**—The Supreme Court ruled that the accused has the right to have counsel present at postindictment lineup procedures.

White v. Reid, **125 F. Supp. 647 (D.D.C.) (1954)**—The court ruled that juveniles could not be held in institutions that did not provide for their rehabilitation.

Wilkins v. Missouri, **109 S.Ct. 2969 (1989)**—The Supreme Court decided that the death penalty was appropriate and sentenced Wilkins to die. The Missouri Supreme Court later upheld this decision.

Name Index

A

Abadinsky, H., 324n.4
Abrams, L. S., 242, 245, 256nn.18,26
Ackley, E., 300n.61
Adams, B., 46n.10, 150, 151, 157, 163nn.12, 13,15
Adams, W. T., 226, 235n.43
Addams, J., 320, 321, 326nn.72,83
Addie, S., 150, 151, 157, 163nn.12,13,15
Addington, L. A., 344n.10
Adkins, C., 280
Adler, F., 77, 88n.34, 300n.61
Ageton, S. S., 36, 37, 40, 47nn.18,23,30, 69n.66, 70n.71, 325n.16
Agnew, R., 52, 68n.16, 88nn.26,30,33,41,43
Aichhorn, A., 56, 69n.31
Aickin, M., 40, 47n.32
Akers, R. L., 68nn.8,11, 12
Albert, D., 147–148, 163n.7
Alexander, J. E., 207n.18
Alford, A., 279
Allen, E., 75, 88n.20
Allen, R., 280
Alper, B. S., 274n.31
Altschuler, D. M., 252, 256nn.7,19,30, 257n.40, 306, 325nn.8,10,18
Anderson, C. A., 332
Andrews, D., 256n.14
Armstrong, G., 114n.22
Armstrong, G. S., 225, 235n.39
Armstrong, T., 28n.39, 170, 171, 185nn.10, 252, 256n.7,19,30
Arner, W., 203
Ashcroft, J., 115n.74
Augustus, J., 10, 28n.16
Austin, J., 28n.22, 163n.29, 208n.60

B

Bachman, J. G., 89n.52, 114n.14, 305, 309
Bailey, W. C., 260, 274n.4
Baird, C., 233n.1
Ball, R. A., 186nn.30,31, 301n.74
Ballard, D., 325n.28
Barker, G. E., 226, 235n.43
Barksdale, D., 280
Barlowe, D. B., 208n.46
Barnes, R., 161
Bartol, A. M., 69n.26

Bartol, C. R., 69n.26
Bartollas, C., 88n.47, 114n.1, 186n.28, 207nn.1,7,10, 224, 225, 226, 227, 231, 235nn.37,40,41,42,47,48,54, 269, 270, 275n.43, 344nn.22,27
Bartollas, L. D., 280
Barton, W. H., 234n.11
Basena, M., 326nn.56,77,91
Baskin, D. R., 65, 70nn.81, 82
Batani-Khalfani, A. S., 299n.9
Battin-Pearson, S. R., 300nn.47,49
Bauzer, R., 114n.24
Bazemore, G., 23, 28n.39, 185nn.11,12
Beal, M. R., 326n.87
Bearch, L. R., 68n.7
Beazley, N., 159
Beccaria, C., 49 50, 68nn.3,5
Beck, A. J., 227, 235n.51
Becker, E., 208n.49
Becker, H., 61, 63, 69nn.59, 61
Bell, D., Jr., 131, 143n.45
Bem, D., 275n.50
Bender, K., 326n.88
Bennear, L. S., 208n.59
Bennett, W. D., 143n.38, 326n.54
Bentham, J., 49, 50
Beres, J., 196, 207n.40
Bernard, T. J., 13, 28n.23, 69n.64
Bernstein, N., 322, 326n.92
Beyer, M., 73, 87n.6
Bibb, M., 207n.9
Bilchik, S., 300n.39
Binder, A., 142n.4
Bishop, D. M., 89n.72, 143n.36, 228, 229, 234n.8, 235nn.58,59
Bjerregaard, B., 293, 301n.66
Bjornstrom, E., 70n.89
Black, D. J., 114nn.19,20,21
Black, T. E., 143n.37
Bloch, H. A., 283, 299n.19
Block, D., 285
Bloom, B., 74, 85, 87n.11, 89n.85
Blumstein, A., 40, 47n.28, 315
Boldt, T., 208n.63, 275n.40
Bonczar, T. P., 256n.16
Bonta, J., 256nn.14,15
Borduin, C. M., 172, 325n.40
Bortner, M. A., 136, 143nn.54,55
Bottcher, J., 70n.80, 84, 89n.79, 234n.13
Botvin, G., 207n.22

Note: The locators followed by "illus", "b", "t" and "f" refer to illustrations, boxes, tables and figures cited in the text.